Road romances at a glance

600,000
Number of Western women (esti mated) who have engaged in travel sex, 1980 to 2005 *page 41*

G000136900

3,500
Number of U.S. women a year who bring home non-Western husbands, fiances *page 182*

... ot U.S. women have had sex with a stranger *page 180*

Triple
The divorce rate for women married to foreigners vs. compatriots *page 190*

1 in 200
... of husbands in New York state is a foreign man marrying a female traveler *page 188*

7
Number of main reasons women engage in travel sex *page 85*

1 in 250
... of young females traveling solo take a foreign man as a new lover *page 40*

3
Number of French women for every 2 French men who marry foreigners *page 185*

Among female sex travelers:
1 in 7 are married or have a boyfriend *page 45*
1 in 30 turn holiday affair into long-term relationship *page 47*
1 in 50 engage in lesbian activity *page 47*
1 in 1,000 contract HIV *page 47*

3 in 5
... of women who frequently visit Jamaica take local lovers *page 45*

Hall of Fame sex travelers

- Over the course of five months, a tourist woman in Belize took seven lovers *page 47*
- In six days in Greece, an American woman had three lovers *pages 16-26*
- In Jamaica, a tourist woman in one night took three lovers *page 47*

- In the Dominican Republic, in 14 days a German woman took 18 lovers *page 100*
- In Egypt, a traveling Scotswoman had sex with her lover seven times in one day *page 101-02*

Romance
on the Road

Traveling women
who love foreign men

by Jeannette Belliveau

BEAU MONDE

Baltimore, Maryland
www.beaumonde.net

Published by Beau Monde Press

Copyright © 2006 Text, charts and maps by Jeannette Belliveau

Photographs by Jeannette Belliveau unless indicated otherwise. Cover design and photos by Jeannette Belliveau.

All rights reserved under International and Pan-American Copyright Conventions.

Published in the United States by:

Beau Monde Press
P.O. Box 6149
Baltimore, MD 21231-6149
www.beaumonde.net

Publisher's Cataloging-In-Publication Data
(Prepared by The Donohue Group, Inc.)

Belliveau, Jeannette, 1954-
  Romance on the road : traveling women who love foreign men / by Jeannette Belliveau.

  p. : ; cm.
  Includes bibliographical references and index.
  ISBN: 0-9652344-1-X

1. Women travelers--Sexual behavior. 2. Sex customs--Cross-cultural studies. 3. Tourists--Sexual behavior. 4. Visitors, Foreign--Sexual behavior. 5. Women--Travel. I. Title.

HQ29 .B45 2006
306.7/082   2005909964

Manufactured in the United States of America by Lightning Source of La Vergne, Tenn.

Grateful acknowledgement is made to the following for permission to reprint previously published material:

The Estate of Peter Hujar, courtesy Matthew Marks Gallery, New York, for Hujar's photograph of Anne Cumming.

Neil Libbert, for his photograph of Fiona Pitt-Kethley.

James Hamilton, for his photograph of Lucretia Stewart.

Editions JC Lattès, for a photograph of Claude Bergeret.

Irving Hexham, for his photograph of Karla Poewe.

Marcus Robbin, for an image from an interview with Cleo Odzer in the documentary *Last Hippie Standing*, by Tangiji Film.

James Sinclair, for his photograph of Mohiuddin Hossain Meerza and family.

Contents

Sexual geography

Where straight women go: See pages 135-36, 210, 329

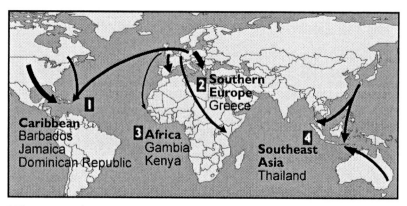

Where straight men go: See pages 135-36

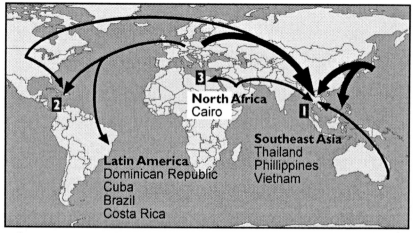

Where gays and lesbians go: See pages 48-49, 290, 298, 327-29

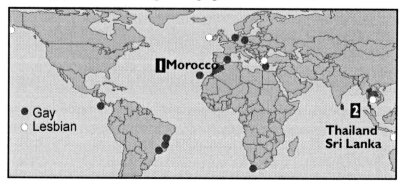

Wanderings of a sex pilgrim

When I became interested in the topic of traveling women who romance foreign men for this, my second book, I counted my luck in knowing an experienced Sex Pilgrim.

This East Coast woman, now 51 and happily remarried, was a leading participant in casual travel sex, and a particularly unlikely one at that.

A veteran traveler, she had taken foreign lovers on three different continents. She could describe what it's like to engage in anonymous sex within five minutes of meeting a man ... to enter affairs while living as an expatriate ... or to pick and choose a lover for the night from a flock of handsome Mediterranean peacocks.

Further, the Sex Pilgrim had married and divorced a foreigner. She'd established platonic relationships with island men too mild-mannered to make an overt proposition, played games that stopped short of full intercourse in areas of high HIV, and worried about pregnancy after impetuously not using condoms.

Sex Pilgrims, especially female ones, can be elusive creatures, yet she was available and nearly a perfect interview, her life a blueprint for the who, the where, and the whys of love under a foreign moon.

She intermingled the rectitude of Roman Catholic schoolgirl and the innocence of bygone America with an awareness, gathered as an adult expatriate in Europe, of an Old World pragmatism toward casual sex and a Continental penchant for travel that released inhibitions. And she shared the ethnicity of the women who pioneered sexual exploration of the Caribbean: the French Canadians, who for two generations have impressed their lovers in Barbados and elsewhere as unapologetic, fun-loving, generous and skilled.

The Sex Pilgrim's flings took her from Greece on a trajectory to the

Virgin Islands, the Bahamas and ultimately Brazil. This pattern unintentionally followed the overall history of female travel romance, which was born in the Mediterranean, became wildly popular in the Caribbean and now flourishes in much of the world. This pilgrim was willing to be quoted and had given some reflection to her adventures. She could articulate reasons for her behavior, motives that had evolved and expanded as she passed from her late 20s to her 30s and early 40s.

Her pilgrimage, she felt, had been a tough but perhaps unavoidable journey, one that unfolded in its own curious fashion.

A marriage breakup shocking in its swiftness started the process of unraveling the thick hawser that once welded intimacy only to love. Foreign men sliced away the final strands.

If the Sex Pilgrim's lovers stood together in a line-up, the parade would include a tall Athenian with a dark moustache, a laughing slim Mediterranean wolf-boy, a commanding French naval officer, an Amazonian Indian, an olive-skinned Brazilian teenager and most of all, black Caribbean islanders, the most indelible a confident, muscle-bound lobster fisherman.

Total strangers, most brown skinned, some barely of legal age, anonymous yet innately chivalrous, provided her satisfaction first, theirs second. And in the process, they helped rebuild the poise punctured by a collapsed marriage.

These strangers shared their bodies with the open delight any man brings to sex, and a bit of their buoyancy and élan rubbed off.

The Sex Pilgrim struggled back on her feet, and though frightened, reconnected sex and love — this time with a man from her home state who found nothing whatever unnatural about her experiences, for to him sex that didn't harm either partner was without question a good thing. One way or another, her pilgrimage brought her together with a man of color, who looked as exotic as a pharaoh but could discuss her hometown sports teams — a fortunate combination.

The Sex Pilgrim proved to be an ideal informant, one that trusted me to report on her odyssey without distortion. The only awkward problem: learning about this Sex Pilgrim involved interviewing an earlier incarnation of ...

... myself, the Jeannette who wandered lonely through a dozen years between first and second marriages.

Some romantic history

Growing up in Rockville, Maryland, in a blue-collar neighborhood in the overwhelmingly affluent Washington, D.C. suburbs, the idea of meeting an exotic Englishman in romantic San Francisco and later marrying him seemed utterly outside the realm of possibility.

Yet at the tender age of 22, wanderlust led me to visit the city by the bay while between jobs. Within five days, at my boarding house I met a 6-foot-2, green-eyed man with thick brown hair, a beautiful voice and a sense of humor that provided pure delight. We fell in love walking along the Pacific.

Adrian made me laugh and thrilled me in some almost mythic sense. He possessed the wit and accent of the Beatles, who had potently imprinted preteen female Baby Boomers with their first sexual yearnings. He was handsome in the intelligent way of the British Isles actor, with the expressive eyes of Pierce Brosnan or Alan Bates, more compelling than the Hollywood plasticity of Robert Redford or Brad Pitt.

For two years, we visited each other, taking intensely romantic trips to the Loire Valley in France and England's West Country. Then we got married and began living in Maryland.

The end came not via infidelity, drug or alcohol abuse or financial woes — painful problems but at least clear-cut and amenable to advice columnist solutions. One October day, after less than two years of marriage, angry criticism of the United States and my faults suddenly filled the air. Welcome to having a manic-depressive husband, yet not knowing it at the time. A husband who six months later, without telling me, flew home to England, then in air-mail letters dangled the idea of reconciliation.

Out of misdirected devotion, I made plans to move to England. Yet as I handed in notice at my newspaper job and sold my car, my estranged husband's behavior grew critical and unpredictable again. By the time I actually arrived in London, I had decided that my marriage had to end for my own emotional survival.

A post-divorce shell

Meeting an Englishman had nudged me down a new and different road. I lived (estranged from my husband) and worked in Britain much longer than I had planned, for three years. From there I visited Greece, where I began experimenting with casual foreign affairs. When I left England I traveled for 100 days in Asia, creating the foundation for my first book, *An Amateur's Guide to the Planet*. My marriage to Adrian had for all its hurts expanded my horizons and changed the young woman who knew little beyond Rockville into someone far different.

Yet while I became a competent explorer of mysterious lands and seas, it was the world of men that I couldn't navigate. Everyone takes divorce hard, but I felt a certain humiliation for having been so naively unquestioning of the mental stability of my white knight in shining armor. Others saw warning signs where I saw only perfection. (Ever after, I could see the rationale for arranged marriages — or at least getting outside feedback from family and friends on one's romantic choices.)

After spending £35 on a British divorce, uncomplicated by children or joint property, I withdrew into a shell around available men. My confidence in reading and responding to their signals was simply gone.

Clever married men moved in, for they smell isolation in the way sharks smell blood and move in on the aloof single woman. My relationship mistakes became compounded as I moved through my late 20s, 30s and early 40s. It was a hell of a lot of time to misuse.

The psychic dislocation of divorce explains much of why I did what I did with foreign men. Travel romance led to my first marriage to a foreign man met 2,400 miles from home, and travel romance provided a road to healing from that marriage's ashes. Many other women have followed a similar path, as the pages of *Romance on the Road* will show.

Does the author know what she is talking about?

So, to answer a reader's very first question in picking up a book about women sharing intimacies with foreign men met on their travels, "Has the author herself tried this?"

... the answer is "yes."

Of course, the perils of "coming out" as this Sex Pilgrim would be risky. These included:
- my mom.
- the automatic and profound negativity of critics to female sexual memoirs.
- the trickiness of segueing from somewhat voyeuristic but useful descriptions of personal experience to examining female sex travel as a social phenomenon.
- and again, the perils of my mom, my mom and my mom.

For I know I absorbed most of my mother's values and am fortunate to have done so. I respect fidelity, the family, marriage, commitment, honorable behavior and sturdy morals. Yet needs for closeness, for the sex connection as a part of basic humanity, instinctively told me what to do to emerge from my lost period — and overpowered the conventions I had been taught.

With apologies to Mom, "Intermarriage Jeannette," my former self, had racked up experiences critical to an understanding of modern female loneliness and of travel as a way out of a tough-to-escape prison. These first-hand encounters with foreign men gave me personal understanding of the transportive ecstasy and redemptive healing of wild nights with a near-stranger.

Feel free to just read "the dirty parts," like a *Playboy* subscriber dedicated to study of the centerfold. (These are the chapters entitled "Discovering the Nymphomaniac Within," "Ready, Willing and Able: Caribbean Men" and "Instant Sex, Amazon Style.")

Or conversely, censor the racy bits and read just the chapters on what's happening and what it all means.

My hope, however, is that you the reader will benefit from a synergy between the personal and the universal, for the first has illuminated how to organize the second.

For example, *Romance on the Road* visits Southern Europe first, the Caribbean second, and Latin America later, mainly because that is the order that reports of female travel romances surfaced — yet also because my own experiences fell in that sequence.

In addition, *Romance* catalogs seven reasons for romances on the road, ones I lived through in chronological order from the ages of 28 to 40.

And finally, *Romance* will take issue, again based on extensive personal experience, with errors and negative judgments in academic reports on female sexual behavior while overseas. Killjoys see travel sex as exploitation of poor men and damn an older woman for taking a youthful lover or decry liaisons that fulfill mutual racial fantasies. One wonders if these judges have themselves ever been as lonely as a divorced Western woman or as lacking in hope for the future as a Caribbean man facing high regional unemployment. Further, have these judges ever themselves possessed the playfulness or the intellectual curiosity (or colorblindness) to lie down in bed with a lover of a different race, age or income?

In the same vein, *Romance* will challenge a miscellany of other misperceptions that cropped up in the research of others and prompted me to shake my head and smile:

• that women are nearly incapable of instant sex.

• that (all) Caribbean men are lousy and selfish in bed.

• and that sexually free Western women are an unmitigated danger to the social fabric in traditional societies (read: a challenge to a long-standing order where typically men make decisions and local women are close to invisible).

These are the ways personal experience has shaped my telling of the overall story of women who travel for love.

Also, in early drafts where I tried to camouflage my own participation, this book proved impossible to write, because ... such things can't be hidden successfully, for the reader correctly demands, What do you really know? Why are you so passionate about this, as to write a book?

Why do we care about romance on the road?

This may be your, the reader's, next question.

Travel intimacy is important for a number of reasons:

• From 1980 through 2005, perhaps a cumulative 600,000 Western women have dared to pursue carnal closeness with foreign men, yet public awareness of the phenomenon is spotty even after the release of popular books and movies on the topic.

• Physical intimacy with a poor or non-white foreigner undermines fundamental assumptions about what a woman looks for a man. And the thousands of resulting marriages sledgehammer a full century of academic theories about mate selection.

• Casual travel sex is a leading indicator of the state of feminism and real increases in female power. Impromptu liaisons with foreign men began to flourish during feminism's first wave in the 1840s and re-emerged in the 1960s, tracking wider social change with exactitude. And as roughly 10,000 Western women a year marry foreign men — as they bring holiday lovers home to their own countries — they exercise a power reserved through history for male military conquerors.

Why write this book?

On sporadic occasions for more than a dozen years, intimate adventures while traveling provided some of the most vivid experiences of my life. Eventually, I began to suspect that out of the public eye, many other women must be secretly been having their own emotionally powerful, unforgettable affairs — ones that a lot of them kept carefully concealed.

Romance on the Road seeks to normalize the experience of travel liaisons, which for American women especially may create anxiety and feelings of confusion, unnecessary shame and secrecy.

Any female traveler entering a sexual relationship can now learn that she is:

• not the first to ever do so (by 150 years).

• far from alone (an estimated 24,000 women a year also indulge).

• and not crazy (at least seven compelling reasons make unanticipated sex likely for many traveling women).

Romance on the Road should permit Western women who get close to foreign men to look at themselves as fulfilling normal human desires for a closeness often blocked by obstacles in their home society.

Women are entitled to know the long history of their experimentation with travel sex and the geographic near-universality of the phenomenon.

Female hedonism on holiday may seem to be a niche topic. But the scattered but valuable components of this story — the women's memoirs, academic reports, movies and novels — deserve comprehensive reporting and build a picture of an important change in female pursuit of intimacy, mating and companionship.

The microcosm of road romance tracks important changes in the macrocosm of overall female sexual behavior, including a exponential increase in women's sexual freedom to a level likely unprecedented in civilization for at least three millennia and possibly throughout all human experience.

Hunting down the story

During radio interviews for my first title, *An Amateur's Guide to the Planet*, phone-in listeners often often asked, "Why did you write your book?"

My reply was, "You always write books because no one else articulates your vision."

The same motivation drove this writing of this book, also. Where was the big book measuring and explaining sex travel (by women), describing experiences similar to my own? At first, the sum total of information seemed to be the description of a "zipless fuck" on an Italian train in the 1973 novel *Fear of Flying*, at its core a mere six paragraphs of fantasy that launched a useful phrase into public consciousness. In 1996, the novel *How Stella Got Her Groove Back* further publicized holiday carousing — but captured only a slice of what was going on around the world with hundreds of thousands of women.

In 1999, five years after a Brazil trip provided what would be my last instance of casual sex, I began to dig further.

I interviewed female travelers and expatriates, from as close by as my soccer teammates in Maryland to as far away as Germany. I commissioned a statistician to help determine from immigration data for the first time where U.S. women go to bring home foreign husbands.

And I found a cache of writings going far beyond the "zipless fuck" and the restoration of Stella's groove.

Each trip I made to the U.S. Library of Congress, Baltimore area libraries and other motherlodes was like passing through a gate to a magic garden. I took my magnifying glass and dug up more than 800 pieces of the puzzle, often in obscure sources.

On their own, the puzzle pieces sat quietly, barely touched, on library shelves, in immigration datatapes, at specialty video stores, in handwritten, never-published diaries recording love at first sight between Indian nobles and pretty Englishwomen. Entire memoirs devoted to recounting sex travel (most published in Europe, and many not in English) came to light, as did anthropologists' confessional remembrances, social science reports, histories of the Raj in India, Victorian travel writing, literary criticism, articles in medical journals, and more.

Dusted off, held to the light and seen in their totality, the puzzle pieces came together and revealed patterns. A rich story unfolded about Western women and foreign men, both willing to address a worldwide Affection Deficit Disorder with exotic and surprising mates. A quiet revolution had begun, likely in a bedroom in Rome in 1840s, and this female rebellion had grown over a century and a half to encompass experiences ranging from quick sex on sandy Barbados beaches to marriages that changed history.

Travel sex by women is revolutionary yet also understandable, a vivid life event yet one barred from polite conversation, and a phenomenon now even reaching obscure fishing towns in Central America and hamlets in the Himalayas, yet misunderstood and incompletely chronicled.

In effect, traveling women have been stumbling into a major life experience without a map, in a situation comparable to having one's first period with no preparation from Mom.

How to structure the assembled puzzle?

As with my first book, *An Amateur's Guide to the Planet*, *Romance on the Road* will be organized by geographic region, and every region will be followed by a related theme. In addition, the chapters on Southern Europe, the Caribbean and Latin America are preceded by narratives of personal experiences.

Where I have only a few anecdotes about an area, these are incorporated into the regional chapter. In Africa and Oceania, I have been leered at or propositioned; in China and Borneo, admiring of handsome men but too timid to make the first move; and in Bali in Indonesia, able to observe gigolos in action first hand. In what I call the Zone of Sexual Winter, I can report the discovery, made also by most all white female expatriates, of a place where we utterly lack the appeal so hailed to the skies by most of the world's other men.

In only two areas of the world have I not had at least some suggestive interactions with men, and these would be the Near East and Antarctica, two areas I have not explored unless a refueling stop in Dubai counts as a Persian Gulf visit.

The ordering of regional chapters follows roughly the timing in which each became known for casual travel sex. Where regions differ little in the arrival of erotically adventurous women, areas with greater numbers of holiday liaisons appear first. Thus *Romance on the Road* visits in succession Southern Europe, the Caribbean, Africa, South and Southeast Asia, Latin America, the Middle East and the Maghreb, Oceania, and the Zone of Sexual Winter. Asia and the Middle East appear somewhat out of order to allow other regions introducing crucial thematic chapters to appear first.

The three biggest theme chapters, What's going on, Reasons and Experiences, appear early in *Romance on the Road*. These are followed by themes on History, Portrayals in literature and film, and Sex, power, ethics and etiquette.

It's human to seek intimacy

For American women in particular, an utterly unanticipated seduction by a polished Don Juan, seasoned by success with worldly European tourists, has the potential to create upset and disorientation.

Yet the seduced tourist is not a freakish nymphomaniac.

My hope that women will better understand their own liaisons as normal and understandable, particularly for women at certain stages and in certain situations.

To that end, *Romance on the Road* will attempt to describe the full saga of women who travel for love: their experiences, overall numbers, history over several centuries, destinations, motivation, outcomes and depictions in the media.

And *Romance* will go a step further, grappling with the health and

safety issues, ethics and etiquette of road romances, with a hope of providing some guidance as well as information.

So let's normalize this behavior, but not too much, for sharing the bed of an exotic paramour also needs to continue to be daring and thus, to thrill.

Jeannette Belliveau
Fells Point, Baltimore,
Maryland, USA
Oct. 5, 2005

The author poses beside her map of the Yucatan.

Women, men, travel and sex

Romance on the Road examines Western female travelers who have sexual encounters, either casual or longer term, with foreign men involving a significant cultural leap and often hedonistic behavior.

Within that definition, I have made some inclusions and exclusions.

Including women who live overseas

As well as travelers, *Romance* includes anthropologists, expatriate women and daughters of colonial settlers, who confront as much or more than the vacationer the question of whether to take up local companionship. These women face potentially more ostracization than tourists if they defy taboos against fraternizing with local men of dark skin or exotic ways.

Further, resident white women especially in Africa and India have usually led holiday visitors by at least a year or two in shattering color barriers. Memoirs by residents (especially anthropologists) provide valuable insights into the mental calculations of any woman who decides to share the bed of a foreigner.

Including sublimated attraction

Some descriptions of non-sexual relationships shed useful light on how admiration and friendship can lead a Western woman to become attracted to a foreign man. In the 19th century, European women began to praise the moral character and looks of foreign men, taking tentative steps along a road to physical intimacy.

Including lesbians

For traveling women, most encounters are heterosexual. Yet lesbian experiences and destinations will be included, particularly to note interesting differences between heterosexual and homosexual women.

Including men

No study of travel sex can ignore men, for they obviously make up half the story.

Romance on the Road will describe:

• where men go for travel sex or foreign wives, and how women prefer different parts of the world.

• how shortages and surpluses of men in various areas of the globe contribute to female travel sex.

• how mutually negative views that Western men and women hold toward each other, and similar conflicts between non-Western men and women, accentuate the appeal of a stranger.

Including gay men

No discussion of fleeting travel encounters, a defining aspect of gay male identity, can afford to overlook homosexual men.

In fact, the histories of gay men and straight women intertwine:

• In the Victorian era, both groups in significant numbers departed the same country (England) to the same destination (Italy) in search of sexual options and to flee sexual prohibitions.

• Nowadays both share many of the same commercial sex zones (Thailand, the Dominican Republic, Sri Lanka and other countries) in search of beautiful available men.

• Gay men and straight women have written many of the core works on the significance, extent and benefits of romance on the road.

In sum, an examination of sex travel by women will be complete only if studied alongside the behavior of straight men, homosexuals and lesbians.

Excluding sex at trade conventions

This book excludes sex at conventions and between backpackers. Such liaisons are perhaps the most frequently occurring forms of travel sex yet by the same token are, obviously, commonplace.

Instead, we will learn about more controversial forms of travel sex that challenge taboos, including:

• crossing racial and color barriers.

• choosing a man from a vastly poorer area as a permanent mate.

• and partaking of pure hedonism (such as instant sex, sex in public or with multiple partners during one holiday).

Relationships must involve: significant cultural leaps ...

Romance on the Road will stress encounters between Western women and the men of Southern Europe, Africa, Asia, the Caribbean, Latin America, the Middle East and Oceania.

A real-life example: Swiss boutique owner Corinne Hofmann falling in love with a Masai warrior while in Kenya with her boyfriend.

This radical change in selecting sex partners and mates rejects homophily, defined as social pressure to date and marry someone much like yourself.

Western women falling for Western men met while traveling will not be a focus, with two exceptions, involving France (prior to World War II) and Japan.

In France, from the 1880s through the Jazz Age, young American women living in Paris created scandal back home for their affairs with French and other foreign men — "Italians, Russians, Roumanians, Greeks" (Levenstein 207). These well-documented affairs will be included because though they occurred in a Western city, at the time they represented both a cultural leap and social rebellion.

And Japan, though a modern nation, presents a bizarre situation between Western women and local men so unlike the rest of the world as to merit discussion.

... and social rebellion

Women also rebel in a second dimension when they not only lie down with a culturally different lover but later become seriously involved with him.

And women rebel even more when they indulge in hedonistic behavior forbidden at home, such as instant sex, sex with a near-stranger, taking different partners each night, paying for sex or procuring men based on characteristics including physical endowment.

What will be of interest, in ascending order of social rebellion, will be examples of:

• **Sexual encounters leading to serious relationships,** especially where a Western woman eventually brings her foreign lover home. This alters a status quo over the millennia where international marriages usually involve a male soldier or traveler bringing a foreign woman home. Today a woman's personal wealth and her membership in the vibrant Western economies confer on her the heretofore-male prerogative to select and bring home a foreign spouse. **Real-life examples:** Each year, 3,500 American women bring husbands and fiances from Southern Europe and the developing world into the United States. In France, more women than men now bring home foreign spouses.

• **Anonymous travel sex. Real-life example:** Anne Cumming (*Love Habit* 135), an upper-crust Englishwoman, explored Egypt's Pyramids on horseback with an Arab guide and immediately allowed him to penetrate her from behind.

- **Love 'em and leave 'em. Real-life example:** Post-loving, English poet Fiona Pitt-Kethley made her breezy exit from an Italian rock musician who wondered what he was going to do without her: "Presumably he was going to do very nicely without me like I was going to without him" (*Journeys* 174-75).

Note that these situations represent women behaving in a way that was once almost exclusively seen as male.

Definitions

Romance on the Road employs the following definitions.

Encounters

Travel sex: Range of intimate activities, primarily sexual intercourse, but also its preliminaries. To borrow from Patricia Anderson (4), a scholar who studies the Victorian era, "I need to say plainly what I mean by 'sex.' Not only does it signify the act itself but also what comes before — initial attraction, flirtation, falling in love, and courtship."

Casual travel sex: Marked by an emphasis on physical attraction swiftly consummated. Examples include instant, fleeting or anonymous sex, and holiday flings of a recreational nature. No-strings fun, in some cases, later evolves into a long-term relationship.

This definition by a Swedish medical researcher (M. Arvidson, et al., "Risky Behavior" 419) offers useful elaboration: "Any history of sexual intercourse on a journey abroad with a man previously unknown to the woman, a contact that did not lead to a steady relationship."

Anonymous sex: Spontaneous encounters where the participants don't learn each others' names prior to the act. **Real-life examples:** English writers Anne Cumming with her Arab guide on horseback (*Love Habit* 135), Fiona Pitt-Kethley with a newly met Greek motorcyclist (*Pan* 151).

Travel romance: Holiday relationship with significant component of sweet declarations of ardor, where the man is viewed as at least a temporary boyfriend and a means of entry into local culture. **Real-life examples:** Many of the relationships between Western tourist women and Jamaican men.

Platonic friendship: Relationship involving a foreign man marked by inviting a tourist woman to meet or dine with his family or his gentlemanly provision of transportation to buy necessities or see local sights. The foreign man may purchase small gifts of soft drinks or coffee and later write letters to his tourist friend. Can have high culture-brokering component. **Real-life examples:** My own relationships with Alain Hodge

Acknowledgments

Profuse thanks to **Mary Ann Constantinides**, a family therapist in Baltimore, Md., who counsels many urban women battling loneliness. She read the entire text and provided insightful editing suggestions as well as crucial encouragement. And to statistician **Anamaria Kazanis**, who extracted immigration data on foreign husbands and wives brought to the United States.

Numerous scholars, listed below by chapter reviewed, made suggestions of tremendous worth:

Southern Europe: Dr. Eugenia Wickens of Buckinghamshire Chilterns University College in England, author of several journal articles on female hedonists in Greece, and **Dr. Erik Cohen** of Hebrew University in Jerusalem, perhaps the world's most eminent researcher on the sociology of tourism.

What's Going On: Dr. Michael Bloor of Cardiff University in Wales, an expert on HIV-related risk behavior, who has conducted the only random survey of young sex travelers.

Caribbean: Suzanne Lafont, co-author of the landmark study "For Love and Money: Romance Tourism in Jamaica," and veteran Caribbean travel writer **Marianne Ilaw**.

Reasons: Dr. Laura Juliano of American University (identity loss) and Dr. Bloor's Cardiff University colleague **Dr. Michelle Thomas** (identity loss and the search for healing and love); Baltimore hairdresser **Maya** (connoisseurship and fantasy fulfillment); **Dr. Scott J. South** of the State University of New York-Albany, premier sociologist on family and marriage issues (man shortages and a revolution in mate selection); **Dr. Denise A. Donnelly** of Georgia State University, research pioneer on involuntary celibacy; famed anthropologist of human sexuality **Dr. Donald Symons** of the University of California-Santa Barbara (mate selection); and therapist **Mary Ann Constantinides** (the dating war).

on St. Bart's and Yutong Chen in China.

Participants

Sex tourist or sex traveler: Man or woman who anticipates sexual encounters during travel, even if this is not their primary goal, or eagerly embraces sexual opportunities after arrival. **Real-life example:** Women visiting the Dominican Republic carrying recommendations from girlfriends on men reputed to be good lovers.

Culture broker: A man who can heighten the apparent authenticity of a woman's vacation by providing glimpses of how local people live, by translating and by helping her negotiate logistics and customs. Modern version of the Eastern Mediterranean's dragomen of the Victorian days. **Real-life examples:** Margaret Fountaine's Syrian boyfriend Khalil, Lady Jane Digby's Bedouin guide and later husband, Medjuel.

Africa: **Catharine Cooper,** a former Peace Corps volunteer in Kenya, and **Carr** and **Elizabeth Kizzier,** former residents of Kenya, now a Baltimore area teacher and a development officer with the Johns Hopkins international maternal health program. **Experiences: Dr. Ron de Graaf,** senior researcher at the Netherlands Institute of Mental Health and Addiction (types of sex travelers, and their HIV and mental health risks); University of Michigan statistician **Anamaria Kazanis** (immigration data); and **Mary Ann Constantinides** (mental health aspects). **Asia: Dr. Petri Hottola** of the Finnish University Network for Tourism Studies and the University of Joensuu, author of a book on backpacker behavior in South Asia. **History: Dr. Maria Frawley** of George Washington University, author of *A Wider Range: Travel Writing by Women in the Victorian Era,* and **Jane Robinson,** author of *Unsuitable for Ladies: An Anthology of Women Travellers* and *Wayward Women* (Victorian female travelers); independent scholar **Christopher Buyers** (Indian maharajas), who maintains a comprehensive Web site, The Royal Ark: Royal and Ruling Houses of Africa, Asia, Oceania and the Americas (http://4dw.net/royalark/index.html). **Latin America: Elizabeth K. Hilton,** a former Peace Corps volunteer in Honduras and graduate of the Johns Hopkins School of Nursing in Baltimore, Md. **Middle East: Athena Kellner,** a former English teacher in Syria. **Oceania:** Hawaii-based **Shereé Lipton,** veteran traveler in the remote South Pacific and author of *Fiji I Love You, Full Speed.* **Portrayals: Dr. Susan Blake** of Lafayette College in Pennsylvania and **Dr. Jessica Rabin** of Anne Arundel Community College in Maryland. **Sex, power, ethics and the future: Mary Ann Constantinides.**

Ready to talk frankly now? To get down to the nitty-gritty of travel sex? Then let's hear of a real-life experience, as our Sexual Pilgrim journeys to Greece.

Understanding citations in text

Works cited appear in brief shorthand in the text, in the form of, for example, (Stafford) if an entire work is cited, (Stafford 15) giving a page number if a specific passage is quoted, paraphrased or summarized, or (Hoyle qtd. in Stafford 25) if secondary sources are used. These citations and the bibliography are in the style of the Modern Language Association.

If just a page number, such as (144) appears, this refers to the author most closely preceding the page number.

Full publication information for cited works appears alphabetically by author in the bibliography at the end of this book.

Discovering the nymphomaniac within

At the age of 27, I made the first of three visits to Greece. At the time I worked as a copy editor on a health journal near London, was separated from my first husband, a resident of Surrey, and was dating another Englishman.

APRIL 1982

On the clock of the sexual revolution, it was 10 minutes before midnight. Soon everyone would hear of a sickness called AIDS that could kill the too-reckless pleasure seeker.

However, on my first visit to Greece, I was innocent of the knowledge of killer viruses — and a lot more.

I was becoming an experienced traveler, with solo trips in the United States, Britain, France, the Netherlands and Belgium, often as a lone bicyclist going from campground to campground. But I had no interest in casual sex and did not take flirtatious men met on the road seriously. I was up for wanton behavior, except for one minor detail: it had to be within a framework of knowledge, liking, affection and love born of time.

As I cycled chastely around Northern Europe, however, thousands of Scandinavian, British and other women were heading, as they had since the early 1960s, to destinations all around the Mediterranean for vacation flings.

So by the time I, a naïf despite my fashionably tight short shorts, followed in their footsteps to Athens, the stage was set for the taking of an innocent lamb.

A lifelong dream of seeing the Parthenon and the islands brought me to Athens airport. I had no thoughts at all of having to deal with Southern European men. I had a boyfriend, new love at its most delicious, so therefore I wasn't looking. My ability to be faithful had always arisen naturally, or so I thought, from an unswerving character.

The incessant hounding that followed began to change my outlook. Preposterous come-ons from dozens of little and ugly men brought about a paradox: Their words made it clear that anything goes, and their numbers indicated the law of averages might send along an attractive fellow who could manage a stylish seduction.

In Greece, a woman can go from choir girl to veteran sex tourist at the snap of the fingers.

And no one would have to know.

I sensed that copulations of convenience, while tawdry in the context of being flat drunk in a college fraternity house, would possess a certain zing performed in exotic settings.

Unlike many of my vacations to follow, this time randiness from prolonged celibacy did not heighten temptation. Yet for a different reason I was more alive to enticing suggestions, for I just embarked on a new physical relationship in Britain, which brought a certain sparkle to me that only served to draw yet more swains. The short shorts, which I wore as did many 1980s American women without a thought in the world, underlined an unintended message of invitation.

Of course Greek men thought I a prime sex tourist (although probably any female falls into that category). A woman of 27! Wearing short shorts! Boyfriend not with her (= nonexistent). I had booked the solo trip and then fallen for my boyfriend. Rather than his arrival in my life inoculating me against mischief, the opposite happened. I so glowed in the good mood of early love that I probably projected triple my normal appeal.

This was bad.

I had wandered into a scene that Northern European women already knew was always one step away from an impromptu orgy. If you didn't ration yourself you could have three men a day. And even if you were uptight, selective and prone to religious guilt, this universe of available men times their persistence equals a good chance of a quick trip to bed.

My first evening stroll took me from my hotel, near Syntagma Square and within sight of the Parthenon, into the Plaka, the old town. My bouncy demeanor based on newfound love was more than evident. Men from Greece, men from Iraq, men from elsewhere swarmed around like bees, new ones zooming in when the old had been swatted. "My name is Demosthenes," said one, impressing me with the local alternatives to John and Michael.

Within minutes, however, the aggressiveness and sheer numbers of men badgering me began to be rattling. Block by block I devised new stratagems:

"I am married."
"I am meeting my boyfriend."
"Watch out, my boyfriend will get angry at you."
"Buzz off."

Then:
Angry silence.
Passive silence, worthy of a deaf-mute.
Willing these men into invisibility.

It takes no great sex siren to draw men like a magnet. I am 5 feet 4, brown hair, blue eyes, less than buxom, decent legs ... here's a picture of me at the time:

A taverna keeper took notice from his doorway. He ushered this flustered new arrival into his haven. To my relief, he was not using a ruse to hit on me.

"The men think you have come here for them," he explained simply, beckoning me to sit, have a drink and calm down. "We get many Swedish and Norwegian women who come here looking for sex because their men are so cold."

In my provincialism and knee-jerk feminism, I didn't believe him. "That's what these guys want to believe," I thought. "They strike out 100 percent of time." Further, weren't Sweden and Norway zones of free love, with hunky blond men for the taking?

Me, at Athens' Parthenon. Dressed in these short shorts, I must have appeared to be a prime sex tourist to Greek men.

As it transpired, the taverna keeper was correct. Later in the 1980s, academic journals, popular movies and TV documentaries would rain down tales of these surprising Scandinavian women. Maybe their own men were indeed boring. So in reality, the come-ons by Greeks had a fair chance of success.

Earlier in the day I had wandered the back streets of Athens on my own, photographing the sights, far enough from tourist areas to be more of a curiosity than a target. Veiled widows moved like shadows, as though in Saudi Arabia. Men and only men whiled away the time in jammed cafes. Boys played soccer. Girls remained in the clasp of their mothers.

In public the sexes, even children, conducted no joint activities. No young men and young women strolled together. No wonder the local men bothered the tourists.

On my second day of walking around, a businessman from Baghdad named Adnan treated me to lunch and then made a dignified proposition on the rooftop of his hotel. "Aren't you married?" I asked. He seemed a nice guy, a bit shorter than me, and had a dark moustache and intelligent eyes. I pictured him having a pleasant wife.

"Yes," he said honestly. The question must have perplexed him, given both the near-irrelevance of marital status for prowling men in Europe and nearby regions, and the widespread belief not without foundation that "American girls are easy."

The poor guy. He had run into me a little too early, in my last moments of rectitude.

Ticket to ride

At Syntagma Square, a half-Greek man, his 5-foot-10 stature and mesomorph physique attesting to a Swedish mother (was he the product of a travel tryst himself?), asked me a few unmemorable questions. A handlebar moustache graced his smooth face, not gorgeous but certainly handsome. He had all the time in the world and offered a ride along the beautiful coast east of Athens, to the end of the Attica peninsula. I agreed, placing the invitation in the category of Intrepid Traveler Gets to Meet the Friendly Locals.

The cassette player of his convertible provided perfect scene-setting music, the trilling bouzouki that hints of the exotic Oriental bazaar. Near the ride's end, at Cape Sounion, we parked along a secluded beach. Cliffs guarded a narrow strip of sand, out of sight from the road. Offshore rock sentinels resembled those of a less grand Big Sur.

My escort noted it would be fun to bath nude. I had a notion now of our situation, and his motivation for being so generous with his time became clearer. Yet some out-of-body person took control and agreed it was the most normal thing in the world to strip in front of a total

Cape Sounion as it looked on my second trip, in 1988. My earlier interlude took place, I believe, on the shores below the mountain at right.

stranger. (In fact, it is easier in some ways to act with license when a relationship lacks any baggage whatsoever.)

He was powerfully built, not as burly as a wrestler but quite thick through the chest.

After bathing, I lay back on my towel. My nakedness would have been mortifying anywhere in the United States, but somehow I carried it off as though I was a German nudist who dishabilled all the time.

The half-Swede emerged damp from the Aegean, backlit by the low late afternoon sun. He transited from walking to kneeling to love-making in one seamless motion.

The absence of preliminaries must sound well short of five-star fornication. Yet our swift intro was not a drawback. The setting, its fantasy feel, the lack of the slightest obstacle to physical union, even the briefness and unremarkable mechanics of the encounter, added to the raw naturalness of the act.

We drove back, sometimes quiet, sometimes chatting. Mostly I just listened to the music, unruffled by my remarkable change in personal behavior. Both of us were clear that what had just happened was an experiment for me, a not-so-rare event for my driver, and not the start of any grand amour.

Thus did I put my toe in the water of random sensuality, which I always have considered entirely out of the question at home (with the exception of a single lapse, involving resentment at my first boyfriend, that had seemed unreal). No question, however, that away from home, the experience made me quake with a heady sense of being able to act on my most impulsive desires.

Six years after the beach encounter, despite no expectations to revisit

Greece, I sailed along the same coast in a chartered yacht, as Sounion's cliffs and the lapping Aegean turned blood-red once more in a lowering sun (*Amateur* 161).

The memory of my first act of raw hedonism on the sand returned to grip me, powerfully. My mind became agitated. I almost wanted to point to a spot at the harbor's western edge and blurt out, "Years ago I just went right ahead and had sex with a Greek guy over there. It was an important and strange event for me." My yachting companions would have thought me demented.

My fling at Sounion began to betray the fact that my separation from my first husband had taken a sledgehammer to an idealistic goal of unswerving loyalty to one soul mate. Underneath the glow of a new boyfriend was another layer: raw pain dating back exactly a year to the breakup. For 12 months, my period had disappeared; body and mind mourned.

My idealistic and sensual sides still wanted great lovemaking with a harmonious man, improving and deepening with time.

But a competing attitude had emerged. Now purity of feeling was a con, romance was suspect, the notion of a perfect kindred spirit was for starry-eyed youth.

Battle scarred and less devoted to the linking of sex and love, I changed. Now buried aspects of my identity surged: atavism to my French ancestors and their pride in practicing the erotic arts, further inflamed by the pagan fire of my Irish Celtic half.

Round two

In for a dime, in for dollar. The Cape Sounion escapade was only the beginning.

A night later in Athens, while eating dinner at a hole-in-the-wall eatery, a wiry young man, a Turk-Greek mix with a corona of long curly hair, sat beside me. He had the dark, wolfish look of a Barbary pirate, a bad-boy appeal reinforced by an opposite quality, boy-next-door good looks and an innocent smile.

After just a few words, we began kissing. Almost immediately we could feel each other's heat. He glanced down at his trousers. A rock-hard outline had emerged along his right groin. It revealed something I immediately wanted. "Well, look here," his laugh said, and he shrugged.

We taxied through nondescript neighborhoods to his cinder-block flat God only knows where.

The square single room consisted of two twin beds on either wall, a table bearing a neat, 4-feet-high pyramid of empty Marlboro cigarette packs, and a hot plate and sink. My lover-to-be's bed was nearest the door. A roommate pretended to sleep in the other bed, three yards away.

With mutual smiles, we stood facing each other and took our clothes off as though we were a familiar but still playful long-time couple. We needed no Barry White, no four-star cognac, no slow stroking of hair or unrushed kissing.

He smiled and stepped out of his underwear. His complete readiness was evident. The sight scorched me. With this available male stranger, what I had often been famished for at home, before and after my brief marriage, was going to happen with dreamlike ease.

I dropped my own clothes to the floor and stood before him with far less inhibition than I would feel with a man I cared about. Again I was naked, as at Sounion, without shame. He gazed at me, still wearing his gentle smile. He was about three inches taller than my 5 foot 4 self, and young, perhaps in his mid-20s.

We got into the bed. He moved with the subtlety of a construction worker jackhammering concrete. This hard banging style doesn't provide a lot of latitude for feedback to a man on how far along a woman might be. But as always, my body whooshed forward taking care of itself, a smooth machine able to keep up with or race past even the fastest male sprinters, and unfazed by what amounted to a relentless pounding of pelvic bones.

He dozed. I lay absorbing the experience, then and always unable to sleep beside a new body. He stirred with another lazy smile and glanced down, again directing my eyes with his, saying plain as words, "Look! Time for more!" He placed my hand on his shaft. Round two differed in no detail from round one.

His roommate muttered something. My bedmate said, "My frien', he want to make love to you."

"Mmm, no," I said, passing on a chance to re-shatter my personal record for shortest time between lovers, namely the 30 hours elapsing between the earlier beach frolic and this two-man bedroom. Even my newfound nymphomania determined that, having had successive days involving two men and three acts of coitus, a third man and a fourth sex session were surplus to requirements. I need to recharge for at least a little while. So I passed on the chance to have two men within minutes of each other. Yet the offer itself was still noteworthy, an example of the kind of sexual experience undreamed of at home yet utterly possible via travel.

I felt a bit sorry for the roommate, who must have been raring to go given local virility levels and his proximity to our brazen monkey lust.

Just before dawn, with both men sleeping, I dressed and slipped out unnoticed to find a taxi back to my hotel. There I breezed just after sunrise past the desk clerk, a potential source of real-world condemnation if he cared to put two and two together. Yet I had not a whit of guilt or caring about what had to be a conspicuous case of Tourist Woman Runs Wild. I was now officially an easy American lay and unworried by the fact.

Some, perhaps most, of you readers are doubtless thinking, "How stupid. One of these guys could have been Ted Bundy or the Hillside Strangler. Didn't you ever read *Looking for Mr. Goodbar*?"

Though naïve, on some level I was not a complete fool. With each man I sniffed the air and detected only straightforward lust identical to my own. Maybe my confidence was misplaced, but this was not the United States, which for some is a country of tormented sexuality driven underground and twisted. This was Greece, a land of quite horny and forward men.

It's tough to get strangled by a normal guy looking forward to non-deviant fucking. And it's not easy to be raped if you the woman want it bad.

Veteran status

Waves lapped the black sands of Santorini, a stunning half-volcano once home to the Minoan civilization. Away from Athens, three days of rest and celibacy settled me. I rented a moped and explored every monastery and archeological excavation. Left unchaperoned with my jolly and aboveboard official guide at a complex of ruins, we managed to not copulate. My explorations reverted to a more typical tameness, due to fatigue and a lack of interesting pickings.

Going from soul-mate seeker to wild thing had taken two days. Now I was a veteran. I knew the ropes as well as the Scandinavian girls.

One unwritten rule seemed to be that with so many men eager to offer their services, one could be picky. While watching the sunset from a taverna nestled in the cliffs of Santorini, an overweight middle-aged man in naval cap whose stomach pushed out a sagging blue sweater made an uninspired overture. He seemed like no more than a dirty old man. After a glance of assessment I spurned the offer, as if telling a waiter, Coffee? No thanks.

Exploring a new universe

On my return to Athens airport, the half-Swede, who had agreed to meet me, was nowhere to be found. That just increased my liberty to have new escapades.

Back at my first hotel, my pheromones must have been obvious. Under the grape arbor of the rooftop bar, a handsome waiter named Satoris showed me his name inscribed on a silver plate bracelet. His dark eyes bored into me. Would I go out with him later? We could go to his place in the northwest part of the city.

I had the bit in my teeth. Satoris was very attractive. But could I do even better, in this separate universe that offered women any pick of her choice? "Maybe I'll be back, I'm not sure though," I replied. "It's my last night here, and I want to wander in the old town."

Satoris looked disappointed. He had been put on standby at best. Off I went, down a narrow street in the Plaka flanked by open-fronted restaurants, most with bouzouki dancers breaking plates in traditional style for benefit of the tourists.

I wove my way to a seat in a taverna crammed with small, round tables topped by white cloths. One would meet one's neighbors with little effort.

Two French naval officers drank ouzo at the next table. The stumpy one had a pug nose in a ruddy face. His trim friend sported short brown hair, perfect teeth, the broad shoulders of a baseball slugger and the quick-study eyes of a thinker. Charisma shone from him. It sounds implausible, but imagine a European with a body of Marine Corps steel somehow resembling a young Jack Kennedy.

We chatted *en français*. Their submarine, the *Redoubtable*, was moored in Athens' port, Piraeus, while they roved on shore leave.

We drew our astrological signs on a paper napkin: I a *Taureau* (bull), the handsome man, Jean-Marc, a *Belier* (Aries the ram). The stubby sailor, already a fifth wheel, did not record his star sign.

We three left and went for a walk.

Out of nowhere, Jean-Marc grasped me and pressed my back against an ancient whitewashed wall. He ground his full white trouser front against me with the same mercuric ardor of my previous two lovers of the week, with added urgency born of the deprivation of a tour at sea. His alignment and motion created a white-hot sensation of near unbearable intensity. If he felt like me, in a few seconds we had both made it nearly to the brink.

The friend stood off a few yards waiting, staring into the middle distance.

Jean-Marc consulted briefly with his friend, who then departed in an air of mild resentment for a lonely submarine berth. Back at my hotel, we learned guests could not be admitted. This rule came as big news to me and I raised a fuss, though I knew it was fruitless. Why did Greek men run rampant with tourists but all of a sudden, desk clerks enforced a rule against guests?

We tramped the city looking for a room to rent together, moving west through Athens and encountering several receptionists with no vacancies. The delay felt excruciating. One can't be sure without first-hand knowledge but I think I can match or surpass a horny teen-aged boy in blind lust. At least I can't imagine anyone being even more impatient to proceed. The sight or feel of a male erection cues me right up.

Around 2 a.m., on our umpteenth try, we found a hotel and checked in to a modestly sized room with two beds.

Jean-Marc stood between the beds and lowered his trousers a foot, revealing himself in full glory, disproportionately huge for a 5 foot 8 man. I was gleeful in anticipation of experiencing a French lover but the battering ram endowment came as a happy bonus. With confidence he swung right away toward my mouth, which made cooperative and eager contact with his tip.

Leaning back on the bed, I watched with some detachment as Jean-Marc twisted my hips at an angle, arranged my legs a certain way, and commenced the first segment of the night's performance involving full contact. He mapped out a campaign for three unrushed episodes, each involving a variety of novel, often asymmetrical couplings selected by the creative maestro himself from what seemed to be an extensive repertoire. Each Kama Sutra position appeared to ease transition from one angle of attack to the next.

While so far this week, the styles of couplings could best be described as tally-ho straight to orgasm, with Jean-Marc came a new approach. Without words, he would mastermind an exquisite, deliberate, magnificent tryst.

If anything, my French naval officer proved too brilliant in the bedroom arts. He made me feel like a kindergartner sitting in at the Sorbonne. This feeling of inadequacy crept into my thoughts despite having had, to say the least, an imaginative and robust private world with my English ex-husband.

I couldn't match Jean-Marc's talent. Truth be told, I also achieve satisfaction with such ease that prolonged stimulation seems a waste of sleeping time. Yet as a French Canadian I felt reflected glory upon confirming the French reputation as premier lovers. And like a tourist photographing a leopard in the Serengeti, I felt I had bagged a different sort of travel experience, one crucial for a female connoisseur: a rendezvous with a Frenchman.

And some meanings lay almost too deep to be plumbed in the psyche of an American Roman Catholic woman who had shared a hot interlude with a JFK lookalike. The moment Kennedy's afternoon assassination had been announced loosed a nightmare upon Catholic school-children. Now a martyr whose death had been announced to my miserable fourth-grade class seemed to metamorphose into a smiling man so alive he could provide all-night amours.

In the morning we stepped into the Aegean sunlight. I grasped Jean-Marc's reluctant hand, instantly dashed by his distance.

Intimacy lesson: Real intimacy lies not in copulation but in touching, kissing and sleeping beside another, feet in light contact.

Of the trio, the slender Turk-Greek won lifelong space in my vault of fiery fantasies. His pneumatic drill attack lacked beauty or subtlety but by Zeus he was harder than granite, a powerplant of ferocious stimulation, a masterpiece of raw maleness, and a throwback to a pagan nomad doing exactly what made his body feel divine. He disappointed me in nothing.

The moment of untruth

Oh yes, I remember now ... the English boyfriend. He greeted me with flowers at Gatwick airport. "I can't believe you didn't feel tempted to make love to the men over there," he said.

I stopped breathing for an instant. I didn't anticipate this challenge to my faithfulness. You like to think that you project the image of steadfast loyalty.

But this man believed that erotic tension underlay most relationships between a man and a woman. And being well traveled, he had an inkling of what could happen over in Greece. By nature he had the European practicality verging on cynicism about sex and knew nothing of American idealism regarding faithfulness. And maybe he detected a difference in me.

"If I had," I replied with great care, eyes latching on the flowers in my hands, "it would only have been because I was thinking of you."

Wisely, he didn't try to tease out more information.

What could I tell people of what I did on that trip to Athens? I shared my tale of promiscuity in a letter to just one girlfriend, who demanded warning labels on the outside of any future bombshell missives.

For the next dozen years, I visited exotic lands. Upon my return, people would ask, "How was your trip?" I toyed recklessly with the idea of saying, "Oh, I had three lovers in seven days," to see how well disclosing the inner nymphomaniac would go over, especially in the sterile, dessicated no-sex atmosphere at work.

In the end, every time I would answer in niceties, but red-hot images saturated my memory.

Southern Europe

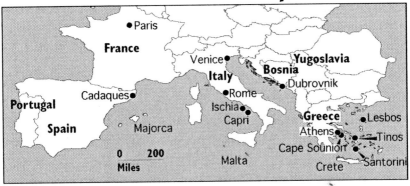

My 12-year odyssey as Sexual Pilgrim began fittingly in Greece, today's top European destination for the love-starved lady.

However, it is really Italy that, from the earliest leisure travel in the 1600s, held an iconic place in the imaginations of Northern Europeans (Littlewood 24). The peninsula provided modern history's first erotic services to tourists, both male and female.

Bedrooms in Rome likely became the first sites where women explored the delights of *amours de voyage*, and the earliest documented pioneers were an American journalist and an English aristocrat.

Let's visit the cradle of the Mediterranean, a decade after Queen Victoria took Britain's throne.

History's top destination for women

ITALY

> Italian lovers, you realize, are as easy to pick up on Ischia as ceramic ashtrays painted with lemons.
>
> Laura Fraser (195)

Lady wanna guy?

> Naples man poking his head under umbrella of Beth Ann Fennelly (26)

The year was 1847, and the place, appropriately, was Rome.

Massachusetts-born feminist writer Margaret Fuller fell in love with a Roman marchese a decade younger than herself. She became pregnant, later married him and had his son.

Two years later, again in Rome, Lady Jane Digby romped with an Italian artillery officer, an army captain and a diplomat's son over the course of a brief visit (Lovell 137). This oft-married, sexually adventurous

Englishwoman appears to have led the way in what was likely the first instance of casual travel sex.

By the 1880s, many nouveau riche young Americans had followed in Fuller's footsteps, documented by public clamor surrounding the Henry James novel *Daisy Miller*, set in Rome. Lesbians settled on the island of Capri, near Naples. Gay men, including sexual renegades among the British literati, gratified themselves in Venice and Rome (Aldrich 6, 134).

As the year 1900 approached, steady improvements in steamer and train links made getting to Italy ever easier (164). Remarkably, women not escorted by men (Pemble 78), many seeking romantic possibilities, came to predominate among foreign visitors in Italy (and in Greece and Paris, as well), John Pemble notes in *The Mediterranean Passion* (77):

> ... by the end of the nineteenth century women were outnumbering men among the tourists in Southern Europe. [E.M.] Forster wrote of encountering 'stacks of females' in Italy in 1901 and 1903; [Arnold] Bennett noted that in the drawing-room of his pensione in Florence there were fifty ladies, and a single man in a corner 'like a fly on a pin'; and women without men constantly figure in the pages of other late Victorian and Edwardian travel writers.

And these women found limitless opportunities to take Italian lovers. In the Sicily of 1896, English entomologist Margaret Fountaine (*Love Among* 87, 91) fended off numerous suitors. An Englishwoman who married an Italian of low station inspired E.M. Forster's first published novel, 1905's *Where Angels Fear to Tread* (Beauman 124).

During the Jazz Age, the shenanigans of expatriate women, straight and gay, on the island of Capri inspired two novels by Compton Mackenzie (*Vestal Fire* and *Extraordinary Women*). And by 1930, women paid Venetian gondoliers for physical intimacies, as D.H. Lawrence recorded in his most famous novel, *Lady Chatterley's Lover* (260).

By the 1950s, the Vatican museum, of all places, had become "an excellent cruising ground for the capture of foreign female tourists with time to spare and dreams of Latin lovers" (Cumming, *Love Quest* 85).

The continuity of liaisons with Italian men remains unbroken from the era of Fuller and Digby right up to the present. Today, finding an Italian lover remains effortless, as attested to by female travel writers who find lovers in Naples, the Amalfi Coast and, time and again, Venice, Rome and Capri.

During the course of two visits to Italy, British sex traveler Fiona Pitt-Kethley managed encounters with eight local Romeos. Her tally confirms that Italian men, like American women, are easy.

Journeys to the Underworld, Pitt-Kethley's "sexual Baedecker to the

Italian male" (P. Howard), describes seven weeks of encounters, involving two guides at ruins, a rock musician, a train ticket agent and a bank manager. (Three more Italian lovers appear in her 1994 followup, *The Pan Principle*.)

Why Italy's pre-eminence as a free sex zone? Numerous British essayists have tackled the question. Pitt-Kethley finds the simplest answer: the Italian man, if not a great lover, is at least available: "more willing than the British, but then everybody is" (*Journeys* 10-11).

Two other Britons, both expatriate writers, decided that Italian men are practical and flexible (even as regards sexual orientation) when it comes to intimate relations. Anne Cumming felt that "most Italian men are slightly bisexual and even the real homosexuals often finish up married. They move very easily from one way of love into another in Latin countries; no one takes a particular stand on sexual issues" (*Love Quest* 94). And Compton Mackenzie similarly believes that "the Latin individual is capable of what seems to the Anglo-Saxon a cynicism in sexual relations utterly beyond his comprehension" (*Vestal Fire* 208).

On my own trips from 1984 to 1998 to Italy, Spain and Portugal, I have always had a husband or boyfriend alongside and thus cannot speak directly about casual lovers there.

Yet it was apparent that Italian men would offer the most aggressive pursuit of a tourist female outside of Greece. In Italy alone did I find suitors materializing the instant I stepped away from my boyfriend to buy a map or oranges, a testament to the willing role for centuries of Italian men in providing free love for foreigners.

Harpooning foreign women
GREECE

Dating foreign women has become the "national sport."

Eugenia Wickens ("Review"), a sociologist studying Greek men

We can neatly place the first recorded incident of a Western woman romping in Greece in the year 1852, courtesy of the aforementioned Lady Jane Digby, who three years after her Italian flings arrived in Athens. There both Lady Jane and her maid had affairs (not without recriminations) with the same Albanian general.

Today, Greece appears to have surged past Italy and Spain as the Mediterranean's leading destination for women seeking foreign lovers, judging by copious media coverage, particularly in Britain, and a survey by a popular magazine, which found that "the most popular locations for a holiday romance were Greece and the Greek islands, followed by Spain and the Balearic Islands" ("That Holiday Romance"):

Nationality of lovers for British women having holiday affairs

British	55%
Greek	6%
Italian or American	5%
French or Spanish	4%

Source: "That Holiday Romance"

By the time of my first visit to Greece, in 1982, 130 years after Lady Jane and her equally adventurous maid, casual sex involving foreign women had long been a huge and controversial phenomenon. By the late 1980s, a Greek television documentary on the phenomenon was filmed but was "considered to be scandalous, and abruptly removed from the air halfway through" (Zinovieff 205).

And not everyone was as naïve as I about the local men, called *kamakia* or harpoons. Greek men said that American women are "direct and straightforward and may play the kamaki themselves" (209).

By the 1990s, female European tourists had become as sexually opportunistic as American women. Europeans even had their own pick-up lines: "Look at what my mum has bought me" (showing a packet of condoms to a potential sexual partner) and "I've got to use all of them up, before I go home" (Wickens, "Licensed" 157).

A Swedish 19-year-old told of how she dreamed all winter of her Greek holiday (158). "Greek men always volunteer for sex," she said, adding, "No I wouldn't do this at home, never, ever, ever. You have your reputation to think about."

In 1989, the film *Shirley Valentine* was released, depicting an Englishwoman dissatisfied with her marriage departing for a holiday fling to Greece. There a man named Costas seduces her on his boat after a little set speech about how he wouldn't dream of doing such a thing.

The release of *Shirley* made a huge impact on the popular imagination of Europe, where "Shirley Valentine" became headline shorthand, in newspapers and journals, for the lovelorn female traveler. A captain in Cyprus even named his love boat, used to seduce tourists, the *Shirley Valentine*.

Real-life Shirley Valentines negotiate a different course with Greek men than my own; they gravitate to Greece with plans of having a fling and take package tours to resorts full of experienced kamakia:

Travelers expecting a new romance

PERCENTAGE OF THOSE WHO VISITED:

Greece	19
Spain	11
Other parts of Europe	6
U.S. or Canada	3

Source: Adapted from Bloor Feasibility Study sec. 12.19

Yet not all women who visit Greece for sex seek men, as we will see now.

Sapphic love in tents

LESBOS

> **Lesbos? ... about a zillion women ... go there looking for Sappho. ... It's practically a pilgrimage. ... there are so many dykes there at the height of the season it looks like the Dinah Shore Open.**
>
> Michael in the novel *Sure of You* (45)

Some women who visit Greece seek other women, generally other tourists rather than Greeks.

In the 1970s, the island of Lesbos, appropriately enough, began to attract lesbians "in groups, in couples and alone" (Herman 242). They stayed in tents on a gray beach near Skala Eressou, birthplace of an ancient Greek poet who celebrated love between women.

By the late 1980s, novelist Armistead Maupin chronicled Lesbos as an emporium of ready sex, where both a heterosexual mother and her lesbian daughter achieve satisfaction.

A decade later, "the scene has passed from tents and campfire cooking to studio apartments and beachfront tavernas," related Deb Herman (239-40), who learned about Lesbos from Maupin's *Sure of You.* "This, unsurprisingly, has led to a warmer welcome from the locals; modern Greece is not noted for sexual tolerance, but money has a most persuasive voice ... . [Locals] vary in their acceptance of their queer clientele from slightly hostile to positively welcoming."

"Sleek, fashionable" German, Dutch and British couples predominate, with some also from North America, as well as Britons on singles tours (Herman 240, 242; Errington; Maupin 155).

Many backpackers posting on the Lonely Planet Thorn Tree (Skala Eressos; Lesvos) rank Skala Eressou as a top destination for lesbian women and a "bubble world" filled with beauties, but a dissenter (Shame on) described her disgust at unhygienic conditions around the lesbian campsite and in a showering block provided by the Greeks.

In September 2000, lesbians went a little too far in local eyes by distributing a flier for a package holiday advertising a "wet pussy" pool party and "lesbian Olympics on the beach." The mayor threatened to bar women on this British tour (Theobald) until organizers agreed to drop some of their events. The controversy split the tiny village (population 1,300), as hotel owners eager for pink money confronted a majority of traditional older residents upset by lesbians engaged in public kissing, hugging and even sex (Z. Williams).

For all its ups and downs, Skala Eressou may rank as one of only three visibly lesbian foreign travel destinations (the others being in Thailand — Pattaya and to a lesser extent Bangkok), and the only one not shared with gay men.

The men just keep on coming
SPAIN, YUGOSLAVIA, PORTUGAL

What about other Southern European men?

• Somewhere between Italy, the historical cradle of travel sex, and Greece, quite likely the current leader for tourist women, lies **Spain**.

English translator Lucia Graves, who grew up in Majorca, watched mass tourism arrive "almost overnight" in the mid-1960s, transforming "every available stretch of Mediterranean Spain" (149-57). Suddenly the plazas in Palma in Majorca were filled with Scandinavian girls and Spanish boys, the women wanting Latin Lovers and the Latin Lovers, engaged but celibate, wanting a way out of their "sexual misery."

In the 1970s, English translator Anne Cumming also took full advantage of the pent-up libidos of young Spaniards, of which more below.

In recent years, growing numbers of female expatriates (Lynch; Balentine) have had their fun with Spanish mountain shepherds, such that their resulting essays constitute a minor genre of travel writing.

• **Yugoslavia** garners a mention or two for having youths participating in Greek-style, organized cruising for foreign women (E. Cohen, "Arab Boys" 226; McElroy 191).

• **Portugal** receives only passing mention by one female sexual adventuress (Cumming, *Love Quest* 143). But I would be very surprised if the appealingly handsome young men who do folkloric dances at hotels along the southern Algarve coast don't end up with admiring tourists.

Two of the world's leading sexual adventuresses, both English writers, have tales to tell about holiday lovers in Spain, Italy and Greece.

Profiles of adventurous women
The grande dame
Anne Cumming, 1917-1993

ENGLISH WRITER, FILM PUBLICIST, ACTRESS, TRAVELER
CASUAL AFFAIRS, MOSTLY IN THE MEDITERRANEAN, NEAR EAST AND THE UNITED STATES, FROM 1952 TO 1986

In 1972, a publicist for a film company arrived in Cadaques on Spain's Catalan coast northeast of Barcelona. A veteran of 20 remarkable years of fleeting travel romances, Anne Cumming, 55, hadn't had a

young man since an affair in London ended
badly. Evenings she sat on the seawall, reading
Spanish literature aloud.

One evening, a handsome, 20-year-old policeman asked if she was all right. After debating
politics, she invited him to sit down (*Love Habit* 211).

"You are not like a Spanish woman," he
said. "A Spanish woman would be afraid to sit
alone with a man."

"Really? Well, now, I'm afraid to sit alone
without a man," she replied.

Anne Cumming

© The Estate of Peter Hujar, courtesy
Matthew Marks Gallery, New York

Cumming was the experienced sex traveler, Manuel the innocent fly
in the spider's web. She admired his uniform, running her finger up his
thigh. He took off his revolver and ran his hands under her blouse and
over her nipples.

Back in her hotel room, Cumming discovered Manuel "hadn't had a
woman for a long time," witness sex six times by 10 p.m. "I don't know
whether centuries of keeping women out of reach has anything to do with
it — but the pent-up sex drive of the Spaniards is almost alarming" (215).

Cumming couldn't say Manuel's "love-making was inspired or imaginative, but what it lacked in quality, it made up for in quantity. ... He
was very handsome, I was very lucky, and we were both happy" (214, 216).

Manuel had encountered a woman of historic stature in the annals
of sexual adventuresses. She loved young men and knew exactly how
to steer them. Perhaps it is no accident that one of the many career hats
she wore was as a translator. With Mediterranean males, she knew how
to open a conversation and drop hints, and the magic of a gentle touch.

Cumming bridged four decades of romance on the road, active
before and during the 1960s sexual revolution and continuing into the
era of AIDS. She describes first having casual travel sex in 1952 (*Love Quest*
13) at the age of 35 in Morocco, vowed in 1966 that all her sexual relations would be casual (*Love Habit* 2-3) and gave up sex in 1986 (Kenny) upon
being diagnosed HIV positive.

Her erotic travelogues, *The Love Habit: The Sexual Confessions of an
Older Woman* (1977) and *The Love Quest: A Sexual Odyssey* (1991), establish her as a pioneer. She could knowledgeably compare men (including
bisexuals) from New York to Rome, from Portugal and Morocco to Iraq
and Egypt.

Cumming was a rebel in the conformist 1950s, and though we live in
more licentious times, even today her equal doesn't seem to exist.

Married, with familial ties to the Royal Family, and the mother of
two children, Cumming would not at first seem a likely candidate for

What is it about Walton-on-Thames?

Felicity Anne Cumming was born in 1917 in Walton-on-Thames (Pulsifer), a city southwest of London in Surrey.

Curiously, fellow travel sex celebrant and famed novelist E.M. Forster was also born in Walton-on-Thames, in 1879, and in 1984 I myself lived there. The town has a rail station, nice shopping district and pretty homes, none of which solve the riddle of why any sex travelers at all would spring from this comfortable commuter suburb for London stockbrokers.

sexual adventure, yet as is often the case money and the slack moral standards of Britain's upper crust played a role.

"Most women have neither the support of a treasured nanny nor the private means" to behave in such a manner (Kenny). Few would have a tolerant husband comparable to novelist Richard Mason, who while Cumming was in Morocco availed himself of sex-loving South Pacific beauties in their grass huts (Love Quest 53).

Yet even Mason eventually concluded of his wife's Morocco excursion (featuring four new lovers), "I think that sort of behaviour is very admirable in a woman, but not in a wife" (qtd. in "Anne Cumming" Times of London obituary).

In 1993, at the age of 75, Anne Cumming became the oldest female in Britain to ever die of AIDS (Kenny) as well as the second noted travel writer (after Bruce Chatwin, who died in 1989). Not wanting sympathy, she told no one of her illness.

Thus we have no details of how she contracted HIV, an obvious question for any woman wondering if casual travel sex equals a death sentence.

Though travel sex would be one possible vector for infection, one can infer an equal risk from gay lovers Cumming described taking on home turf during residencies in New York (Love Habit 264) and Rome. For example, beginning in Rome, she had a long-term relationship with Austrian set designer Beni Montressor (Kenny), depicted as the bisexual Rudi in her books.

Despite her illness, Cumming ran an energetic salon in London (Twedwr-Moss), attended by poetess and fellow sexual adventuress Fiona Pitt-Kethley, in many ways her heir apparent.

The court jester
Fiona Pitt-Kethley, b. 1954

ENGLISH POET, ESSAYIST, TRAVELER
CASUAL AFFAIRS IN GREECE AND ITALY IN THE 1980s AND 1990s

Fiona Pitt-Kethley

© Neil Libbert

One would have loved to be a fly on the wall at Cumming's London salons attended by Fiona Pitt-Kethley. Despite being two generations apart, both surely talked about how much they took pleasure in both the sex part of travel and the writing about it.

Unlike many other travel writers, Anne and Fiona express no solemnity in retelling their romps with foreign men.

Pitt-Kethley doesn't regard herself as unique in relishing carefree holiday behavior, noting of the English, "Booze and casual sex are a must for both men and women" *(Journeys 7)*.

This free spirit seems to have a knack for hooking up with those Italian and Greek men most likely to take her to an uncomfortable place and to barely last two minutes. In Greece, for example, the first man she met, Spiros, "was awfully quick about it" (8). Nick "had slightly more staying power than Spiros, but not a lot" (60). A motorcyclist named Giorgio had problems with his aim so that things started painfully but "we managed a very brief fuck" (52).

Pitt-Kethley found Southern European men to be available but at times indifferent in skill and stamina (for additional discussion, see the Portrayals chapter). Let's look now at an overall scorecard for the region.

Following your yearnings to Europe

DRAWBACKS

• **The whore label.** A female traveler may run into the hypocrisy of a Southern European male who woos her and then dismisses her as a slut. In the Eastern Mediterranean, harsh attitudes toward loose women date from Old Testament times.

A Greek gigolo "will rarely establish a real relationship with a tourist woman, and in extreme cases he may reject her after the first night. ... Once conquered sexually, she has become equal to a prostitute" (Zinovieff 210).

Similarly, Anne Cumming was called a "whore" by her Spanish lover just for receiving a platonic male visitor (*Love Habit* 220-21). Cumming reacted with a level, experienced head. "There was no reason to try to work it out. I didn't feel guilty. We had served each other's purpose, and now the romance was over."

Southern Europe timeline

1847-Jazz Age: Italy (Aldrich 164-65) and to a lesser extent **France**, especially **Paris** (Levenstein 205-08), become the prime destinations for solo women from Britain and the United States seeking romance.

Around 1900: Lesbian colonies spring up on **Capri** (Aldrich preface, xi) and in **Paris** (Levenstein 203-04, 245).

1954: British writer, actress and traveler Anne Cumming relishes short-term but searing fornication in **Italy** (and later **Spain**, in **1972**), as well as numerous additional sites in the Near East. Her two landmark books provide the earliest first-hand accounts of casual travel sex after World War II.

1960s: "Intimate relations between Western European and Scandinavian tourist girls and local youths can be found in sea-resorts all around the Mediterranean, in Spain, Italy, Yugoslavia and Greece" (E. Cohen, "Arab Boys" 226), notes the earliest social science report on female travel sex. "Most of these are short-lived, intensive but shallow adventures, often seemingly initiated by the girls, mostly for kicks. The local boys, though they probably enjoy it, take the flow of foreign temptresses rather nonchalantly in their stride."

1970s: In a town on **Crete**, about 9 percent of marriages involve foreign women who had originally arrived as tourists (Kousis 230).

1975: Lesbian scene in **Greece** begins with a tented community near a village on Lesbos (Z. Williams; Herman 239).

1977: On out-of-the-way **Malta**, a local Don Juan-type emerges, as young men "become more aggressive toward unaccompanied female tourists, many of whom admittedly hold more permissive standards than Maltese girls. But the behavior of Maltese men is still timid by Italian standards" (Boissevain 534).

1982: Author swarmed by kamakia on unescorted visit to **Athens**.

1985-1987: Travel sex in **Greece** draws more interest than ever:

• Often poorer than the rest of the community, Greece's kamakia do not appeal to local women, who looked at them as losers (Zinovieff). They live in a macho culture that limits contact sexual or otherwise with unmarried females. Affairs with tourist women solve the men's problems.

• In **1986**, an American anthropologist (Dubisch) finds that her divorce and greater insight into her relationships

---

She left a note for her lover at his favorite restaurant, reading: "Dear Manuel, Don't think all foreigners are whores. When you're older, you may be more tolerant of me. Thank you for bringing me back to life, and I'm sorry if you feel I brought you lust without love. It's not strictly true."

• **Resulting marriages may not work.** Many of the marriages ensuing from holiday romances appear to be of poor quality. Details will be explored in the Experiences chapter.

with men allow her to take a local lover while doing fieldwork on Tinos in **Greece** — an action that would have been inconceivable during her 1969-70 stay.

- In **1987**, novel *Sure of You* (Maupin) chronicles lesbian sex travel on **Lesbos**.

1988-2002: After a century and a half, **Italy** continues to lead as a sex destination, as measured by female travel writers reporting travel affairs (Pitt-Kethley, *Journeys, Pan*; Fellner; Fennelly), incandescent romance (di Blasi; Fraser) and incessant offers (Fennelly 26; Fraser).

1988: In **Yugoslavia**, the "Dons" of Dubrovnik, "handsome young men in throaty shirts," sell "their bodies to foreign tourists," often Nordic ones. An African-American poet reports being approached by a thin young version of Robert Redford who thrust a rose in her hand, saying, "Please, for you, madame" (McElroy 191, 193).

- On my third trip to **Greece** (Belliveau *Amateur* 147-66), two sinister kamaki approach a female companion and me at a marina near Athens. My brother (burly and aggressive) responded to my calls and waves, and his fierce glare moved the men away rapidly.

1989: Film *Shirley Valentine* boosts popular awareness of dissatisfied English housewives who acknowledge traveling to **Greece** to meet men and have sex.

1991: Real-life Shirley Valentines in northern **Greece** include older married women seeking escape from "domesticity" and "family life" (Wickens, "Consumption" 820). By 1995, young ravers aged 17 to 23 also visit, in search of "one-night bonks" (Wickens, "Licensed" 158).

1993-97: British Embassy in Athens registers 22,000 citizens in **Greece**, most of them young females staying on after a holiday romance in Crete, Corfu or Rhodes. Many additional women go unregistered (H. Smith, "Paradise"). On Rhodes, 4,000 foreign women are married to Greek men (Selanniemi). Irish women marry notable number of men on Crete (Comerford).

Late 1990s: Lesbian scene on **Lesbos** moves upscale, with women now staying in hotels and guest houses.

2002: **Italy** still appears in the top ranks: Venice's gondoliers agree to a code of seduction for female tourists, with Australians and Canadians said to be easiest: "Australians will give in to seduction after one ride" (Kurosawa).

Advantages

- **Payment not expected.** Unlike poor men in the Caribbean and sub-Saharan Africa, the men of Southern Europe generally will not maneuver for cash, meals or other gifts in return for sex.

"Few kamakia are gigolos (i.e., are paid for their services by usually older women), but in some cases the hope of receiving presents, a ticket to travel, or hospitality abroad is a powerful motive" (Zinovieff 217).

While a few youths may be interested in a Western girlfriend as a means to emigrate, the vast Greek diaspora (Belliveau, *Amateur* 148) speaks to a great resourcefulness in getting abroad without the help of a Shirley Valentine.

• **Health risks lower than in Caribbean.** AIDS rates remain lower in Southern Europe than in the islands, but women *have* become infected with HIV and other sexually transmitted diseases by Greek and Cypriot men, including several who knew of their infection.

• **Promising destination for women of color.** While African-American women are most often mentioned entering holiday affairs with men in the Caribbean and West Africa, they also have many admirers in Southern Europe, in Rome (Romano 11) and in Paris as well (McElroy 188). In Dubrovnik in Yugoslavia, for example, Colleen J. McElroy, a poet with striking eyes, sculpted cheekbones and luxuriant hair, was handed a red rose by a youth. Later during travels in Italy, she received a public plea on bended knee from an Italian who begged, "*Amore,* come with me, I will make you chief dancer in my harem."

One day a handsome Bosnian Muslim sat by her on a bus, announcing, "I feel as if I know you. That I am here for you." He cast flower petals in the wake of her ferry as she departed for Italy, and they embarked on a two-year affair taking them to beaches "in Finland, Hawaii and the Northwest" (206-09).

§§§

Now let's look at a topic that follows from our visit to Southern Europe, the birthplace of modern travel sex by women. From its earliest beginnings in Italy, how extensive has sex between female travelers and foreign men become today?

What's going on?

We're on a voyage from Southern Europe, the apparent birthplace of romance on the road, to the Caribbean, also awash in foreign women enjoying holiday trysts with local men.

But before we land on Jamaica and other islands popular for sex holidays, let's broaden our focus for a moment to the world and address a question at the heart of this book:

Just how many women find new holiday lovers?

And who are they?

To quote Marvin Gaye: What's going on?

> **It's common knowledge that many thousands, perhaps tens of thousands, of women from western Europe and North America travel to the Caribbean with the specific purpose of finding a virile young sexual partner.**
>
> Lord Monson to Britain's House of Lords

> **Half are doing it and the other half wish they were. How many times are you going to be able to act on an impulse to get it on with three matadors than in the heat of a moment of your trip to Spain?**
>
> — Michael E., a Maryland traveler

My friend Michael's off-the-cuff estimate that "half are doing it" is not so far off the mark. Tens of thousands of Western and Japanese women, often as many as two in three of solo travelers in congenial destinations such as Jamaica, have intimate relations with a new partner during overseas travel.

In this chapter we will take a look at:

• How many North American, European, Japanese, Australian and New Zealander women engage in romances on the road.

- What kind of woman indulges in holiday liaisons and how many partners she has.
- The shifting extent of lesbian involvement in travel sex.

How many women engage in romance on the road?

Of solo female travelers under the age of 35, one in 250 have sex with a new, foreign partner while on vacation, indicates the most reliable figures available, obtained via a random telephone survey in Britain by social scientist Michael Bloor (adapted from "Differences").

For women above age 35, solo visitors to tropical resorts and women working overseas, the rate skyrockets. As many as two out of every three women on a repeat visit to the Caribbean take local lovers.

How do we know? By the early 1990s, medical researchers in Europe, the United States and Asia concerned about the spread of HIV began to measure the extent of casual travel sex. Social scientists curious about why so many Western women romanced men in the developing world — and how tension and dislike between the sexes fueled these encounters — conducted additional surveys.

The 21 surveys conducted to date show anywhere from 2 percent to 62 percent of women reporting travel sex. (These are described in the companion to this volume, entitled *Sexual Geography*.) The lowest figure, 2 percent, from the Bloor survey, provides the best overall estimate for female travelers and can be broken down into 1.6 percent having sex with fellow travelers and 0.4 percent (one in 250) with foreign men.

The highest figure, 62 percent, represents women who frequently travel to Jamaica interviewed in a smaller, less statistically valid survey (Sánchez Taylor, "Dollars").

Sexual Geography estimates conservatively that 8,000 American women each year engage in casual travel romances with foreign men. This figure derives from applying the 0.4 percent in the Bloor survey, with some adjustments, to the number of U.S. women who take solo leisure trips each year.

Global estimates

Can we similarly guesstimate figures around the world? Yes, by taking the 8,000 figure for U.S. women having casual travel affairs with foreign men each year and applying it to other Western nations known to have female sex tourism, in proportion to their adult female populations.

Obviously the totals charted below do not account for different age structures and cultural attitudes, so are only approximate at best.

**Female travel romances by nation, estimated,
with foreign men annually**

NUMBER

United States	8,000
Japan	3,685
Germany	2,384
Italy	1,683
France	1,670
U.K.	1,662
Spain	1,172
Canada	924
Scandinavia *	666
Australia/New Zealand	661
The Netherlands	459
Portugal	298
Belgium	287
Switzerland	209
Total	**23,761**

* Denmark, Sweden, Finland, Norway

Source: Calculations based on *The World Factbook* populations. Detailed explanation can be found in *Sexual Geography* (Belliveau).

A figure of nearly 24,000 female sex tourists per year may strike an observer as low, given the pervasiveness of the phenomenon.

Yet let us look at cumulative figures. If 24,000 women per year experiment with travel romances, during the past quarter century 600,000 women worldwide have so indulged. In these aggregate figures, we see the power of a social trend that has spawned bookshelves of women's memoirs, breathless coverage in British tabloids, medical research propelled by fears of disease spread, and evidence of a radical shift in sexual behavior and mate selection by many Information Age women.

Of course, let me be the first to repeat, before any horrified statistician does, that these figures are educated guesses, based on assumptions outlined above and elaborated in *Sexual Geography*.

Looking at these figures, for example, one can readily argue that fewer than 300 Portuguese women are sex travelers, based on only one fleeting mention (Ridout 595) that I found in a vast sea of research.

But other figures may be close approximates or in fact underestimates.

Why these figures may be reasonable — or low

• Again, 3,500 or more U.S. women bring in non-Western husbands and fiancés each year, which would suggest they are part of a large pool of women exploring foreign men in an intimate fashion, yet I am listing a figure of only 8,000 for U.S. women.

• Government officials in a West African nation renowned for sex tourism state "that many of the 130,000 tourists who visit the Gambia every year are women seeking sex with young men" (Jammeh). Here we have one nation estimating visiting females in the tens of thousands, enough to account manyfold over for our estimate of almost 24,000 female sex tourists per year worldwide.

• In Greece alone, young females, many staying on after a holiday romance, make up the bulk of 22,000 Britons registered with their embassy in Athens (H. Smith, "Paradise"), a hefty cumulative figure that would more than account for the worldwide figure of 1,662 for U.K. women.

• In Japan, the phenomenon of young women seeking foreign lovers has received intense national publicity (Yamashita, *Bali* 100-01), suggesting that indeed each year 3,700 or more Japanese women — or many more — are involved. Further, Thailand reports that more than 40,000 female Japanese tourists each year visit the sex island of Phuket alone (Vorakitphokatorn 66).

• German, Italian, French and Dutch women receive frequent mention in the literature, again suggesting that their behavior is so readily visible to outside observers because it involves thousands of participants.

• It is quite likely that more than the estimated nearly 700 Scandinavian women, nearly 700 Australians and more than 900 Canadians (especially French Canadians) encounter foreign lovers in their travels, based on extensive global reports by social scientists.

• A figure of around 200 women from Switzerland seems credible — if a Swiss woman (described in the Africa chapter) has written an entire book about her romance with a Masai warrior, surely each year hundreds of other Swiss women find foreign lovers too.

• Spanish women are indeed becoming known as sex tourists, with Internet bulletin boards discussing Cuban men as especially favored.

The weight of anecdotal evidence

A body of documentation — 800 works consulted for *Romance on the Road*, including the stories of many women, and my own observations and interviews — support estimates of travel romances involving tens of thousands of women each year, perhaps at levels far higher than the estimates I have given. Here are just two indications:

• Let's take just one tiny slice of reality: the noon hour on Valentine's Day, 2001, on one little Caribbean island, Tobago, at a table at the Trinidad and Tobago Taxi Cooperative, a beachside café. In the space of just minutes, my husband and I observed a beach boy preparing to meet his Swedish long-distance girlfriend and the same man trying to establish a quick relationship with a German woman pushing a rented bicycle. Meanwhile a couple at our table said that their breakfast companions, three young British women, had spurned beach boys seeking payment for sex the night before.

Moments later, when briefly stepping away from my husband, I received a pointed greeting from a dreadlocked, muscle-bound beach paddleball player.

This swarm of mating behavior could be seen in one afternoon on one part of one beach on a remote island attracting nowhere near the visitor totals of the Caribbean's tourism giants. One can multiply by hundreds of thousands the incidents we observed at a Tobago café to gauge what has happened since the 1960s in resorts worldwide.

• Many nations have created new slang words for participants in sex tourism, and such expansion of the tourism lexicon suggests a sizeable social phenomenon at work.

The men who chase tourist women are *kamakia* ("fishing harpoons," Greece), sharks (Costa Rica), rent-a-dreads, rent-a-rastas, rent-a-gents and the Foreign Service (Caribbean), Kuta Cowboys or *pemburu-bule* ("whitey hunters," Bali), Marlboro men (Jordan), bomsas or bumsters (the Gambia), sanky pankies (Dominican Republic).

The tourist women are Shirley Valentines (if British), longtails (Bermuda), yellow cabs (Japan) and, in Jamaica, either milk bottles if newly arrived, ultra-white and in need of filling, or Stellas if black. Female sex tourism in Barbados has been dubbed "Canadian secretary syndrome."

Martinique's national airline has been nicknamed "Air Pussy" for the tourist women it brings (de Albuquerque, "Big Bamboo" 84).

Which woman is most likely to have a travel romance?

Now that we have discussed the overall scope of this phenomenon, let's discuss the individual woman who finds herself in bed with an exotic lover. To generalize, she is more likely to be in her 30s or 40s, white or Japanese, adventurous of spirit and in a faraway locale.

Whether she is attractive and beautiful or overweight and plain, she lacks a man at home, looking at her lonely face in the mirror and wondering why her life doesn't include love. Her lack of male attention will change dramatically as soon as she lands at a distant airport — where she will become recipient of far more sexual attention than she is used to receiving (de Graaf, "Underlying Reasons" 662).

Let's look at the details. The female sex traveler is likely:

• to be from any nation in the West or Japan. In the 1960s, Scandinavians and French Canadians dominated, judging by mentions in academic and popular literature. Today, American, Japanese, German, British, Dutch, Swiss, Italian, French, Belgian, Spanish, Australian and New Zealander women also participate, and even Portuguese, Venezuelan, Korean, Taiwanese and indigenous Indonesian women have been mentioned.

• to be in her 30s or 40s (Sánchez Taylor, "Dollars" 752; Gagneux 17), although women from their teens to their 60s have been seen having travel affairs.

• to be white (77 percent in one U.K. study, Mendelsohn 44) or Japanese, though there are also some sex-seeking black females visiting Jamaica and Southern Europe.

• to be in any income range — that of a hairdresser, office assistant, nurse, postal worker, teacher, artist, entrepreneur, journalist or waitress (Gorry 76, 89), yet somewhat likely to be professional and better educated (M. Arvidson, et al., "Risky Behavior" 420; Pruitt 427). Some female sex tourists are lawyers, corporate executives, business owners (Phillips) and university professors (de Albuquerque, "Sex, Beach Boys" 95), with female anthropologists especially forthcoming about their liaisons conducted during fieldwork.

• to view herself as "attractive" and good at establishing contacts (M. Arvidson, et al., "Risky Behavior" 420).

• to have an adventurous and risk-taking attitude (de Graaf, "Sexual Risk" 1180).

• to have a history of broken relationships (94 percent in one study: M. Arvidson, et al., "Risky Behavior" 419).

• to smoke cigarettes (Bloor, Feasibility Study sec. 12.12) or marijuana and to use more alcohol than others (M. Arvidson, et al., "Risky Behavior" 420).

• if she is a Continental European, to have entered casual relationships at home (Gagneux 17) and have a history of many sexual partners, group sex or infidelity (Hellberg 143).

• if she is American, she may not believe in having casual sex and may shock herself by swiftly falling for a foreigner. For example, of 50 tourist women (including many Americans) in a survey who described being involved with local Belizean men, none traveled seeking a relationship (Gorry 76).

• if she is British, to fall somewhere between Continental Europeans and Americans. A British woman may either have many sex partners at home (Gillies 340) or conversely, be acting out of character, having much more sex than usual (Carter 337). She may also consider alcohol and casual sex an integral part of holidays abroad (Pitt-Kethley, *Journeys* 7).

• if she is Japanese, to be consciously rebelling against limited opportunities in her home society and to be seriously considering marrying a foreign man and living abroad (Kelsky, *Verge*; Ma; Yamashita).

What situation is she in?

A female sex traveler is likely to be:

- at a beach resort, especially in Jamaica, Barbados, Mexico, Greece, Africa, Thailand or Bali — and not in China, Japan or Korea.
- on a repeat trip (Gagneux 19; Sánchez Taylor, "Dollars" 753), a lengthy trip (Bloor, "Differences" 1666) or living overseas (de Graaf, "Sexual Risk" 1179).

Survey results in Jamaica and the Dominican Republic, below, indicate that repeat visitors agreed to an islanders' suggestive invitation on their first visit or warmed to the idea on their second trip. Also, women who view propositions as harassment may refuse to return to Jamaica, further concentrating sex tourists among the repeat visitors.

Repeat visitors

PERCENTAGES OF WOMEN ENGAGING IN CASUAL TRAVEL SEX

	NUMBER OF VISITS TO COUNTRY		
	1	2-4	5+
Jamaica	7%	44%	62%
Dominican Republic	18%	23%	39%

Source: adapted from Sánchez Taylor, "Dollars" 753

- not married or without a steady boyfriend (de Graaf, "Sexual Risk" 1175, 1181), though one in seven women entering liaisons do have husbands or boyfriends (M. Arvidson et al., "Types of Journeys" 410; de Graaf, "Sexual Risk" 1179).
- more likely to be on a charter or backpacking trip than on an educational program or language training assignment (M. Arvidson, et al., "Types of Journeys" 491; Hawkes, "HIV" 249).
- not traveling with a husband or boyfriend: either solo, with girlfriends or as part of a charter. (There are exceptions to this observation, however, among married women who have been reported to sneak out on their husbands for trysts with shopkeepers and beach boys.)

If I had to guess, I would expect solo travelers are most free to pursue hedonistic inclinations, a result found in some surveys (Gagneux 19; Gillies 340). A woman on her own, it seems obvious, would be readily approached by strange men and might also have an adventurous, risk-taking nature that applies to sex as well as travel.

Yet the picture is not so simple. More precisely, a woman traveling without a sex partner is most likely to respond to the attractions of a stranger (Clift, "Factors" 282; Gillies 340).

That could mean women traveling solo, in pairs or in groups, or even with children! For example, a Scottish woman, Rosemary Long ("Holiday Love"), traveling with her (grown) daughter met a new lover in the Gambia, as did a woman traveling with her 19-year-old son in Belize

(Gorry 45-46) and another with her teen-age daughter in Bali (Dowling 278).

In fact, a mother trekking in Nepal asked her sirdar (trek leader) to sleep with her teenage daughter, so that she would have an exotic and romantic introduction to sex. The sirdar (married and a father) rounded up an unmarried and more-than-willing cousin for the task (Adams 59).

• Among British women, those who traveled with friends were actually more likely than those who traveled alone to report a new sexual relationship (Bloor, Feasibility Study sec. 12.15).

This may reflect Britain's "Shirley Valentine" syndrome of women traveling to Greece with a friend or two for flings that lack stigma. Indeed, Greek men and Thai beach boys seek out women in pairs or groups, betting that these women feel more secure and thus open to overtures that might threaten solitary females (Zinovieff 208; Vorakitphokatorn 74).

By comparison, an American might enter such liaisons only with reluctance and discretion — in other words, without a girlfriend present.

Expatriates

Women who live overseas may be most consistently adventurous of all, with at least one in three taking a local lover. An extensive study of U.S. Peace Corps Volunteers found even higher rates: 39 percent reported sex with foreigners in their posting area.

Of sexually active Peace Corps volunteers, those reporting sex with locals in host nation

1,018 SURVEYED IN 28 COUNTRIES IN 1991

BY REGION

Eastern Europe	52%
Latin America	43%
Sub-Saharan Africa	36%
Asia/Pacific	32%
Overall:	**39%**

Source: J. Moore 797

Similarly, one in three Dutch expatriate women report sex, either casual or steady, with locals in their host nation (de Graaf, "Sexual Risk" 1163).

One group of female expatriates — anthropologists — has written numerous essays and books about relationships with foreign men, and their stories will be found throughout this book: Jill Dubisch in Greece, Jean Gearing in the Caribbean, Joana McIntyre Varawa in Fiji, Helen Morton in Tonga, Karla Poewe and Jacqueline Roumeguère in Africa, Donna M. Sherpa in Nepal, and Cleo Odzer in Thailand.

How does the female sex tourist behave?

• She is most likely to take one lover, though one in four sex tourists, the true veterans, take two or more foreign men to bed during a vacation (Sánchez Taylor, "Dollars" 753; Mendelsohn 44).

One woman in Belize had sex with seven local men in five months, acknowledging that "I must look like the town whore ... but I feel like this is my last hurrah" (Gorry 91-92).

In Jamaica, one woman reputedly took three different men in one night (Noakes 322). And some veterans of "fucking trips" to Belize would arrive with "lists of who to sleep with and who not to, who was good in bed" (Gorry 118).

• If she is a solo traveler, she is more likely to report four or more sex episodes on a holiday (these can be with one man or several, see Bloor, "Differences" 1666) than those traveling with friends.

• She provides meals, cash or gifts to her lover in the Caribbean or in Africa, and sometimes in Asia, but not in Southern Europe.

What happens after her trip?

• One woman in 30 establishes a long-lasting relationship with her holiday lover (Hellberg 145). Looked at another way, a bit less than 1 percent of all U.S. marriages and cohabitations began with meeting on vacation, according to a national sex survey (Laumann 235).

• One in perhaps 1,000 in high-risk areas contracts HIV. In sub-Saharan Africa, one or two expatriate or Peace Corps women out of every 1,000 display the HIV virus (Houweling 257; Bonneux 581; Eng 175), a figure that rose to one in 100 among women reporting sex with African partners (Houweling 256).

• Some number of women get pregnant and return home with their babies (Meisch 459; Pruitt 435; Odzer 272) though the number is difficult to quantify. For example, four tourist women had babies by local men during one researcher's year-long stay on a Belizean offshore island (Gorry 92).

The puzzle of lesbian travel romances

Lesbians may participate in holiday flings at levels similar to straight women. Around 1.5 percent to 3 percent of traveling women report same-sex experiences, a level a bit higher to their percentage in the general U.S. population of 1.1 percent (Laumann 304).

Though survey results indicate (indirectly) that travel romances involving lesbians occur at the same rate as those involving straight women, there is some reason to think lesbians actually shy away from casual sex, whether at home or abroad. Many lesbians I have interviewed have said they don't look for pickups when they travel.

Further, documented cases of Western lesbians hooking up with foreign women while traveling in the developing world are quite scarce. I could find only a handful of instances: primarily in Bali (Nilan, "Young People" 19; Craft 56; Runciman 159) and Thailand (Nilan 19; Hector; Houellebecq 77), but also in Kenya (Lightfoot-Klein 210, describing a part-English woman named Rocky), Ghana (T. Shaffer 40-47, describing a Dutch volunteer) and Sumatra (Blackwood). A passing reference in Maryse Holder's sexual tour of Mexico (79) indicates "only the dykes" approach beautiful Indian girls on the beach in Acapulco. Two additional reports describe instances of overtures from local lesbians spurned by Western women: in Paraguay (Grossman) and on the Caribbean island of St. Lucia (R. Jones).

One might speculate that many of the reasons motivating straight women to have casual sex overseas, especially a dating war with men, may be non-existent for lesbians, and further, that lesbians face a mighty challenge in tracking down a miniscule population in the developing world of women who love other women.

Yet even as this book goes to press, accounts of lesbian vacation affairs are growing. I have just read the first inference that lesbians have joined the sex free-for-all that is Jamaica's beaches (Bindel) and an additional confirmation of a tiny number of lesbians visiting Thailand for sex that typically does not involve payment ("Preconceptions — Removed").

Even though their liaisons may involve a slow process of seduction, single lesbians do travel to meet similar Western women. Their three leading foreign destinations are Lesbos in Greece, and Pattaya and Bangkok in Thailand. Some women seeking women also sign up for goddess tours to Greece and Ireland, take lesbian cruises in the Caribbean, hike the Appalachian trail and visit Alaska.

Though cruising may be out of favor with some lesbians today, once upon a time, lesbians did look for pickups — and they may be returning to the practice gradually. Cruising may be partly a historical legacy of the 1970s, when more than one-third of lesbians surveyed reported sex with strangers (see the Experiences chapter), a figure astronomically higher than that for straight women.

Maryland clinical psychologist Barbara R. Slater wrote to me that "in the '60s and early '70s there were few athletics, music groups, hiking groups and other organizations. For many lesbians the bars were the main means of social contact. Lesbians met other lesbians and they sometimes went home together."

Two generations later, some lesbians may be returning to their 1960s ways, by cruising — and some may be, for the first time, purchasing intimacy from foreign women.

Remarkably, at the time of this writing, the first reports of paying lesbian sex tourists are surfacing. Some German, Danish and French lesbians (see Nilan and Hector) seeking companionship have gravitated toward taking advantage of the sex market, primarily set up to service male customers, provided by female prostitutes in Thailand and Indonesia.

One can speculate that lesbians, as do straight women, confront times of loneliness due to mate shortages and that more and more they will leverage their affluence to purchase sex as a commodity. If so, lesbians can be expected to be a more visible presence as consumers in the existing all-purpose pleasure zones of Southeast Asia and the Dominican Republic.

Women's behavior in focus

An estimated 24,000 or more women engage in sex overseas with a local man they barely know each year. The elusive true figure may be manyfold higher than this educated guess. Thus a large company of women, equal to the population of a small city, each year pursues recreational sex in a way long forbidden to women.

Situations almost dictate whether women will shun pick-ups or embrace (by the thousands) the experience of travel romance.

For a happily married woman traveling with her husband in, say, China, the likelihood of a travel fling may drop to near zero.

For lonely divorcées from big European or American cities with significant gay populations, traveling solo on a repeat trip to the Caribbean, sex may be almost a certainty.

For example, I recall chatting in February 2001 with a beach boy on the Caribbean island of Tobago. Wayne had to be at the nearby airport at 4 p.m. to meet a Swedish woman returning to see him. Their holiday romance had evolved into a long-distance relationship (though almost certainly not exclusive on Wayne's part). In fact, in one survey (Bloor, Feasibility Study sec. 11.8), 5 percent of women described vacation sex that involved visiting a long-term foreign boyfriend.

"We look at solo travel, by any solo traveler, whether married or not, as being a risk factor for casual sex," says Susan Petry, a nurse practitioner who provides medical advice to prospective international travelers. "It's a red flag. You're in a new situation, and especially if there is alcohol involved, attraction blossoms.

"Some percentage in the vicinity of 20, 30 or 40 percent sounds about right," Petry added, speaking of unattached women in resorts. "Men too find sex less intimidating with the local women. But the surprise is the number of women travelers involved."

Now let's visit perhaps the world's hottest, in several senses, destination for female sex tourism: the Caribbean. Our Sexual Pilgrim will now provide dispatches on her experiences in the islands.

Caribbean men: Ready, willing and able

St. Bart's, Jamaica, St. Martin, Tortola, Bahamas

A decade spent wandering the desert of sexual exile is a long time for a healthy woman. If you pride yourself on your edgy wit and explosively responsive body, and once upon a time had an appreciative husband who was smart, sensual and the stuff of dreams, being without sex feels like a prison sentence. In a vicious circle, ebbing confidence gradually dampens the formerly electric spirit.

I knew I could cook, give massages, keep myself in reasonable shape, and provide inventive intimacy and wide-ranging conversation and decent jokes. I wanted to be a good companion, a buddy, to my man. (My father told my first husband, "You're going to have a lot of fun.") A life with no chance to extend affection seemed a waste.

My story is also that of perhaps hundreds of thousands of women worldwide, a story of anomie — of women disoriented, anxious and isolated. Many professional women live in sexual exile, with fragmented social connections. In my particular case, much of the time I worked on a city newspaper's copy desk on nights and weekends, or as a graphics editor putting in long days plus a commute from Baltimore to Washington. Ladies, know one thing: You need to get married before going into a consuming job, because finding someone while you are in a perennial state of near-collapse will not happen. Well, you may find a married guy, yes, someone at work, a time waster, and then, after a year or two or three, you will be farther away than ever from sexual stability

At age 31, after 3½ years in England, I returned to the United States. For the next 10 years, periodically I had boyfriends, often I did not. Most of the time I wandered a desert of Sexual Exile.

Caribbean islands offered occasional oases from this desert. Over seven years and five men, I found companionship that escalated in intimacy over time, from the platonic to the purely physical.

Thus my Caribbean encounters quite accidentally followed a steady course toward post-divorce healing. One could also argue that I moved from tentative, private enjoyment of black men to public endorsement of them, for at age 41 I married my second husband, a mixed-race fellow.

I really don't think, however, that I have a special attraction to black men — fine men of any type appeal. What really happened, I believe, was that I learned (on a very slow curve) that many black men seemed to like and loudly express an appreciation for headstrong, bantering, athletic and financially sound women.

And a woman needs to be good to herself, responding to men who like her rather than pining for men who are fixed on the Britney Spears of the moment. A full-figured female athlete friend of mine, with a beautiful Italian face, big brown eyes, luxuriant hair and top-rate grooming, finds herself only attracted to tall blond men, despite realizing she is a near-goddess to black men. She fears rejection by her New Jersey-based family if she reciprocates black interest.

A woman needs to know who she is, learn the leanings of the men she spends time with, and stamp out counterproductive preferences for uninterested men and petty family objections.

Slowly, my travels in the islands taught me this.

Mon bon copain Alain

St. Bart's, January 1986

God put Alain Hodge on my road.

We met on St. Bart's, one of the whiter, most French and relaxed islands in the Caribbean, a compact speck of eight square miles. My first night there, I discovered that I had forgotten to pack a hairbrush and began walking in search of a shop.

A red Isuzu pickup rolled to a stop. The driver, perhaps 5 foot 10, of medium-brown complexion with a neat goatee, insisted on helping.

I hopped in. From the first instant, we felt like old friends.

As dusk fell, he followed switchback mountain roads to village roadside stalls that sold candy and smokes. He called out in the darkness and received soft answers from female vendors. No hairbrushes.

"God put you on my road," he said. He spoke simply, with overtones of the King James Bible, and no trace of flirtation. He resolved by the next morning to find out where to buy toiletries: "I will study on it."

We returned to my lodgings. "What time do I pick you up tomorrow?" my already solicitous friend asked in a courtly way.

At 10 sharp, he arrived the next morning, having just completed delivering fresh water around the island, a job he began daily before dawn. He took me to three pleasant beaches, where he sat motionless

Alain Hodge poses in front of boats in the harbor of St. Bart's capital, Gustavia.

under shady shrubs, forearms crossed over his knees, the picture of platonic devotion while I snorkeled and swam.

"You don't mind waiting?" I asked. His generosity was invaluable, but our arrangement shouldn't resemble a neocolonial mistress idling the time away while her retainer stood by at attention.

Alain assured me he was happy. He sat still as a rock, as though a Buddhist in meditation, but with a soft look to the eyes and a bemused smile. With Alain staring at oceans of free time, my value lay in providing him with something different to do.

We went for lunch to the Santa Fe Restaurant, breezeswept on a mountaintop with views of St. Kitts and distant Nevis, a magical spot Alain suggested, and one not mentioned in guidebooks focusing on Jimmy Buffet's nightclub.

"Why are you so quiet?" Alain asked.

"I'm quiet when I'm happy."

Alain took me to dinner at his home in St. Bart's principal town, Gustavia, where he lived with his siblings. His sister, Maryse, cooked. A brother, a carpenter, worked in idyllic surroundings: He labored on sunsplashed sawhorses under a tree bearing large iguanas. Once sensed that race was immaterial in their dealings with others. They smiled warmly to see me and spoke knowledgeably about regional patterns in the Caribbeam and the international movie stars who lived on St. Bart's.

After dinner, Alain drove uphill to the edge of Gustavia, stopping at a weatherbeaten house, once his mother's and still in the family. We looked around, tiptoeing over the cracked floorboards of the porch. I took in the shuttered windows and gray, sunbleached planks and thought of how the house would look with a little work.

Alain painted me an unspoken picture. He as much as said: I am employed, available, of good family, and own property that could be made livable. I am not flashy. I am solid and undemanding. I do not hound white women; I have lived in Paris and am used to them. Nor am I a snob, expecting you to fall all over me.

He seemed to offer much and ask little of a woman except that she be comfortable in his company.

I stood on the porch as my mind projected scenes from a future on St. Bart's with Alain. He would provide a tonic after a divorce from a difficult, complex Englishman. And under Alain's wing, I could certainly get a lot of writ-

I smile for Alain in the dazzling light of Gustavia on St. Bart's.

ing done in quiet Gustavia. His solicitude touched me, gently fanning an attraction that was more encompassing than just the sexual.

My thoughts remained just tendrils of imagination, however.

When traveling in repressed societies, such as in Arab sections of Israel and in China, women often find themselves in platonic relationships with men thirsty for both knowledge of the greater world and female companionship. Platonic relationships in the Caribbean orbit are not unheard of, either, for on the tinier islands, a man's romantic choices are limited, and a tourist woman offering him conversational variety is better than nothing.

For a year after I returned home to suburban Maryland, Alain shipped me bottles of a yellow liqueur from Curaçao, one we had enjoyed together. It didn't taste as nice away from the islands.

Yet Alain put me on my road, one that led after many meanderings and reversals to another generous brown man with a goatee, my second husband. And Alain demonstrated that attractiveness of a nurturing man to a woman feeling neglected at home.

Good time Charlie

I'm not sure who put Charlie Wilson on my road, but I doubt it was the Supreme Deity.

Light-skinned, about 5 foot 7, with a devilish smile, fluffy hair and a handsome moustache, he worked at La Semanna, a resort favored by Jackie Kennedy and former *Washington Post* editor Ben Bradlee. After I flew from St. Bart's to the northwest corner of St. Martin, we kept running into each other in various small eateries, where he would invite himself to sit down and join me.

Charlie offered to take me around the landscaped grounds of the exclusive hotel, which I would have never set foot in otherwise. Like Alain, he drove me from one beach to the next. Unlike Alain, when I bent over to grab my beach towel out of his trunk, he managed a sly grab of my ass. As I lay on the beach, eyes shut, he silently crept up and tickled my lips with his moustache.

Despite my distaste for his tactics, he certainly got me hot. I lacked the nerve to do anything but fantasize about him later in bed alone. It seemed unfair that nice, handsome Alain was so proper, and devilish Charlie so forward.

Why had I renewed prudery after my binges in Greece? After all, I had already crossed a huge Rubicon for a Roman Catholic woman by dabbling in sex travel. I think, however, that I never really acknowledged this side of myself. Greece felt like an alternate reality where I could do what I wanted, fueled by a sexual confidence traceable to a new boyfriend. Meanwhile, to an East Coast American, the Caribbean was less exotic (I had periodically visited there since the age of 18), and my confidence had fled.

Driving me to the airport to leave, Charlie reached over to the passenger seat and played his fingers in a naughty place. He eased a sizable boner out of his zipper and , with only fleeting assistance from me, came. (Are these Caribbean Don Juans not getting laid? He popped like a sailor on shore leave.)

"Drink the milk," he offered without a speck of shyness, waving his hand to his crotch, his sex organ on full display. I declined and hopped out to catch my plane. But I was a step closer to rediscovering my Greece-era hedonism.

'Hey baby, wanna get laid?'

Now I was 35, eight years after my Greek bacchanalia, four years after a perfunctory hand job on St. Martin, a few weeks after breaking up with a brief Stateside boyfriend. Time to take things a step further.

I arrived via a combination of flight and ferry on Tortola, a center for yacht charters, one day earlier than my friends for a week's sail around the British Virgins.

From the dock at Roadtown, I strolled inland, casting a glance at a baseball night game under the lights. Players wore pro-style uniforms, dreadlocks over pinstriped shoulders, red garters over immaculate white socks.

"Hey baby wanna get laid?" came ringing over the field the instant I gazed at the players, to soft laughter from the team. The ballplayer presented no hazard, only a healthy availability.

I continued inland, not a tourist in sight, to an inexpensive hostelry catering to workers from other islands.

The innkeeper scowled at her lone white guest. I felt it unfair for her to judge me by first sight as a swiper of island men. Within minutes, however, the innkeeper would guess better than I myself what I would and wouldn't do.

On the landing to my second-floor room, two construction workers chatted. Both perked up at my arrival. It dawned on me, a bold thought I hadn't thought I'd been thinking, that I could have my pick. I liked the looks of the stern, slimmer, taller fellow, but the rotund, shorter man with a goatee proved easier to maneuver to my room.

A new bold Me invited the rotund islander in "for a drink."

Our interaction did not follow the more typical island pattern of a calculating beach boy carefully chatting up a reluctant tourist for possible sex that night. No, now I was a veteran. I made it much easier for the man. Up the stairs, sweep into the room, and right away have sex!

The goateed worker stood beside a clothes bureau, sideways to me, laying his underwear on the back of a chair. In profile he exhibited a big thick organ that pointed almost straight up and then curved back toward his ample stomach.

As usual after a dry spell, the entrance of a male member stimulated an orgasm pronto. Seeing him aroused had almost been enough.

There was still the matter of waiting for him. Like some other black men, he found pleasure in taking a while, and not just to help the woman along, but to just feel good, stroking his cock inside. I got on top for a while, where it was difficult to straddle his girth without straining my pelvis.

After, he told me he was married, with a wife "down island." They had no children, one miscarriage. I invited him back the following night. Like clockwork he returned and tapped on my door, but I didn't feel like trying to sleep around a huge wet spot for a second night in a row. I laid quietly, pretending I was out.

Still, the moment felt like a wasted opportunity. I thought of my interminable dry spells at home. It seemed that post divorce or post breakup, I wasted months feeling sad and clueless as to what to do. The more breakups piled up, the less I even understood how to find and assess male companionship prospects. Lonely weekends stretched into lonely seasons, times when an island handyman would have come in very handy indeed.

Loneliest men in the Caribbean

With my extracurricular mating a secret, the next day I met my friends and we began a standard sailing route, from Roadtown to Peter Island and Virgin Gorda, and thence Jost Van Dyke.

On our visit to Jost Van Dyke, I would really learn, as the men I met on St. Bart's and St. Martin seemed to indicate, that for all the Caribbean reputation as a place of underage, easy and promiscuous sex, on many islands plenty of men lacked potential partners. Only later would I learn that women around the world tend to depart rural areas for cities, in search of service and technical jobs. On the smaller islands, men who stay behind to fish have a job but no mate. Later I would meet dive boat workers on Bahamas outislands who headed to Grand Bahama on weekends, in search of women.

Jost Van Dyke rose from the sea shaped like a steep crashing wave frozen in rock, cooled lava that curved back over three minuscule settlements on its sheltered southern shores.

We anchored at the easternmost bay and made our way to Foxy's, an open-air calypso bar, well known to yachties.

Strolling around, I met Foxy Callwood's relation, Godwin, a short man with a round forehead. He invited me for a boat ride and a drink. We raced in his motorboat to the next bay west, and he casually tossed the anchor in the surf without looking. We waded through knee-deep water to the shore.

At the White Castle hotel bar, Godwin met two friends. Joe, midnight black, not tall, resembled a later-period Marvin Gaye, with his fine nose and a trimmed beard. Noah was taller, with rounded, more African features.

Godwin bemoaned the lack of women on Jost Van Dyke. There were 110 people on the island, he said, almost all men.

Joe agreed with a shy little smile: No women. Godwin teased him about how little sex Joe was getting: "It's so hard in the morning, it's knocking your forehead." My mind wandered directly to how mutually agreeable it might be to wake up with Joe.

Joe and Godwin merrily demonstrated a risque parlor trick. They bent matches carefully into various shapes and dropped water on the joints, making the figures move. After an innocent flying bird, they made an ingenious match man who when moistened pumped a reclining match woman.

Next they debated infidelity. "Any women having an affair with a married man is looking for a husband," Godwin said. I listened with keen interest, turning the words over, for I had just split up with a married man. Maybe Godwin's words were serendipitously directed at me, to understand deeply hidden desires.

"The Bible says it's wrong," Noah countered with vehemence. Here in the languid tropics, where the very moistness of the air suggested making love with anyone not grossly unsuitable, Noah preached religious-based monogamy.

Godwin motored me back to his home anchorage. He showed me his bungalow, front and side doors open to all, breeze riffling the yellow gauze curtains, two shelves of paperbacks on the wall.

He said, hinting at a past romance with a visiting tourist, that he had a daughter in Vermont. The door to his bedroom stood ajar, but I didn't agree with the Vermont woman about Godwin. As with Alain and then Charlie, my tastes ran to the handsome gentleman (Joe) and not the more-than-available alternative (Godwin).

Oh, Danny Boy!

OCTOBER-NOVEMBER 1993, THE BAHAMAS

On this late season visit, the Bahamas sat at their least inviting, cold, gray, forlorn. Early storms swept from the Carolinas to these islands, disrupting the annual autumn migration south of sailboats from Annapolis, Newport, Marblehead and other East Coast sailing centers.

Once again, four years after my British Virgin Islands sail, I was:
- alone.
- awaiting the rest of a sailing party.
- and staying in a local hotel on an all-black island!

And: kidding myself that I expected nothing to happen.

Had everything gone to plan, I would have met my friends and had a (sexually) uneventful trip. But the storms delayed their planned arrival on northernmost Walker's Cay. I hadn't budgeted for land accommodation, so I went to seek out cheaper lodging on the adjacent islet, Grand Cay, strictly a community of black workers with no resort facilities.

After landing on Grand Cay, I received (another) frosty reception from a female hotel staffer, this time at Rosie's Island Bar and Hotel. She was completely uncommunicative as to whether I could stay. I decided to wait for the owner, Roosevelt Curry, on a balcony outside Room 6 of his attached hotel. I sank into a white plastic chair.

A jukebox and TV blared up from Rosie's bar. A power saw whined and a jackhammer slammed away as workers added stairs to the restaurant dining room and a new stretch of sidewalk.

The unfriendly island woman made me feel uncomfortable. Poor weather, a stalled search for lodging, missing friends and no messages on what had happened seemed to sink my vacation into the toilet.

I considered making an immediate return to Walker's Cay, where it would be more expensive to wait out the weather. But that seemed like surrender, a white tourist unable to abide being a minority of one on an island of 300 black people.

A tall, solidly built, barefoot man arrived to let himself in Room 6. At first he masked his expression, surprised and therefore guarded on seeing a lone white woman on the cay. His gaze then softened and he introduced himself.

"Hello, I'm Danny ——— Jr.," he said in a deep voice. Joon-yuuhh, it sounded, so resonant it became the name of an Ashanti chief. He reminded me of former basketball star Charles Barkley. Thick bone and rounded muscles, boulder-like shoulders, a deep chest, a spherical head, a true Charles Barkley power ass and sculpted calves, partly covered by long shorts. Danny's white muscle shirt, on him, truly lived up to its name.

Clipped grooves formed a complex pattern in his hair. "I ask for a road, they give me a highway," he pretended to complain, when later in bed I rubbed my hand over the outline and complimented it.

"Today is my 33rd birthday," he said. Friends had flown in to celebrate, but he was tired of their company, especially the females who hadn't given him the good time he wanted. He wanted to get them on the 4 o'clock flight from Walkers Cay back to Freeport.

"I'm always ready for anyt'ing," he said, as if discussing the weather, and promptly pulled condoms from his back pocket. "I'm careful."

"But condoms aren't 100 percent effective against AIDS," I said, the cerebral, statistic-spouting American for a moment.

"No!" he barked, as he would many more times. You always knew where you stood with "Joon-yuuhh," as his Mom calls him. "They are 100 percent. If you use them right. Not 100 percent if you stay in ... ."

Danny pantomimed how you had to grasp the base of the shaft and withdraw right away.

He certainly could suggest possibilities, and without wasting a moment.

Maybe Danny knew that talking breezily about male readiness would set me alight after yet another stretch of frustrating celibacy.

Danny ran off to find a room for me. Soon Rosie, a quiet giant, arrived. Danny, now part of my parade, walked with us to a more secluded annex, a separate compound of rooms.

In silence Rosie handed over a key. He stayed outside my room, busying himself fixing a patio light and lining up the room's satellite TV connection. Danny departed to check out of Room 6.

I zoomed into my room, shut the door, lay on the bed facing the wall, and touched myself to rapid relief, perhaps in hopes of calming down so I don't feel compelled to go to bed with a stranger. Somehow just landing in the tropics after a year or so of celibacy sent me wild. I had nothing physical going on in my life at home. Even my last stretches of iffy sex, offered by a married man and a single but sexually dysfunctional fellow, were receding into the distance. A hellacious job at a newspaper drained my libido, in fact all my energy.

Trying to be nonchalant, as though I hadn't been up to anything, I then stepped out to the patio table. Danny joined me in proprietary way. In the island worldview, clearly I was in need of a man, as was any lone woman. He staked his claim, for otherwise, "Other men will bother you."

I felt self-conscious because our sexual tension must have been obvious to Roosevelt Curry, Sphinx-like as he soundlessly tinkered next with a replacement bulb.

Danny laughed suddenly. He'd noticed stubble on my legs, which I shave on an erratic schedule.

"I'm sorry," he said, but "I loves hairy women. I see you are sticky there. It turns me on. I'm sorry."

I felt molten. To my surprise, as so far our minutes-long courtship had been leading to a classic Caribbean quickie, first we took a walk. Danny conversed at length. One of 11 kids, he said he weighed 13 lbs. at birth, the biggest child of all. He was the third son and fifth child of the kids "inside." His father also had an unknown number of children "outside" his marriage. Many Caribbean families thus describe legitimate and illegitimate children.

We returned to Rosie's redoubt, where Danny picked up two diet soft drinks for me at the bar and some bottles of Guinness for himself. Back in my room, he switched on the horror movie channel and, utterly transfixed, watched a poorly produced film. He sucked on a Guinness, reclining on the twin bed nearer the door.

"When I finish this," Danny announced, "I will lie with you."

If I were back home with a man I'd known for a couple of hours, I would have felt compelled to refuse sex on general principles. But here, sex was no big deal, a pleasant way to pass an overcast autumn after-noon in the Caribbean. The ease of intercourse was part of the culture, and though with local women intercourse might come with a burden or two involving finances for resulting children, a man felt no fetters at all attached to sex with tourist women.

I glanced over in silent assent.

Danny brought two pillows over to my bed. He took off his muscle shirt and curled his body around mine, straying his hands over my nip-ples and crotch. I ran my hands over his burly chest, with its few tightly curled hairs.

"You have a great body," I told him.

"Any woman would find my body everything she wanted," he said, in a tone of no brag, just fact.

I took my clothes off. "Babes!" he called out. (He never did take the time to master my name.) He lavished praise on my body. He loved the fact my breasts weren't mammoth, like island women's.

Then Danny got down to business. He left off foreplay to expertly stack two of the pillows, placing my ass on them. He kissed my breasts and began to head downward, but I was beside myself (it had been a while for both of us, it seemed). I urged him back up with my hands on his hips, and he was persuaded to speed up what he wanted to take his time over.

He slid in, and I came as soon as his ball-bearing hips began to gyrate.

Fabulous motion marked Danny in action. Not the in-out of the white man who operates like a piston, but a swivel hips, the merry-go-round carousel of the black man.

He came with a deep island moan. "Baby oh baby." But he kept stroking. I came a second time (a third, counting the warm-up vainly intended to prevent orgasms two and three). Continued pumping, he said, was called in local parlance "helping her along" — as in, helping a woman to climax.

For 48 hours, we spoke of our different worlds. He mentioned his first daughter, whom he'd never seen, born when he was 14 of a girl, 16, who had left the island suddenly after they'd begun sexual relations.

Later, two more children came along. Then he took a wife, a waitress in Freeport, not mother to his children but with four kids of her own.

He couldn't believe I was 39, that my breasts still stood up and that I didn't have kids. To my protest that there are plenty of people on earth already, he replied forcefully, "The Bible says, you should be fruitful and multiply.

"I would love to have another baby. I love them from when they are born until they are five. I love to holds them and cuddle them and kiss them and play with them. Then you have to take control of them.

"If you were with me for t'ree mon's," he added, "and you weren't pregnant, then there's sometin' wrong."

Danny took me dancing at the Fishnet, a reggae disco. He danced bent over, his ass in my crotch as his powerful arms stretched toward his ankles, his white muscle shirt gleaming in the near dark. He bounced his ass in big loops against me. Then he danced what Americans call the Freak and islanders call wining, grinding his crotch into mine until he was semi-erect, his cock tip tapping on me so that (even after a three-orgasm day) I was again feeling thrilled. The low light of the disco turned his powerful physique into a manly dark silhouette.

This stud is my sex slave, I thought.

This isn't real, it's an lust-driven daylong sex dream.

I ground and bounced right back. "Babes," Danny announced later, "the men say you are a very good dancer."

During our two days together, we spent an impressive amount of time, for two people primarily interacting as no-commitment sex partners, actually walking and talking around the minuscule island. Gran' Caws, the locals pronounced it. Homemade cement sidewalks led to abandoned shacks by fingers of water or to random promontories. Plywood, the construction material of choice, gave the occupied homes a shantytown ambience. Some of the sidewalks made logical circuits, and others shot off to mysterious dead ends in the mangrove. Grand Cay seemed like a worn-out miniature golf course with no tees.

Some women gave me sharp looks, some men, leers. They wanted to shame me, and I didn't give a damn. After all, it was one of their own laying the pipe to yours truly. Send your sharp looks to us equally, I decided, or just to him, or stop it altogether.

Between our walks, on my laptop computer I wrote an outline for what would become my first book. For two days, this pleasant interlude of writing, eating grouper, walking, talking, watching NFL football and sex brought me contentment.

Danny asked what the laptop was for. I showed him the word processing program, then the spreadsheet software I use to balance my checkbook.

"I don't need that," he barked, with typical certitude. He grasped in a flash how a spreadsheet worked and that he would never need one.

As a lobster diver, Danny could keep all his financial reports in his head: "I need $500 each season for petrol for my boat, $300 for lobster pots." He reeled off the sums needed for boat repair and equipment and projected revenue.

His stories intrigued the amateur ethnographer in me, but time with Danny was no perfect idyll. Even in 48 hours, he got drunk, was overbearing and told me he hit women, citing the Bible, "which says women should obey."

He freeloaded. I ended up buying our last dinner of grouper fingers, soda and beer. As we ate at the table in my room, he commanded, "Pass me the can opener." I flashed with annoyance at how I was paying for everything and yet Danny tried to order me around.

Still, his role as an easygoing provider of hot sex won the day. Our second and last night, he had waited patiently until I finished watching another NFL game. I felt pleased, a bit like a sultan with a harem girl ready to please at the snap of the fingers.

In anticipation, he remained partly aroused as he waited for the game to end. I glanced over at his swelling package with a feeling of happiness and control. After I turned off the TV, he had unzipped his red-orange shorts, took his long-staying erection to full salute, and peeled off his shirt. I sucked him and then obliged his favorite position, woman on top. First I bent down flat and took my pleasure, then sat upright to provide him his.

He curled his body around me. "This is how I like to sleep, to cuddle," he rumbled in his rich baritone. "In case I wants a midnight snack," he laughed.

When younger, I had been so idealistic about sex, thinking it was best allied to love and got better over time. I didn't pretend to love Junior. I didn't even pretend that I wasn't using him, as he used me for free meals. But the freedom to just have fun together was intoxicating.

The next morning I didn't touch him. I only kissed him, once on the chest. One strange aspect of the wildest casual sex can be the coolness of the partings. In one sense it stung a bit, reminding me that this fun interlude had hit a wall. It would not lead to a long happy companionship. We had talked a bit about him visiting me in Baltimore, where he could have provided another oasis for a Sexual Exile. He seemed hopeful that I might have conceived, but our awkward impulses toward real intimacy ran aground. Yet the cool parting bespoke a freedom to to give, to take and to leave.

Still, Joon-yuuhh could move his hips like a carnival ride. Glancing down on his blackish skin as he pumped my forbidden white body thrilled. Flying home, changing flights in Orlando, I studied my daytimer calendar over and over, worried that our unprotected sex might well have made me pregnant. In which case, I wondered what I would do — maybe have the child, as I was not getting any younger.

One thing I remember Danny saying:

How when he was first married, he washed his wife's back, would cook if she was tired, and paid the electric bill and helped with the rent. In his own way, he must have been trying to say, a bit like Alain's hints, that I'm not rich, I'm not educated, but I am capable of giving affection and being loyal to someone tender.

"For me, the first year, I didn't see other women," he said of his marriage, a loyalty that dissipated once she began nagging him. He readily reverted, it appeared, to the typical island pattern of multiple partnerships designed to provide children to care for one's old age.

How does your gardener grow?

WALKER'S CAY

Of course, Danny Jr. was man enough for one's entire vacation. Yet more temptation came right along, and I saw no point in resisting a little dessert after the main course.

After two action-packed days and nights on Grand Cay, I headed back to the marina hotel on Walker's Cay for news of my friends, to learn only that they had radio'd that they were "having problems" before the airwaves went dead. Indeed, later I learned that they had gotten caught in a gale and limped their broken boat into South Carolina.

My sailing vacation had disappeared.

To pass the time, I signed up for diving lessons, and spent my days looking at barracuda, huge Nassau grouper, bull sharks, nurse sharks and eagle rays. My dive instructor, the Jeri-curled Barry Albury, was a dear man, who declared affably that he greatly liked the ladies but was now married. That was fine. It seemed I was back to Situation Normal with men, that is, unexpected sex not lurking around every corner. Walker's Cay seemed to offer a chance to compartmentalize. On Grand Cay the time-space continuum briefly allowed casual coupling, and Walker's was a return to the real world, "back to work," no hanky-panky, or so I thought.

After a few evenings of good behavior, I watched Monday Night Football in the lounge, having to head home the next morning without any sailing.

A hotel gardener, a short dark man in a knit hat, sat down beside me. Happy, carefree and almost simple minded, he seemed like Adam before the Fall, innocent in his pursuit of desires.

He gave me a playful noogie in ribs, and we left to take an impromptu tour of the gardens he tended. We walked up some flagstone steps in the dark to a hilltop. He turned and pressed his front against me, suddenly breathing sharply, diamond hard pressed against my lotus. I didn't object. I was beginning to savor the idea of instant carefree union. There was mighty power in saying to society, "These are MY rules, and I can do what I want with a man."

"You go back to the room, I'll go back a different way," he said, indicating that as a staff member (no pun intended), he couldn't openly visit guests in their rooms. "I'll knock in five minutes."

He arrived as promised. I let him in. Soon he was wearing nothing but his big smile. He stood in the dark beside the bed as I pulled the cover out of the way and leaned back on the sheets.

We were Adam and Eve, no sin, no obstacles, straight to physical satisfaction. Well, one minor delay. The gardener, of small endowment, balked mildly at the condom I provided, but eventually rolled it on.

He climbed aboard. Despite Danny's services earlier that week, I came so quickly, it startled him.

He felt the snapping hard grips, the pussy like a clamp. He rose up slightly on his arms. "Already?" he said, his voice rising in an adorable tone of confusion and delight. "Yes," I nodded with a little grin.

He took much longer. I ended up drenched by the sweat pouring off him, feeling mildly annoyed and thoroughly selfish — once I was satisfied, I thought he should hurry up and do the same before perspiring rivers over me.

When he finished, I all but pushed him out the door, laughing nonetheless, and raced for the shower. Thanks for excellent physical release, and you can go now. I wanted (at the time) a man in my bed but not in my life, as my girlfriend Kasey once said. I didn't want to sleep with him. And because of him I slept well.

At breakfast the next day, the gardener greeted me with an overjoyed grin and handed me a passport-sized photo of himself, taken at a machine kiosk.

Now I wonder if the gardener and the handyman and Danny and Charlie only episodically had sex, because their bodies had seemed so starved for a woman. Or maybe having a white female tourist who required absolutely no courtship or seduction just made their day.

But Caribbean men, whether I can name them all or not, kept me "in the game" during my Sexual Exile. Alain treated me like a lady, and Charlie began to tickle my sensibilities. The handyman did the job, confident and opinionated Danny shared his body and his stories, and the gardener delivered simple and straightforward satisfaction.

God put them on my road, and eventually that road would wind its way out of the lonely territory of Sexual Exile – but not without one more round of shenanigans, in Brazil.

The Caribbean

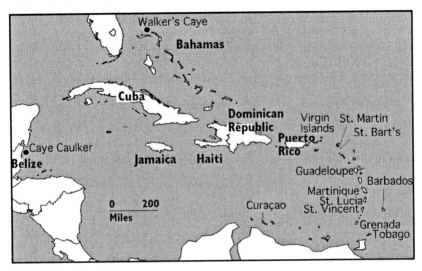

Enter into the spirit of life on the island, Mrs. Amron!

West Indian man seeking sex from an American woman (Marshall 423)

My oh my, whatever obstacles exist to ready sexual gratification back home certainly tumble for the tourist woman in the heady atmosphere of the Caribbean.

Today, these New World islands lead the globe for female sexual adventuring, with more than half of repeat visitors to Jamaica, for example, indulging themselves with local men. Tourist women from lonely Western cities discover an alternate cosmos brimming with almost limitless sexual opportunity.

How do my encounters in the 1980s and '90s with five Caribbean and Bahamian men fit into a larger picture?

First, my liaisons materialized nearly a full century after the first visits to the Caribbean by affluent white women seeking discrete servicing by local men, and decades after numbers of female sex tourists began to build in the 1960s and 1970s.

Second, the fact that my frolics began in Southern Europe and progressed to the Caribbean parallels, by happenstance, the order in which female sex travel appeared in these regions.

Third, my preference for Caribbean sailing destinations and French-influenced possessions took me far from the Big Three Destinations for road romances: Barbados, Jamaica and the Dominican Republic. So I only learned later, as I began research for this book, that thousands of other women romped in the Caribbean, usually with lovers lacking an education and a job. Yet even away from the Big Three, I readily managed to encounter lovers, not one a beach boy, ready to show a foreign woman a good time.

And fourth, I unknowingly demonstrated some sort of ancestral memory by flying to the Caribbean to indulge (even unintentionally) in vigorous, uncomplicated coupling — for French Canadian women in the 1960s appear to have spearheaded travel to what would over time become a booming region for romance on the road.

In this chapter, after a historical note, we will look at the Big Three destinations and then explore the situation on less-touristed islands. Finally, we will see how sex with local men may offer the female visitor her most facile means of exploring the authentic culture of these islands.

Risky business a century ago

In the late 19th century, we hear the first whisper of naughty behavior in the islands, as:

> ... older white women [came] to winter in Bermuda, the Bahamas, and the U.S. Virgin Islands. The stuff of island legend, these well-heeled women arrived with steamer trunks, took up residence in large quarters, and tapped young black males to service them discreetly for the duration of their stay. (de Albuquerque, "Big Bamboo" 83)

Oral history holds that these older women took great care to draw "minimum attention to themselves and their companions."

Apparently they succeeded in their quest for secrecy. While the historic record shows many instances of Victorian ladies more than a century ago permitting the men of Southern Europe, the Near East and Asia to take liberties, further information on the Caribbean proves difficult to obtain. Possibly this reflects modest tourism in the islands prior to the Jet Age, whereas Victorian Englishwomen and Americans swarmed into Southern Europe and more distant lands in great numbers. Another factor, given how pioneering female sexual explorers in Eurasia and Africa tended toward princes, counts, chiefs, rajas, nawabs, sharifs and sheikhs, may have been the obvious absence of royalty and a warrior class among the Caribbean's slave descendants.

When the Jet Age began in 1958, however, one group swiftly made the Sunny South their own playland: Women from Quebec, an easterly Canadian province that appears to empty each winter and send much of its population to Florida, Belize and the islands proper.

Foopin' with French Canadians

> ... French Canadians, about whom there has been considerable research, consistently demonstrate [sexual] attitudes that are more accepting and permissive than other Canadians. ...
>
> Barrett (333)

> ... Beach boys in the Dominican Republic reported significant nationality differences with the French Canadian women being the easiest to meet and also the most liberated in terms of sexual values and sexual practices.
>
> Herold, "Female Tourists" (985)

> [For Caribbean hustlers,] a wealthy attractive French Canadian in her 30s tops most lists.
>
> de Albuquerque, "Big Bamboo" (84)

> "Quebec women think we are better at sex."
>
> Dominican Republic beach boy qtd. in Herold, "Female Tourists" (982)

The men of Barbados knew an opportunity when they saw one.

In the 1960s, young men began to prowl the beaches. They avoided young, white Americans, who tended to be ignorant of the rules of the game: cash, gifts or meals in exchange for sex (Karch 257).

Instead, they pursued a more promising target: the sporting *française canadienne*:

> Dem girls does come down here specially for fun and games. Dem girls does boast to their friends back home of the sweet foopin' we guys does give dem. (Island man qtd. in Karch 252)

Other Caribbean men told one researcher that French Canadian women have "prodigious sexual appetites and a correspondingly inexhaustible supply of gifts." In fact, the beach boys of Martinique termed Air Canada *Air Couconne*, or Air Pussy (de Albuquerque, "Big Bamboo" 84).

This French Canadian playfulness with black men seems quite plausible. Random examples of such liaisons cropped up constantly during my investigation for this book — even a case of a Zulu prince who unlearned African male chauvinism from a French Canadian lover (Patta). And of course, my own marriage also reflects this compatibility.

American, British and German women swiftly caught up with French Canadians and now dominate mentions of sex travel in the Caribbean.

Italian, French and Scandinavian women, as well as Spanish, Japanese, Belgian, Dutch, Swiss, Australian and New Zealander females, have all been sighted with Caribbean men.

Female journeys in search of loving echo travel patterns based on geographic proximity (such as Americans visiting the Bahamas) and colonial ties: the English going to Barbados and Jamaica, the French to Martinique, the Dutch to Curaçao (Pattullo 9) and the Spanish to Cuba.

Bopping with black Americans

JAMAICA

Not long after French Canadians paved the way in Barbados, African-American women made Jamaica their sexual playland.

"For years, since way before Stella got her groove back, women have been traveling to tropical islands for some R&R only to find themselves swept up in a crazy fling they swear they'd never let happen in their 'real lives,' " Jeannine Amber (102) wrote.

"Even Mrs. Brown, my friend's mother, tells me she got it on with a beautiful Jamaican man in 1974. Back then, Mrs. Brown says, 'Everyone knew Jamaica was the place for women to have affairs. I had propositions all over the place and flattery, flattery, flattery.' "

Beach boys make the popular resort of Negril their headquarters. Here author Terry McMillan found herself a real-life husband (see timeline in Reasons chapter), though he was a hotel worker rather than a beach boy. Her novel *How Stella Got Her Groove Back* boosted visits by black Americans (de Albuquerque, "Big Bamboo" 85). Black women still appear to make up a significant portion of sexual adventurers in Jamaica, perhaps one in five (O'Connell Davidson, and Sánchez Taylor, "Fantasy" 54).

As of today, Jamaica attracts not just women from North America but also women from much of Europe and Japan, suggesting that the reggae island rivals Italy as a hedonism destination for women.

Today the scene at Negril sounds a bit out of control. A hotel frequented by German women includes a male "guide" in the room price, and a glass-bottom boat driver procures men for tourists who "tell me what he should look like, smell like, even fuck like" (Bindel).

To many tourists, the Jamaican man represents "the archetypal masculine," and black women further see him as "the black man who stands closer to his African heritage, in this case embodied in the Rasta identity" (Pruitt 430). He loves sex, fathers children and projects an image as a raw, natural man, happy to express his attraction to a woman. As reggae star Peter Tosh sings in "Glass Houses," "Respect the Rastaman, 'cause he's the only man left on creation."

Caribbean men: How good in bed?

After Barbados and Jamaica comes the final island of the Big Three: the Dominican Republic, North America's answer to Thailand, where beach boys push themselves to establish a reputation as the best lovers in the world.

Happy women spread the word. For example, a hotel manager reported receiving many faxes such as this addressed to his staff:

> **Dear Pablo,**
>
> **I had such a great time. Hope you can show my girlfriend a similarly nice time when she comes to the DR on vacation next week.**
>
> Forsythe, "E-Mail"

Tourist women would return "from vacation and [refer] their girl-friends toward certain men [with whom] they could engage in sexual relationships during their vacation" (Forsythe, "E-Mail"). The fact that the Dominican Republic receives a good number of purposeful female sex tourists may explain why more of its first-time visitors (18 percent) enter into new sexual relationships with local men than in Jamaica (7 percent, adapted from Sánchez Taylor, "Dollars" 753).

This is not the only regional vacation spot where visitors share recommendations: on Belize, some tourist women also arrive with fuck lists (Gorry 118).

The Dominican Republic's many Pablos specialize in good oral sex. They "attempt to provide the woman with the 'best sex' she has ever had:"

> They want the sexual encounters to be a truly memorable experience for the tourists. Consequently, the beach boys focus more on sexually pleasing the tourist than on pleasing themselves. For example, they may perform all night with the goal of giving the woman several orgasms. (Herold, "Female Tourists" 988-89)

These remarkable sexual athletes raise an overall question: How good are Caribbean men in bed?

Based on the experiences of many Western women, island men at minimum provide robust sex the moment you want it. And many know inventive techniques and have physiques designed to impress. The only island that tends to draw steady complaints is Jamaica, where tourist women report having to teach local men oral sex and the fine points of foreplay (Bindel).

Caribbean women, however, find their own men wanting, which has misled many academics into generalizing that even non-Jamaicans are lousy lovers who, for example, don't provide oral sex (despite abundant evidence to the contrary, especially in the Dominican Republic). Below, you can view a profound disparity below between quotes by tourist women compared to those from academics and Caribbean women.

West Indian lovermen: Terrific ...

When we made love, I realized that his fantastic "skills" probably had never been appreciated before. I still find his tender messages on my answer machine, and I think that I will go back to Guadeloupe, ASAP.

Susanne K., describing her Martiniquan lover to the author

... Women told [the Dominican Republic beach boys] that they have never had such enjoyable sex in their lives ... . The beach boys view providing pleasurable sexual experiences as another means of encouraging the women to fall in love with them.

Herold ("Female Tourists" 989)

Handsome, physically fit, 27-year-old, honest, proud, serious, family man, excellent lover.

Tourist describing her Jamaican boyfriend (qtd. in Sánchez Taylor, "Tourism" 47)

[If] Caribbean men are so bad in bed, why is it that beach bumming is an occupation that brings droves of foreigners to our shores every year?

Bajan man (qtd. in de Albuquerque, "Sex, Beach Boys" 102)

Affectionate ...

Three women describe their boyfriends on Caye Caulker, Belize (Gorry 158):

When I sleep with Clide he's always reaching out to touch me, to hold my hand. He'll hold it all night long. — Karen

We always fall asleep hugging each other. — Julie

I really like my Rasta friend. He's not the best lover I've had although it's good with him, but I just like him. [We] spent a whole month together and made love at least two times a day, more than once each time. — An American woman

Improving ...

Changes in heterosexual practices are ... taking place. ... Today the missionary seems to be the preferred position, but one cannot be too sure.

With the spread of VCR technology and exposure to the influence of blue movies, many Jamaicans are experimenting more.

Chevannes (38)

Mechanical ...

He knows a lot of positions but there wasn't much caring in it — at one point he was telling me to do this and that and I just said, stop, this isn't working; there's no emotion here.

Sharon describing her boyfriend on Belize (Gorry 52-53)

... or lousy?

They have this big thing but they don' know how to use it.

Trinidadian woman named Gina (qtd. in Stewart, *Weather* 14)

Like most West Indian males, beach boys prefer straight sex; few deviations from the missionary position, and no cunnilingus. ... Foreplay is limited. The sexual service provided is clearly permeated with emotional indifference.

de Albuquerque ("Sex, Beach Boys" 102)

A reality check on sexual mores in the Caribbean — these are predominantly male-dominated, sexist, homophobic societies that consider anything but straight heterosexual intercourse dirty. So the "big bamboo" is probably all you get. The men in Jamaica refer to sexual prowess as "kill dem wid it."

Letter to the author from a researcher

In general, men feel a desire to please when they receive tender attention and encouragement, rather than criticism and rejection. A poor Caribbean man, considered one of life's losers by his own women, may pour his best efforts into pleasing a wealthy tourist for whom his financial status is of much less relevance.

As my husband Lamont says, "The most important part of sex is not oral sex or technique. The most important part of sex is that the person you are with is really into it."

He added: "On any island people are bound to get sick of each other due to a lack of [a pool of] potential partners."

Thus female tourists and Caribbean women may both be correct in their views of Caribbean men, who only assume a role as hot lovers with the tourists, much as the tourists only assume the role of eager, confident, highly sexed women with their Caribbean men.

Wayne's world

Beyond the Big Three sex destinations, Barbados, Jamaica and the Dominican Republic, women carouse abundantly even on islands where holiday affairs are not quite so flagrantly public.

I have described my own romps on St. Martin and Tortola and in the Bahamas. Other women and social scientist observers describe dalliances on Cuba, Virgin Gorda, St. Vincent, Bequia, the cays off Belize, Grenada, Martinique and Guadeloupe (Belliveau, *Sexual Geography*).

In February 2001, my husband and I visited one of the Caribbean's more quiet and traditional islands, Tobago, where Lamont's mother co-founded a community college.

A bike ride away from my mother-in-law's home, along a south-westerly peninsula beside Storefront Bay, we viewed low-key hustling, more muted than found in the Big Three.

Around noon on the day of our first visit, we saw three fairly typical beach boys, with either dreadlocks or super-tight Speedos or both. One man in his late 20s, however, chose a more conservative image.

Wayne K———, professional and polished, wore neat, short hair, a polo shirt and well-tailored, knee-length shorts.

"Do you want a guide to the island?" he asked us, handing over a well-organized photo album containing his own snapshots of natural splendors on Tobago, the blossoms of its immortale trees a screaming red. One picture showed him in a skimpy bathing suit, laughing as he stood in a crashing waterfall hugging a grinning blonde woman in a bikini. The clear implication: that he could fill a female tourist's island fantasies.

Still, he seemed to find the option of guiding us, a married couple, around for the day preferable to negotiating a more complex relationship with a single female.

For once, in dealing with a Caribbean man, I had a husband right by my side. This did not entirely keep Wayne from a tiny touch of flirtatiousness in his sales pitch, which I sidestepped with a proposal of my own. "We're OK with riding our bikes and taking buses around the island," I told him. "I would like to talk to you about ... being a beach boy."

"She's writing a book about men and tourist women," Lamont said with a wry smile at how, turning the tables, I had put Wayne on the spot.

Wayne took a breath and with admirable candor replied, "It takes a big man to admit that he's a beach boy. You can take me to dinner. I like lobster."

We all laughed. For all my adventuring in the Caribbean, Wayne was my first up-close look at a proper beach boy. As it turned out, we didn't need to wine and dine him to learn how he operated. Wayne stayed in character, zipping away briefly from our small talk to chat up a short, heavyset German woman with limp hair and a plain face, who smiled at Wayne's attention.

On our second visit to Storefront Bay, Wayne greeted us with warmth and recognition. He sold us discounted tickets for a boat ride to the (ruined) offshore reef. He mentioned that he had to leave at 4 p.m. to meet a Swedish girlfriend arriving at the airport. He planned to take her to a lovely, secluded hideaway: "We'll go to my grandmother's house on King's Bay."

Lamont teased him about the rendezvous. "Now you're saying things about me!" Wayne hollered to his appreciative friends under the beachside trees.

"Oh no," I told him, "we heard only that you are a choirboy."

"He was pretty slick, carrying his presentation around of him and women," Lamont reflected later. "The message was, 'I'll show you around and then I'll have a little fun.' "

Apparently Wayne had company in his professionalism — and Tobago had more sex tourism, involving European and North American women, than met the eye. "The trade is run with business-like efficiency by 'tourist agents' and unlisted guest houses, with advertisements in European magazines announcing 'package deals' including the services of a local male or female" (Gibbings). In 1995, a Swiss visitor known as Simonetta was deported "after announcing on the local television news that she was HIV positive and had engaged in unprotected sex with numerous local men."

On little Tobago, once little touched by HIV especially compared to nearby Trinidad, reports linked female sex tourism to the appearance of HIV in almost very island village. Yet without good medical detective work, one had to wonder whether this claim (also made, and disputed, in Kenya) holds up.

Still, romances on the road here (as elsewhere) have resulted in at least some local benefit. My mother-in-law, Dr. Cynthia Harvey, told us of a student at her community college whose much older foreign girl-friend pays his tuition.

Sexual geography: Language and intimate encounters
ENGLISH- AND SPANISH-SPEAKING ISLANDS

The early island leaders in female sex tourism, Barbados and Jamaica, are English speaking and "predominantly Protestant countries, where males and females come of age in their early teens and sexual mores are more relaxed" (de Albuquerque, "Sex, Beach Boys" 94).

Until recently, the Spanish-speaking islands, "sexually more restrictive Catholic countries," serviced male sex tourists only, but anti-government campaigns against gay sex tourism seem to have left beach boys who became homosexual mainly for economic reasons no choice but to switch their attentions to tourist women, who report overwhelming flattery on Cuba, "an island full of gorgeous men calling you *linda* [pretty]" (Griest 48).

Fidel Castro's Marxist experiment, and Cuba's economic ruin, drew notoriety in the 1990s as it became one of the cheapest places in the world for male sex tourists.

Now female tourists, especially from Britain, Germany and Italy (Sánchez Taylor, "E-Mail") have also discovered Cuba. They share stories on the Lonely Planet Web site's Thorn Tree discussion area.

One British woman (Yes It's Sex), who described herself as average looking and in her 30s, posted that she visits Cuba twice a year to look over the island's young men, finding a different partner each time.

A Spanish woman (Sex ... or a Misplaced Need), in her 40s and self-described as a veteran of casual affairs in the Caribbean, chimed in to say that the women of her country find Cuban men extremely attractive, and told of her holiday flings with two gorgeous men, one in his 20s and one in his 40s.

She suggested delicately that the younger man in particular had a lot to offer.

Another Spanish-speaking island, Puerto Rico, falls into a category of its own. "There is a small but vital gay scene," Marianne Ilaw told me ("Interview"). Heterosexual women are able to find holiday sex, she said (stressing that she does not take up offers due to fears of disease and potential heartbreak), but out of pride Puerto Rican men do not expect dinner in exchange, as on poorer islands.

Spanish is also the language of the popular Dominican Republic, although many of its beach boys are actually French-speaking Haitians, dark black "Greek gods like Michelangelo's David," a female Dominican consular official told me.

And what about the ...

French-speaking islands?

Four main islands remain not only French-speaking but also under overseas French administration: Martinique, Guadeloupe, St. Bart's and the western half of St. Martin.

Only a tiny number of beach boys conduct business on these four islands, according to women I interviewed. But as I personally found on St. Bart's and St. Martin, propositions still stream in from men with decent jobs not involved with tourism.

In the spring of 2001, Susanne, a 45 years "young" international recruiter in Dusseldorf, Germany, spent three weeks in Guadeloupe. She e-mailed me that, as one of the few single women visitors in the off-season, she would have expected to monopolize:

> the entire interest of beach boys (as I experienced it in Jamaica), but there were very few — only about five in three weeks. Their approach was very courteous and therefore much harder to refuse than the Jamaican bluntness. When they invite you for a drink, they will pay (don't forget, it's France!).

Affluence in part explains these islands' relative invisibility on sex tourism maps. As with French Polynesia compared to other South Pacific entities (Belliveau, *Amateur* 134), heavy subsidies prop up relative prosperity in the French Caribbean, which enjoys a standard of living as good as or better than Barbados and Trinidad and far above that of Jamaica, Cuba, Haiti, St. Lucia and the cays off Belize.

France's islands are known for modern hospitals, better roads than in the rest of the Caribbean, finer food and a high cost of living. Islanders are citizens of France, eligible for many social services. On St. Bart's, my escort, Alain Hodge, told me his brother was flown to Paris for leg surgery.

Marianne Ilaw, who has visited most of the Caribbean, told me ("Interview") that although the men of Martinique rank high "in terms of sheer beauty and attraction," American women will find Martinique "not very welcoming," especially compared to Jamaica and Dominica.

"It's hard to get to meet people, unless you speak French and have French ancestry. The men don't flirt with you, they expect you to fall all over them." She said a woman could expect to "have exquisite meals and no one to talk to," unlike the "places you are guaranteed to meet men," including Jamaica and Barbados.

She found much to admire, however, on French-speaking St. Lucia. The men, she had written earlier ("West Indian Men" 137) "were pretty smooth; well, you know, those Creole cultures have that extra little continental twist. I met men who would bow at the waist and kiss my hand, a guy who crooned to me in French under a palm tree one evening, and a bunch of mannerly teenage boys who plucked hibiscus blossoms and fresh coconuts for my approval."

Now that we've looked at scenes from many of the islands, let's turn our attention to the resume of another British woman who, like her sisters Anne Cumming and Fiona Pitt-Kethley in the Mediterranean, kissed and told and thus offers us details on Caribbean sexual sociology.

Profiles of adventurous women
A blonde busy
in the Caribbean
Lucretia Stewart, b. circa 1954

Lucretia Stewart

© James Hamilton

ENGLISH JOURNALIST, TRAVEL WRITER, NOVELIST
CASUAL AFFAIRS IN THE CARIBBEAN, FAR EAST

In England, when journalist Lucretia Stewart told her male friends that she was Caribbean bound, they responded with "expressions of prurient complicity and nervousness" (*Weather* 71).

Clearly Stewart's friends knew, better than she herself, what truly lay in wait (no pun intended) for an unaccompanied, 40-year-old white woman with a sensuous mouth and a shock of platinum blonde hair.

She soon fathomed the "apparently indiscriminate desire, of black men for white women." A Frenchman on Martinique told her looks and age didn't matter, "what really interested Martiniquan men was that I was a white woman" ("Weather" 145).

First came Alec, a Grenada man marking his 65th birthday. (One begins to wonder, as Danny told me the day of our meeting was his 33rd birthday, if this is a Caribbean pickup line.)

She told him 65 was too old for her. He replied that "an old gun could shoot just as well, the bullets went just as straight" (49).

During an evening stroll, they kissed, and "desire became imperative. I untied the sarong from my waist and spread it, like a sheet, on the grass." She learned Alec had been correct: "An old gun could shoot just as well" (50).

Next up: Theo, a handsome male nurse on Martinique (140-43). Touring the island together and swimming in the ocean in the rain dissolved into an almost wordless agreement to have sex in a secluded mountaintop house.

A restaurant proprietor named Raoul on Marie-Galante, south of Guadeloupe, provided fiercer sex. As with Alec and Theo, negotiations were minimal. Raoul came to her hotel and announced "that he had something he wanted to show me" (170).

Stewart involved herself as well with Neville, an islander of Italian or Spanish descent (87-88). "It was rapidly becoming clear to me that West Indian men, black or white, were quite unlike the sort of men that I was used to. They combined ease and an immediacy about sexual matters which was incredibly relaxing, although there was a veneer of gallantry and romanticism which concealed a hard core of chauvinism."

Stewart does not display the casual ésprit of two other English sexual adventuresses, Anne Cumming and Fiona Pitt-Kethley, who prowled Southern Europe and the Middle East.

In fact, she expresses an unintentionally humorous determination not to be lumped in with the dreaded lower orders, the female sex tourists.

She told an interviewer (Rogers), "I loathe the idea of sexual tourism, and there was no exploitation of any sort on my part. Everyone I went to bed with was middle class; there were no fishermen or anything like that."

It's as though she slaps down the fastidious dating rules of Home Counties Britain onto a vacation spot. Thus Stewart finds a 50ish Finnish woman on a Bequia dance floor to be out of bounds and harshly compares her to a reviled plant: she "twined herself like poison ivy around a young black boy" (71).

Later a fantasy moment presents itself when a youthful Anguillan on the beach brushes off her declaration that she is too old for him (93). He stalwartly replies that older women are "more sensually experienced."

She sends the lad packing. "That's very kind, but I don't prefer younger men."

One wonders, what is the point of having sex in the Caribbean with middle-class, middle-aged (or even elderly) men? It seems positively bizarre to sleep with a 65-year-old man given the universality of choices in the Caribbean. As my husband Lamont said when told of Lucretia and Alec, "You don't order a New York steak in Italy."

Stewart's acceptable partners seem to be a more dissolute bunch than the spurned young Anguillan. They slam back rum (49-50), seem to hate women (175), resemble "a Mafia hit man" (88) or take her to a squalid house for afternoon sex (142).

Still, Stewart picks up the local sociology well, encountering three themes conspicuous to any female tourist in the Caribbean:

• Sex is a natural act, marked by "ease" and relaxation.

• Sex is unrelated to love and marriage. She detected no notion of a conscience in sexual matters, "Or rather the idea that love and sex might be connected was alien" (42).

• Sophistication rules on the French islands: Nudity is acceptable, unlike on "the Anglophone islands, where Christianity had dictated that nudity was provocative and offensive (a modesty that had no apparent effect on the sexual mores of the people)" (130). And unlike men on poor islands, concerned with survival, Antillais can afford to be interested in "clothes, jewellery, cars and white women" (180).

Sex with Caribbean men might feel like "a radical act," Stewart felt, but it was also easier and more relaxed than with American or British males. She noted the hallmark of Caribbean sex: its spontaneity.

> With West Indians I didn't feel judged and found wanting. Because sex appeared to be so casual, so much more spontaneous (rather, I imagine, as gay sex was supposed to be before AIDS), it didn't seem to carry with it the weighty implications demanded by more lengthy courtships; sex was part of life and a pleasure ... . (89)

As other women have noted of Brazil, "Male lust rarely felt threatening — and this was the reverse of what I had expected. If I wasn't in the mood, someone else would be."

Views on sex: Barbadian men

"A natural act."
"I think it is natural."
"It natural."
"A man want sex and he get sex."
"You do not have to be married to have sex, because it is natural."
"I personally think it is clean, it's a wonderful, it's a beautiful thing, and there shouldn't be any limit at all."

Dann (48)

Jamaicans

Sex is independent of marriage.
Sex is independent of love.
Sex is natural.
Sex is healthy ...

from Chevannes (5-6)

Vincentians

Sex provides a release from hardship and a source of pleasure, and is one of the most positive things life offers.

Gearing 191

Intimacies in the islands

DRAWBACKS

• **Beach boys want control** of the sexual encounter, to take charge of the vacation and maneuver a woman via flattery into giving them money, meals or gifts (de Albuquerque, "Sex, Beach Boys" 109).

• **Men vary in sexual skill,** as is to be expected in a region of 37 million people. Tourist women in Jamaica now report that drug and alcohol abuse impairs the performance of some rent-a-Rastas and indicate that other men now sport bald Michael Jordan pates to distinguish themselves as clean and high performance (Bindel).

• **Men want money.** Unlike the men in Southern Europe who chase tourists, one-third to two-thirds of Caribbean hustlers (Sánchez Taylor, "Dollars" 754) receive money or other gifts from tourist women. In Jamaica, one source ("Where Men Are for Sale") reports a going rate of an hour of sex for $20 to $30 and a full night of ecstasy for $150. Another report holds that a night costs anywhere from the cost of a hot meal to $100, with oral sex included at $150 (Bindel). Women who anticipate that they would quickly tire of a foreign man sponging off of them should only visit islands administered by France or the United States.

• **Men may behave unacceptably,** drinking to excess and seeing no problem in striking women.

• **Locals feel negative impact.** Female sex tourism in the Caribbean has been linked to tourist harassment, rising HIV rates, family destruction and resultant hostility of black women towards white tourists.

• **Heightened HIV risks.** While 0.6 percent of the adult population in the United States (0.3 percent in Canada) live with HIV or AIDS, the rate zooms to 3.5 percent in the Bahamas, 2.5 in the Dominican Republic and Trinidad and Tobago, and 1.2 percent in Jamaica and Barbados (UNAIDS). Condom use is imperative for the female sex tourist.

ADVANTAGES

• **A good time is had by all.** Most holiday affairs prove to be mutually beneficial (de Albuquerque, "Sex, Beach Boys" 87).

• **Attractive, interested men abound.** The phenomenon of vacation liaisons has spread to every Caribbean island, large and small, and even to nearby Bermuda, the Bahamas and Belize. This creates a heady, take-your-pick atmosphere. On islands administered by France, however, men may show little interest in women unless they speak French.

• **Older women can find sex.** Women in their 50s and 60s are seen with younger men, a phenomenon also seen in Africa but not so much in Southern Europe. One woman in her 60s, who'd lived for seven years in Belize, noted "I once had this 20-year-old ask to walk me home. It was the best sex I'd ever had" (Gorry 86).

• **Islanders want to pleasure women,** as seen in the Dominican Republic.

• **Sweet talk serves as a balm.** Though this was not the case in my

Caribbean timeline

Circa 1890s: Older, wealthy white women begin to arrive in the Caribbean and the **Bahamas** for discreet relationships with young black men (de Albuquerque, "Big Bamboo" 83).

Early 1960s: Oral history in the English-speaking islands dates contemporary female sex tourism to "the planeloads of French Canadian women who visited the Caribbean on charters" (Pattullo).

1969-71: Already, some hotels and apartments on **Barbados** had tired of beach boys on the premises begin to refuse reservations to single women (Doxey qtd. in Momsen 116).

• Theme of island men cynically seducing white women pops up in two works by West Indian writers: a short story about **Barbados** (Layne) and novel set on fictional island (Marshall).

1970s: Word gets out among African-American women about ease in meeting men at **Jamaican** resorts (Amber 102).

1971: First performance of Trevor Rhone (119-24) play, *Smile Orange*, in which Ringo, a waiter at a **Jamaican** hotel, coaches Cyril the busboy how to wear deodorant, chat up North American tourists, have them drink "two liquor," take the tourist and his kneepads to "di sand," and "give dem a sob story" to get money.

1975: A **Barbados** newspaper editorial, "Leave the Women Tourists Alone," deplores increase in taxi drivers, waiters and beach boys molesting visitors: "It is a grave error to assume that every female visitor is coming to Barbados only to hop into bed with some native as part of her vacation experience" (Matthews 60).

1977: By now, "many of the resort areas of the Caribbean ... have been able to throw up a large cadre of gigolos," notes a tourism report, citing the **Bahamas** as well as **Barbados** and **Jamaica.** The author decried the "dudish, pimpish image that one gets from able-bodied young men who should be doing something constructive" as a new "minstrelsy mentality" (Nettleford 33-34).

1981-82: Female sex tourism becomes a spectacle on **Barbados**, where social scientists study the modus operandi of beach boys (Karch) or "rent-a-gents" who "cater to North American women who have been steeped in the myth of black virility and come to the Caribbean to experience it" (Manning 13-14). Islanders express "deep moral concern over the social impact of tourism."

1983: Female sex tourism becomes obvious even on less well-known islands:

• White tourist women on the 80-passenger ship *Flying Cloud* descend on

experience, other women receive outrageous flattery from Caribbean men and bask in the feeling of being admired quite absent at home.

Perhaps the most important advantage
• Sex with local men is one of the few means of cultural exploration.
Walled hotel compounds and off-limits tourist beaches keep the foreign

tiny **Virgin Gorda**, population 1,500, every Wednesday night and dance with local men at the Bath and Turtle Pub, flirtations that in some cases "undoubtedly lead to sexual liaisons" (Lett, "Yacht Tourism" 52).

• On **St. Vincent**, beach boys succeed with visiting European and American tourists (Gearing 195-96): "Many of the blond young Scandinavian women seemed particularly attracted to the young Vincentian men, the darker-skinned the better." Yet so many tourist women came "looking for sexual adventure" that "men did not take seriously tourist women's refusals of sexual contact, and this in turn led to several incidents of sexual assault."

1987: The How to Be Jamaican Handbook describes the "North Coast Hustler," shirtless to show off muscles, behind mirrored sunglasses, sending "greetings to the daughters" ... "two fat-thighed school teachers from Iowa or the lab technician from Hamburg" (K. Robinson 39, 40).

1992: The **Dominican Republic** government discourages rampant gay sex tourism, so beach boys, known locally as sanky pankies, turn their focus instead to servicing tourist women (de Moya 135, 137; Cabezas 100).

1995-96: Romances with **Jamaican** men attract wide notice as a landmark study by social scientists (Pruitt) probes the motivations of female tourists and as the novel How Stella Got Her Groove Back becomes a best seller.

1998-2000: Thriving female sex tourism boomerangs at the top two destinations, as reports of harassment escalate.

• Jamaica's prime minister warns that "people are going to refuse to come to **Jamaica**, resulting in a virtual collapse of the tourism industry because of harassment," including badgering for sex (McDowell). To avoid incessant advances, one African-American travel writer dressed in "roots" fashion: "long dresses, flowing African garb and headwraps" (Cummings-Yeates 314).

• On **Barbados**, female tourists, particularly solo travelers, endure persistent badgering on beaches and in bars. Some men even masturbate in front of them (de Albuquerque, "Tourist Harassment" 487).

2001, 2005: Author and her husband find sex tourism involving female tourists highly conspicuous even on little, out-of-the-way **Tobago**. On several southwest beaches, on two separate visits, we often saw pairs consisting of a white woman sitting quietly under a beach umbrella with a local beach boy.

woman distant from any islanders except service workers — unless an island man offers to serve as guide and culture broker (and lover). Further, sex, as a central focus of Caribbean life, almost begs to be experienced to attain fuller understanding of the islands.

As seen in the previous chapter, "Ready, willing and able: Caribbean men," black islanders offered a window into a different world, one where life's focus revolved around sex.

Conversations (in my experience) might dwell on morning erections, how some island women braided their pubic hair, varying vulva shapes or how the Bible calls for fertility.

A drink at a hotel might include a demonstration of how to make matchsticks into a copulating couple, and a ride to the airport might entail providing an impromptu hand job.

Amorous island men also offered me a glimpse of everyday life: a carpenter brother cutting wood under trees bearing iguanas, a fisherman who didn't need a spreadsheet, a gardener who smiled his way through women and work.

The vast majority of non-sex tourists have a difficult time getting below the surface of the Caribbean. Many tourists stay in a gated resort community with guest-only beaches, where no islanders circulate except as staff.

In fact, visitors to Jamaica will often find local friends barred from entering their hotel grounds (Cummings-Yeates 316).

Authors ... have described Bahamian tourism as "enclave tourism," as illustrated by the Cable Beach "strip" of hotels and casinos, with the best example being that of Paradise Island. ... The very nature of enclave tourism discourages cross-cultural understanding by clearly demarcating the tourist from the local, the hotels from the homes.

Palmer (795)

Tourists who venture off-resort encounter the dirty little secret of the Caribbean: anti-white hostility (author's observations on Jost Van Dyke, also see de Albuquerque, "Sex, Beach Boys" 94; P. Thomas 589, 592).

Because of this, a local man, guide and sex partner may be a near-necessity for departing the tourist ghetto and seeing island life without nasty encounters.

Some female travel writers (Noakes; P. Thomas; Cummings-Yeates) have managed to have cultural intercourse rather than sexual. But Lucretia Stewart noted accurately how attraction drenches interactions between men and women in islands where steaminess marks both the weather and the sexual climate. Physical union seems a logical route to knowledge.

"I didn't set out to have these encounters," Stewart told an interviewer (Rogers), "but if you're any good as a travel writer, you have to be a chameleon, and the Caribbean is a sexy place. To experience it, this is how you have to behave."

Let's look now at a question posed by the huge numbers of solo tourist women in the Caribbean: Why do they enter these liaisons?

Reasons

Casual sex is never pursued in a vacuum. It is influenced by development, personal appeal, sex ratio, cultural traditions, legal sanctions and the strategies pursued by others.

Buss, *Evolution* (95)

Next we will visit Africa, where Western women pursue some of the world's most exotic men.

But first let's examine the reasons why women take new lovers met on vacation. This topic follows naturally from our discussion of the Caribbean, which neatly illustrates several of the most important factors.

This book and especially this chapter attempt to figure out why tourist women and foreign men land in bed together.

In my personal experiences, described so far in Greece, the Caribbean and Bahamas, my behavior deviated so sharply from that at home that I shocked myself. A completely new woman whom I'd never met hand-picked men, as she were an empress in a palace of willing lovers — and at the time, with no self-awareness as to why.

My search for an explanation has led into the fields of economics, demography, psychology, sociology and anthropology. In fact, there are so many forces creating the potential for road romances that it is a wonder that any unattached traveling women have not indulged.

I will try to demonstrate that for the vast majority of female travelers, psychological reasons motivate holiday liaisons, and for older women, profound social forces create an added impetus.

Psychological, social and economic reasons

For example, in my own case, travel flings first occurred in my 20s in Greece for psychological reasons, mainly identity loss created by an alternate reality. Two other factors also came into play: sexual curiosity and a search for healing precipitated by divorce.

Later, as I entered my 30s and traveled in the Bahamas and the Caribbean, physical desire became overwhelming, the result of extended celibacy during much of a decade wandering in sexual exile.

But celibacy was only a manifestation of an unseen hand dimly sensed, affecting millions of women. An array of formidable social imbalances has created a shortage of marriageable men for women above the age of 35, women living in cities and black women.

This man shortage, which arrived in Britain and New England in 1850 and in the overall United States in 1950, has altered society. Women unable to count on a husband coming along found it necessary to attain higher levels of education and income (Guttentag 32; South, "Sex Ratios" 20). Feminism arose to act essentially as a "labor union" representing these working women's interests (Grossbard-Schechtman 388). Increased female incomes gave women, especially those single and divorced, the ability to travel. It is no surprise that today unmarried women make up an estimated half of adventure travelers (T. Edwards).

In time, these traveling women joined in the heretofore male activity of taking foreign lovers and in some cases paying for sex. And feminism led to altered sex roles and ultimately a dating war that made exotic foreign men seem more appealing than domestic brands.

So sex ratio imbalances, or more precisely, a lack of marriageable men, created a chain reaction: better female education, higher female incomes, feminism, altered sex roles, a dating war, more travel by Western women and more travel sex.

Global economics, while not a reason per se for casual travel sex, certainly serves as an essential prerequisite. The Industrial Age in Britain and the ascendancy of the U.S. economy created the pioneers of travel sex in the Victorian era. For the past 150 years, a traveling woman has found that while her professional achievement and impressive life experiences have lowered her pool of suitable mates at home, her money makes her spectacularly attractive to poorer men overseas.

Conversely a foreign man rejected as lacking means and thus unmarriageable by his own women may find a holiday affair his best opportunity for a better life. Men in Java, in Tobago, in the Gambia often find "sugar mamas" who provide them with a car or a Jet-Ski, capital to start a business or money for their college tuition, or in the most sensational case a gift of hundreds of thousands of dollars, as in the case of the young Jamaican man who inspired a real-life hit novel and film, *How Stella Got Her Groove Back*.

Sweeping social forces encourage the female tourist to embrace a foreign man — and she may be his best hope of economic advancement.

Making sex available as a commodity, something that is bought and sold subject to market forces, at a stroke gives almost any salaried Western women options for short-term, no-obligations companionship — if she travels abroad.

In sum, we shall explore ...

Seven reasons for casual travel sex

PSYCHOLOGICAL REASONS

1. Identity loss
2. Sexual connoisseurship and fantasy fulfillment
3. Search for healing, affection, sexual worth and love

DEMOGRAPHIC AND ALLIED SOCIAL, PHYSICAL AND ECONOMIC REASONS

4. Man shortage and a revolution in mate selection
5. Widespread, involuntary female celibacy
6. Dating war
7. Commodification of sex and culture brokering

Reasons the foreign man approaches the female tourist

Most if not all of these seven reasons also motivate the foreign man.

For a tourist woman and a foreign man find themselves in bed together to meet many needs that are reciprocal and mutually beneficial.

Together the couple in a holiday affair escapes a worldwide dating war and addresses a domestic shortage of members of the opposite sex. They exchange what they have for what they lack: her material wealth and sexual availability for his good looks, fine body, attention and of course affection (real or feigned).

Each meets physical urges, experiments with a new identity both more hedonistic and more affectionate, explores sexual curiosity about the other and lives out a mutual fantasy.

Both may yearn for a better future — the woman seeking a long-term companion, the man, economic prospects — a fantasy that may become a reality for one couple in 30.

Even two motivations that would seem exclusive to the female tourist — identity loss and ending a period of celibacy — may also apply to her foreign lover! A foreign boyfriend may be free to try on a new role as a tender, romantic, sexually skilled, highly desirable man, a role denied him by local women, as is sometimes seen in the Caribbean. And incredibly, many foreign men may endure prolonged celibacy, as we will discuss later.

Though the women is more likely to ache for sex after a long dry spell, there are many cases where her lover similarly lacks access to caring forms of sexual release. In much of Africa and the Islamic world, young women marry older men, leaving men under 25 high and dry except for visits to prostitutes.

Not every single factor that lands a tourist woman abruptly in the arms of a stranger is reciprocal. Only she is on unfamiliar ground, so that the opportuning men have the upper hand. Beach boys experienced in seducing newly arrived tourists may play a big role in her first instance of travel sex.

Other reasons for men to seduce female tourists include:

• male competition, "whereby men without material and social status establish other grounds for prestige" (Zinovieff 203).

• antagonism toward the West. Greek men who seduce tourists "may see themselves as belonging to a poorer, inferior society, and by lying to, tricking, and sexually conquering foreign tourist women from the supposedly superior societies, they have some revenge" (203). The ex-wife of a Greek man confirmed to me that "the taller, the leggier, the blonder the tourist the better, and in the process they enjoyed taking her from, for example, German men." (I may add that during my trips to Greece, antagonism in the form of anti-Americanism was rampant, as expressed by for example tour guides to classical sites that would gratuitously begin trashing NATO.)

• and a desire to "change their lives, to escape, or to take material wealth or prestige from the West" (203).

Let's begin our look at reasons by examining a psychological phenomenon of paramount importance.

Identity loss

1. Travel creates an alternate reality. A woman suffers loss of her "home" identity and assumes a new, sexy and free persona.

> **For the archetypal voyager the promise is that somewhere — in the bleakness of the Arctic night, the loneliness in mid-Atlantic, the blinding heat of the desert — they will be stripped of their protective layers of civilization, freed from boredom and routine to discover an alternate reality.**
>
> S. Cohen, and Laurie Taylor, "Escape" (137)

> **You must have seen what happens to the women when they come here [to Belize] — morals, standards, regrets — nothing matters.**
>
> German woman (qtd. in Gorry 163)

In an e-mail to me, Susanne K., 45, a German international recruiter, hits the nail on the head:

> Reasons for holiday romance: To me that is quite easy — I'm in a holiday mood far away from the social control of my everyday life and in this sit-

uation, I can do what I want. For example, I remember that I had a wonderful love affair with an illiterate farmer in Jamaica — unconceivable at home in Duesseldorf!

One journalist puts it this way: "[A] woman I know has a rule: Anything that happens in another time zone does not have to be recorded in the history of your life" (Spano, "Romance").

Hundreds of women have told researchers that on vacation, they can act differently than at home (see, among many others, M. Thomas; Gorry; Amber; Eiser; Lett; Mewhinney; Phillips).

In fact, the deliberate shedding of a home identity — especially one forged by suffocating restrictions — motivates thousands of Japanese women to enter Study Abroad programs, work overseas and take sex trips to Thailand and Bali. It seems Japanese women must leave home and travel to discover themselves, for they cannot do so within the strictures of the Japanese family and economy (Kelsky, *Verge* 9, 16).

It's easy enough to conclude that female travelers generally have lowered inhibitions and a greater willingness to take risks (Vorakitphokatorn 58). Yet this pat answer scarcely captures the wholesale revision of behavior, the jettisoning of all home values by some women. Pointing to "lowered inhibitions" does not fully explain how someone as mild-mannered romantically as myself, for example, found herself in Greece taking three lovers in a week.

So we know that a woman will behave differently away from home, but we still wonder exactly why: How can she become such a different person as to astound herself with her sudden sexual license?

One answer comes from a school of psychology that holds that situations, rather than personality, determine behavior.

And the ultimate in changed situations is travel.

The power of a new situation

In the modern West, women and men like to think that they have a strong, steady, reliable personality. "The assumption of cross-situational consistency is virtually synonymous with the concept of personality itself" (Bem 506). To have character is good; to be wishy washy is bad.

Yet do we truly have fixed identities?

Prior to the 18th century, the self was thought to be "an outward and visible thing constructed of the reflections of others," Eric Leed wrote (283). Though Romanticism created "the notion of an inner, natural self, distinct from society and its attributions," travel subverts this idea "that an individual has one, real, consistent persona and character" (276).

The realization that we behave differently because we *are* different in a novel environment should provide an "ah-ha" moment for many a

'Who am I?' through history

As early as the Victorian and Edwardian eras, a heyday for female travelers, women grappled with identity loss while on the road.

In 1913, Sylvia Leith-Ross canoed up a Nigerian river with a British colonial official. Despite the obvious difficulty in dressing for dinner, a custom more appropriate to London society, the pair prepared for lamp-lit dinners on the sandbanks by changing a shirt here, a blouse there. Leith-Ross showed great awareness of assaults on her home identity, and less willingness to abandon them than many a more hedonistic later traveler:

> When you are alone, among thousands of unknown, unpredictable people, dazed by unaccustomed sights and sounds, bemused by ways of life and thought, you need to remember who you are, where you come from, what your standards are.
> (qtd. in Strobel 10-11)

Another sort of lady explorer, however, deliberately "left Britain in search of a new definition of herself" (Birkett, *Spinsters* 78-80). Thereupon she might enjoy great freedom and adventure on her own in Africa or India — until running into a male colonial, who would force her back into her home identity (again, holding up a mirror, one insisting that she be helpless). Even "one white man could nevertheless constitute that same society and the restrictions it implied."

One of the richest explorations of identity loss brought on by travel can be found in the novel *Black Narcissus* (Godden). In it, a group of European nuns travel to far northeast India to set up a convent school, and the exotic East infuses their lives with palpable sexuality. Their identity as Western nuns seems to dissolve as the women fixate on two virile men, an Indian general's son and an English expatriate, plant riotous gardens and think suddenly of old boyfriends.

woman who lets loose on vacation. At home, she looks in the mirror of family, friends and co-workers and feels an onus to be respectable. On vacation, local men hold up a different mirror, and she behaves in accordance with her transformed reflection. Now she is a queen in a world where sex is fun and natural and where men, willing and eager, line up on the beach to sing her praises.

Unfortunately for those who value character, some psychologists have found almost no consistency in the human tribe across situations for even simple behaviors such as being punctual, friendly, dominant, talkative and honest — even for people *not* traveling! Situations can account for up to 11 times more variance in behavior than personality (Hunt 82). In fact, "without such adaptability human survival would be difficult indeed" (Mischel 176). In everyday terms, if a woman behaves the same way when flirting in a bar, when being interviewed for a job, and when threatened on the street, she simply will not survive. She must adapt to each situation.

So when a tourist woman impulsively has sex with her guide on the jungle floor (Gorry 86), she takes a promising situation and improvises, as the human race has always had to do to survive, to meet her physical, psychological and even spiritual needs.

Evidence exists that women, more than men, need the alternate reality of travel to engage in sex with a large number of partners. A survey of 20,000 Britons found:

Three or more partners in previous five years

	STAYED AT HOME	OVERNIGHT TRAVEL
Women	12%	21%
Men	25%	25%

Source: Johnson, *Sexual Attitudes* 141

"It appears that social constraints may have a greater effect on women than women," the survey authors concluded.

Local men skillfully insinuate women into an alternate reality. Their pressure often arises from the assumption logical outside (and often inside) the West that any single woman is looking for a man, as Deborah Elliston found while traveling in the South Pacific:

> I met a man on a ferry boat who, after only a short conversation about Tahitian culture ... asked me to sleep with him, even to come and live with him. I said no: I'm here to learn about Tahitian culture. He said that's nice, and reiterated his desires for me. (qtd. in Kulick 7)

Pressure from local men to alleviate one's single status can reach comical proportions, including serious offers of marriage. One Edwardian era traveler, the unmarried Edith Durham, repeatedly had youths ceremoniously presented to her in her travels in Central Europe: "Five offers in twenty minutes is about my highest record" (qtd. in Birkett, *Spinsters* 80).

Another angle men pursue is that of ostensibly playing bodyguard (in the most literal sense). As Danny Jr. told me in the Bahamas: "Babes, if you don't have me all the other men bother you."

The receptive expatriate

Women vary in the extent of their receptivity to sexual overtures while traveling. Most receptive will be the woman who perceives a holiday situation as quite different to home (Eiser) and one who responds to "situational and interpersonal cues" by tailoring her behavior to her audience and environment (Snyder 1281).

This suggests that a woman adaptable to the folkways of her host culture — such as a female expatriate, anthropologist or independent traveler — may have a mindset that while ostensibly requiring her to "blend in" with locals remains paradoxically open to sexual overtures, particularly in an exotic setting. She may head overseas determined to be proper in her interactions with locals, as a sign of respect for their ways, and can shock herself with intimate behavior.

In particular, female anthropologists seem talented at self-diagnosing identity loss, because it poses a tricky problem for an observer who must cling to her Western, professional perspective while adapting to a different society. (For examples, see among many others Markowitz 167; R. Jones; Dubisch 35; Wengle 369-77).

Many fight the temptations of sexual offers and the concomitant transition away from their old self.

Others acknowledge their loss of identification with Western people and their attitudes toward sex, taking a new self into explorations of intimacy with local men. One anthropologist, Karla Poewe, who wrote under the pseudonym Manda Cesara, took Zambian lovers. "Confronted by the existential vacuum of a lost identity, Cesara had attempted to establish an alternative identity through the affair" (Wengle 377).

In some posting areas, expatriates go through a "process of habituation to the freer sexual morality" of the local population (de Graaf, "Underlying Reasons" 654-55), losing the Western idea that sex needs to be invested with a meaningful relationship to one's partner.

As a former expatriate myself, living in Britain from 1981 to 1985, I can attest that my American identity felt under constant assault — my vocabulary, my voice volume, my attitudes didn't make sense to locals. And in turn, I couldn't decipher the oblique, subtle suggestions of British neighbors and work colleagues (Belliveau, *Amateur* 99-100, 115).

During this period of disorientation, men in my life acted both as guides and contributors to a mid-Atlantic identity, an Anglicized veneer that made my friends and colleagues more comfortable.

A role for personality?

We are not purely reactive creatures, however, with a new setting dictating our behavior. While many psychologists emphasize situations, others emphasize the personality, and most see an interaction between the two.

Believers in personality argue that particularly in the modern West, people can pick their situations. Here we can argue that a female college student entering a bar in Florida knows full well that spring break is a notorious time for student promiscuity (Mewhinney).

Similarly, a package tourist to Greece, Kenya or Jamaica, especially one familiar with the films *Shirley Valentine* (in Europe) and *How Stella Got Her Groove Back* (in North America), may set out to find a new man — her adventurous, thrill-seeking personality at work.

The primacy of personality may be most visible among the worldwide club of sex travel veterans, including French Canadian women on Barbados, Swedish women in Greece, Italians in the Dominican Republic, and German women in Kenya. These specialists select destinations based on reports about the men from girlfriends (Phillips 189; S. Forsythe, "E-Mail") and even pay to procure men based on appearance, smell and penis size (Sánchez Taylor, "Dollars" 759, Bindel), scarcely impulsive acts. In such cases, the new situation enables promiscuity but did not create the original idea of giving in to hedonistic impulse.

Even a woman traveling solo to the Caribbean ignorant of the availability of men, as I was on my first trips in the 1970s and 1980s, may not be innocent of desire, deep in the psyche lying unexplored and unacknowledged, to find sexual freedom in a novel situation. A woman traveling to a new place has, intentionally or not, drawn new boundaries on the types of sex partners she will encounter (see Laumann 257).

A sense of obligation to the man back home

Although one might assume that travel per se liberates a woman to have casual sex, because she enters an alternate reality where restraints are dropped, the case is not so simple.

"The type of travel engaged in, the life situation of the individual, travelling companions, situational factors in the host destination and opportunity to engage in sexual contacts" influence the traveler (Black 254).

Put another way: "The nature of a woman's needs — whether she feels loved and valued at home, or whether she needs to feel loved and valued — is likely to be a strong determinant of whether or not she succumbs to the tactics of hustlers" (Gorry 244).

Indicating that women do not always fully abandon themselves to a new situation, this alternate reality does acknowledge relationships at home. Situation does not fully override a personal sense of obligation or conversely resentment. Thoughts of a husband or boyfriend left behind can spur feelings of affection or anger, steering a woman's decision to pursue new men. "Such pre-existing relationships appeared to cross the boundaries between holidays and everyday life and acted as both a deterrent and a motivating factor in decisions regarding sexual intercourse" (M. Thomas 206).

For example, a married anthropologist, Rose Jones, while working in the Caribbean on her own, was pressed by island women to take a quasi-husband, or at least a male lover to make babies with, and failing that, a lesbian companion. Despite the overwhelming belief by local women that she needed sex and children pronto, from someone else if her husband was not available, she refused, loyal to her marriage vows and apparently not tempted in the slightest to follow local mores.

By contrast, one woman who had sex on spring break "explained that since her relationship with her boyfriend 'was on the outs,' she was able to justify her actions" (Mewhinney 283). The popular film *Shirley Valentine* similarly explores the tale of an Englishwoman, resentful of her husband, deliberately flying to Greece to find a lover.

Paradoxically, if a woman has boyfriend at home only recently acquired, she may be most likely of all to have flings. She seems to find herself both armed with new courage with men and ready to temporarily forget about the boyfriend. Lucretia Stewart, for example, arrived buoyant in the Caribbean (Weather 37, 143). Han Suyin fell in love in Nepal and returned giddy to Delhi, where she "spent the next several days not quite knowing where I was, exuding radiance, since several men suddenly fell in love with me" (House 109). And see my own earlier tale, "Discovering the Nymphomaniac Within."

Women in happy relationships still fall prey to deep infatuation, especially it seems in the South Pacific, but despite the siren song of travel romance man they find creative ways to avoid the Act itself:

• One happily married California woman danced with and kissed just once a tattooed Tahitian who recorded songs for her, made her a leaf tiara and called her beautiful (B. Clark).

• Another woman wanted to stay faithful to her "nice boyfriend" yet burned with curiosity about sex with a Trobriand Islander. She persuaded a female acquaintance to seduce a bartender and report back to her (Ferrin 90-91).

• A third went to great lengths: getting herself pregnant by her Australian boyfriend before a posting to Tonga, where she had been seduced before (Morton 168).

You are entering the Liminal Zone

Social scientists use a fancy word for an alternate reality: a "liminal zone," a place where a person "is unconcerned with the basic economic and political events and processes of day-to-day existence" (Lett 44-45).

In a liminal zone, a woman may suddenly:

• view others as social equals.
• view herself as anonymous.
• banter suggestively with strangers.
• and engage in sexual excess.

Travel and 'coming out' for lesbians

Many lesbians do seem to find that foreign travel plays an important role in acting on sexual impulses toward other women. Novelist Rebecca Brown ("Foreword" ii-iii) recalled a 1974 study trip to Europe as a high school senior.

"I'd never had sex before that year. Maybe it had to do with the women I met. ... But I also believe it had to do with the place. It had to do with not being in my native land, with being foreign. None of the people there had known who I was before. They didn't know who my parents were or the daughter I had been. I felt free to act like I hadn't before.

"Like Stein, Toklas, and other women who have traveled away from home, it took leaving my native land to realize I was a lesbian."

Brown does not state it, but much the same was true in the early 20th century of E.M. Forster and other British homosexuals in the arts, who found the Mediterranean a congenial place to explore acts illegal at home.

An electric charge of eroticism zaps the liminal zone. Travel, the arrival of a stranger somewhere new, is inherently sexy, even when the whirlwind romance is with a paradoxically prosaic lover. As one woman posted online (Ç'est la vie!): "I fell in love, got engaged, then got married, all in about two weeks. The funny thing is that I had to travel half way around the world to meet a man who lived 15 mins. away from me here at home." Similarly, in the novel *Backpack* (Barr), protagonist Tansy Harris encounters the love of her life, Max, an fellow Briton, but must suffer a rough trip to Vietnam to find him.

Paul Theroux once wrote of Eros even in the act of a young landlady leading him upstairs to his room: "We would enter, breathless from the climb, and stand next to the bed somewhat flustered" (*Kingdom* 95).

Arriving in the Caribbean, which combines the inherent sensuality of travel with that of the tropics, may be the sexiest of all. Female charter yacht tourists "commented upon their increased sexual appetites in the British Virgin Islands" (Lett 50). Another female traveler noted that "everything in the Caribbean seems to vibrate with a sensual energy" ... birds, sudden showers, bright hibiscus, perfumed flowers and reggae ... but "unless you are given to picking up strangers, this is not the place to holiday on your own" (Dougary).

In fact, the sexual exploration of others may be one of the few forms of adventure into the unknown available in today's well-charted world.

Alas, one definition of a liminal zone is that it is doomed to end. A typical woman (except for the one in 30 who pursue a serious relationship, see Hellberg 145) simply returns home after her sojourn in Sexlandia, holding her secrets. Lucretia Stewart enjoyed encounters in China and elsewhere in the Far East "and, when I was back in England with its monochrome colors and its gloomy climate, I would take out and examine my store of such memories much as a miser might gloat over a secret hoard" (Erogenous xxiv).

> **In Rome, the traveler must do as the Romans do, but must at home stop doing it, even if the Roman custom seems better than the local one.**
>
> Leed (277)

Sexual connoisseurship and fantasy fulfillment

2. At least a few women believe great sex has an important place in life, along with great food, great art, great music. Travel offers a way to explore fine lovemaking with men more varied than those at home.

Because I love sex.

Fiona Pitt-Kethley describing her motivation for casual travel affairs (*Journeys* (9)

For women, extensive sexual investigations at home will lead to the slut label, so travel romances provide a more discrete way to experience a variety of men.

The female connoisseur compares male lovers in many ways — by nationality, race, lovemaking skills, stamina and physique. She may also experiment with new situations such as anonymous intimacy, should she begin sex wordlessly at first sight of a stranger. Waterfalls, moonlit ruins or seaside cliffs may serve as the exotic backdrop to romance, as even the setting becomes a part of her sexual adventure.

And she eventually may use her acquired wisdom in a monogamous setting.

Lovemaking skills by nationality ...

I have described Jean-Marc (French) and Danny (Bahamian), who between them demonstrated unique positions and motion as well using props such as pillows.

Anne Cumming, the English erotic travel writer active in Southern Europe and the Middle East, went much further.

Calling herself "a one-woman research team" (*Love Quest* 143-44), she compared the lovemaking abilities of most of the men of the Mediterranean — Italian, Spanish, French, Portuguese, Greek, Jew and Arab:

> The Greeks and the Portuguese are generally rather ugly men with short legs and moustaches, so they don't waste time at their tailors' or their mir-

rors. They concentrate on performance rather than looks. This makes them the most virile of the Europeans. (*Love Quest* 143)

She enjoyed uncircumcised Latins (*Love Habit* 217), young men (264), and most of all Arabs. She sampled four Moroccans, an Egyptian horseman guiding her around the Pyramids and an Iraqi kept in Baghdad by a gay older man and molten at a rare chance for straight sex:

[Khalid] came back and undressed and lay beside me with no shyness or hesitation. There is something tragic and fierce about Arabs, with an overlay of softness and tenderness. Courtesy and control are inborn and natural to them and they make the most experienced lovers even without much previous experience. (*Love Quest* 75)

Cumming's heir apparent, British poet Fiona Pitt-Kethley, collected more esoteric tidbits. She learned in her travels that "Greeks take an average of two and a half minutes for sex, and that includes bargaining time and undoing their flies" (*Pan* 208). Italians, she found, enjoy outdoor sex (*Journeys* 11) and "have an annoying habit of wanting to be masturbated or masturbating you through clothing. It must do a lot for their dry-cleaning bills" (*Journeys* 10).

(Note: Xaviera Hollander, with a perspective of a prostitute rather than a sex traveler, also compares men by nationality. The author of *The Happy Hooker* (191-97) found Irish-Americans, Greeks, Italians and Spaniards excellent, Asians "clean and simple," and "quick." French men often had hygiene issues but could be "cute lovers if I can coax them into the tub before bed.")

... by race ...

White women from Europe, especially Scandinavia, and North America, as well as Japanese women, use travel as a chance to explore black men. British women head to Barbados (Phillips 191), while other females travel to Belize (Gorry 118) and the Dominican Republic (Herold, "Female Tourists" 984) with "fuck lists" of talented local Creole and Afro-Caribbean men.

An Englishwoman (Stewart, *Weather* 89) compared sex with a black man to "the loss of a second virginity," and a Japanese woman (qtd. in Kelsky, "Intimate" 471) felt that "the thing that black guys have that other guys don't is strong thrusting motion and a sense of rhythm."

Other women find Asian men intriguing and different:

The boys, such pretty enchanting silken-skinned boys, they sang to you and shopped for you; white girls would say once you'd had a Balinese lover you'd never want anything else, and they asked for little: meals, petrol, a souvenir. (Baranay, *Saddest* 31)

A woman (Asian lover) married to a Thai man believed Asian men to be the most beautiful race of men, with distinguished features and able to perform wonderfully in bed. She did not provide specifics, but I can say having watched a live sex show at a bar in Bangkok, that the men showed prodigious stamina. One assumed a tabletop position (torso in air, face up, supported by his arms and legs), allowing a woman to ride on top of him. Another managed sex standing up, one leg wrapped around his partner. Of course, this was paid entertainment, and not likely to be indicative of routine Saturday night lovemaking.

Does size matter?

Manly endowments also intrigue many women: "They are different one from another, straight and crooked, long and short, thick and thin, endless fascinating at rest or attention" (Juska 4).

The wife, mentioned above, of a Thai man noted that she had no complaints about penis size, stating that Thais, Filipinos and Indians tend to be bigger than Japanese and Chinese and about the same size as the average European.

An anthropologist (Odzer 241) who took a Thai lover or two decided the men are "a bit [smaller] and narrower" than whites.

Anne Cumming noted for posterity that an Egyptian horseman had a purple penis (Love Quest 135) while a Moroccan had "remarkable equipment ... nearly a foot long" (118).

While some sociologists presume that all white women visit Jamaica and the islands for the "big bamboo," the vast majority of female tourists to the Caribbean actually tend to say little about organ size or even lovemaking skills, stressing their men's attentiveness or affectionate gestures instead. Similarly, Japanese women who pursue foreign men describe their appeal in terms of kindness and chivalry, rather than lovemaking skills or endowment (Kelsky, Verge 138).

This "attentiveness is what we lack in the U.S., because we have no time," family therapist Mary Ann Constantinides told me. "Society is so technological and busy, we have not put time into the art of lovemaking. The effort goes after the initial passion, which quickly turns to flatness. Part of being a good 'sexpert' is having time to relax."

A perfect body

A woman seeking a sensational male physique, who doesn't have groupie access to the world of professional athletes, can find what she wants in much of the developing world.

The example I'll provide is of a man I encountered in the company of my husband.

We stayed with family in Tobago in February 2001, and our host took us to King's Cove, where we met a man cleaning a bonito under the palm trees.

The barefoot fisherman, wearing only a skimpy green Speedo, could have been an instructional poster of human musculature. Trapezoids, delts and quads popped in rippling perfection.

His flawlessness was arresting. I opened my notebook and wrote:

> chiseled shoulders, perfect shoulder blades an anatomy lesson.
> arc to hamstrings, sinews in calves visible.
> dark ebonywood skin, small padlock key on chain on neck.
> 5'10" 160.
> impossible not to stare.
> goes and trims a coconut for kids.

Lamont noticed my notekeeping. I looked up and said: "No one, no man in the industrial world is as buff as he is."

I expected Lamont to tease me, but even he, as a semi-pro soccer player conscientious about conditioning, found the sight of zero body fat on another male impressive.

"You could stay in a gym every single minute," Lamont agreed, "and you wouldn't look like him."

"He's not coming on, either," I said.

I noted how much more powerful he was than the beach boys elsewhere in Tobago. Yet he displayed neither arrogance at his manly strength nor self-consciousness at baring his skin in the tropical air. He had conversed courteously with us about his catch and treated a family of tourists kindly. This only increased his appeal.

"I bet the fisherman attracts a lot of attention, too," as compared to the beach boys, Lamont reflected later. "He looked ... perfect."

Women do notice a fine build. A writer visiting the Peruvian Amazon drank "in the beauty of the guides, their stone hard thighs, as they carry the dugouts over their heads and lead us back to camp," and was seduced by the most intelligent one with "smouldering good looks" (Stanton 87-98). A friend of mine seconded the pleasures of the Latin American body, "amazing, with little hair and smooth skin."

An arresting face

In 1987, Corinne Hofmann landed with her Swiss boyfriend in Kenya. In Mombasa, they found themselves on a ferry, where a Masai warrior stood out from the crowd.

Corinne's first sight of Lketinga left her "breathless" (Blanche 9). She couldn't keep her eyes off this "young god" (8). Photographs show him to have the typical slender, long-limbed look of East Africa's cattle herders, accentuated by a red woolen blanket, ochred hair and beaded decorations on his forehead, neck and shoulders. With his pleasing, warm brown face decorated with white striped paint and a Michael Jordan-style short moustache, one can readily imagine how arresting a first glimpse of him must have been.

"His face had a beauty so harmonious that one would almost say it belonged to a woman," she felt. But "his proud gaze and his powerful musculature left no doubt of his virility" (8).

Hofmann dropped her boyfriend and pulled up her stakes in Switzerland to marry her Masai warrior and live a life of near-squalor in the African bush — all for a pretty face. In photos taken among Africans, trim and graceful Corinne stands out as having an opposite but equal beauty, with porcelain skin, blonde wavy-curly hair past her shoulders, a tilt to her head and a smile.

Lketinga proved at least initially to be something of a bust in bed, in terms of skill if not frequency, but this dazzling man passed on his share of attractiveness to their daughter, as a photo on Hofmann's Web site attests.

Luxuriant locks

As Diane Ackerman (190) writes, "One may love the whole person, body and spirit, but hair becomes the fetish of that love ... Hair is sacred to lovers."

One morning in a temple resthouse in Calcutta, a Sikh religious warrior, sword at the ready, removed his turban and shook out his hair.

A traveling Englishwoman watched, while pretending to read a book. "He rubbed [his hair] with coconut oil, combed it again in long slow strokes from the back of his neck, twisted it into a rope and tied it in a double knot on top of his head."

The traveler was moved by the Sikh: "his tenderness, his simplicity and his beautiful eyes."

And by his hair. "Beauty is a great robber of my common sense," Sarah Lloyd (*Indian Attachment*, 4) acknowledged.

Much like Corinne Hofmann, Lloyd lived for nearly two years surrounded by filth, disease and obnoxious neighbors to be with a man she loved and whose beauty initially attracted her. Both white women fell in love with handsome warriors from tribes of elegant bearing, armed with weapons of a simpler time.

In the stories of Sarah and Corinne, we see the specific turn-ons that they responded to in a foreign man:
- facial beauty.
- exotic hair fashions.

- spears, swords, machetes as accessories.
- proud carriage.
- and traditional ideas of masculinity.

You could almost write a formula on what Western men need to do differently to appeal to Western women!

Experiences: exotic settings ...

Foreign men have surprised me with searing, out-of-nowhere arousal while hanging onto a boat in the Amazon, lying on a sandy beach by the Aegean sea, grinding against a wall in old-town Athens, strolling along a lazy stream near a Brazilian bird sanctuary and in a Caribbean hotel garden.

It goes without saying that beautiful scenery acts as a powerful aphrodisiac for the woman seeking romance.

For other women, beaches, mountainsides, jungles and deserts prevail — most anywhere will do.

The pinnacle of such exploits involves women who make love with their Sherpa guides during treks to Nepal (Spano, "Trekking"), as well as on smaller mountains in Grenada (Stewart, *Weather*), Italy (Fennelly) and especially Spain, where tales of sex with shepherds on hillsides abound (Balentine; Lynch).

In Africa, women conduct their affairs in huts (Rosemary Long, Corinne Hofmann, Cheryl Mason), tents (Mirella Ricciardi) or chiefs' palaces (Claude Bergeret). Anne Cumming had sex riding on horseback around Egypt's Pyramids (and in the Near East, in a train compartment bound for Baghdad).

Fiona Pitt-Kethley's back has graced the slippery marble floor of an art museum (*Pan* 44) and, following Sicilian custom, a compartment in the parked-trains section of Messina station (266).

Female travelers posting to the Lonely Planet Thorn Tree chat site (Sex on the Road) described trysting in the jungle with a guide, with a handsome young Greek among Hellenistic ruins and on a deserted island off the coast of Sumatra.

... wild or spontaneous encounters ...

The connoisseur understands that a casual coupling can be one of life's most remarkable experiences — and ultracasual sex, conducted anonymously, especially so. If you want to attain a peak of sensuality, the equivalent of a symphonic crescendo by Mozart, a foreign stranger in an exotic setting may fit the bill. Burning excitement makes a travel fling, particularly with a near-stranger, a thrill quite unlike any other. Camille Paglia (60) understands this principle:

Stranger sex will never be risk-free; it is just as challenging an exploration of hazardous nature as cliff-climbing, sailing, car racing, big-game hunting, bungee-jumping, hang-gliding or parachuting. The thrill is partly due to the nearness of disaster or death.

"Some of the most intense and poetic and intimate experiences of my life were one-night stands," gay writer Edmund White noted. Female sexologist Susie Bright (141) adds:

Sex with a stranger can be extraordinarily satisfying. The highly condemned "anonymous" sex — with someone whose name you can't remember afterward, or perhaps only for forty-eight hours — cannot only result in an orgasm or two, but can be a meeting of spirit and body, a kinship that's all the more intense because it happens so fast. Sex with a stranger persists, despite all its risks, because there is a special kind of lust that only happens when one's lover is unfamiliar.

The exhilaration of picking a partner from among a number of suitors and the freedom to have several lovers during a week (or day) appeals to some connoisseurs, such as a German woman who bragged to a Dominican Republic beach boy that in 14 days she had taken 18 men (Herold, "Female Tourists" 984).

In exploring exotic sexual experience, female travelers follow in the footsteps of homosexuals. Gay men have long made instant, near-anonymous sex a signature act, and some female travelers have also dipped a toe into this torrid experience.

For example, Anne Cumming (*Love Habit* 265) once shocked a psychologist friend who burst in on her as she enjoyed instant sex with one of his clients. The psychologist found their coupling "clinically interesting. You seldom see heterosexual relationships skipping even a token courtship period. There is usually at least a short verbal exchange, although my homosexual patients tell me they often get down to it without a word being spoken."

Similarly, Lucretia Stewart (*Weather* 89) found sex with West Indian men "so casual, so much more spontaneous (rather, I imagine, as gay sex was supposed to be before AIDS)."

Fantasy fulfillment

Women no longer stop at merely fantasizing about the exotic — they act on their deepest desires.

The reality of romance on the road fulfills several of the most common erotic dreams held by women, including:

• acting as a Wild Woman. "Casual, anonymous, sometimes raw sex is the norm for women who take on the Wild Woman role in their fantasies. This role gives women a chance to enjoy sex without rules, limits or commitments" (Maltz 32).

• playing the Dominatrix — another role in which a woman "actively initiates the sexual encounters she wants for her own pleasure" (36).

• indulging in taboo forms of sex, including anonymous liaisons that "free a woman to take what she's always wanted sexually, taking it the way she's always wanted it" (Friday, *Secret Garden* 93); enjoying the taking of "big black men" who "reek of sexuality" and can take you to "the most absolutely orgasmic time it is humanly possible to experience" (171-72); or "young boys" (175). Or all three.

In the generation between Nancy Friday's first book on women's secret scenarios, *My Secret Garden*, and her most recent, *Women on Top*, she notes that fantasies involving both anonymity and control have become even more prevalent. A desire "to initiate and control sex — indeed to continue sex until the woman's full sexual appetite is satisfied — is the underlying theme of these fantasies." Today's women describe how "their favorite erotic scenario is not about their husbands or lovers but about a man they will never see again, someone with whom there is no relationship" (*Women on Top* 62-63).

Both parties, the man as well as the woman, in a holiday romance may seek to fulfill fantasies of sex between a white or blond woman and an Arab, Indian, Polynesian or black lover. In fact, the 1970s-era fantasies of *My Secret Garden* now read less like taboo longings and more like a blueprint for action in the real world.

Having lots and lots of sex

As mentioned above, a German woman had sex with 18 Dominican Republic men in two weeks — an impressive accomplishment, though one that would qualify as overdoing it for many women.

American writer Hanny Lightfoot-Klein, multi-orgasmic and "having all my life suffered from an unassuaged sexuality," took advantage of travels in Africa and Israel to sample men. But it was on a side trip to Europe that she met a Cockney truck driver, a huge bear of a man named Roy, whom she assumed would be merely a comforting, calm sleeping companion. After his 10th orgasm, and her umpteenth, she gasped, "no more" (122). Travel sex had finally provided her with a man with stamina to match her own.

Scottish traveler Trudy Culross (244) described an Egyptian lover named Hafez: "I remember one day, he walked in on me in the bedroom, when I'd just finished dressing to go out. I was minus my clothes in no time and the sex was great, as usual. Twenty minutes later, I was dressed again and just stepping into my shoes, when he strolled out of the bathroom, fixed me with that look I'd come to recognize ... and I was minus my clothes again. The sex was still good. ... The scene was repeated seven times, believe it or not."

From fantasy to actuality

How many female sex connoisseurs might there be? Possibly many thousands or tens of thousands, worldwide. For example, a quarter of female sex tourists take more than one lover during a vacation. Some of these women may be into quality as well as quantity.

Further, French Canadians in the Dominican Republic (Herold, "Female Tourists" 986), tourists in Jamaica (Sánchez Taylor, "Dollars" 759) and Belize (Gorry 118), and Americans in Greece (Zinovieff 209) and Nepal (Ortner 224), as well as women elsewhere not documented by observers, initiate sex with local men, indicating an aggressive curiosity about bedroom escapades.

For Japanese women, connoisseurship of an almost materialistic variety may be pivotal in driving encounters with foreign men. Young single females generally live at home and have the nation's highest disposable incomes, making extravagant consumption the order of the day for many.

Japanese women's search for aesthetic purchases "went beyond mere shopping and entered the realm of connoisseurship," and by the late 1980s Japanese products had been exhausted. Young women became "connoisseurs of the West" and began to "cross Japan's borders in search of the 'gaijin lover,' the exotic sexual experience that represented the final frontier of the foreign left to consume" (Kelsky, Verge 135-36).

Yes, traveling women by the thousands are moving exotic, erotic daydreams out of the realm of unattainable fantasy and into reality, a reality that is easy to access in vast parts of the Caribbean, on Mediterranean shores and to a lesser extent Africa and Southeast Asia.

However, this begs the question, as a fantasy is by definition an improbable situation residing only in the imagination, of what becomes of a once-taboo desire when it can be effortlessly realized for the price of a package tour to Jamaica, Greece or Kenya.

As female veterans of sex travel demonstrate, women who readily fulfill fancies and whims evolve into sexual connoisseurs. Such women will hold a less giddy impression of travel sex, no longer exclaiming, "Wow! I can't believe I'm making love to an Arab sheikh." Connoisseurs deliberately seek encounters, achieve them and can act out playing the part of a harem girl.

As accomplished sexual adventuress Fiona Pitt-Kethley (Pan 91) described herself and her young Greek lover: "We were both firmly convinced that fantasy was a bad thing. Probably a lot of people indulge in it, but I think they're missing out on the real situation. It's a kind of betrayal of your partner too."

Sex orientation reversal

Experimentation may even take the form of testing a new sexual orientation. Some homosexual travelers experiment with heterosexual relationships while traveling. A lesbian friend of mine took a New Zealand Maori as a lover. And a gay man (Fallowell) in St. Petersburg wrote of going along with an overture from a Russian female prostitute.

And straight women may experiment. In Paraguay, Peace Corps volunteer Sarah Grossman (119) found "doubting women" who, far from home, stirred by "the heat and humidity and abundance of passion fruit and papaya," would embrace her under a mosquito net ... "adding our tryst to their list of new things experienced in a foreign country."

Expert men also compare women

> **Bajan women can't fuck, and they doan even wanta suck you. You got to beg she to do it ... . Now a white woman, you gotta beg she to stop!**
>
> George, a Barbadian (qtd. in Phillips 192)

Foreign men who cater to tourist women also become connoisseurs. As discussed earlier, many Caribbean men prefer a French Canadian woman in her 30s for good times and good tips. Barbadian (Barbados) men enjoy white women because they will give them oral sex (Phillips 192).

Bali's Kuta Cowboys prefer a wealthy Japanese woman (Harvey) or women from Hong Kong, Taiwan or Korea who have more money to spend than Europeans (Best to Avoid).

Mexicans like gringas because of a belief that they "keep better than tropical women" (Holder 156). Costa Rican men often find white women pretty for their wide variety of hair and eye colors (Kimball 3, 9). Further, they find their own women to be quite jealous, while "foreign women are much more relaxed in relationships, leaving much more space and making far fewer demands."

In Belize, beach boys "find themselves in [a situation] of not being constrained in their pursuit of sexual variety" (Gorry 113-14).

And Solomon Islanders find white women to be more vocal and to move more during sex (Irvine, *Faraway* 290), displaying a "wriggle and gasp" not found locally. Similarly, a Balinese prince once told a British-American woman that her hips were "what our men admire most. You see, when we walk there is nothing to get excited about. When a white woman walks it is different" (Tantri 37).

A payoff at marriage?

People who are having lots of sex with more than one partner are usually more sexually sophisticated. To learn about sex we need to be intimate with more than one person.

Dodson

Travel sex while unattached can be a good way to reconcile the urge to experiment with a later goal of a monogamous marriage bound together partly by imaginative sex.

Travel sex offers the single or divorced woman who wants to be good in bed and ultimately settled with a nice guy a good way to achieve both goals.

Further, travel sex allows a woman to "stay in the game" when prospects for sex partners are dim at home. "Sex without love has a purity which can lighten the heart," wrote Duncan Fallowell (46), a gay man with an insight equally applicable to women. Though "sex in a loveless life can be a reminder of inner bleakness," it is "much better than nothing at all. It keeps you in shape for love."

British poet Fiona Pitt-Kethley noted that "the sowing of my wild oats lasted slightly over 20 years, during which time the nearest I came to having 'family values' was enjoying three handsome brothers one after the other." She was seeking in a man "good looks, intelligence and good sex all in the same package. It took me half a lifetime to find it" ("20 Years"). The alternative would have been lengthy celibacy.

Overall, I am glad I engaged in travel sex in the dozen years between my marriages when action just about slowed to a stop!

Lucky the man or woman who marries a connoisseur for whom travel sex was an interim arrangement before committed love. In more autobiographical works, the novelist Paul Theroux hints at such a progression in his life.

In fact, one of the more well-known, Victorian era sexual adventurers, Isabelle Eberhardt, enjoyed vigorous sex with working-class Arabs. Yet when she settled down with an Algerian sergeant, they engaged on both physical and spiritual levels. She appeared to acknowledge drawing on her hedonistic history to enjoy even finer sex when at last she really loved her lover. Describing her own acquired sensual wisdom, she wrote (81) that "the only true and honest knowledge must have been imparted heedlessly by the one person I had truly loved and who had loved me as well; for the miracle of love — one could say the sacrament — is accomplished only when love is shared, and not one-sided."

The United States may be particularly open to the merger of Madonna and Whore in one woman, as measured by the yardstick of pop culture. Our movie heroines and their sexual auras tell us a bit about mythical cultural ideals. A study (Wolfenstein 20) found that American films, more so than the British or French, revealed a culture that valued in a woman "the exciting qualities of the bad girl and the comradely loyalty of the good one — in one prize package." The U.S. film heroine seems promiscuous, but "sexual wickedness" becomes "a forepleasure stimulus to wholesome love" (Wolfenstein qtd. in Wasserstrom 105).

Among connoisseurs, the proportion stockpiling bedroom tricks in hopes of eventually thrilling a longed-for "wholesome love" may be a small, wistfully idealistic subset of a whole consisting of women just out for a good time. Or it may not be a rare occurrence at all, given how Isabelle Eberhardt traded wild freedom for even better loving sex. Certainly, travel sex does provide avenues to both knowledge and healing, as we shall see now.

Healing and the search for affection, sexual worth and love

3. After a breakup, women may find a love cure with a foreign man. Holiday sex may also become part of a spiritual search for what is valuable for a good life.

> **Many people travel to heal a broken heart. They want to find proof that others don't view their faults quite so seriously as do ex-loved ones. Perhaps they wish to reaffirm their sexiness through blind encounters, to heal themselves, to forget. Some of them even fall in love and return with acceptable partners.**
>
> **... Traveling for love. Or else, why travel?**
>
> Chapple

At the head of the line for candidates for romance on the road must be women who go through a shattering surprise divorce.

"Let's say your husband leaves you. He leaves you like husbands always leave in bad novels, abruptly, with a trail of lies that are impossible, after all those sweet years, to believe."

When the disaster described above befell Laura Fraser (4), a San Francisco-based writer, she felt broken hearted and could barely eat or sleep. She booked a flight for Italy and wondered whether "an Italian man might not be such a bad idea, either."

She found her Italian man, half-Arab actually, a professor. At the beach, he placed a warm rock lightly on her back. They spent four days swimming, eating and making love.

Over two years, they rendezvoused periodically until one day the professor announced that Fraser, once heartbroken, was now "ready to fall in love" (221), and the author herself could finally agree.

One intriguing aspect of Fraser's story that resonated with me (having been through a similar experience) was her need to begin picking herself up after an initially romantic marriage broke up with sickening swiftness. In my case, it was the abrupt onset, in our 15th month of an idyllic marriage, of irrationality and incessant criticism.

In Fraser's case, her husband just went and fell in love with someone else.

"All those bright, soft moments of falling in love are buried by divorce now, under shovelfuls of shit" (129). Only her travel affair could begin to soothe her and move her from heartbreak to healing.

After a similar crushing breakup, Katya Macklovich (237) also went to Europe, feeling 35 and frowsy. "All I do remember is my friend Debbie telling me that if I wanted to regain my confidence with men, I needed to parade myself down the boulevards of Paris, tout suite, and let the men follow me like poodles in heat."

As with Laura Fraser, she began her trip in a romantic spot weeping for her lost boyfriend. When she called a friend of a friend, however, her luck turned. Drinks led to dinner with a handsome Englishman who spooned ice cream into Katya's mouth. Along the Seine they began caresses in public, to "whistles and applause" from passing tourist boats.

They spent three days eating, visiting bookstores and making love in their hotel and in hidden corners of Paris.

Marlena di Blasi (98-100) a chef, learned during her second pregnancy that her psychologist husband had no feelings for her or their children. When she then fell for another man, her husband left her three days later. And when she told her new lover they were free to be together, he muttered, "Fool."

Decades after this series of emotional traumas, during a business trip to Italy, a banker in Venice fell in love with her at first sight, embraced her on their first stroll together, and arrived to visit her in St. Louis two days after her return home. Their mercurial decision to marry and live in Venice shocked others, but in the way of many second marriages between mature adults, to di Blasi it seemed like the only calm and correct romantic decision she had ever made:

> I never felt the earth crack open. Never. What I felt, what I feel, is quiet. Except for those first hours together in Venice, there has been no confusion, no confounding, none of the measuring and considering one might think to be natural for a woman up to her knees in middle age who thinks to jump the moat. ... This does not feel like a new perspective but the first

and only perspective that has belonged only to me. ... (34)

Di Blasi concludes, "too often it is we who won't let life be simple." Laura, Katya and Marlena are far from alone. Writer Lucretia Stewart (Weather 37) left England "consumed with fear and unhappiness" about being 40 and facing the loss of attractiveness. A little sex in the afternoon, island style, put her right: "I felt refreshed and alert, languorous and ravenous. ... It seemed to me that I felt better in the Caribbean than I had ever felt in my life" (143).

Women traveling with British-based Aphrodite Tours, which ferried them to Cyprus for some healthy Mediterranean flirtation, told proprietor Patricia Cowley "if they had known about her company, they could have saved a fortune on therapists" (Theodoulou).

As for women not divorced but in mediocre or teetering unions, the film *Shirley Valentine* and the E.M. Forster short story "The Obelisk" illustrate how travel sex can even revitalize the married woman, helping her put zip back into her relationship.

Perhaps the most brutal kind of breakup is the permanent loss of a lover. Lisa Bay (144) wrote of going to Egypt and stepping aboard a romantic *felucca* (Arab-rigged sailboat). The robed captain, Ahmed, "turned his attention on me. And from the moment he did, I realized he was the brown-skinned incarnate of my first lover, a man who had been killed when I was seventeen. Within a few minutes, repressed tendrils of longing became a siren song."

Sometimes the foreign man is the one healed by the female traveler. Anne Cumming (Love Quest 75-76) met an Iraqi man, Khalid, who wanted to know a woman's body but was kept out of circulation by his poverty, which kept him dependent on an older gay sugar daddy. In a brief hour before she departed her Baghdad hotel, she gave him a guided tour, and he responded with tender curiosity, vigor and multiple positions, "bursting into real tears at the final orgasm."

Some women seek healing in a more cosmic sense. They:

- **want a return to nature.** Western women often express awe towards a man who can simply climb a tree and bring down a coconut.

- **seek a sense of community.** Women have moved to Nepal, the Gambia, Belize, Fiji and many other places where they feel more connected to others than they do at home. Three hundred Japanese women, for example, have married Balinese men and moved to the paradise island, calling the Indonesian jewel "cozier" than home (Yamashita 96). Travel in general and travel sex in particular may be an attempt to transcend everyday isolation and join an emotionally rewarding community (Pearce 62).

- **desire a life of less materialism** and with a more spiritual focus. One Englishwoman (Lynch) left an aggravating job, selling everything to live in rural Spain and settle into a quiet romance with a shepherd.

Another Englishwoman left her businessman husband, posh home with swimming pool, and BMW to move to Gambia, where she opened a clinic on an impoverished island and gradually came to love a Gambian long-term friend, 15 years younger (Chalmers).

A third Englishwoman, Sarah Lloyd, lived with an impoverished Sikh for 18 months, and acknowledged that fantasy played a role in her decision to live in India. She knew what she really wanted:

> To indulge my nostalgia for English village life fifty years ago, a life arranged not by machines but by nature, where people and animals lived in close contact, where every tool was comprehensible and the earth was held sacrosanct. (*Attachment* 40)

She is not alone. Scottish traveler Trudy Culross (230), tired of an empty life as a London executive, briefly considered becoming the second wife of Bedouin in the Egyptian desert: "it would be comforting to be under the protection of a man who took upon himself all the worries and problems. My days of being alone and self-sufficient would be over at last." Women do indulge in "nostalgia for a pre-industrial past" (Gorry 246) and a belief that "men who live removed from centers of industry are more in touch with their bodies and emotions and, therefore, more representative of man's original state."

The man in pre-industrial society is a master of his environment, be it the flanks of the Himalayas or a Pacific reef, in a way lost to a Western man, worrying about his future and trapped in a changing world of capricious bosses and stressful deadlines that defies mastery. "Guys back home who are always worried and anxious are less attractive by comparison, even if they drive BMWs," anthropology professor Donald Symons e-mailed me.

Perhaps somewhat paradoxically, given the general perception of readily available sex in the developing world, tropical men can sometimes be much more marriage-minded than men in the West.

I believe that part of the reason many Western men are commitment-phobic is that mothers (and sisters) think no one is good enough for their son (or brother), and so men feels no family pressure to marry — in fact, the pressure may be to delay.

In contrast, female travelers in Fiji, to take just one example, report constant serious marriage offers (Stanley).

One visitor, Joana McIntyre Varawa, wrote an intriguing book about being proposed to within days of her arrival. The reason: A chief instructed his son to marry her and thus help the family materially.

The motive may sound unromantic, but social pressure does create men who seek mates, not just lovers, and a genuine marriage offer still may be the surest way to regenerate a woman's feelings of attractiveness and completeness.

> ... The subject of love and tourism appears to have no place in the minds of social scientists. ... Yet the study of love, in all its variety, is an area rich and ripe for furthering the understanding of human psychology, in general, and the behavior of pilgrims/tourists, in particular.
>
> Singh (261)

> To have sexual intercourse with an attractive and popular male [while on vacation] was seen as a positive reflection on the woman's own desirability. This reinforcement of sexual attractiveness was perhaps particularly important for those women whose trip had been motivated by a bad or broken relationship at home.
>
> M. Thomas (206)

While away from home, a woman may enter into a carefree sexual relationship for pure enjoyment. An unexpected cultural fit may shift her and her lover into an entirely different mindset: that of seeking a mate.

Two men in Barbados report how real feeling crept up on them. A beach boy named Mark recalled, "At first we weren't anything" but over time, his vacation lady began staying with him longer and longer. "Now I only got she one, and I does go up and she does come down" (Phillips 195). And a man named James noted: "People fall in love despite not wanting to. Sex is a powerful thing. You start off, maybe you want a fucking, before you know it there is a feeling there."

Yes, sex is a powerful thing.

We've examined a trio of psychological reasons for holiday flings. Now let's begin to look at social forces that also contribute.

These apply in the main to older tourist women, above the age of 35, and to younger foreign men, under the age of 30.

Man shortages — and surpluses

4a. World demographics explain much of the world's Affection Deficit Disorder. A man shortage prevails in the West, while a man surplus can be in much of the developing world.

> ... Given the imbalance in sex ratios, individuals may very well react to this situation by breaking the age or social class constraints by taking a mate outside the usual bounds.
>
> Guttentag (175)

... The pursuit of exotic sex [is] bound up with [desire] which must at some level spring from a dissatisfaction with home.

Littlewood (185)

If a person goes overseas to have sex, that reflects problems in the home society.

Lamont W. Harvey, author's husband

When you have too many unattached men in one area and too many unattached women in another, travel may provide a much better opportunity for meeting a potential lover than staying at home.

In the West, for more than a century, women have been traveling to escape man shortages.

For example, by the 1850s, male emigration to the colonies resulted in 104 women remaining in Britain for every 100 men (Strobel 25), a figure that worsened steadily through World War I. No surprise then that the Victorian and Edwardian eras were a golden age of female travel and female emigration, with numerous marriages of Englishwomen to maharajas in India, Malays in South Africa and minor royalty in Italy.

Currently in the United States, among white, unmarried college-educated heterosexuals, for every 100 women aged 35 to 44, there are (in theory) 98 men, a figure that skids to 77 men for every 100 women aged 55 to 64.

The picture worsens dramatically for unmarried black college-educated women. For ages 35 to 44, only 69 black men can be found for 100 women. For ages 45 to 54, the figure plummets to 53 men for 100 women — one available man for every two women.

Yet these figures do not capture a phenomenon that further reduces the mating opportunities of older American women: the tendency of divorced and widowed men to marry women significantly younger than themselves.

A shortage of available educated males

UNMARRIED COLLEGE-EDUCATED PEOPLE, U.S. MALES PER 100 FEMALES, 2000

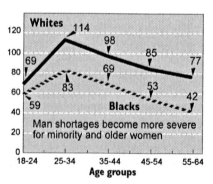

Source: Data adapted from U.S. Census Bureau, Educational Attainment, corrected to remove 2.6 percent homosexual men and 1.1 percent lesbian women per Laumann 304

Men take younger brides

MEDIAN AGE AT MARRIAGE, 1990

	GROOM	BRIDE	YEARS YOUNGER, BRIDE
First marriage	26	24	2
Previously divorced	37	34	3
Previously widowed	63	54	9

Source: U.S. Centers for Disease Control, "Table 9"

For example, men in their 40s or 50s or 60s who become divorced or widowed will seek younger women to remarry, reducing the pool of possible mates for women of their own age bracket. Therefore there are even fewer unmarried males who are actually interested in females their own age.

Put another way, the older a man gets, the more his universe of potential wives expands, while the reverse is true for women, creating a double whammy for women above 40 (mitigated by at least some younger men who demonstrate interest in older women, see Laumann 252-53).

If a woman married in her 20s or 30s selecting from a good pool of suitors becomes divorced or widowed in her 40s, at the other end of the tunnel she emerges to a much tougher market, and one she is less likely to approach with sunny optimism.

For women in large cities, two other factors also worsen the marriage squeeze:

• Women dominate urban populations in the developed world.

• Women find the limited pool of potential urban mates further constricted by disproportionate numbers of gay men.

Shortages of straight men in urban areas

Around the world and from the Middle Ages to the present (Guttentag 58), unattached women have flocked to cities in search of better-paying jobs and a more varied pool of potential mates — a migration paralleled by gay men, who also find urban living congenial (Laumann 308).

Thus women in large cities around the world confront a shortage of both men and of male heterosexuals.

This will come as no surprise to observant women who live or work in the Big Five gay centers in the United States — New York, Washington, D.C., Miami, San Francisco and Los Angeles.

Let's try to arrive at figures capturing the extent of this dynamic:

Percentage reporting same-sex partners in last year

SELECTED DATA BY PLACE OF RESIDENCE

	GAY MEN	LESBIANS	NET GAY MEN
Top 12 cities	10.2	2.1	+8.1
Next 88 cities	3.6	1.2	+2.4
Rural	1.0	0.6	+0.4
Total	2.6	1.1	+1.5

Source: Adapted from Table 8.1, Laumann 304

In the top 12 central cities, if we subtract the 10 percent (using rounded figures) of gay men from the marriage pool, and the 2 percent of urban lesbians presumably not interested in husband hunting, we find that homosexual men create a net decrease of 8 percent in the pool of marriageable men.

How does this play out in the marriage pool in the largest U.S. cities? Cities such as Philadelphia have only 87 men for every 100 women to start with. If Philadelphia has a typical net decrease of 8 percent in its marriageable man due to its gay population, 100 women are then left with just 80 straight men. Washington, Detroit, New York, Chicago and other cities also become deserts for single women, especially as they get older.

Thus women in Philadelphia, Washington and New York may face slightly better luck finding an eligible male in, of all places, San Francisco than at home — the City by the bay (see chart, right), is not only full of men, but its straight male component has been boosted via the technological ascendancy of nearby Silicon Valley (Conlin). (A side note: I can attest to finding my first husband in San Francisco and my

Males per 100 females

12 LARGE U.S. CITIES, 2000

	CENSUS FIGURE *	LESS HOMOSEXUALS **
Philadelphia	87	80
Washington, D.C.	89	82
Detroit	89	82
New York	90	83
San Antonio	94	86
Chicago	94	87
Miami	99	91
Los Angeles	99	91
Houston	100	92
Dallas	102	93
San Francisco	103	95
Phoenix	104	95

* Source: U.S. Census Bureau, *County and City Data Book*

** 8 percent lower than Census figures, based on Laumann 304

second in Washington, D.C. Though both men lived elsewhere, this demonstrates that even large cities with significant gay populations are good places to meet men, even if the men are not permanent residents.)

Black women, already facing a dearth of eligible educated men, discover especially dramatic shortages in many mid-sized cities. Areas with more than 130 black women for every 100 black men include Buffalo, Cincinnati, Jackson, Miss., and Birmingham, Ala. (Lyons). No wonder at least some African-American women who travel to Senegal and other roots areas return with husbands.

Demographers also report a feminization of many European cities such as Paris and London, where women predominate and many — 20 percent of French professional women, for example (Clarke 36) — live alone.

A number of writers (for example, Paul Theroux and Karla Poewe) have addressed the topic of sexual loneliness in the West. As the weight of numerical evidence demonstrates, sexual loneliness is neither a figment of the creative imagination nor an isolated problem. Rigid, unyielding numbers, combined with social forces for men to marry younger women and for gays to migrate to congenial cities, work against the chances of even kind-hearted, loving women, who could appeal to male counterparts also scorched in the dating wars, of finding a mate near home.

> **Among their reasons for travels, the women list sudden loss of a romantic partner or close friend, a sense of closing possibilities due to advancing age, and a general sense of isolation and unhappiness at home.**
>
> Gorry (74)

> **I see so many truly nice women and so few truly nice men.**
>
> Mary Ann Constantinides, Baltimore family therapist

We have been discussing the male shortage in the developed world. Now let's examine the male surplus in the developing world.

Oodles of tropical men

> **West Indian men are great — they're sexy, sweet, charming and attentive. ... And there is no man shortage in the Caribbean.**
>
> Ilaw, "Men" (133)

While an older urban woman from the West confronts a man shortage at home, she faces anything but that if she visits the Caribbean, Africa, the Mediterranean or the Islamic world.

In these areas, significant numbers of men under the age of 25 are unattached, the result of either personal choice, older men marrying many of the young women, outmigration of more women than men, or exceptionally low marriage rates across the board in their society.

The chart on the next page shows, by age groups, the ratio of unmarried men to women in four centers for female sex tourism. Greece shows an incredible surplus of single men in their 30s, and Cuba of men in their 20s. Single men under 40 also abound in St. Vincent.

These young men lack access to women their own age, who are much more likely to be already married. Indeed, men known to chase tourist women are generally described to be under 25 in the Gambia (N. Brown, 363); under 26 in Sri Lanka (Beddoe 47), 17 to 25 in the Dominican Republic (Herold, "Female Tourists" 982), in their teens, 20s and 30s in Thailand (Vorakitphokatorn 67) and 16 to 35 in Barbados (Karch 251; Phillips 186).

Perhaps it is no accident that many of the leading destinations for female sex tourism score extremely highly on demographic measures that point to large numbers of unattached men.

And where can we find especially high numbers of unattached Western women? It will come as little shock to check marriage figures for Sweden, home of the West's pioneering sex travelers and also the Western nation with by far the lowest proportion (84 percent) of married women in the age bracket of 45 to 49. (For comparison, the United States is 94 percent, and Britain, 95 percent.) In fact Swedes are almost as marriage shy as many Caribbean peoples, making the older Swedish woman and the younger Jamaican man who meet via tourism quite likely to be looking for a partner.

Let's examine what is going on by region:

The Caribbean: The top islands for female sex tourism also have the world's lowest marriage rates. Many couples live in informal arrangements including children, and have children by more than one partner, which while not affecting sex ratios points to a culture where males and females often roam, and sometimes into the arms of tourists. In Jamaica, 48 percent of men are still unmarried at age 50, in St. Vincent and the Grenadines, 39 percent, Barbados, 37 percent, and Belize, 24 percent (all marriage percentages and median age differences in this section unless otherwise specified are from the U.N. Population Division, World Marriage Patterns).

Jamaica and Dominica also have the world's highest mean age at marriage, 35 years for males and 33 years for females.

Barbados, Antigua, Grenada, Guadeloupe, St. Vincent, the Virgin Islands and other nearby nations follow just behind, with male ages at first marriage right around 32 to 34 years.

(Again, Sweden, with a similar emphasis on cohabitation and men

Island surpluses of single men

NUMBER OF UNMARRIED MEN FOR 100 WOMEN, MOST RECENT YEAR AVAILABLE

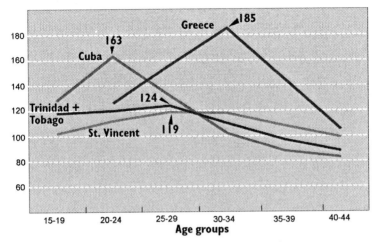

Source: adapted from U.S. Census Bureau, *International*

not getting married until a mean of age 34 and women at 32, mirrors the Caribbean and demonstrates why its women are so prominently mentioned in sex tourism literature.)

We also saw in "Discovering the Nymphomaniac Within" many more men than women living on the tiny island of Jost Van Dyke. This demonstrates how "sex ratios may be so unbalanced among small local populations that they provoke social instability" (Clarke 36).

The Gambia: Africa's top destination for female sex tourism has the world's highest gap in ages at first marriage — men are typically 9.2 years older than their wives, again placing young men out of the running for mates their own age. Of persons under age 25, 82 percent of the men are single and only 20 percent of females. Single young men end up turning to unattached older women who arrive by the planeload from Britain and Scandinavia (Aziz 12).

Greece: Like a minor version of the Gambia, this Southern European nation has Europe's largest gap in ages at first marriage — nearly five years, again leaving lots of young men on the loose for tourist women.

This marriage age gap statistic tallies with another measure for Greece (U.S. Census Bureau, *International*) showing an incredible 126 unmarried men for every 100 unmarried women aged 15 to 24, and 185 unmarried men per 100 women for ages 30 to 34! No wonder Greek men show a keen interest in visiting tourists.

Further, looking specifically at its rural areas, Greece also features an excess of young single men, with 115 men for every 100 women, higher even than found in rural Jamaica and St. Vincent:

Surpluses of rural single men

RATIO OF MEN TO 100 WOMEN, MOST RECENT YEAR

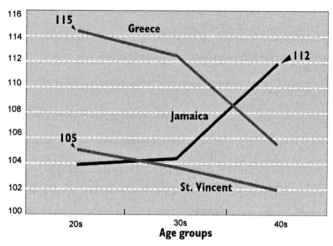

Source: *United Nations Demographic Yearbook*

Morocco and Tunisia: Islam's strong proscriptions against extramarital sex and its required chaperonage of unattached females give special incentive to single young men (85 percent of males under the age of 24 in Tunisia are unmarried, according to the U.N. Population Division) to seek out foreign tourists for sex.

Kenya: Fear of HIV has prompted many men in sub-Saharan Africa to seek women on average six years younger (the highest regional marriage gap in the world) and to marry ever-younger women (Saardchom 31, 21). One could wager that tourist women, who frequent Kenya's beaches and safari routes, similarly represent a safer and thus more appealing outlet for sex than local women.

One caveat must be noted about all the figures in this section: women may be undercounted in much of the developing world, and men (especially black men in the United States) in the developed world (South, "E-Mail"). Such census errors could render man shortages in the West and man surpluses in the developing world just a bit less acute than depicted here.

The many available young males in the developing world, and the many lonely older women in the West set the stage for a transformation in the way women select their companions.

4b. The man shortage has contributed to a revolution in mate selection by many Western women.

I was working on my dissertation in divinity at the University of Chicago, and he was a [Nepalese] yak herder with a fourth-grade education. But on the way down [from a trek], I got this incredible rush of oxygen. I was in an ecstatic state just breathing, and our plane was delayed for three days. So I said, "Oh, who cares?" and got involved with him.

Barbara Pijan Lama (qtd. in Spano, "Trekking")

Intercultural marriage "spoils" the matrimonial order that all societies have established. It increases in societies of higher geographical and social mobility as international relations develop ... .

Barbara, "Mixed Marriages" (577)

These are times that confound observers of the human mating dance, as wealthy Silicon Valley bachelors go unclaimed while women of means pull up stakes to join impoverished African tribal dancers.

The Old Testament is rife with warnings against marriage outside the tribe (Deuteronomy 7:3, Ezra 10:2-3). Since ancient times — and especially in the past century (Russell 33) — the vast majority of women have picked partners, for dating or marriage, of similar backgrounds to themselves, especially in age, education, race, religion and ethnic background. Other areas of similarity tend to be, in order, attitudes, opinions and world views, intelligence, socioeconomic status, physical attractiveness, verbal abilities, personality and family size (Buss, "Human" 49). Couples even tend to share less desirable traits: criminality, alcoholism and psychiatric disorders (Rushton 31).

The fancy word for this is homophily, or the process of mating with others much like oneself. To some extent this may reflect comfort with or greater exposure to members of one's own "tribe."

More precisely, homophily probably involves a compromise between desire for a mate "better" than oneself — taller, healthier, wealthier, better looking — and the reality of one's mate value to others, which brings one back down to Earth, to a spouse similar to oneself. Donald Symons, an anthropology professor and leading scholar on mate selection, drily explained to me the concept of mate value, as developed by social scientist Erving Goffman, as "a characterization of a marriage proposal as being a suggestion by a man that the woman to whom he is proposing is not so superior to him (in some market basket of mate relevant-qualities) as to preclude a merger between them. He added wryly that "Jennifer Aniston and Brad Pitt are not together because they are the only ones who will have each other."

Homophily sounds unromantic, given that society tends to view "choosing a partner ... as a highly personal decision" (Laumann 225, 266), yet "the vast majority of sexual partnerships originate within tightly circumscribed social settings" ... and this applies even to short-term liaisons!

Casual travel sex thus may be one of the few settings where personal preference truly prevails, and with a vengeance. This again demonstrates the importance of the loss of one's socially defined identity as a reason for holiday love affairs.

Surveys indicate that even among domestic U.S. couples who live near their families and their concomitant pressures, homophily is eroding slightly — particularly for women above age 30 (Lichter). As women progress in their careers and their reproductive cycles, homophily may become difficult, irrelevant or actively rejected by women seeking mates.

Surveys also show that homophily weakens as liaisons become less formal, so that couples living together involve more disparate individuals than might be found married (Blackwell). Couples living together are especially likely to involve people of different religions (Laumann 255).

Obviously travel sex falls at an even farther end of this continuum, being just about the least formal sexual liaison possible and, unsurprisingly, in many cases between partners with little in common.

High-status women may be most in need of revising what they are seeking for in a casual or permanent lover. Preferences for a super-successful man dictate that "as a woman's socio-economic status improves, the playing field of acceptable men shrinks considerably" (Batten 82).

The capable, prosperous woman may reach a dating dead end sooner than her middle-of-the-road sisters and feel even more pressure to seek romance on the road. Evidence of this can be seen in female university professors, heiresses, executives and entrepreneurs found in Caribbean love zones.

So weakened homophily appears working in tandem with several other motivations for casual travel sex:

• **Identity loss,** which permits a woman to jettison the social rules of home.

• **Female sexual connoisseurship,** a deliberate pursuit of the exotic and different.

• **A search for healing,** whereby a woman may need to undertake a revitalizing brief affair. Discretion mandates finding a partner outside of one's network.

• **The man shortage,** which gives some women a stark choice between obeying the homophily rules and thus having no partner at all, or rejecting homophily.

- And **the dating war,** which may reclassify the men in one's in-group from potential partners to "the enemy."

Today a mate may be met far away ...

Take geographical homophily. In 1940, more than three out of four marriages in New Haven, Conn., involved couples living within 20 blocks apart of each other (R. Kennedy). In 1950, the median distance between the birthplaces of husband and wife, at least for those studied in a Michigan city, had increased a fair bit, to 110 miles (Spuhler 235):

> Conceptions of romantic love aside, the 'one and only' typically lives within driving distance: it is naturally easier to become intimate with someone who is close by. (Buss, "Human" 48)

Now romantic love flourishes between couples a long-haul flight apart, with partners less alike and the Western woman feeling less constrained by the "homophily rules."

As seen in the earlier discussion on identity loss, distance from home directly impacts behavior. For example, higher distances from one's family are linked to greater interracial marriage, witness high rates in the American West among blacks who moved there from the North but not those born in the West. Researchers "suspect that this is a function of the enduring familial and community control over mate selection behavior" (Tucker 214) — a control weakened by far-flung voyaging.

This linkage between greater distance from family and greater inter-racial marriage of course can be applied to romances on the road. Take as one example a Maryland friend of mine, Rachel Saidi, who met a man from Tanzania (almost 8,000 miles away) while working in the Peace Corps and later married him.

As Rachel's experience shows, a woman who travels or works overseas enjoys a redrawn propinquity: now within 20 blocks of her lodgings, she rubs shoulders with exotically different men, her world no longer automatically segregated by race or income.

Further, an expatriate such as Rachel not only enjoys propinquity with exotic men, she works with them — and workplaces are (at least back home in the United States) where 15 percent of married couples first meet (Laumann 235). Given that fewer than 1 percent of married couples meet on vacation, one might make the bold prediction that the expatriate is 15 times more likely than the traveler to find a permanent mate. We don't have figures to prove this, but coincidentally, among surveys collected in *Sexual Geography* (Belliveau) as many as 30 percent of expatriate women participate in travel sex, and as low as 2 percent of women on short-term travels — exactly a 15-to-1 ratio.

In this vein, Scott J. South, a noted scholar of demography, e-mailed me to recall "the rise in women's labor force participation (including professional occupations where travel is more common) and declines in the sex segregation of occupations." These suggest another reason "why casual travel sex might be on the rise — simply put, the opportunities for women to engage in these types of relationships (at least through their work) have increased." This observation would especially apply to expatriates, he noted, whose romances may "grow out of fairly routine, workaday activities."

Obviously, an increase in the total of Americans undertaking overseas leisure travel from virtually no one in the wartorn early 1940s, the time of the New Haven study, to 20 million today (Belliveau, *Amateur* 1) has vastly increased the presence of distant foreigners in the mating pool for U.S. men and women. As Professor Symons e-mailed me, "I'm sure you'd agree that the huge effect of propinquity on mating is not the result of people sampling every potential mate in the world and finding that they prefer those who live within 20 blocks, but simply the result of being more likely to encounter people who live nearby."

To extend this logic, phenomena today such as binational marriages really reflect, fairly perfectly, the expansion of women's travel opportunities since the 1940 New Haven study. Women still met "nearby" men, but jet travel created new "neighborhoods" with new neighbors — the Sherpa ahead of you on a trail, the Jamaican squatting by your beach towel, the Greek at the next table in an Athens café.

... a mate may be of a different race ...

Homophily began to lessen in the 1960s, and in the 1980s markedly dipped across all sex, educational and racial groups. White and Asian-American women and black and Hispanic men, particularly those with better educations, have proved especially willing to marry outside their group (Qian 265).

More U.S. women now marry outside their race: Figures rose from 0.4 percent in 1960 to 2.6 percent in 2000 (U.S. Census Bureau, *Abstract* 47).

And women in the United States and Western Europe now marry outside their nationality: Figures now range from 6 percent to 8 percent of all marriages.

White women's preferences regarding intermarriage may be "contingent upon the social status of the potential nonwhite spouse" (South, "Sociodemographic" 938). At home, white women often marry nonwhite men of higher educational attainment.

And even for romances on the road, there is often some truth to the statement that "women, whether rich or poor, prefer high-status males" (Batten 91). Western women have, for example, married dozens of Indian rajas and Italian marchese, a Cameroonian chief (Njiké), Nepalese, Thai and Zulu princes (Basundhara, Sanidh and Mwele), sons of Fijian chiefs (Malé and Epi) and Tibetan rulers (Tenzin Choegyal), and the Sherpa nephew (Lhakpa) of the first Everest conqueror, all discussed later. Preferences for aristocrats illustrate not only the evolutionary preference for high-status males but also the magic of meeting a real-life prince (even a non-white one), the stuff of romance novels and fairy tales.

One curious fact: "while white women are more likely than white men to out-marry, they state that they are less willing to do so" (South, "Sociodemographic" 938). Thus white women tend to shock their own selves with curious pairings during vacation, for they readily do what they thought they would never try.

Dozens of white women have landed extensive media coverage and book contracts (in Europe mainly) for their travel sex stories, telling tales that demonstrate white female outmarriage and with sales that demonstrate how their novel mate choices intrigue readers.

This gap between what white women will say and what they will do casts doubt on the predictive worth of surveys measuring mate preferences rather than actual marriages. For example, female medical students and college undergraduates prefer, even more than other women, to find higher-achieving husbands — but of course, actual marriages always reflect what's available rather than the embodiment of an ideal, especially when Mr. Perfect is in short supply.

... a husband may be less educated ....

The female desire to "marry up" to a more educated man is becoming somewhat more difficult for white women (Guttentag 237) and markedly more difficult for black women, giving a loss that began in 1980 of male dominance of college enrollments (Fonda).

Women born after 1976, who have come to dominate the ranks of college graduates, may also see wisdom in modifying their elders' preferences for men of equal or higher education. For these women, there are now only 68 unmarried white educated males (and 58 black males) for every 100 similar females (as seen in the chart on page 110).

Despite the example that opened this section of a woman with a doctorate and her Nepalese husband with a fourth-grade education (not that unusual among the annals of such tales), not all travel romances involve men with only rudimentary schooling.

In fact, Western women (such as anthropologist Jean Gearing or travel writer Robyn Davidson) often take foreign men of erudition as lovers, and higher education becomes the couples' primary (but ample) area of homophily.

For white women, who tend in the United States to marry up educationally when they marry minority men (South, "Sociodemographic" 938), their "marketability" may be greater to a man of higher learning overseas than to white men at home. In both cases, women trade the status of being white for the foreign man's educational, economic or royal status.

Older women are now appealing ...

An erosion of age homophily in short-term mating can be seen most starkly in countries including Kenya, St. Lucia, Morocco, the Gambia and Sri Lanka, notable for the numbers of visiting female tourists in their 50s and 60s or even 70s seeking the companionship of younger men.

Even in the West, the preference of men for younger spouses has shown some signs of weakening, a fortunate development — for if men would begin to prefer women circa five years older than themselves, the marriage squeeze for older Western women would be eliminated (Davis 505).

In three developed nations, Ireland, Iceland and Israel, age differences are close to disappearing (less than 1.6 years in all three), suggesting that a good number of marriages there involve brides older than their grooms.

In the United States, despite the fact that on the mean, husbands in first marriages are 2½ years older than their wives, in 9 percent of marriages (about 5 million in total) the husband is two to five years younger, and in 3 percent (almost 2 million) the husband is six or more years younger:

Emergence of older wife, younger husband

Age difference in years, U.S. husbands and wives, 2001 (Millions)

Female 6 or more years older	1.9
Female 2-5 years older	5.1
Within 1 year	18.0
Male 2-5 years or older	20.5
Male 6 or more years older	11.0

Source: Fields

Looking at lovers instead of spouses, the sex partners "reported by women over 40 are about equally likely to be older or younger" (Laumann 252-253), in sharp contrast to women under 40, who tend to take older men as lovers.

So the model of older woman, younger man, exists not only in poor countries hosting lonely female tourists but to a growing extent in Western nations as well.

And a woman past menopause, as well as today having better chances with younger men (due to changing preferences and a larger available pool), may also place greater importance on her spouse's companionability than heritable traits or money (Essock 20). Finances and genes are less important factors when not planning to have and raise children. Many women past their child-bearing years who have married younger foreign men, including Lady Jane Digby in Syria, Joana McIntyre Varawa in Fiji and Rosemary Long in the Gambia, illustrate this point.

How does a foreign man excel?

The main requirement for many a traveling woman: That a man possess appealing personal qualities rather than impressive attainments and wealth.

In place of a formal education or high job title, women find pleasing such virtues as practicality, confidence and prowess in the physical environment.

• **Kindness and intelligence.** When measuring personal qualities, foreign men can readily compete with or surpass the "boy next door" on personal qualities high on the list of characteristics prized by women, such as kindness and intelligence (Buss, "Human" 50).

Many a traveling woman will have been impressed by tropical men's superior awareness, spatial intelligence, mental speed and practicality, all traits that I have long admired. To select an example of such competence even among a young male, a boy of 12 years competently guided me through Borneo's poorly mapped upland jungle (Belliveau, Amateur 66-69).

Even Western men have noticed the gifts of foreign men:

> From the very beginning of my work with New Guineans, they impressed me as being on the average more intelligent, more alert, more expressive, and more interested in things and people around them than the average European or American is. At some tasks ... such as the ability to form a mental map of unfamiliar surroundings, they appear considerably more adept than Westerners. (Diamond 20)

• **Sweet talk, romantic gestures.** Despite his relative poverty, a foreign man can also compete with or surpass a Western man in displaying affection and generosity (with what little he has), as well as physical domination, good health and vitality (B. Ellis).

Most of all, a poor man can often project self-confidence, romantic expressiveness and masculinity. "If you versatile with the language you can pull women easy," one Barbadian man said, while another noted,

"Them done know that we are kings. We are kings, creatures of the earth you understand" (qtd. in Phillips 197).

**Report: Economically Disadvantaged Men
More Skilled at Communicating Attraction to Women**

headline in The Onion

A foreign man who listens to and praises a Western woman, it seems, can leapfrog a more accomplished but remote Western man — for the modern fellow's admirable ambition also leads him to work so hard that his energy for love, kindness and sensuality dissipates.

The heart of the long-neglected female tourist can be won by the smallest gesture, from a Sherpa guide bringing tea to her tent in the morning (Spano, "Romance") to a Caribbean man who can cook her dinner or sew the strap of her sundress (Amber 104).

I've written of a young Chinese student, living on a monthly allowance of $6, who staggered me by treating me to a Coke for 75 cents (Belliveau, *Amateur* 51). His generosity touched me deeply.

Sometimes too the foreign man makes truly grand efforts, as travel writer Robyn Davidson found when an Indian friend and later lover drove 500 miles straight to assist her through her travails. Narendra soothed her by saying, "Just leave everything to me ... Don't worry. Everything will get sorted out" (*Desert Places* 32, 107, 123).

Illustrating that romantic eloquence is apparently only essential for men who need to compete for women's attentions, we see sweet talk mastered in the earlier eras of male surpluses: by the real-life models for Cyrano de Bergerac, in love letters written by the hopeful suitors of the Victorian era and scared soldiers of 20th century world wars, and in the modern Caribbean — and not so much in the modern West.

A new homophily: seeking someone nice

Especially for divorced women whose husbands were both accomplished and capable of falling right out of love with them, homophily, when not combined with a careful character check, may be looked at as a failed and almost dangerous strategy.

A woman may look instead for one overriding criteria in a mate: niceness.

Or put another way, a faithful heart. The literature of travel romance describes many examples. A shy Venetian man asked Marlena di Blasi, after falling in love with her from afar, if she believed in true love (13). A powerful and confident Sherpa enjoyed a blind woman's complete trust as he carried her over Nepal's icy streams, and won the love of an observer, her deeply impressed companion (Brook 163, 172).

The search for healing, illustrated earlier in this chapter in the cases of di Blasi, Macklovich and Fraser, may force a woman in the interests of self-preservation to jettison the pressures of homophily, for she may have found homophily alone does not protect a woman from wrenching heartache.

Thus the search for love and healing, an individual motivation for travel sex, intersects with a social trend, the revolution in mate selection. Suddenly, a women looks at a foreign man with new eyes, thinking, "That's a nice, gentle guy," and not thinking, "I wouldn't dare become romantic with someone so different."

On a visit to Fiji, Joana McIntyre Varawa, divorced and in her 50s, received a marriage proposal within days of arrival. She admitted, "I knew that Malé did not love me. He was following his father's wishes. But he was kind and attentive, and seemed solid inside" (*Changes* 19).

In my own case, after a divorce and broken engagements to tall, witty but critical men, with the help of a social worker I gained determination to avoid continuing the same mistakes. I ruthlessly reprogrammed myself to respond to acts of kindness, ignore height and to drop men at any hint of sarcasm or edged criticism.

My second husband meets the "nice" criteria but not the homophily rules: he is younger, better educated and of a different race and religion, though having grown up 40 miles apart in Maryland, we do share geographic propinquity.

In her search for male kindness in places farther afield, a female traveler can find herself drawn to foreign men who innately and perhaps because of cultural training pay more genuine courtesy to women than men in the West.

Further, a divorced woman's revised homophily rules may involve seeking men of shared interests rather than backgrounds and attainments. Both partners in a holiday affair, by virtue of finding themselves in a geographically attractive locale and being willing to initiate conversation with a stranger, may by definition be culture brokers, romantic in nature, active and mobile and adventurous, passionate and in search of spiritual connection, and open to creating a relationship melding disparate worlds.

Whereas home, school and church traditionally "bring people together physically [and] facilitate the acquaintance process by creating shared interests and experiences" (Laumann 229), nowadays experiences themselves — trekking in mountains or desert, snorkeling on a reef, studying folk dancing or viewing animals on safari — perform the function of joining the like-minded but socially dissimilar.

A revised homophily for travelers rests partly on love of a place, shared between a tourist woman enthralled with Italy, Kenya, Nepal or Mexico, or seashores, deserts and mountains, and a man of the treasured spot. From the very earliest travel romances in the 1840s onward, women met men as they explored landscapes they loved — Margaret Fuller in Italy, Lady Jane Digby and Margaret Fountaine in Syria and Isabelle Eberhardt in Tunisia.

How they created an alternative to marrying a man living 20 blocks away.

In many international marriages, homophily may be present in many areas other than nationality and background. Women interviewed in studies of crosscultural marriages stressed common interests (R. Lewis 70), their husband's intelligence and his warmth or sense of humor — "the same personal qualities [sought by] those who do not marry out" (Khatib-Chahidi 53).

Another good example of how the new homophily can be little different from the old homophily comes from a study of Indian-Western couples (Cottrell, "International Life Style"), many of whom considered themselves committed internationalists, with one respondent noting, "I would have so little in common with a parochial Indian." Many of the more than 100 couples interviewed could "be seen as marriages within communities [that] happen to transcend national boundaries such as religious groups, international organizations, the scientific community. ... Although all the couples in this sample are cross-national, they are not necessarily primarily cross-cultural."

Measuring the mate revolution

Social scientists and feminists have attempted to foresee a potential for women as they become wealthier to seek men who might be fun rather than prosperous (Buss, "Evolutionary" 313).

Immigration data provided in the Experiences chapter measures the number of U.S. women who marry non-Western men. These figures challenge the conclusions of studies relying on interviews with young professional women who indicate a continued preference for homophily. As mentioned above, female medical students (Townsend) and college undergraduates (Wiederman) have declared that even more than other women, they would prefer higher-achieving husbands.

Older women, however, cast a wider net. In 1995, April Gorry began 12 months of study in the tiny Central American country of Belize interviewing unattached female tourists.

She spoke to 32 women who indeed rejected homophily in favor of selecting poor men who offered them attention and affection and who demonstrated a manly masterly of the natural environment of Belize's offshore islets. She noted a revolt that had been growing worldwide:

> The mating behavior of Western women tourists visiting Greece, Indonesia, East Africa, Jerusalem, Jamaica, Ecuador, Barbados, Hawaii and Belize poses a problem for scientific and intuitive models of human sexual psychology. Many of these women enter into sexual relationships with low status local men they barely know. The phenomenon of romance tourism violates ... expectations that women will prefer to mate with men they have had time to assess and who are resource rich, in the Western sense. (vi)

Tourist women, Gorry concluded, were wowed by the "social ease, laidbackness, and sexual and romantic expressiveness of island men ... because the larger-scale industrial societies the women originate from do not tend to encourage strong expressions of these traits" (vii). Further, "conditions at home ... lead some women to seek a sexually and socially affirming experience abroad."

Gradually over time, from the 1840s to now, women at home and abroad have redrawn age-old rules of mate selection, because as a woman gets older, to seek a resource-rich Western man has become a long-odds chase for the unavailable and uninterested. For the unattached woman living in a Western society that equates sex with happiness and fulfillment, an interested foreign man may fill the bill.

"... Neither male sexual prowess," Gorry concluded (2) "nor a nostalgia for a pre-industrial lifestyle can fully explain the appeal of the 'man of the tropics.' Behind the myth of female lust is a set of male qualities that appeal to more than just white Western women travelers ... competence, self-assurance, sexual directness and devotion."

Widespread, involuntary female celibacy

5. *After an extended time without sex, a tourist woman may leap at the chance for an affair.*

> **Many tourists experience sexual encounters simply because the opportunity arises or because the meet like-minded individuals. ... In other cases, they simply feel lonely and sexually deprived.**
>
> Oppermann, "Sex Tourism" (256)

> **I faced the twin problems of loneliness and sexual frustration. ... Under such circumstances, why not respond to the advances of local men?**
>
> Dubisch (38)

To speak of an "unseen epidemic" is to verge on cliché, but celibacy among unattached women certainly qualifies. Each year, a remarkable number of Western women have no sex — about one-third of those who are single, divorced, separated or widowed.

In the United States, of women who are not living with anyone:

- 32 percent report no sex in the past year.
- another 23 percent say they had sex only "a few times per year" (Michael 116).

So more than half of all non-cohabiting U.S. women have very little sex. Add to this that one in seven married women also reports sex not at all or only a few times a year.

In fact, sex travel connoisseurs — women who love sex the most — may be most likely to suffer stretches of celibacy if they are either not yet married or between marriages. One historical example was the North African sex traveler Isabelle Eberhardt, who more than a century ago "led a divided life: Those who lived alongside her knew that she went for long periods without sex, as she had in the Sahel, if you call two months long, but from the sleazier parts of town would come rumours from people who knew she had indulged in orgies of kef-induced eroticism" (Kobak 100).

Similarly, British poet and sex traveler Fiona Pitt-Kethley ("20 Years") captured the harsh reality of being a "swinging single." She noted at the time of her 1995 marriage that "TV researchers asked me if I was a 'sex addict.' I pointed out that a promiscuous woman is never that. She often has to endure periods of celibacy in between partners. Sex addicts are all married, wedded to their pusher."

One can assume that the vast majority of women not having sex are involuntary celibates, victims of the dating war, the man shortage and their own fading youth rather than women obeying religious vows or making a personal pledge to abstain. Sociologist Denise Donnelly defines an involuntary celibate as "one who desires to have sex, but has been unable to find a willing partner for at least six months."

Even with the man shortage we have described, the scope of physical deprivation among unattached women (and even some married women) seems enormous. Consider divorced American women aged 45 to 59: More than half report no sex in the previous year (Laumann 189).

Residents of U.S. cities report higher rates of celibacy for at least one year than suburbanites (T. Smith, table 11), a finding consistent with plight of urban women who vainly seek heterosexual men to date.

Family therapists in cities see first hand the pain of celibacy among their clients. "I see so many nice, beautiful, smart women locked into points of view, who have not opened their own mind into other possibilities," Mary Ann Constantinides, a Baltimore therapist, told me, indicating that the women needed to look more flexibly at potential mates.

Let's look at percentages of women in the West who report no sex over the course of a year:

Women reporting no sex in past 12 months

	U.S.	U.K.	France
Not cohabitating	32%	38%	35%
Married	3%	3%	3%
Aged 45 to 59	26%	19%	8%

Sources: Michael 116; Laumann 189, 190; Johnson, *Sexual Attitudes and Lifestyles* 453, 454; Spira 121

In the United States, the United Kingdom and France, one-third or more of non-cohabitating women report no sex in previous 12 months, as do 3 percent of married women — figures that hold remarkably constant across countries. In the United States and the United Kingdom, the rejection of older divorced women as sex partners seems more acute than in France. (Clearly older women in France maintain their desirability, as is readily apparent for anyone who has spent an afternoon in Paris or admired the aging actress Jeanne Moreau still successfully playing the vamp. Yet a competing explanation could be that older French women are more likely to resort to casual travel sex and report their activities to survey takers, thus lowering their celibacy figures. One can also read the chart above as indicating that that older British and American women are more likely than French women to be in need of casual travel sex.)

What is remarkable is that so many women even confess to celibacy to a survey taker (the U.S. women were interviewed face to face, and the French women via telephone), for "celibacy is a taboo subject ... according to society, something's wrong with you if you're not having sex" (D. Williams 35). A celibate woman can be labeled unattractive and undesirable, and feel shame, despair and depression (14-15). Thus one can reasonably wonder if surveys actually understate the extent of involuntary celibacy among women.

Small wonder that a foreign man who seems to drop out of the sky to announce "you are beautiful" and that he wants "to make you happy" may find a long-celibate woman receptive. As one of my friends on a world tour described it, she found herself in the "danger zone" because "it had been too long" and allowed a Maori man "with a lovely face" to join her in a clawfooted bathtub surrounded by lit candles.

Violent love comes "by the visitation of God," as our juries say; the man or woman must satisfy it or die.

Duff Gordon (*Egypt* 138), on encounters between colonial Englishwomen and Egyptians

Indeed, of Dutch and Swedish women who take holiday lovers, one-quarter to one-third report no steady partner at home (de Graaf, "Sexual Risk" 1177; M. Arvidson, et al., "Risky Behavior" 419).

One writer, Maryse Holder, perhaps one of history's most tormented practitioners of casual travel sex, noted an incredible three years of celibacy (94) and rejection in New York City, which she described as a "paunch and fag death scene:"

> ... It finally occurred to me that I am leading this greedy whore life — drunk and dancing every two days at Chololo, eating men up with my eyes and my body on the beach and in town — because of the life I led in N.Y.; what an unreal existence! No sex, a manless world. So of course here [in Mexico] seems like a last chance at love, intensity of feeling. (50)

Yet most other women seem to go out of their way not to cite celibacy as a motivator in holiday affairs. This may be in part "due to gendered expectations that men 'must' have sex, but that women can do without it more easily" (D. Donnelly, "Review").

For example, older tourist women in Belize willingly discussed their loneliness and sense of closing opportunities, but none gave the impression of the sex-starved tourist (Gorry 69), perhaps because to acknowledge being celibate is an acutely embarrassing admission in an era when sex plays an important role in Westerners' self-esteem.

Sexuality, appropriately expressed, is our main source of happiness ... .

Reich (paraphrased in Giddens 160)

For people in all cultures, sex is ... most commonly associated with seeking comfort, finding pleasure, and survival.

Ross (107)

British women who had engaged in travel sex were more open (M. Thomas 205): "Sexual desire and the urge for sexual fulfillment were often mentioned as motivating factors. Indeed some relationships appeared to be based primarily on a strong physical attraction and a resultant desire for sexual pleasure."

The British novelist E.M. Forster ("Kanaya" 230) once wrote of travel sex that it is "the companionship one really seeks, although it presents itself as a physical urge." In the reasoning of some women reticent to acknowledge sexual need, the ranking could be reversed: The physical urge may present itself as a desire for companionship.

Involuntary celibacy is only beginning to receive public discussion, via a fledgling Web site (Boltwood) and via focused scholarly investigation (Donnelly, et al., "Involuntary").

My sense, based on personal experience and essays by others (Fraser; Dubisch; Gornick 198), is that for divorced women more than singles, involuntary celibacy is a painful and difficult situation and a powerful motivation to travel sex. Why? As my father told me once, describing his Army service in postwar Germany, lack of sex was a bigger problem for married GIs than single ones, because it was the husbands who were accustomed to a steady supply! Similarly, a cutoff of ready intimacy should be a source of greater frustration to divorced women.

In my own experience, celibacy has played a great role in making the gravitational pull of casual travel sex impossible to try to resist, particularly with Danny Jr. and other Caribbean men. Even during my trip to Greece, when I had a new boyfriend, quite probably I felt the echoes of celibate periods during college and marital separation and wanted to "make up for lost time."

As seen in the preceding section on the man shortage, widespread involuntary celibacy follows inexorably from aspects of Western social structure, especially the tendency of men to marry younger women and high divorce rates. "Older heterosexual women of the baby boom generation, [despite] sexually liberated attitudes and behaviors," face a dwindling supply of men (Gillmore 103), and thus must "accept serendipitous sexual encounters or affairs with married men because it may be their only opportunity for physical intimacy."

And what could be a more serendipitous sexual encounter than a vacation romance?

Celibate men?

Do you realize how difficult it is ... for a Senegalese man to have sex with a Senegalese woman? Basically, he has to marry her.

Sumner (60-61)

As far as dry spells go, might both the tourist woman and her holiday lover be feeling deprived?

For one example, my friend in the "danger zone" was told by her Maori that he hadn't been with a woman in 18 months.

One might dismiss this as a come-on line designed to indicate sincerity, a man trying to say, "I'm selective, lonely and not exposed to disease."

And it seems ludicrous to imagine that a Caribbean beach boy juggling demands from a harem of new and returning female tourists (and perhaps a wife and local girlfriends) feels sexually deprived at all.

Yet I suspect, even in the Caribbean, some truth to these claims when made by men who are not beach boys and who are not married. Even in cultures with freewheeling attitudes toward sex, the man may also have been, if not celibate, at least mildly deprived for some time.

A woman has a fair chance of meeting a long-celibate man:

• in China, India, Iran, Taiwan and Indonesia, four countries that rate chastity highly (Buss, "Sex Differences" 11).

• in countries such as the Gambia, Greece, Morocco, Tunisia and Kenya, where young women tend to be married and young men tend to be single.

• in areas where women live segregated lives from men, as in the Islamic world and Southern Europe.

• and in resorts surrounded by poverty, for a poor man is often rejected by his own women.

Other situations can also lead to male celibacy. Black men in a Latin country may come up empty (Gorry 109). I have also mentioned sexual overtures received from a French naval officer on a tour of duty, a Caribbean guest worker distant from his wife, and men living on tiny islands with few female residents.

So we can see that a woman deprived of sex for a lengthy period, especially if she lands in the sensual tropics, may find overpowering urges to take a lover — and in fact, local suitors may feel just as deprived.

Dating wars

6a. Western women and men alike flee a dating war in their home countries and seek lovers from foreign lands.

> **I've been a relationship coach 10 years, and I've never seen things so bad. The misunderstanding between the sexes is tremendous. The women are very tough on the men. They're constantly finding reasons to not like them. And the men, who are some of the nicest guys in the world, think that women just don't want nice guys.**
>
> Julie Paiva (qtd. in Nieves)

> **Something must have occurred, so that the Westerners do not manage any more to sleep together ... .**
>
> Houellebecq (250)

Everywhere around the world, it seems, women and men are angry at each other and seeking greener pastures with foreigners.

What lies at the root of the dating war in the West? "Men and women compete for jobs and advancement at work — and they may find this competition spills over into personal relationships," therapist Constantinides told me.

Dates may become screening interviews about salary and career. Women hire private detectives to investigate their boyfriends. No level of personal attack is off-limits in child custody battles. One in three men and women report that their partner competes with them (Laner 185).

Add to competition the problem of chaos in the aftermath of women's changed sex roles, "the single most important social change to have taken place in the United States over the past 40 years" (Fukuyama). Some women revel in deliberately confusing men, wanting it both ways: using either feminism or conversely femininity — whichever gives them the advantage — to win their goals and to manipulate men (Young 7).

As Constantinides and others have pointed out, a loved one may not offer much solace from workplace strife. "Despite romantic ideals, conflict in close heterosexual relationships is pervasive" (Buss, "Married Couples" 663) and includes condescension, insults, infidelity, physical abuse and power struggles (Glickauf-Hughes).

With so much discord at work and home, "the normal individual ... is in the dilemma of needing a great deal of affection but finding difficulty in obtaining it" (Horney 287).

Today, tens of thousands of lonely Westerners seek affection at the other end of an airplane journey. For:

> When an existing social order fails to provide for the emotional needs of large numbers of people — fails to provide them ways to meet social expectations and to feel loved — significant social movements with emotionally loaded mass appeal may ensue. (Buck 52)

How should men and women interact?

Social upheaval regarding sex roles may be yet another manifestation of the West's man shortage (Guttentag 166-67), as women with poor marriage prospects adopt feminism as a means to attain higher wages in job markets.

As women demand more money and power, they also demand men to be more sensitive and nurturing.

Yet a Western man ends up in a no-win situation: "If he lets go of the traditional masculine style completely, he may find to his terror that he is becoming invisible, unsexy and unworthy in the eyes of most women" (Goldberg 163). And "as men become the New-Age sensitive guys women want, some women are less able to find them sexually attractive because they strike too many feminine chords" (Ackerman 155).

So men end up thoroughly confounded on whether and how to approach capable females. To cite again my correspondent, Susanne K., the 45-year-old international recruiter:

My (dis)satisfaction with German men: Indeed, it is difficult to find a German man who accepts an independent, professionally successful woman. The few men who are singles are at first very much attracted but then afraid of starting a relationship. All my girlfriends share this experience. Consequently, my girlfriends at least enjoy a holiday affair with a good-looking local man.

Indeed, from the male point of view, feminists have created the New Sensitive Man, then set upon him viciously and ultimately dumped him for the Macho Foreigner.

One female travel writer unintentionally crystalizes this viewpoint in describing a trip to Sicily: "I want to know brute male strength and masculine essence. So lonely in America, so tired of men who are afraid of their essential selves, I am like a panther in heat, craving" (Rigoglioso 130).

Over and over again, women echo this preference for confident and attentive men:

Guys at home are so confused, they don't approach women directly very much. But you come down here [Jamaica] and the men are dropping out of the trees like mangoes.

Canadian woman (qtd. in Pruitt 426)

... Japanese males are just too awful: I guess what it amounts to is this: any man is better than a Japanese.

Japanese woman (qtd. in Kelsky, *Verge* 81)

[Belizean men are] very confident about their masculinity — not like the guys in the States who are unsure whether to be manly or something else. The men here know their place [sphere of activity] and how to act. They've done it for years and they're very strong.

Jennifer, a foreign resident (qtd. in Gorry 176)

In Silicon Valley, home at the height of the dot.com craze to legions of well-off single men, the mating game even perplexed newly minted millionaires, who by rights should be date magnets. Some hired image consultants and matchmakers to learn how to dress and how to greet women (Nieves).

Compare these men's lack of savoir-faire to the assurance of Caribbean men who do not hesitate to yell out, "Hey baby, wanna get laid?" Western women go wild when complimented or openly propositioned on island beaches, praising beach boys' masculinity while pigeonholing kindred behavior in Western men as sexual harassment.

As Western women seek the proud traditional male, meanwhile Western men mourn a lessening of traditional femininity. Other men have become so hostile to women it's almost scary. A sampling of international opinion:

- German men on German women: "very cold, very authoritative ... self-centered ... in marriage they are two equal persons, or like two men in the house" (Cabezas 111).
- An American tourist in Bangkok: "American women are fucking bitches and idiots compared to these [Thai] women" (qtd. in the 1995 film, *The Good Woman of Bangkok*).
- Australian men on white women: "white bellies, creatures who are deemed to be spoiled, grasping and, above all, unwilling or inferior sexual partners" (Kruhse-MountBurton 197) and "incredibly obnoxious, dominating, demanding" (Iyer 58).
- An English character in a novel about the bars in Bangkok: "Fucking a white woman is a step away from homosexuality" (C. Moore 107).
- A man, operating a Web site offering mail-order brides, on American women (repeating a joke about the difference between heaven and hell): "Heaven is having a Japanese wife, a Chinese cook, a British country home and an American salary. Hell is having a Chinese salary, a British cook, a tiny Japanese house and an American wife" (Gary Clark qtd. in Bowden).

In sum, men and women around the developed world are in conflict, with perhaps the most severe problems in Japan followed by Australia, where reports persists of dissatisfied Australian women taking desperate interest in foreign men. "The Aussie male is ... almost totally devoid of charm. He is biased, bigoted, boring and, above all, brutal," travel writer Robyn Davidson (*Tracks* 34) observed, indicating the fever pitch of the Antipodean dating war.

Hyperfeminine women, hypermasculine men

The men go to Thailand and the women go to Jamaica.

Saying in Germany (Pruitt 425)

It's true, it's striking, inevitable: The white women prefer to sleep with Africans, the white men with Asians. I need to know why ... .

Houellebecq (243)

The entire West (and perhaps the world?) seems to suffer from Affection Deficit Disorder.

What do Western men do about it? They seek the archetypally feminine woman in Southeast Asia, Latin America and other areas.

Meanwhile Western women seek the archetypally masculine man, often from Africa and its New World diaspora, or Southern Europe or Polynesia.

Japanese women seek British men and Americans, both black and white, as well as Southeast Asians (Kelsky, *Verge* 6). Japanese men seek Filipina, Thai and Chinese women (256).

In their search for a masculine man, Western women even accept domination from a foreigner that they would vociferously reject from a Western man. "De white boys are more laid back and take de orders, de black boys now does give them the orders" (Barbados man qtd. in Phillips 197).

For all the bossiness of Caribbean men, white women feel valued by them and "are offered a stage upon which they can ... reject the white men who have rejected them" (Sánchez Taylor, "Dollars" 760).

Tastes of Western white men for the thin and the "attractive" in a narrow sense, as defined by leading models and actresses, also translates into a feeling of rejection. Full-figured women who visit, for example, Africa and the Caribbean pass under a magic wand that transforms them instantly from pig to love goddess.

"So if you have been a neglected woman in civilization, when you come down here [to the Dominican Republic] ... they are going to wipe you off your feet," one American female expatriate in her 50s said (O'Connell Davidson, "Fantasy" 51).

In their quests, men and women alike seem to be searching not only for tradition but also romance, defined for centuries as the knight in shining armor rescuing the damsel in distress, a symbiotic scenario difficult to achieve in an androgynous society.

> **There seems to be ... a near-perfect match between the Western men, who are unappreciated and get no respect in their own countries, and the Thai women, who would be happy to find someone who simply does his job and hopes to come home to a pleasant family life after work. Most Western women do not want such a boring husband.**
>
> Houellebecq (132)

Some Western women flee the androgyny of the modern era to explore the world's most traditional societies. Sarah Lloyd, an English architect, followed an impoverished Sikh named Jungli to a religious community in north India. Jungli helped her with household chores out of kindness, not nagging, and Sarah reciprocated. Traditional sex roles, she felt, eliminated confusion and bickering and dignified how the couple interacted. Lloyd concluded, "India taught me to be a woman" (210).

Lloyd's sentiments echo the conclusions of a top scholar on the neurotic personality. Back in 1937, Karen Horney foresaw the downside of blurred sex roles: "If an individualistic competitive spirit prevails in any society it is bound to impair the relations between the sexes, unless the spheres of life pertaining to man and woman are strictly separated" (197).

6b. Foreign men also flee their own dating wars by taking tourist lovers.

It is only logical that men who are shut out of mating opportunities in their own community for social and economic reasons will seek emotional intimacy with a sexually desirous and appreciative "other."

Gorry (71)

Caught up in examining conflict and competition in the corporate suites of the West, we tend to overlook that even in simple societies, dating wars rage rampant.

Deep levels of distrust and suspicion exist between the males and females of the Caribbean (R. Jones 30, Campbell), Thailand, Greece, and other areas, so that in Belize for example, both tourists and local males "sense that they are isolated and undervalued at home" (Gorry 128).

In the developing world, at the root of the dating wars lie issues other than personal conflict and workplace competition. Caribbean women want a man of means, Thai (and Japanese) women resent male control, and Mediterranean women kept under wraps until marriage feel rejected by their men who chase tourists in the meantime.

Palestinian girls, left at home "while their male contemporaries and future husbands run around with shapely and well-dressed European girls," wonder if they are no good (E. Cohen, "Arab Boys" 229).

In Barbados, Indonesia and Belize, many beach boys no longer have relations with local women (Phillips 198; Dowling 278; Gorry 110). Likewise Indian men in Rajasthan discover a new universe of sex, neither rushed nor hidden in the dark, with white women (Martin).

The Caribbean epitomizes the dating war as played out in the developing world. Local women seem to find their own men overbearing, tiresome and unable to provide material comfort: "They abuse us and we start hating black men because we come to Negril and see white guys, they treat us like princesses" (Campbell 151). The women also come to favor Japanese men: "them nice."

Caribbean men shoot back in the dating war: The white women they meet on the beach "compare wid the people that from your country they more nicer, they more friendlier, they even help you more than your own" (Phillips 188). White female tourists praised their lovers while island women said they were lousy in bed.

Derided as "white bellies" and sexually cold by Western men, white women win high praise from other men the world over.

They are "more sexy, more adventurous, friendlier" than Barbadian women (Phillips 198), "more tender and emotional than Jamaican women" (Pruitt 428) and "better educated, wealthier and more worldly" than Belizean women (Gorry 85).

La Ronde, updated

The pervasiveness of dating wars around the planet can be demonstrated in the chart below, a roundup of documented examples. As in the 1950 Max Ophuls movie, *La Ronde*, which depicts a woman who pursues a man who prefers another woman who prefers another man in a chain of unrequited attraction, so goes the world. Let's look at how one woman's trash in another woman's treasure:

	ARE DISLIKED BY:	AND ARE LIKED BY:
Thai men	Thai women [1]	Japanese women [2]
Western men	Western women	Thais, Filipinas, Russians, Cubans [3]
German women	German men	Greeks, Africans, even Irishmen [4]
American men	American women	Japanese, [5] British women [6]
American women	American men	British, Caribbean men
Caribbean men	Caribbean women	U.S. black women [7]
U.S. black men	U.S. black women	European women [8]
Japanese men	Japanese women [9]	Filipinas, Thai, Chinese, [10] Jamaican women [11]

Sources: [1] Odzer 303 [2] Vorakitphokatorn 72 [3] Wilson 14, 115, 147 [4] H. Robinson 248 [5] Kelsky, *Verge* [6] Wilson 61 [7] Amber 162 [8] What Is It [9] WuDunn [10] Kelsky, *Verge* 256 [11] Campbell 151. Uncited portions of chart are discussed elsewhere in this chapter.

Even in Italy, historically the world's leading travel sex destination, British and American women still take local consorts, but Italian women apparently find them wanting and sample men on the tiny Caribbean island of Bequia (N. Price; Stewart, *Weather* 68).

Maybe it's time for a truce in the dating wars. If every man or woman in the world seems capable of having at least one foreign admirer, every man or woman must have some appealing characteristics that could be appreciated at home as well.

Still, it's easier to make a match with someone who reciprocates your interest, so sex travel may be with us for some time.

Tourist women are also "more beautiful" or "more intelligent" than Greek women (Zinovieff 212), and apparently cleaner: "When a kamaki approaches a woman who turns out to be Greek, he may return to his friends, and say disparagingly, 'she smells of sheep' " (216).

Tourist women also give poor men a second chance, for they ignore "the local status system; to them, all these people are relatively poor," anthropologist Donald Symons e-mailed me, citing the work in Belize by April Gorry.

"What they see," Symons wrote, "is the hustlers' social and physical confidence, their lack of worry (tomorrow will take care of itself ... it always has), how good they are with children, how they know every-body, etc. etc. So it's not that status isn't important — it's just that these hustlers don't exhibit cues that trigger the perception 'low-status man' in tourist women's brains, but they do trigger that perception in the brains of local women (who want to marry an ambitious man who will start his own business and get ahead)."

Symons' observation of the hustlers' lack of worry, blended with supreme manly confidence, is echoed in Grace Jones' song, "My Jamaican Guy," whose central lyrics describe a man who is laid back, not worried, not thinking (that is, overanalyzing), "never holding back."

Given that the lives of women are so arduous in many tropical regions frequented by tourists, a Western woman even if older may be more vigorous and well-groomed than local women and thus appear to tropical men as a paragon of health, education, cleanliness and wealth — with a brave and intrepid spirit to boot. For example, my exception-ally well-traveled friend Jane noticed her guide's interest in her in Madagascar and wondered to me: "Is it that we American women are so different from the locals, especially those of us traveling alone?"

6c. Sometimes the dating war resembles a covert operation, marked more by indifference than outright hostility.

When California writer Laura Fraser met a man in Italy who made her feel relaxed and romantic, she noted ruefully that "there don't seem to be any men like that in San Francisco" (63).

For her, the dating war means living in a "desert for dates" (71) with a quiet but pervasive feeling of being disregarded as a woman. She longs to visit Italy, just for a bit of male attention. "Italian men, unlike American men, like to flirt even when there's no chance of any tangible outcome. They just like to let you know, in restaurants and on the street, that they appreciate women."

As for American men, "either they want to sleep with you, and they open doors and pay for meals and do all that, or they don't, in which case you hardly exist any more as a woman — you become a buddy or a business associate, a kind of honorary man" (64-65).

In a word, she feels "invisible."

Thus, for many women, the dating wars smolder without bursting into flames. For an urban woman in particular the war between the sexes consists of ... indifferent men not even seeing her as date material.

That is, until the invisible city girl goes overseas and suddenly a magic red carpet unrolls at her feet.

Commodification of sex

7a. *For perhaps the first time in history, women are willing and able to buy sex — principally from foreign men met while traveling. And the poorer the country visited, the more likely even elderly female tourists can hire or even marry attractive local youths.*

> **As women devote themselves more to their professional life, to their personal projects, they will also find it simpler to pay for sex; and they will turn to sexual tourism. Women can adapt to male values ... .**
>
> Houellebecq (154)

> **Sex for resources, or resources for sex — the two have been exchanged in millions of transactions over the millennia of human existence.**
>
> Buss, *Evolution* (86)

By the time the Beatles released "Can't Buy Me Love" in 1964, for more than a century many Europeans and North Americans had viewed romantic love as essential to a happy courtship and marriage.

A more relevant song today might be titled something like, "Can Buy Me Affectionate Sex." Well-to-do Western women now travel and pursue pragmatic exchanges with sex partners in the developing world, where foreign men provide compliments and romance in a transaction designed to appear less cold than Western prostitution.

Still, in sex tourism zones, affection and sex have become commodities, bought and sold and subject to market forces, as are eggs in a grocery aisle. Tangible estimates of the commodification of sex, such as the global value of the sex industry, run to an estimated $20 billion ("Sex Industry"). The proportion of women thought to be among European sex tourists: 10 percent (Berer).

Thailand and the Dominican Republic, which explicitly offer sex for sale to both men and women, straight and gay, serve as paramount examples. And today poor men actually emigrate in search of wealthy female tourists: from Java and Sumatra to Bali (Fickling, and online posters on bali-travelforum.com) and from Haiti to the Dominican Republic, according to a Dominican diplomat friend of mine.

Though the fact that some vacationing women pay cash for sex with foreign men will come as shocking news to 99 percent of the world, the idea has been around for many years.

Swedish women in the Gambia and French women in Senegal began paying for sex as early as the 1960s, according to one report (Wagner 48).

But even further back in time, the novelist D.H. Lawrence described, with great plausibility given copious reports on Italy as an early female destination for travel sex, the gondoliers of 1920s Venice eager for tips from the ladies. Giovanni "was perfectly ready to prostitute himself" to Lady Chatterley and her companion, "as he had been devoted to cargos of ladies in the past:"

> He secretly hoped they would want him: they would give him a handsome present, and it would come in very handy, as he was just going to be married. (Lawrence 260)

A real-life Giovanni would have been providing an extra fillip to well-established commercial relationships between journeying women and Venetian men. In *European Travel for Women*, published in New York in 1900, author Mary Cadwalader Jones stresses the importance of hiring a gondolier while visiting Venice and provides a daily rate of $15 (in current U.S. dollars) — with a $3 tip.

Back in the 1880s, rich young American women married titled but poor European foreigners in arrangements with specific terms. One such wife (qtd. in Sherwood 689) spelled out the details: Her foreign husband would not talk about money. He would not get on her nerves. He would be complimentary and pleasant in conversation. And he would "at least pretend to love me; he will make me very satisfied with myself; he will make me comfortable. I shall buy respect and graceful attendance."

Yesterday's Victorian heiress discovered the sexual zone where pragmatism begins to shade into commodification. Today's Western woman may not gain a title and its privilege from marriage to a foreign man, but he can still offer her satisfaction and comfort.

Measuring the phenomenon

A sex survey in the United Kingdom yielded rows of "not applicable" when women were asked if they paid for sex in the past five years (Johnson, "Sexual Behaviour" 1839), while U.S. and French studies made no mention at all of this question.

In measures of men's use of prostitutes, "the corresponding numbers for women were so low that they are not even reported as significant sexual outlets for women" (Buss, *Evolution* 85).

Yet overseas, 65 percent of women visiting Jamaica and 39 percent in the Dominican Republic offered cash, gifts or meals to their local lovers (Sánchez Taylor, "Dollars" 754).

So the number of Western women paying for sex is not quite zero and includes some part of the 24,000 women estimated to engage in travel sex annually. Though some women are willing to pull cash from a handbag, many seem to prefer to reward men with gifts, so that the transaction outwardly more resembles buying a boyfriend a birthday present.

For the women who do purchase sex, they do so while traveling overseas, although tiny numbers of women also purchase sex when at home (Haddad), generally in the guise of gifts given discretely to gigolos (Macy 266-67).

And neither traveling men nor traveling women, despite payments for sex, view their vacation lovers as prostitutes or gigolos or themselves as sex tourists (Sánchez Taylor, "Dollars" 750; Forsythe, et al., "Paradise" 279).

Love, romance and cash

That women could come to treat sex as another item in the supermarket trolley is not such a leap, perhaps, given that many economists believe that:

• singles compete in "marriage markets" for others of similar intelligence, education, height and so forth (Becker 832).

• if singles have high socioeconomic status they seek to "exchange" their resources "for a spouse with valued qualities" (South, "Sociodemographic" 937).

• the time taken in finding a mate and the standards set for one depend on supply and demand (Oppenheimer).

• and the gains from a potential marriage for the man and the woman can be predicted by elaborate formulae (Becker 832).

Of course such a framework seems utterly unromantic to the typical Western reader, but "in countries such as Japan and India marriage market awareness is a fact of life," with marriage fixers, newspaper advertising and local marriage bureaus (Grossbard-Schechtman 391). Yet the British expression that a single woman is "on the shelf" acknowledges the link, even to Westerners, between a mate search and shopping.

Buying intimacy

In Southeast Asia and the Caribbean especially, the transaction lacks the coldness of Western prostitution, as attested by how, despite the initial intentions of both parties, love can blossom, with one in 30 liaisons perhaps becoming long term.

So in fact, what is being purchased is something that can't be bought in the West, or satisfied via masturbation: not so much sex per se but companionship, much more attainable with a Thai woman or a Jamaican man than by picking up a streetwalker or bar patron at home. People engage in sex tourism in developing countries "where their money supposedly can buy not only more sex, but also more tenderness on the side of the prostitute" (Oppermann, "Sex Tourism" 255).

A woman in a holiday affair, with her money and her ultramasculine lover, may enjoy the best of both worlds: "She adopts the masculine role of economic provider yet also explores the traditional feminine role thrown off by the feminist movement" (Phillips 198).

Relying on female tourist money

At least some poor adults have come to terms with providing sex as a commodity and will fight for the right to maintain contact with tourists. In the Gambia, for example, (male) elders frowned on the cultural taboo of local beach boys going with older female tourists when the liaisons began in the 1960s (Harrell-Bond). By the 1990s, however, mothers of beach boys protested government attempts to crack down on their son's main source of income: services to foreign women (N. Brown, 365-66, 368).

Journalists and academics who disapprove of sex between older, paying female Westerners and Gambian youths often dwell on the fact that the Gambia is one of the world's poorest countries. A caveat needs to be applied. The Gambia's per capita income is 50 percent higher than the mean for its West African neighbors (Population Reference Bureau), indicating perhaps that grateful white women, happy to buy sex as a commodity, have played some small role in lifting the Gambians' lot far past that of residents of Benin, Nigeria and Burkina Faso.

Such payoffs mean that most governments (as well as their citizens) in the developing world come to accept sex tourism as a valuable genesis of airline and hotel receipts. In the Caribbean, for example, government-paid advertising to foster tourism, highlighting sun, sea, sand and friendly locals, indirectly promotes sex tourism as well (Mullings 236-37), given the tight weave of sex and travel in the tropics. And those amiable locals include taxi drivers, waiters and Jet-Ski rental agents willing to befriend tourist women.

Most observers conclude that these relationships are mutually beneficial, although at times one partner or the other becomes hurt or exploited. This aspect of holiday affairs will be explored in the Ethics section.

Whether to categorize the commodification of sex as a cause or an effect of casual travel liaisons would be difficult to say. It seems clear, however, that either way, wealth plays a defining role.

Gambian teenagers, for example, would never consider marrying a Gambian woman two generations older, but in a significant number of real-life cases, they have indeed married white, moneyed European grandmothers (Aziz).

What is being traded

Let's see what both parties to a typical vacation affair bring to the table, taking an American woman as an example.

U.S. women,

PER CAPITA INCOME BY OCCUPATION

IF SHE IS A:	... SHE EARNS ANNUALLY ABOUT:
Technical or sales worker	$26,000
Professional	$29,000
Nurse (L.P.N.)	$31,000
Administrator	$43,000

Source: U.S. Census Bureau, *Occupation*

If, for one example, an experienced nurse earning $40,000 a year goes on vacation to the following countries, she earns at least double what typical local men do:

Female sex tourism destinations,

PER CAPITA INCOME, 2001

Greece	$17,200
Barbados	$14,500
Thailand	$6,700
Dominican Republic	$5,700
Jamaica	$3,700
Morocco	$3,500
Belize	$3,200
Indonesia	$2,900
Kenya	$1,500
Gambia	$1,100

Source: *The World Factbook*

In fact, the gap between the Western woman's income and her foreign lover's is likely to be far greater than these figures would indicate. If her lover is a beach boy, for example, he probably has little education and few personal assets except charm and beauty, and thus earns less than the national median. In fact, he may earn close to nothing at all. If he lives in the Caribbean, he likely belongs to the ranks of the region's 15 percent or more unemployed. If her lover is a Masai tribesman or a similar man in a subsistence economy, he probably ekes out at most a little beer money by performing dances for tourists or selling crafts.

Ultimately, in extreme cases, a tourist woman could earn 1,000 times a year more than her foreign man.

Going rates for sex with foreign men have been reported as anywhere from $30 for an hour (Jamaica) to $150 to $225 for a full night of top-end sex (in Jamaica and Bali). With the average per capita income of both Bali and Jamaica hovering around $10 per day, men must be pleased to earn as much as 20 times a typical income — by getting laid.

What does the foreign man bring to the exchange? A more relaxed view toward sex, an appreciation for most female body shapes, and an interest in older women based on a view that either they are more sensual, wealthier or better able to help him improve his lot in life.

In sum, the foreign man has only to peddle sex and affection to potentially reap cash, meals, drinks, gifts, tuition money, air tickets abroad, business capital or other considerations. Even on remote Lombok, deep in the Indonesian archipelago east of Bali, "the female tourists are regarded as potential business associates who bring in the money to start tourism enterprises on the island" (Dahles, "Entrepreneurs" 288).

Simply put, for unemployed men, loving a tourist woman is "a job they can do" (Gorry 114).

In fact, sometimes the poorer the man, the better: "Women of all ages and social backgrounds tend to view kamakia [gigolos] as being inferior or inadequate men, who are unable to find Greek women" (Zinovieff 205). Yet these men may be more desirable to a tourist woman, who "may have come to Greece with notions of romantic simplicity, and ... if her holiday lover is a fisherman or a waiter rather than a doctor or an architect, this fits her preconceptions better" (210).

Practical views toward sex prevail in many poor areas. In the Caribbean, men of many islands offer the same refrain, "Sex is natural." Not sacred, not too precious to be shared without love, just natural. An unemployed beach boy who receives a car radio or a motorcycle in return for sex fulfills natural desires via a natural act and receives a reward.

Similarly, female bar girls in Thailand bring a certain practicality to their calling. Due to a "much higher degree of ambiguity" in Thai culture, "love and money are in the West mutually exclusive [while] in Thailand they are not. While it may be too gross to say that in Thailand love can be 'bought' by money, it can certainly be 'earned' with it" (E. Cohen, "Bangkok" 232, 226).

Money buys control

In the developing world, a Westerner buying sex exercises much control over the encounter (Wheat), a feature that may be especially appealing to those feeling vulnerable after recent romantic setbacks. As one male correspondent, a music producer, e-mailed me:

I think the issue [in sex tourism] is subservience, not masculinity and femininity. Yes, we are worn out and seek relief and "unencumbered" companionship — but what we really want is what we want, period. And that's (theoretically) what you get when you're calling the shots. ("Re: Pleasantly Surprised)

Paying for sex means "there can be no real intimacy and so no terrifying specter of rejection or engulfment by another human being" (O'Connell Davidson, "Fantasy" 40).

A San Francisco prostitute, Carol Queen, put it somewhat differently and more positively:

> We create sexual situations with very clear boundaries, for ourselves and for our clients. In fact, one of the things that people are paying us for is clear boundaries. It's like the person going to the massage therapist; you're paying to be touched without having to worry about intimacy, reciprocity, and long-term consequences. (Chapkis 77)

Similarly: "why would a rich, handsome, famous man pay a woman $1,500 for sex when he could walk into any bar in Beverly Hills and go home with a very attractive young woman? The answer is that he was not paying the prostitute $1,500 for the sex per se; he was paying her $1,500 to go home afterwards" (Salmon 48-49).

In the late 1970s, at a San Francisco bordello, call boys serviced female patrons. The women in a sense purchased confidentiality: They described a need for discretion to protect their careers and marriages (Haddad 58).

The San Francisco bordello is not the only example of women buying sex from men who are not poor. Japanese women, buoyed by a strong yen, purchase sex from local playboys in the Waikiki tourist strip east of Honolulu. Their support of Hawaiian men reveals commodification at its clearest, for they provide:

> ... payment of the costs of the affairs, cash gifts, loans that were rarely repaid, payment of the foreign male's rent, upkeep, outstanding debts, and finally, material gifts of designer goods, watches, jewelry, and in a few cases, cars. (Kelsky, Verge 136)

As seen earlier, in the discussion of healing and seeking a sense of sexual worth, road romances often appeal to women who have been through breakups, some of which are particularly brutal in the details of how their man took leave. Obviously, a woman may take seriously the need for "very clear boundaries" — to resume her intimacy with the world of male lovers in a way that guards a bruised psyche.

Even without paying for sex, in my personal experience I have exercised control over my encounters. I have rejected a repeat visit from a lover (Tortola), quietly left a man's apartment when my desires had been satisfied (Athens), asked a man to leave my room, again when I was sated (Walker's Cay) and refused proceeding from foreplay to intercourse (in St. Martin, and in Alcântara in Brazil).

My opinion of my lone experience with an economic exchange, that of being expected to buy Danny Jr. meals on Grand Cay, was negative. I resented being looked at as Santa Claus — he expected to be treated, though I was meeting his needs too — and had I any illusion of keeping him somewhere in my future, that vanished. Perhaps the fact that he had a job and that the Bahamas are prosperous relevant to the Caribbean islands (making Danny appear a bit of a lord, or a scrounger) played a role.

Even without money changing hands, the female tourist can define boundaries, difficult to negotiate with men at home, to her holiday affair, such as limiting it to a short-term liaison.

7b. Many foreign men offer services to Western women as a culture broker, either as part of friendship or as a paid guide, in a relationship that may evolve to include sex.

Yanis, familiar with anthropology and my own research, frequently offered information and comments which were of direct help to me in my work.

Dubisch (45)

With the development of tourism [Gambian] youths have had immediate, massive and direct contact with another social world, such as never before experienced. [They] have adapted economically to these changes, demonstrating the entrepreneurial talents typical of a culture broker.

N. Brown (369)

Another relationship found at the nexis of sex, travel and money is that of a woman with a man who initially serves her as a local guide.

More than a century's worth of traveling women have relied on their culture brokers: Margaret Fountaine and the Syrian Khalil Neimy, Emily Hahn in Shanghai with Sammy Zau, Robyn Davidson and her Indian guardian angel, Narendra Bhati Singh, and many more.

Culture brokers, also known as fixers, go-betweens and in the Middle East as dragomen, have proven almost essential to many female anthropologists (Gearing; Cesara; Dubisch) and to Caribbean travelers otherwise trapped in tourist ghettos (Pruitt; Gorry 42-43), where a local man "serves to ease her experience in the society and provide her with

Reasons timeline

1840s: Man shortages appear in both England and New England, followed by a first wave of **feminism** and **contraceptive improvements**, creating conditions that contributed to the earliest instances of modern women engaging in casual travel sex.

• Sex pioneer Lady Jane Digby travels and undertakes casual affairs, for reasons including **a need for healing, sexual connoisseurship** and requiring **a culture broker**.

1900: English entomologist Margaret Fountaine, in an early example of the **dating war**, sees no appeal in her countrymen, writing in her diary, "I suppose that Englishmen do make love sometimes, too, though I can't imagine what it would be like. I don't understand the material they are made of, and I never did get any distance with one, and I never shall" (*Love Among* 124). She exuded a great appeal for foreign men, however.

1914: Not long after Fountaine complains of British men, a British man fires back with **complaints against Western women.** As bisexual English poet Rupert Brooke dallies with traditionally womanly Tahitian beauties, in letters home "he returns to his dislike of the sort of modern women produced by Europe and America, most of them, it seems to him, 'spoilt by feminism and riches' " (Littlewood 174).

1921: Embodiment of **female sex fantasy** arrives on the silver screen in the form of Rudolph Valentino as *The Sheikh*. Valentino's "role as the dark foreign lover who sweeps the civilised western woman into a world of dangerous passion tapped a vein of fantasy that for most female tourists

had to wait another half-century before it could be tested against reality" (Littlewood 100).

1920s: Companionship becomes **commodified** for American women visiting Paris, who can hire gigolos, often Russian men, for dancing and being squired around town at a rate of $10 a day (Josephy 231, 233).

• Meanwhile in Venice, gondoliers offer female tourists a range of **services for sale** including sex, according to D.H. Lawrence's 1930 novel, *Lady Chatterley's Lover* (260).

1937: Dating war — conflicts between the sexes related to competition — identified as problem by noted psychologist (Horney). In **1946**, anthropologist Margaret Mead notes escalation in conflicts and confusion in a lecture series that later became the book *Male and Female*.

1939: Identity loss created by women who travel to a more sensual culture explored in popular novel *Black Narcissus* (Godden).

1950s: The United States registers for the first time in its history **a surplus of women to men**, with the following ramifications. As in the first wave during the Victorian era, feminism and improvements in contraceptives appear, in a second wave commencing in the early 1960s. In the 1970s, complaints about rampant sex role confusion, adversely affecting men (Goldberg), appear and accelerate a **dating war**.

1960s: Psychologists gain ground in demonstrating that **situations determine much of behavior** (Hunt; Mischel).

1966: Sociologist in Israel begins to

investigate how **lack of access to women** motivates youths to seek out tourists (E. Cohen, "Arab Boys"), in this case, Palestinian males who forge relationships with Scandinavian females.

1974: Swedish sociologist first to note contemporary tourist women **providing cash or gifts** to young men (Wagner, "Out of Time" 48), in the Gambia; quotes colleague who found that in Senegal, women **paid around 100 French francs a night** for male companionship (52).

1986: In a frank and rare acknowledgement of the role of **extended involuntary celibacy**, female sociologist (Dubisch) reports sexual frustration and loneliness as factors in taking Greek island lover.

1990: **Income from female tourists** becomes important in West African town's economy. Gambian mothers, dependent on their sons' earnings as beach boys, protest a government crackdown (N. Brown, 365-66, 368).

1995: A famous author's relationship epitomizes several contributing factors for casual travel sex — **shortages of eligible U.S. black men**, the **confidence of young Caribbean islanders** in approaching tourists and the **role of money**. After receiving a huge payday from a film deal for her novel *Waiting to Exhale*, Terry McMillan took the first vacation of her life, visiting Jamaica's top resort (Patrick 195-230). There she met a young man named Jonathan Plummer, and their love affair inspired her novel *How Stella Got Her Groove Back*. She brought him home to California, shared with him some portion of the many millions in royalties for *Stella* and married him in 1998. In 2005,

she filed for divorce, alleging that Plummer was actually gay.

Late 1990s: Income from lesbian sex tourists buoys economy on Greek island of Lesbos, so that business owners come to extend a warmer welcome to same-sex partners.

2000: Sociologist (Gorry) describes how tourist women in Belize take impoverished local men as lovers, defying scientific thinking on **mate selection**.

- *Platforme*, a French novel, provides a cunning analysis of the **commodification of sex**, for male and female tourists alike, in Thailand, the Caribbean, Africa and ultimately the world. Protagonist Michel declares, "For my part, I had no objection to sexuality being subject to market forces. There were many ways of obtaining money, honest and dishonest, cerebral or, by contrasts, brutally physical. It was possible to make money using one's intelligence, talent, strength or courage, even one's beauty" (212).

2001-02: The commodification of travel sex for women becomes more nakedly evident:

- Going rate for night of oral sex for female tourists visiting Negril Beach in Jamaica hits **$100**; most clients are American women in their 40s from large cities (H. Campbell).

- Going rate for upscale gigolos on Bali in Indonesia reported at 600,000 to 2 million rupiah a night, or **$67 to $222** (Harvey).

- Organizing themselves as would-be tradesmen, 30 of Venice's gigolos who work St. Mark's Square band together, share via cell phone alerts of Western women arriving (Owen).

increased access to the local culture" (Pruitt 426).

Obtaining a culture broker may be a necessity for women traveling or working in remote areas — anywhere that she cannot simply melt into the crowd. Karla Poewe's reliance on a local official in Zambia to meet important people (Cesara) serves as a case in point. If a woman receives favors from a knowledgeable or powerful local man, she may be favorably impressed by his resources, grateful for his aid and eventually find him an appealing lover. Again, an element of transaction, of intimacy for assistance, becomes evident.

Not all culture brokers (for example, Alain Hodge, my companion in St. Bart's) proffer sex or seek money. Many culture brokers are female. In *An Amateur's Guide to the Planet*, I described important female brokers in Kenya, Bora Bora, Borneo and Madagascar. Some culture brokers are even well-traveled Western women, or foreign women married to Westerners, as I found in Brazil, Borneo and Japan.

In my experience, female culture brokers tended to be providers of lodging. Male culture brokers tended to be guides. This points out the key role that owning transport (or being strong and savvy enough to lead jungle hikes), in many places a male prerogative, plays in getting to meet and spend extended time with tourists. This is why men often dominate culture brokering for the traveler on the move and why vehicle owners and jungle guides often figure in travel sex stories.

Culture brokering often grows from legitimate relationships. If the man should be a hired driver or paid snorkel instructor, any resulting sexual liaisons occur in an already established commercial framework. The foreign man ends up paid for his full range of services, from travel arrangements to companionship.

Romance as part of authentic travel

From leading a woman through the jungle or mountains to sharing her tent can be a short step. "What could be more backstage, and [seemingly] offer a more intimate experience of a culture, than being invited into someone's bedroom and bed?" (Meisch 452).

As a means of distinguishing real "independent travelers" from mere tourists, intimacy with the locals is gaining currency – in fact, becoming a cliché – as being almost as important as dressing appropriately and learning the language. Many female travel writers have asserted that sex is the way to local knowledge: "Let me tell you how to travel. Making love is the way to get to know. Making love is the way to meet. Making love is the way to see the real" (Baranay, *Saddest* 10).

Sexual explorer Anne Cumming, who wrote, "Don't forget that fornication is communication!" (*Love Habit* 215), had rich historic precedent. In the Horn of Africa, Sir Richard Francis Burton spurned formal language tutoring, believing "it was more useful to follow the ancient and proved adage that the best way to acquire a language was in bed, and so Burton took up with some of the Somali prostitutes in Aden and quickly obtained proficiency in their tongue" (Rice 236). Paul Theroux noted of prostitutes in Uganda, "Many spoke English better than my [university] students" (Vidia 73).

More reasons than not to have a fling

Anne Cumming described four main reasons for younger men to explore sex with a traveling older woman (The Love Habit 315):
- Money. "She pays for the things he needs ..."
- Propinquity. A young man finds himself with an older woman. "He has no one else to turn to, and his youthful sex drive urges him on to the point of no return. He enjoys it and finds her a convenient and problem-free sexual outlet."
- Class or color. "They don't see that you are old; they only see that you are a princess and/or white!"
- Need for "a mother figure."

As for her own motivation for travel antics, she explained (264), "Young boys make me feel young. That's all there is to it."

Cumming the pioneer identified reasons for romance on the road: the commodification of sex, man shortages and surpluses and fulfillment of racial fantasy. Initially, she also needed to enter an alternate reality (Morocco, Iran, Egypt, and to an extent Rome) to be naughty to her heart's content. She also epitomized the female sexual connoisseur seeking skilled men in exotic settings and then rating them.

With so many psychological reasons (identity loss, sexual curiosity, the search for healing) and social reasons (man shortage, a revolution in mate selection, widespread involuntary celibacy, a dating war and commodification of sex), no woman should feel mystified — or alone in her behavior — for falling out of character during a holiday fling.

Sub-Saharan Africa

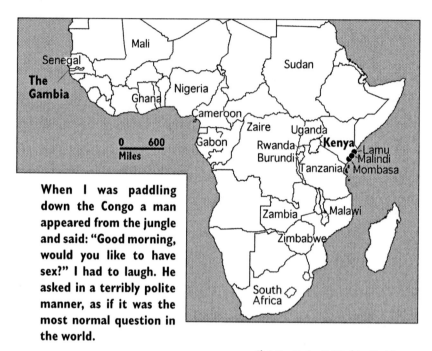

When I was paddling down the Congo a man appeared from the jungle and said: "Good morning, would you like to have sex?" I had to laugh. He asked in a terribly polite manner, as if it was the most normal question in the world.

Christina Dodwell, "Pushing Back"

T he phrasing of the proposition Dodwell received is slightly more formal than the Caribbean variant I became familiar with ("Hey baby wanna get laid?").

But the straightforward availability of men is the same in Africa as in its New World diaspora.

A steady stream of memoirs and press coverage of white women who marry chiefs, dancers and warriors tell us that the African man has appeal as well as availability. He is often attractive, physically strong, interested, possessing a pleasant vocal timber, available and appreciative of women.

Carina Marong (208), an office manager in Scotland, described trying to ignore the flirts on a Gambian beach, yet one man, Lie, caught her attention and made her laugh. She "turned to look at him and saw a supremely confident man, whose eyes were intelligent and full of life."

When she returned home, letters started arriving: "Instead of requests for expensive electrical items, he sent thoughtful words and gifts, along with pressed flowers still holding the scent of Africa."

African males and Western females form a mutual admiration society of long standing. Colonial women from the 1860s on have written paeans to black men. And from Senegal to Somalia to South Africa men return the interest, relishing women in all colors and forms, such that even women who prefer other women have commented on feeling appreciated. One lesbian studying dance in Senegal and Guinea stated, "Africans feel a love for the very nature of women that doesn't match my experiences with American men" (Allegra 145).

The continent showcases some of the greatest extremes in modern travel sex. African men reside on the globe's poorest continent (Belliveau, *Amateur* 183), often in the bush with limited exposure to modern ways. Africa is where:

• white women in their 50s, 60s and, incredibly, their 70s buy sex from African men — some of whom are teenagers.

• women from Britain, Germany and Switzerland, among Europe's most modern nations, marry tribesmen and live with them in huts.

• two sexual freedoms from the beginning and end of history converge: the license of the modern Information Age woman and that of the polygamous, cattle-herding man.

What prompts Western women to jump this cultural canyon, vaster than that between them and the men of the Mediterranean and Caribbean? To live, for love, in some of the world's rudest dwellings?

The starting point seems to be the exotic good looks and warrior mystique of many African men, notably the Masai and Samburu in Kenya, the Wollof in the Gambia and Zulus and Xhosa in South Africa. Married for eight years to a Wollof man, Scottish journalist Rosemary Long ("Lovers") recalled, "Like a lot of African guys, Ray was extremely beautiful, well put together and muscular. I loved his eyes and his voice."

Back in the 1860s, European women first wrote appreciatively of good-looking African men. Sexual contact gradually followed.

In South Africa, by the 1860s European women who emigrated as domestic servants began to break the color barrier by marrying Malay men (emigrants from Asia, see Duff Gordon, *Cape* 31). By 1913 the truly forbidden line had been transgressed: More than one mistress had initiated "intimate relationships" with her South African servant (Strobel 25). These were frowned upon by colonial societies and seen as "going native."

In a testament to taboos against interracial intercourse, south of the Sahara there is little evidence of the steady incidence of travel trysts by Victorian and Edwardian era women elsewhere, in Italy, the Near East and India.

But in the mid-1960s, the world changed, and barriers fell with a vengeance. In East Africa, safari drivers said tourist women were "always after them" (Theroux, *Vidia* 28). In Kenya, two professional, married white women entered affairs with local tribesmen. In the Gambia in West Africa, Scandinavian women began to arrive on sex charters; a neighbor of mine, an Africa hand, heard these were called "Black Cock Tours."

Tourists in greater numbers began to arrive, not only in the Gambia and Kenya but in less-visited Ghana, Zimbabwe, the Sudan, Gabon, Mali and Malawi. Today's travel fad for European and North American women is for transient relationships, that is, to "sample" local tribesmen as part of their safari experience (Hofmann, *Blanche* 45; Brueggemann), for a "souvenir so exotic it will fill their dreams for the rest of their lives" (Weaver).

And Peace Corps workers, documented in novels, essays and medical journals, loved local men in Cameroon, Tanzania, Senegal, Nigeria (Hirsch) and undoubtedly more out-of-the-way places. A former volunteer who served in Gabon a few years ago told me, "The men are very hard to resist. I knew of three pregnancies when I was there."

As in the Caribbean, female tourists can find male companionship options ranging from polished gigolos in resorts to freelancers almost everywhere. When a woman is on vacation, she can be assured of attention and devotion from a beautiful African man for the length of her stay.

And as in Greece and Israel, Scandinavian women on charters to Africa led the way in pioneering liaisons faster than you can say "package holiday."

A special refuge for older women
THE GAMBIA

> **Did I go to The Gambia, as I suppose some European women do, just looking for a scorching sexual experience far from home and inhibition? The answer is absolutely no.**
>
> Rosemary Long ("Holiday Love")

> **"We are not sex machines. I want that to be clear to whoever comes here purposely for sex."**
>
> Lt. Yahya Jammeh, Gambian ruler

In 1910, Australian traveler Mary Gaunt departed London for a solo trip to West Africa. She arrived first in the Gambia. Though she decried "mingling of the races," in the process she backed into an acknowledgement that "tall, stalwart, handsome ... is many a negro" (16).

Little could Gaunt foresee that more than a half-century later, tourism to the little "groundnut colony" would bring European women who would happily mingle with a "stalwart negro."

The scene began in the early 1960s when a Swedish tour operator began to offer affordable trips to the fine Atlantic beaches of the Gambia. By 1973, 20,000 tourists a year, including Swedish women arriving by charter flight, were visiting four Scandinavian-operated hotels (Wagner, "Charter" 41).

Female tourists befriended Gambian males, often a generation or even two younger. Even more urgently than their counterparts in the Mediterranean and Caribbean, Gambian beach boys pursued romances with emigration the goal. Older women, some in high-status jobs, might provide them with air tickets to Sweden, where many youths foundered but a handful succeeded in their dream of obtaining a higher education (Wagner, "Gambians"). Eventually African-American women became a significant proportion of visitors to the Gambia (Ebron 238).

By the 1990s, in response to a situation seen to have grown out of hand, police challenged boyfriends and even the husbands of white women. Problems arose for Long (Baobab 43), who began to feel that "people are looking at me and saying, 'She's one of those women on holiday'."

"I feel like wearing a placard around my neck saying I'm a properly wedded woman," Long said ("Stay Away, Gambia Warns"), "not just someone shacked up with a Gambian or a woman who comes over once a year for a bit of nookie. But men go out to Thailand for that reason, so who can blame some women for doing the same thing?"

Likely because the nation's Muslim culture proscribes extramarital relations, the Gambian government appears to be the world's first to condemn the female sex tourist. To date no national officials in other hotbeds — Greece, Jamaica, Thailand and elsewhere — have declared opposition to comparable situations, though local officials along coastal Kenya have tried to forbid youths from propositioning visitors.

Reporter Anne Barrowclough compared female sex tourism in the Gambia to that in the Mediterranean: "... The difference in the Gambia is that the women coming here for sex are not 20-year-old post-adolescents out on their first adventure, or even Shirley Valentines on the verge of middle age. They are women in their 50s, 60s and even 70s, who will shell out hundreds of pounds for sex. What is even more extraordinary is that so many are taken in by the proclamations of love from boys decades their junior — boys they meet offering sex on the beach — and go on to become their wives, living in the most desperate poverty and squalor."

Gambia's lone wedding registrar said, on a day when he performed five mixed marriages: "They all fail" (Barrowclough). On one occasion, he said he had refused to marry a 14-year-old local to a 67-year-old tourist.

By 1994, Gambia's new military leaders decried female sex tourists and said their behavior would not be tolerated.

"We are Africans, and we have our own moral values," Lt. Yahya Jammeh said. "Any trade that is based on sex is immoral, and we cannot condone that." Gambian officials claimed "that many of the 130,000 tourists who visit Gambia every year are women seeking sex with young men." The government began to throw beach boys into jail for a night and to shave their heads.

Yet in one Gambian town, such crackdowns drew wrath from the beach boys' mothers, who appreciated the income and prospects female tourists offered to their sons (N. Brown 365-66).

Spending by female tourists is no small matter in a country with an annual per capita income of $1,100 (The World Factbook), and where prospects for betterment must be seized without hesitation given a life expectancy of 52 years for men.

For connoisseurs: World's most exotic men
THE MASAI OF KENYA

> [Masai youth] spend an enormous amount of time preening and grooming themselves and each other, and generally just stand around looking outrageously beautiful. There are few style-queens in the world who could even hope to lick the bootstraps of a Masai or Samburu moran [warrior] in full cry.
>
> Weaver

> ... Masai warriors wear bright, red-colored wrap clothes and carry spears. I found their appearance striking; they were among the most beautiful people I'd seen anywhere in the world.
>
> Brueggemann

> To outsiders [Kenya] seems like ... a place charged with a kind of sexual energy that seems to trigger something in people who normally wouldn't behave with such abandon and a kind of innocent promiscuity.
>
> Marciano (qtd. in Ricciardi, Visions 261-62)

In the Gambia, European women indulge in the fantasy of a holiday romance.

Four thousand miles east, the dream becomes even more exotic for tourists who pursue a tribal warrior, with his spear, red cloak, face paint and colorful beaded regalia. The trend began way back in the early 1960s (if not earlier), when an Englishwoman lecturing at a Uganda university ran off with a warrior living near Tanzania's Ngorongoro Crater and had a long-legged daughter by him (Theroux, *Vidia* 37).

Today, liaisons that would have led to ruinous scandals during colonial days are chalked up as part of the "tourist experience." And the Masai are just as interested in experiencing tourists. "Masai used to have to go and kill a lion as an initiation into manhood rite," said Catharine Cooper, a Peace Corps volunteer in Kenya from 1997-99. "That's no longer legal, and now they travel to the coast and 'bag' exotic white women."

In Britain, tabloids led by the *Daily Mail* pump out tales of how female hairdressers, caterers, garden consultants and travel agents meet gorgeous Masai men on their holidays. Headlines run along the lines of, "We may look an odd couple, but my Masai warrior is no sex slave" (C. Mason, "Sex Slave").

In addition to British tourists, many German, Danish and Swiss women also dally with men on Kenya's coast. In 1995, nearly one-third of German women interviewed in beach resorts near Mombasa, Malindi and Lamu reported flings with local men (Kleiber 245).

In Malindi, as in the Gambia, some holiday romances involve significant age differences. One study (Peake 212) found beach boys taking older, paying women as lovers in secret. As for younger tourists, the men willingly escorted them in public and paid for them at discos.

Unlike in the Caribbean, where men regale visiting tourists with romantic speeches, some Masai warriors apparently just stand around looking beautiful while women fall at their feet. One warrior, Lketinga, won Swiss tourist Corinne Hofmann's love just by being in her sightlines on a Mombasa ferry; Daniel Lekimenju appealed to English hairdresser Cheryl Mason for his dancing and ability to listen, not to woo.

Masai and Samburu warriors looking for a cash windfall ride two to three days by bus from their home villages to Kenya's coast to find work, either dancing in shows or escorting tourist women. Local coastal men themselves also find favor. "Lamu was popular," said a Kenya development worker, "because it feels so remote, and the Swahili men are a beautiful mix of Arab and African — intelligent and beautiful men."

Back on their home turf, in the interior savannah, warriors also encounter willing Western females who pass through on safari. In 1997, Seattle-based photographer Rudy Brueggemann visited the Serengeti in Tanzania, at the southern edge of Masai lands. His guide, Timothy, told Brueggemann that AIDS had taken a toll on the Masai and blamed French and Italian women on overland tours. Though Brueggeman notes that Masai liaisons with bargirls are the more likely HIV vector, the guide's remarks do underscore the frequency of casual tourist sex.

Timothy reported that overland groups would camp outside game parks, "occasionally receiving Masai visitors. The mzungu (White) women would sleep with the Masai warriors for the novelty." In addition, a guide at a Masai cultural center in Kenya's Hell's Gate National Park told Brueggemann how "three warriors from his village had married British women in recent years."

A Washington, D.C.-based safari operator told me in September 2001 that her clients, more likely those in their 30s and 40s, coupled with Masai men, offering a rare report of American women involved with the exotic tribesmen.

While the paucity of reports on American women reflects their relatively low tourism to Africa (Belliveau, *Amateur* 95), other factors may also be at work.

Scandinavian women in the Gambia have been accused of being fetishistic in seeking sex with black men (Aziz 18), making the African man into a fantasy toy in a way that would appear dated in the contemporary United States, with its growing number of genuine love matches reflected in black-white marriage statistics. The same dynamic may be true in coastal Kenya, where more than 5 percent of tourist females, led by German and Swiss women, are estimated to arrive seeking sex (Pohl).

Four women dared, early on, to get involved with African men.

Profiles of adventurous women

JACQUELINE ROUMEGUÈRE
FRENCH WOMAN, BORN IN AFRICA, MARRIED MASAI WARRIOR

MIRELLA RICCIARDI
FRANCO-ITALIAN WOMAN, BORN IN AFRICA, AFFAIR WITH SWAHILI YOUTH

KARLA POEWE
CANADIAN OF PRUSSIAN EXTRACTION, AFFAIRS WITH ZAMBIAN MEN

CLAUDE BERGERET
FRENCH WOMAN, BORN IN AFRICA, MARRIED CAMEROONIAN CHIEF

Earlier we looked at sexual adventuresses, all British, in the Mediterranean (Anne Cumming, Fiona Pitt-Kethley) and Caribbean (Lucretia Stewart).

In Africa, we have perhaps the world's richest lode of memoirs, now told with a French or Italian accent, by women who loved exotic men. The tales of these four women include sneaking through windows and into hidden palace buildings, and cheating on their husbands (in three cases). Two agreed to polygamous marriages. Only Ricciardi, however, appears to have thrilled to tasting forbidden fruit, as the other three women felt more comfortable with black men, due either to self-identifying themselves as quasi-African or positive childhood experiences with African-American soldiers (Karla Poewe).

• The earliest trailblazer, **Jacqueline Roumeguère**, epitomizes patterns also found in other early white women who loved African men. She is African born of French heritage (as is Claude Bergeret; Mirella Ricciardi is of Italian-French descent), an anthropologist (as is Karla Poewe) and her first marriage was to a Westerner, with whom she had children (the same story applies to Bergeret and Ricciardi).

Roumeguère, grand-niece of an earlier exotic sex trailblazer, North Africa traveler Isabelle Eberhardt, met the Masai warrior she would later marry in essentially the same way of many a typical couple: through work. However, her work was unusually exotic. As an anthropologist, she studied Masai tribal rituals. In 1966, a Masai elder adopted herself and her children and entrusted them to a warrior named Ole, who "performed his mission so well that 22 years later we are still inseparable" (*Python* 234). In 1987, they married officially after the death of her first husband, Pierre (207).

One combs through the pages of Roumeguère's memoir, *Quand Le Python Se Déroule* (*When the Python Unrolls*) looking for racy details or descriptions of troubles the taboo-defying couple encountered — especially given the catalog of disasters that beset later white women who married Masai men.

Instead Jacqueline recites in a matter-of-fact way the twosome going about their business together, traveling to France to enter Roumeguère's daughter in school and to look at cattle to potentially export to their Kenyan farm.

After they had been together a decade, Ole wanted to take his first of eventually seven additional wives (C. Roumeguère, "Growing Up"). "I hid in the forest to cry hot tears," Jacqueline recalled (*Python* 235). "It seemed I could never accept this sharing."

Yet eventually she took sympathy on her newer co-wife, a 14-year-old waif relocated hundreds of miles from her Samburu home in the north. She served as confidante to the youngster and then to Ole's subsequent wives.

After balking initially, Jacqueline came to have no quarrel with polygamy, coming to believe it offers advantages to women, including shared child-rearing responsibilities and "solidarity between the co-wives [who] form a bloc to obtain what they want from the husband" (*Python* 237). Ole has fathered "30, maybe 40," children, according to Jacqueline's third child, Carolyn ("Style"), an international model and jewelry designer. (Pierre is the father of all three of Jacqueline's children.)

In 1968, Jacqueline found a beautiful spot on the banks of the Mara River and a decade later completed a cottage on the site. Carolyn lives nearby in a hut on the river's edge, when not traveling in the West selling her bead jewelry to actors and jet-setters.

Meanwhile, Ole lives on his cattle ranch, where his wives have their own houses. His stepdaughter Carolyn ("Growing Up") says, "This wise and gentle man brought me, my brother and my sister up like his own children. He looked after us so well then and he still does." Carolyn appears to be a living testament to tangible benefits of a mother's "romance on the road." She considers herself a French Masai (Ricciardi, *Visions* 267); she mixes tribal and classic Western fashion, in a manner she learned from her mother, and speaks English, French, Italian, Swahili and Masai.

Jacqueline simply doesn't seem to view her second marriage as controversial or unusual. Roumeguère's Swiss-French grandparents performed mission work in Mozambique, as did her parents in South Africa, where she was born in the Transvaal. "Her mother ... showed her that there was no inherent conflict between her native French and her acquired African identities" (D'Elia 348). At the age of 5, Jacqueline was permitted to spend days in the dance of the python, an initiation that included sex education for unmarried girls of the Venda tribe.

For Jacqueline Roumeguère, romance with a Kenyan brought her happiness and molded her children into far different people than they would have been growing up in Paris. She found a middle way, preserving certain French elements — wearing Chanel, insisting that her children respect education and display excellent table manners and grooming — while making her peace with Masai polygamy, diet and other customs.

• One can scarcely imagine a romance novel lustier than the real-life affair between **Mirella Ricciardi** and the young fisherman who sneaked into her bedroom in the dark of night.

As with her friend and contemporary, Jacqueline Roumeguère, Ricciardi's work brought her in contact with African men. While her nominal husband roved far with some of Europe's greatest beauties, in 1967, at age 35, Ricciardi began two years of travel for her photo essay book *Vanishing Africa*, crisscrossing Kenya to take photographs of traditional tribes from Lake Turkana to the shores of the Indian Ocean.

On the coast, one photograph shows an attractive, dark-haired woman in a simple wrap, smiling on the deck of a wooden boat. Behind her is a tall, slender man, looking his 19 years, his face a Swahili blend of Arab and African features.

Mirella had met Shaibu while relaxing on the beach. He came to show her shells. "I saw the most beautiful black face I had ever set eyes upon," Ricciardi recalled (*Saga* 167). She wanted to touch his skin. Shaibu stayed close, building her a shelter each night and sleeping on a straw mat at her feet.

"One day I caught myself looking at him, not as a black man, but simply as a man," Ricciardi recalled (287). Her attraction caused her anxiety, and she spoke to an Italian friend who warned her, "Be careful. You will upset the natural ecology of his life, while you yourself have nothing to lose."

Both lived in an era of severe colonial taboos against mixing. Yet she proceeded. One night in her tent the lamplight played on his calm face and naked chest, and very nervously she "embarked on the most exciting love adventure of my life" (288).

Forbidden fruit tasted very sweet. "At one with him," she reflected, "I was at one with Africa, an experience which never repeated itself in sheer physical intensity. Making love to him, I felt, was making love to Africa" (290).

Mirella hired Shaibu as an assistant during her photo safaris. He entered her world in an awkwardly limited way, and with internal conflicts between his healthy sex drive and Muslim proscriptions against extramarital sex.

During periodic visits to Mirella's parents' farm to repair her vehicle and develop film, Shaibu lived in the servants' quarters and found his way into Mirella's bedroom at night. Mirella knew that if her Neapolitan father found them out, "he would have shot Shaibu, and probably me and then himself" (289). Yet her husband took her affair with a black man in stride. "So what? Invite him to dinner," he said. Lorenzo and Shaibu even became fishing buddies.

When Mirella departed for a year to England to see her book to press, Shaibu's parents begged her without success to take their son along. "He will die if you leave him here. He is your child now," they told her (290).

The affair eventually spelled doom for the young black man. After Mirella returned to Kenya, she visited her former lover. Fat, his face swollen from drinking, Shaibu now transported illicit ivory. He had begun, Ricciardi wrote, to pursue liaisons with white tourist women "in an attempt to maintain the lifestyle I had introduced him to; he never returned to his simple life as a fisherman" (*Visions* 55). He contracted AIDS and died aged 35 in his village.

As Ricciardi learned, love does not conquer all. Romance alone does not always offer a road to understanding.

The tragic outcome casts a pall over her affair. Still, Ricciardi's reaching out to Shaibu illustrates a progression from first- to second-generation white Africans, such as occurred with Jacqueline Roumeguère's parents, who encouraged their daughter in pursuing an African identity.

Circa 1923, Mirella's mother, Giselle, "spent long periods in North Africa drawing and sculpting the people in the streets" (*Saga* caption 26), and later created illustrations of East Africans.

"Ever since I could remember," Mirella recalled, "my artist mother had pointed out to me the beauty of black people. She ... made me aware of the way they walked, the way they stood, the way they moved their hands and held their heads" (*Visions* 51).

Giselle may have planted an unintended seed. In the course of photographing stunning young Kenyans, her daughter vaulted the gap from admiring the men in an ornamental sense to discovering their sexual allure. Giselle and Mirella personified a progression to intimacy seen on the African continent from the Victorian era to the 1960s.

• In the winter of 1945, a young girl in East Germany, a refugee from the Nazis, screamed and bit a white soldier attempting to rape her mother (Cesara 190). A black American soldier rescued the mother, wiped her tears and asked, "Alright?" "No wonder I have always loved Africa," the daughter, **Karla Poewe**, wrote later (Dresden, introduction).

The girl grew into a beautiful blonde model and a hostess for Air Canada, and later an anthropologist. After marrying a colleague, she departed in 1973 for Africa to conduct fieldwork.

Poewe's work in Zambia brought her in contact with a helpful regional official she dubbed Douglas Kupeta. She began to explore Zambia with him. He admired women and, driving from village to village, took her to visit powerful females among his friends (Cesara 58).

One evening they visited a candle-lit bar, talking past closing time (55). By unspoken agreement, they then returned to her room in a resthouse. "He leaned against the frame. Not a word was said and yet I had already invited him in. I looked at us, looking at one another, and I experienced a deep sense of peace. It enveloped us like a soft blanket."

Karla seemed to be entering a dream where intimacy became easy. Unburdened of marital strife and the cerebral West's various obstacles and complications, sex now entailed just walking into a room together after a pleasant dinner and conversation.

Unlike Ricciardi with Shaibu, Poewe's affair with Kupeta would have no sad endings, only insights into culture and sex.

In a letter to her mother, she mused on the gap between Africa and North America, even with a sexual revolution well underway in the West:

> But what is sensual indulgence? It's hardly what we have in the West. ... Why are we such despisers of the body? Have we forgotten that our virtues grow out of our passions? ... The West is hardly sensual in comparison to [Africa]. (54)

Karla Poewe

Photo by Irving Hexham

Poewe described her experiences in *Reflections of a Woman Anthropologist*, appearing in 1982 under the pseudonym of Manda Cesara. The memoir's academic publisher shied away from giving Poewe's real name, most likely because intimate relationships between anthropologists and their research subjects were and remain a controversial issue (Poewe, Re: Reflections).

While Western men kept their distance from Poewe's imposing intellect, Zambian men felt no such intimidation. They appreciated her conversation and energy and showered her with attention.

"Why this open and relaxed expression of feelings of romantic love?" she asked. She put her finger on the reason for Africa's being a sex playland for visiting Westerners, male and female. "The explanation must be that there are no solidly bounded marriages here. The boundaries were fluid. Exclusiveness as established between couples in the West was simply absent. ... A man was not restricted to only one woman any more than a woman was restricted to only one man. It meant, therefore, that the sexes felt quite free to express their interest in one another" (Cesara 126).

One day, a young fisherman named Kosa complained about a negative aspect of his culture's open sexuality: "Ah, our women, they can't be trusted. Today they love you and tomorrow they throw you out" (72-73).

Poewe decided to pose a few questions, asking Kosa whether he would like to be "married to one and the same woman your whole life and not sleep with others? ... Would you like to take your wife to friends, beer drinks, dances and hold her hand and show the world you love her?"

Kosa became alarmed. "No, if I took my wife, I could not talk with other women. I could not explore what others are like."

"You see," Poewe told him, "in our society many are lonely, sexually frustrated because one man and one woman are each other's exclusive and private property" (73). She stepped into a world where men loved women, where sex was natural and healthy, and where women slept with appealing males without confusion, guilt or self-punishment.

Her words echo those of American novelist Paul Theroux, who while in Africa during the 1960s also complained to Africans of the sexual loneliness of the United States.

As a side note, romantic expressiveness, which wows female tourists especially in the Caribbean, seemed to have its cultural roots in the African motherland. Primary school teachers told Poewe that Zambians "enjoy writing love letters. One teacher mused that the easiest way to teach young men how to write was to let them write love letters" (126).

• One day in 1976, a white teacher at a mission school for girls in Cameroon attended a local festival.

Claude Bergeret abruptly fell in love with Njiké Pokam François, the district chief for Bangangté.

At the festival, she found herself enthralled by his dancing, with its movements of "sweetness and power, joy and might" (164).

She was "hypnotized," "bewitched." She couldn't wait to see him dance again. She tossed without sleep that night. She had been divorced from her husband for quite some time (their two sons in France joined her for their vacations). She knew she had fallen in love, but argued with herself that a relationship would be impossible for two such different people (165).

Claude Bergeret

Photo courtesy Editions JC Lattès

"No question, I was not the kind to be only one of his numerous and ephemeral mistresses," she recalled thinking. "What then? To marry him? ... If he asked officially for my hand, how would I definitively break with some two millennia of a civilization, a culture, a religion that forbade me polygamy?" (166)

How indeed could a missionary's daughter marry a man with multiple wives?

The chief, also smitten, visited her house at night. On an early visit, he made a lunge for her. Despite her infatuation with him, Claude rebuffed him. He took care on subsequent trips to provide more courtly attentions.

To learn what she would be getting into if she really wanted to marry the chief, the teacher decided to observe life in his harem. She undertook a renovation project in his palace compound, where she found the women engaging and warm. (Their exact number seemed difficult to pin down, given the chief's blend of long-term, short-term and truly brief liaisons.) Claude began to think she could live in a polygamous arrangement.

Finally, Njiké sensed the time was right. The chief visited Bergeret, embraced her and declared, "I want you to be my wife. I want to have children with you." Unable to speak, Claude nodded yes.

One evening two weeks later, Njiké made his move. He may have been able to smell or otherwise detect her periods and by inference her fertile days (255). He drove up to Bergeret's house at 9 p.m. and said, "Come in two hours to my house" (177).

Bergeret parked away from the main buildings of the chief's palace and with a "tranquil heart" made her way without a lamp to his private sleeping house.

"He brought me in, embraced me, caressed me, undressed me, but with much more tenderness than two years ago at my house" (178).

As if that night had never occurred, the chief continued to visit Bergeret at her home for French lessons. A month later, Claude discovered she was pregnant. Six months later, they married.

As with Jacqueline Roumeguère, Claude Njiké-Bergeret found advantages to polygamy, especially the co-wives' help with child-rearing. Unlike Jacqueline, she recounts a firestorm of dismay greeting their wedding, including efforts by her family to force her repatriation to France (237).

Bergeret (and Roumeguère) had not only been born in Africa but, in contrast to many other expatriate children, essentially grew up among local children. Until the age of 13, Claude played with local children and learned their language. When her family returned to Cognac, her grandmother forbade her to speak Bangangté and scolded Claude and her two siblings, fresh from the open spaces of Africa, for being noisy and uncivilized. At school, she felt no rapport with teachers and students. She felt like "a small Negress difficult to restore to civilization. ... The little African was caged, and she was no longer even African" (62).

With such a powerful African identity, no wonder Bergeret returned to Cameroon, married a chief, had two children by him, and befriended her co-wives. "As for jealousy in love, I always was unaware of it. None of my co-wives seemed to me a 'rival' in the heart of our husband" (231).

Instead, she perceived the household as powerful, united group. "All that I can affirm having lived it, is that love can exist between a woman and a man who has married others. And that the friendship can be deep between this woman, her co-wives and their children. Children who sometimes had better relations with other women than with their own mother. [I belonged] to this great family with whom I shared work, the joys, the sorrows: a family, not an indistinct mass."

After the birth of their second child, the relationship between Claude and her husband began to fracture. Njiké drank to excess, and all the women of the household felt his unwarranted rages. After being beaten after an unreasonable argument, Bergeret, at age 40, told the chief, no more sex, just friendship (268). After Njiké died of a liver disorder in 1987, Claude chose to stay in Cameroon. With the help of her sons, she runs a small farm about 12 miles from Bangangté.

At the beginning of her memoir, Claude described her relationship with her husband simply: "Why did I choose to marry the traditional chief of Bangangté? Because I loved him, that's all. No one really thinks too much about these things in my country, in Africa."

Following in the footsteps of these four pioneers, even more memoirs have followed. Tourist women from Europe have written or given copious press interviews about their marriages to the men of the Gambia and Kenya. Their stories will be discussed in the next chapter, Experiences, for the light they shed on relationships facing extremely long odds of success.

Making out in Africa

A century ago, the prospect of sex between white female travelers and African men was remote beyond all realms of imagination. Over time, such encounters became:

- remotely conceivable but still forbidden by society (Mary Gaunt).
- intriguing (Mirella Ricciardi).
- natural (Karla Poewe).
- a fitting part of a permanent bond (Roumeguère, Bergeret).
- and just another travel trend.

This evolution in attitudes and deeds accelerated from the late 1960s onward.

Road romances in sub-Saharan Africa display two distinguishing characteristics compared to the Caribbean and Mediterranean:

- Formal government opposition to female sex tourism (in the

Gambia and coastal Kenya).

• And support for tourist liaisons by the mothers of the beach boys, who in the Gambia have protested arrests and harassment of their sons as they try to earn money (N. Brown 365-66).

As a practical matter, how does sub-Saharan Africa rate as a sex tourism destination for women?

The regions' advantages and disadvantages, arrayed below, stem from the fact that, as in the Caribbean, sex is viewed as natural.

Zambians, Poewe noted, view sex as containing elements of joy, rejuvenation, health, warmth, enjoyment, affection, ease and relaxation (Cesara 146). Sex is pleasurable and "not at all possessive and grasping."

Such relaxed views makes Africa the world's sexiest continent. Sex drenches the landscape. All creatures great and small mate quite publicly, and tourists wonder about the proper etiquette when viewing elephant erections and hippo humping and even duck love (Belliveau, *Amateur* 76).

More somberly among humans, heedless copulation has spread dire viruses, born in the isolated Congo, along the Continent's trucking routes and into many African bodies. So much sex everywhere has its good points and its wrenching repercussions.

DRAWBACKS

• **Sub-Saharan Africa has the world's highest HIV rates.** In Kenya, 15 percent of adults (an astronomical one in seven) live with HIV or AIDS, a figure that should give the female sex tourist cold shivers. In the Gambia, the figure is 1.6 percent, obviously lower than Kenya but still almost three times the U.S. rate of 0.6 percent. The continent's highest rate is in Botswana, at 40 percent.

Frankly, as much as *Romance on the Road* portrays sympathetically travel affairs that heal and rejuvenate the lonely Western woman, the female tourist in Africa would be well advised to abstain. The thought of making merry with locals during my trips to Africa frankly petrified me despite the beauty of the continent's young men — the Masai with their sculpted Picasso faces and Madagascar's Malagasy looking like princes of a lost Atlantis between Borneo and Mozambique.

Barring abstention, a female traveler should avoid temptation in the worst countries (see the statistics at www.unaids.org), and if she must have sex, be utterly meticulous about carrying condoms made in the West, insisting that her partner use them and rolling them on her partner correctly. Be wary of the man sneaking them off during intercourse.

Traveling Western women who do not inject drugs should be aware that sexual contact in sub-Saharan Africa is their most likely vector for acquiring HIV and AIDS. Medical literature reports European expatriates and U.S. Peace Corps women developing AIDS as a result of exposure in sub-Saharan Africa.

"Anybody who goes to Africa in this day of AIDS for sexual adventure has some serious screws loose," a female author of Africa travel books, who sampled the men there in earlier decades, e-mailed me.

• **Many disastrous marriages arise from holiday liaisons** — unless both parties show exceptional maturity and ability to negotiate, rather than merely cope with, a profoundly different culture.

In fact, in Sweden the divorce rate is 20 times higher for marriages involving a Gambian and a Swede (see Experiences chapter) than for marriages of two Swedes.

Western women have described physical and mental abuse stemming from alcoholism (Claude Bergeret) and tears over their husband's polygamy (Jacqueline Roumeguère) or philandering.

Marriage involving relocation to the bush may also create health risks; for example, Corinne Hofmann suffered from anemia and malaria. In other words, Western women find themselves, like local Africans, exposed to many frightening tropical diseases and with little access to health care.

• **Some men may require tutoring to sexually please a Western woman.**

As in the Caribbean, African men receive mixed (in fact, frequently negative) reviews as lovers. Often women are taken, not pleasured.

In Kenya, Corinne Hofmann reported intercourse to be vigorous but almost instantly over. She first made love to her husband-to-be, Lketinga, on a camp bed at the hut of Lketinga's aunt, Priscilla. "Suddenly, everything happened very quickly. Lketinga pushed me on the bed and, already, I sensed his virility in full excitation. Before I could have determined if my body was ready, I felt a pain, I heard strange sounds, then all was finished. I could have cried, so disappointed I was, I had imagined other things" (Blanche 26).

By the night's third or fourth coupling, one after the other, she gave up on trying to prolong matters by kisses or caresses. Her warrior seemed displeased by foreplay.

The next morning, Corinne learned from Priscilla that she been initiated into normal Masai sex, complete with its shortcomings in pleasing the woman. "We hear that the whites are good with women, in the night as well," Priscilla acknowledged.

For the Masai, however, the mouth was only for eating, and hugs were repellent. "A man can never touch a woman lower than the belt, and a woman does not have the right to touch the sex of a man. The hair and the face of a man are equally taboo" (28).

"I didn't know whether to laugh or cry," Hofmann wrote. "I desired a very beautiful man, and I didn't have the right to touch him."

Corinne could have sex with her romantic idol but she couldn't stroke or caress him. Orgasm eluded her for a good while, not a surprise, but eventually arrived one evening at a lodging house (122). Over time Lketinga began to greet Corinne with a full kiss, and we can infer that she coached him in other ways as well.

Similarly, Washington, D.C., writer Marita Golden (51, 53) described her Nigerian fiancé's lovemaking as "fervent, blunt, like being swept up in a hurricane." He had to learn how "to make love to me instead of taking me."

One American woman noted that Kenyan men needed a lot of teaching, as they were not aware of the "Kama Sutra" of sex, viewing sex more as a bodily function to be relieved.

But other African cultures tutor males extensively on specific skills.

"Before their first 'marriage' young men are taught various ways to enhance a woman's sexual pleasure," Poewe recounted of Zambians. Elders tutor a young man to "drop everything and engage in sexual intercourse with his wife when she desires it, no matter what time of day" (147). And Zambian men "know that women can have multiple orgasms" (149).

A Tutsi doctor told me in June 2001, on a visit to a Baltimore medical university, that, "In Rwanda, they used to have a practice whereby the old aunties told the young men how to please a woman. He would learn how to last through the night and other secrets. The practice is coming back now."

ADVANTAGES

- **An African man may provide a positive experience for women interested in short-term, recreational sex**. Handsome, happy, strong, confident, playful and supremely interested in women, of all shapes, sizes and ages, an African man may have the confidence to be unfazed by a woman of intellect and attainment.

As Karla Poewe found, "In conversation, most [Zambian] men related toward women with an easy warmth. Where at home men usually found me forbidding or unapproachable, or where they fidgeted or otherwise displayed uneasiness while talking with me, here both they and I enjoyed talk" (Cesara 126).

"Women are swept off their feet by their 'worldly' seeming man," said one former Peace Corps volunteer in Africa. "He knows more than three languages and understands the sheer mechanical workings of life, such as how to fix a car, collect food, start fires. He's completely at ease in this life. How many Western men have such calm assurance and know their place in life. Confidence is *very* sexy!"

Africa timeline

1966: In **Kenya**, anthropologist Jacqueline Roumeguère admires and falls in love with a Masai warrior assigned to guide her. In **1967**, photographer Mirella Ricciardi falls for a young fisherman.

• In the **Gambia**, Scandinavian tourists begin to arrive and take local youths as lovers. A report later notes that "male prostitution among young Gambians is rampant. Middle-aged Scandinavian women, the age group which predominates among tourists, openly solicit" (Harrell-Bond 52). Youths seek not only cash but a chance to emigrate to Scandinavia.

• In **Uganda**, novelist Paul Theroux observes Land Rovers heading into the bush. "These African drivers tell me that the women tourists are always after them," Theroux (*Vidia* 28) tells visiting professor V.S. Naipaul. And Theroux (37) describes an English feminist history lecturer who some years earlier abandoned her husband to have a brief affair and a child with a Masai warrior in Tanzania.

1973: During fieldwork in **Zambia**, Canadian anthropologist Karla Poewe conducts affairs with local men.

1974: Claude Bergeret returns at age 31 from France to **Cameroon**, the country of her birth. She falls in love with a traditional, polygamous chief.

1978: U.S. retired teacher Hanny Lightfoot-Klein begins years of travels in the **Sudan**, finding intimate fun with an art teacher under a tree by a creek and with a West African diplomat (90-93, 128-29).

1982: Publication of first memoirs about affairs with African men: Mirella Ricciardi's *African Saga* and Karla Poewe's *Confessions of a Woman Anthropologist*.

1988: Belgian researchers find 14 women among 56 HIV-positive expatriates, including many who returned from **Rwanda**, **Burundi** or **Zaire** (Bonneux 582). Nine of the women reported sex with African men.

• Third memoir published: Jacqueline Roumeguère's *Quand Le Python Se Déroule*.

1989: Along coastal **Kenya**, the author visits Lamu where she is propositioned by a 40ish man with oversize, crooked and stained teeth who said, "European girls find it easy to get pregnant here." A year later, rising numbers of beach boys spur town authorities to forbid "young local men from talking to visiting women" (Hilsum 275). In Malindi, youths spirit elderly female sex clients out of town to avoid being seen with them (Peake 212). Older clients might be damaging to the youth's image yet were also the "most common sponsors" to set the youth up with a dreamed-of business.

1992: In the **Gambia**, sex scene continues into fourth decade. In the beach town of Bakau, multilingual males aged 16 to 25 still seek the "ultimate prize:" an airline ticket to Europe via "a sexual relationship with a female tourist, particularly a wealthy, middle-aged female" (N. Brown 364).

• A year later, an visiting American celebrity, black American writer Alice Walker (53), tried to go swimming but "was driven back to the hotel by the hordes of intrusive men on the beach." Local men "treat women as if they have no other role in life but to respond to any inane comment any man makes to them ... There's no such thing as a woman having a quiet moment on the beach alone."

1993: White tourist girls in **Malawi** and nearby countries sleep with local truck drivers to obtain their full "African Experience" (Murphy 224).

1994: In **South Africa**, radio reporter Debora Patta, of English-Italian parentage, begins to date Zulu prince Mweli Mzizi. A white bull is slaughtered at their royal wedding, attending by 750, including Nelson Mandela. "African men were fine about my marriage," she noted (par. 9), "but African women gave me a lot of very standoffish, 'you've stolen one of ours' comments."

1995: Scene in **Ghana** resembles the Gambia. At Labadi beach in Accra, Denise Roach (248), whose family moved from Jamaica to Britain, reports that "pleas to 'take me to England' ... came thick and fast as soon as I stepped on the beach. The cheeky calls to 'unite the diaspora' did impress me however — I'd never heard the phrase used in that context before."

• At least five female Peace Corps volunteers contract HIV while serving in sub-Saharan Africa, with at least one case involving a volunteer who served in **Cameroon** (Eng 176).

• Along coastal **Kenya**, nearly one-third of a group of 65 German women interviewed report flings with local men (Kleiber 245).

• Novel *Polite Society* describes male **Senegalese** professors "waiting for the Peace Corps to send them a fresh batch of American girls" who would fall for "the flowery French" and the "exoticness of a black man" (Sumner 60).

1997-2000: Avalanche of press reports about European women and **Kenya's** Masai men: Scottish garden consultant Aneris Sullivan, 35, meets Pakori, a 6 foot 5 warrior, at a bar near her hotel and sends him a promised air ticket (Long, "Lovers"), but Kenyan authorities refuse to let him leave the country. A Welsh vacationer, Lyn Davies, marries a man she meets in Mombasa, Kenya, "but it was over in weeks" (Mason, "Our Bizarre Love" par. 42). Failed marriages by Corinne Hofmann and Cheryl Mason draw extensive publicity, as does the swindling of Debbie Hulme.

1998: In **Zimbabwe**, far from coastal tourist resorts, "easy thinking" Japanese, Australian and English tourist women take local lovers, bringing them back to shared dormitory rooms or taking part in public sex at hotel swimming pools (Shibuya). By 2000, older Scandinavian women roam Zimbabwe's capital, Harare, arm in arm with dreadlocked youth, provoking anger from local prostitutes who find that their former customers are now being paid themselves for sex (Shoko).

• In **Mali**, first of two reports surfaces of a Western woman marrying a Dogon prince (Nozedar; Art and Adventure).

2000: Ten years after first crackdown on gigolos in Lamu, officials elsewhere along the **Kenyan coast** plan additional crackdowns. An estimated 5 percent of female tourists, especially Germans and Swiss, visit for the sex trade (Pohl). In **2001**, a world traveler (Richardson) reports female sex tourists with young males in Zanzibar, off **Tanzania**.

- **A full-figured woman can find genuine admirers**. As in the Caribbean, a woman considered heavyset by Western standards may be a beauty goddess in Africa. Based on her experience of the Yoruba culture in Nigeria, African American writer Andrea Benton Rushing noticed an "accepting attitude toward women's bodies of every size and shape. ... In a society where most women are producers (rather than consumers), tall, large-boned, full-figured women are the ideal" (24).
- **Gentle men provide mythic healing**. As described above, Karla Poewe felt profound gratitude to a black American soldier who stymied the rape of her mother. Hanny Lightfoot-Klein (130), a retired teacher, similarly found strength from a black orderly who took her hands during the excruciating labor attending her son's birth in the United States. Each women, during times of danger experienced prior to travel, had felt deserted by distant whites and rescued by decent and tender blacks.

Years later, affairs with African men carried special resonance, a soothing of the soul at its most basic. Lightwood-Klein, for example, slept one night with a small, intelligent West African diplomat, and every time she awoke, "I felt him tenderly stroking my face, stroking it with love and caring, as a mother strokes the face of her sick child, as my own mother never stroked my face" (129).
- **An older or even elderly woman can have a last hurrah sexually**. Again, as in the Caribbean, joblessness in Africa makes the continent a promising venue for even grandmothers willing to reward young men with cash or gifts.

I must admit that photographs published in U.K. tabloids and women's magazines of grandmothers well past their prime, kissing young black men, take me aback (see Aziz and a discussion in Ware). So it is possible to appreciate the viewpoint of academics and other observers who decry the elderly female sex tourist as a pathetic exploiter of impoverished youth.

Still, at some level we are being cruel to these lonely women, harsh on them for no longer being beautiful, and unthinkingly condemning women for behavior judged more benignly when practiced by elderly men. This double standard makes less and less sense in terms of today's women with their money, control of child-bearing and role in society.

§§§

Let's look now at the types of experiences traveling women may encounter with foreign men, a topic that follows logically from many of the extremes found in African relationships.

Experiences

Love, marriage, childbirth, migration, illness, death, renewal, recreation, divorce, rape, confusion, joy — sex travel opens the door to a spectrum of dramatic experiences.

This topic follows logically from our discussion of Africa, the continent hosting the greatest range of outcomes for sexually adventurous women. There a woman faces her highest risk of contracting a fatal virus, being asked to join a polygamous household or to live in the world's most primitive environments. And in the Gambia, she has the best chance, even if she is in her 70s, to lie with a willing man.

South of the Sahara, and around the globe, encounters range from instant and anonymous to the beginning of lifelong togetherness.

When love arrives, women may relocate to remote corners of the planet or try to bring their foreign man home to the West. And some of the world's most exotic children are forged, such as international fashion model and jewelry designer Carolyn Roumeguère, a white woman whose French mother and Masai stepfather raised her in both cultures.

Other women with bicultural influences wield some influence over world affairs. The daughter of British and Arab parents, Jehan Sadat, married the future leader of Egypt, set up village cooperatives for peasant women, reformed divorce laws and campaigned for feminist causes.

Many other Western women — Emily Keene in Morocco, Sonia Gandhi and Sally Holkar in India, Aimée Dubucq de Rivery in Turkey, Hope Cooke in Sikkim, Queen Noor of Jordan — who married foreign leaders have similarly dedicated themselves to helping their adopted homeland, via improving education and health care, creating export markets for cottage industries, strengthening ties to the modern world or politicking actively. K'tut Tantri, a British-born American who in the 1930s became the mistress of a Balinese prince, played a role in

Indonesia's drive for independence, much as Fanny Knox, after marrying a provincial governor in the 1870s, worked to convert Thailand from an absolute to a constitutional monarchy.

Foreign frolics can also have negative consequences. Marriages break up at three times the average divorce rate — in some cases, even higher. Four out of five marriages between Nepalese men and American women fail; in the Gambia, "they all fail," a wedding registrar said of unions entered by female tourists.

Western women may find themselves without rights and captive to a husband in a Muslim nation. Many thousands of children of binational parents are abducted, to the point where French women, for example, had to fight for a government treaty with Algeria to have their snatched children returned home.

And situations linked to sex travel can kill:

• In October 1975, Southern Californian **Jennie Bolliver** was found dead in the shallow water near Pattaya, Thailand, after dancing seductively at a party hosted by serial killer Charles Sobhraj (T. Thompson 330-35).

• There is every possibility that the unsolved 1976 murder in Mexico of a near-nymphomaniac, **Maryse Holder**, arose out of a dangerous liaison, though it must be noted that she courted humiliation and self-destruction.

• And in July 2000, Englishwoman **Lucie Blackman** vanished from her bar job in Tokyo and was drugged, raped and dismembered by a Japanese serial rapist, who has also been indicted for killing an Australian woman (Sheridan).

• Frommer's travel guide writer **Claudia Kirschhoch** disappeared while on assignment at a resort in Negril on Jamaica. She was cast by local media as an adventure seeker, a depiction disputed by her New Jersey-based parents (Fineman). Kirschhoch was last seen in the company of local men in this famed sex travel destination. Much was made of her admiration for novelist Paul Bowles, who wrote *The Sheltering Sky* — about an American woman who disappears with North African nomads.

• AIDS, quite possibly contracted while traipsing the world, led to the deaths of two British travel writers, **Anne Cumming** and **Bruce Chatwin**, with a foreign vector acknowledged in some accounts of Chatwin's condition and not in others (Shakespeare 490-91).

This chapter will examine the gamut of experiences related to romance on the road, describing:

• **Six types of women** open to overseas sex adventures. Women vary in levels of experience, from novice to veteran.

• **Instant and anonymous sex.** This form of travel encounter represents a higher degree of social rebellion against convention than more measured, gradual affairs.

- **Marriages.** The main focus will be my original research on U.S. women who marry foreigners, followed by prognoses for such marriages.
- **Risks of sex travel,** including threats to physical, mental and community health.
- And **benefits** of filling the basic human need for at least occasional rambunctious physical revelry.

How experiences define female sexual adventurers

SIX TYPES

Not only does travel romance lead to all kinds of outcomes, levels of experience also vary, from Novice to Connoisseur.

Two researchers have created groupings to categorize expectations and behavior for female sexual adventurers, focusing on tourists (Klaus de Albuquerque) and expatriates (Ron de Graaf). A third researcher, Julia O'Connell Davidson ("Sex Tourism in Cuba") examined male sex tourists.

I have tried to blend their typographies, guided by real-life experiences of myself and others, to come up with six categories:

- **The Novice.** This category applies to a woman who is flabbergasted when an opportunity for vacation sex appears — and when she assents.

> **You are approached with a kind of affection you are not familiar with. I am 50, and if I met a 30-year-old man here [in Europe], I would never think that anything was going to happen. But Tanzanians are very nice, they think you are beautiful, all kinds of things many white women are no longer used to. So it's hard to resist the temptation.**
>
> Dutch female expatriate qtd. in de Graaf, "Underlying Reasons" (662)

For the tourist Novice in, say, the Caribbean, her initiation may begin at a club with drinks, marijuana and dancing, including close grinding, with a foreign man (de Albuquerque, "Sex, Beach Boys" 100). This "primes" the neophyte who, after listening to the man's sob stories about sick mothers and hungry children, becomes aware that she will be paying for drinks, food and transportation in return for gratifying her now-inflamed lust.

In Greece, Bali and other locations, initiation may begin with an offer of a car or motorbike ride to a remote beach (as I described my first casual travel liaison, in Greece; see also Dahles, "Entrepreneurs" 282 and Gough, "Bali Moon"). Beach boys and playboys seek out novice foreign women, and tour guides, bell-boys, waiters, taxi drivers and hotel recreation directors often have the tourists literally fall into their lap.

For the expatriate Novice, boredom, loneliness and sexual desire increase over time. Back at home, she had a small number of sex partners, always "in a framework of intimacy" (de Graaf, "Underlying Reasons" 653). She either never imagined a reality of bold offers from legions of eager, attractive men or had a low opinion of licentiousness in general.

Eventually, the expatriate becomes aware of a "freer sexual morality ... with a large sexual supply" (654), yet her first tangible offer of sex comes as a surprise.

• **The Intermediate.** The expanded sexual opportunities intrinsic to travel come as no shock to Intermediates, who do not travel "with the specific intention of buying sex but avail themselves of the opportunity when it arises" (de Albuquerque "Sex, Beach Boys" 95). An Intermediate takes conscious advantage of looser sexual mores overseas. She may offer her lover meals or drinks but does not view herself as a sex tourist conducting an economic relationship.

The Intermediate could be either an expatriate or a situational sex traveler, who may find herself attracted to a man who is not a beach boy and spend her entire vacation with him. In this case, companionship and genuine feeling, rather than drinks or dancing, become central.

• **The Unaffected.** This woman behaves the same at home as while traveling. For example, a Maryland acquaintance of mine let lust erupt with an Egyptian, having sex with him while standing in the Red Sea, yet considered her behavior no different from what she might try at home. In other words, unlike the Novice or Intermediate, the Unaffected does not need the alternate reality of travel to pursue opportunistic sex.

Some Unaffected women view "engaging in sex as part of getting to know a new culture" but keep "control of their sexual and relational life abroad" (de Graaf, "Underlying Reasons" 659-60). They are not as impulsive as Novices.

• **The Veteran.** Likely to be older, Veterans account for about one in four traveling women bedding foreign gents, as discussed in the What's Going On chapter. Veterans "travel explicitly for anonymous sex and usually find multiple partners" (de Albuquerque, "Sex, Beach Boys" 95).

"For the veteran female sex tourist," Klaus de Albuquerque wrote (100), "adept at being picked up or picking up beach boys ... preliminary conversations are predictable and amusing. Such women are not averse to cutting the conversation short and getting down to business or, if the first beach boy is not to their liking, inquiring about another who may have caught their fancy."

Veterans dispense with preliminaries except a few drinks. After sex, they may offer the man a generous gift couched as a payment for a meal and a taxi.

Female veterans act like male veterans, so perhaps I can borrow an articulate passage from the de Graaf study ("Underlying Reasons" 657) describing Dutch male expatriates who — after a bad divorce — became fanatics about foreign casual sex. Their split from their wives "had meant a breaking point in their sexual development, from sex in a relationship to sex just for the fun of it with casual partners." Caring and sex had been uncoupled, as it were, yet sex may eventually serve to heal the casualty of a terrible break-up.

These Dutch male fanatics (like female veterans) may have started "unprepared for the freer sexual morality, but immediately perceived it as attractive. It did not take them long to get used to it" (658).

Another type of veteran, more refined and less of a fanatic, would be:

• the female **Connoisseur,** who frequently seems to be a writer, generally English (Anne Cumming, Fiona Pitt-Kethley, Lucretia Stewart) or a former resident of England (myself, now retired).

The connoisseur tends to sample men:

• outside of resort circuits and without paying for sex. For example, while Englishwomen on package tours pick up the waiters at the hotel, Pitt-Kethley noted a personal preference during a trip to Italy for guides and archeologists met at ruins. Connoisseurs may also cruise in search of a lover.

• on more than one continent.

• and because so many of them are writers, on trips primarily aimed at collecting material for a book.

• **The Returning Girlfriend.** She flies in to spend time with a boyfriend met on an earlier trip (de Albuquerque, "Sex, Beach Boys" 95-96). As mentioned in the What's Going On chapter, about 5 percent of young solo travelers surveyed who reported meeting a lover abroad were reuniting with an existing boyfriend or girlfriend. Returnees bring gifts, are met at the airport by their man and stay at his home, a guest house or small hotel. Most likely the woman is mature and more economically secure.

A woman can graduate through several categories in one vacation. For example, in Greece I began as a Novice and within a span of six days (remaining celibate on only three of them) graduated to an Intermediate and then, on my last night, a Connoisseur. I have also traveled overseas to visit boyfriends in Britain, making me a Returning Girlfriend, so the only category I claim to never have experienced would be "Unaffected."

An anthropologist's story

A CHANGE OF HEART POST-DIVORCE

For all Britain's stories of Shirley Valentines, and for all Sweden's and Quebec's primed sex travel veterans alighting at tropical airstrips, other more innocent women travel with no intention to have vacation sex, have never heard of such a thing and find banal come-ons by typical foreign men preposterous and harassing.

Thus for these women, most likely American, the categories above do not fully capture an experience involving:

• accepting foreign men's offers with great reluctance, after weighing concerns about reputation.

• being responsive to seductive overtures mainly because a tough divorce had weakened idealistic notions of love.

• and being shocked by one's own hedonistic behavior.

The Reluctant Divorcée, as I will dub this seventh category, contains some elements of the Novice expatriate, surprised by her first offer of sex, mingled with the Veteran's more casual (and slightly bitter) views of sex and love post-divorce. She is the opposite of the Unaffected, because accepting a no-strings offer of bedroom or beachside recreation is for her a major decision that conflicts with her morally grounded preference for committed sex.

I am not sure how many women fall in this category, but at least myself and Arizona anthropologist Jill Dubisch do. Since (significantly) we are both American, perhaps we should call ourselves the Reluctant American Divorcées. Let's look at Dubisch's story.

In 1969, Dubisch began fieldwork in Greece. She arrived on the island of Tinos a married woman in a village that had no contact with tourists. She was determined to "cause no scandal or gossip" (29) and was very careful in her behavior with men.

When she returned in 1986, much had changed. She was now divorced, and the little village had grown into a busy touristed town. Despite being a professional who spoke Greek, she still had to wonder how "to respond to the island kamaki [gigolos]" (38).

Over time, she watched happy couples and families on the island every day and became lonely and sexually frustrated: "Under such circumstances, why not respond to the advances of local men?"

Yet Dubisch was reluctant:

• She had no interest in nor experience with pick-ups or one-night stands.

• She did not want to be viewed by island men as just another "available foreign" woman, like those who would view "a sexual adventure with an exotic Mediterranean male [as] exactly what they are looking for as an added spice to their holiday" (36).

• Anthropologists are supposed to avoid getting involved with informants or other locals.

She decided eventually that she was worrying too much. A shopkeeper named Nikos asked if he could treat her to coffee. (As Fiona Pitt-Kethley, *Pan* 91, also found in Greece, "So seldom is coffee given without intent that it almost ought to go down as a synonym for sex in every language.")

After their coffee, Dubisch agreed to meet Nikos later in the evening. "I had no illusions about what I was agreeing to, but I also felt that it was, in some sense, 'safe.' I was leaving, there could be no repercussions for my fieldwork" (42).

Though she awoke the next morning "with a sense of anxiety," she had more than survived her initiation into casual sex, feeling sad about leaving the island yet also "pleasure that I had spent my last evening" with Nikos (43). On a return visit she paired affectionately with another man, an Athenian fellow who spoke excellent English.

Dubisch had discovered Mediterranean pragmatism about sex, where men would typically believe that "our being a man and a woman was sufficient basis" for an encounter. Nobody needed to display an "interest in each other that went beyond sex" (44).

Among other epiphanies, she learned that her authentic self was a sensual woman. Dubisch concluded that she did not begin treating Greek men as equals until she responded to them (as friends or lovers) as sexual beings.

The uncommitted sex offered by a foreign man seems shocking at first. As Dubisch noted, "for me our encounter was something different and daring, for Nikos it was almost routine, given his regular contact with female tourists of all ages and nationalities." (In a similar vein, no doubt my three lovers in Athens have not given a second thought to our encounters, while I found the experiences so vivid that they inspired this book.)

Over time, however, the Reluctant American Divorcée decides that accepting a proposition (if it is not too crass) is a practical way to avoid loneliness. In reacting in an adult way to Nikos' proposition, for example, Dubisch avoided extremes reported by other women: angry rebuffs (Fennelly 26), playing the sexual aggressor herself (described in Zinovieff 209), a devil-may-care eagerness for even awful sex (Pitt-Kethley, *Journeys*; *Pan*) or investing her encounter with exaggerated preciousness (Fennelly 31).

In a novel and tricky situation, Dubisch may have found the happiest of mediums, neither giddily romantic nor calculating.

Veterans and instant sex

> There's nothing better than two strangers in the night. It's happening as frequently even though not as safe.
>
> A globetrotting, female travel agent in Maryland

> **... Relative anonymity ... diminishes the reputational damage incurred by casual sex. Geographic mobility lowers the restrictive influences that parents often impose on the mating decisions of their children.**
>
> Buss, *Evolution* (95)

British poet Fiona Pitt-Kethley alighted from a ferry to Greece, walked a few blocks, and ran into a man named Spiros who offered her coffee (*Pan* 4-7). After dinner and kissing on the beach, they went to his flat to have sex.

He appears to have been about the very first person she laid eyes on after standing on Greek soil.

The history of women having sex with strangers long predates Pitt-Kethley's 1994 trip. At the beginning of the Roman Empire just before the birth of Christ, Augustus Caesar's daughter Julia, tired of a string of political marriages arranged by her father, took anonymous lovers in the evening shadows of the Forum ("Hail Caesar").

Today, for the female veteran of sex travel, things can move quickly. Even waiting until the same night, as Pitt-Kethley did above, counts as a lengthy courtship compared to more tempestuous couplings. My personal bests for time from meeting to intercourse, as best as I can estimate, include probably a bit over an hour (Grand Cay in the Bahamas and three times in Athens) to under a half hour (Walker's Cay in the Bahamas, in the Amazon in Brazil and on Tortola in the Virgin Islands).

Though 1 percent of U.S. women admit to having sex with a stranger (see table below), the fact that women could be capable of this level of lusty spontaneity seems unimaginable to many researchers:

- "For most women, sex after just one hour is a virtual impossibility" (Buss, *Evolution* 78).
- "I don't believe tourist women respond favorably to direct sexual come-ons" (Gorry 70).

While the capability of straight women for mercuric mating remains largely denied, homosexual men seem to be recognized far and wide for their capacity for instant and anonymous sex, adopted perhaps as a protective mechanism against "blackmail and unwanted public disclosure" (Bell 101). Prior to the AIDS epidemic, sex with strangers was a signature act for homosexual men (308), joined by more than a third of lesbians:

People who have had sex with a stranger

FROM A U.S. SURVEY:

Men	7%
Women	1%

Source: Hollander (228)

White gay men	99%
Black gay men	95%
Black lesbians	44%
White lesbians	38%

Source: A.P. Bell, *Homosexualties* 308, a 1978 study. Post-AIDS studies have consistently shown decreases in numbers of anonymous partners reported by gay men, according to Gillmore (102).

For traveling women, instant and anonymous sex paradoxically confers protection from the slut label among her peers, much as sex with a stranger protects gays from blackmail and outing.

Western women, even when they aren't having sex within 30 minutes of first hello, often by nightfall find themselves granting intimate favors to a foreign man on the sand or in bed.

Beach boys in the Dominican Republic reported that one-third of the time, they made love to a female tourist the day they met, one-third said two or three days later, and one third said longer than that (Herold, "Female Tourists" 988).

Even the most reluctant women may soon succumb with out-of-character haste. Scottish grandmother Rosemary Long took just days to agree to tiptoe with a young Gambian suitor to his bedroom:

> Our first time making love was the night before I went home, in the least romantic of circumstances. When we got to his room — the size of a cupboard and separated from his parents' room by a thin plaster wall — a cousin was sleeping in his bed. We evicted him in whispers. ("Holiday Love")

Chef Marlena di Blasi briefly met a man in Venice and 18 days later got to know him a little bit better in her St. Louis boudoir, an intriguing example of sex with a virtual stranger delayed until post-trip.

By contrast, for couples who meet at home, the physical side often takes time to develop. Among married Americans, only 10 percent of had sex within one month of meeting, and almost half waited a year or more (Laumann 241).

While just 1 percent of U.S. women admit to actually having sex with a stranger, 10 percent of women under the age of 45 secretly like the idea of anonymous sex:

Having sex with a stranger

Idea is "somewhat or very appealing"

Ages:	Men	Women
18-44	34%	10%
45-59	25%	5%

Source: Michael (146-47)

Cruising

Another behavior shared by gays and some traveling women is that of cruising, or visiting an area in a selective search for a lover. Lesbians in the 1970s bar era cruised for sex. And even heterosexual traveling women sometimes dump one man for another who seems more desirable (de Albuquerque, "Sex, Beach Boys" 101; Phillips 191; Pruitt 435). Scottish traveler Trudy Culross (153), once part of a London trio of women called the Stormtroopers who aggressively chased and discarded men, described cruising the bars in Cadiz in Spain: "I need company ... and I knew better than most women how to set about getting it."

Fiona Pitt-Kethley was once stood up in Italy and then embarked on a manhunt (Journeys 62): "I started to consider my options like a couple picking a restaurant. 'Shall we go Chinese tonight, or do you fancy an Indian.' " She spurned an American and "settled for French in the end."

§§§

We've been talking about instant and anonymous sex. Next let's look at more permanent relationships: marriages between traveling women and foreign men.

Marriages to foreigners

Each year 8,000 women in the United States and 24,000 worldwide — based on *Romance on the Road's* conservative estimates — find travel flings irresistible.

And about 3,500 American women per year bring home spouses and fiancés they first loved in either Southern Europe or the non-Western world, based on U.S. immigration figures analyzed for the first time here.

Nearly 2,000 husbands and more than 1,500 fiancés arrive yearly from Southern Europe and non-Western areas to marry American women they truly love, for a total of about 3,500 such relationships.

How many Western women worldwide marry non-Western men? Perhaps 10,000, three times as many as the 3,500 in the United States, based on relative sizes of adult female populations in other Western nations known for female sex tourism.

Romance on the Road's study of immigration data quantifies marriages and enables a test of three concepts presented in the Reasons chapter, namely:

• That a backlash to the dating war has led Western women to prefer hypermasculine Caribbean and Mediterranean men, and Western men to prefer hyperfeminine Asian and Latin American women.

• That traveling women have undertaken a revolution in mate selection, rejecting social rules that they marry someone of like background.

• That women in large U.S. cities feel most acutely the shortage of heterosexual, available men.

For detailed information on how the data were obtained and analyzed, especially on how sham marriages were removed, see *Sexual Geography* (Belliveau).

Do U.S. women bring home masculine men?

American women, and likely Western women in general, gravitate to the masculine men of the Mediterranean, Caribbean and Africa while U.S. men feel attraction to the feminine women of Asia and Latin America. Anecdotes abound of how dating wars drive Western men and women into the arms of foreigners who still preserve traditional sex roles — observations now concretely supported for the first time by this exclusive analysis of U.S. immigration data.

For example, three of the world's top female sex tourism destinations (the Dominican Republic, Greece and Jamaica), all known for macho guys, appear on a list of top four source countries of husbands for U.S. women. (The lone exception is the Philippines, which has extensive ties with the United States not based on tourism.)

(A) Top 4 source countries of husbands for U.S. women

500 OR MORE HUSBANDS, SUM OF YEARS 1972, 1980, 1990, 1996

Dominican Republic	1,320
Philippines	1,156
Greece	599
Jamaica	576

Overall, seven out of 10 binational marriages involve a foreign woman and an American man. Yet the remaining marriages buck this trend. Where does it happen that men hold special appeal for American women? Five nations with macho cultural attitudes provide more male than female spouses for Americans and (with the exception of Argentina) display highly visible sex tourism by females:

(B) Top 5 source countries, more than half of spouses male

250 OR MORE HUSBANDS

	PERCENTAGE MALE SPOUSES
Jamaica	59
Greece	57
Israel	54
Trinidad and Tobago	53
Argentina	51
Average, all countries	31

Chart **(B)** above lists countries with significant numbers, 250 or more, of husbands for Americans. Chart **(C)** below lists the nations with the highest percentages of husbands among foreign spouses of Americans, even if the total number of husbands is less than 250, and reveals six island nations, all described earlier in the Caribbean chapter as known for their masculine, flattering, confident men:

(C) Highest proportion of male spouses

FEWER THAN 250 SPOUSES

	PERCENTAGE MALE SPOUSES
St. Lucia	70
Barbados	68
Grenada	60
Netherlands Antilles	60
St. Vincent and the Grenadines	59
Bahamas	56

Do U.S. men bring home feminine women?

Meanwhile, U.S. men seek hyperfeminine women. Chart **(D)** and Chart **(E)** demonstrate that American males bring in Asian and Latin American brides:

(D) Top 5 source countries of wives for U.S. men

1,000 OR MORE WIVES, SUM OF YEARS 1972, 1980, 1990, 1996

Philippines	4,647
Korea	2,759
Dominican Republic	1,660
Thailand	1,277
Vietnam	1,118

(E) Top 7 source countries, 75 percent or more of spouses female

250 OR MORE MARRIAGES

PERCENT FOREIGN SPOUSES WHO ARE FEMALE	
Ryukyu Islands *	99
Vietnam	98
Thailand	95
Korea	95
Taiwan	87
Panama	86
Philippines	80
Hong Kong	76
Average, all countries:	69

* Japanese prefecture including U.S. Okinawa base

The tables above, listing Asian nations mostly, paint a picture of the American male response to changed sex roles. The Far East provides women that appeal to U.S. men who wish to reject the assertive female. Yet Asian nations do not appear to produce men who appeal to American women. Japan's southern Ryukyu Islands and Vietnam portray this principle most dramatically, with 98 percent to 99 percent of U.S.-bound spouses being female.

The dating war and man shortages: worse in Europe?

Throughout history, military men have returned home from foreign campaigns with wives and consorts.

Yet now U.S. women bring in nearly two out of five (38 percent) of all foreign spouses (and 31 percent of Southern European and non-Western foreign spouses). These may be seen as a high proportions, given the extreme rarity of traveling women even having intimate relations with foreign men prior to the Victorian era.

Let's examine five other nations for purposes of comparison. Incredibly, in France, more women than men marry foreign spouses, and in Germany women comprise almost half of those marrying foreigners. Japanese women constitute an overwhelming proportion of marriages to Westerners:

(F) Women as percentage of those marrying foreigners

	PERCENTAGE
Japanese (marriages to Americans, Britons)	94
French	60
German	48
Swedish	42
American	38
Japanese (all marriages to foreigners)	26

Sources: Adapted from Månsson, *Cultural Conflict* 104-05; Barbara, *Frontiers* 8; Roloff, "Marriages" 328; Kelsky, *Verge* 255-56

What stories lurk in these statistics? Japanese women's dissatisfaction with their home society and their own men dwarfs that of North Americans and Europeans. European women may be more adventurous, more likely to travel, and more interested in sexual connoisseurship than American women. French women in particular gravitate to Italian, Algerian and African men as husbands (Barbara, *Frontiers* 35), displaying a certain flair for the exotic partner also seen in French Canadians.

European women may also be more dissatisfied with their men than American women are with theirs (a view made clear to me in Athens by a Greek shopkeeper, described in the chapter "Discovering the

Methods of studying foreign marriages

University of Michigan statistician Anamaria Kazanis at my direction extracted marriage counts from U.S. immigration datatapes for the years 1972, 1980, 1990 and 1996.

I began my analysis of the spreadsheets of raw data she created by counting the total number of husband immigrants for each year. Then, to focus on marriages involving a cultural leap, I removed almost all Western nations from these totals.

Finally, I discarded a portion — 50 percent — of the marriages as being shams, steps all described in *Sexual Geography*.

All data in this section, comprising charts A through I, with the exception of parts of Chart F:

- describe spouses from Southern Europe and non-Western nations.
- include legitimate spouses only, 50 percent of the raw total.

Nymphomaniac Within"), or they could facing more acute man shortages.

Is a revolution in mate selection measurably underway?

At first glance, the revolution in mate selection can be looked at as a tiny drop in the bucket, involving only 3,500 traveling women out of 2.3 million marriages annually in the United States.

Yet this figure of 3,500 counts only the most culturally challenging engagements and marriages, involving Southern Europeans and non-Westerners. Nor does this figure include American women who marry and live with foreigners overseas.

Yet over time, even in the United States, small trends build, so that ultimately hundreds of thousands of traveling Americans are choosing foreign spouses instead of domestic ones, spouses often at a great cultural remove.

The table below calculates cumulative numbers of Southern European and non-Western foreign spouses brought in for the 30 years from 1972 through 2001, during the time when sex tourism for men and women began to accelerate:

(G) Southern European and non-Western spouses brought to U.S., 30-year aggregate total

	MALES	FEMALES
Average of 1972, 1980, 1990, 1996	2,472	5,580
Cumulative estimate, 1972-2001 (average multiplied by 30)	74,160	167,400

These cumulative figures tell a story of many U.S. men and women (enough to populate a city of almost 250,000) emphatically rejecting the homophily rules, that is, the social pressures to marry someone of your same background.

Let's look now at the estimated cumulative numbers of all foreign spouses, not just Southern European and non-Western ones, brought in for the 30 years from 1972 through 2001:

(H) All foreign spouses brought to U.S., 30 years

	MALES	FEMALES
Average of 1972, 1980, 1990, 1996	6,000	9,914
Cumulative estimate, 1972-2001		
(average multiplied by 30)	180,000	297,420
Percent of total	38%	62%

These figures show that near a half-million Americans, likely travelers, over the past generation and a half have married non-Americans.

The actual annual figures for all binational marriages are much higher than the nearly 16,000 shown in table **(H)** above, closer to 200,000 or 8.6 percent of all marriages.

Why? The figures in table **(H)** include only foreigners brought into the United States on marriage visas. Additional binational marriages are forged involving foreigners who entered the United States on a fiancé, visitor, student or working visa and later happened to meet and marry an American citizen.

These binational marriages (all involving an adjustment of immigration status), added to the husbands brought in on marriage and fiancé visas, brought the total in the year 2000 to 197,525 (U.S. Immigration and Naturalization Service 36), or 8.6 percent of the 2.3 million annual U.S. marriages (U.S. Centers for Disease Control, Marriage, Fastats A-Z).

This percentage is approximate given that some of the binational figures include marriages in an earlier year receiving immigration adjustment in 2000.

In both the United States and Sweden, about one in 12 marriages involves a foreigner, as the chart below reveals:

Binational marriages

AS PERCENTAGE OF ALL MARRIAGES

United States	8.6
Sweden	8.0
France	6.5
Japan	4.5

Sources: Barbara, *Frontiers* 8; Månsson, *Cultural Conflict* 106; Curtin

The bottom line? In many parts of the developed world, one in 20 marriages, or more, represents a revolution in mate selection, uniting a man and a woman from two different nations.

Urban American women appear to lead way

Finally, the U.S. immigration data yield information on which states have the most resident women bringing in foreign husbands.

To make this data proportional to varying state populations, I have made the number of foreign husbands brought in per state a proportion of annual marriages:

(I) Ratio of women bringing in foreign spouses by state, 1996

NUMBER OF FOREIGN HUSBANDS
AMONG EVERY 1,000 NEWLYWED MEN

New York	5.0
New Jersey	3.6
District of Columbia	3.1
Hawaii	2.6
Massachusetts	2.5
Rhode Island	2.4
Connecticut	2.4
California	2.3
National average	1.3

Source of overall marriage figures: U.S. Centers for Disease Control, Table 3

The table above, I believe, really tells a story about U.S. cities, not states: a tale about New York, Philadelphia, Washington, D.C., Boston, Los Angeles and San Francisco.

We saw earlier in the Reasons chapter the contribution that urban man shortages make to the loneliness of older women in the West.

The table above includes:

• New York, New Jersey and Connecticut, states with female residents who work in New York City, which has (among heterosexuals) only 83 men per 100 women. Women in New Jersey also work in Philadelphia (80 men per 100 women).

• Washington, D.C., with 82 men per 100 women.

• Massachusetts and Rhode Island, whose women may work in Boston (85 men per 100 women). Note also that the New England region saw significant man shortages from at least the Revolutionary War onward (Guttentag 136), long before a nationwide man shortage appeared in 1950, and with residual effects still being seen today.

• California, with the urban giant of Los Angeles (91 men for 100 women) and many female adventure travelers in the Bay Area.

Hawaii stands as the only anomaly, explained by the likelihood that many of its Asian-American women bring in Asian husbands.

Now that we have tried to assess the numbers and significance of marriages to foreign men, let's look at the quality of these marriages.

Do marriages to foreign men succeed?

My outburst was cut short by the strength of Moody's clenched fist, catching me full on the right side of my head.

Mahmoody (*Daughter* 101)

"What about Thai men and farang [foreign] women?" I asked.

Tom guffawed at this. "You're joking right? That doesn't last one week. A Thai man thinks he can slap girls around. First time he hits a farang, she's gone."

Odzer (151)

[My Cameroonian husband's] fist struck me a great blow, right in the face, so quickly that I had not been able to make the least gesture to absorb the shock. ... Blood ran from my mouth, my nose.

Njiké-Bergeret (253-54)

What is (literally) striking about Western women's stories is how often a foreign men hits them and they separate, divorce or plot to escape, often in great secretiveness if they have children they wish to take with them.

Betty Mahmoody, author of *Not Without My Daughter*, told of being pounded and kicked in the back by her Iranian husband. Other blows have been landed by husbands and lovers from Thailand and Cameroon (cited above), as well as men from Greece (H. Smith, "Paradise"), the Gambia (Mackay), Nigeria (Golden 204-05) and India, especially with Sikh men (Lloyd, *Indian Attachment* 115, 204; Baer 251).

The acceptability of hitting a woman, close to nil in the West, is a male prerogative in many other places. Observe the lyrics to a Shabba Ranks hit in Jamaica: "If she try to rule me, me have contention. She could get a broke foot and get a broke hand" (qtd. in Pruitt 435).

Getting beaten up poses perhaps the most stark risk for a Western woman involved with a foreign man.

Sometimes, however, the abuse goes in the other direction, as in the case of English hairdresser Cheryl Mason and her Masai husband, Daniel Lekimenju. Mason ("How I Killed Marriage") acknowledged that her verbal abuse spelled the end of their years together.

The answer to the question above, "Do marriages to foreign men succeed?" is:

Although many marriages do work, the couple faces odds of divorce typically three times higher than marriages between couples of the same nationality, because of such obvious cultural differences such as the acceptability of physical abuse.

In some cases, marriages between Western women and Africans are 20-fold more prone to divorce. One African-American woman (Golden 205) in Nigeria, married to a local man, described a chilling scene as she visited a fellow American woman's spare room "filled with a dozen trunks, suitcases and boxes of varying sizes and shapes" — all being held for friends forced to flee home abruptly to the United States.

Studies in Australia and Hawaii (F. L. Jones 213) have found higher divorce rates among ethnically mixed marriages.

European and Japanese statistics most starkly demonstrate higher divorce rates in binational marriages. The divorce rate for German women married to foreign men (many of whom are Turkish or Yugoslav) is nearly 30 per 1,000, more than triple the rate for marriages involving two Germans. Nearly the same picture prevails in Sweden and Japan:

Divorce rates in Germany, Sweden, Japan

PER THOUSAND

German woman, foreign man	29.5
Swedish woman, foreign man	28.5
Japanese woman, foreign man	24.5
German man, foreign woman	15.0
Swedish man, foreign woman	19.5
Japanese man, foreign woman	29.8
Two Germans	7.5
Two Swedes	9.6
Two Japanese	1.9

Sources: Roloff, "Marriages" 332; Månsson, *Cultural Conflict* 110, 111; Ma, 286

In Japan, a quarter or more of binational marriages do not succeed, regardless of whether the foreign spouse is male or female.

In Sweden and Germany, divorce rates are much higher for women than for men who marry foreigners, as two surveys presented in the chart above (buttressed by copious anecdotal evidence) reveal.

An explanation may lie in how marriages that follow the tradition of the man as the breadwinner have a greater chance of success. A foreign man accustomed to a traditional role as "boss" falters when he tries to tell a salaried Western woman what to do. She begins to doubt their relationship, which unravels as he, out of his element in a strange place, feels stranded in circumstances where he lacks leverage.

Sven-Axel Månsson, author of the Swedish study, concurs ("E-mail"): "The main conflict behind the divorces seems to arise from the fact that the men have a hard time [adapting] to the new situation with their women entering the labor market and becoming influenced by Swedish policies and practices of equality between men and women.

"[This] conflict is very likely to appear in a binational marriage between a Swedish woman and a foreign man, given the fact the man persists in imposing his (traditional) values and practices on her."

Juliane Roloff, author of the German study, adds ("E-mail") that fraudulent, short-lived marriages may inflate the figures for German women's divorces from foreign men.

Månsson's study of Swedish women also tallied divorces by nationality. Greater cultural gaps appear linked to higher divorce rates, with marriages involving a Gambian or Muslim man relatively more fragile than those to Greeks or Spaniards:

Divorce rates for Swedish women

1981

PER THOUSAND

Woman married to man who is:	
Gambian	229.9
Turkish	139.5
Iranian	129.9
Algerian	93.5
Greek	58.6
Spanish	53.1
For comparison:	
Swedish man and woman	9.6

Source: Selected countries from Månsson, *Cultural Conflict* 111

Faced with such statistics, and additional interviews with men in mixed marriages, Månsson (*Cultural Conflict* 103) began to "wonder about whether the mixed relationship, without exception, is a more 'crisis-inclined' cohabitation relationship" than one between people of the same nationality.

One woman married to a Nepalese Sherpa "estimates that only 10 of the 50 or so mixed marriages she's seen in the U.S. have survived" (Spano, "Trekking"). An American woman who married and then divorced a Jamaican decided, "it's really impossible for these relationships to last," given differing cultural expectations (Amber 104).

In Barbados, marriages often end if the couple moves to the tourist woman's home country (the same is true of marriages involving a

Jamaican, see Pruitt 434). Marriages that survive "do so when the female decides to live in Barbados" (Phillips 195-96), indicating that Information Age women are (slightly) more able to adapt to a traditional society than traditional men are able to cope in a modern nation. Jamaica may be a tougher case, where even marriages involving a foreign woman moving to the island may dissolve in beatings (Bindel).

Some marriages represent pure lunacy on the part of participants, notably a 12-year-old English girl who met a Turkish waiter, 18, while on vacation with her family. Her parents permitted her to marry him at 13. She had a child at 14 and returned to England at 15 (Hancock).

In general, even more suitable marriages based on vacation romances have obvious potential points of conflict, based on different incomes, ages, education and views of the role of women.

Of marriages that do last, especially those based on vacation fantasies, some are of poor quality. When a woman succumbs to the "attractions of a stranger," she is drawn to her partner "in the realm of imagination ... . This imagination realm is a free space where illusion and reality are not always distinct" (Barbara, "Mixed" 577).

For example, although some marriages of tourist women to Greeks "are successful, a number of the wives themselves suggest that, in the unsuccessful cases, there had been a large degree of fantasy and illusion in the beginning. For these women, it had been a question of falling in love under romantic circumstances in a foreign country, perhaps with men who could not speak their language" (Zinovieff 217).

Thus reality can come as a shock. When a woman from the less patriarchal West moves to her husband's homeland, where typically men are more dominant, she comes unprepared for "her primary role in a traditional society, that of mother and wife" (Cottrell, "Review" 157). She will have to confront the matter of which culture to transmit to her children and cope with a "high degree of gender segregation."

Yet many a special couple, often involving a man who is especially considerate and a woman who is adaptable and enthusiastic, do very well, and no doubt benefit from the unique zing of how "opposites attract." For example, a sample of European women in intercultural marriages included many whose unions stood the test of time, including one woman married for 40 years (Khatib-Chahidi 64).

Other potential problems

In addition to physical abuse, other difficulties may include:

• **Unfaithfulness.** Greek, Caribbean and African men who chase tourists often keep up the habit after marriage (Phillips 195; Zinovieff 219; Borzello 629). Some tourists fall in love with a foreign man who has a hidden wife or children (for an example reported in the Gambia, see Long, *Baobab* 106-07).

- **Polygamy.** Claude Njiké-Bergeret in Cameroon willingly joined a polygamous household. But in Kenya, Jacqueline Roumeguère had the idea sprung on her mid-marriage, and Corinne Hofmann on the night before her wedding (*Blanche* 118). An American woman who could not bear children found her Nigerian husband pressured by his family to take a second wife (Golden 140-01).
- **Drugs and drinking.** A recurrent theme in marriages to Africans that end in separation or divorce include a husband's excessive reliance on alcohol (Long, "Lovers"; Njiké-Bergeret 233) or alcohol combined with narcotic weed (Hofmann, *Blanche* 80).
- **Isolation.** Wives of Greeks report lack of a support network and a struggle with the fact that "to the Greeks around her she will remain a stranger ... for the rest of her life in Greece" (Zinovieff 218-19).
- **Poor quality marriages.** And many foreign women who marry Greeks find themselves in a twilight zone, away from their own families, out of the Greek mainstream, dealing with men who continue to hound foreign women, yet not getting divorced (216-19).

One female travel writer observed, "the few women I have encountered who have married Greeks don't seem very content, having little choice but to fit into their husbands' lifestyle, the extended family, the cooking, sewing, gardening, washing and having babies way of life that Greek women lead" (Zoro 185).

Similarly, Western women married to educated Sudanese were said to congregate in Khartoum bemoaning their husbands' indifference; local expectations held that men preferred each other's company while "wives were expected to find their interests and emotional support at home and among other women" ... all this in an alien, restrictive society (Lightfoot-Klein 179).

- **Husband's dependency.** For couples who relocate to the West, a man tough and capable at home may find himself both isolated and in a new role of dependency, a role the reverse of that in his home country when he squired his tourist woman around.

"With the man's role as culture-broker and guide no longer necessary, educational, age and racial differences which seemed inconsequential in the host country are magnified" (Pruitt 434).

Men from Nepal, the Gambia, Belize and Barbados have all been reported stuck in a woman's apartment, in Chicago or Stockholm or elsewhere, without language skills or job prospects, watching alone as snow falls outside the window (Spano, "Trekking"; Wagner, "Going North" 208-09; Gorry 107; Phillips 195).

- **Unrealistic expectations.** English hairdresser Cheryl Mason's marriage to a Masai tribal dancer lasted seven years (about the same as Rosemary Long's, discussed below) — all things considered, a remarkable span given that he relocated from the Kenyan bush to England's Isle of Wight.

Yet both Cheryl and her husband, Daniel Lekimenju, seemed to have brought overly high hopes into their marriage.

Mason implied that she expected almost as much in terms of earning power from Lekimenju as from an Englishman. Meanwhile, Mason said, Daniel expected to remit cash to his Kenyan kin, but "because English is not his first language, Daniel can't get a well-paid job — he works in the delivery department of the local supermarket." She concluded that a binational marriage:

> isn't glamorous and the odds are stacked against it. Women have this image of an idyllic relationship with a gentle caring man and often the Masai men think they will be able to come here and send money home to support their vast families. It isn't like that. ("Our Bizarre Love")

Loss of legal rights to travel and child custody. Corinne Hofmann and her daughter could not leave Kenya without her Samburu husband Lketinga's signature on a permission slip, a difficult proposition as their marriage deteriorated and he had reason to suspect they would leave forever (Blanche 337).

Women in binational marriages may be shocked to learn how little help they can receive from their home government if they or their children want to depart their husband's country. Kenya is far from the only example. Problems have also cropped up in Spain (Toynbee), Greece (Spathias) and throughout the Islamic world.

A classic example is recorded in Betty Mahmoody's *Not Without My Daughter*, later made into a film starring Sally Field. More than 1,000 women are said to be held against their will in Islamic countries (419), and about 1,200 children are internationally abducted annually.

In 2004, in fact, the Vatican warned Roman Catholic women to exercise caution in marrying Muslims, calling women "the least protected member of the Muslim family" and citing the "bitter experience" Western Catholics had with Muslim husbands, especially if they married outside the Islamic world and later moved to the man's country of origin (Darlington).

Western women may find their children by a foreign husband abducted either during a visit to the father's country or from their home country.

This partial list of countries reporting abductions also provides a rough scale of which Western nations lead the way in international marriages:

Top 10 countries reporting international child abductions by parents, 1996

RANK	COUNTRY	NUMBER
1.	United States	367
2.	England and Wales	206
3.	Australia	104
4.	Germany	84
5.	Canada	59
6.	Netherlands	56
7.	Ireland	47
8.	Spain	45
9.	France	38
10.	New Zealand	32

Source: Lowe (149)

Political changes in Europe may increase these figures, as economic unification has allowed single, Northern European women to work in Southern Europe, where many stay and get married (Ackers).

Englishwoman Barbara Gregory, who lost her two sons to abduction by her Spanish husband despite a U.K. custody order, came to a stark conclusion (Toynbee):

"I'd advise British women never to marry a foreigner but, if they do, to make sure their children are born in Britain. After all, marriages between people across cultures are more likely to break down and no one should risk having their children stolen from them."

A former teacher in the Middle East quoted a U.S. embassy staffer on an unwritten rule for American women: Cultivate an embassy contact if you are being held against your will. She added her advice for Western women married to Middle Eastern men: "Never go to the home country, ever. If he says, 'Let's go visit my parents,' don't. If you do, leave the children at home because you may find yourself being held against your will without resources or support."

Con men. One European woman followed an Indian musician she met in Madrid back to Ecuador and had a baby with him, after which they got married. He "took every cent of the couple's savings, abandoning Sara and the baby," and left for Argentina (Meisch 459).

In one year, a Tunisian hotel worker married two Englishwomen, each on the rebound, one from a divorce and another from a broken relationship, and was convicted of bigamy ("Romeo Waiter").

Similarly, a British woman, Lindsey Mackay, married a Gambian, not knowing he had another girlfriend in Shropshire. Mackay had two daughters with the Gambian and eventually saw him walk out of the family's life after a series of arguments.

An English travel agent was swindled by a Masai con man in Kenya. Eventually left penniless and homeless, Debbie Hulme acknowledged how the alternate reality of relaxing in Kenya led her to let her guard down: "When you are living in paradise, with the ocean lapping on a sandy shore and someone showing you this much attention, it's enough to turn the most sensible girl's head. Believe me, it could happen to anyone."

She had sold all her property in England and invested in a bush taxi with her Masai boyfriend. Only later did she learn that he had an English wife, an African wife, other European girlfriends and contact with prostitutes, and had similarly swindled another Englishwoman.

These experiences should be a lesson to other women to look before you leap, for con men have identified the single female traveler as a juicy target (du Cros 48-51).

Negative aspects of casual travel encounters

The negative potential for women of impetuous couplings include a trio of health problems:

- **physical health problems**, including AIDS, other sexually transmitted diseases and tropical disease, and rape.
- **mental health problems**, including fear (of harassment), anxiety (about physical diseases), and perhaps emotional disorders for which promiscuity is a symptom.
- and broadly speaking, the **disruption of community health**.

Physical health problems

INFECTION WITH HIV AND OTHER SEXUALLY TRANSMITTED DISEASES

Certainly at the most negative end of the spectrum of outcomes for sexually receptive female travelers would be to contract a fatal illness.

Each year, up to five Peace Corps volunteers, females and males, come home with HIV, according to a source. Most served in Africa.

Over time, "I wouldn't be surprised if there haven't been 15 to 20 seroconverters [people whose blood tests positive for HIV] among former Peace Corps volunteers in Africa," another source, a former volunteer in Gabon who is now an HIV researcher, told me. "They are mostly women who have taken French and end up in West Africa, an area where there are fewer men from their own culture. I knew of three pregnancies there. It's hard to resist the men."

Two additional sources, both former Peace Corps volunteers in Africa now studying nursing in Baltimore, told me of three HIV-positive female PCVs in Malawi and a fourth who served in Burkina Faso.

These reports gathered by the author appear to jibe with a five-year study of PCVs returning from Africa that found two HIV-positive women (Eng), a rate if applied to the 40-year history of the Peace Corps would produce 16 HIV-positive female volunteers. Another study (Moore) through 1993 also found that six female (and four male) PCVs were believed to have acquired HIV during their Peace Corps service; all but one had served in Africa.

World totals are anyone's guess, but with German and Swiss women prevalent in Kenya's major sex resorts, perhaps 50 or so Western women a year contract HIV from travel liaisons, including U.S. women who are not in the Peace Corps. (The author would be very interested in hearing from women who have contracted HIV/AIDS in the course of overseas travels.)

> **Almost every sexual revolution in history has had significant disease consequences for the populations breaking free of sociocultural restraints.**
>
> Pirages

> **... All sexually active persons should be warned forcefully of the dangers of casual sex, particularly if they are young, traveling without spouse or partner, and going to countries where the sociocultural context is conducive to risky behavior.**
>
> Mulhall (461)

Though sub-Saharan Africa is the main risk area, HIV can be contracted almost anywhere (except perhaps Mongolia, which as recently as 1999 reported a rate of zero, though it's a long way to travel for safe unprotected sex).

In Cyprus, for example, in the mid-1990s an Englishwoman contracted HIV from a fisherman who was later jailed for deliberately infecting her (Hellicar, "AIDS"). And an HIV-positive waiter had sex with a Norwegian tourist, also without informing her of his condition, and faced jail (Hellicar, "Waiter").

In poor areas, such as the Dominican Republic, Costa Rica, Morocco, Egypt, Thailand, Sri Lanka and coastal Kenya, where bisexual gigolos service both male and female tourists, women also face increased risks of contracting HIV.

In the Dominican Republic, for example, in the 1980s up to half of gigolos "had sexual relations with male tourists," a figure that dropped a decade later to one in five, "largely because of homophobia reinforced by fear of AIDS" (de Moya 130). Still, a rate of one in five gigolos offering bisexual services should raise a high level of alarm in the female tourist who wishes to remain HIV free.

Even where bisexual gigolos are not prevalent, note that the HIV figures for adult infection charted below may be higher among men who initiate sex with tourists, in other words, near resorts, than in the population at large.

Assessing HIV risks. A woman can check the Web site www.unaids.org for the latest statistics. Figures in the table below should help inform the female traveler of risks by destination:

Popular destinations for female sex tourism

	HIV-INFECTED ADULTS PER 1,000
Kenya	150
Bahamas	35
Dominican Republic	25
Belize	20
Trinidad and Tobago	25
Thailand	18
Gambia	16
Jamaica	12
Barbados	12
World average	12
Brazil	7
Nepal	5
Mexico	3
Greece	2
Morocco	1
Indonesia	1
Israel	1
Egypt	0.1

Source: UNAIDS

Let me emphasize and repeat what the chart above says: Kenya is by far the most dangerous of popular sex destinations for the female traveler. If an unexpected opportunity for Masai sex occurs during your safari, realize that it is really more important to avoid risky partners than to live out this particular fantasy. If you proceed, use condoms every time, condoms brought from your home country, and you be the one to put them on the man. Even if you don't plan so much as a kiss on your travels, it's best to bring condoms. Few women anticipate their responsiveness to a new man in a beautiful place.

OTHER STDs

Tourist women can catch all kinds of things from gigolos who may service 10 visitors a year (Herold, et al., "Female Tourists" 988) and may carry on additional sexual contact with male tourists, local prostitutes during the off-season (Hellberg 147) or a local girlfriend.

Among Swedish women in a survey (table IV, Sikstrom), 47 percent of those with cervical human papillomavirus infection had engaged in casual travel sex overseas, vs. 27 percent of women who had not engaged in this activity. Female sex travelers also had higher rates of gonorrhea and chlamydia, attributed to sexual risk-taking both at home and abroad (Mardh).

TROPICAL DISEASES AND UNSANITARY CONDITIONS

When Swiss traveler Corinne Hofmann moved with her Masai husband Lketinga to his home village in the Kenyan bush, she lived in a micro-sized, smoky hut with his mother and sister. Malaria, kidney malfunction, anemia and pregnancy complications plagued her.

Similarly, Sarah Lloyd, who lived with an Indian Sikh in an impoverished village, also contracted malaria and battled worms, lice and dysentery. Rosemary Long, after moving to the Gambia to get married, suffered skin disorders.

Both Hofmann and Lloyd put up with squalor, walking out of humble dwellings to ground littered with excrement, a telling detail of how far they were willing to depart from Western standards to be with their man and of the overall health risks of such a decision. Their willingness to live so poorly almost suggests esteem or depression issues, of which more below, rather than romantic dedication.

RAPE, ATTEMPTED RAPE AND ASSAULT

Writer Ellen Sussman was 18, living a life that was "impossibly wonderful," when on a foreign journey she was raped and left to die. She had just discovered sex, and considered herself tough and fearless. All that changed at a stroke.

Statistics for attempted rape and rape of female tourists are alarming in both scope and rate of increase, with multiple reports from Lamu in Kenya (Hilsum 395; Lightfoot-Klein 203); Colombia (Jansz, More Women Travel 151); Chiang Mai, Krabi and Ko Samet in Thailand (Coates); Goa in India (Kay), Ecuador (Meisch 455) and many other places. In the Caribbean, tourist rapes have been reported on St. Lucia and Jamaica, as well as in the Bahamas (G. Lee).

One report cites 36 British women being raped in Turkey, 26 in Spain, 21 in Greece, and three in Cyprus (Simons), with additional rape claims in Cyprus by four Norwegian women (Free Holidays).

In St. Vincent (Gearing 193-96) and the Gambia (Harrell-Bond 52), assaults have been linked to men who interpret loose tourist morals as a blanket invitation to pounce on any Western women.

For information on how to avoid rape, please see pages 372-73.

• **Gang rape.** Misplacing her trust, Anne Cumming agreed to visit an apartment in Cairo with five men, who took turns with her. She told a friend of the experience with remarkable equanimity:

> I shrugged my shoulders, not with shame but with a kind of resignation as I told Max about it the next day. "I suppose it had to happen sometime. If you behave like a whore, someone is eventually going to treat you like one," was my only comment. ... In spite of this unfortunate experience, I could not be expected to give up all contact with the male sex. Resilience was my middle name. (*Love Quest* 139)

HARASSMENT

In much of South Asia and Latin America, Western women run into men who follow them and try to enter their rooms, to touch them and to confront them aggressively. Violent harassment has been reported in South India and Sri Lanka (Crossette). In Northern India, even local women fear being rubbed on public buses (Lloyd, *Indian Attachment* 148).

Contributors to a travel essay collection, *More Women Travel* (Jansz), also listed harassment in:

• **Islamic and African lands**, including Turkey, Morocco, Pakistan, Sumatra, Iran, Egypt, Nairobi and the Kenyan coast and Mali.

• **Latin America**: Colombia, the Dominican Republic, Mexico, and Costa Rica.

• and **Southern Italy** and **Sicily**.

Contributors even found it notable when they were not harassed, citing Ireland, China and Haiti as relaxed areas.

The fact is that tourists who decide in favor of a few days of sex play with a foreign guy seem to pave the way for harassment of women who arrive in subsequent years and who are not interested. My own experiences in Greece, recounted earlier, point to the circularity of this reinforcing cycle. At first I was appalled and disbelieving at the smothering level of harassment I encountered in Athens. Then I succumbed to these temptations, with the likelihood that my sex partners became further convinced of about the ease of seducing any lone Western female tourists to later cross their paths.

The combination of sexually liberated women in the bygone age of the hippy trail [through Pakistan] and widely circulated Western pornography make up a formidable myth of the Western woman ...

Wetherall (373)

We could do little [in Egypt] to dispel the myths which abound

about foreign women (amply reinforced by imported American films and television programmes).

C. Bullough (201)

... Public opinion [in an Ecuadorian mountain town] holds that "gringas are putas (sluts)."

Meisch (459)

Mental health problems

POST-SEX ANXIETY AND GUILT

In the cold light of day, women may view their impulsive decision to have casual sex with ambivalence, with guilt toward their regular partner, fear for not having used a condom, or so negatively they vow never to repeat the experience (de Graaf, "Underlying Reasons" 655-57).

One British woman (Mackay) described walking to a secluded beach with a Gambian man. "We got carried away with each other and had sex there and then. There's no way I would have had sex with somebody straight away normally, let alone without a condom. But I just found myself going with the moment. It was only afterwards that I thought, 'Oh my God, what about AIDS?' "

Young Canadian women surveyed at dating bars who went ahead with casual sex tended to feel guilty, especially compared to men (see table below). One might surmise, however, that casual sex conducted anonymously overseas leads less often to guilt given the more forgiving alternate reality of travel overseas.

Casual sex attitudes

	MEN	WOMEN
Always enjoy casual sex	25%	2%
Feel guilty about casual sex	32%	72%

Source: Herold and Mewhinney, "Gender Differences" 39

ABASEMENT AND SHAME

Mental health problems can also be linked more sinisterly with promiscuity, as seen in the case of Maryse Holder. In 1976 and 1977, this New York part-time academic made a tormented odyssey of alcoholism, bulimia and ultimate self-destruction in Mexico (177). For Maryse, casual sex with randy Mexicans contained elements of abasement, of giving herself to macho men who would discard her after one night.

Thousands of women have grabbed the same freedom and returned home changed positively, but Holder's is a cautionary tale of risks for the traveler who grapples with grave underlying insecurities.

Similarly, Victorian sex traveler Isabelle Eberhardt may have desired her sex with a dash of sadomasochism: "literally violent lust ... would sometimes tip over into brutality. ... It was this which sometimes made her feel ashamed afterwards of her sensual life, seeing it as a separate, unworthy part of her" (Kobak 9).

MOOD DISORDERS

Thousands of women each year suffer relationship setbacks. Those who take a vacation for consolation often cheer up in the sun and more than regain their usual confidence, so that they embark on a wild affair.

This pattern suggests that big mood swings may be either a cause or an effect of holidays that include carnal pleasure with a near-stranger.

One can see perhaps self-medication at work in female travelers who, in place of light-box therapy, sign themselves up for a sunny vacation. They boost their endorphins — pain-relieving compounds that act as natural opiates — via hiking, trekking, snorkeling and sailing. After a few happy days or hours, their uplifted souls encounter ego-boosting males with healing ways, men who listen well and serve as ad hoc therapists. No wonder moods become expansive!

Do trysts in the tropics suggest that a woman from northerly latitudes enters a natural euphoria that mimics the exaggerated high spirits and sexual excess of mania?

Consider the official symptoms of a milder version of bipolar disorder called cyclothymia: "episodic promiscuity" and "repeated marital or romantic failure" (Akiskal, Khai and Scott-Strauss qtd. in Jamison 264), symptoms that describe with eerie precision the life stories of some veteran female sex travelers.

I do not declare here that any woman whose vacation evolves into a sex holiday is manic depressive, only that real life has demonstrably hammered numerous women with crushing lows followed by the buoyant high of "getting your groove back" with a foreign lover. It is possible though that some depressed women, who feel trapped and unable to find love in more comfortable climes, have been among those who live in punishing circumstances with foreign lovers.

Women who actually do suffer from clinical depression, that is, a more lasting down state than the blues stemming from a minor breakup, as well as those with attention deficit disorder or mania may undertake increased, adventurous or addictive sexual behavior (indicated in Myers; Spalt). In fact, the drugs themselves that women take to treat depression may increase desire, arousal and sexual activity. These side effects are more likely with Wellbutrin, also called Zyban, but may also occur after taking Paxil, Prozac or Ritalin (Elmore). Wellbutrin has also been linked to spontaneous double orgasms (which one patient described as pleasurable, see Labbate).

So mood lowered either by relationship problems or by faulty brain chemicals can ultimately spur female sexual adventuring.

The fact that "episodic promiscuity" and "romantic failures" can be found in some female travelers and in mild manic depressives suggests to me that holiday affairs can be a sort of beneficial, self-aware form of temporary madness designed to throw off the old bad times, live in the present creatively, complete a necessary cycle of personal growth and return to confidence.

"I suspect either one party or the other [in a travel romance] is manic," Baltimore therapist Mary Ann Constantinides told me, when I mentioned how frequently the foreign lover in women's travel essays gives early, obvious signs of alcoholism, irrationality or madness. "After all, romance is based on illusion."

> **The lingering warmth and light of the Mediterranean never failed to intoxicate minds numbed by the dark and cold of an English November or December.**
>
> Pemble (150)

> **That strange second life, the life of voluptuousness, of Love. The violent and terrible inebriation of the senses, intense and harrowing, contrasting with my everyday existence, so calm and pensive . . . what intoxications! What drunken love under this hot sun!'**
>
> Isabelle Eberhardt, unpublished story (Kobak 100)

MENTAL HEALTH BENEFITS

Most women, however, find holiday affairs a net plus, as African-American poetess Colleen J. McElroy describes:

> I have learned over the years that adventuresome love, love caught on the run while I was traveling from one place to someplace called home, hardly ever greeted me directly: It sidled in, stumbled in, tripped me up, and left me confused and happy. (189)

Though sexual excess may indicate a delicate mental state in some traveling women, in many others it is part of the swagger and confidence of an adventurer.

Over the course of dozens of encounters, the British sexual explorers Anne Cumming and Fiona Pitt-Kethley safely conducted their assignations with strange men, with the one untoward event, a gang rape in Egypt described above, no laughing matter but somehow taken in stride by Cumming.

Pitt-Kethley observed, "Everywhere I went in Italy I was told that it's bad to travel alone. I see no evidence for this."

Some of her confidence came from weight training and being muscular. This assurance and a belief in equality led her to a conclusion (*Journeys* 10) that "all the human possibilities are open to a woman," including travel and choosing sexual partners, including strangers.

Unlike in the early days, when sex travelers such as Maryse Holder and Isabelle Eberhardt felt mental torment following their behavior, today's sexually assertive women (more in the mold of Pitt-Kethley) may be quite comfortable and confident in seeking multiple experiences (Seal 164) and view her earthy explorations as yet another exciting facet of adventure travel or life abroad (M. E. Jones 99).

In fact, even as early as 1906, a writer in *Ladies' Home Journal* (Stapley 16), decrying the extensive fooling around by young, female American students in Paris, noted grudgingly that most likely to entertain foreign men was a certain kind of lively girl: "the bright interesting ones, with alert minds open to every impression the new life holds for them — those who, to sum it up, have temperament."

Women who find romance on remote roads may often be (obviously):
- attractive (Mikach 142).
- sexually confident (Seal 164)
- adventurous and pleasure seeking (M. E. Jones, "Expatriate" 99; T.M. Wright).
- independent, active and curious, with an interest in exploring novel situations, strong feelings of desire and a more positive attitude toward sex (Apt 320, 322).

The confidence of today's female traveler is often obvious. Finnish travel researcher Petri Hottola (*Intercultural* 285) noted that his impression of backpackers in India was "not that of helpless victims, the women of victim feminism, but that of strong independent women who are capable of caring for themselves, the women of postfeminism."

A STRONGER SEX DRIVE?

Part of the sexual confidence of many traveling women may stem from exposure to the hormones androgen and testosterone, which may in fact prime them to desire and to succeed in finding casual lovers.

"Yes, I would expect to find that women who engage in casual travel sex would have stronger sex drives (linked to levels of testosterone or ovulation times) than other women," Dr. Lee Ellis, author of *Sexually Aggressive Women*, e-mailed me. "Keep in mind that testosterone does not only affect behavior in terms of the amount circulating in the brain at a given point in time, but also perinatally, when the brain is basically being 'sexed'."

Women who display behavior thought of as typically masculine may have been exposed as fetuses to another hormone, androgen, which also masculinizes the brain (Mikach 149).

Research also suggests that as "women become more sexually experienced, they [show] an increase in 'masculine' social and sexual behaviors and a decrease in 'feminine' social behaviors" (Whitley, qtd. in Lucke 276). Women open to casual encounters may have been tomboys and then display masculine behavior as adults (Mikach), a nexus reported in the erotic traveler Isabelle Eberhardt, who wore men's clothing as she traveled, sex disguised, across North Africa.

Now let's widen our focus from the physical health of the individual to look at community health — that is, the impact of mass numbers of Western women descending on tourist areas and taking lovers.

Community health

Female tourists and expatriates have been blamed for men abandoning their families in Jamaica (Amber 162) and Nepal (Spano, "Trekking").

One travel writer's indiscretion disrupted a delicately balanced small community (Dea Birkett on Pitcairn Island), and a photographer crushed a young African man's spirit when she left him behind (Mirella Ricciardi in Kenya).

Western females during tourist season also usurp local girlfriends all around the Mediterranean: in Israel (E. Cohen, "Arab Boys" 229), Malta (Boissevain), Spain (Graves 154) and Greece (Kousis 230-31).

Sometimes foreign women tar all Western females with a reputation as man-stealers. In Nigeria, a large network of foreign wives have formed an organization, Nigerwives (Bryce 351), which also serves as a refuge for single expatriates in need of support and viewed suspiciously by "married middle-class Nigerian women who see [them] as a threat" to relationships with their own men. (Costa Rica may be an exception, where young women tend to seek older, employed men for dating and are unbothered to see young surfers with gringa tourists; see Kimball 5).

Family disruption can also run in the opposite direction, as foreign men swipe tourist women from their husbands (Lindsey Mackay in the Gambia and arguably Cheryl Mason in Kenya) and boyfriends (Corinne Hofmann in Kenya). For example, the captain of the pleasure boat *Shirley Valentine* was convicted in Cyprus of assaulting a British retiree who protested the Cypriot's seduction of his wife (H. Smith, "Man Jailed").

The most disruptive change wrought by Western tourists, male and female, is how their needs create, for tens of thousands of foreign men, a new role as freelance hustler with sex offered as part of a smorgasbord of services.

While history has always had its fixers, touts and dragomen for people on the move, today, as one traveler in India noted:

> You see them in every town — veering toward you on the streets, calling out from the doorways of souvenir stands. They speak English, maybe a little French, a sprinkling of Italian. Their behavior is so suggestive, so forward, they seem to be a breed of their own — sprung incongruously from the traditional culture that surrounds them. (Dreir)

Female sex travelers, we see, can have profound impacts on local communities, often disruptive in the short term — and sometimes positive in the long run.

Free and easy lady travelers, whose behavior may appear as amorality and an affront to the old ways, actually relieve the pressure-cooker celibacy and unemployment for unmarried males in many countries, and serve as the thin edge of the wedge for another change, that of local female emancipation.

For example, the disregarding of restrictive Latin codes for women by Scandinavian tourists spurred the arrival of the sexual revolution in Spain and to a lesser extent in Greece and Mexico.

Finally, female tourists, in the name of authenticity, also tend to latch onto more exotic minority groups, such as the Masai in Kenya, Otavalo Indians in Ecuador, Palestinians in Israel, darker-skinned Balinese, Sikhs in India, Sherpas, Kami and Tamang in Nepal, and lowly regarded members of society, such as fishermen and porters, the world over.

This creates consternation among larger rival groups who control power. I have examined this phenomenon elsewhere (see "Dayak culture faces assaults from many fronts," Belliveau, *Amateur* 61), to my mind a delightfully subversive move on the part of travelers.

Sometimes internal problems alter a community, with repercussions for female tourists. For example, a frightening increase in harassment for women visiting the Hindu holy city of Benares in the 1990s was linked mainly to a changing student body at the local university, where an influx of "eve-teasers" arrived from backwards areas holding views of women as "no more than chattel ... and a foreign woman is even less than that" (Mishra, *Ludhiana* 227).

How will you shape your experience?

Women can make what they will of overtures from exotic men, rejecting overtures that seem risky and embracing others that seem potentially rewarding. Recreational bedroom exploits can often create a short-term mutual benefit for both holiday lovers.

When it comes to marriage, however, a woman enters riskier territory. While the rejection of homophily may be exciting and even essential to short-term liaisons to avoid discovery by judgmental peers, the likelihood of ultimate failure is greater. Even among U.S. residents, a difference in race (let alone nationality) is enough to increase the risks of divorce from 40 out of 100 to 47 out of 100 (and to 54 out of 100 in the case of black-white marriages; see table 21, Bramlett).

Compensating factors must be present to better the chances of lasting binational marriages. Some examples:

- Both the traveling woman and her fiancé are internationalists, with extensive intercultural experience (Romano 13-14; Cottrell, "Extension").
- One is fluent in the others' culture (for example, Marlena di Blasi in Italy).
- Shared values cement their union (Romano 41-42).

Intercultural marriages that work meld the excitement of a relationship that offers personal growth, a delicious sexual frisson along with the security of more typical unions — and perhaps offer greater ultimate rewards for the lucky.

Even if divorce eventually happens ...

... it doesn't take away from a life containing special years of romance and exotic experience.

For example, Scottish journalist Rosemary Long made a fateful decision in January 1989 to take a vacation with her daughter to the Gambia. Separated from her husband and celibate for year, she "went on holiday to avoid men," she recalled, "but I ended up with a new husband."

Long stopped one day at a beach bar for a beer. Her daughter asked the serious young barman, "How many wives have you?"

"No wife," Ray Faal replied. "But maybe today I have met the woman I should marry." He referred not to the daughter, but to Rosemary herself.

"Oh yeah, just what I, a granny, one year off 50, needs," she thought: "a black toyboy with a beach bar made of palm leaves" ("Holiday Love").

Ray, 26, was "short and slim as a whippet, with fine cheekbones and gentle, sad eyes," she recalled. The trio left for a walk. "I know it sounds corny," Long wrote, "but I felt the most powerful attraction between us. I was terrified."

Ray pursued her, and Rosemary found she enjoyed talking to him and soon felt a consuming commitment to him. She moved to the Gambia and learned the Wollof language. On land she bought, they built a house and guest huts. Ray took to guiding tourists to nearby Senegal, though he tended to rush home to be with Rosemary (Baobab 145). She felt cherished and attractive.

After Ray's drinking led to the end of their marriage and Rosemary returned home, she was philosophical about her decision to marry an African man met on vacation: "I believe every woman has somebody else inside who wants to throw off her inhibitions. It was like that for me" ("Lovers").

Counting the cost of love

Similarly, American chef Marlena di Blasi had friends who frowned on her whirlwind romance with a reticent banker met on a working visit to Venice and her decision to uproot and join him. One female friend, however, offered her different counsel:

> Take it in both your hands and hold tight to this life. If it comes, it only comes once. ... If this is love , if there is even the possibility that this is real love, what do you care? What will it cost you to live it out? Too much? Everything? (57-58)

One last example: English architect Sarah Lloyd lived with an impoverished Sikh, named Jungli, in the north of India for 18 months. Over time, her lover's opium addiction and non-Western reasoning brought the relationship to a close.

Yet Jungli exerted a permanent influence. Lloyd wrote: "He lived a life of absolute simplicity, preferred to eat and drink from his own hands, had no sense of personal territory and owned nothing that wasn't immediately essential" (Indian Attachment 69).

"There was indeed pain for both of us, but maybe also much enrichment," Lloyd e-mailed me. "Jungli was what I would later become, so he must have been important for me. ... what I mean is that later on I too renounced, and now live a much simpler and more spiritual life."

§§§

Now let's visit Asia, the world's center for sensuality for sale and the epicenter of the dating war.

South
and Southeast Asia

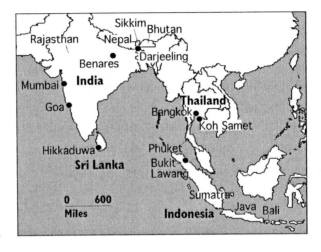

In keeping with Asia's reputation among backpackers as simply the world's most colorful, exciting and vibrant destination, the flavor of sexual opportunity here takes on added exoticism compared to the Mediterranean, the Caribbean and Africa.

Female travelers tell of elegant erstwhile lovers out of *The Arabian Nights*, reclining on cushions and clapping their hands for tea (Davidson, Desert 4) and of being the bride in an opulent, weeklong royal wedding in a Himalayan kingdom (Cooke 108). From the Victorian era to the present, female travelers have been attracted by the kings, princes and minor royals of India, Bali, Thailand, Nepal, Sikkim and Indonesia.

Yet the story of travel amours in Asia is one of extremes. Today, women are as likely to pick a pauper — a Sherpa mountain porter, Indonesian gigolo or Sri Lankan teen-ager — as a prince. A contributor to a travel Web site (Sumatran Men) was staggered as he traveled around Indonesia at the number of Western women dragging around beach bums and unemployed young men vs. a normal Asian guy.

Indeed, Western women don't seem to go out with "normal Asian" guys. Clean-cut guides in Indonesia know they lose out in seducing female tourists: "Maybe I look too decent and too serious. I wear my shirt in my trousers, my hair is neatly cut and I am clean. Maybe women think I am not interested in having a relationship" (guide qtd. in Dahles, "Entrepreneurs" 283).

In this respect, Asia resembles the scene described earlier in Africa, where tourist women also gravitate toward chiefs or conversely penniless but exotic warriors.

Other aspects of female traveler's behavior in South and Southeast Asia are significant:

 • Women as well as men now visit Thailand, the world's leading sex boutique, demonstrating how affectionate sex has become a commodity for both sexes.

 • When Japanese, Korean, Taiwanese and Hong Kong women alight at the airports of Southeast Asia, they demonstrate he universality of how women in all the developed countries in the Northern Hemisphere (and Australia and New Zealand as well) gambol with foreign guys. The simple geographic pattern is one of women from cold northern nations flying south to tropical resorts with available men. As Europeans go to Greece and Africa and North Americans to the Caribbean, affluent Asian women head to warmer climes and hot gents.

 • With female travelers now famous, in both mountainous Nepal and remote Sumatra's jungle, for affairs with locals, Asia also demonstrates the spread of holiday liaisons outside of beach resorts.

 • Most important, Southeast Asia is Ground Central in the dating wars. Western men rejecting their own women have long explored Thai and Filipina beauties. Now rebellious Japanese women crowd Thailand too, their unhappiness directed at their constricted options in their home society.

A history without a hiatus

Asia has the world's longest uninterrupted history of female sexual exploration, with steady reports over parts of three centuries, from 1859 to the present. Other regions have at least some gaps from 1900 to 1960, as wars, depressions and postwar domesticity curbed female travel in general.

In 1859, a mere decade after Margaret Fuller and Lady Jane Digby put Italy in the record books, Miss Henrietta Melvina Hodges, who was likely an American born in India, married the raja of Kapurthala in Northern India.

Many, many marriages between other Western women and Indian nobles steadily followed, even during the 1930s buildup of tensions toward World War II. And even during the war, intrepid Western women stayed near Asian men they loved until the Japanese invaded, with examples including Emily Hahn in China and K'tut Tantri on Java, who was imprisoned.

In most of the rest of the world, World War II and the 1950s was a slow era for female sex travel, reflecting society's overall chaos followed by stasis.

However, Asia knew no such hiatus. In the late 1950s, a number of American women visiting Himalayan Asia and Thailand began to marry local princes. Hope Cooke, educated in Virginia and New York City, married Chogyal, Sikkim's philandering leader. D'Lynn Waldron of New Jersey married Nepal's Prince Basundhara, who would shortly replace her with live-in love Barbara Adams of Virginia. In Thailand, Prince Sanidh married his second Western wife.

Let's examine the current situations in South and Southeast Asia, beginning with the curious case of India, followed by Sri Lanka, Nepal, Thailand and Indonesia.

From maharajas to pests
INDIA

Much has changed since the days of the maharajas. After the heyday of the 1960s hippie trail through Asia faded, replaced by a stream of more middle-class backpackers, India seems to have become just about the only nation in the world where erotic options for traveling women flourished more before the mid-1970s than after.

Ironically, given India's historic reputation for sensuality (see History chapter), now most traveling women seem to find the subcontinent more threatening than alluring. Finnish researcher Petri Hottola, who has studied backpackers in India and Sri Lanka, e-mailed me to note that "the maharajas have lost most of their wealth and fame ... and hippie idealism has faded."

Today, India, the north in particular, is moving into another column — as a zone of harassment, along with Pakistan. And once women are harassed enough, they "close themselves from the local people," Hottola added in his e-mail. While some backpackers still pursue romances with Indians, most shun them, tired of unwanted sexual advances (Intercultural 309, 313, 363).

Canadian travel writer Tim Ward (67) observed his sexy Austrian girlfriend adopt a harsh, unsmiling tone toward Indian men as they traveled together. He began to appreciate her "daily battle ... . Her yellow hair was a candle for over two hundred million sexually repressed male moths. Beating them off would be an exhausting task."

Benares, a center for Hindu pilgrimages and major tourist attraction, nosedived in the early 1990s, becoming known as a "molesters' paradise." Tourist women reported overwhelming harassment, their bodies grabbed, the propositions non-stop, men flashing their penises on streets with a 30:1 male:female ratio (Mishra, Ludhiana 218-26). Indeed, Indian men are seen as pests. Perhaps it is no wonder, given that India has a surplus of 32 million men (U.N. Statistics Division) — yes, that is 32 *million* — that they seem so desperate for female company, a desperation made keener by the deprivation that even married Indians face. Conjugal sex is said to be "with the lights out, over in moments and very physical" (Martin). In rural areas couples sneak out to fields, away from jammed households and prying eyes.

Indian men find Western women, in comparison to their wives, "to be sex goddesses; powerful, experienced, ready and available, and equal to men in sexual relations [compared to wives who are] passive and submissive" (Hottola, *Intercultural* 315).

Desperation seems nationwide, from Rajasthan, where youthful "Casanovas ... have had a little taste of white flesh and can't get enough" (Martin) to Mumbai (Bombay), whose hopeful "studs" place personal ads — for tourists! For "the dream of many young Indian men involved in tourism is to meet a white woman who will rescue him from his prison of caste culture and poverty" (L. Daniels) — and sexual unfulfillment.

Even Mumbai's playboys, with millions of beautiful Indian women to choose from, seem to find greater potential for "hot" and "sizzling" sex with tourists, as these personal ads attest:

> From: The Stud of the Heart
> hi wanted girls/women /tourists for discrete fun. Total confidentially guarantied and expected. I have chocolaty looks am handsome work for multinational

> From: Hottest Stud in Mumbai
> Looking for HOT!! SIZZLING!! female tourists !!!!
> Hi there darlings. If you are hot ... sizzling (or think you are!!), of the female sex (only) and are visiting Mumbai then let this 6.1, athletic, well endowed (nice term!!) and passionate (of course!!) man show you the sights around Mumbai!! Needless to say, you will be very well looked after (chivalry is not dead - yet!!) and thoroughly spoilt!! (Ranny)

In fact, in a 180-degree reversal of the days when Western women swooned over rich, sexually athletic maharajas, today the shoe is on the other foot. Indian men love looking at Western women and fantasizing about them, for "much like the hippies believed the Orient to be a realm of superior spiritual wisdom, many Orientals seem to envisage the West as a realm of superior sensual pleasures" (Hottola, *Intercultural* 385).

In addition to Mumbai and its playboys, other areas of India report at least some female sexual adventuring today:

- the hippie and rave enclaves at Goa (Hottola, *Intercultural* 283; O'Connell Davidson, Goa 17-18).
- many towns visited by tourists who shop for rugs and paintings, which have spawned local playboys (Dreir).
- Darjeeling and the surrounding area under the gleaming mountain Kanchenjunga in far northeast India, mentioned in the novel of Western sexual hysteria, *Black Narcissus*; site of the seduction of American socialist Hope Cooke by the ruler of Sikkim; and where writer Barbara Baer encountered a magnificently ardent Sikh of film-star looks.
- and the deserts of Rajasthan (Martin), where Western tourist women enjoy sex with camel drivers, "enticed by the magnificent turbans worn by proud Rajasthani men," who sing them traditional love songs under the stars (L. Daniels).

The camel drivers have very limited sexual knowledge and experience prior to their tutorials with Western clients. Similarly, a novel by Pankaj Mishra, *The Romantics*, describes a young Indian in bed for the first time, with a Frenchwoman named Catherine. Samar simply doesn't know any women outside his family, has paid little thought to romantic love, and though avid has no real idea how to make love: "the first nervous explorations, the fumbling with buttons and hooks, the awkward impasses and the shameful lonely climaxes" (127).

A remarkable travel book by an Englishwoman who fell in love with a poor Indian provides even more insight into the entire question of male sexual naïveté.

Decades of virginity

In 1978, an impoverished Sikh, Jungli, fell in love with English architect Sarah Lloyd as she traveled in India. She decided to take him up on an invitation to his home village.

They shared a room in the house of Jungli's family. Though very attracted by this man with long, glossy raven's hair and a warrior's sword, Lloyd recalled that "respectful of Indian traditions, I was careful to avoid any physical contact with Jungli and did nothing to attract it" (14-15).

After a week of constant companionship, Jungli lost some of his physical shyness, even though Sarah reminded Jungli that his religion prohibited extramarital sex.

"Oh one or two won't matter," he replied.

"When he touched my arm, awkwardly, woodenly, as if I were a goddess and above that sort of thing," Lloyd wrote, "I realized that this was the first time in his life. I was thirty-one and so, near enough, was he."

While living with Jungli for 18 months, Lloyd uncovered some reasons for male inexperience.

Villagers were "extraordinarily ignorant about sex. Young men would be told what to do on their wedding day by their elder brother's wives" (58-59). They accepted their doctors' advice against more than two instances of sex a month "or a man wouldn't have the energy to plough his fields. And unmarried men kept jugs of cold water beside their bedsides because 'you'll never be able to satisfy your wife if you do that' they warned. Jungli never had done."

She noted that village life suppressed the individuality and freedom of children and the sexual energy of adults, even the married, who had so little privacy that some met in the surrounding fields for sex (56-59).

Given this level of inexperience, it is not surprising that some Indian men who do get to know Western women find them intoxicating.

Elsewhere in Asia, we find instead men with extensive sexual experience and skill. For example, off India's southern coast lies a teardrop-shaped island. Sri Lanka, known more for gay orgies and Western grandmothers who buy sex from teens, could not be more different than innocent, desperate India. Let's visit there now.

A secret sex Shangri-La

SRI LANKA

For India, Nepal, Thailand and Indonesia, a student of female sexual geography can readily piece together a solid picture of what's going on from a wide variety of sources — personal observations, newspapers, magazines, scholarly journals, dissertations, books, films, novels and sometimes even plays.

Sri Lanka is another story entirely. Here, secretively, gay and bisexual men from Europe predominate as they pursue liaisons, often with young boys. Some foreign residents conduct orgies with the handsome locals ("Cycle"). This shadowy world has received only scattered news reports — tiny items in Berlin newspapers, for example — and hints on gay-oriented Web sites.

I first became aware of Sri Lanka as a destination of interest to homosexuals quite some time ago, in 1982, when I lived with a young gay housemate in a mock castle in rural England. My housemate and his uncle, also gay, took a trip there together.

Without divulging any juicy details, they returned to say they absolutely loved the place. I thinking at the time, "Why Sri Lanka?" For they both were architecture fiends and India, Thailand and Indonesia seemed better bets for fascinating temples. Now I believe I understand better their choice of destination.

By the mid-1990s, women also began to take advantage of Ceylon as a sex emporium. French and German women aged 50 to 70 wintered with teen-aged boys in their family homes ("Reisenotizen;" and Sri Lanka Ministry of Health report, qtd. in Beddoe 49).

Wealthy widows showered gifts on favored youths. At the beach resort of Hikkaduwa, "The women befriend boys aged between 16 and 19 hawking shells or ornaments and stay in the teenagers' homes, with their parents' trust, and ask if their sons could sleep in the same room" (Kennedy).

These huge age gaps — Sri Lanka teens with women pushing 70 — are certainly an extreme example of female sex tourism, one that is also found, however, in the Gambia in West Africa.

For their services over the three months of northern winter, the teens receive watches, clothes and radios and televisions.

One Sri Lankan hotel, the Ranmal near Hikkaduwa, warns its female guests of a cadre of slightly older beach boys, aged 18 to 25, laden with gold jewelry, who aim to get 50 female tourists in bed per season. The gigolos service young women for free and expect older women to pay.

Young men combine sex work with other jobs, including tour guide, bell-boy, waiter and taxi driver (Ratnapala 217). They "can easily recognize those women who are seeking sexual adventures. Sexual activity takes place in hotels, on the beach, on an arranged trip, or even in the houses of sex workers themselves."

Even before the 2004 tsunami, hookups between European women and Hikkaduwa men were "no longer popular according to several people I talked to," my brother-in-law reported after a 2003 business trip. "We spent the day in a resort just north of there and saw only one interracial couple but did notice a popular massage place for French women. Apparently the civil war has changed a lot of tourists' minds."

With its tropical beaches, Sri Lanka joins the Caribbean and Africa as a warm-weather resort where tourism and sex travel arrived hand in hand. Now let's examine a very different geography, our first example of amours at altitude: Nepal, where feminism brought women into mountaineering and eventually into the tents of sexy Sherpas.

Princes and porters in mountain kingdoms
NEPAL

Before the tourism boom, Sherpas were universally described as shy. "But what are you going to do when a woman climbs into your sleeping bag?"

Brot Coburn (qtd. in Spano "Trekking")

Love is glandular. And mountain air is wonderful for one's glands. A woman always vibrates more in the mountains.

Suyin, *Mountain* (257)

In the late 1950s, Nepal's Prince Basundhara began a series of marriages, legal and de facto, with Western women. And a 1958 novel by Han Suyin, *The Mountain Is Young*, portrays romances thriving at that early juncture between numerous Western women and dashing royals and professionals of Kathmandu.

By the 1960s (Ortner 221-22), a different trend appeared, one that did not draw the same amount of attention from society columns. The counterculture brought footloose women to Nepal, where at least some female hippie trekkers initiated sex with Sherpas, a local ethnic group accustomed to altitude and thus often employed to guide trekkers and climbers and carry their gear.

The trend intensified in the 1970s, as more female mountaineers arrived, their sights set on some of the world's highest peaks on the Nepal-Tibet border.

In the 1980s, women began to give personal accounts of falling in love and getting married. In 1984, Elaine Brook guided a blind woman, Julie Donnelly, to an 18,000-foot summit. Their climb was assisted by Lhakpa, the nephew of Everest conqueror Tenzing Norgay.

During the trek, the trio came to a halt at a frozen river, with torrents of water rushing under the surface. "No problem," Lhakpa exclaimed. Brook (163) recalled how the Sherpa "hoisted Julie onto his back and to my amazement leaped from rock to slippery rock with her. He left her on the far bank and came back for the rucksack."

At that moment Brook "began to fall in love with him, as he muttered his catch-phrase, 'No problem' " (Melchett 205).

Brook admired not only Lhakpa's strength and competence but also his simple, family-oriented life, enjoying a visit to Lhakpa's uncle's house, a spartan large single room where "the whole family lives, works, eats, sleeps and prays ... it seems very natural, very human" (Brook 111). And Lhakpa had come to understand Western ways, as from the age of 14 he worked for expeditions. They later married and formed a trekking company, splitting time between England and Nepal.

In 1988, American teacher Donna M. Sherpa met a guide on trek and later married him. She wrote later (86) of "a strict code of honor among the Sherpa who participate in the treks and expeditions. It is quite positively understood that no Sherpa is to step over his bounds of friendship with the foreigners."

In the 1980s, despite a decade or two of discrete fraternizing, both Elaine Brook and Donna M. Sherpa still had to make the first move with their shy admirers. Over time, as trekkers followed mountaineers to Nepal, more women fell for their intelligent, joking Sherpas, "strong, handsome men, generous and warm. They seem to have all the values our culture lacks" (Covington, qtd. in Spano, "Trekking").

By 2000, however, Sherpas had progressed from standoffish "honor" to a shy responsiveness around women, and ultimately to bold, Don Juanish propositions (Spano, "Trekking").

Later romances often proved more complicated, particularly in cases where the guide already had a wife and children and abandoned them. Local women came to fear losing their husbands to a rich foreigner. In one case, a Sherpa man left his wife and children to live with a Japanese-American woman, who later jilted him. He reportedly committed suicide (Spano, "Trekking").

Despite such risks, the Sherpas know that romance could also eventually lead to an invitation to the United States, where they could find casual work for a few months and return with thousands of dollars (Spano, "Trekking"). Given the promise implicit in working with female tourists, one Sherpa joked that for a women's trekking expedition, "I work for free" (Ortner 223).

By the 1990s, tourists and tour operators described Nepal as the women's equivalent of men's excursions to Thailand — a "sexual vacation," with tales of Western women having sex with Sherpa guides now "rampant" (V. Adams 56).

Yes, Nepal has become a woman's version of Thailand — but guess what? Thailand itself had evolved into a sexual paradise for female travelers.

The revenge of the Japanese women
THAILAND

For centuries in the Land of Smiles and in fact throughout much of Asia, brothels have served the common man (Thanh-Dam 535) — and by all accounts Thai men still lead the way as the top customers for paid sex in their homeland.

The Korean and Vietnam wars first brought non-Asians into this established sex economy. When these conflicts wrapped up, the part of the Thai sex industry oriented to foreigners began to attract civilians, mainly from Japan, Germany and Holland (C. Michael Hall).

After 1990, away from Bangkok's bar district, an astounding new client — the young Japanese woman — showed up. Her destination was Phuket, a giant island at Thailand's southwest edge between Phangnga Bay and the Andaman Sea, with an undulating coast of scalloped bays fringed with beautiful beaches.

Belying their (outdated) reputation in the West for soft, feminine subservience, the Japanese women arrived at their tropical hotels armed with steely confidence, lots of cash, annoyance with the men at home —

and an openness to suggestive proposals from slender Thai windsurfers and beach vendors.

While in the 1990s public awareness was starting to build, at least in Europe, of slut-for-a-week behavior by female tourists in the Mediterranean and Caribbean, this confounding move by Asian women eluded detection at first. So did the activities of blonde Swedish and Norwegian women frequenting Koh Samet, an island in Thailand's northeast, to find Thai boyfriends (Odzer 269, 272).

Thailand's tourism minister, apparently unaware of the existence of female Japanese sex travelers, called for women to visit and "see what their men get up to and how they have exploited uneducated women and children" (Viravaidya qtd. in C.M. Hall 157). And a political economist declared in error that "Japanese women do not travel in large numbers to countries described as sex markets" (Leheny 380). Yet, as we say in the United States, the horse had already left the barn.

It almost seems as if no one wanted to look into the spike of female tourist arrivals on Phuket and figure out what was going on — except a lone Thai demographer. Sairudee Vorakitphokatorn (66) discovered that during the years 1990 to 1994, numbers of female Japanese visitors to Phuket soared from fewer than 4,000 to more than 40,000, and they began to outnumber male Japanese tourists. Beach boys reported that Japanese women, usually aged 18 to 27, comprised 70 percent of their clients (72).

Vorakitphokatorn documented that the Japanese women hooked up with beach boys, youths in their early 20s renting scooters and offering Jet-Skis, parasailing, diving, snorkeling and boat rides.

Her message was not popular with, paradoxically, Japanese women themselves, who feared (more) discrimination if they were shown as being sexually loose. Her findings provoked a storm in Japan, where women in denial "fiercely protested the report and demanded an apology from the doctor" (Ma 68).

What exactly was going on here? The trend was so prevalent that the tourist women were dubbed "yellow cabs," ready to ride with anyone anytime. Why were Japanese women now sex tourists, not only in Thailand, but also Indonesia, Hawaii, Britain (Kelsky, *Verge* 134), Nepal (Spano, "Trekking") and Jamaica (de Albuquerque, "Sex, Beach Boys" 91)?

A battle zone in the dating war

Dating wars, in both the developed and the developing worlds, propel romances on the road. Thailand serves as a case in point.

• Japanese women feel "desperation and rage" at a society that essentially offers them no options but dead-end jobs or marriage to a childish, unhelpful and rarely at home man (Kelsky, *Verge* 8-9). Hence the dominance of women in Japan's Study Abroad programs and traveling abroad, and the controversial trend of seeking relations with foreign men — as demonstrated on Phuket and even within Japan, as expatriate Western men became much sought after (Iyer 78, 296).

Of all the women in the developed world, Japanese women may have the most cause for anger at their home society's circumscription of their role. Paradoxically, despite having low-level jobs, they often have sufficient disposable income to travel because they live at home.

This makes Japanese women perhaps the most representative of those women who fling themselves into holiday liaisons as a critique of their home societies and their own men. Free love for them may, even more than for other women, involve the forging of a new identity and exploring "the liberatory potential of the West" (Kelsky, Verge 4, 8).

• One group of Thai women, the bargirls in Patpong Road (Bangkok's collection of sex clubs), rendered by the demands of their profession confident, independent and vocal,"could express their anger at the way society fashioned Thai men — an outlet for revenge where women could reject them, at least verbally" (Odzer 303).

• And Westerners also fight a dating war in the Thai battle zone. American anthropologist Cleo Odzer, in the course of research in 1988 on Thai prostitutes, was told flatly by a sneering expatriate that Thailand was "not the place for a Caucasian girl, you know. ... I've seen newlyweds come here and the wife ends up flying home alone" (57).

Profiles of adventurous women
An out-there anthropologist
CLEO ODZER, 1950-2001
NEW YORKER WHO BECAME HIPPIE, DRUG RUNNER, SEXOLOGIST

A petite, lovely blonde who grew up in New York City, Odzer possesses a sexual résumé that seems have been at the cutting edge of many trends from the 1960s through the 1990s. She was model, a rock groupie (with Keith Emerson of Emerson, Lake and Palmer), a hippie and drug runner to Goa in India, a travel sex connoisseur, and finally a cybersex celebrity. She died of a stroke in Goa in March 2001, according to Marcus Robbin, who filmed her for the documentary *Last Hippie Standing*.

After her near-fatal drug phase, she pulled herself together and went to New York's New School of Social Research to obtain a doctorate in anthropology. In 1988, she headed for Bangkok to interview bar girls for her dissertation. Thai prostitutes, she found, could be spotted at a distance, for far from being exploited and kept down, they had more brashness and confidence than other, more demure women. She conducted affairs herself with a pimp and beach boys. Her favorite was Toom, a windsurfer on the island of Ko Samet east of Bangkok, who called her "Creo, my honey bunches" (271).

Cleo Odzer

"Since my research dealt with Western men who paraded their Thai girlfriends as prizes of womanhood — women who knew the real way to treat a man — being with Toom afforded me revenge," she recalled (270). "I knew the Western guys on the beach watching us wouldn't approve. Ko Samet was loaded with Western women with Thai boyfriends. I loved it. What a switch!" In a hut in the exotic jungle near Burma, around a dying fire, Odzer enjoyed a final liaison with a Chiang Mai trail guide. She concluded, "Thailand was a paradise for Western women too" (305).

Where lesbians gather

Evidence is mounting that in Thailand's three main districts offering sex shopping for foreigners — Bangkok, Pattaya and Phuket — Western lesbians are the latest customers. And the Thai bargirls they hire may themselves actually be true lesbians themselves rather than heterosexuals willing to service lesbians (Derr).

Less-than-flattering reports out of the northeast resort of Pattaya describe "fat eighty-year old German lesbians with fifteen-year old Thai girls" (Hector; also see Houellebecq 77).

Observers suggest that lesbians also buy sex in Phuket (Phuket Thailand — A Newbie Guide) and Bangkok:

> Many Western women can be seen in go-go bars and other establishments in Thailand, apparently in a voyeuristic role observing male sex tourist behavior. [Also,] female tourists are to be found in massage parlors perhaps testing out their lesbian nature. (Latza in Oppermann, "Sex Tourism" 253)

In Bangkok, quite apart from the massage circuit, a private lesbian scene exists: "while the male gay scene is very much in your face, the lesbian scene is less evident and the venues much more dilute. The scene centers around groups of friends with no specific lesbian areas in the city" (Bangkok by Night).

The Utopia-Asia Web site (Thailand Lesbian) lists popular nightspots for Thai lesbians, whose toms and dees tend to correspond to the Western styles of butch and femme, but warns Westerners that "foreign women may find that language and their own ambiguous gender style (not femme enough to attract toms, and not butch enough to attract dees) to be challenging hurdles."

One academic researcher in Australia has noticed increasing lesbian activity in not only Thailand but in Indonesia.

She e-mailed me to note that she was "quite convinced from my own observations that there is a steady trickle of German and Dutch lesbians who seek out non-Western women while tourists in South-east Asia, but this is a very secretive and closeted community, so I haven't been able to get very far in to find much out in a formal sense. My understanding is that these are 'romantic' rather than commercial liaisons, very much like the ones heterosexual women often make with young non-western men" (Nilan, "E-mail").

The themes of an emergent lesbian clientele and a continuing dating war between Japanese men and women will stay with us as we move south into Indonesia.

'Want banana, Miss?'

INDONESIA

Once upon a time, Western women's affairs with local Indonesians remained discrete.

In the Bali of the 1930s, many expatriate artists and visitors, including two women, found themselves roused by the comely and sensually refined locals (the island remains a notable destination for sublime massage). One woman, a Briton who lived for long stretches in the United States, assumed the Indonesian name K'tut Tantri. She became the incredibly close friend of Balinese Prince Anak Agung Nura.

The prince's daughter confirms Tantri as her father's concubine (Lindsey 31). Tantri insisted, however, that the relationship was platonic (Tantri 55). Had she acknowledged an affair, her book *Revolt in Paradise* could have made a fortune as a Hollywood screenplay (Lindsey 31).

And lesbian anthropologist Jane Belo, wife of the gay composer Colin McPhee (author of *A House in Bali*), quietly became intimate with female Balinese village dancers (Runciman 159; Craft 56).

No such delicacy surrounds the all-too-obvious sexual relations between female tourists and Indonesian men today. One indication of how times have changed is this blatant proposition from a Javanese gigolo: "Want banana, Miss? Indonesia banana small but hot!" (qtd. in H. Dahles, "Entrepreneurs" 267).

We will focus on female tourist behavior at Kuta Beach on Bali and at a nature reserve in Sumatra. (For more information on gigolos on Java and Lombok see Dahles, "Entrepreneurs" and "Birds".)

The Kuta Cowboys

The first gigolos I ever noticed in the course of my world travels were the Kuta Cowboys, lined along the wall at Peanuts Disco in southern Bali during my 1985 visit there. They had long hair, trendy sunglasses and affected Mick Jagger expressions of sultry arrogance, an unintentionally comical stance in an island whose appeal to foreigners lay squarely in the genial, unaffected charm of its inhabitants. Other observers have even termed a minority of the cowboys as "markedly sinister" (Wolf 16).

Young man on the beach in Bali. His expression is less modest than that of a typical non-beachboy.

They did nothing for me, a veteran of holiday misbehavior in Greece, and an aficionado of more powerful, athletic men, but by other accounts these skinny dudes had since the early 1980s found willing Australian women.

By late 1980s, Japanese women also arrived. Today an estimated 400 of them are married and resident on the spectacular isle (Yamashita 94-96). The overwhelming majority are from Osaka and Tokyo and are said to be fleeing urban life. Many of the women's attitudes imply a rejection of Japanese men, as they never considered marriage until meeting a Balinese man.

For the most part, however, the Kuta Cowboys represent commerce, not romance: "I like the older women because they have more money. We say, 'No money no honey,' said one 'cowboy' " (qtd. in Dowling 277).

No wonder Bali began to attract economically desperate emigres from Java (Wolf 17), who along with local Balinese men, "follow the money," pursuing not only Europeans but also Japanese, Hong Kong, Taiwanese and Korean women, thought to have more spending power (Best to Avoid).

The October 2002 disco bombing in Bali had caused virtually all tourists to vanish, in turn leading to the complete disappearance of the Kuta Cowboys. One vendor said, "There is no one for them to gigolo with" (Baker). We can now reverse the observation of the Kuta Cowboy, quoted above, from "No money, no honey," to "No honey, no money."

Hindus on Bali apparently have second thoughts about their tolerance of prostitutes and gigolos, connecting an acceptance of vice with the bomb disaster, and would love to see the gigolos never return (Baker). And west of Bali, among tourists themselves, rages another debate, perhaps one of greatest in female sex tourism.

The Bukit Lawang controversy

A nature preserve in Indonesia's remote backcountry may seem an unlikely hotspot for sex travel.

Yet the remote Sumatran village of Bukit Lawang, next to an area set aside for orangutans, has managed to ignite one of the most savage debates over the sexual mores of traveling women.

An outraged discussion (Sumatran Men) on the Lonely Planet Thorn Tree, a chat room aimed at independent travelers, brought to the fore once again that Southeast Asia, as mentioned in this chapter's opening, is ground central for the world's dating wars.

The controversy ignited in August 2001 when a woman described sleeping with an Indonesian man on her weeklong jungle trek around Bukit Lawang. She wondered if other ladies could report similar experiences.

Vitriol sprang immediately from dozens of critics perhaps prompted in part by male anger at female interlopers in Asia's sex playgrounds, long the preserve of the male sex tourist.

One poster, a long-time traveler to Thailand and Indonesia, said he frequently would see intelligent-seeming Western women with some local male, a walking mess, in tow.

Another man described 99 percent of Western women as ugly, fat pigs, who did not compare favorably to slim, elegant, beautiful Asian women. Others attacked female travelers in Sumatra as terribly naive and lacking taste and discretion — sluts and losers who jumped into the lice-infested bed of the first guy they saw strumming a guitar.

The Bukit Lawang playboys, described as festering maggots by one poster, allegedly swapped tourists among themselves for 50,000 rupiah (about $5 at the time), and returned to their wives and children at night, laughing at Western whores.

Western women would obviously be wiser to show more selectiveness in their selection of foreign men, avoiding those who offer sex with a healthy dose of contempt.

Amorous in Asia

DISADVANTAGES

• **High HIV rates.** While Asia overall is not so dangerous overall as sub-Saharan Africa, the rate of adult HIV infections in Thailand and to a lesser extent India still proves worrisome. A woman from North America will encounter an HIV rate in Thailand triple that of home, six-fold higher for a Western European. Before my most recent trip to Thailand, my traveling party was warned by a doctor at an international health clinic, "Don't even get a manicure in Thailand," for fear that cuticle tears would expose us to the virus.

HIV-infected adults per 1,000

Thailand	18
India	8
Nepal	5
Indonesia	1
Sri Lanka	less than 1
For comparison:	
North America	6
Europe	3

Source: UNAIDS

Note: Special warnings have also been issued regarding increasing rates of HIV in Goa in India, a popular site for rave pilgrimages (D'Cunha)

• **Faltering marriages, split families.** As noted in the Experiences chapter, the vast majority of Sherpa-tourist couples living in the United States fail. Poor judgment involving tourists who take up with married Sherpas has led to suicide and abandoned families.

In Indonesia and Thailand, local men may become fathers to children raised in distant Europe, with few chances to visit their offspring. Cleo Odzer (272) relates a sad tale of a youth on Ko Samet in Thailand whose holiday girlfriend returned to Sweden, bore twin girls, and found a new Swedish boyfriend.

The Thai youth sold his belongings to fly halfway around the world to see his daughters and was only permitted a few minutes with them. Another man in Java sees his half-Austrian son just once a year (Dahles, "Entrepreneurs" 285).

• **Slut label in Muslim areas.** In Bukit Lawang, we see a combination of cautions for the female sex traveler. Even though the briefness of her visit confers some anonymity, she may still become an object of contempt, if Western men and judgmental locals are nearby (and don't forget, Sumatra is the most fundamentally Muslim area of Indonesia).

For example, one women posting to the Lonely Planet Thorn Tree site (Sumatran Men) described becoming pregnant by a Bukit Lawang man. She spoke fluent Indonesian but wrote that she wish she didn't after hearing what was said about her.

• **Stuck-up men, coarsening approaches.** I sensed an arrogance in the Kuta Cowboys, an arrogance not even partly justified by any special handsomeness or fineness of physique. By comparison, other foreign men who pursued me, in Southern Europe, the Bahamas, the Caribbean and Brazil, seemed not full of themselves but merely eager and vigorously pro-sex.

The Kuta Cowboys' attitude of "I'm God's gift to women" holds little appeal; even less so, the jungle playboy's creepy willingness to go behind a woman's back to sell her availability to friends.

That is the "yuck" factor of Bukit Lawang, and a measure of a certain coarseness now confronting the female sex traveler. Older female friends of mine who had extensive expatriate experience in the 1960s and 1970s, in the Caribbean and Asia, recall fondly an earlier era marked by a smooth, sophisticated seduction dance between women working overseas and discrete, suave foreign men. Today however we see the worst of the Indonesian gigolos comparing unfavorably to foreign men of a generation ago and even to their contemporaries, such as the Sherpas.

• **Rising prices for high-end sex.** "White girls would say once you'd had a Balinese lover you'd never want anything else, and they asked for little: meals, petrol, a souvenir" (Baranay, *Pleasure* 31).

As writer Inez Baranay notes, in the 1980s, Balinese men did not ask for much. By 2002, however, the going rate for upscale gigolos on Bali was reported at 600,000 to 2 million rupiah a night, or $67 to $222 (Harvey).

At a price, Bangkok agencies offer male escorts for women (Odzer 208). "Exclusive bars for women" are said to "provide contacts with attractive young men; middle-aged women often 'patronize' young male performers in traditional theater arts. Many Western female tourists engage in liaisons with Thai men, which inevitably have a commercial or financial aspects" (Hamilton).

Cleo Odzer (100) once paid the "bar fine" (allowing a client to take a sex worker away from a go-go for the night) to interview a gay dancer, and reported the going rate in 1988 at 200 baht ($7.50) — cheaper than the bar fine for a woman. Bar fines do not include the payment made directly to a partner for their companionship.

In Thailand, with about double the per capita GDP of Indonesia, men in resorts outside Bangkok may pay for dates: "Ko Samet boys adhered to the belief that a man should pay for a woman. [They] did accept gifts from women, though, which left them dripping with jewelry and trinkets ... and possessing colossal assortments of stuffed animals" (Odzer 271).

• **Rising reports of rape.** At press time, Japan's government was weighing the idea of warning women to avoid Bali in wake of five assaults and a lack of arrests ("Japan Mulls"). Similar problems have been reported in Chiang Mai, Krabi and Samet in Thailand (Coates) and Goa in India (Kay).

ADVANTAGES

• **Sex like beautiful music.** In Southeast Asia especially, we lack the graphic, incendiary reports women provide of wild sex with African, Caribbean or Arab men. Here reigns Passion Lite, expressed with

South and Southeast Asia timeline

1879: Fanny Knox, half-English and half Thai, marries a **Thai** provincial governor named Pra Preecha. Later she advocated Siam's evolution from absolute to constitutional monarchy (Minney 368, 372, 380; Terwiel 231).

1902: Dr. Malcolm Smith, attending to the health needs of Thai royalty and European expatriates, notes traits that presage the coming domination of **Thailand** as a sex market: "Sexual indulgence by the Siamese is carried to a degree that to most Europeans is incredible. Between the ages of eighteen and forty, it is the over-mastering passion of their lives" (qtd. in Hunter 23).

1912: **Thai** Prince Rangsit Prayurasakdi marries a German woman, Elisabeth Scharnberger. In **1946**, their son, Prince Sanidh Rangsit, marries Amelia Montalti. In **1959**, Sanidh takes as his third wife another Westerner, Christine Clerc. Another pair of Thai princes, Chula and Bira, marry Englishwomen met in Britain and in **1938** honeymoon together in Thailand (Hunter 195).

1930s: During the interwar period, bohemian Western women on Indonesian island of **Bali** enter affairs with local princes; one lesbian frolics with village dancers (Lindsey 32; Tantri 106; Craft 56).

- Around **1930**, at age 16, French colonial Marguerite Duras embarks on affair in **Vietnam** with a young Chinese heir, a liaison to appear later as a reworked autobiography in the book and film *The Lover* (Adler 348; Duras, *The Lover*; *The North China Lover*).

- In **1932**, a British-American artist who later became known as K'tut Tantri meets **Balinese** prince Anak Agung Nura. Her account that the relationship was platonic (Tantri 55) has been disputed (Lindsey 31). Other sources attest that "she slept with all her male Balinese servants" (Bagus footnote 47).

- In **1935**, American writer Emily Hahn meets and later becomes the concubine of **Shanghai** aristocrat and publisher Sammy Zau (Cuthbertson 140-66; Hahn, *China to Me* 56-57 and "Big Smoke").

1939: An early look at Asia as a realm of sexual awakening for women (rather than just men) appears in the novel *Black Narcissus* (Godden), featuring a handsome, young Indian general's son whose sensuality begins to

greater delicacy of expression, as women in their own first-hand accounts focus on kissing along romantic moonlit beaches (Gough, "Bali Moon"). Cleo Odzer (116) recalled of her first instance of sex with a Thai lover, "His gentleness made me think I held a cloud, and I lost myself in a blend of East and West."

In this fictional but quite plausible account, a female character in an Inez Baranay novel compares sex with a Balinese man to the hypnotic, eddying sounds of a gamelan orchestra:

It's all so non "exciting," she would think, excitement had nothing to do

unhinge a convent of nuns assigned to the Himalayas.

1946: Balinese Prince Anak Agung Made Djelantik (169, 181), son of the last raja of Karangasem, marries Astri Zwart, a Dutch nurse, riding to their ceremony in Amsterdam in a horse-drawn carriage. Back in Bali, Djelantik's father hosts a second wedding with 5,000 guests.

1956: In **Nepal**, the Chinese-Dutch writer and medical doctor Han Suyin meets and instantly lusts after Vincent Ruthnaswamy, an Indian engineer in charge of building the first paved road connecting the mountain kingdom to India (*House* 106-07). (How perfect that the road builder, opening Nepal to the outside world, should himself enjoy romance on the road.) They became constant companions and married in 1971. Suyin recorded their romance in her autobiographical volume, *My House Has Two Doors*, and in her novel *The Mountain Is Young*. Coincidentally, D'Lynn Waldron, see next item, worked on a movie treatment for *Mountain*, and Suyin also encountered Emily Hahn, above, in her travels.

1958: Basundhara, the "playboy prince" of **Nepal**, takes D'Lynn Waldron of Cleveland, Ohio, as his third wife. In **1961**, with Waldron out of the picture, Virginian Barbara Adams visits Nepal with her Italian husband of two years, falls in love with Basundhara and stays and lives with him for a decade (Stephens 175-83). The prince later took a French mistress.

1959: Jennifer Kendal, part of an itinerant British family troupe performing Shakespeare in **India**, marries the incorrigibly handsome Shashi Kapoor, destined to be a great Bollywood star. They later starred together in early Merchant-Ivory productions.

1963: American Hope Cooke, educated in Virginia and New York, marries Chogyal, the crown prince of **Sikkim**. Given the strategic importance of the mountain kingdoms of Sikkim and Nepal to India, China, the Soviet Union and the United States, Cooke (87) and fellow American Waldron ("War") were subject to paranoia that they were part of CIA plots.

1965: Indonesia's playboy president, Sukarno, visits Cambodia "accompanied by a very beautiful American

with it. For most men, sex is this build-up to a final crescendo and then it's done. This is so different. It's like the music ... that absolute music, that feminine music, music without the western anticipations, without regularity, without climaxes, without resolutions, without finales. (*Bali* 195-96)

The culture of the rice-growing lands of Southeast Asia, which often blends social cooperativeness with Buddhist gentleness and avoidance of extremes, affects sexual style.

• **Handsome men.** In Thailand, a female sailing buddy and I, as an exercise, decided to evaluate male attractiveness. At an outdoor eating pavilion near Bangkok's airport, we concluded that one out of every

girl" (Suyin, *House* 373), suggesting some truth to the view expressed by Hope Cooke (87) that "Asian men are ridiculous about American girls. I think because they've seen so many American movies they think we must all be loose."

Mid-1960s: Counterculture Western women exploring **Nepal** initiate sexual relations with Sherpa men (Ortner 221-22).

1973: The erotic film *Emmanuelle* (see Portrayals chapter) explores the idea of the East, and **Thailand** specifically, as a place of sexual awakening for women.

1978: English architect Sarah Lloyd and Australian travel writer Robyn Davidson (in **1979**) meet **Indian** men at either extreme of the income and status scale, later write books about their experiences.

Early 1980s: Numbers of Australian women visiting **Bali** for liaisons with beach boys increase (Ryan *Sex Tourism*, preface xiii).

1985: In **Bali's** Peanuts discotheque, Indonesian youths — with hair past the shoulders and sunglasses, open-necked shirts and tight pants — strike rock-star poses as they look over

tourist women (Belliveau, *Amateur* 210). These Kuta Cowboys are "on the lookout for Australian girls" (Mabbett 86-87).

• Lisa Van Gruisen, an Englishwoman active in publishing and wildlife conservation, marries a man she met in **Nepal**, Tenzin Choegyal, son of eastern ruler of Tibet (Stephens 190, 198).

Late 1980s: Young single Japanese women travel to **Bali**, U.S. military bases in **Japan**, **Hawaii** and other destinations to seek out Asian, white and black men for casual sex (Kelsky, *Verge* 134).

1989: Anthropologist Evelyn Blackwood enters relationship with a woman in rural western **Sumatra**, a rare and early example of a lesbian bedding a Third World lover. In her essay on the affair, Blackwood described some dissatisfaction with their sex life, as her lover, Dayan, wanted to play the man in lovemaking and Blackwood herself rejected "male-defined and hierarchical sexuality" (68).

1991: Prince Dhirendra of **Nepal**, nephew of the above-mentioned Prince Basundhara, marries Canadian

two men qualified as extremely handsome, with beautiful faces, pleasing brown skin and ravens' hair (Belliveau, *Amateur* 140). (We made no move, however, past admiration at a distance.)

The former wife of a Thai man posted on the Web her opinion: "I personally think that Asian men are the most beautiful race of men. They have very distinguished features" (Asian lover).

Balinese men (away from Kuta Beach) and the Javanese are captivating in a different, almost feminine way. In Java, a guide I hired rotated his hands as he walked, practicing ancient temple dances (Belliveau, *Amateur* 206). In the town of Mas on Bali, my travel group watched local men

woman, Shirley Greaney, and lives with her on the Isle of Wight (North).

1992: Australian writer Inez Baranay depicts the **Indonesia** scene in *The Edge of Bali*. The novel describes a naive tourist who returns to find her lover involved with another Western girl, and a second tourist who enjoys rapturous sex with a charming dancer of royal lineage.

1996-98: In **Sri Lanka**, tourist women, most French and German, pay beach boys for sex (Beddoe 49; D. Kennedy).

• Tourists and tour operators now describe **Nepal** as the women's equivalent of men's excursions to Thailand — a "sexual vacation" (V. Adams 56).

• Street guides flourish in Yogyakarta, on the Indonesian island of **Java**. Long-haired young men "looking like a hybrid of Michael Jackson and Prince" (Dahles, "Birds" 38) target younger women. Other men project a polished, businesslike look and pursue more affluent women in their 30s, 40s and older.

• In **Thailand,** female tourists patronize exclusive bars for women, where they can meet and offer patronage of various sorts to young male performers in traditional theater arts (Hamilton 146).

• In **Malaysia**, men ("Local Casanovas") prey on Japanese tourists with promises of marriage.

1999: Kuta Cowboys, visible on **Bali** for nearly 20 years, actively solicit tourist women (Dowling).

2000-01: In **Sumatra** in Indonesia, gigolos appear in Medan and Lake Toba (Indonesian Diversity). A village, Bukit Lawang, where tourists begin treks to view orangutans, becomes a hotbed of female sex tourism and earns the sobriquet "Bangkok in Reverse" (Bukit Lawang).

• Single American women, particularly lonely professionals, continue to flock to **Nepal** to find romance with strong, handsome, generous Sherpa men (Spano, "Trekking").

• Lesbians reported in bars of **Bangkok** and in dance clubs on **Bali**, picking up local women (Nilan, Bali 19).

2002: An American documentary filmmaker (personal correspondence with the author) in **Cambodia** finds evidence of Japanese female tourists marrying local men met on trips to Buddhist temple at Angkor Wat.

---

pass idyllic days painting or carving masks, making them seem 100-fold more at ease with their world than are many Western men in theirs (211).

• **Variety in men.** As some men love to envelope petite women, women themselves may enjoy a man likely to be less tall, bulky and hairy than their fellow Westerners. Cleo Odzer wrote of her first Thai lover, "I loved the feel of him; his shoulders seemed the width of mine. ... I hated being with someone a head taller and twice as wide. Jek had been perfect" (116, 151).

"I explored the shape of his body which felt different from farang [foreign] men in ways I couldn't identify. He smelled different too. ...

Young men play soccer on Kuta Beach in Bali. Many youths appear to strike poses to appeal to visiting Australian female tourists.

His kiss felt like a kiss, though, and as he moved on top of me I thought some things were just the same, except he felt very light."

Opportunities for older women. In Sri Lanka, as in the Gambia in West Africa, women up in their 70s can procure teen lovers for the holiday season. And on Bali and Lombok, women in their 30s and 40s and possibly older will be courted by teen-aged boys in search of a better life — in the form of an air ticket to Europe or Australia (Dahles, "Entrepreneurs" 284).

• **Measures of normalcy and delight.** Some women who choose to marry Asian men, especially in Bali, seem to enjoy happy and comfortable lives, in marked contrast to the absolute squalor, previously discussed, endured by some Western wives in Africa and India, and the social isolation of wives in Greece.

Japanese women particularly seem to enjoy their new lives married to Balinese men. Said one: "If I am in Japan for about two or three weeks, the energy I bring back from Bali disappears, and I begin to think that I've had enough. Bali is a much cozier place to live" (qtd. by Yamashita 96).

§§§

Next we'll visit Latin America, Polynesia and the Near East, but on the way, let's look at another important aspect of sex travel by women, touched on above in our discussion of Asia: its long history.

History

Mohiuddin Hossain Meerza, his wife, Nora, and their daughter, Zena.

On a Sunday a century ago, a young aristocrat named Mohiuddin Hossain Meerza rode a fine chestnut Thoroughbred on the route to Darjeeling.

Grandson of the last provincial governor, or Nawab Nazim, of India's eastern provinces of Bengal, Bihar and Orissa, Mohiuddin traveled north, in India's far highlands. Along the road, Mohiuddin's gaze fell on Nora Partridge, daughter of the local pharmacist, on her way back from church with her family.

Mohiuddin "raised his hat and wished her well as she blushed coyly from beneath her parasol," their daughter, Zena Meerza Sinclair, later recalled in her memoirs ("Petals").

He "had fallen in love at first sight" — a literal case of romance on the road.

Mohiuddin wanted to court the porcelain-complected beauty and learned that Nora taught the piano and mandolin. He applied for lessons, and not long after, Nora's parents granted him permission to take their daughter's hand in marriage. "He was such a nice little fellow," they thought, though other family members were "not much in favour of a mixed marriage."

The Meerzas were married "and didn't give a damn" about outsider disapproval, comfortably moving in both the British and Indian circles that coexisted under the Raj. "They loved each other dearly and that was what counted," their daughter recalled.

"As far as they were concerned, the difference in the colour of their skins (Papa was quite dark whilst Mama was fair-skinned and blue-eyed) did not matter one bit."

Stories such as Nora Partridge's, which her grandson James Sinclair carefully preserved as a manuscript in his South London home, come as a pleasant surprise to somewhat like myself, a child of the 1960s and '70s who recalls interracial dating occurring at my Maryland high school — but not without attendant controversy.

How, one wonders, back in 1907, did blue-eyed Nora dare to love the richly brown Mohiuddin, despite no cultural winds blowing at her back, as in the modern era with mixed-raced entertainers and athletes dominating *People* magazine's Most Beautiful lists? She displayed a quiet bravery that astounds in the current day, when some families continue to view crosscultural marriages with alarm.

But Nora Partridge was far from alone in marrying a foreign royal, and in surprising numbers, equally daring women preceded her.

A hidden saga

Perhaps the discovery I least expected to make in researching this book was that from the 1840s on, Western women not only had the courage to conduct traditional courtships with foreign men but even at times aggressively sought lovers (especially Arabs) for the rawest of raw sex.

For example, in the 19th century, in Egypt, Lucie Duff Gordon wrote home that "English maids ravish the Arab man so continually" (*Egypt* 187). Meanwhile, over in Tunisia and Algeria, a young woman named Isabelle Eberhardt supplied hurricane-intensity lovemaking to enthusiastic young North Africans.

A fruitful conversation opened my eyes to this earlier era of female sexual adventuring. In May 1999, Jan Brown, compiler of a bibliography of female travel writers, invited me to speak to a meeting of Women Outdoors in New Hampshire.

After my talk, I mentioned to Brown my research on traveling women and foreign men. She told me about *Love Among the Butterflies*, the edited diaries of English butterfly collector Margaret Fountaine, whose flirtations with a parade of Mediterranean suitors culminated in a torrid affair with a guide in Syria. Her romance occurred in ... 1901.

Fountaine's diaries inspired a hunt for other early adventuresses.

Ultimately I found that documented romances involving traveling women began in the 1840s, coinciding with the flowering of the Industrial Age rather than the 1960s era of Flower Power.

Yet outside of a few scholars who study the travel writing of Victorian women, few seem aware of sexual adventuring by women before Swinging Sixties, let alone the extensive record of such activity.

Thus women have had no knowledge of their sweeping history of sex travel, nor the extent to which such encounters have for more than 150 years reflected a natural response to social turmoil.

The story of this early era can be assembled via numerous but wildly scattered accounts — biographies of some of the women, once-popular novels, Victorian history, women's travel essays, archives in London's India Office, academic journals, unpublished memoirs, missionary correspondence, and articles, book reviews and letters to editors hidden in microfilm of aging magazines.

This chapter will attempt to integrate for the first time the totality of knowledge available on travel romance by women prior to the 1960s.

From pioneers to package tourists

If we were to sketch an outline of the history of romance on the road for the last century and a half, a simplification would show three eras:

• **Victorian era through the Jazz Age**. In the earliest stages, beginning in 1847, pioneers became amorous with men in Paris, Italy, Greece, Syria, North Africa and India. Their travels and loves owed much to the first wave of feminism in the 19th century. As remains the case today, the women came from a gamut of backgrounds: aristocrats, heiresses and scientists; writers and daughters of the middle class; and (especially) maids, domestic help, dancers and bar girls.

• **Between the sexual revolutions**. From the late 1920s through late 1950s, world turmoil followed by Eisenhower-era quietude limited travel and travel romances — with some notable exceptions, most in Asia. In Thailand, India and the Himalayan kingdoms, royals continued, as much after the Jazz Age as before, to marry Western women or invite them into harems. And five idiosyncratic authors — Marguerite Duras, Emily Hahn, K'tut Tantri, Anne Cumming and Han Suyin — detailed their love affairs in (respectively) Vietnam, Shanghai, Bali, much of the Arab world and Nepal.

• **1960s to the present**. With no fanfare, in the '60s Scandinavian women began taking charter flights to find short-term holiday lovers along Mediterranean coasts and in West Africa, while French Canadians hastened to Barbados. Away from these resort romps, anthropologists and missionaries' daughters took lovers among remote tribes in Africa, Latin America and the South Pacific.

By the year 2000, female travelers from all the nations of the developed world had appeared at the side of foreign men in the vast majority of the world's sun, sand and sea destinations as well as in remote bush country.

In this chapter, we shall examine:

• the social conditions that led to traveling by Victorian era women, and the little-known but profound sensuality of that era.

• the Seven Pioneers: adventurous women who forged the earliest history of travel liaisons.

Milestones prior to 1960s

Many of the pioneers shown below are only the earliest of numerous women in a specific country to love foreign men.

In 1837, in Karnal, India, the adopted daughter of a Maj. Gen. Sir John Adams married Bahadour Khan, son of Dirbija Singh, raja of Sis Kotumba (Wilmshurst, "Mixed Marriages," citing the Eastern India Register and Directory of 1838, 2nd ed.). I am reluc-tant to list this as an early travel romance unless I can track down the daughter's name and ascertain she was a non-Indian. If substantiated, the general's daughter would place the start of travel romances a full decade earlier.

Readers are welcome to contact the author with additional information on earlier historical reports than those given below.

BY FIRST REPORT IN HISTORICAL RECORD

YEAR	AREA	WOMAN
1847	Italy	Margaret Fuller
1852	Greece	Lady Jane Digby
1854	Syria	Lady Jane Digby
1859	India	Henrietta Melvina Hodges
1864	Egypt	Sally Nedrett
1873	Morocco	Emily Keene
1879	Thailand	Fanny Knox
1890s	Caribbean	Various dowagers
1897	Tunisia, Algeria	Isabelle Eberhardt
By 1913	South Africa	Various mistresses of servants
After 1925	Polynesia	Unnamed anthropologists
1930s	Vietnam	Marguerite Duras
	Bali	K'tut Tantri, Jane Belo
1953	Iraq	Anne Cumming
1956	Nepal	Han Suyin

• the thousands of beautiful, unreserved American girls who conquered the male aristocrats of Rome and other European capitals, and the backlash against them.

• and showgirls, dancers, itinerant performers, nurses and others who pushed further east to India to marry princes.

But first, let's try to discover to what extent Victorian women recaptured personal freedoms vanished in the dim mists of time.

The big, big picture through history

To understand how revolutionary were the Victorian women as they traveled away from home and explored sensual pleasures, we need to place their wanderings in the grand scheme of human history.

In essence, these brave ladies cast off at least 3,000 years of government limits on female freedom.

Their sexual independence reclaimed an era lost since early civilization. In the nomadic and primitive agricultural societies extant prior to the first cities in the Fertile Crescent (from Egypt to Iraq), women reveled in their desires, and sex was celebrated in pagan rites. In fact, some American Indian tribes permitted travel sex by women (see timeline).

And an enduring view of sex as natural and good for men and women, though repressed as civilization arose, endured uninterrupted from early history to the present in rural Africa and in her New World diaspora.

Why did women's sexual freedom diminish as civilization grew? An anthropologist, Martin King White (156-182), links control of women's sexual choices to the appearance of a simple implement: the plow.

In sparsely populated places, with limited harvests from crops planted via digging sticks and hoes, women exercise freedom to travel, to market goods and to own property, he found in a study of 185 pre-industrial groups. With land plentiful in low-population areas and controlled by clans, a daughter's impetuous conduct and a resulting pregnancy did not pose a catastrophe.

The arrival of the plow in the area where Europe meets Asia made the difference between day and night for women. Populations soared, unclaimed land became scarcer, and owning property and draft animals became crucial to status. Male heads of family rather than clans controlled property, and marriages were arranged to preserve wealth. Young, exuberant daughters racing into the fields with comely youths could wreck parental plans. Rambunctious sex lives for young women simply would not do anymore.

For a time, early civilizations such as that of Assyria (in what is now northern Iraq) continued celebratory attitudes toward the joy of sex, evident in the prestige of temple priestesses who engaged in cultic rituals (Lerner).

In the year 1080 B.C., however, as intensive agriculture created dense populations, the world's first veiling law appeared, distinguishing wives (made to cover their hair) from prostitutes (made to go bareheaded; see Passman). Now the public could clearly see which women were under the control of a man. Now controlling female sexuality was the business of the state rather than the clan.

The idea of controlling girls and women spread next to Assyria's Near East neighbors, and later to Hebrews, Christians and Muslims. Audacious women became condemned as harlots by Old Testament prophets.

Men from ancient times through the Victorian era not only controlled the sexual activity of women, they also defined travel as a male activity. Societies used immobile women as one means to control territory while men sallied forth to hunt and do battle. "During a long and significant period of human history, a period of the growth of patriarchal civilizations, travel was thought to demonstrate a particularly male character, antithetical to a femininity rooted in place, in soil and gardens, in the very material qualities of the earth" (Leed 117).

Only the appearance of powered machines — the dawn of the Industrial Age — would shatter the fetters of women shackled by the plow's arrival. Female travelers born of the Industrial Age close a circle, reclaiming a bit of pre-civilization paganism, carnality and free movement. Women today who astonish themselves with their own licentious behavior on vacation may be at some level returning to a wisp of a memory of how women in precolonial Africa, pre-Columbian America, Polynesia, ancient Babylon and Egypt felt free to behave.

The amount of freedom that Western women on vacation in tropical settings have to act on their sexual inclinations is undoubtably greater than that experienced by the average female member of a hunting and gathering, horticultural, agricultural and even industrial society.

Gorry (241)

Along comes Queen Victoria

The constrictions of life under the veil began to lift as the Western world moved from agriculture to industry, beginning in the 1700s in England and Scotland and spreading to Western Europe and the northeastern United States by the 1850s.

The Industrial Age weakened sexual controls on women. Agriculture had declined in importance, political systems begin to emphasize egalitarianism, and new occupations emerged that (unlike farming) did not require strict sexual controls on family members (Whyte 182-83).

As steam engines, power looms and iron-making furnaces began to dot the landscape, equality between the sexes zoomed. During the time of Queen Victoria (1837-1901), economic opportunity burgeoned. British and American women won growing rights to enter contracts, own property, to work outside the home, to decide what to do with their earnings and to get divorced (Purvis 76; J. Lewis 78; Whyte 181).

The Victorian era saw not only legal but also social changes that affected women's options. As soon as Victorian ladies began to work outside the home, they pursued an additional level of freedom: to travel. Leaving the home for work evolved into leaving the country.

Events now began to move swiftly. As if on cue, the Industrial Age spawned female travelers, and those travelers immediately showed a keen interest in foreign men.

At first, the middle-class women of Britain and the United States began to venture abroad with a view toward learning, shopping or having fun. By 1855, demand by restless Englishwomen to see the sights on the Continent helped spur Thomas Cook to offer the first package tour (Enloe 28; "Thomas Cook").

Though many women signed up for Cook's tours of Europe and the United States, most Victorian females traveled unaccompanied by men, even as far afield as Africa and India (Pemble 78; Frawley, *Wider* 23). In 1857, Emily Lowe, author of *Unprotected Females in Norway*, wrote that "the only use of a gentleman in travelling is to look after the luggage, and we take care to have no luggage" (qtd. in J. Robinson, *Unsuitable* 12).

Surely the fact that, by the 1880s, more female travelers than males explored Continental Europe shows a mindboggling change from all previous history, a migration never before seen of thousands of women traveling without male escorts — thus free to engage in conversation and deeper intimacy with foreign men, principally guides, aristocrats, soldiers and high officials.

The sexy Victorians

That female sex travel (notwithstanding Indian tribal and Turkish women traveling minor distances to find new lovers) really began during Victorian times may astound many readers, given that the era's image is one of prudery.

Part of the problem is that people tend to look through the wrong end of the telescope. The Victorian woman may not seem quite as wild as the girls on *Sex in the City*, but when compared to the shuttered women of classical Athens and the peasants of medieval times, she clearly knew how to swing.

Further, in recent years, many scholars have unearthed contrary evidence demonstrating that the 19th century in fact shared with the 20th century a fascination with sex (M. Mason 3).

Victorians revered sex as having a "mystique of acutely pleasurable naughtiness." Women in England, riveted, watched men bathe nude. Many reaped the benefit of having skillful husbands advised by marriage manuals to "practice in lawful wedlock the arts of the seducer," as three-quarters of the women in one survey reported attaining orgasm (8, 15, 88).

A myth of repression, stemming from Victorian use of euphemism instead of clinical language, as well as less public discussion of sex, became widespread after World War I (M. Mason 10). New scholarship published from the 1970s onward revealed the lustiness of the Victorians but has yet to alter popular misconceptions.

That the first recorded instances of traveling women and foreign men tumbling into bed together appeared by the mid-19th century provides further evidence that the era has been misinterpreted.

Uninhibited admiration

If anything, the Victorian era may have been a sexier time, in terms of intensity of feeling, than our own. The vitality, exuberance and "special poignancy" of sex has declined as "legislators, doctors, educators, Freudians and the like ... analyzed, labeled and discussed it" (Anderson 1). Over time, ardor lost out to abstraction. This loss goes to the heart of why the modern woman feels drawn to men from simpler cultures.

Passion of the keenest sort bursts from the writing of Victorian female travelers, as Isabelle Eberhardt described nights of "furious lovemaking" with her Algerian sergeant paramour.

And the shy Margaret Fountaine noted with charming delicacy but unmistakable electricity the morning her Syrian guide first "laid me on my bed, and when he lay over me the weight of his body was sweet to me now, because I loved him" (*Love Among* 148).

It may take a while to get used to the idea of the Victorian era as a sexy time, perhaps even lustier than our own.

Indeed, back in those years when longing for sex while waiting for marriage must have honed desire to a fever pitch, Victorian women expressed keen appreciation for the physiques of exotic men with a vigorous eloquence that can scarcely be matched today. In keeping with mores of the time, they borrowed from classical mythology, rather than today's more anatomical terminology, to heap their praises.

Victorian era traveler Lucie Duff Gordon (*Egypt*), a translator of German born of accomplished parents in London, termed male Egyptian friends "graceful," "sweet-looking," "lovely to behold" and, in neatly calibrated assessments, either "handsome," "very handsome," "prodigiously handsome" or (in the case of several Ethiopian merchants) "handsome as the Greek Bacchus."

Mary Thorn Carpenter (21) drank in the sight of a Turkish soldier headed to watch Cairo's races, "dressed in an embroidered red and gold costume marvelously combined with silks and silver, producing a harmonious effect at once beautiful and splendidly savage."

And as continues to be true today, Victorian women became positively weak in the knees for virile, masculine warriors, especially rulers.

Saudi leader Ibn Saud impressed Gertrude Bell (qtd. in Winstone 189-90) as a man "of splendid physique, standing well over six feet, and carrying himself with the air of one accustomed to command. ... He has the characteristics of the well-bred Arab, the strongly-marked aquiline profile, full-flesh nostrils, prominent lips. ... His hands are fine, with slender fingers."

How truly innocent can it be to describe Ibn Saud in terms of a romance novel hero? One waits for the other shoe to drop, for kisses from those full lips and and caresses from his skilled fingers.

Certainly, if a male writer were to describe a woman's mouth and breasts and hips, no one would assume that he was doing so in only a chaste, clerk-of-record fashion.

Yet in letters to me, scholars of Victorian-era travel by women tend to downplay the significance of these paeans to foreign male beauty.

Maria H. Frawley, author of *A Wider Range: Travel Writing by Women in the Victorian Era*, wrote that the women were "experimenting with ethnographic discourse," that is, simply describing people of a different culture in the fashion of an anthropologist. Jane Robinson, author of *Wayward Women* and *Unsuitable for Ladies*, felt that many of these women considered exotic men only "animate art," but acknowledged that "even looking created a sexual frisson deliciously wicked to the pure-minded."

Perhaps a reader could read little into these countless descriptions of foreign men as "beautiful" or "handsome" — if one assumes Victorian women indeed denied some part of the humanity of the Zulu chiefs and Turkish soldiers they praised so effusively, and only thought of them as objets d'art, comparable to an exquisite statue by Michelangelo.

Yet female travel writers in earlier times also admired the Turkish, Egyptian, Syrian, Kuwaiti and other men they encountered for their characters. They cited sterling qualities of courtesy, hard work, good cheer, honesty and bravery (J. Robinson, *Unsuitable*). Those who fell in love with their guides — notably Jane Digby and Margaret Fountaine — succumbed gradually to outpourings of quiet devotion, illustrating the role of nurturing in love and affection.

Reputable foreign guides readily met Victorian standards of honor. Further, these men were complicit in rebellion against traditional women's roles, willingly leading female travelers to desert antiquities and jungle interiors — in a way, proto-feminists themselves, expediting greater women's independence over the objections of European males.

Thus Victorian women responded to foreign fellows as real men — not only as sex partners, but as essential accomplices to genuine exploration — and even as husbands of superior quality. Emigrant British women to South Africa often married local Malays instead of fellow colonials, and got "thereby husbands who know not billiards and brandy — the two diseases of Cape Town. They risked a plurality of wives, and professed Islam, but they got fine clothes and industrious husbands; ... and the real Malays are very handsome" (Duff Gordon, *Cape* 31).

'Splendid young Hercules'

What is most telling to me personally are Victorian women's unstinting raves for black Africans, viewpoints that must have required some daring to express in colonial Britain.

Even in the 21st century I find the quotes selected below remarkable. Allowing for some element of embellishment, nonetheless travel writing by Victorian women provides a rare counterpoint to reigning views portraying Africans as degraded, pathetic, inferior beings, suitable only as objects of ridicule.

In South Africa, in the 1860s, Lucie Duff Gordon described the lads of the Xhosa tribe as "splendid young Hercules" (Cape 31, 93).

In the 1870s, Nile river traveler Amelia Edwards (274) remarked on a pair of brothers from Khartoum: "Their small proud heads and delicate aristocratic features were modeled on the purest Florentine type; their eyes were long and liquid; their complexions ... were intensely, lustrously, magnificently black. We agreed that we had never seen two such handsome men. They were like young and beautiful Dantes carved in ebony."

In the 1880s, a missionary's wife described the famed Zulu chief Cetshwayo as "a fine, tall handsome man" (Wilkinson qtd. in Stevenson 62) and without blushing confessed she found Zulus to be "so handsome and so well made, it is a pleasure to look at them."

In the 1890s, intrepid explorer Mary Kingsley (328-29) found among the Fans of West Africa "magnificent specimens of human beings, both male and female. Their color is light bronze, many of the men have beards. ... Their countenances are very bright and expressive. ... The Fan is full of fire, temper, intelligence and go."

One must add a caveat here, because when Kingsley heard of a Sierra Leone lawyer marrying a white woman, she felt "mentally sick," and she believed in separation of the races (Birkett, *Spinsters* 157, 201). A similar line between admiration and consummation restrained Mary Gaunt (16) when she visited the Gambia. She noted with candor that Africans were attractive but dalliances carried huge social costs: "Tall, stalwart, handsome as is many a negro, no white woman may take a black man for her husband and be respected by her own people."

Yet Kingsley and other female travel writers admiring forbidden fruit betray unacknowledged sexual impulses in their writing, marked as they are by a "language of restlessness, longing and desire. ... its cumulative effect is to link travel with the acting out of an irrepressible physical and, by implication, sexual drive" (Frawley, *Wider* 113).

Seven early pioneers

Indeed, other feisty women left home and, lacking Kingsley's and

Gaunt's inflexible views, pursued grand amours. Some were highly sexed and aggressively pursued lovers (Digby, Eberhardt, Nedrett). Others were shy and rather plain yet drew men to them by their exotic, intriguing independence (Fuller, Keene and Fountaine).

Back in 1842, forerunner Lola Montez, a woman of Irish descent, grew up in India and the United Kingdom. She eloped with her first husband, who was posted back to India. There the maharaja of the Punjab, Ranjit Singh, lavished presents on her (J. Robinson, *Wayward* 55-56); his grandsons would actually marry white women. After Lola's marriage, she arranged adulterous affairs with aristocrats in London, Brussels and Bavaria.

Montez's adventures don't fit the focus on cross-cultural liaisons in *Romance on the Road*, for she frolicked with upper-crust Northern Europeans. Yet her activities set the stage for women later in the same decade who posed greater challenges to social norms by romancing men across vaster cultural gaps.

Let's look at the women who truly comprise the Seven Pioneers.

Margaret Fuller (foreign love affair in 1847, Rome). Though largely forgotten today, Fuller, a Massachusetts-born teacher and journalist, was the "first American to write a book on equality for women and men" and said to have "laid the groundwork for the feminist movement" (L. James 3). Fuller arrived in Rome to file dispatches on Italian unrest and launched an affair with a marchese, a younger man described as thoughtful, handsome, gallant and attentive to her needs (Stern 279). They got married when she was 37 and he, 28 (Chipperfield 261), and she bore her husband a son. The young family, headed for a visit to the United States, perished when their ship foundered off Fire Island.

As a foreign correspondent, a feminist and an independent woman, she perfectly crystallized both the broad drive toward women's rights in her time and how individual women exercised a new freedom to travel and thence to love younger, foreign men.

Lady Jane Digby (1849, Rome). After a youthful marriage, this wealthy aristocrat, granddaughter of a Norfolk industrialist, launched a series of intrigues, à la Lola Montez, with Northern European royals. Yet her affairs were just a warm-up for hedonistic, exotic wanderings and a marriage far more controversial than Margaret Fuller's, making her perhaps the true pioneer of female travel sex.

During a stay in Rome, one account holds that Lady Jane juggled three squabbling suitors at once (Lovell 137), and tales of her adventures grew into a myth that she had "six Italian husbands" (Schmidt 150). In Athens in 1852, she found comfort in the arms of an Albanian general.

Two years later she toured Bedouin country and frisked in her tent with first one guide and then another.

It was a third guide, a Bedouin named Medjuel who led her to Damascus, who gradually won her heart for life. A fine conversationalist, Medjuel knew the romantic sagas of the Bedouin tribes and related them to Sir Richard Francis Burton, who captured them as *The Arabian Nights* (Oddie 271).

Medjuel himself bestowed his own romantic, Arabian nights flourishes. He presented Jane with a fine Arab mare and then proposed. Jane was flustered at the thought of marrying a man so different than herself and nearly two decades younger than her 47 years. But Jane found Medjuel's kisses remarkable and followed her heart. In Syria, in 1855, she took the plunge.

It appears that Medjuel and Lady Jane first made love on their wedding night (Lovell 191), an extraordinary wait given Digby's sexual appetites. Medjuel's affection and Lady Jane's girlish body led to years of mutual delight.

Jane and Medjuel were together until her death. On the day of her funeral, one report has it that in grief Medjuel galloped on his finest horse to her grave (Blanch 203).

The significance of Lady Jane Digby cannot be overstated. In flamboyant fashion, she used travel to reclaim the sexual freedom long curtailed by humankind's adoption of complex agriculture.

With supreme irony, the ancient world, home to the earliest restrictions on women's sexuality, became the first documented zone of free sex for modern female travelers, as Lady Jane Digby cut swathes through Italy, Greece and Syria.

For 3,000 years, Mediterranean and Near Eastern men did such a good job at restricting their own women indoors and away from unsanctioned sex that even a proper Victorian Englishwomen must have seemed exotic — so free that she took their breath away. One can scarcely imagine what a man like Medjuel would have thought of Lady Jane, wealthy and considered one of the great beauties of her day, arriving like a bright sun in his desert world, a romantic figure to rival those in *The Arabian Nights*.

Further, the Englishwoman was an "outsider," and thus the Mediterranean male could consort with her without facing the dire consequences of unofficial liaisons with local females.

Margaret Fuller and Lady Jane Digby personified radical new freedoms for women to decide how to use their income, to travel, to select men as casual lovers and to choose younger husbands outside their ethnic group. Many others would follow shortly.

Even today, were she alive Lady Jane's behavior would shock, landing her on the cover of *People* magazine. Imagine a sock-o combination of Lady Di, Zsa Zsa Gabor and Queen Noor of Jordan — a wealthy, titled English lady who ran off to live with a desert Arab, leaving behind three living ex-husbands, all aristocrats.

Henrietta Melvina Hodges (1859, India). Little is known about Hodges except that she married Randhir Singh of Kapurthala.

As with Margaret Fuller, who married a marchese, Henrietta found a noble title attractive — Randhir Singh was a raja, or chief. Hodges, likely an American born in India, inaugurated more than a century of similar liaisons with Indian royalty.

Sally Nedrett (1864, Egypt). As the maid to Lucie Duff Gordon, Sally (whose surname is variously given as Naldrett in Frank 211) accompanied her ailing employer to warmer climates, including South Africa, France and ultimately Egypt.

In Alexandria, Duff Gordon hired Omar Abu Halaweh, a dragoman, that is, translator, guide and fixer, to arrange a trip up the Nile. At the beginning of the voyage Omar and Sally "became great friends" (*Egypt* 46). In April 1864, Sally suffered a fainting spell that frightened Omar. No one suspected morning sickness, or even pregnancy, which the 30-year-old Sally hid from everyone almost to the moment of her child's birth in early 1865, on a boat "at midnight in the middle of a desolate place" (165, 187, 189).

Omar was the picture of remorse. His apology to Lucie implied that Sally was a woman of hearty appetites and little inhibition, with a thing for Arab men: "By God, if an English girl comes to me and pulls up her shirt before me again, with the permission of God, I will slap her face, though I am only an Arab and she English" (165, 189-90).

Lucie indicates that Sally was sent home to England and that Omar and his Egyptian wife kept his child.

It is not out of the question that Omar and Sally were emboldened by reports of Lady Jane Digby's marriage to a Bedouin sheik, which spread like wildfire through the Middle East and reached the ears of British expats in Egypt, including Duff Gordon's friends (Frank 276).

Emily Keene (1873, Morocco). Born to a middle-class family in South London, in her early 20s Emily Keene traveled with friends through Spain and to Morocco. In Tangier, she took to bathing in the sea each morning, unaware that Hadj Abdeslam, the religious leader or shareef of Morocco, watched her with interest. One morning, her horse bolted, and a "tall, black bearded Moroccan" steadied her and set her on the ground.

Over the course of watching Emily from a distance, especially as she brushed her long, thick brown hair, Abdeslam had developed feelings for her. As had Lady Jane's husband Medjuel, before declaring his intentions the shareef took care to divorce his previous wives. After several marriage proposals, Emily finally agreed.

They had two sons, and though their marriage was troubled in later years, Emily was called to console Abdeslam on his deathbed. Keene is credited with encouraging religious tolerance and greater public health in Morocco (Emily; U. Hall).

Emily Keene

From My Life Story

Isabelle Eberhardt (1897-99, Tunisia and Algeria). While Lady Jane's intimate encounters (except for a wild spell in Italy) often resembled serial matings, as a young woman Isabelle Eberhardt pursued more casual, no-strings-attached relationships.

The wanton writer serves as a prototype for the true hedonist of the 20th century, the female who capers, sometimes anonymously, with multiple partners.

Isabelle's father, a Russian anarchist, seems almost to have deliberately crafted his daughter, born in Geneva in 1877, to become a mold-breaking sexual pioneer. He demanded she perform hard physical labor outdoors, to speak and read many languages, including Arabic, to dress as a man and to be indifferent to public opinion (Bowles, *Oblivion* 8).

If Margaret Fuller was an intellectual who wrote about equality between the sexes, Eberhardt was a more aggressive type of feminist, a woman of action who simply went out and smashed stereotypes.

At the age of 20, Eberhardt went to North Africa. In Tunis, "at night she could be found lying on the floor of some native café smoking kif [marijuana] or wrestling with the soldiers from the barracks. Often she took one of them home with her to spend the night" (Bowles, *Oblivion* 9).

Eberhardt craved "brutal, uncommitted lovemaking," was "indefatigable" in bed and periodically fell "prey to a literally violent lust" (Kobak 83, 99). "Her sexuality was in a sense masculine — which is why she preferred making love with Arabs, or in working-class areas: she wanted a very physically active role in it, and to be able to make love without any responsibilities, even without love, just 'for the love of making love'."

She explored the desert, wrote evocative stories of its magic and studied mystic religion, eventually settling down to some extent with

Slimane, a young Algerian sergeant.

In 1900, during a stay at El Oued in Algeria, Isabelle and Slimane partook of "nights of love and absolute security in one another's arms; enchanted dawns, calm and pink, after nights of Ramadan prayers. ... The last night I was destined to pass under my own roof was the mad night of 28 January, which was spent in furious love-making" (Eberhardt 77).

With Slimane, Eberhardt had evolved from blind lust, with its echoes of the ancient world's cultic sexual rites, quenched by soldier strangers, to a heightened sensual world explored by true lovers.

Margaret Fountaine (1901, Syria). Older, full of poignant longing for a man's arms, and perhaps the shyest of the Seven Pioneers, Fountaine was a butterfly collector who traveled much of the world. Like Lady Jane, Fountaine hailed from Norfolk in England and possessed an annual income (Fountaine's was more modest). Also like Digby, in her middle years, Fountaine found the love of her life in Syria.

> **I remember when I was quite a small child I told my mother one day: "Mamma, when I grow up, I mean to be a loose adventurer," and I could imagine why my mother rather reproved me for the remark.**
>
> Margaret Fountaine, *Late Loves* (22)

As she roved abroad, Fountaine elicited streams of flattery and propositions from, among many others, a Corsican gypsy, a baron in Palermo, and a tall young entomologist from Budapest who stirred her heart strings. She accepted the roses he picked and the strawberries he plucked. Infatuated and in her 30s, she wrote in her diary wistfully of "wandering through the sunny woods among the butterflies, often with the longing which all women must sometimes have to feel strong arms around me and a man's heart beating against my own" (*Love Among* 117).

As she grew older, she grew more attractive to men. En route to Greece, at the age of 38, she wrote: "I am in a better position in the game of life, I have even climbed a rung or two of the ladder of — shall I say fame? My relations with men have advanced considerably, in spite of the great burden of years I drag behind me" (117, 125).

In 1901 in Damascus, a Syrian, Khalil Neimy, served as her dragoman. As were Margaret Fuller and Lady Jane Digby, she was older than her swain, 39 to his bare 24 years. Neimy brought her bunches of flowers, kissing her hand ardently.

She didn't react well. She wrote of the man who would be her lover for nearly three decades that she had never "come into contact with quite such a weak, contemptible character before" (117, 133, 137). Over time, however, she "began to find [Neimy's] untiring devotion and constant adoration decidedly pleasant."

Their growing intimacy she described with euphemisms charming in their transparency. She allowed him to kiss her hands and arms "as I felt in a thoroughly 'loose' mood that day." Then she felt the "weakness of human nature." Under the shadow of mountain rocks, she recalled, "I sank lower than I had ever sank before; the very audacity of the man overcame my sense of all that was right and proper" (135).

One night they stayed in a Latin monastery. "When Khalil came in next morning and folded me in his arms — my whole heart went out to him." They lay together, and "his body was sweet to me now, because I loved him" (148).

In social encounters with English couples, Fountaine noted with pride that, compared to other husbands, Neimy was handsomer, younger, more devoted and a better listener. He proved more fluent in everyday life, delighting the locals on trains and in desert camps by chatting in Arabic about the Koran.

They were together until 1928, when Fountaine was 66 and Neimy, 51. Her lover eventually felt compelled to return alone to Syria, ostensibly to care for his mother.

Fountaine basked in continued male attention during travels to the Amazon and other distant points. Her adventuring only stopped when she died of a heart attack, aged 78, on a monastery path on Mount St. Benedict in Trinidad while walking to collect butterflies.

In February 2001, my husband and I visited the spot where Fountaine collapsed, still strewn with butterflies. At the Pax Guesthouse, a man guiding a birding tour showed us a plaque, commissioned by a local women's club, reading:

In Loving Memory of
Margaret Fountaine
English Traveller
and butterfly collector
Born 1862
died at Mount St. Benedict 1940

Though it took her time to get used to the idea, Fountaine could appreciate — five long generations ago — a foreign man with particular mastery of his environment, as Neimy displayed in their travels. She blazed a trail for those women today who also admire the ability and masculinity of the foreign man.

More merry maids

From the 1830s until World War I, another stream of single British and Irish women traveled, not for leisure but for economic survival, emigrating to the colonies in search of domestic work and higher wages (Strobel 25-27; Duff Gordon, *Cape* 107).

They left not the record, in society columns, essays and diaries, of the Seven Pioneers. Yet many readily consorted with foreign men, sometimes with resulting good fortune. The woman who truly hit the jackpot was Miss Florry Bryan, elder sister of a stable master, who married an Indian maharaja.

The lustiness of Europe's maids became notorious, especially in Egypt. After Lucie Duff Gordon sent home Sally Nedrett, a German replacement named Marie was sent packing for loose morals almost as soon as she arrived. Lucie concluded that the maids had not been corrupted by the East; rather, they arrived predisposed to Arab men.

Sally and Marie were far from isolated cases. American missionaries in Egypt gave up hiring Western women and switched to local men and boys for domestic work. And a young, handsome dragoman named Ali told Lady Duff Gordon that he refused to work for foreign ladies, "because where there are ladies there is a maid, and I fall in it somehow. If I refuse her she tells lies of me all the way, and if I do as she likes, there is some mischief" (*Egypt* 253-54).

Biographer Katherine Frank (294) perceptively notes that Duff Gordon "could never acknowledge — perhaps even to herself — the fact that she was jealous of Omar and Sally's intimacy." Currents of subterranean attraction appear evident in Duff Gordon's admiring descriptions of distinguished Egyptian men.

Maids, domestics, bar girls and prostitutes also took an aggressive interest in the men of India and Burma, with nothing to lose and much to gain given man shortages and limited jobs available back home in Britain.

In South Africa, Duff Gordon, who had a keen eye for maid behavior, described a Mrs. D—, who headed to Cape Town to find replacement servants, her "Scotch girl having carried on her amours too flagrantly," as well as a Malay waiter who married the "ladies-maid to the Governor's wife" (*Cape* 112, 158).

The minuets between ladies and their maids and foreign men displayed a certain "Upstairs Downstairs" quality. The maid Eugenie greatly distressed the noblewoman who retained her for most of her life, Lady Jane Digby, by also snaring Jane's own lover in Athens, the Albanian general.

More typically, however, the lines between upper crust and lower orders remained firm, as Lady Duff Gordon in Egypt and wives of Raj officials in India considered local men intriguing but off-limits. Lady Betjeman, married to Britain's future poet laureate, "thought that although Indian Princes would have liked affairs with lady sahibs, [Raj officials] did not allow their women to flirt with anybody" (Morrow 256). And a Lady Birdwood stated that "no girl of good family would have become involved with an Indian."

India's princes were supposed to set their sights lower, on the daughters of tutors, landladies and pharmacists ... or maids.

The last Nawab Nazim, or governor, of the giant, rich territory of Bengal, Bihar and Orissa, Mansur Ali Khan, was almost fetishistic about servant girls and maids. In the 1840s, Mansur Ali mowed his way through four of his mother's attendants (Mirza 77), most African concubines, and three wives, before taking as his fourth Sarah Vennell, 17, a parlormaid at his hotel in London (96), who bore him six children. (While Mansur Ali seduced his Englishwomen outside of India, and thus the maids were not actually involved in romances on the road, his story does offer insights into the chemistry between poorer white women and rich men of color.)

When Mansur Ali moved into cheaper lodging in London, he promptly seduced the maid there, who bore him two sons (Mirza 104, 112; J. Sinclair, "Meerzas"), part of an eventual brood of 100 children.

This maharaja of a vast swath of northeast India, a certified sexual athlete who took a substance that was the Viagra of the day (Mirza 111), came to desire women he could talk to (96). His mother's non-Western servant girls were too intimidated by his presence to say much more than "dinner is ready." In London, his housekeepers were accessible conversation partners.

For their part, these young girls with their aprons, caps and feather dusters could scarcely believe their luck. For example, Sarah Vennell "was no doubt overwhelmed by the wealth and charm of this Eastern potentate" (96). Or put another way, as an India scholar e-mailed me, "few if any" of the maharaja's consorts "were, for want of a better term 'the top drawer.' So fame and fortune beckoned strong."

Titled ladies had much to lose, and housemaids had everything to gain, by ignoring barriers of color and caste. Yet both joined the vanguard of sexual adventuring.

The floodgates open in Europe

Perhaps, if Lady Jane Digby had been the only woman of her kind, her pioneering escapades in Rome, Greece and Syria could have been dismissed as just another instance of a bed-hopping, decadent aristocrat.

And if we knew of only the Seven Pioneers and the lusty maids described above, we could assume that only this handful of exceptional women dared to travel for love prior to the 1960s.

Yet the truth is quite the contrary. In the blink of an eye — within the dozen years after Fuller and Digby made sexual history behind closed doors in Rome — many thousands of American and British women had begun to sweep through European capitals, the Near East and India, taking foreign lovers in such numbers that their home societies took outraged notice and white men mounted a backlash (see timeline).

A New American Woman, often unchaperoned, descended upon Paris, Berlin and Rome. In the 1850s, she would have noticed an equal numbers of American men and women visiting Europe's cities; by the 1890s, however, she dominated the ranks of the unaccompanied in Paris (Levenstein 119, 185).

The New American Woman was likely to be one of "the daughters of the self-made," the newly wealthy entrepreneurial class, or she could be of modest means, having saved her earnings for years or received small loans from friends to study science or art in Europe. She might be single, married yet on her own, or widowed — in any case, traveling solo (Hoxie 477; J.P.T. 355; I.M. 258).

Whatever her background, the American woman's vibrancy and ease at dealing with men wowed her hosts. These young ladies seemed almost an entirely different and new sort of "Miss." Exaggerated accolades rang down around their heads. They were an entirely new and wonderful representative of humanity, the hope of the future.

British and French social observers noted with approval that American girls were livelier, handsomer, brighter, more deft, more adaptable, and more independent, self-reliant and able to decide matters for themselves than women elsewhere (see an excellent discussion in Wasserstrom 3; also Kelley 269; Hoxie 476; Mackenzie, *Vestal Fire* 156).

In the latter 19th century, American women (and many Englishwomen) created a love migration, visiting Italy by the thousands; and tens of thousands more landed in England and France (J. Miller 200; Sherwood 681).

This sparkling creature, pointing her umbrella boldly at Rome's sights and curious to meet new people, immediately drew Europe's faded aristocrats seeking to parlay a noble title into creature comforts:

> There is one fact which the American girl can be sure of: she is at present the most talked-of creature in the world. Never before did the women of one nation so successfully invade all nations and, reversing the Sabine legend, carry off the most able-bodied warriors. The march over England and the Continent by the American girl is a triumphant one. It is a great

story of conquest. These lovely Amazons do not stop for ocean, river, or geographical boundary. (Sherwood 689)

In her enchanting diaries, heiress Julia Newberry described how at hotels on the European grand tour, flocks of interested gents enjoying her consummate ease in conversation called on herself and her sister.

She did not consider herself a flirt, but clearly she greatly appealed to men, including the dishy colonel Jerome Napoleon Bonaparte Jr., "the most magnificent figure I ever saw" (81, 86). In 1870, at the young age of 16, Julia made a 29-name list of "My Particular Male friends as they stand up to the present time."

Any later diaries Julia Newberry made of her continued travels in Europe or Egypt, or possible amours along the way, have not come to light. Malaria contracted in Rome ended her life at age 22, likely depriving her of a future as notable writer, one with potential for romances on the road. For she was a rich, quick-witted, charismatic and multilingual expatriate who had thought through the essentials for true love and could never "say I have been much in want of attention from the opposite sex" (104, 157).

An obituary of Julia's death, melded with the tale of another American girl known to be free-spirited with Italian royals, likely inspired the popular 1878 novel, *Daisy Miller*.

Because Yankee girls in Europe dazzled male observers (and scandalized their female expatriate sisters), *Daisy Miller* was part of a huge body of commentary — including three other major novels by male writers — sketching the portrait of a New American Woman finding adventure abroad.

Julia Newberry

True stories of monied American and British women courted by the fallen aristocracy of Rome also inspired *The One Fair Woman* (1876, Joaquin Miller) and *Where Angels Fear to Tread* (1905, E.M. Forster).

And during the Jazz Age, Compton Mackenzie's *Vestal Fire* (1927), also set in Italy, sketched traveling American women as vigorous vixens up for anything involving a foreigner in pants.

In *Vestal Fire*, a Miss Hannah Bilton, of dark brown hair, a fine profile and "vivid hot blue eyes," bursts upon the swinging expatriate community on the isle of Capri. At parties at the island's villas, Italian men readily steer her into the shadows for quickies:

> Her appeal to a libertine was always immediate, because she had the charm of having evidently never experienced love with all its irksome implications of emotional standards. ... Sentiment was wasted upon Miss Hannah. ... When a woman only draws near to men by the high-road of sex, it is not astonishing that she should become inured to heavy traffic. (292)

When Miss Hannah traveled on to the Far East, wagging tongues told of the unsentimental traveler "in the harem of a hospitable potentate" and permitting "familiarity with the Chinese coolies" (321).

We can take our "unsentimental" traveler as a colorful personification of real Jazz Age women flooding Europe and Capri in particular (documented in Aldrich, preface, xi-x; Levenstein 245).

From the Victorian era through the Jazz Age, the New American Woman spread her wings and began to fly, setting out for foreign shores. *Daisy Miller's* author, Henry James, surmised that the American girl, so unlike every other woman in history, became "most interesting when she left her native land for Europe" (Kelley 270).

Via Julia Newberry's life as transmuted in *Daisy Miller*, a national debate on romance on the road ignited in the United States.

A crescendo of criticism

Novels about traveling women and the social reaction they provoked prove to be a gold mine for the travel sex researcher.

A segment of the U.S. population defended the New American Woman and her freedom to be natural and friendly with men. Yet many women's magazines and literary journals attacked the real-life Daisy Millers as scandalously independent. Agitated talk about the New American Woman's overseas adventures had impressive staying power, kicking off before the Civil War and continuing until the Jazz Age.

By 1859, Dr. William Sanger, a Victorian sexual historian, fired the first salvo. He warned that many American women might find themselves returning home from Europe with minds culturally improved but morals corrupted, for "a portion of our female society are ardent admirers of everything foreign, be it a lord or a lace veil, and these delight in an intrigue because it is an exotic" (569-570).

From the 1880s through 1906, more criticism arrived of solo female travelers "not at all [well-]bred, not at all repressed," "journeying about Europe with more money at their disposal than discretion." Young American women arriving in Paris as art students entertained, in their rooms as late as 2 a.m., Frenchmen, "Italians, Russians, Roumanians,

Greeks — everything" (Sherwood 681; *New York Times* qtd. in Stafford 103; Stapley 54).

The novel *Daisy Miller* especially ignited debate across the United States: "society almost divided itself into Daisy Millerites and anti-Daisy Millerites" (Howells qtd. in Stafford 111-12). A backlash occurred. From the mid-1880s until the early 20th century, many young American women now had to travel with chaperones (previously a Europe-only custom; see Hoxie 483-84).

As late as 1906, a disapproving piece in *Ladies' Home Journal* described young American women studying music, art or French in Paris who had kept foreign men in their rooms until the early morning hours — "men whose attitude toward sex is as unlike an American's (in his own country) as one could possibly imagine" (Stapley 54).

By dividing into two camps over Daisy Miller, American society a century ago demonstrated a far greater public awareness than seen today of young women's pursuit of foreign affairs, paradoxical given Baby Boomers' conviction that they created sexual openness in the 1960s. (For a wonderful roundup of reaction to *Daisy Miller* over more than seven decades, see Stafford, sections III and IV.)

After all the controversy attending the Victorian traveling women and their foreign lovers, the topic faded. This early history essentially sunk from view, and we lost much of our understanding of the search by modern women for physical freedom.

Harem fantasies — and realities

Meanwhile in Britain, emigrating women upped the ante. While some Victorian women became betrothed to the minor, often struggling royalty of Europe, their even more intrepid sisters ventured to India.

There many travelers and émigrés and expatriates married maharajas, true Oriental potentates in eye-popping estates, with such large palaces that some forgot about entire rooms full of dusty boxes of priceless, surplus jewels.

American and European fun-time gals, including disproportionate numbers of cabaret dancers, arrived singly or en group to join royal harems. They lived one of humankind's most enduring sex fantasies, popular from the 19th century through today and expressed in erotica, oil paintings, romance novels, Rudolph Valentino films and even pornography (Opposite of Progress): That of the fair princess ravaged as a harem slave by a dark monarch .

Even for women not susceptible to *Arabian Nights* fantasies, India's rajas exerted the appeal of being simultaneously rich, exotic, fluent in English and French — and in many cases, easy on the eyes.

Sikh appeal

Hands up, ladies, if you agree with me that a handsome Indian man can be one of the world's most captivating sights?

Especially the majestic Sikh, whose last name, Singh, means "lion." He follows a 500-year-old religion that stresses meditation and bravery, lives in the northerly state of Punjab, and dominates India's army.

The traditional Sikh is not permitted to cut his luxuriant hair, wears a ceremonial sword, and in not-so-far-off history flexed his virility with multiple wives and a religion-endorsed station as eminent over women.

Something about a Sikh — the hair, the sword, the turban, beautiful eyes and confident masculinity — seemed to have an almost fetishistic appeal to Englishwomen. In 1901 in London, where these troops were posted, Lord Curzon (qtd. in Ballhatchet 119) noted, "English women of the housemaid class, and even higher, do offer themselves to these Indian soldiers, attracted by their uniform, enamoured of their physique, and with a sort of idea that the warrior is also an oriental prince."

Even today, Sikhs have been depicted as striking figures with majestic manes — including Jungli in Sarah Lloyd's memoir, *An Indian Attachment*, and the bomb-defusing Kip in the film *The English Patient*.

In bygone times, Sikh maharajas dripped with priceless jewels, carried themselves as warriors, shopped for presents such as stupendous tiaras for their favorite wives, and competed among themselves as lady killers.

In India's Sikh princely states, Kapurthala and Patiala, princes sported turbans with gigantic topazes, necklaces of rubies the size of pigeons' eggs, and pearls insured by Lloyd's for a million dollars.

Their sex appeal magnified by lives larger than life, the Sikh princes supported huge harems long after they had disappeared from much of the Arab, Turkish, Chinese and Thai palaces. (Quite a contrast to the inept man of today's India, by and large shunned by female Western travelers as a pest, as described in the Asia chapter.)

Kapurthala's Sikhs, smooth and silky

The first raja documented to taken a foreign wife, Randhir Singh, must have seemed resplendent to the chosen young woman in his district, Miss Hodges, with his sarpesh (jewels decorating a silk turban), choker, brooches, necklaces and medals.

Miss Hodges, at the age of 18, consented to be the third bride of the lion of Kapurthala (whose name is also spelled as Rundher Singh), with his hooded eyes, wax-tipped curled moustache, powerful chest and trim waist. On May 16 of 1859, as recorded in the New Calcutta Directory (Wilmshurst, "N.C.D."), they exchanged vows:

At Kuppurthala by Rev. J. S. Woodside of the American Mission, His Highness the Rajah Rundher Singh Allowalia of Kuppurthala to Miss Henrietta Melvina Hodges, eldest daughter of the late Robert Hodges Esq. of Kuppurthala.

Randhir Singh, maharaja of Kapurthala

Hodges, likely an American born in India, would inaugurate a century and a half of similar liaisons, involving not only Americans and Englishwomen but also French, Italian, Austrian, Russian, Spanish and Australian women.

Randhir's grandson, Jagatjit Singh, an even more dashing and sybaritic figure, certainly raised the bar in terms of his involvement with great numbers of women.

While the comparatively easily pleased Randhir stuck to just three wives, Jagatjit (descended from Randhir's first wife, an Indian) collected 300 women, but somehow managed only four official wives and five official children.

Jagatjit modeled himself as a French monarch and, accordingly, European women were part of his fantasies. Like many other maharajas, he had top tutors and became multilingual, in English and French as well as various Indian languages. He exchanged vows in 1908 with the Spanish dancer Anita Delgado, variously described as his third or sixth wife (Buyers, Kapurthala; Younger 78, 87), who eventually ran off with the son of one of the maharaja's older mistresses. In 1942, the Czech Eugenie Grosupova became European Wife No. 2. When Jagatjit's gaze lingered on newer fancies, she killed herself by jumping off a tower with her little dogs (Younger 88-90).

Of Jagatjit's wives and mistresses, many from France, Italy and Britain, "only the Europeans made trouble" on the occasion of being either isolated in the *zenana* (harem), retired or sent away from the palace (Morrow, chapter 6).

Next, Jagatjit's first son, the crown prince Paramjit, fell head over heels for an English cabaret dancer, Miss Stella Mudge, when he saw her perform in Italy, and made her his third wife. And in 1922, Jagatjit's second son, Amarjit, married Sophie Adjemova in Paris.

The house of Kapurthala was not the only harem welcoming white women. Princes of nearby Patiala, just north of Delhi, also found European ladies attractive.

The playboy princes of Patiala

From generation to generation, the rulers of Patiala handed down "a diamond breastplate, its luminous surface composed of 1001 brilliantly matched blue-white diamonds."

One sporty tale, perhaps apocryphal, holds that the prince would "appear once a year before his subjects naked except for that diamond breastplate, his vital organ in full and glorious erection" (Rohit).

The first maharaja to abandon the practice, Rajendra Singh, instead directed his vital energies to pleasing his wives, including his second, Miss Florry Bryan, elder sister of his stable master.

British colonial society sniffed at the match. "The idea threatened the racial and social hierarchy in various ways," for the pair were not only of different colors but also classes (Ballhatchet 116). Nothing in the record indicates Rajendra or Florry cared.

Much like his brother Sikhs in Kapurthala, Rajendra, in the first generation to intermarry, added a Western wife to an existing Indian one, while his sons assembled spectacular harems including white girls.

Rajendra's notorious eldest, Bhupendra Singh (born of Florry's Indian co-wife), considered absurdly handsome by many, was a contemporary of Kapurthala's Jagatjit Singh and became his rival in bedroom exploits. Bhupendra gave British colonial administrators far more cause for alarm — while titillating many of their wives — than his father did with his marriage to Florry. At Simla, a hill station and summer retreat from lowland heat, the maharaja struck the assembled Europeans as "a sensation, a superb dancer, a sexual athlete" (Morrow 230, 95).

His retinue included a goodly number of his 10 wives and concubines, housed in cottages decorated by red satin hearts with purple arrows, pictures from the Kama Sutra and copies of the erotic carvings at Khajuraho (232).

In Simla, the six-foot maharaja, clad in a bright tunic and white buckskin trousers, certainly set the flesh of high-station ladies to tingling, including none other than the woman of highest rank, Lord Curzon's wife. The vicereine of India, Mary Curzon, an American heiress, in the fix of Bhupendra's vivid dark eyes "succumbed to the sensuous pleasure of being wrapped in a crinkling silk sari by the Maharajah of Patiala, who excitedly fished out his best jewels and covered her in rubies, emeralds and diamonds and heavy gold ankle bracelets" (230-32).

Lord Curzon was outraged later on hearing of the subversively intimate encounter. He sensed quite correctly that for the memsahibs, wives of the colonial officers, "in the fantasies of at least a few he [Bhupendra Singh] was a tiger of a man." The maharaja was banned from Simla after making advances on Englishwomen, and from that point, making little headway with expatriate ladies of high station, he made trips to London to restock his harem.

Sir Bhupendra Singh "the Magnificent" fathered 88 children (Buyers, Patiala). Lists of his sons' birthdates look nothing short of bizarre, as groups of his wives and concubines often came to term in the same calendar year. For example, his English-nicknamed sons "Brian" and "Bobby" arrived two months apart, and three months later "Mervyn" joined them.

Western women elsewhere in India

Outside the Punjab, many other princes also followed suit by taking non-Indian wives.

In Indore, northeast of Bombay, Sir Yeshwant Rao Holkar became adverse to things British in the 1920s when as teen he attended the exclusive private school Charterhouse and received galling mistreatment from faculty and fellow students.

He developed a "consuming passion for all things American," including women. In 1938 Marguerite Lawler became his second wife, later walking out with all with her jewels (Copland 194, 212d). In 1943, Fay Crane became Wife No. 3.

His son, Richard, also married an American woman, Sally, whom he met at Stanford University and married in 1966 (Morrow 72; Copland 212, 194; Buyers, Patiala).

The chart below details a fair number of known marriages between Indian princes and white women, yet historians hint at a number of additional women not documented.

"There were said to be white women, both officially and unofficially, in India's royal harems — the Australian Ethel Anderson writes a fictive short story of a 'Begum Jane,' for example," Sanjay Sircar, an independent scholar in Canberra, Australia, e-mailed me. "Look at the Aga Khans ending up as white men as a result of marrying foreign wives."

And even far from royal harems, colonial observers (such as Henry Beveridge in his travels in Bengal) often encountered blonde wives, their names lost to posterity, also suggesting a broader sprinkling of Western women out of the spotlight.

Indian princes and descendants with white wives, mistresses

RAJAS (SIKH)	SOURCES
Jind	Younger 67-73; Ballhatchet 17
Patiala *	Younger 58-66; Strobel 4; Morrow 95
Kapurthala **	Wilmshurst "N.C.D."; Morrow 56-67; Younger 74-90
RAJAS (HINDU)	
Narzigunge, Purnea, Bihar	J. Sinclair, "Interesting"
Pudukkottai	Allen 192; Younger 115-30
Indore **	Buyers, Indore; Younger 147-59; 189-200
Udaipur	Morrow 216
Jodhpur	Morrow 87
Cooch Behar	Morrow 207; Younger 95-99
Nawanagar	Morrow 254
Porbandar	Buyers, "E-mail"
Tikari	Younger 99-109
NAWABS (MUSLIM)	
Bajawalpur	Morrow 96
Bengal, Bihar and Orissa **	J. Sinclair, "Interesting"
Murshidabad	J. Sinclair, "Interesting"
Bhopal	Morrow 96
Palanpur	Allen 192; Morrow 14

* Two generations of intermarriage
** Three generations of intermarriage
Note: Some introductions occurred in Europe

Echoes of Sikh splendor

The appeal of the noble Indian man and his world touched by fantasy has great staying power with traveling women. For the spirit that joined Henrietta Melvina Hodges and Randhir Singh, and Mohiuddin Hossain Meerza and Nora Partridge, continues to live in recent times.

• In the mid-1960s, American writer Barbara Baer chanced upon a Sikh hotel keeper in Darjeeling. Though he looked like a cross between a Bollywood star and Alain Delon — "his eyelashes were so long, he was so good-looking, I trembled" — "in bed, he was modest, unaware of his beauty" (246, 249). Vikram hit Baer when she received a letter from a male friend, ending after three weeks a whirlwind romance involving daily gifts in Kashmiri boxes, Hindi love poems and good loving: "Sikhs were a warrior caste, the fiercest men in India, and the most ardent lovers, I could attest to that. I hadn't known such a ravenous desire, almost too much attention to pleasure and to me, in my life" (249).

• In 1978, Australian travel writer Robyn Davidson, upon landing in

India, encountered by chance a congressman of noble birth named Narendra Bhati Singh.

Indian aristocrats still knew how turn a fine figure; Narendra was "a personification of elegance dressed in black jodhpurs, black kurta [tunic], black sunglasses and black moustache." And charm: Narendra had read Davidson's first book, *Tracks*, and invited her to stay in a cottage on his property (*Desert* 3). "How odd that you should arrive here," he said, "just as I was thinking of writing to you."

Made a guest at his farm with its large, red stone house, she plunged into the exotic. Its main room included "a wall-to-wall mattress covered in embroidered bolsters and cushions. Narendra is half reclined on the bolsters and clapping his hands like something out of *The Arabian Nights*. Tea does appear and is placed on squat, octagonal tables ... edged in silver" (4).

Narendra became her nurturing angel during a hellish trip through India. As of 1996, they still maintained a long-distance love affair between the subcontinent and London (Birkett, "Journey").

• And 1980s Scottish traveler Trudy Culross (313) was impressed to arrive in Rajasthan and note its men a breed apart from the small, thin Indians of the south: "here the men frequently topped six feet, were muscular and fit, with skin the colour of bronze. Their eyes carefully made up with kohl, their ears festooned with crescent moons, while heavy bracelets and anklets tinkled merrily ... they really were the most amazing-looking men. Sporting luxuriant, dropping moustaches, their eyes flashing wickedly from beneath their ... multi-coloured turbans."

They sound little changed from Randhir Singh.

The Jazz Age

After World War I, with its curtailment of all leisure travel, reports of flappers with foreign admirers resurfaced during the Jazz Age.

Paris now drew American and English women explicitly seeking male companionship. Indicative is the 1929 guidebook, *Paris Is a Woman's Town*, with a remarkable roundup of places to go have a good time and which foreign men to pick up. On the first page, the authors related their initial fears that Paris "was full of apaches ... lying in wait to rap over the head any unwary woman who ventured out alone ...

"It would have been impossible for us to believe than that a nice woman could, with perfect propriety, accept the invitation of a strange man to dance, much less pay him for asking her" (Josephy v).

In a milder version of international man ratings by sexologists Anne Cumming and Xaviera Hollander, the authors of *Paris* (153-60) comment that "an Englishman is impossible unless he has enough money," that Swiss men are faithful and marriage-minded, and "the aristocratic Italian

. . . is adorably sweet and understanding and can be an ideal lover."

Italy, in the Jazz Age as well as before and after, remained a sex travel capital. D.H. Lawrence briefly described gondoliers eager to service visiting females in *Lady Chatterley's Lover*. And the isle of Capri served as a sex haven for lesbians and straight women alike.

After the pioneers

Now that we have explored this era of women's sexual history, we can see continuities from the Victorians to our own day. For example, Daisy Millers still overrun Europe's capitals each summer.

And in some cases, the line from the past to the present is exceptionally direct — involving descendants of early female adventurers.

In 1960s Kenya, Isabelle Eberhardt's great niece, Jacqueline Roumeguère Eberhardt, married a Masai warrior.

Lady Jane Digby's descendants would include Pamela Harriman (née Digby), wife to a Churchill, to a Hollywood producer and to an ambassador, and lover of many powerful men. A devotee of serial power matings, Harriman admired Jane Digby and "had the same disregard for public opinion as her ancestor" (S.B. Smith 115).

As we've earlier discussed, women today forge new identities by traveling overseas and permitting themselves revels with foreign men. And so did their great-great-grandmothers who so captivated the European male. We also see a constancy in the hearts of women, from the Victorian era to the present, as they seek more sensual identities denied them at home and permitted overseas.

Travel sex as indicator of feminism

Most important, casual sex involving traveling women serves as a leading indicator of the state of feminism in general.

A first wave of feminism appeared in the 1840s; a second in the 1960s. Female sexual explorations flourished during both eras. With perfect synchronicity, just as feminism first appeared in the 1840s, American journalist Margaret Fuller and English aristocrat Lady Jane Digby arrived in Rome to tantalize eager beaux.

Feminism in both eras also benefited from advances in birth control: condoms, sponges and pessaries in the Victorian era, and the Pill in 1960s. And better birth control led to eras of free and easy attitudes toward sex, in the England of the 1860s and early 1870s and throughout the West in the 1960s (Anderson 57; M. Mason 120-22).

As noted in the Reasons chapter, today profound man shortages motivate a nation's females to look for greener pastures. Similarly, the 1891 census returns for England and Wales showed 900,000 more women than

History timeline

1080 B.C.: Government begins to control female sexuality, as women in **Assyria** become first to have to wear veils to differentiate virtuous from fallen women. Status of temple prostitutes plummets. Later, Old Testament prophets decry "harlotry."

1st century B.C.: During beginnings of the **Roman Empire**, aristocratic women ignore constraints and travel for love and to fornicate with strange men. Cleopatra departs her home in **Egypt** for Asia Minor to seduce Marc Antony. Julia, the daughter of Augustus Caesar, takes anonymous lovers in the Forum.

Middle Ages:

- **8th century:** St. Boniface decries English women who in course of religious pilgrimages turn their attentions to more earthly delights. "There are few cities in **Lombardy**, or **France**, or **Gaul** in which there is not an adulteress or prostitute of the English nation" (Littlewood 4).

- Compelled travel sex occurs as captive women taken from conflict zones in **Africa**, **India** and the **Middle East** move to slave markets (Tolmacheva 124). There they stood a chance to become concubines, affording them a measure of comfort and influence. In a technical sense the women would be sexual travelers, lthough not voluntary ones.

- Well-off Muslim women **travel for pleasure** as well as to make pilgrimages to Mecca, the North African traveler Ibn Battuta (1304-77) observed (Tolmacheva 127-28). No record of trysts exists, yet it remains worth noting that at this quite early date we see free movement by wealthy women.

Pre-Columbian America: In the first examples of voluntary travel sex by women, unmarried Navajo girls "had the right to establish a house of their own where they were able to welcome male visitors. Such women could move from settlement to settlement seeking out bedmates, responsible to no one but themselves" (V. Bullough 10). Papago and Pima Indians had similar practices.

Circa 1580: Pirates deliver a Venetian noblewoman to the harem of **Turkish** sultan Murad IV. Two centuries later, Algerian pirates deliver French colonial Aimée Dubucq de Rivery to a later sultan's harem.

1717: Women in **Turkey** travel cross town for adulterous sex, using their veils to avoid detection, in a delightful subversion of the purpose of veiling laws. "You may easily imagine the number of faithfull Wives very small in a country where they have nothing to fear from their Lovers' Indiscretion," Lady Mary Wortley

---

men in a total population of 29 million and "the imbalance was particularly high between the ages of twenty and thirty" (Anderson 150; Strobel 25).

As late as 1912, Australian traveler Mary Gaunt called England "a manless country" (J. Robinson, *Unsuitable* 194). Exacerbating the man shortage, some Englishmen proved reluctant to marry (Anderson 151-52) — shades of today's commitment-phobic male!

"Travel was a means of escape for so many Victorian women — not

Montagu observed (qtd. in J. Robinson, *Unsuitable* 113-14). "Upon the Whole, I Look upon the Turkish Women as the only free people in the Empire."

1837: Victoria takes the British throne, Industrial Age accelerates social changes that spur travel by women.

1847: In **Rome**, American journalist Margaret Fuller falls in love and marries a young Italian aristocrat.

1849: Lady Jane Digby takes lovers in **Rome, Greece (1852)** and **Syria (1854)**, then marries sheikh 20 years her junior **(1855)**.

After 1858: R. C. Chandra, first **Bengali** student to qualify for medical service exam, becomes commissioned officer, marries a British woman (Crawford qtd. in Chandrika Paul footnote 48).

1859: This year was a busy one in the history of romance on the road:

• In Kapurthala, **India**, Miss Henrietta Melvina Hodges weds the local raja; many binational marriages follow.

• **Beginning of criticism of traveling women**. In the United States: Dr. William Sanger fires first salvo criticizing American women cavorting with **European** men.

• Beginning of backlash by white men against dark men who might want to become involved with white women:

In **India**, a Eurasian physician in India, Dr. Gillies, was accused of touching an English woman's body during childbirth, underscoring both professional jealousy by British physicians and a general view of "Hindu men as lascivious" and attractive to Western women (Strobel 5-7).

1861: In **South Africa**, English and Irish immigrant women marry local Malays (Duff Gordon, *Cape* 31, 158).

1864: In **Egypt**, maid Sally Nedrett aggressively seduces a guide and has his baby the next year (Duff Gordon, *Egypt* 187-90).

1873: Emily Keene marries religious leader of **Morocco**.

1879: Fanny Knox marries **Thai** provincial governor.

Circa 1890: First whispers circulate that American women visit the **Caribbean** in the winter and take young local lovers.

1892: In Murshidabad in **Bengal**, Henry Beveridge (345) of the Indian Colonial Service meets a family consisting of an English lady "very large and blonde," who had born her husband, a "Mahomedan," 10 children.

1893: In a letter home, Mary Kingsley recounts marriage between white

just something they elected to do because they had the opportunity and the money," Jane Robinson, a leading authority on female travelers of the 19th century, wrote to me. "It was often a question of needing to get away from the social, cultural, political, or emotional circumstances at home."

The Victorian ladies "were travelling away from things, as well as towards them. ... If they subsequently discovered sexual choice and excitement, that just proved how right they were to have gone in the

woman and prominent local lawyer in **Sierra Leone** (qtd. in Birkett, *Spinsters* 157).

• Despite objections of British snobs, maharaja of **Patiala** marries Miss Florry Bryan, elder sister of the raja's stable master (Younger 58-66; Strobel 4; Buyers, Patiala).

1896: Margaret Fountaine courted in **Italy**. In **1901**, she takes a long-term lover, her guide in **Syria**.

1897: Isabelle Eberhardt takes legions of lovers in **Tunisia** and later **Algeria (1899)**.

Circa 1900: Backlash by white men continues, as **South African** officials forbid intercourse between black men and white women (in the main, prostitutes), fearing such intimacies would spark a "Black Peril" of sexual assaults on white women.

1902: In **Italy**, novelist E.M. Forster eavesdrops on gossip of a visiting Englishwoman "who had married an Italian far beneath her socially and also much younger" (Beauman 124), inspiring his running theme of how British society erected obstacles to pursuing true love outside one's class — and how travel could destroy such obstructions.

• A barmaid named Miss Matheson draws attention of colonial officials in **Calcutta** for "her liking for coolies";

they conclude "it must be a case of nymphomania" (Ballhatchet 139). European prostitutes abound in Calcutta and Bombay (Younger 24).

1900: Olive Monalescu, daughter of a **Bombay** barber of Rumanian ancestry, marries Ranbir Singh, raja of Jind, in secret ceremony (Buyers, "E-mail"; Ballhatchet 117; Younger 67-73).

1909: Australian actress Elsie Thompson marries Gopal Narain Singh, or "Rajie," maharaja of Tikari in **India** (Younger 94-114).

1915: Maharaja of Pudukkottai in **India** marries Esmé Mary Sorrett, an Australian born in Melbourne (Buyers, "E-mail"; Allen 192).

1905: While traveling in Aleppo in **Syria**, English traveler Gertrude Bell (268) comes upon "a pleasant little lady from Brixton" in South London, married to one of Bell's friends, a Turkish pasha. The "little lady" had met the pasha during a trip to Constantinople and they married there.

1907: In Darjeeling in **India**, Nora Frances Partridge, an Englishwoman, meets, later marries the grandson of the last Nawab Nazim of Bengal, Bihar and Orissa (Z. M. Sinclair, "Petals").

By 1913: Some white housemaids in **South Africa** become sexually involved

first place!" Robinson added:

> Far from being a casual thing, sex was a means to an end: an expression of their physical and spiritual potential. Despite growing awareness of feminism, women at home — spirited women — did not in general have the power to choose the course of their lives while still retaining their essential femininity. Travel could change that.

with black male colleagues (Strobel 27).

1926: Backlash by white men continues, as the lieutenant governor of **Papua New Guinea** signed the White Women's Protection Ordinance, which required the death penalty for rape or attempted rape, though there were no cases of such crimes. The ordinance was not repealed until 1958.

1929: Publication of *Paris Is a Woman's Town* marks end of an era of scolding of young American women traveling in **France**, instead describes characteristics of various datable European men.

1930s: Marguerite Duras in **Vietnam**, K'tut Tantri and Jane Belo in **Bali**, and Emily Hahn in **Shanghai** pursue affairs with local men (or in Belo's case, local women).

• In **India**, Englishwoman Muriel Ray, of Calcutta, married Waris Ali Meerza, who was to become the last Nawab of Murshidabad; in 1932, he had divorced Moselle Meyer (Mirza 345). Around the same time, Trudy Lal married the son of raja P.C. Lal of Narzigunge, Purnea, Bihar (J. Sinclair, "Interesting").

1938: In **India**, Marguerite Lawler of Fargo, North Dakota, marries 12th maharaja of Indore, Yeshwant Rao Holkar (Copland 194; Buyers, Indore). In

1939, Joan Alice Falkiner, an Australian, marries the Nawab of Palanpur (Buyers, "E-mail").

1941: Urdu poet Faiz Ahmad Faiz marries Alys (or Ellis) George of London; her sister marries Muhammed Din Taseer; both men hail from Lahore in modern-day **Pakistan** (Jayawardena 227).

1948: In **India**, Hanwant Singh, maharaja of Jodhpur, marries Sandra McBryde, 19, of Scotland, who worked in an Indian nursing home and met the prince at a party (Morrow 87, Younger 218). Maharaja of Cooch Behar marries Nancy Valentine, later divorces her and in 1956 marries Gina Egan (Buyers, "E-mail").

Late 1950s-early 1960s: Royals in the mountain kingdoms of **Nepal** and **Sikkim** marry American women (see Asia chapter).

• In **India**, Bhagwat Singh, maharana of Udaipur, marries Annabella Parker, a British colonel's daughter who met him while visiting friends in India (Younger 230-42; Morrow 218, caption following 210). In **1954**, the maharaja of **Porbandar** marries Annette, widow of resident of Ceylon, believed to be English but possibly of Dutch and Ceylonese descent (Buyers, "E-mail").

Next let's visit the remaining world regions — Latin America, Polynesia and the Near East — to see how female travelers are getting along. But first, our Sexual Pilgrim, already heard from on Greece and the Caribbean, recalls her exploration of Brazil and its men.

Instant sex, Amazon style

My Sexual Pilgrimages began in Greece and continued over the years in the Bahamas and the Caribbean.

Finally, in Brazil, I discovered a place where the promise of al fresco intimacy sambas along the breeze, with no more preamble than the time it takes to minimally rearrange a garment or two. A man and a woman could be upon each other in acts of purest spontaneity.

If travel sex elsewhere allowed a woman to reclaim pagan freedoms lost since the advent of civilization, in Brazil's wild places she could strip away the very last drop of inhibition ever known to humankind. She could discover something more basic than her pagan self: the naked primate, grabbing at whim a moment of pleasure.

'Do you swim naked?'

By the time I was 40, I had visited five continents, all except Antarctica and South America. I decided to go next to the warmer of the two destinations.

The time seemed ripe to explore Brazil, which had always intrigued me for its beautiful music, wild jungles and considerable African heritage. In August 1994, I explored five contrasting areas of the South American giant (described in my first book, *An Amateur's Guide to the Planet*).

Midtrip brought me to Manaus, in the middle of the vast Amazon basin. The owner of an Indian-run company picked me up in the dark of night at the airport and sent me east via taxi and bus. By midmorning, I found myself at a collection of wooden shacks beside a landing on the river.

An *African Queen*-style riverboat took aboard myself and nine other tourists from Europe and North America. Our Indian crew blasted the music of Foreigner as we chugged along under picture-perfect blue skies and fluffy clouds.

Twelve miles later, as farms gave way to jungle on the riverbanks, the thatched buildings of a simple camp appeared, bounded by two channels of water. I was issued a hammock and found a rudimentary shelf for my backpack.

We tourists changed into bathing suits to head back out on gentle tributaries of the Amazon. All the others left paddling dugouts. An Indian I had briefly noticed on the riverboat, named Tim, offered me a ride in a motorized canoe.

My guide glided into the igapó, a seasonally drowned forest that felt like a cypress swamp. Green-black water rippled in an almost syrupy way.

I got a better look at Tim, less handsome than the other Indians involved with the camp, with his protruding lower jaw, a bit apelike, and a low growling voice. After we reached a distant, private corner of the igapó, he lowered his thin brown body over the side to swim, inviting me to follow. We dogpaddled toward a tree trunk and clung to it, Tim indicating that I should hold onto his back.

He then reached behind to my legs, grasping the ankles and wrapping them around his waist. You had to hand it to Tim for confidence in dealing with the opposite sex.

As bizarre as this may seem — allowing a strange man to thus arrange my limbs, in what would be an unspeakable outrage outside of this patch of jungle — I scarcely even analyzed the situation. We acted as two creatures of the water at innocuous play. His back felt strong, and it was fun to get wet, baptized by the Amazon. We clung together in quiet, the river noiselessly lapping at the trees, punctuated by the occasional bird call.

Though Tim had set us on a course to full intromission, for the moment he pressed no farther. We climbed back into the canoe and motored a bit farther into the jungle. After what seemed like a few minutes, Tim cut the motor, backed up to a trunk and tied up the canoe. He turned around and sat facing me.

Like a pair of shameless monkeys

In full view was the distorted front of his light blue, knit bathing trunks, poked out and up by a bony flagpole, less imposing in size than the thicker bamboo Made in the Caribbean but no less ready and eager.

I made no move toward or away from him. After glancing at his triumphant arousal, more suggestive clothed than had he been naked, I stared at the bottom of the canoe. As an exercise, I became deliberately passive, wondering what sort of gambit he would try so as to advance his plans for action. Nothing seemed obvious: Lying on the bottom of the canoe would be uncomfortable. Kneeling would be unsteady. The drowned forest had no shore.

He came up with a serviceable line: "Do you swim naked like Indian?"

"Yes," I decided.

Tim stripped and stood for a moment in side profile, his baton narrow and medium long, but jutting out as unselfconscious as a monkey's, in a most enflaming way to the female audience. Where the baton led, pointing overboard, I would follow. Unconcerned about modesty, I stepped out of my swimsuit and lowered myself in the water. Tim handwalked down the side of the canoe and again reached behind him to wrap my legs around his back. Then he reversed his handholds on the gunwales to face me. The moment we clung front to front, brazenly I reached down to grab him and yanked him into me.

I came instantly. I was 40, my body primed but starved for sex, able with such incendiary provocation to climax at the speed of light.

My partner remained still in the water.

"Are you OK?" I asked. "Mmmmm," Tim assented, a bass sound from deep in his chest. We must have both convulsed in one powerful spasm, mine so overwhelming that I couldn't feel his.

An impromptu, emotionless, keenly exciting monkey fuck in the Amazon.

One in which I had without any tenderness or restraint grabbed a man and rammed him where I wanted. Was that why Tim and I achieved an orgasm not only simultaneous but instant (one for the scientific record, perhaps)? I would have thought he shagged tourists regularly, given his ready access to them and his assured moves of seduction. Yet if he lacked deprivation, he really should have a bit of staying power.

But maybe the situation had seemed just as intensely stimulating to my Indian guide, as raw as a male could ever dare to desire. Maybe humans immersed in water had sex in the manner of whales and guppies, who lacking the purchase of land just maneuver into position for a very brief "money" thrust.

We got back late to the village to innocent queries from others as to where we had been for so long. I guess we had spent far more time than I realized dipping in and out of the dark mirror of the Amazon. As we had dragged the canoe up on the shore, Tim had still been semi-hard. His bathing trunks hid nothing. I hoped no one would notice.

I blithely answered that we had done an extensive tour of the igapó. Upon our return from the bubble world of wild nature, we had been promptly challenged on our whereabouts. It was as if, even in a spare society of leafy huts, the others had to uphold social no-no's against frantic coupling between strangers.

Outside of the moment, it is difficult to comprehend how swiftly hikes, swimming and rides involving canoes or motorcycles or horses evolve from distance between the male guide and the female traveler to frantic coupling. But travel sex proceeds on its own set course, the only rule being that there are no longer rules impeding near-immediate intercourse. Only in retrospect does it seem obvious that a male guide's suggestion for a solo excursion is bound to be an invitation for sex. (Lady travelers, take note.)

I had packed condoms on this trip, just in case, but scarcely thought to have taken them on a quick canoe trip sans luggage. Another lesson for readers: You may need those condoms when you very least expect to; keeping them bedside may not be enough. I wondered if the noted acidity of this Amazon tributary, thick with tannin released by its floating leaves, would control sperm as well as it did mosquitoes.

Would I be protected from pregnancy and disease by the fleeing nature of the act?

I hoped so.

This behavior later struck me as insane, when I voluntarily took an HIV test prior to my second marriage and spent a week in the torment of waiting for the results.

Over the next few days, Tim kept to the kitchen hut, while I went off with my little group, hiking or canoeing under the care of another Indian. During a single brief moment of slight proximity in the kitchen, our eyes didn't meet. Yet there was no forced avoiding each other or pretending we had something to cover up.

As for our monkey fuck, we had a monkey's ability to attach a simian's amount of importance to it.

Though in retrospect, as a connoisseur of men and travel, I did feel as though my first instance of sex with an Indian counted for something, at least as another ethnic notch on the bedpost (or canoe paddle). American Indians have an excellent reputation as lovers (based on a stream of endorsement letters years ago from women to Dear Abby), though I certainly couldn't generalize based on microseconds of dangling in a world-famous river.

Happy trails

Four days later, a thousand miles east of the Amazon, I opened my travel notebook. I sat at a desk in a spacious room in a plank-floored former brothel, now an inn overlooking the quiet square of a faded coastal town, Alcântara. I caught up with recording my Amazon adventures.

The atmosphere of a lost era of prosperity clung to the quiet streets of pastel-colored homes and roofless churches. Goats cropped the grass outside what had been a slave market.

Alcântara was the most serendipitous and least known of my destinations in Brazil. A ticket agent for a Brazilian airline had heard of provincial efforts to restore the colonial city and suggested visiting it when I told her my trip goals were "photography and adventure."

After breakfast, I walked out of the town square and down a cliffside path to the local beach, the Praia de Baronessa, to photograph a handful of scarlet ibis scouring its mud flats at low tide. I had gasped when I first spotted them circling over the harbor on my arrival by ferry from nearby São Luis. They gleamed with a brilliant red of otherworldly intensity. The sight of them could leave you disbelieving your own eyes.

On my walk back, I took a leftward branch off the path and got off track. Here was a pretty little marsh, with tall grass and bushes and brooklets surrounded by soggy silt. Thick gluey mud encased my sandals and I began to clop along, my feet heavy.

Suddenly I found myself face to face with a boy the color of a golden tan, with thick, curly black hair, about my height, 5 feet 4, his strong body clad only in magenta cutoffs. I rolled my eyes and grinned, acknowledging the absurdity of being a tourist lost on the mud flats.

The boy looked 14, so he was probably 16 or a year older — many Brazilians seemed, like the people of Portugal, their cultural parent, short of stature.

The bare-chested youth took my sandals, pinching the straps between his fingers, and gently swirled them in a brooklet until they were clean, then followed me uphill on a path back to the town.

He murmured softly but urgently. I stopped and turned to catch his words. "*Transar? Entende? Comida?*" came a proposal in musical Portuguese. The gist of his comments seemed clear without even understanding the exact words. I memorized his little speech and later verified he had asked, "Have sex? You understand? Eat me?"

He touched me, then his zipper, finally his lips. "*Boca?*" he asked. Mouth. Did I want to go down on him?

"No," I replied.

"*Ese pequino*," he said. It's no big deal. Meaning both — let's have some fun — and — I'm not pressing you.

Under his zipper, this boy-man's virility was fully alive. Even more swiftly than Tim the Indian, the boy was completely excited. To what extent should I, as a 40-year-old woman, regard as a personal compliment the creation of powerful instant erections? Gifts from strange men in Athens, in the Bahamas, in Brazil?

My father likes to say you can judge the state of a marriage by the state of the penis; in other words, erectile dysfunction tells you something, most probably, to be nicer to your man outside the bedroom.

So the erection is the ultimate compliment to the wife.

But creating burning excitement in a *strange* man without touching him graces a woman with a different kind of erotic power, more magical and mysterious, one granted mainly to the beautiful actress, the provocative stripper, the shapely high school French teacher of schoolboy fantasy.

Was I really so attractive? Not especially on that trip; certainly not in the same way I had been in Greece a dozen years earlier, radiating the charisma of entering a new romance, young and slender at perhaps a lifetime best of attractiveness. In 1994, stress tore at me at work and tagged along on this vacation, with its tiring middle-of-the-night flights around Brazil's interior. I was also taking an anti-malarial drug later shown to drive some people to madness, one that made my face in the mirror often look anxious and sad.

No, men saw not great beauty but a female adventurer, alone in a wild place, and Nature abhors a sexual vacuum. Nature allows some of our animal kin to mount each other at whim, and she even allows humans to reclaim this abandon — right here in Brazil's rivers and marshes. Minutes away might be a town with buildings and small roads and civilization's statutes, but one could escape all that with a few steps into this moist hothouse teeming with life, including an ibis blazing the scarlet of burning passion.

Here in nature, a boy and a woman might explore any pleasure that would delight their rushing blood.

The prospect of instant, anonymous sex sets off sirens screaming through the nervous system and scorched the minds of my foreign male admirers as much as myself. The boy's body had readied itself in a rush. Something in our past evolution must have required a capacity to mate swiftly, for we retain this skill despite society's preference for slow courtship. In a fashion, God finds our lust necessary and beautiful in Creation, for we need it to survive. Egyptians believed that "violent love comes by the visitation of God" and "the man or woman must satisfy it or die."

"How big are you?" I wondered out loud. My hand stroked the answer, a splendid shaft that his cutoffs strained to contain. His magnitude pleased me. An old stereotype seemed at work: Tim the Indian (ultimately Asiatic) less blessed than this coastal boy with a trace of African ancestry.

Undeterred by my demurral to pleasure him by *boca*, he pointed to a rectangle of grass between the path and the overgrowth where we could lie together.

I certainly longed for real sex, full knowledge. Yet this was no longer 1982, when on a trip to Greece I'd discovered the nymphomaniac within, minutes before the AIDS clock would strike midnight and fear began to surround hedonism.

A dozen years later, a traveling woman moved in a different time, in the second decade of a killer microbe that cursed sensualists in pleasure-lands such as Brazil and Thailand. The virus was more likely in men's bodies near the coast, with its foreign commerce, than at an Amazonian camp — though both places hosted tourists, a possible vector.

Unwilling to accept risky penetration — for I had not anticipated bringing my condoms on midday bird-watching stroll, as I hadn't for an Amazon canoe ride — I grasped his rod through his cutoffs.

He unzipped. "How old are you?" I murmured to myself in English. He was young, but fully a man below the waist.

He still wanted to lie together, as demonstrated by touches belonging to bedroom repertoire. He kissed me gently like the nuzzling of a horse. As my hand grasped him, he stroked me in return. He's so mature with the little kiss and the fingering, I thought. The boy of the marshes offered more gestures of affection than had the man of the Amazon. This youth would make someone a nice lover when he was older, for he hadn't just stood there lost in his own pleasure.

He glanced up the path, his largish cock hanging out in the sunshine at full salute. He lasted about 10 firm strokes.

Drenched in the noonday sun under Heaven, standing in the middle of the path in full view, nothing deterred us from satisfying our curiosity and lust.

Despite his youth, he already had been winning sexual favors for some time, perhaps even from older women. I wondered about his flashes of knowing talent. Nothing could be ruled out in this tiny place. My stroll the preceding evening had offered glimpses into the open doors of small homes, where teen lovers flirted and chased each other. And some of the most confident, sassy women working in their garden patches, who drew me in conversation, had seemed to be older and available, depths of experience and confidence in their eyes.

Perhaps the mature women and youths of razor-edge potency in this little out-of-the way town had ways to make their own fun. Alcântara, like other more derelict towns throughout the Latin Caribbean, seemed frozen like Macondo in *One Hundred Years of Solitude*, a town notorious for how generations of precocious adolescent males in the Buendía family sought out the hammock of an aging but bawdy and extremely fertile fortune teller.

Perhaps all the men and women of Brazil had knowledge in their eyes.

I was glad he came so quickly without discovery. "OK, you feel better?" I asked him rhetorically. "*Ciao.*"

I continued on my way back to the hotel.

Our stroking near the stream had begun three or four minutes after first sight. This was an example of perhaps the wildest variant of sex with a stranger: completely anonymous and immediate. A man-boy made a suggestion, "mouth," he touching two gentle fingers to his zipper and then lips. No small talk, no coffee, no names, no histories, no hello, no farewell, no thank you, no I'll call you. No preliminaries, except "Have sex? Understand?"

Afterwards I had just walked on as if nothing unusual had happened. Yet this could not be an everyday occurrence even in the magic realism of Latin America. A hypothetical passer-by could have rounded the path to see in plain view a youth standing erect, his sizable organ shooting an arc of ejaculate courtesy of a bemused and game tourist woman.

Yet again, erotic fire lives in its own logic, of the hot body locked in the imperative of moving toward orgasm, all else be damned.

I felt in retrospect I handled the situation well, again by the rules matrix governing travel sex. I had not:
- reacted in a shocked, prudish way;
- been raped. Being a bit taller than him and most of this nation, even at 5 feet 4, probably had given me a bit of freedom to do as I wished and rebuff him if I had chosen to. I did have confidence in my strength and will.

- had unprotected sex and the resulting worries about AIDS or pregnancy.

I had enjoyed stroking him, grasping him, handling a man's hidden instrument of amusement, playing with a woman's most enticing adult toy, a pulsing magic wand taken out of the darkness and into the brightness of day. How interesting civilization would be if you could always just reach out and grasp a strange male, a ritual permitted in Nature.

Memory would smile on the sweet boy on the path, a reality purer than fantasy, insistent and uninhibitedly touching me. I still wanted him after I walked away.

What I wouldn't have given that HIV did not exist. Or that we could follow our marsh encounter with him arriving undetected in my graceful room in the former bordello. A studly Brazilian boy-man would probably be the ultimate in quick recycling between climaxes.

And on that fantasy, after our encounter, did my inflamed imagination dwell alone back in my elegant, spacious whorehouse room.

A professional woman who wanted to personally lower the celibacy statistics among unmarried older females could in a vacation week or two harness the boundless erotic energy of Brazilian puberty. What the golden youth managed on the path hinted at prodigious indoor stamina.

Sex was there for the taking in Brazil, in a way comparable to the Caribbean, but if anything even more pervasive and more gently inviting, for it was less insistent. So many of the men seemed interested and available. With little or no English, they communicated with fingers on the zipper, or wrapping your legs where they wanted.

On the ferry to Alcântara, Toquino, tall, European looking and in his mid-20s, had collected my ticket, hitting on me as just another tourist. After debarkation, he followed me to a restaurant, and sitting across the table, raised fully his shirt to reveal a giant tattoo of a snarling, clawing panther across his back. His anthracite eyes glittering, he told me slowly in English, "I. Like. You." I didn't. Like. Him. Yet I felt fire, a desire to ride that savage big cat.

Brazil floated along like a surreal phallic fantasy, part Fellini, part Dalí, part Robert Mapplethorpe. During street parties in Salvador, the African heart of this musical country, a woman could play voyeur. At a thundering drum concert, I inadvertently glanced just away from the main plaza at a long wall, to see rows of long black dicks hanging out, belonging to beer-drinking concertgoers, just peeing but still an impressive display of endowment.

A woman wanting momentary, undemanding company need not go

to a well-known resort, where the men catered to tourists, or even to the beaches in Rio. A canoe ride, a stroll to watch birds, would bring an encounter, like the omnipresent harmony of guitars and tambourines riding on the breeze.

Local men are said take rebuffs with good grace, for another woman, Brazilian or tourist, will soon come along who will say yes.

Brazilians seemed sexy not in the elegant and virtuoso French way, or the affectionate and imaginative British manner, or the athletic African style. The men seemed to offer themselves lightly, to emerge from river and stream like male mermaids. Sex was as easy a decision as breathing.

Love talk with Zinha

That evening in Alcântara, I wandered to the front of the inn and sat under a Cinzano umbrella at one of the tables.

The proprietor sat drinking her preferred Guaraná soft drink. Zinha, 38, a Susan Sarandon lookalike, owned the inn, a pizza stand and sundry other properties around the town square. She specialized in love talk, in expounding on her well-developed *philosophie d'amour*.

She gestured for me to sit down and have a drink, and without hesitation began divulging her life story, most notably her acquisition of seven husbands. Zinha seemed to rack up husbands in roughly the same quantity as I had acquired men for travel sex.

Zinha's first, a pilot looking like Tom Cruise, she married when she was 15. "Tupp Gawn!" she exclaimed. Her "top gun" had been a handsome man, she said, who had died in an airplane crash when she was 18. Zinha's subsequent husbands had been *suisse* and Spanish and more than one, if I followed her correctly, had been named Marcos.

As can suddenly happen during a long trip, scraps of vocabulary finally came together with a click. I uttered my first sentence of Portuguese.

"*Voce gusta omes lindos,*" I said.

In Portuguese, she replied, "I am not beautiful." She was too tough on herself. Zinha had the kind of appeal that is equally looks and vital energy and intelligence.

"But" (she confirmed my observation) "I like handsome men."

Only two years apart in age, we thought on the same wavelength, as women getting older who had had to come to grips with some hard luck, losing our first mates, hers especially brutally.

I'm through with love, Zinha said. She liked one of NASA's Americans working at a rocket-launching base near Alcântara, but he was "friend only." She too seemed to have distanced herself from pain and decided on more recreational arrangements for her physical needs. Especially, we both appreciated good-looking gents. Always had, always would. (I sensed we were in the minority of women in pitilessly appraising male appeal, in the same way men rated women as attractive. Most other women seemed instead to seek good providers.)

But this connoisseurship had its cost. I had found myself wandering the desert of sexual exile due in part to tall, good-looking men who were mentally unhealthy, or married, or otherwise hurt me and left me ever less confident of finding healthy companionship.

This was about to change.

After my Brazil vacation, as the days in my rough, draining job drew to an end, my physical vitality returned and my mental outlook changed. With the help of a social worker, I accepted that only one criteria mattered in a man: He needed to be nice. I let go of wanting a handsome man. I was one step away from release from limbo.

But I get slightly ahead of my tale. Let's go back to that conversation in Alcântara.

Zinha and I liked handsome guys, wanted our fun, and fretted over disease. We discussed reports that the local AIDS rates ranged from 10 percent to 20 percent.

Nose wrinkled in disgust, Zinha exclaimed: "Men in Brazil, sexsexsex." No translation necessary. Part of the truth of this was crudely visible. In public, Brazilian men and boys handled themselves continually. Waiting for buses, having a coffee, sunning at the beach, a Brazilian male "will habitually affirm his manhood by performing a continuous testicular jiggling routine," a book on the men of Rio noted.

Even with all the public displays of pocket pool, for me, "men in Brazil, sexsexsexsex" was a welcome change from "men in Washington, no sexsexsexsex." And I know that Zinha and I, despite our guardedness, liked nothing better than sexsexsexsex and silently longed to enjoy it again in tandem with lovelovelovelove.

Confessions to Lamont

Early the following summer, I lay on my futon, atop a sheet of hunter green, beside the open window of my Baltimore rowhouse. It was a late Saturday night, early Sunday morning, the comfortable June air moving only slightly. Lamont, my guest in bed for a few nights now, and I had reached the point of relating our *histoires d'amour*, as perhaps many in lasting courtships do ... filling in the arrows that bring a pair from separate lives to a shared one.

An image from that discussion sticks like a photograph in my mind. As we talked, I glanced at his tapering artist's fingers and narrow wrist, resting black against my white hip, bright in the ambient glow of the urban night.

The sight quietly startled me. I really was in bed with a black man. Lamont had a cinnamon face and torso, and we could walk easily in public without attracting much notice. But his arms shaded much darker. To look at his hand lightly on me, Othello skin to skin with fair Desdemona, was to see that we defied race taboos in a way I had not really spent the time to comprehend. Though at some level, I did realize I would now have to dare to be with a black man in my hometown, in public, a braver step than engaging in secret liaisons without potential social penalty in the faraway Caribbean.

Saying goodbye to sexual exile was a delight shot through with paradox. I had traveled the world of foreign men, yet here was a young Marylander who looked as exotic as any of them. People guessed he was South American, or Egyptian, yet he could discuss local sports teams, childhood TV shows and current events in the most comforting and familiar way. We shared giant areas of cultural shorthand.

From dallying with an anonymous boy in a marsh, I now found myself with a friend I had known for two years, with whom I shared a home state and a profession; further, we discovered our parents had also worked together, in a naval laboratory.

And only when I had at last let go of all other criteria except that a man be kind, was I granted the combo package: Nice 'N' Handsome bundled together. As taught in Buddhism, only letting go of attachments led to contentment.

Now there remained the matter of my unorthodox love history B.L., Before Lamont.

We met working together at a newspaper. As an artist who knew me best as a harried editor, of modest dress and demeanor, Lamont could scarcely have anticipated my hidden life as a sex traveler. But he coped well with — nay, enjoyed thoroughly — tales of my escapades in Greece, the Bahamas and the Caribbean. Sex to him was natural, and is for both of us of high interest and a favored conversation topic. On all counts, my stories held his full attention while not stirring jealousy.

However, the monkey fuck in the Amazon was too much.

"I offered to go with you on that trip!" he cried, rising on one elbow. "I don't believe this! You went off with an Indian in the Amazon when I could have been there!"

"I didn't believe you really wanted to go," I replied. Two people who had wanted to go with me to Brazil backed out. I hadn't treated Lamont's offer as sincere, though it was. "Everyone else had blown me off. I should have taken you seriously," I acknowledged. "You would have loved the soccer down there. Would we have become lovers earlier?"

"Maybe I after I scoped out some of the *morenas* on the beach," he said. I had told Lamont, son of a white father and black mother, about the hot reputation (and minuscule bikinis) of Brazilian's mixed-race women. I noted he had a good memory for the term *morena*.

He just couldn't get over my obtuseness to his pursuit. Sometimes you need to clobber me with the obvious. One of my sisters is the same way — she had to be told point-blank about how that pleasant player on her softball team, her future husband, was interested in her. Belliveau women can be oblivious.

Lamont remained flabbergasted. "I can't believe you went without me and had an Indian in the river."

If only I had known sooner. That nice guy at work, who brought me books he thought I would like, who wanted to see my Brazil slides, who took me to a Baltimore batting cage on what I mistakenly thought were non-dates, would marry me less than a year after my Brazil trip.

Had we both known each others' desires, he would have been more than willing to minister to the needs of a woman suffering from a celibacy so interminable that she came after the merest tidbit of intercourse in the mighty Amazon.

He was the adult man promised by the Brazilian boy in the marsh, who had been unafraid of an older white woman, with the makings of an attentive, reciprocal lover. And instead of a panther on his back, as Toquino wore, Lamont sported an Assyrian eagle of his own design tattooed on his shoulder.

Lamont was the rich color of Brazil, a historian well-versed in Portugal's former colonies, an artist with a flair for bringing birds, including the ibis, to life in his sketchbook, and a soccer player of talent and enthusiasm. He would have loved the bus ride from the airport into Salvador proper, past 20 miles of continuous beaches with nonstop *futbol*.

He belonged in my Brazil picture. But Fate sent me there alone, perhaps so I would have a dip in the Amazon some months before saying "I do" on a boat in Baltimore's harbor. Writers seemed sentenced to live through unpredictable experiences that they can use as material when most of the time they just want happiness.

Latin America

The whole country [of Brazil] seems to breathe in time to some original, sensual drumbeat; sex is everywhere ... .

Cripps (65)

As fantastic and almost bizarre as my impulsive adventures in the Amazon basin seem to me, apparently they are rather routine in the eyes of Indian canoeists.

On a visit to Peru, writer Maureen Stanton similarly followed her leader, Angel, when he invited her for a solo ride in his dugout on the Amazon. He dove overboard, nibbled her fingers, tickled her and washed her hair. Later she made her way to join him in an empty hut.

So much for any "specialness" to my radical loss of all inhibition. Animal rutting in the Amazon, which seemed so extraordinary to me (and probably Stanton as well), was simply standard operating proce-dure for our river guides.

Sigh. We tourists may be dupes — our memory of a lifetime merely leaves the river guides smirking, "A canoe ride gets the *gringa* every time." But whatever locker room derision occurs between the Indians out of our earshot, nonetheless, their calculated seductions do inflame us with rank lust. And because men tend to mirror the eagerness of their partner, these bronze seducers do seem to get vastly, genuinely excited during the act itself.

Let's step back now and find out the big picture, of what traveling women can expect in Latin America and these other regions:

- the Middle East.
- Oceania.
- the Zone of Sexual Winter (China, Korea and Japan).
- the Sotadic Zone, and its opposite, Platonia.

Where Indians defeat the conquistadors

THE BEDROOMS (AND CANOES) OF LATIN AMERICA

As mentioned in the previous chapter, my Indian guide Tim apparently is one of a legion of Amazon men whose canoes serve (as was once said of the Model T) as "whorehouses on wheels."

Further, my other encounter in Brazil, involving the golden boy in the marshes, may not be so extraordinary either. In Sambaland, "teenagers make love as soon as their bodies are able, and sex is universally proclaimed as the greatest possible pleasure" (Cripps 65). As with so many travel experiences that seem extraordinary to American eyes, I had merely managed to encounter local, almost everyday, reality.

My personal experiences accidentally illuminate another fact about Latin America: Brazilians and Indians have gentle, unthreatening ways of conversing that tend to please, and not disgust, Western women.

A Peace Corps worker in Ecuador described how a handsome Indian youth suavely told her he wanted a relationship with a gringa and a gringo baby. She demurred but found his approach suave, and much more comfortable than strangers yelling, "Hey baby" (Meisch 455).

Meanwhile, sexual harassment of women, hissing or chanting "*chica chica chica*" in the most annoying possible fashion, and even rape attempts (as evidenced anecdotally by numerous women's travel essays and Meisch 455), tend to come (a) from men in most countries except Brazil and (b) from mestizos, mixed European-indigenous men.

In the hearts of tourist women out for a good time, the sons of the conquistadors lose out to Indians (Dennis; K. Shaffer; Wood; Stanton), from the Amazon's river guides to Mexico's cliff drivers in Acapulco, from gigolos in Puerto Vallarta to Pacific coast surfers in Quepos, Costa Rica.

Online, women debate which Latin men are most attractive (Sexiest Men): Brazilians good looking enough to leave onlookers speechless, and especially Brazilian Indians; Chileans; coastal Peruvians; Argentineans; Colombians from Bogota (dark hair, contrasting blue eyes); or Guatemalans. Trysts have also been reported in Bolivia (Bradt).

In most particulars, female sex travel in Latin America is similar to that of other places:

• Women generally engage in short-term, mutually beneficial liaisons with men, often buying them meals or presenting them with gifts; those that enter serious relationships usually hit a dead end.

• Full-figured women, including tourists, are considered attractive in Latin America (Wood 24; Meisch 443, 456, 451), as they are in the Caribbean, the Islamic world and sub-Saharan Africa.

Because so many of the universal aspects of female sex tourism discovered in earlier chapters also apply in Latin America, we will proceed directly to specific pluses and minuses about this region.

Latin lovers, likes and dislikes

ADVANTAGES

• **For the female sex connoisseur: handsome guys**. As women gravitate toward exotic men with beautiful hair and daggers as travel trophies, scoping out the Masai and the Samburu in Kenya and the Sikhs of India, South America's Indians with their ponytails or braids and their machetes also fit the bill.

Mary Morris, a writer from Chicago, decided one night to go to a party in San Miguel de Allende and noticed the arrival of Alejandro, a craftsman, "dark-skinned with pure Aztec features." He stood "back in the shadows. Yet my eyes landed on him right away. He was tall, slender, and striking in an eggshell-blue shirt and jeans. He had a flat nose and high, sculpted cheekbones, deep-set dark eyes, and thick black hair. There was something about this man which struck me; it was as if a light emanated from him, a warm glow" (57). She was in love.

Some women I have interviewed, however, prefer mestizos to Indians, citing them as "much more attractive," good kissers and taller.

• **Handsome guys ... with money!** Latin America's most prosperous Indians (Englebert) live in Ecuador's Otavalo Valley, where they have attracted huge gringa interest.

Fine woven textiles and money earned from busking Andean music overseas have created "noble savages with a credit card and [an Isuzu] Trooper. ... Some Otavaleños are substantially richer than their visiting gringa girlfriends" (Meisch 455). These indigenes join a select few other solvent men with jobs, including those of Martinique, Puerto Rico and at times Thailand, who can foot the bill for dates with visiting Western women rather than sponge off them. (Of course, maharajas and oil kingdom sheikhs who pamper foreign women are in another world yet, one of great wealth.)

And these musical fellows have the diets and health care to look even a bit more exotically good than their poorer cousins. One American woman (449) gushed: "These guys are so sexy! Long hair, high cheekbones, white teeth, well-built, nicely dressed, friendly. ... Sometimes I just like to sit and look at them. They're Madison Avenue Andean Indians."

• **Sex as a parallel universe of magic.** Maryse Holder (199) describes four days in a hotel room with a Mexican Indian named Miguel, "never any money, sex at any hour, both of us breaking some sort of record." Their near-constant caressing led in and out of sex, either as foreplay or post-play, as they performed a symphony of intimate touch living in "our eternal night ... with the night's deep secret communion, its unquestioned magic. ... All I wanted in [Miguel] was the quintessence of Mexico, of Mexicans more precisely, since I no longer tour countries, just souls."

She later discussed such dreamscapes with Eduardo, another *amor*. "It was the nature of life to be overwhelmed in a three-day love affair. It's one of the best experiences life offers, Eduardo said and added in English, after he said it in Spanish, a gift of the gods" (223).

• **Sex as dark magic.** In the 1970s, UCLA anthropology graduate student Regina Thal, under the pen name Florinda Donner, wrote in the book *Shabono* of going deep into Venezuelan Indian territory to study traditional medicine. In the forest on a trek, she observed her traveling companions, a married couple, having moaning sex yet "the motion of their bodies was so closely adjusted they barely moved." The husband, "not in the least embarrassed, moved out of Ritimi [his wife] and knelt in front of me. Lifting my legs, he stretched them slightly. He pressed his cheeks against my calves; his touch was like the playful caress of a child. There was no embrace; there were no words. Yet I was filled with tenderness" (160).

On another occasion, a shaman who needed "femaleness" in his body gave Thal a dark liquid, saying it would keep her warm. Suddenly "his eyes were so close to mine I saw myself reflected in their dark pupils. I was crushed by the weight of his body and my arms folded beneath his chest. He whispered words into my ears that I could not hear. ... I reached out; my hands grasped leaves adorned with diamond drops. Iramamowe's heavy body held me; his eyes sowed seeds of light inside me; his gentle voice urged me to follow him." Thal had visions of dancing with spirits, singing with birds and jaguars, and experienced "waves of pleasure" (287-88).

Though she represented *Shabono* as her experiences as an anthropologist, many academics suspect her book is a fraud and have termed it "ethnopornography" (Kulick 5). Thal's account may well be fiction, and plagiarized at that, from an earlier, true-life account by a Venezuelan woman (Valero) of being raised by Indians.

Nonetheless, Thal portrays a mystic dimension to Indian sensuality, a sensibility similar to Gabriel García Márquez's portrayal of the Latin Caribbean as a place of tortured lust and everyday occultism. Whether sex magic exists in Latin America outside writers' imaginations is difficult to prove, yet the region's melding of Indian, African and Latin physical vitalities certainly holds out that promise.

• **Good dancers, and more**: One female friend who loves Latin men adds a host of other advantages. They are "excellent dancers," she told me. "They aren't afraid to sing in your ear and dance with you (to merengue, salsa). Gets you all hot and ready to jump into bed. They will die to protect their family. They are very romantic, hard workers, good soccer players." She added that Latin men have cute accents, are nice dressers, and "smell good."

• **Moderate HIV rates**: In Latin American nations known for some level of female sex tourism, HIV rates are generally in same range seen in the United States and Europe, barring the higher figures for Guatemala. Rates are far lower than in sub-Saharan Africa and Thailand.

HIV-infected adults per 1,000

Guatemala	10
Brazil	7
Argentina	7
Costa Rica	6
Colombia	4
Peru	4
Chile	3
Mexico	3
Bolivia	1
For comparison:	
North America	6
Europe	3

Source: UNAIDS

Three caveats must be noted:

• During my trip to coastal Brazil, local people told of much higher rates of 100 to 200 per 1,000 (compared to the official U.N. rate of seven per 1,000 shown above).

While the locals may been exaggerating, there is much truth to the idea of high variation within a country. And the U.N. figure may be low, given the local assertions to the contrary and the prevalence of ads promoting condom use throughout public spaces in Brazil.

• Women traveling to Surinam, Guyana, Panama and other areas off the beaten track face higher risks than elsewhere in the region; see www.unaids.org for exact figures.

• A good number of HIV cases may go unreported, especially in rural Guatemala, Nicagarua, Honduras, and El Salvador, because of a lack of testing facilities and extensive unprotected sex.

<small>DISADVANTAGES</small>

• **Rural men may not live up to the Latin lover stereotype.** "Some are better than others," a 27-year-old Californian development worker who lived in Central America for 2½ years told me, adding that many Latin men are known derisively by expatriates and tourists as "three-pump chumps. Even the gay guys in our group [of Westerners] complained about that." A Western woman may find it necessary to tutor her rural man, she indicated: "They don't understand foreplay. They just dive right into it." She said she had tried to give oral sex to her boyfriend. "He says 'don't do that' because he likes me, and I would be a whore in his eyes if he let me." City men are more modern and seek oral sex and anal sex, which they perceive as available only from female tourists.

• **Men view conquering women, be they local or foreign, as a sport.** Young Costa Ricans "would choose an unsuspecting tourist woman as the goal, and whoever ended up engaging in sexual relations with her ... would win the contest. The more attractive they deemed the girl, the more successful the winner was considered to be" (Kimball 8). My Californian confidante told me, "After they get in your pants they don't want you any more, or the other extreme, they show up every night at your house. ... After a while you realize everybody wants you, even if you are 100 lbs. overweight and have buck teeth. ... Then you realize you're not so special." Further, men may be jealous and abusive.

• **Men insist on a right to have other women** (Litt 4) and many men do not declare they are married. Indians especially get married in their teen years and may not mention the fact to interested gringas. "Also in poor countries," the Californian told me, "you are married if live with a woman in a *union libre*, or common-law marriage. Since technically they aren't married, they think they aren't lying to the gringa."

• As indicated in the observation above, Latin men may have a **breezy attitude toward the truth,** or put more directly, "They lie about everything," as one woman told me. "They'll tell you a sob story about 'I'm married but my wife is blah blah blah.' "

• Though only a minority of Latin men generally seek money from tourists, and "many are willing to provide the tourist women with whatever she desires" (Kimball 9), there are exceptions. In Costa Rica and Ecuador, **women feel used by men** who bring along friends and run up bills (Meisch 456). Even in long-term relationships, with a man earning a living, some women report an attitude of "you rich American," and an expectation that a woman pay for most things.

Profiles of adventurous women
Maryse Holder (ca. 1941-1977)
NEW YORK PART-TIME TEACHER, ERSTWHILE WRITER

As cruel as men can be to an ugly woman, it must be no fun to have a deformed face sagging from nerve damage, to be 60 pounds overweight, to have demons from losing a mother at the age of 2 in the Holocaust — and to want closeness to a man.

After three years of involuntary celibacy in New York City, in 1976 Maryse Holder decamped for the first of two extended trips to Mexico, where she lost weight, exercised, got toned and tan, and scored lots of sex — though at a horrific price.

A posthumous collection editing thousands of pages letters sent home by Holder serves as a grim but rich document of motivations for one-nighters overseas. Holder gave her own take on the dating war. According to a friend, the New Yorker found macho American men unattractive, for they equated sensuality with being a sissy, and they treated her cruelly (177).

Holder had learned that "sexually aggressive women are not rewarded in America by white middleclass heterosexuals, at least not in 'proper' settings." Thus the need to go overseas for the truly adventurous female. Camille Paglia (237) echoes the point: "Being a strong woman, okay, a strong sexual woman, is an absolute horror — because there are very few things that you can do, okay? Really, the number of opportunities for sexual adventurism available to men [and not women] — it's just appalling — through history!"

To be female, hot with bold desire, yet deformed — a disastrous combo in the United States — proves no problem south of the border. In Mexico, a bus driver tells her, "No woman is ugly for us" (Holder 280). Maryse actually begins to feel attractive.

Carlos, Alfonso and Emilio kick off a string of fine-looking, virile men willing to prove the bus driver's observation. Maryse swims in the nude with Carlos: "Saw his body in front of me ... and noticed he had the usual huge easy Mexican erection. I dug giving it to him" (47). The "terrifyingly expert" Eduardo (223) happily disappears below to work magic with his mouth, followed some days later by Eliseo, who loves

1928: Decades after she fell in love with her Syrian guide, at age 66 Margaret Fountaine could still elicit from a man (this time from a **Brazilian** in a riverside hotel along the Amazon) "a look in his eyes which, though familiar enough in the days of my youth I had not seen on the face of any man for years" (*Late Loves* 103). She fled however to her room.

1959: In a **Mexican** village in Guerrero, "boys of all ages, marriageable young men, and occasionally some married men" swarm to the house where anthropology graduate student Peggy Golde lives during fieldwork. She heeds warnings not to engage in intimate relations, "which didn't prevent me from embroidering some fantasies of my own in those occasional cases when I found a man attractive" (85). Her report reveals that Mexican men took great interest in foreign women prior to the 1960s. She accurately forecast that film, TV and the actual sight

of tourists in bikinis would further inflame the "heightened sexuality" of some local men (88).

1968: On an island off **Costa Rica**, anthropologist Ethelyn G. Orso describes responding to aggressive, near-violent courtship by the son of the local patron, who finally takes her standing against an oxcart in a corral (118). The young, pretty fieldworker's experience appears to be one of the first instances of a female anthropology fieldworker giving in to sexual urges.

1975-76: Maryse Holder makes two trips to **Mexico**, engaging in many casual relationships, and appears to have died at the hand of a tough hombre.

1979: Sizable sex migration to **Mexico's** coastal towns becomes quite visible: Young female hippies, "single women in their 30s out for a week's worth of 'good times,' older, divorced and widowed women, seeking some respite from loneliness and their own moral

hugging and turns it into a passionate embrace, a revelation of "the strength of his young arms and in his beautiful back." Eliseo smiles, and comes in her, "unarrogantly huge and easy" (193-94). And Lucio indeed lights up her life with "his extraordinary beauty and youth — a treat, really, for the aging gringa" (65).

Maryse has sex three times with a kitchen helper. She racks up five men in two months. Too overcome with gratitude to be truly aroused, at first she rarely achieves orgasm.

After a sex idyll in Mexico City with an Indian named Miguel who loves her, wants to marry her and treats her kindly, she leaves him (he cries "very voluminous tears," 200) in what seems to be an incredibly destructive act of self-punishment. She hops a bus out of town, drinks more and more, has sex with a 16-year-old boy in a remote coastal town, serves a relatively painless jail sentence for her transgression, records her experiences but comes no closer to transmuting them into great literature. In September 1977, her body is found by the side of the

standards ... come in droves" (Bengis).

1983: Lesbian Peace Corps volunteer Sarah Grossman heads to **Paraguay** with no anticipation of "Latina lovers." Though tempted to come out to two short-haired members of her women's basketball team, she balks, fearful her sexual orientation will jeopardize support for her local projects. She repulses an advance from one of the women, named Marta, but might as well have accepted, as townspeople had seen right through her. Her Paraguayan dinner hosts shriek with laughter one evening when brings home-fried tortillas, for a *tortillera* chef such as herself is slang for "a woman who loves other women" (125).

1985: Gringas visiting **Ecuador** begin in significant numbers to date men in the small city of Otavalo, known for its excellent weaving. Rising income in the area after the mid-1960s had resulted in taller, healthier and better-educated Otaveleños. Some of the locals traveled to Europe and North America, to sell their unique textiles and to busk in the streets. White women began to aggressively pursue these handsome, cosmopolitan and multilingual, yet shy and humble men (Meisch).

1996: Female tourists from North America and Europe visit Margarita Island in **Venezuela** and enter relationships with teen-aged fishermen. One 17-year-old, "Raphael," described his affair with a divorced Swiss woman, 45: "It is normal for boys to have affairs with tourist women, sometimes for love, sometimes for money. The age difference doesn't matter" (O'Connell Davidson, *Venezuela* 22, 12).

• As a newlywed, the author, with bemused husband at her side, endures suggestive leering by local Indian named Suki, clearly used to access to *gringas*, at seaside palm huts in Tulum, on Yucatan coast of **Mexico**.

road, presumably left by a cruel pick-up. She was 36.

In 1979, her letters home were published. A poorly organized book, almost incomprehensible at times, *Give Sorrow Words* explains essential facts either not at all or only in an epilogue. Holder's own letters jump around in time and suddenly introduce new figures by name only. Yet passages describing dynamics of travel sex, especially the discrepancy between an average white woman's sexual magnetism at home and abroad, make Holder's writing canonical for the sexual geographer.

§§§

Now let's visit the world's most complex sexual terrain — lands, some made rich by oil, where men and women struggle today as much as their ancestors did 3,000 years ago with how to handle the bright flare of the sexy woman.

The Middle East
and the Maghreb

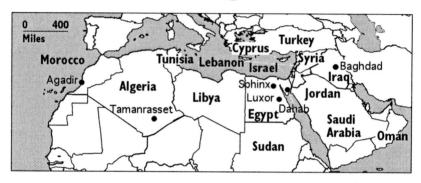

Englishwoman Pamela Windo followed an incredibly handsome, 24-year-old Tunisian boyfriend from London to his home country, where she lived with his family for three years. The year was 1960. She was just 18 but brave and ahead of the crowd. She predated by about seven years the hippie, free love invasion of North Africa.

After three years, she headed west to Morocco. Now in her 60s and a writer living in New York, Windo ("Agadir") recalls an incident from that era. While changing a traveler's check in Agadir, on the coast, a friendly bank cashier in his 30s struck up a conversation, learning that Windo was writing a book and had a boyfriend in Marrakesh. With a mischievous look he asked, "Are you and he lovers?"

Windo admitted, yes. "And was it wonderful?" the cashier said. "Yes," she nodded, smiling.

"I think Moroccan men are very good lovers," he said. Moroccan women, however, were not: "Their husbands have to teach them."

He told her a story about two Norwegian women who had come to his bank to change money. One was in her 50s, the other much younger: "I would talk with them, ask them if they enjoyed being in Morocco. ... One day the older woman told me her watch was broken."

He took the watch to be repaired and refused payment when the Norwegian returned to pick it up. She invited him to dinner in her hotel, not knowing that it was "shameful for us to go to the hotels of foreigners." The bank cashier and a friend took them home for a Moroccan lunch, including couscous and mint tea.

After much laughter, the men drove the happy women back to their hotel. The older woman invited the cashier in for a drink, and this time, he accepted.

He was asked for one more favor: to make love for one hour.

"I felt surprised and shocked, but excited too, and wondered what it would be like. Her age had nothing to do with it. I wasn't in love with her or anything, but I liked her.

"So I took her into the bedroom and it was amazing. She knew many things that Moroccan women don't do, things that made me feel good. It was a beautiful moment. When we finished making love, she looked at me so happy and said thank you, that was the most wonderful lovemaking she'd ever known. She said I gave her more than any man had ever given her. And I wondered how that could be, as she was beautiful and experienced."

The bank cashier knew not the value of his gifts of providing a bit of help, conversation and hospitality, nor the loneliness of many a beautiful, experienced Western woman.

'Ah, the Arabs!'
FINE DESERT STALLIONS, PRIMED TO GALLOP

The knowing Norwegian woman and the vigorous Moroccan fitted together perfectly for one fleeting hour. It's a match often repeated, regardless of age differences, between Western women and Arab men, both parties escaping blandness with their own kind for molten loving.

And many men of the desert draw raves.

As a one-time sexual connoisseur, now retired, it is with some envy I read women's accounts of romps in the Middle East (the area from Turkey and Iran through Saudi Arabia and to Egypt and the Sudan) and the Maghreb (Morocco, Algeria, Tunisia and Libya). I was propositioned once in Athens by a married Iraqi who might have succeeded had he bit a bit taller, handsome and single.

If female travelers are to be believed, men of the rock and sand from Atlantic Morocco to inland Iran can conjure up precious oases of utter sensuality. European ladies have even flown directly into the heart of the Sahara — Tamanrasset in southern Algeria — "to make love in the desert to desert men" (Langewiesche 243). "Ah, if these stones could talk!" mused a local romancer, Addoun, to a visitor.

Put another way: "Ah, the Arabs! They don't last well but there's nothing like them." Sexologist Anne Cumming thus viewed the appeal of the men in Egypt, Iraq, Persia and Morocco she'd taken to bed, and in trains and on horseback (Love Quest 143-44):

"They're tops for size and performance — but it's their attitude as much as their aptitude. ... There's no false puritanism. Have you ever stopped to wonder why the Arab women are so veiled and protected? To protect them from their own raunchy race. The sexual urge is an accepted appetite, to be gratified daily like any other. Women are for that purpose. So if you are alone with a woman for a moment, it is quite normal that you should gobble her up."

Shocking the Sphinx
Morocco and points East

Anne Cumming deftly seduced a Spanish militiaman, described in her first book, *The Love Habit* (read: *The Sex Habit*, described in the Southern Europe chapter).

In her follow-up, *The Love Quest* (i.e., *The Sex Quest*), she divulges dalliances farther afield. In 1950s Marrakesh, she had two lovers daily (17), "Badour the gazelle" to enliven her afternoon siestas, and "Abdelkader the monkey" to clamber over her at night. "They were both neatly circumcised, well hung, and I could not tell their penises apart. Thus they became known as the Heavenly Twins."

A year later she traveled by train to Baghdad, maneuvering her way to stretch out "head to tail" along a bench in her compartment with a Persian as two Turkish men and a parrot slept nearby. She unbuttoned the Persian's fly (59). "Here was one parrot that didn't bite; it leapt into my hand with friendly alacrity, already moist with desire." Despite their awkward angle, the pair enjoyed "pleasurable animal contact" and managed to fulfill each other.

"A country is its people," she concluded, "and you get to know them best in bed." Cumming thought Arab and Persian men made excellent lovers, controlled and considerate, even when they had little prior experience. For example, in 1953, she schooled an Iraqi named Khalid, a virgin whose delirious joy made him a splendid pupil. He managed three orgasms in one hour (75-76).

By 1963 she had moved on to Egypt, again keeping close track (six episodes, three hours) in her Cairo hotel room of the performance of a Cypriot electrician who had arrived to fix the light (132).

At the Sphinx, a handsome Arab horseman in a nightshirt gave her a tour. Mid-ride, out popped his "purple penis, engorged with the excitement of the situation ... under my skirt and between the cheeks of my bent-over bottom." They remained in the saddle for what Cumming rated as "not the most comfortable fuck I have ever had, but one of the most spontaneous" (135).

Afterwards, she raved to her gay male companion, "Max" (actually the American painter Brion Gysin), "Darling, I had almost forgotten how divine the Arabs are! So quick on the draw, so unembarrassed by sex. No puritan ethics to get in the way!"

The Big Four
EGYPT, ISRAEL, TURKEY, MOROCCO

The land of the Pharaohs still rates at the top for traveling women. A woman posting to the Lonely Planet Thorn Tree (Middle East) asked to rate the sexiest men of the Mideast replied, Egypt, without a doubt.

Writer Paul Theroux confirms the keen interest Western women take in the men of the Nile. He met an Egyptian named Ihab, who "knew a thing or two about women, especially foreign women. In his business, which was sales and marketing, he had many sexual proposals from visiting women — all Egyptian men did. Visitors found them attractive" (*Safari* 56).

As an indication of Egyptian allure to foreigners, a guide at Luxor named Salah was able to describe "the distinctive ways in which French girls made love, and German girls and Danish, and English and Canadian ... and Italian, and Dutch, and Lebanese, and of course, American" (Gornick 231; though we must take this report with a grain of salt, as the author has acknowledged fictive elements in elements of her ostensible memoirs — see Kurtz) . And this in 1971 — in the infancy of mass sex tourism by women.

Female travelers posting online (Israeli Men) also praise Israel's high proportion of beautiful men, described as mature, handsome, gentle and romantic, with fit bodies to boot.

California women rave online (Turkish Men) about Turks as gorgeous, romantic, sexy, smart, and among the world's best. A man who described his fellow Turks as romantic sex maniacs got no argument from the ladies.

Some women posting online say Turkish men are talented at oral sex. A friend of mine who briefly lived in Turkey observed that her boyfriend "never did oral — even after I asked ... [laughing out loud] ... poor me. Although I did have a friend tell me her Turkish [boyfriend] would not enter her until she had an orgasm!"

One woman (Middle East) noted good-looking men in Israel, Lebanon and Oman, as well as the Berbers of North Africa.

Morocco, long a destination for gay men, began to draw hippie women in the late 1960s. By the 1990s, older, middle-class Italian and Nordic women arrived, noticed by a gay Italian poet, Aldo Busi (40-41), also lurking on the beaches.

Busi watched a little brunette on the sand with a handsome Moroccan man, muscular and with beautiful teeth, in tow. "He carries her purse, takes the sand off her back, has a deferential attitude — and his prick is always stiff under his shorts." A lot of sex involving foreigners, gays and women alike, Busi said, was conducted hidden in the dunes but "in the open air," a practice also dictated elsewhere in the Islamic world. In Jordan, Annie Caulfield (52) hesitated to offend by openly sharing a hotel room with her Bedouin lover, and they would repair to "the vast, romantic privacy of the desert."

A Manichean choice
SEX IS HEAVEN, SEX IS HELL

In the vast majority of destinations for women seeking no-strings sex — taking Jamaica or Brazil as typical examples — local men are ready partners because they view sex as completely natural: a God-given pleasure both girls and boys may taste early in puberty, continuing for two decades before marrying in their 30s.

In the Islamic world, a different dynamic is at work. Men may well marry in their 30s, but during their sexual prime lack access to release outside of cheerless prostitutes.

Meanwhile, Muslims view the male libido as natural but also capable of exploding into a dangerous wildfire. The Koran describes how man "was created weak" in the flesh (Surah 4:28). In the early Victorian era, English expatriates recorded how Egyptians viewed chastity as difficult for man and woman alike and believed "violent love" arrived by the visitation of Allah and must be satisfied (Duff Gordon, *Egypt* 138). Even today, a Sunni Muslim theologian (Sheikh Yussef Al-Qaradhawi, qtd. in Chancellor) describes male passion as uncontrollable.

Yet any sex play outside marriage is forbidden. "Let those who find not the wherewithal for marriage keep themselves chaste" (Surah 24:33). And even within marriage, women may be too repressed to find enjoyment. Forced to protect their virtue by wearing shapeless clothing, remaining indoors hidden away behind screens, chaperoned outdoors by a male relative, and in the worse case lacking her ritually removed clitoris, the sheltered young Arab woman is not likely to perform harem-girl gyrations in the bedroom.

Concurrently, the intense come-ons of extremely virile men tend to overpower and frighten young female travelers, at least in Morocco. Most of the women who take Moroccan lovers, Windo ("Interview") told me, "are in their 40s, 50s and even 60s. More than anything it is that age. Young foreign women are wary, because the young men there are very eager and potent, very strong seducers, and it can make them nervous. Whereas an older woman is more experienced, she may have gotten out of a marriage" and has less to lose.

When given an opening by older Western females, Arab men apparently turn tigerish. From this ancient region, we can uncover some extraordinary tales of excitement honed to a fever pitch — no surprise when abundant virility is finally permitted an outlet.

Traveling women describe impressively blessed males with insatiable energy. Even Old Testament sexpot Ohol´ibah is quoted in the lively book of Ezekiel (23:19-20) as doting on her Egyptian paramours, for they were hung like stallions ("whose members were like those of asses, and whose issue was like that of horses").

In the current day, we have updated tales of Egyptian men. Scotswoman Trudy Culross got dressed in front of her boyfriend, Hafez, and soon received "that look I'd come to recognize." Clothes off. Afterward, she dressed again and went downstairs. "I saw him looking up at my legs and felt my dress practically removing itself. ... That scene was repeated seven times, believe it or not by the end of which episode, my dress was a crumpled, unwearable heap on the bedroom floor and I wasn't much better" (244).

Similarly, Annie Caulfield fell in love with a Jordanian named Rathwan, with Omar Sharif eyes: "... some days, passion came stinging through the hot air in a passing glance" (15).

Yet a Muslim man feels delicious torment as he reaches for his Christian (or even Jewish) girlfriend, doubly forbidden as an infidel and a woman not his wife (Caulfield 251; Gornick 262). After nights of mingled lust and tenderness, a muscular Egyptian policeman shared his second thoughts with writer Vivian Gornick (131): "I cannot fall in love with an American. I will not fall in love with an American. I am not in love with an American."

Still, a Middle Eastern man has little need to deny his manly urges with a foreign woman, for she is a safe target, unlike a co-religionist. And a foreign woman is "more sexually knowledgeable and uninhibited than Moroccan women" (Windo, "Interview"), knowing all sorts of bedchamber tricks he never imagined.

Further, a foreign woman interests an Arab man on other levels. "The young men feel an incredible need for contact with, and curiosity" toward foreign women, Windo notes, "whether it's for money, for language practice, relief from lack of opportunities in life and boredom," or to gain information about the wider world.

From temple priestesses to carnal gays

Although Italy has the longest contemporary record of congeniality to lonely traveling women, the Middle East has compiled a deep, sweeping history of female sexuality itself.

As mentioned in the History chapter, thousands of years ago, temple priestesses performed cultic sex rites in Assyria. And from Egypt to the Fertile Crescent, vigorous, lusty women, then as now, loved a man in uniform. In the Old Testament, Ezekiel (23:15-17) describes Ohol'ibah, a young woman who, after reaching the age of love, tore up Egyptians, Assyrian warriors and young Chaldean cavalrymen with flowing turbans, who "came to her into the bed of love, and they defiled her with their lust."

Veiling laws and the emergence of Judaism and later Christianity attempted to curb harlots, who nonetheless continued to remain the people's favorites for a long time. When Islam arrived with Mohammed 600 years after Christ, women's status and sexuality were lowered further. Yet Islam coexisted for much of the next 1,000 years with an ever-expanded collection of sexy stories of queens committing adultery with black slaves and lively harem goings-on, burnished by storytellers in Persia, Baghdad, Cairo and Syria to become *The Arabian Nights*.

When Victorian travelers such as Jane Digby, Emily Keene, Isabelle Eberhardt and Margaret Fountaine arrived in the Islamic world, they readily found devoted lovers, men who often divorced or abandoned their Muslim wives faster than you can say "Koran" to demonstrate their willingness to conform to Western expectations of marriage based on mutual respect. The sensual *Arabian Nights* side of their robed desert men blossomed and won over Koranic injunctions against infidels ("the worst of creatures," Surah 98:6) and the perils of lustful women (Surah 4:25).

Even Islam's rulers took an early and continuing interest in Western women. By the 1580s, pirates had delivered a Venetian noblewoman to the harem of Turkish sultan Murad IV. The woman, Sultana Baffa, bore the sultan a male successor. Two centuries later, history repeated itself when Algerian pirates captured French colonial Aimée Dubucq de Rivery on a ship bound from her school in France home to Martinique (Branch 214). Also sold into the sultan's harem, she bore Selim III a male successor (Chidester).

In 1873, Emily Keene agreed to marry a smitten shareef, the religious leader of all Morocco. In more recent times, Egypt's Anwar Sadat married a half-English woman, and in 1980 Lebanon's married leader, Bashir Gemayal, launched an affair with an ABC news producer (Newman). I have a second-hand report from a well-connected freelance writer of Libya's leader Moammar Gaddafi holding a news conference, inviting journalists to his residence, and being taken up by a female Westerner who went over on her own.

"Marriage with foreign women [has] subverted nations and governments," a commentator (Gurumurthy) remarked in the context of the Italian

Sonia Gandhi running for office in India. The reason for his alarm? "The marital bliss that the Arab kings and Sheikhs found in the western women repeatedly proved to be the undoing of the Arab cause."

Clearly, the Indian writer is taking aim at Jordan's King Hussein (as well as other liaisons listed above). Hussein indeed found marital bliss with wife No. 2, a beautiful Englishwoman, and wife No. 4, Lisa Halaby, a beautiful American. And he made peace with Israel. A connection is assumed by critics, who note that his half-Western children speak English as their mother tongue and are imperfect in Arabic.

At least Hussein was open about his preferences for Western women, marrying them rather than paying for sexual services. Over in Saudi Arabia, after the death of the serious-minded Saudi King Ibn Saud (Mather) in 1953, sundry of the thousands of the king's oil-wealthy direct descendants and cousins turned to hedonism, and the term "playboy prince" and "womanizer" became almost synonymous with "Saudi ruling family."

Away from home, they drank and partied and hired European prostitutes in wholesale quantities. Yes, the wider world has for eons been a dire threat to a Muslim man's religious identity.

How Arab men learned of Western love

In the 1930s, Arab literature began to record themes growing from the experiences of men who went off to study in Europe and entered often-complex relationships with Western women (Hopwood 252-73). The authors included Egyptians, Lebanese, Sudanese, Syrians, Libyans and Franco-Algerians.

As happened with scholars from the Caribbean and Africa, expatriate students in London and Paris found themselves in demand as exotic, taboo lovers. For the Arab, however, the experience was likely a greater shock, coming from lands where "no Arab brother would allow his sisters to have a sexual relationship outside marriage" (253).

Well ahead of the video revolution and the international explosion of pornography, Arab men who had traveled and returned home, as shabby students or regal royals, retained confidence in their ability to win over Western females — including tourists.

Fundamentalists were scandalized. And by the late 1970s, at least one man, Osama bin Laden, evolved from just another Saudi playboy prince, admiring the girls on a trip to Sweden and later chasing European blondes in Beirut (A. Robinson; Lines; Mackinnon), to pious Muslim and terror master, with dreadful consequences for the United States.

Bin Laden, who has plenty of money and educated operatives, still needs foot soldiers and popular support. The Arab of pent-up desires cannot find a job, a woman, a future or hope, yet knows the open secret that his nation's playboy princes party with white women. He lashes out at the loved and hated West, and the nexus between terrorism and a lack of physical release becomes stronger.

The sexual frustration is real: Vivian Gornick (137), living in Egypt in the early 1970s, describes how a well-dressed undersecretary shook with a convulsive orgasm as they wrestled and she tried to fight off his crazed attempts to kiss her; later, a married businessman virtually duplicated that first incident of sexual hysteria. On a train ride to Luxor (214-15), she endured eight hours of keen sexual tension in her compartment with a young engineer named Fouad, who begged in whispers, "Stay beside me this night. Stay." A young platonic male friend, Mohammed, admitted, "when I am alone, I think of making love to you. I see you all ways on the bed" (324).

Like many other Egyptians that Gornick meets, Mohammed displays an almost feminine sensitivity and wariness of being used when Gornick confesses to having slept with two other men: "Have you come here to make a sexual study of the men of Egypt?" He senses an affront to his manhood, one that stings because it arrives from a female infidel.

Osama bin Laden, Princess Diana
THE WEST'S SECRET WEAPON: SEXY WOMEN

In the Arab world more than anywhere else, sex with a local man thrusts the lovers into a powerful nexus of politics and history.

Way back in 1966, a sociologist in Israel observed the budding relationships between shy, lonely Arab youths and visiting Scandinavian women and later produced the first social science report ever published on Western female sex adventurers. Erik Cohen ("Arab Boys" 232) presciently noted that tourist girls provided the youths with an alternative to "extreme activism (found in nationalism) and extreme passivity (found in drugs)." Decades before Sept. 11, he identified the life of the unmarried young Arab as a tense, unhappy, "pitiful and eventless," such that just to obtain a blonde visitor's home address offered a shining ray of hope for a decent life — overseas (226, 227).

After the bombing of the World Trade Center in 2001, tabloid newspapers pounced on the topic of sex 'n' terror with articles that seem far-fetched but certainly obey the very real logic of how itinerate females from the West, from backpackers to British aristocrats, blithely subvert Islam and threaten Middle Eastern governments.

Indeed, how much did the stakes escalate when, rather than a passing tourist from Ohio, a British princess — one of the world's most glamorous figures — dated a Muslim.

"Bin Laden Had Diana Murdered," blared one headline (Herz). "Princess was targeted because of her influence on the Muslim world." After her divorce from Prince Charles, Diana dated first a Pakistani heart surgeon and then Egyptian Dodi Fayed, son of a billionaire. Her boyfriends became the talk of the Middle East. Would an Arab man steal a British royal, gleefully trumping a nation of millions of men descended from the Crusaders? Who was more worried about the ramifications: Queen Elizabeth, Israel, or Arab fundamentalists?

A romance that might have resulted in the Queen's grandchildren having a half-Arab sibling has spurred almost as many conspiracy theories as the Kennedy assassination. Bin Laden, Israel's Mossad, and even the CIA have all been implicated in Diana's fatal 1997 car crash.

Princess Diana's post-divorce fascination with Arab men and the attendant controversies, which alarmed both Westerners and Middle Easterners alike, are those of the traveling woman writ large.

"Tourism in its present form is an abomination," claimed the leader of an Egyptian Islamic group, justifying attacks against foreign visitors (qtd. in Hopwood 283). "It is a means by which prostitution and AIDS are spread by Jewish women tourists, and it is a source of all manner of depravities."

In fact, Saudi Arabia and the United Arab Emirates are taking steps to discourage their men from marrying foreign women (Ahmad; Reuters).

A novel by Sulayman Fayyad (*Voices*, qtd. in Hopwood 266-68), dramatically illustrates the threat of a foreign spouse. Egyptian villagers attack the French wife of a man named Hamid. Simone is said to parade around in skimpy clothes, to bewitch the village headman and to agitate men by her free ways. Angry women seize her and cut off her clitoris, a bald metaphor for making the Western woman as incapable of pleasure as the virginal Arab girl.

In the same vein, a British sociologist (Bowman) found real-life anti-Western hostility when he followed in Cohen's footsteps decades later to revisit Arabs and tourists in Israel. A teen-age Arab shopkeeper in Jerusalem, Salim, described how he persuaded a 31-year-old New Yorker to sneak away from her rich, older, sleeping husband at night to meet him. Salim took her to a "a dirty little room," pleasured her (he said) until 5 a.m., and won high praise for his skill and the size of his "Palestinian cock."

Then comes the classic: Salim called her "just a slut" and said "she fucked with everyone in all the countries she'd been in" (86).

The tale novelistically conveys the ancient world, unchanged from the Old Testament and the Koran through the present. The religious man is forbidden to enjoy harlotry yet cannot really resist the opportunity. And once he wins a woman's body, he is consumed by paranoia that this sexy woman is just a whore. Yet the good virgin he must marry, a girl barely out of childhood, is lousy in bed. But who knows if he will marry at all, with no jobs available. In anger and confusion, he lashes out.

Similar echoes of an ancient cult of virginity reverberate in the tale of American writer Mona Simpson (162), who on visit to explore her Egyptian roots had her period arrive, shortly after sex with her tall, thin, teen-aged driver. He became overcome with devotion for this woman he believes to have saved herself for him and wrapped a rose petal around her reluctant ring finger, saying simply, "Marrying."

Divinity and deviltry in desert men

Unless the man is truly unique or truly Westernized, matches of an Arab man and a Western woman can be quite difficult, so much so that the Vatican has even cautioned Roman Catholic women against entered such unions (Darlington). While women marrying Masai warriors in bush country try to bridge a giant gap between pre-industrial and Information Age mindsets, many of those with Arabs seem to face an equally formidable abyss on the question of her actual importance as a human being, one viewed as second class in Islamic law.

DISADVANTAGES

• **Young women may struggle with overwhelming come-ons**. Older women, as noted by Windo, are more likely to have the maturity to nego-tiate an intimate relationship or conversely to steer men away from innu-endo into neutral conversation about culture and history (Hubbard). Parts of the Islamic world, notably Pakistan and Egypt, and to an extent Morocco, have moved into the category of Zones of Harassment for the female traveler. A Maryland mental health professional who traveled in Egypt told me she felt "the eyes of all the men of Cairo mentally undressing her" and considered Egyptian men handsome but unpleasant.

• The flip side of the rugged masculinity of many a Middle Eastern man may be **behavior that borders on the tyrannical**. He may initially trea-sure the independence of a Western girlfriend, and then at engagement or marriage become violently jealous and possessive, attempting to con-trol her every move. As discussed in the Experiences chapter, Western women who live in Islamic states lose rights to freedom of movement and control of children. In Saudi Arabia especially, they may find daily life akin to being in a prison given the almost incomprehensible gap between Western and Saudi laws and customs regarding women (for an excellent discussion, see www.victimsofsaudikidnapping.org).

• **Men display a baffling mix of emotional intelligence and outbursts of displeasure**, often sparked by Western female attitudes. Vivian Gornick

(6-7) described her Egyptian lover Ali Mahmoud as "capable of grasping and describing the elements of emotional behavior with great clarity, great distinction, great detail." His sensitivity gave him the control to wait for meaningful sex. "He was the most sensual man I have ever known — and yet, he had not slept with a woman in more than a year because the sexual directness of Cambridge women shriveled his soul, and muted his desire."

A well-traveled Maryland friend of mine in her 30s, J.S., e-mailed me to say she "loved" the emotional intelligence of the men she met while working as a teacher in Turkey. "I remember being upset one evening and this guy told me, 'You should talk about it — it's not good to keep things inside. What do you want me to know?' Whew! And we did talk — and it was just like talking to a good friend.

"I often felt like I was hanging out with a woman when I'd talk to all the men I knew — much more mature in some ways — but my incredible independence bothered them. I often got the message that I 'didn't know my place' or said what was on my mind way too much."

Middle Eastern men can be torn between modern yearning for a soulmate and desiring a sexy companion with loads of personality in bed, and traditional belief that women should be deferential and his wife must be a virgin, which may require a man in his 30s to marry a 17-year-old (Gornick 261). This conflict, as well as resentment of the West, may eventually cause Arab men to denigrate as a slut a foreign woman who does agree to have sex with him, as mentioned in the case of Salim the Jerusalem shopkeeper (see also Hopwood 258).

• **Men may be shocked by cultural differences.** Many Muslim women use a homemade sugar concoction to "wax" off underarm and pubic hair monthly, often after their periods, according to a friend of mine who has lived in the Arab world. Muslims may perceive Western women as dirty for not waxing (Tournier qtd. by Hopwood 265). In a novel entitled *Women of Sand and Myrrh* (al-Shaykh) — a novel whose credibility in cultural observation is supported by outside observers — a Gulf Arab named Maaz is shocked and a bit disgusted when he first observes his American married lover, Suzanne, entirely naked and with full public hair (211).

My friend J.S. confirmed by e-mail that "they ALL shave in Turkey — pits and pubes. When I asked M. why, he said because he didn't feel clean unless he shaved — to which I exclaimed — 'Oh my god — do you think I'm dirty because I don't shave?' I started shaving that week and kept it up until months after I got home to the USA."

• **Mixed feelings about female passion.** *Women of Sand and Myrrh* (201-02), and *al-Sayyida Vienna* (*The Lady of Vienna*, described by Hopwood 260-61), depict Arab men as excited by bedding an eager and responsive female

— and then becoming overwhelmed. In *Women*, Suzanne keeps moving after her lover Maaz comes first. "Damn your race! You're a devil!" he cried. Maaz accuses Suzanne of doing things for her own pleasure: "You seemed like a man to me, when you were crying out."

Given practices such as the removal of Egyptian women's clitori — "the fear of female sexuality is at the root of the problem" (Hopwood 266) — male schizophrenia about pining for great sex yet being fearful of female lust should come as no surprise.

- **Professional bisexuality**, particularly among men in tourist sectors of Morocco (a huge gay destination) and Egypt (Theroux, *Safari* 34, 56), poses a risk of HIV to reckless women.

- **A need to be discrete.** Women should make an effort not to get their devoted man in trouble. Annie Caulfield (52) and Rathwan stayed in non-touristy hotels in traditional areas of Jordan and had to be careful to return by morning to separate bedrooms.

ADVANTAGES

- **Very handsome men.** Caulfield entitled her book about a romance with a Jordanian *Kingdom of the Film Stars*, a reference to the stunning looks and Omar Sharif eyes of her lover, Rathwan, and his two best friends. Salah and Bashir resemble "two young Italian film stars," flashing "white teeth and [the] glint of glossy black hair" (67).

- **Older Western woman should find excellent options** in the Middle East, especially in Morocco and Egypt.

Muslim men are said to lack hang-ups about age differences: Arab culture, according to more than one woman posting online (Middle East — Mixed Marriages), sees nothing amiss in a sexual relationship or marriage between a young man and an older woman. An older woman's body retains its appeal. In the novel *Women of Sand and Myrrh*, overweight Suzanne describes her lover Maaz as taking "hold of the folds of flesh as if he were snatching up gold in Ali Baba's cave" (al-Shaykh 184).

Further, adherents of Islam cite the example of the prophet Mohammed himself, who in 595 A.D. married a wealthy widow 15 years his senior and enjoyed a happy union for 24 years, until her death.

A Muslim man also sees, in the older female, someone "who has enough money not to be stressed and who's an animal in bed" (DMT, Middle East — Mixed Marriages). Put another way, "most Middle Eastern men prefer foreign older women because the sex is better." However, out of earshot Egyptians may mock older tourists: "In Luxor they have a name for these kinds of women — 'Mummies' " (NileDoc, Middle East — Mixed Marriages).

- Moroccan men pride themselves on bedroom skills, as the bank cashier in Agadir described above remarked matter of factly. They appear to have the inclination, upon escaping cultural prerogatives against pre-marital sex and liaising with tourists, to explore passion and poetry with a woman and become "very, very sexual ... they don't have the repression Western men have," as one Maryland woman who had taught in Syria told me. "It's torrid, it's great, the men are naturally flirtateous."

Another Moroccan man posted to Morocco.com that he did not consider himself a real man until he saw his lady with smiling eyes to express her happiness and physical satisfaction. Asked by his American ex-girlfriend where he learned his secrets, he told her it was a national secret, related to an innately romantic and hot-blooded nature.

Some Moroccan men, however, are gifted physically but not in terms of skills. "While in Spain I dated a Moroccan," my friend J.S. e-mailed me. "He told me how he had to tone things down for Barcelona. Also, he was a terrible lover with a huge cock — but wouldn't let me teach him anything — he was in such a hurry to get it on!"

- **Men in some countries, such as Morocco**, may have limited interest in emigrating; thus their interest in foreign women may be somewhat less calculating and more romantic.

- **Sweet talk comes readily to many Muslims**, raised in a culture that perhaps more than any other treasures poetry, with between 35 and 60 different Arabic words for love, and endearing (though overworked) compliments, such as calling a pretty woman a gazelle.

Despite contemporary repression, the Middle East is after all the home of the bawdy tales in *The Arabian Nights*. In *Women of Sand and Myrrh*, Maaz tells Suzanne his love is as vast as the sand and the sky. "He was like a man worshipping at a pagan shrine, uttering incantations," Suzanne said of Maaz. After they first made love, "he closed his eyes, letting his body go loose, murmuring that now he would welcome the Angel of Death" (183). He wanted no more from life than the bliss of their communion. He would kiss her feet and mutter, "More fragrant than sandalwood or incense." Her skin he called "pure silk."

- **Western women are deeply divided on the merits of marriage to a Middle Eastern man**. On the Lonely Planet Thorn Tree discussion boards, male travelers warn their sisters that they are regarded as a walking passport or cash dispenser (Middle East — Mixed Marriages). However, some women reported being treated like gold by uniquely sensitive men. In the desert a lucky woman may find a true romantic of touching earnestness, a man likely to marry the first girl or woman that he falls in love with. Novels by Arab men portraying romances with Western women have featured the man as highly idealistic and devoted in love (Hopwood 255).

Lebanese men win highest marks as being fairly Westernized and making good husbands for a woman on their wavelength. On the

Middle East and Maghreb timeline

1538-1905: Beginning with the abduction by pirates of a Venetian woman given to the Turkish sultan, through the times of Victorian women who loved Turks, Syrians, Egyptians, Moroccans, Tunisians and Algerians (see History chapter), Muslim men find fascination with exotically free Western women.

1952: British translator and later sex activist Anne Cumming embarks on first casual sexual escapade recorded after World War II — in **Morocco**. She continues through **Syria** and **Iraq (1953)** and **Egypt (1963)**.

1960: Writer Pamela Windo follows lover to **Tunisia**, later moves to **Morocco**, predating the hippie invasion of North Africa.

1961: A British army officer's daughter, Antoinette "Toni" Gardner, becomes the second wife of **Jordan's** King Hussein. In **1978**, American-born Lisa Halaby becomes the king's fourth and final wife.

1966: Sociologist Erik Cohen observes Arab youths pursuing tourist women in **Israel**.

1968: In **Morocco**, an early hippie, Bernadine Coverly, escapes London with her two daughters and meets Bilal, a kind, handsome Berber acrobat. Later, the hippie's daughter, Esther Freud, captures their romance with great sympathy in her semi-autobiographical novel *Hideous Kinky* (1992), filmed in 1998. During the filming, director Gillies MacKinnon shows Esther a photograph of Bilal, saying, "We think he died two years ago. One of the drivers knew him. Apparently at some point he had two American wives" (Freud, "Joy").

1980: A novel by **Syrian** author Shakib al-Jabiri depicts a Western woman telling her Arab lover that "hundreds of my country women are eager for the sun, the sand, and the men of the East" (qtd. in Hopwood 284).

1992: In **Tunisia**, a dramatic film called *Bezness* explores the world of a sea-

Thorn Tree (Lebanese men), one woman described successful marriages involving Lebanese guys and foreign girls, especially if the woman was sympathetic to traditional ways of having the man as head of the family. Many children of mixed-Lebanese marriages also attest to strong unions between their parents at the Web site MarriedtoanArab.com.

When Annie Caulfield wrote of her love affair with a Jordanian man, her goal was to tell "of an exception to all those bleak contemporary tales" of abusive Arab men who abduct their children from the West. Both Caulfield and Vivian Gornick describe deep empathy and uncanny understanding between themselves and their lovers.

• **Low HIV rates**. If there is a silver lining to the cloud of sexual repression in the Middle East, it is low rates for HIV (though syphilis is said to be a problem in Morocco). Be forewarned that gigolos who service women in Morocco and in the feluccas cruising the Nile also trick with gay men, which heightens the risk of illness for the unwary visit-

side gigolo who services Western gays and women. The main character, Rufa, tells French girls he will drive them wild, while keeping his local girlfriend caged from Western influence (she might want sexual freedom too!) and bullying and hitting his independent-minded sister (Hopwood 285).

• Gay men notice they are beginning to share handsome, inexpensive **Moroccan** lovers with visiting European women (Busi 40).

1996: Englishwoman from Liverpool starts Aphrodite Tours to bring unattached U.K. women (most between 30 and 60) to **Cyprus** for romance, in wake of her own rejuvenating post-divorce affair with a young restaurant keeper (Reid; Kemp).

1997: More evidence of tourist women as initiators in **Egypt**: The Red Sea Bedouin village of Dahab attracts hippie women, in a scene reminiscent of Goa in India. "... A substantial number of foreign women ... visit Dahab

regularly in pursuit of relationships with Egyptian men" (Bahbehanian).

• In a testament to the ubiquity of romance on the road at tourist sites, at the remote ruins at Petra in **Jordan**, "Marlboro Boys," young horsemen, make plays for visiting tourist women (Caulfield 219).

2003: In April, an **Iraqi** in Najaf, while welcoming liberating U.S. troops, pithily connects the dots between the West and sexual freedom. He said he believed the Americans would bring "Democracy. Whiskey. And sexy!" (Dwyer).

• Paul Theroux describes a young boatman approaching him to say, "We go. Nice felucca. We find Nubian banana." He demurred but noted "young women, singly or in pairs, being sailed by **Egyptians**, singly or in pairs," putting themselves at the disposal of "these priapic young men. ... The embankments of the Nile rang with the shrieks of Europeans being pleasured on board feluccas" (*Safari* 34, 56).

ing female. A female informant stresses that gay Western tourists and the aversion of many Middle Eastern men to using condoms make the picture riskier than the statistics below suggest.

HIV-infected adults per 1,000

Morocco	1
Israel	1
Turkey	less than 1
Egypt	less than 1
For comparison:	
North America	6
Europe	3

Source: UNAIDS

Now let's go to Oceania, to remote areas with limited tourism and as much sexual license as the Near East has sexual repression.

Oceania

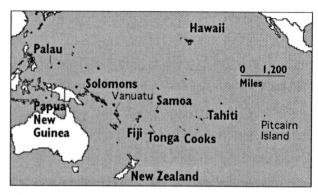

Any reader brought low by combat fatigue in the dating wars can take courage from the story of California-born Joana McIntyre Varawa.

This accomplished sailor lived for 10 years in Hawaii, where she wrote books about whales and served as a harbormaster. In her 50s, she traveled to Fiji, a Western Pacific crossroads between Melanesia and Polynesia. Fijians are a handsome, strong dark people with high foreheads, expressive eyes and hair that often forms a soft, fuzzy corona.

On her third night, Joana met a local girl who asked frankly about her situation (*Changes* 3): "Did I have a lot of money? A little. Was I married? No, not any longer. Did I have any children? Yes, one grown son who was a boat captain and who traveled a lot. Did I want to marry a Fijian?"

Joana considered the out-of-the-blue question seriously. "I had been mate-seeking for years, ever since my marriage broke up, when my son was young. Western men were often eager for bed, but not often eager for marriage."

She replied that yes, she might want indeed consider marriage to a Fijian. Taken to the girl's home village on a smaller island, Varawa was introduced as a woman of means seeking a husband. In one fell swoop, the lonely vacationer ascended from being an unwanted older woman in the World of the Dating Wars to being fought over by rival families to whom she was of great worth.

She became attracted to Malé, like many Pacific people a captivating singer (10). "I looked sideways at him, a handsome man with oblong dark-ringed eyes, luxuriant hair, a broad nose, and a moustache that molded full lips. His brown body, clothed in old rugby shorts and a faded sleeveless T-shirt, looked sleek and healthy."

A day after their first meeting, Malé proposed marriage. Joana was 54, Malé, 22. But what did age matter? Malé's father had advised him that a match would be practical: Joana could buy the family a new boat, outboard motor, fishing net, clothes and watches. As nothing could be more important than family survival, Malé obeyed his father.

Polynesian heirs of these Edenlike bits of geography have an unsettingly pragmatic attitude when it comes to romance, more related to survival of the tribe than to finding "true love."

Kernahan (136)

Joana examined herself realistically, in fact a bit harshly: "I was no beauty, and it was unlikely that anyone would want me for my looks; at least no one had. My body was good, strong and healthy; the sexual desire that had driven me into believing that I was in love with countless men was starting to fade."

She captured the swift and plain-dealing nature of marriage propositions outside of the West. "It all seemed so strange yet so forthright. ... No one in the last twenty years had offered to marry me." She decided love was something that could be constructed over time (*Changes* 23).

They rode a roller-coaster in their early days. Joana wanted privacy to write, her provisions to be hers alone — desires at odds with the communal behavior in many preindustrial societies.

Joana also sought time alone with Malé and romantic gestures from him, yet he vastly preferred to talk to his cousins. When he suffered severe stomach pain, Joana's expensive medicine did not work — only his uncle's patient deep massage.

Over time, she gained insight into the importance of saying yes to Malé's requests to leave her for family activities. Gradually, he began to kiss her on the lips and demonstrate affection.

When women seek romance on the road, a profound paradox may occur. They find true commitment in cultures that really don't believe in romantic love, where attractive, dark, young men will readily marry them — the stuff of purest romance novel fantasy.

The world's greatest diaspora

Out of Southeast Asia, probably via Borneo or other parts of Indonesia, came talented navigators who over the past few thousand years settled the dots of land speckling Earth's largest geographic feature, the Pacific (Belliveau, *Amateur* 117). Canoe seafarers first settled Melanesia ("black islands," or more accurately, islands of dark people) and Micronesia ("tiny islands"), and lastly discovered Polynesia ("many islands").

Let's start with the tiny islands of Micronesia. These islands sweep in a crescent east of the Philippines and host many Japanese tourists,

Postscript to a best seller

Joana McIntyre Varawa updated me via telephone on what happened to the couple after their tumultuous courtship and marriage, chronicled in her 1989 book, *Changes in Latitude.*

Some time after *Changes* was published, they moved together to Hawaii. She edited the *Lanai Times.* Malé received high wages as a construction laborer. One day, a 300-lb. pipe walloped him in the head. He could not work and lost his income.

And Malé entered a love affair with another woman who became his girlfriend, and now he "comes and goes very freely" between the two, Varawa said. But he lives with Joana, and she cares for him now that he is injured and lives in pain.

She says of the arrangement, "It's good in many ways, it allows me room to have a creative life, because he's not around all the time. I have what is best for me at this age. I'm old enough to be amazed he's still with me."

Despite a significant age difference, "the years dissolve," she says. "There's a Hawaiian word: ma'a. What it means you're totally familiar with something, like if you live on a ship, you'd know where everything is in a storm.

"For some reason our attachment is very deep, something hard to attain. Every time I say I can find something better, I get an excruciating feeling in the pit of my stomach. The feeling was so profound, the only I could think of was patching it up.

"He reciprocates in his own peculiar way. I'm his true wife, his real wife." (The arrangement sounds like ones found in sub-Saharan Africa and the Middle East, where the senior wife wields much authority.)

Malé returned home during our long-distance conversation. He chirped in the background to challenge his wife when she described him as not romantic. Joana put her husband on the phone.

In a cordial, direct, charming voice, Malé noted a single, tender gesture. "I came home one day and saw a note that she was walking the dog in the mountains. I brought a drink from ava, a plant, and something to eat."

He spoke of life on Lanai, where he knows only one fellow Fijian. "It's totally different to my culture. It's lonely." Does he miss his family? "Oh yes." He speaks with them sev-

---

particularly divers, which may explain a paucity of female sex tourism mentions in English. I can find only one report, which notes that some Japanese women have married local men on the diving jewel of Palau (Yamashita, Japanese Encounter).

More is known about women's activities south of the Equator, in Melanesia and Polynesia. Let's begin with Melanesia, islands scattered from Micronesia to Australia and New Zealand. Mountainous New Guinea (split politically between independent Papua New Guinea and Indonesia's Irian Jaya province) looms in the west, the Solomon Islands and New Caledonia in the middle, and Vanuatu at the southeast.

eral times a week via telephone.

Joana returned. We were both bemused by Malé's confident way of marshaling a scrap of evidence to support his way of thinking. Joana said he once lectured her that a man should have five wives, such that after each quarrel he could move to the next.

"By the time he got back to the first wife, she'd be glad to see him again."

I mentioned that an academic book on travel writing (Holland), almost comical in its misogyny, had attacked Varawa's descriptions of the buff men in Fiji, specifically a passage lauding "their strong bodies, muscular arms and chests, the seductive careless way they wrap their sulu when they get up, the pervasive courtesy of their talk and motion" (*Changes* 90).

Admiring a beautiful foreign man became, in the words of the academics, "flagrant cultural voyeurism" and "imperialist exoticism. ... Fijians' seductive bodies become commodified objects of desire" (Holland 127, 128).

"They're probably jealous," Varawa said with crispness. "It's the white man's burden."

"They don't have a clue as to what is so delightful about a dark husband," I said, thinking about my own mixed-race husband's warmth and fairness, and quickness to forgive.

"Well they do," said Varawa, "they do have a clue." And they are jealous and at the same time derogatory. "They think black people are never good enough. That thread runs throughout Western Anglo-Saxon culture that white people are better. It's racism."

"Well if it's racism," I said, "it's hiding behind a backdrop of saying that to find dark men appealing and attractive is to turn them into objects." Such reasoning struck me as aligning radical academics with the Ku Klux Klan, as both essentialc ly believed that white women should never stray from their own kind.

Both seemed to find sexual attraction to non-whites damnable, although the academics seemed to go further and just about deem female lust for any attractive man distasteful.

Well fine, we'll have the end of the human race," Varawa said. "That will let the animals live in peace. I think that all those university persons should not perpetuate."

Menace in Melanesia

In the strange islands flung east off the coast of New Guinea, a disturbing shadow of mystery, danger and fear falls over reports of female travelers and men without a sign of tenderness in their eyes. Could it be that some tribal males are simply be too exotic for Western women, even connoisseurs willing to try almost anything?

If so, Melanesians, especially New Guinea's highlanders, would qualify. Their bristly wild beards frame faces painted for ceremonies in cadaverous gray or Satanic red and yellow. They wear gourds on their penises, kus-kus claws or boar tusks in their noses, wigs of human hair, bird plumage on their ears, bubble-wrap breastplates and elaborate headgear out of the wardrobe of Elizabeth I. Some clans cover their skin in pig grease.

With their prominent brows, broad noses, stocky near-naked bodies and woolly hair, highland tribesmen may be too startlingly primitive looking — by another magnitude of order above the Masai or Samburu warrior — to sexually attract the tiny handful of female travelers who happen their way. Highland men appear to lack appeal despite the fact that they take personal adornment and beautification quite seriously (Dodwell, *Papua* 123; Sargent 16; Salak 373) and tend to appear in photographs as keen-eyed, near-naked figures with powerful backs, sculpted buttocks, perfectly bowed quads and chiseled calves, the better to scale the vertical cliffs and raging rivers that isolate many villages.

The lack of interest may be mutual. Dani tribesmen give an impression of possessing "very weak sexual interests" (Sargent 60), perhaps related to a general revulsion toward women. Further, whites ("dim dims") may be viewed as subhuman, ugly and pale (Theroux, *Oceania* 150; Wheeler 242). Tasha Hepworth, the daughter of English settlers, was rejected as wife material when offered by her desperate mother to the son of a Solomon island chief; though white and rich, she was schizophrenic, and thus rated lower than any healthy Melanesian (Irvine, *Faraway* 373).

Still, we have at least one apparent report of travel romance in New Guinea, and quite a curious tale it is. Wyn Sargent, a Quaker photojournalist, visited Irian Jaya, the Indonesian half of the great island. A rather meddlesome idealist, she decided that a marriage feast would unite three warring tribes in the Baliem Valley — and proposed herself as the bride! The powerful, charismatic local chief, Obaharok, readily accepted (201-03). They married in 1973, at a huge feast still the talk of the valley decades later.

Sargent appears to deny consummating the relationship. She declared to Obaharok, "I can't be like your other Dani wives. I couldn't work in the sweet-potato gardens or raise pigs. I have my own work I must do. Things after marriage would be the same as they are now." (This legalistic wording does not entirely rule out premarital intimacy.)

But local tribesmen insist to this day that the pair slept together (Butt 58-60) and that for some weeks the couple lived together happily. Certainly Sargent warmly describes Dani people as handsome and sweet, and the chief as attractive. A photograph of Obaharok shows a striking man with a high forehead, straight nose, and fine cheekbones and temples, wearing a turban topped by fur and feathers, boar tusks through the nose, and a choker and beaded breastplate gleaming white against his dark muscles.

A month after her wedding, Sargent was hounded from the valley by Indonesian authorities, apoplectic that not only that she had begun to protest police brutality but that she had likely had sex with a black man, whom they viewed as unspeakably primordial.

One senses a certain horror among colonial whites (a horror shared by Indonesians) of the prospect of a Melanesian with a white woman. In 1926, the White Women's Protection Ordinance was passed in Papua New Guinea, in response to some incidents of touching between servants and mistresses (Strobel 7). In the 1940s, a young Melanesian boy was "jailed for being on the same path as a white woman," according to an old man living off the coast of New Guinea (Irvine, *Castaway* 244).

In the decades after Wyn Sargent, Western women display no attraction to highland men. Nearly 25 years later, also in Irian Jaya's Baliem Valley, a chief proposed obliquely to a startled married anthropologist, Leslie Butt (55), that she become his seventh wife. She avoided him thereafter.

Female travelers in fact grew to fear many highlanders, with good reason. A quartet of women have written travel books about their time in New Guinea (Christina Dodwell, Isabella Tree and Kira Salak, as well as Sargent). All except Tree, who was escorted by a local official, report some combination of rape attempts, threatening leers and efforts to break into their flea-infested sleeping areas.

Jacket photos reveal that these four writers all fall in the attractive-to-very-beautiful range. Yet while they attracted the crudest of advances, none stirred sincere romantic approaches (Sargent had to propose to the chief, rather than vice versa). White women may hold little serious interest for New Guinea highlanders and for non-Fijian Melanesians, barring the proposal Leslie Butt received.

One imagines that even in the New Guinea highlands, at least one or two Western woman might have partaken of a raw Stone Age encounter, an experiment that makes dalliances with the Masai look like dating an accountant.

Still, the rudimentary culture that makes New Guinea the darling of swarms of anthropologists trying to study pre-metal-working humans may simply put off women sexually.

But gay men are a different story. The best-known sex traveler to Melanesia would be New York artist Tobias Schneebaum, who explored ritual homosexual sex along the south coast of New Guinea with the lowland Asmat people. He learned that Asmat men had not only wives but also male partners for the exchange of semen, which is believed to have magical properties. In one village, 14 men took him into their private lodge and each sucked Schneebaum's nose, fingers, penis, nipples, chin and earlobes. In another, a married friend named Akapitsjin,

"Aipit," took off his clothes and entered Schneebaum's sleeping area for a "balanced" semen exchange, where the white man was the first active partner, the tribesman the second (*Spirits* 186).

A documentary on Schneebaum's life, *Keep the River on Your Right*, showed him returning after two decades to Asmat's muddy capital. By coincidence he ran into Aipit, who greeted him with a kiss. Now in rags and with few teeth (though he did have a kind expression, if one could get over his unhealthy appearance), Aipit seemed unimaginable as a potential bedmate for a Western woman.

In New Guinea, barring Schneebaum's singular experiences, one does not find travel tales of emotional healing or rambunctious fun. In fact tourist couples have faced sexual horror. In April 2000, an American woman camping on an island was gang-raped by armed robbers as her husband looked on helplessly (Ricketts). And reportedly, in another incident involving a Swiss couple, the *husband* was violated (Salak 379).

The travel sex researcher perceives a rawness, a gulf between one stage of human development and another, a violence of *Clockwork Orange* proportions allied to sex in New Guinea. Perhaps a tourist woman senses correctly that sexually transmitted diseases have been rife in Melanesia for more than a century; that some STDs are rare ones little found outside Papua New Guinea — that rough sex is not uncommon, and hospitals treat women whose vaginas are torn (Caldwell 10-11). Here women are often regarded as unwholesome, evil and poisonous (Dodwell, *Papua* 137; Salak 307-09).

A female writer who lives in Hawaii, Sherée Lipton, shared with me her personal tale of not resisting rape by a New Hebridean warrior.

Hers may be the only known and confirmed case to date of sex with a Melanesian living in a Stone Age village, given Wyn Sargent's coyness on her "marriage."

Lipton (*Island Dreamer,* forthcoming) visited an island called Malekula near Vanuatu to stay with the isolated Big Namba people. What struck her about the local men was their hairiness, "with wiry curls on their chests and backs. They probably shaved the pubic area around their penis wrappers for that was free of hair." Their open hostility, distrust of each other, and sense of perpetual anger were also apparent: "Usually when you look in someone's eyes, you see something of yourself, you see a common emotion. [Yet] when I tried to develop any kind of rapport, they averted their eyes. It was never one soul looking into another and the other looking back." She gazed across an incomprehensible gulf.

In her hut one night, without prelude or flirtation, her guide "put the flat smooth palm of his hand over my mouth. He then waited to see what I would do."

She surrendered to the inevitable as thoughts raced through her mind:

I admit to being curious. I wondered how it would be to make love with an ex-cannibal. How were we similar, how were we different in this intimacy? I even thought, "What would happen if a child was born of this union? How much of me would the child have? How much Namba? How much would be recognizably heir to a Euro-Russian culture, and how much identifiably of a primitive Stone Age tradition?" All this went through my mind as I lay perfectly still ... .

His breath was sweet. His teeth were even. He attempted a kiss and touched my body as I imagine he touched the loins of one of his precious well-nourished sows. ... In the end, it was quite ordinary and very quick. There was no foreplay. No heavy breathing, and no spontaneous gesture at climax. He seemed disciplined and abbreviated in his rhythm.

Her guide had "slid on and off my startled length as quietly as a mouse, like a sliver of bamboo shoot in a banana leaf sheath." Afterward, the warrior never mentioned their coupling.

In Melanesia lies an eerie blend of sexual ennui and violence, as well as a zone of sexual license: the Solomons.

Choices in the Solomons

Moving from New Guinea to islands to the east, Melanesian men immediately zoom higher in level of attractiveness, by Western standards. Lucy Irvine, a blonde British woman living for a year on tiny Tuin Island in the Torres Strait (between New Guinea and Australia), described "attractive young men" (Castaway 173, 176). One, stirred by her scantily clad presence, acknowledged, "You make me want to give you one."

Irvine certainly serves as the major source of sexual research for the region, having garnered one best seller, Castaway, from her 1981-82 sojourn in the Torres Strait, and a second, Faraway, from temporarily living in the Solomon Islands beginning in 1998.

In Faraway, Lucy Irvine chronicled the history of the Hepworth family, who settled on Pigeon Island. There, an Englishwoman named Sally Pierce hired to run the Hepworth shop found afterhours repose in the arms of an island man of huge stamina named Ossi, who pleasured her "behind an old dugout half hidden under skeins of trumpet-petalled purple convolvulus [and] in the lap-lapping water" (282).

The Hepworths' mentally impaired daughter fell in love with another islander, Nokali, leaning back with him in the gentle surf, in a leaf-lined cave and in her bed. Tasha was said to be insatiable at certain times of the month and to let Nokali's friends climb on top of her, as long as Nokali hugged her first and last (277).

Irvine herself, libido raging in the tropical air, came to notice Matoko, "one of the most attractive men" around. "How would it feel to be pressed down onto a pile of banana leaves deep in the bush, legs parting under the doubtless corkscrew efficiency of that hard copper body?" (257) She faltered, however, when she foresaw an inevitable lack of mental communion.

Outside of Irvine's reports, we have only a few additional anecdotes:

• In the sexually notorious Trobriands in the Solomon Islands, Lynn Ferrin (91), at the time experimenting with monogamy, talked an Australian tourist into sampling the "smooth copper youth" who tended bar at her lodge. The tourist reported, "Pah! Not worth all the effort. All he knew was the missionary position."

• Decades earlier, travel publisher Tony Wheeler (242) noted contrary information. Trobrianders, he wrote, enjoyed side-by-side sex in crowded areas, such as in huts, or the preferred position of the male squatting on his heels while the woman on her back spreads her legs over his hips, to give both partners maximum freedom.

That is about all the information we have. Yet opportunity must certainly present itself to a greater extent than captured above. For after all, the startling extent of Trobriand sexual permissiveness — including wild promiscuity during yam harvest festivals and female rape of males (Tree) — launched the careers of many famed anthropologists. Even today, Ferrin reports, island boys in the Trobriands "would stand in the road as our bus approached, point down into their laplaps, grin and gyrate their hips" (90).

Let's migrate east in search of more benign settings, following those canoe navigators who departed Melanesia for Polynesia.

Titillation in Tahiti

Polynesia stretches in a rough triangle from Hawaii at its topmost point, southwest to New Zealand and southeast to Easter Island.

These islands have the longest history and most visible examples of female involvement with Oceania's men. Margaret Mead noted, a bit vaguely but we still get the idea, that from the 1920s onward confident Polynesian men felt no caste obstacles to forming intimate friendships with European women ("Field Work" 322). Hiding behind this uncharacteristically coy remark, Mead seems to have been referring to herself. Her biographers note persistent reports that during her 1925 field work in Samoa, she took as a lover a local man, perhaps inflamed by her questions about Polynesian sexual behavior (J. Howard 85, 366). Mead denied all, though the Samoan bragged of a conquest to others.

In recent times, Fiji seems to lead the way in relationships, as reported over the past three decades by Varawa, Laurie Gough and Joanne Rymell (Norfolk), who like Varawa married a chief's son. Even earlier, in the late 1960s and early 1970s, Sherée Lipton (60-78) describes an idyllic marriage to Lepani, who worked on a cable vessel, in the Lau islands of Fiji. Her photos of the striking islander reveal a man of physical near-perfection, tall, muscle-bound and with a gentle intelligence to his countenance.

Other women report flirtations in Tahiti, or more properly, French Polynesia (B. Clark; Salak 7-10); marriage to a Samoan (Calkins); aggressive propositions in the Cook Islands (Kernahan); and affairs in Tonga (Morton), New Zealand (with Maoris) and on isolated Pitcairn (Birkett, *Serpent* 219-20). No organized gigolo scene exists, barring one involving non-Polynesians: Japanese women pay for white and black men on Waikiki in Hawaii (Kelsky, *Verge* 142-43; Ma 69).

In terms of my own friends in Maryland, for some reason the leading men for their own adventures have been Polynesians. Two friends on separate visits to New Zealand took male Maori lovers . One was a lesbian "experimenting with bisexuality," as she put it. Another, staying at a hostel, allowed a beautiful warrior into her claw-footed bathtub, surrounded by candles to celebrate her birthday. A third described an impulsive romance with a Fijian during a trip to Hawaii. "He did have an incredible aura of peace, was a great lover, and we had one night on the beach with a full moon — the Pacific lapping at my toes."

I myself had a near-miss in Tahiti. I stayed on the jewel-like island of Bora Bora with a local family for many days (Belliveau, *Amateur* 118-22), and one morning quietly freeloaded onto a snorkel boat operated by Club Med. We anchored at a tiny motu (islet), and I stretched my towel on a remote stretch of beach.

One of the snorkel guides, a gorgeous Tahitian — like a tanned Clark Gable — sought me out. He sat beside me on my towel. This

Tahitian troubadours serenade tourists on a snorkeling trip.

bronze Adonis sported a short moustache, matinee idol eyes and cheekbones, a strong jaw, and wavy hair longer than his shoulders, parted on the left. He had a swimmer's strong chest and trim waist, set off by a white tank top, and a chestnut streak in his black hair that attested to a life spent in the sun. I had to give the guide about 99 out of 100 points for looks and athletic build.

His index finger brushed my upper arm lightly as he talked. My body was trembling, almost throbbing. I cast an anxious glance at the palm trees in the center of the motu, gauging our privacy to be precarious should any of the Club Med'ers decide to explore for sea shells.

The snorkel guide got called away by a distant voice. Yet even before that, his small talk — "You have bruddah? You have sistah?" — delivered in a lazy monotone attested to both slickness and a lack of conversational depth. His was the sort of ubiquitous, autopilot patter one must endure on every bus, ferry and train in China, Southeast Asia and the Pacific. And such predictable (and non-pillow) talk dampened my reckless willingness for another impromptu shag on the beach, as I had earlier enjoyed on the Aegean.

Only now, in the course of researching *Romance on the Road*, do I learn that in Polynesia (and perhaps in most of the world), a woman who goes to a beach, a trail or anywhere alone is automatically considered to be looking for hot action (Kernahan 67-68).

Later I saw the snorkel guide jogging at night on the main road, north of the village of Vaitape. A local cautioned me that the Tahitian Clark Gable made a practice of seducing American women. Perhaps I sensed in the guide's clunky conversation a lack of any special interest in me as a person. He seemed to exemplify what anthropologist Margaret Mead (qtd. in Lapsley 174) found in Samoans: the "impersonality of sex attraction."

A delicately balanced world

With about 8 million people, Oceania is by far the tiniest region, in terms of land mass and population, described in this survey of female sex travel. Even the Caribbean is more than four times more populous.

For the most part, the story of sex under the Southern Cross is a brief one, that of just a few scattered anthropologists, writers and backpackers falling for traditional village men and telling the tale in individual memoirs.

Outside of Waikiki in Hawaii, the region lacks critical mass for gigolo scenes and in fact is little touristed, for reasons of distance and expense — and growing political chaos.

For underneath the travel-brochure beauty of Oceania lie failing economies, rising crime, a total lack of health care in some areas and endemic rape. Australia's aid policy analysts and media are sounding a panicky alarm, little heard elsewhere, on Pacific turmoil (Caldwell; Perry; Ballantine).

Few North Americans or Europeans may be aware of these issues or many others, including genocide in Irian Jaya; political chaos in Papua New Guinea and the Solomons, about to totter into rogue state status; racial strife in Fiji; abandonment of scores of islands by migrants to Australian and New Zealand cities; and skyrocketing AIDS in Papua

New Guinea's capital, Port Moresby (Caldwell 18).

Traveling women tend to steer clear of evident danger. And stressed communities not only see fewer female tourists but also may experience heightened paranoia about outsiders in general.

Island ecologies, particularly the tiny isolated dots in Oceania, are much smaller and more fragile than continental ones (Belliveau, *Amateur* 25-28). Fragility extends to soil, plant cover, animal species — and family survival. A Western woman can offer economic comforts, but she may later threaten a tiny village with the loss of an able-bodied man to the bright lights of her home in the West.

After all, there are only 800,000 people in all of Fiji, 450,000 in the Solomon Islands, 235,000 in French Polynesia and 170,000 in Samoa. Palau has a paltry 20,000 residents — and reports of Japanese women taking local husbands!

In the Cook Islands, between Tonga and Tahiti, Mel Kernahan learned that when an island woman got pregnant via a white fellow, "the baby grows up on the island and helps with the fishing and planting and takes care of the old people when that time comes." If the baby's father was intelligent, "then the baby inherits that as well as all the brains and skills of his Cook Islands ancestor" (146). Further, the itinerant father offers an alternative, a broader gene pool, for a local woman who has little choice but to lie with men to whom she is likely to be related in some way.

A tourist woman, however, may go "away and [have] the baby overseas and it's lost forever to the Islands." She may take her man as well, and then "he's lost to the family too, because a European wife would not let her husband send part of their money home to his family."

Two female outsiders poisoned their relationships with South Pacific communities in other ways, one (Laurie Gough on Fiji, *Kite Strings* 365-69) by fomenting opposition to her boyfriend's uncle, another (Dea Birkett on Pitcairn Island) by spurning a man who was kind to her in favor of the island Lothario, married and a chaser of white women.

Birkett managed to vindicate Oceania's residents in their suspicion of outsiders. She lied to receive permission to land on what is virtually a closed community. She then misjudged island reality, a reality that allows no one enough privacy to escape indiscretion, even a single, quiet one-night stand. On an island with just 38 people, and exactly two other single available women, she created uproar in the way of Wyn Sargent but on a more minor scale.

Island men, loved and left behind

Further, Birkett (*Serpent* 114-15) managed to re-break the heart of her pal around the island. A local man named Dennis had loved an earlier visitor, an artist from Kansas City named Mary. They were to marry, and Dennis began to build them a house. But when Mary went back to visit her parents, her letters got colder and colder, and she finally informed him she was not coming back.

A Western visitor's departure from the remote Pacific is tantamount to her dying in its finality (indicated in Theroux, *Oceania* 150). When a Western woman leaves a fiancé and gets cold feet as she wonders how to fit him into her world, her man can only accept his powerlessness to Fate.

Men have cause to fear abandonment. Another case in point would be Bressin Hepworth, the son of Diana and Tom Hepworth on Pigeon Island (Irvine, *Faraway* 322-25). Though the son of English parents, he grew up and identified with Solomon Islanders and eventually found himself in exactly the same boat as other islanders in remote Oceania.

Bressin met an American girl while working at a hotel in the Solomons' capital, Honiara. He invited her back to Pigeon. Under the stars, he paddled her silently to tiny islets, laid down a piece of calico, and kissed her. He stroked her instep and waited for her to be willing, as his brother and his island friends had coached him. Bressin asked Angela to be his future, and after her departure waited vainly as mail ships came and went, until he, like Dennis, received a painful letter.

The Reasons chapter discussed earlier how Western women can sow community disruption in traditional areas of West Africa, the Caribbean and the Middle East; in Oceania, their disruption often extends to heartbroken individuals.

No wonder that on Fiji, Malé Varawa must have felt both hope and cold fear when, after he first met and proposed to Joana McIntyre, he took her to the airport for her (temporary) return home to Hawaii. "Be sure to come back," he said. "Come back, Joana, please come back." He stood, clinging to the chain-link fence around the runway, until her plane took off (*Changes* 20-21).

Oceania for the She

Both the pluses and minuses of love with a Pacific islander can be seen in the tale, which opened this chapter, of Joana McIntyre Varawa.

Her experience is really that of most Western women who find themselves involved with men of the South and Western Pacific. These rugged men are thoroughly enmeshed in their huge, extended families and villages. To marry the man is to marry the family.

Such marriages are a two-sided coin. A woman escapes the impersonality, disconnectedness and solitude that can make the Western single person feel like an atomized fragment beset by a difficult world. She gains all the company, generosity and kindness of the extended South Pacific clan — and kinship obligations and a total lack of privacy that can just about drive her nuts.

On a positive note, struggling couples can count on strong support. "One of the great things about this kind of marriage instead of the romantic, personal marriage is that everyone around you is trying to keep you together," Varawa told an interviewer (Shapiro). "Everyone told me it would take a long time, that Malé had never been out of the village and my ways were just incomprehensible to him. Everyone said wait, wait. The whole family was holding us together when we weren't able to hold ourselves together."

For most women, unwritten social codes may be difficult to accept, flying in the face of Western common sense.

In her book *My Samoan Chief*, Fay Calkin describes having to give away her sewing machine when her mother-in-law requested it using the imperative form (!) of "please" (66-67). Her family finances dwindled to nothing as relatives, as well as farm laborers (and all their relatives), ate produce before it could be taken to market. Obligatory, financially draining feasts doomed Calkins's attempt to create profit-making enterprises such as food co-ops and exporting of fine mats.

Calkins and her husband, Vai, built a mountaintop home and watched as "cases of food, tools, clothes, and sheets seemed to vanish from whichever direction I turned my back. Without walls, doors, or locks, I felt completely defenseless. ... I could see that our house would soon look like every other *fale* in Samoa, open, cool, neat as a pin — and devoid of furnishings" (95).

Similarly, Calkins made a speech to an island village pitching a taro co-op, noting that at some point production had to match consumption. She was addressing a sea of incomprehension (83). Much the same litany — a loss of privacy and possessions — appears in "My Chastity Belt," a description of marriage to a Tongan by anthropologist Helen Morton.

The strain of kinship obligation can be fatal to a marriage (as it was in Morton's case), in Oceania and elsewhere. A university official of my acquaintance, who had been in the Peace Corps, eventually married a woman from, as I recall, Cameroon. They divorced when he could no longer abide the unending demands of her extended family for money.

Another evident parallel between sub-Saharan Africa and the South Pacific is discrete but casual sexuality. Land in both areas tends to be communally owned, making illegitimate children unthreatening to inheritances (though many anthropologists and travelers in Oceania note a surprising lack of pregnancies arising from teen promiscuity, perhaps due to a diet rich in yams, see Tree, Culture Shock). Both Africa and

Oceania also require extensive help to kin, stifling incentives for individual success because acquired possessions are virtually stripped away.

• **Outsiders are feared and lied to.** Western women, younger ones in particular, and especially writers who try for insider status but are suspected of not having their heart in staying, should not be too surprised at lies designed to create distance.

Travel writer Laurie Gough, who had an affair on Fiji with a singing youth named Laudi, ultimately concluded that she could "no longer ignore things that go on here, the deception that follows every footstep, the half-heard whispers, the doctrine of mass conformity, the terrible misunderstanding between the sexes, all the things I know I could never permanently endure" (*Kite Strings* 330).

In the Trobriands, Paul Theroux observed, "an island of traditional culture can never be idyllic. It is, instead, completely itself: riddled with magic, superstition, myths, dangers, rivalries, and its old routines ... The key to its survival was that it laughed at outsiders and kept them at arm's length. ... I could now see the utter impossibility of my ever understanding the place" (*Oceania* 150).

Islander fear is legitimate and stems from the social fragility, mentioned above, of micro-communities upended by the arrival of a white female tourist. For example, Wyn Sargent, who married a New Guinea chief and brought nothing but trouble to her Dani "friends," remains disliked today (Butt 61-62). It would be difficult to top chief Obaharok's experience for anyone looking for grounds why Oceania's residents keep outsiders at arm's length, as his family lost its wealth and fortune in the wake of Sargent's meddling.

Some sense of the disaster she could bring about may have helped Lucy Irvine manage to restrain herself from having sex with an attractive Solomon Islander. A liaison could have jeopardized her book project — and like Gough and Sargent, she would have to leave if she destroyed the frail equilibrium on Pigeon island, a speck of land just 1,000 feet wide.

As seen with Dea Birkett, transgressions may force the tourist's departure.

• **Women face a risk of rape**, including gang rape. The police chief of Port Moresby in Papua New Guinea lambasted the violent residents of a squatter settlement, in words that should give the erstwhile female tourist pause: "This is the worst pack rape nation in the Pacific and you're teaching your children to rape, too. You are all title-holders in pack rape. You're raping anything that moves" (J. Wright).

- Also, **situations may arise that a Western woman views as a rape attempt** but the male islander does not. In much of Oceania, women simply should not walk alone at night and possibly not in daytime either.

Here is the flip side of easy-going sex. Men are used to access and to dominating their women. When a man make advances on a local woman, he is facing a powerfully built, confident adversary who can handle herself and either rebuff him or threaten dire retribution from her huge family. Even so, rape of *local* women occurs in New Guinea and on Fiji (Perry), and not uncommon on Tonga, either (Morton). On Vanuatu, local women avoid going anywhere alone.

A less than gigantic Western woman, sans male relatives or even companions, exploring by herself, may find herself a helpless target.

"With our people, when a Tahitian girl goes alone to a lonely place, it's a signal she wants boom-boom," a planter remarked in the early 1980s after a Parisian woman, sunbathing nude with her legs spread, was accosted by a fisherman (Kernahan 67).

On Badu Island, in the Torres Strait between Australia and New Guinea, Lucy Irvine decided to stroll alone to an isolated stream and sunbathe nude. Soon her local guide, Albert, appeared. He lured her into swimming nude and grabbed her by the waist from behind. She told him no; he toyed with the idea of rape but finally backed down, apologizing, "I feel little bit wild" (*Castaway* 250).

One evening while walking home on Rarotonga, in the Cook Islands, author Mel Kernahan (139-41) was attacked by a man and fought her way loose. The police took the attitude that if she hadn't been raped, they would just lecture the youth's father. She was also told local girls, being strong, knew how to break the head of any boy who tried to rape them.

Other annoyances may lurk. While at a dance in the Cook Islands, Kernahan recalled "being grabbed by another local with an erection ... and fuck-danced to the pounding drums and electronic excess of the guitars" (137).

Don't go overboard with fear, however. Barring my Tahitian Clark Gable, other guides were gentlemanly, even on solo hikes up Bora Bora's mountain. Similarly, Kira Salak (10) describes receiving a coconut oil massage from a Tahitian who took no for an answer, even though she was in the nude and responsive to his stroking of her thighs. He managed to just smile and say in French, "You have fear." (As a side note, Salak's actions, a clear "yes" to intercourse in 99.999 percent of the world, could hardly be riskier.)

- Many places outside the West offer **no privacy** for a Western woman

Oceania timeline

1925: Margaret Mead works in **Samoa**, may have accepted overtures from island men. She later wrote that while in most of the world, "tribal men are constrained by caste barriers" from approaching a female anthropologist, "the kinds of culture contact that have occurred mean that Polynesians will not hesitate to approach a European woman." She attributed this to islanders being "sophisticated peoples whom the Europeans have found sexually attractive" ("Field Work" 322).

1926: White Woman's Protection Ordinance passed in **New Guinea** in response to colonial women being touched in their bedrooms by male servants (Strobel 7).

Circa 1972: American writer on **Rarotonga** eagerly enters lusty, nightly relationship with island rugby player, who seduces her via the Polynesian custom of "night crawling." She described, in a personal communi-

caion, how "when a man sets his sights on a woman, he crawls up to her cottage at night and slides the end of his personally carved stick through her window or wall since the buildings are often thatched. She can tell whose stick it is by fingering the distinctive carving. If she is interested, she pulls the stick in and the man may then enter. If she pushes the stick back out, he is sent away, often to the laughter and derision of his friends who have come to see the outcome of this sport."

1973: In **New Guinea** highlands, Wyn Sargent marries a striking chief.

1985: Author propositioned by a gorgeous **Tahitian** on a remote stretch of beach on a fairy-tale islet off Bora Bora. In **Fiji**, Joana McInytre meets Malé Varawa, and the couple enter one of the classic travel romances of the modern era.

Circa 1990: A lesbian friend of the

to think or to get to know her guy (Varawa, *Changes* 93). Oceania is no exception. Typically, an entire village of adults and children will provide a rapt audience 24/7, including when a woman answers calls of nature (Salak 157, 164).

• **Men and women live separate lives.** Laurie Gough wrote of her Fijian boyfriend, "He's such a loving presence while we're alone, filled with stories and quirky passions, questions, and musing. But as soon as one of his male cousins or male friends appears, I vaporize" (*Kite Strings* 106). Joana McIntyre Varawa also reported a lack of kissing and open affection. In fact, "For the longest time I had no idea who was married to whom, for I rarely saw a man and wife together" (*Changes* 97).

Though the feeling of abandonment can be tough on a Western woman, with her notions of companionship, such differentiation can be positive, heightening sexual interest and ultimately avoiding conflict.

In the West, "Egalitarianism has changed roles so that men are no longer romantic," Baltimore family therapist Mary Ann Constantinides told me. "The perception of separate roles is special and was seen as something admirable. With lack of differentiation in roles has come a

author's, on a trip to **New Zealand**, explored heterosexual sex with a Maori. A decade later, another girl-friend, heterosexual, enjoys the attentions of a Maori in a clawfoot bathtub.

1998: Japanese women reported to engage in relationships with men in **Palau**, east of the Philippines, with some resulting marriages (Yamashita, Japanese Encounter).

• Author Lucy Irvine travels to remote Pigeon Island in the **Solomons'** Reef Islands to write family history of the Hepworth family, notes propensity of white women to find great favor with local island men, including the Hepworths' daughter and a former cook from the south of England (*Faraway* 277-290).

1999: In the **Trobriand Islands**, off the coast of New Guinea, Lynn Ferrin became curious about local men after noting that children begin sexual play early, encouraged by adults, who themselves enjoy many lovers before marriage and orgies during the yam harvest. She encouraged an Australian friend to seduce a bartender. Her friend reported only routine, missionary position sex.

2003: A career businesswoman from suburban London travels to **Fiji** and, following in the footsteps of Joana McIntyre Varawa, falls in love with Epi Bolones, a chief's son. Joanne Rymell sells her car and £250,000 house to go live with him and get married (Norfolk).

• Meanwhile, Moon Handbooks' *Fiji* goes so far as to note in its section on customs, "Women should have few real problems traveling around Fiji on their own, so long as they're prepared to cope with frequent offers of marriage" (Stanley). Perhaps every Fijian male yearns to be the next Malé or Epi?

loss of sexual attraction."

Such differentiation also allows both Varawa and Gough to forge excellent friendships with the local women they spend much time with.

ADVANTAGES

• **Tremendous learning to be had about life**. Varawa learns to accept that her island man prefers joking with his cousins to arguments and nagging; at first she is jealous because "his happiness does not derive from me, but from his own sources" (*Changes* 121). She comes to see that blaming a lover for her own moments of unhappiness and thus distancing him is no good. Malé's purity, for want of better word, means that "he has little skill or interest in the complicated psychological game Americans often mistake for relationship ... he just goes outside" (122).

Sleeping together under the tabua, a heavy polished whale's tooth joining couples, she becomes more appreciative of what he can give — a morning cup of coffee, a beautiful song — and she begins to find the solution to the West's dating war. Her island man simply does not know how to retaliate and always de-escalates confrontations, so she learns ... to take care of herself, and him, with calm loving.

Her tale serves almost as a blueprint for how to avoid the dating war: by sharing, letting go of grievances against her man, and allowing him his prized camaraderie with his mates.

• **Low HIV rates**. Rates are officially the world's lowest, though on the rise in Papua New Guinea and likely underreported in Samoa and other places (Susman).

• **Beautiful voices and singing**. I was moved to tears by the lovely singing at a Sunday Mass on Bora Bora. Other women describe more intimate experience of Oceania's men who sing and whisper softly just for them.

When Joana McIntyre first met Malé Varawa, she remarked on his pidgin English delivered an "accent pure and soft, reminiscent of an English university. It fascinated me to be sitting on the stone foundation of a grass house talking with a muscular, barefoot Fijian whose voice sounded like that of an educated English poet" (11).

A happily married woman (B. Clark 138) who visited Tahiti found her vows sorely tested by a "hard-muscled, sun-bronzed" man named Hiro. "His English was rhythmic, poetic, especially when he sang to me. ... I was obsessed with Hiro's voice." She realized she had a crush and didn't act on it — but kept a cassette of her tropical temptation's serenades.

• **Aura of peace**. I will never forget spear-fishing on Bora Bora with Fredo Doom — a calm planet of a man (Belliveau, *Amateur* 120, 122), a Polynesian giant at home in the water. When he invited me to traditional dances or to accompany him on his bus driver errands, words came out slowly, one at a time, stolid and nonchalantly soothing. Other men of Oceania also display this tranquil side. Varawa wrote of Malé that he possesses "innocent goodness ... deep love of his family ... I have never met a man who could so easily forgive and forget, who did not gather his grievances and use them as weapons" (104).

Laurie Gough, an Ontarian in her 20s, summed up the pluses and minuses of love with her "sweet and sexy and fun" Fijian man: "On the nights Laudi sings to me under the stars, I can almost forget everything else — the chauvinism, the adolescent inclinations — and let his voice drench through me so that the other things don't matter" (*Kite Strings* 106).

§§§

To complete our sexual geography of the world as experienced by traveling women, we will quickly visit three more places: the Zone of Sexual Winter, Platonia, and the Sotadic Zone.

The Zone of Sexual Winter

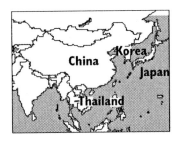

Some Western executive women in Japan eventually go home, relentlessly rejected by local men. One American editor in her early 40s described Japan as "sexual Siberia."

Ma (202)

To Tibetans, "foreign women are incredibly ugly, with flanks like horses and eyes like dead people. It's the blue eyes that are really scary" (Teasdill 608).

To one Japanese man, American women "are not in the least attractive. ... They're just large [and] unrefined" (Hasegawa Katsuyuki qtd. in Kelsky, *Verge* 180). Another admitted, "When I think of a middle-aged Caucasian woman, the first thing which comes up to my mind is a large chunk of boneless ham" (Wagatsuma 421).

And Indian and Sri Lankan men, as well as Japanese, may find Western women too mannish (Hottola, *Intercultural* 315-16; Therival 270).

Though white women are lust objects for men across most of the world's surface, they find themselves rejected in Japan, China, Korea and Tibet. Westerners working in the Zone of Sexual Winter will be ignored both by local men and fellow expatriates. Loneliness prompts many to leave job assignments in, for example, Japan, which poses similar dating problems to those in New York or Washington, if not worse.

Japan

Social scientists and long-term observers note why romantic options are severely limited in Japan:

• Japanese men perceive many Western women as big, frizzy-haired and unattractive. A female English teacher on the Lonely Planet Thorn Tree (True Confessions) posted a feeling of being typed as a hulking, defeminized, Caucasian giantess. Salarymen — Japanese office workers — also feel pressure to conform to social expectations of taking a Japanese wife and further consider Western women to be off limits.

• Western women, while finding some Japanese men attractive, do not like their attitudes toward women or find them to be spoiled by their mothers. While "the pairing of Western men and Eastern women [is] as natural as the partnership of sun and moon" (Iyer 79), there seems to be little or no fit between Asian men and Western women.

• Western male expatriates are interested in Japanese women, not other Westerners. This dynamic appeared just as soon as American women arrived as members of the Occupation staff in postwar Japan. They had come in search of husbands and "were dismayed to find so many of their men under Japanese women's spell" (Kelsky, *Verge* 69).

Yet a very determined Western female can achieve desirability. Well, at least one did. An American anthropologist named Liza Crihfield Dalby (108-18) succeeded in becoming the only woman to join the ranks of geishas, women skilled at pleasing Japanese men, and looks remarkably like the genuine article in photos of her clad in traditional robes, with white make-up and elaborate hairdo. She seemed to have an innate love of Japanese culture, dating from a year spent there as a teen-ager, which must have helped.

Many Western women find employment at a far more basic level of male entertainment, as bar hostesses in Tokyo's entertainment district, Roppongi, a job that can shade into becoming prostitutes for those Japanese men who do fancy English women (McVeigh).

Some signs of thaw have been seen in the sexual winter in Japan, as men become more curious about foreigners. (For an indepth discussion of recent changes, see Ma 199-215). Most likely to be accepted by Japanese men are petite, dark-haired women fluent in Japanese, such as Liza Dalby. As another example, a well-traveled former housemate of mine, a public health master's degree student, dated an attractive, young Japanese man. My friend had two things going for her: being half-Japanese and speaking the language. She also had one strike against: She was very strong and athletic, and she said that made her boyfriend feel inadequate.

Another indicator of change is evident as Japan's young men seem to be transmuting before our eyes into taller, handsomer fellows with wonderful glossy hair and fine cheekbones. One flounders in explaining how the sons of plain men blossom, but maybe the broadcast of Keanu Reeves movies magically constructs golden-skinned, almond-eyed cuties.

My former housemate's boyfriend certainly was Joe Cool, his exotic, healthy good looks in photographs accentuated by his trendy eyeglasses and flowered swim trunks. And in the course of visiting university libraries around the Baltimore area I've noticed striking Japanese males on campus. If these exchange students bring home new tastes in dressing and acting to impress Western women, their domestic cousins will become the latest travel trophies.

In fact, some travel researchers think the sexual winter is more a matter of indifferent tourist women than repulsed Asian men. Tourism professor Chris Ryan of New Zealand e-mailed me to say it is "likely that Western women are not overly interested in Asian men." Especially Australian women, he noted, may show little interest in Japanese males, for reasons "that might include a lingering hostility from the treatment of Australasian prisoners of war by the Japanese — even 50-60 years on this is, for an older generation, a sensitive issue."

China

The Middle Kingdom also seems to be a "sexual winter," although men desperate to emigrate will pester Western women for marriage.

Kerry McKibben (137) fended off an inept proposition in a village in Yunnan province. Her guide James suggested, "Ka-ree, perhaps we can become special friends. We can write to each other. Then one day, we can get married like my friend. He met a Dutch girl here. Now he has his own car and apartment in Amsterdam and his wife is still a modern career woman."

If James's mention of the Dutch woman is true, we have one, just one, documented case of a travel romance, in a nation of more than 1 billion people, including millions of unattached and surplus males.

"While a fair number of Chinese women marry foreign men, the reverse is not so," Alison Saheed found in Hong Kong (202). "In general, Chinese men are not particularly attracted to European women, which leaves you free from any harassment at the office or in the street. It also enables you to function freely at work, deemed as you are as sort of sexless."

I can attest to the lack of appeal of the Franco-Irish complexion in China, where children in one restaurant cried at the sight of my (demon's) blue eyes and reddish-brown hair.

But attraction is a two-way street, and the men of China, for their part, rarely strike women as attractive. Marguerite Duras, the daughter of French expatriates raised in Vietnam, made a mint by writing about a Chinese heir who seduced her (her hit book *The Lover* was made into a movie) and making the relationship wickedly erotic. But apparently she liked only his money and found Leo himself "ugly. [Marguerite] didn't find him attractive. How could she overcome his lack of appeal? ... The first kiss is described like a rape: 'He caught me off guard. I cannot describe how repulsive it was' " (Adler 60).

One exception to the rule of plain Chinese men was so singular I mentioned it my first book (Amateur 34). With my weakness for exotic handsomeness of any type, I fantasized on a riverboat in South China about the first mate, with his American Indian looks. But China, damp, cold and dirty in early spring, completely sapped my libido.

No other men on that trip appealed.

Korea

An acquaintance of mine, Kevin Ross of Baltimore, spent a year teaching English south of Seoul. All the guys at the school, with one exception, had Korean girlfriends, he said; none of the female teachers did.

"If you asked Korean men about it," Ross told me, "they would say matter of factly, Asian women are more attractive, and Korean women are the most beautiful women in the world. White women are too tall, too bigboned and too loud."

Korean men, used to being in charge, also knew that "you couldn't just tell an American woman what to do," Ross recalled. And yet: "American women did interest them — especially anyone blonde. They would ask blonde women, 'Are you an actress?' They would find them interesting and beautiful in a way but not attractive — in the same sense as if I were meeting someone like Katherine Hepburn."

Thailand

The Land of Smiles can also be a sexual winter for, if not Japanese women, certainly white women shunned by their fellow expats. "Phuket thoroughly demoralized me," Linda, a blonde in her early 30s who worked on sailboats, observed (Odzer 33). "I'm going home to crawl under a rock for being the wrong sex, the wrong nationality, too big, too liberated, too curly. I can't bear the sight of one more foxy Asian girl."

From the Zone of Sexual Winter, we can proceed to Platonia, an overlapping area.

Platonia

Yutong Chen shows me around the gardens of Suzhou in China.

Yutong Chen shows me around the gardens of Suzhou in China.

Platonia is the land of the isolated man. He likely does not have sex with a tourist woman, yet he treasures her for knowledge she brings of the wider world.

China and the Middle East are the two most obvious areas of Platonia, marked by courtliness to the Western female guest mingled with intense curiosity about "the outside," especially salaries and living standards. Platonia thrives in areas of political repression, sexual suppression and restricted information.

I have had two major platonic relationships with foreign men. In Suzhou in China, I met Yutong Chen (Belliveau, *Amateur* 51), who gallantly came to my rescue after I had a verbal scrap with a nasty ticket seller at a city garden. Yutong vaulted swiftly to top place as the handsomest Chinese man I had ever seen, tall, well-proportioned in stonewashed jeans that showed off his lanky legs, with pleasant features.

We embarked on a four-year correspondence. I received elaborate, beribboned Christmas cards. How did he get them in an atheist society? Yutong wrote poems in Chinese about a person missing his "friend," signed "Faithfully yours."

Yutong clearly loved his homeland and wanted to improve it, and was singular among Chinese I met in not pestering me on how to become a student in the United States. In the skies over Borneo, I wrote Yutong first. In my letter, I enclosed Chinese stamps, pretending they were "extra," that I'd purchased to keep in touch with him.

Yutong even visited me in Baltimore one summer evening, part of a business trip. By then, I sensed Yutong had moved on. He was going places fast with China's giant arms-making company, and an American girlfriend had probably become a non-starter.

I described earlier my other platonic friend, Alain Hodge on the Caribbean island of St. Bart's, an honorable soul with none of the craftiness of the Jamaican rent-a-dread. Living on a tiny island favored by the rich and famous, he thoroughly lacked the crassness that comes from picking up package tourists. But like men on Jost Van Dyke, another small Caribbean rock, he lived in a sensual region but in a sector with limited dating opportunities. I hope that both Alain and Yutong have found wonderful women.

Above all, Platonia can be found in the Middle East, paradoxically among sensual Arab men. Three decades ago a tourism researcher (E. Cohen, "Arab Boys") described how Palestinian youths brought Swedish woman to their parents for home cooking and to converse about life in the West .

In Platonia, the tourist women meets the parents and family. I was invited to Alain's home and met his brother and sister, who cooked us dinner. And Yutong regularly asked about my parents and siblings, and I always sent sincere greetings for his mother.

In the Middle East, even when Arabs manage sex with tourists, they prize talk, the signature activity of Platonia. In Morocco, "sex I think goes hand in hand for young men in learning about the wider world," Englishwoman Pamela Windo told me. American writer Vivian Gornick (255) found Egyptian men "to be filled with an enormous intuitive intelligence. ... They approach me in order to make love, but in reality they wish to talk more than they wish to make love. ... The talk comes pouring out of them as though they have been locked away from the world for centuries with no one to talk to, certainly not each other."

Baltimore therapist Mary Ann Constantinides recalls having to answer questions about the mores of the United States from isolated men in northeast Greece and in Egypt. Due to media propaganda, the foreign men thought 13-year-olds having babies, surrogate motherhood and various bizarre episodes were the norm. She had to explain that most Americans live conventional lives and get ahead by hard work.

"These people are continually brainwashed towards America," Constantinides noted. "Their world is twisted badly. In Islamic countries an American woman is the most fantastic thing to the most repressed people on the planet."

In some swathes of the globe, the man senses that he is being lied to, and asks the tourist woman where to find truth. She shines, for she is information, she is light.

Finally, let's visit the opposite of Platonia: the Sotadic Zone.

The Sotadic Zone

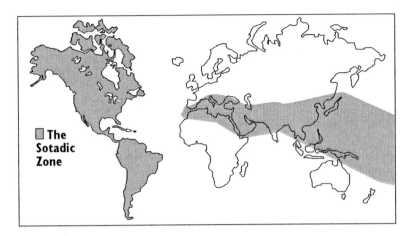

The Sotadic Zone

A map showing today's zones for sex travelers, for men and women alike, would center on the tropics and the near tropics. These areas were also identified more than a century ago as a homosexual sex zone, in the only major effort to develop a worldwide sexual geography.

The so-called Sotadic Zone was the brainchild, in 1886, of Sir Richard Francis Burton, an English explorer, writer and self-taught ethnologist. He coined "Sotadic" from the name of the Greek poet Sotades, creating a new term for gay love. Burton "may be regarded as the founding father of that strand in modern anthropology [that] specializes in the close study of 'primitive' sexual behavior" (McLynn 369).

Burton's experiments with sexual knowledge began with his voyage to Pakistan, aged 24, as a soldier of the Honourable East India Co. Prostitutes helped him become fluent in local languages. An officer in Karachi feared that three bordellos containing eunuchs and boys would corrupt his troops. Burton was sent to visit the bordellos, confirming with perhaps excessive zest not only the boy-man action but adding salacious details. (It is difficult to argue with biographers who believe that Burton was bisexual and active with men, see McLynn 368. Certainly few heterosexual men could be dragged to a gay whorehouse.)

After this initial assignment, Burton became perhaps the world's most broadly traveled (and experienced) sexual anthropologist. The English explorer perceived a geographical pattern to acceptance of "the Vice," anal sex. He presented his ideas in section D, "Pederasty," in the Terminal Essay in volume X of *The Book of the Thousand Nights and a Night*, now known as *The Arabian Nights*. The essay, written to defend

Nights against charges of gratuitous pornography, is perhaps the only detailed, global look at the interplay of sexual practices and geography.

Burton examines the social repression in far northern and southern latitudes and the greater freedom in the tropics. The Sotadic Zone, Burton said, comprised all Mediterranean shores, running east through Asia Minor, through modern Iraq, Afghanistan, Pakistan, the Punjab and Kashmir. "In Indo-China the belt begins to broaden, enfolding China, Japan and Turkistan," he wrote. "It then embraces the South Sea Islands and the New World, where, at the time of its discovery, Sotadic love was, with some exceptions, an established racial institution.

"Within the Sotadic Zone, the Vice [anal sex] is popular and endemic, held at the worst to be a mere peccadillo," he wrote, while in temperate latitudes, men "practise it only sporadically amid the opprobrium of their fellows who, as a rule, are physically incapable of performing the operation and look upon it with liveliest disgust."

Now, why exactly are men of the tropics and near-tropics fond of anal sex with other men?

Burton surmises that people of the Sotadic Zone reflect "a blending of the masculine and feminine temperaments, a crasis which elsewhere occurs only sporadically. ... I suspect a mixed physical temperament effected by the manifold subtle influences massed together in the word climate. Something of the kind is necessary to explain the fact of this pathological love extending over the greater portion of the habitable world, without any apparent connection of race or media, from the polished Greek to the cannibal Tupi of the Brazil."

The sexual explorer never quite pins down how geography, especially climate, determines sexuality. Yet Burton's observation of more feminine men in the tropics seems apparent in Thailand and Indonesia, where many of the slightly built men are involved in dancing, wood carving and other artistic pursuits (Belliveau, *Amateur* 206, 211), and jibes with a sociology study (Meisch) noting that Western women melt at the gentle advances of Ecuadorian Indians.

In Bali, androgyny is apparent. "A Balinese male," Margaret Mead wrote (*Male and Female* 122-23), "is almost hairless — so hairless that he can pluck his whiskers out one by one with pincers. His breasts are considerably more developed than are a Westerner's. Almost any Balinese male placed in a series of western-European males would look 'feminine.' A Balinese female, on the other hand, has narrow hips and small high breasts, and almost any Balinese female placed among a group of western-European women would look 'boyish.' "

And indeed, Balinese boys have been favored since the 1930s by expatriate gays. Novelist Inez Baranay (*Bali* 94) depicts the youths, though treasured by Western homosexuals for their beauty, as not really gay themselves, coming by a count of seven and then falling asleep.

The Sotadic Zone theory does not account for men triple the size and strength of the graceful Balinese, the rugged men within the tropics including the fishermen of the West Indies, Polynesia and Micronesia.

Another discrepancy involves sub-Saharan Africa, where anal sex is abhorrent but Westerners may readily enter casual relationships with locals. The true variable, only indirectly linked to climate, may be whether an agricultural region employs the plow, thus leading to restrictions on female sexuality, a theory given in the History chapter. The link between climate and development, intrinsic to Burton's hypothesis, is a vast subject explored by Jared Diamond in *Guns, Germs and Steel* and countless others, with plenty of disagreement to go around.

The Sotadic Zone at least attempts to provide a structure for pondering striking differences between European sexuality and that of the Orient and tropics. Further, Burton's work shows again the parallels between gay men and heterosexual women in their search for congenial climes for sexual fulfillment. Both must discover attractive and accommodating people with pragmatic attitudes toward sex and money. From the Victorian era to the present, heterosexual women have followed gay men into Italy, Morocco, Thailand and the Dominican Republic. Barring areas of war and of Sexual Winter, much of the Sotadic Zone overlaps with areas that are pleasure goldmines for the modern female traveler.

Romance on the Road posits that sex zones for traveling women are close to universal outside of developed West and the Zone of Sexual Winter, and that even East Asia may one day evolve from a Siberia to a Sexual Summer. Sexual free zones for women do appear quite often in warm climates but a generation ago also sprang up in the mountains of Nepal and Ecuador as well. Burton was broadly correct in describing a geographic component to sexuality; however, level of development, especially whether a society practices simple or complex agriculture, rather than climate per se seems to be the intervening variable. As explored in the Reasons chapter, men in developing countries happily entertain female tourists from the developed world for such reasons as demographics, economics and the commodification of desire.

§§§

Now let's look at various portrayals of women who travel for love, in literature, movies, plays, music and more.

Portrayals:
Literature and Film

The year was 1956, and the place was Kathmandu in Nepal. Dr. Elisabeth Comber, part Belgian, part Chinese, a medical doctor and a writer, attended a royal wedding festival.

Unhappy with her English husband, this woman of many facets had a complicated marital history and sex life, and spent long stretches of her married life markedly indifferent to bedtime congress. Yet she could write knowingly of passionate love, for a few years earlier she had had a brief but most fulfilling affair with a newspaper reporter who died in the front lines of Korea. Under a pen name, Han Suyin, she transmuted the affair into the autobiographical novel *A Many-Splendoured Thing*.

At the palace, the author caught sight of a man with blue-black skin, standing with a whiskey by a grand piano. She was introduced to Indian army colonel Vincent Ruthnaswamy, an engineer bringing the first road to Nepal.

Comber was thunderstruck by the tall man's beauty:

"Then and there I fell out of frigidity into the most blazing need to put my hands on him, to hold him, to want him to make love to me. Heaven — how was this possible, and so swiftly? I stared at him and my legs were unsteady, and all the juices of my body started to pour" (*House* 107).

Their torrid affair inspired her next novel, published in 1958, *The Mountain Is Young*. Vincent and Suyin became the characters Unni Menon and Anne Ford.

The protagonists stroll in a rural valley of Nepal and watch a male bluebird's frantic mating dance (*Mountain* 312). The next thing they know they are on the ground, tearing each others' clothes off. Anne burns as she feels "his swift entry, pleasure so intense that she heard herself cry out ... 'I am going to die, I am dying, I am'." They climax wildly, as Anne feels "the lovely shock of his coming, more pleasurable than hers."

With her daring to verbalize the delirium of being mounted by a man, Han Suyin became the first female novelist to graphically portray the arousal created by the provocative travel encounter. For its daring, Mountain "was declared 'hot stuff,' the equivalent of today's porn," the author later noted (*House* 216).

With two hit novels in the 1950s, the first also made into a popular film, just prior to the true Baby Boomer era Han Suyin gave women a notion that women engaged in exotic romances. This chapter will examine how, for 150 years, literature, films, plays and poems have both depicted and influenced women's vacation romances. The red-hot travel lover has been sketched as vibrant and amusing, doomed or lonely, or simply untamable. Meanwhile female authors themselves have suffered merciless criticism — in some cases compensated for by oodles of royalty money — for tackling the topic of holiday romance.

Millions of women ponder the zipless fuck

Around 1961, three years after *Mountain's* publication, a beautiful, blonde upper-middle class New York City girl — perhaps she had heard of Han Suyin's novels? — arrived in Florence. "There, having gone to study Italian, I studied Italians instead, learning what so many American girls learned, that sex was better in a foreign tongue because guilt could be left at home" (Jong, *Fifty* 122).

Erica Jong, then 19 years old, was the latest of thousands of English-speaking women from the Victorian era onward to worship at the phallus of the agreeably pagan Italian male. She breathed in the experience of romance on the road. A dozen years, two husbands and numerous lovers after she arrived in Italy, she breathed out her idealized version of travel sex: "the zipless fuck," life's purest form of human intercourse. Clothes melt away, tongues intertwine, sex begins without talk, and ends with never meeting again.

On page 11 of her debut novel, *Fear of Flying*, Jong dropped the zipless f-bomb on the 1970s zeitgeist. With swift animality, an amorous widow and a strange soldier pleasure each other in a train tunnel in Sicily. In millions of female minds was planted the picture of overseas places and situations where one could screw wildly with strangers.

The fantasy passage may have remained merely an implausible yet indelible image for 99 percent of its readers. (Some of my high school girlfriends and I discussed the zipless fuck in admiring tones.) But for a few bold souls, Jong's imagined scene was something that they had already tried — *amours de voyage* by then had become rampant in the Mediterranean, East and West Africa and the Caribbean, and even the precise variant of train compartment quickies was documented (Theroux,

"Strangers on a Train" 129). Or the z.f. was something that sounded farfetched to the reader but maybe, just maybe, might be potentially intriguing.

The next year, 1974, the erotic film *Emmanuelle* arrived, immediately reinforcing the appeal of the zipless fuck, airplane style. Emmanuelle, a French diplomat's wife, enjoys sex with a sultry-eyed stranger while flying to join her husband, Jean, in Bangkok. After landing, Jean encourages her to continue her ziplessness with European men, European women and Thai kick boxers, but the film's larger point may be that social restraints dissolve the instant one leaves home airspace.

It was Jong's novel that had the sturdier legs culturally, eventually selling 12 million copies worldwide. Baby Boomer women adopted the book as their own. *Flying* was an anthem of early feminism and earthy female sexuality, and it was the zipless fuck that grabbed specific attention.

Thus *Fear of Flying* was sort of a particle accelerator — a scientific instrument that increases the kinetic energy of charged particles — for changes in female conduct. *Flying* both reflected and affected popular behavior. In her novel, Jong, herself unknowing of unpublicized but rampant female casual adventuring outside Italy, captured a trend little known to the general public and (in cahoots with a slew of social forces) inspired more women to partake of that reality.

"Novels do augment this process [of social change]," Jong believes (Templin 146), "and change what people think."

"Sometimes people will come up to me," Jong recalls (Templin 178), "and say, 'I remember where I was when I read *Fear of Flying*. I was traveling through Europe; I had just met this Greek boy, and I was wondering whether or not to sleep with him, and then I read your book, and I did.' "

Similarly, a Baltimore friend in her late 50s told me she read *Flying* and thought vacation carousing "would be something fun to try." On a trip to London, she embarked on an affair with a scholar from the Horn of Africa. "Erica Jong's timing was perfect," the friend said. "Han Suyin was too early."

A reinforcing trend

Female sexual adventuring grew in popularity, which launched new super-accelerators, the films *Shirley Valentine* (1989) and *How Stella Got Her Groove Back* (1998). The movies had documentable impact on female purchases of air tickets to Greece and the Caribbean (Faul; Trescott). For example, black women packed swimsuits and condoms and jetted to Jamaica in the wake of *Stella*. Their return towing shiny new island boyfriends put novelist and poet Ishmael Reed in the mind of a famous slave ship: "These women are bringing so many Jamaican guys back here it's almost like *Amistad*" (Patrick 217). Meanwhile in Europe, Willy Russell's play (and later movie) made "Shirley Valentine" synonymous with middle-aged lonelyhearts headed to Greece. Reality imitated film. A captain in Cyprus named his love boat after Russell's heroic Everywoman — and seduced the much younger wife of a retired Englishman (H. Smith, Shirley Valentine). The tale of a frustrated housewife even broke up marriages, according to Pauline Collins, star of the movie. The actress received five letters from women saying they had decided to leave their husbands after seeing *Shirley Valentine* (Maddox).

Once you articulate a form of sexual activity with a catchy name (a zipless fuck) and make its participants household words (Isadora Wing, Stella Payne, Shirley Valentine), you have no doubt planted a seed in the minds of many readers. Only on my final rewrite of this chapter did I have the following epiphan. Although my first casual travel sex experiences shocked me at the time, and I thought I had never heard of any else succumbing to instant slut syndrome, they occurred nine years after reading *Fear of Flying*. A tendril of memory from pages 11 to 15 may have been subliminally whispering to me.

At this moment sitting at my iMac computer, I even recall for the first time in more than two decades, my silent and deep disappointment at taking a luxurious private sleeper on the overnight train from Paris to London with my first husband, who was too tired for sex. This tall green-eyed looker, who shared the first name and the nationality of *Fear of Flying's* British sex object, Adrian Goodlove (and only momentarily Goodlove's lack of good loving), couldn't have known the utter necessity of showing more effort with a reader of Erica Jong.

Only intra-marriage did I have my zipless fucks, most classically along a marshy stream in Brazil. Jong described the z.f. as a fantasy, a dream, "rarer than the unicorn. And I have never had one" (Flying 15). Note to Erica: The fantasy has been made real. A number of women as well as myself have ridden the unicorn, including one, remarkably, prior to *Flying's* publication. In 1953, Anne Cumming took her ease with a strange Iraqi in a train compartment shared with others. And Cumming's poet compatriot Fiona Pitt-Kethley burrowed right under the zipper with Greeks and Italians, including a Sicilian in the compartment of a parked train in Messina, following local custom.

Yes, the injection of writers as participants in and later publicizers of casual vacation merry-making allowed the trend to reinforce itself endlessly.

A turn to the memoir

However, if *Flying* inspired behavior, it curiously did not create much of any literary trend in fiction. Henry Miller ("Two Writers") predicted incorrectly that the novel would "make literary history ... because of it women are going to find their own voice and give us great sagas of sex, life, joy and adventure."

Instead of great novels, first-hand accounts flourished. Particularly in the 1980s and 1990s, as travel sex became a more popular topic, women's travel books and essays (I have surveyed about 66) came to outnumber novels by female authors (eight, though I am bound to have missed something) by an 8-to-1 margin. (In addition to *The Sheik*, *Mountain*, *Flying* and *Stella*, the other four major female-authored novels are *Black Narcissus* by Godden, *Women of Sand and Myrrh* by al-Shayk, *The Edge of Bali* by Baranay and *The Lover* and *The North China Lover*, very similar and counted as one, by Duras. A pair of more tangential works include *Polite Society* (Sumner) and *The Chosen Place, The Timeless People* (Marshall).

The memoir, perhaps epitomized by Joana McIntyre Varawa's intrinsically dramatic *Changes in Latitude*, seemed to become the superior vehicle, with real life providing entertaining narrative tension between a middle-aged female traveler, easy for many readers to identify with, and her untamable (in this case Fijian) man. True stories so imitated romance novels that fiction almost became superfluous; hence the lack of Jong protegées and the modesty of Jong's post-1970s career.

Still, novels do continue to appear. Three decades after *Flying*, Frenchman Michel Houellebecq's *Platform* depicts a cold new world, one where Jong's licentious widow on a train, essentially a free spirit looking for quick fun, multiplies exponentially. In the process she evolves into a figure both more despondent and more daring in her taste, dropping the Italian for the ultra lover, the son of Africa, the black man: "laid back, virile, they have a sense of fun; they know how to enjoy themselves without getting hung up on things; you never have any trouble with them" (167). The Western woman, marooned now by dating wars and man shortages rather than literal widowhood, is now portrayed en masse as lonely and looking to buy a smile from willing tropical men.

In similar contrast to the 1970s early feminist zeitgeist that midwifed *Fear of Flying*, the tale of Stella Payne's lost groove tells us that in the yuppie and buppie 1990s, women were celibate, angrier and materialistic — yet searching for something radically opposite to the zipless fuck, namely, conventional marriage against all emotional and demographic odds.

How Stella Got Her Groove Back leaves itself wide open to criticism on its literary merits, blemished by its narrator's scatterbrained, endless internal monologues and her shallow fascination with expensive brand-name possessions. For the sexual historian, however, *Stella* is a document of enormous value, for along with *Shirley Valentine*, it swings the spotlight from the spoiled Isadora Wing to Everywoman (black or white), from Old Europe to package holiday sites (Greece and the Caribbean), and from adultery to wreckage post divorce. Isadora Wing vaults effortlessly in and out of marriages mocked by her adulterous yearnings; Stella Payne and the real-life ranks of the formerly married exhibit no such frivolity, as the man shortage makes having a boyfriend let alone a second husband an uphill task. Angst and doubt attend even simple decisions on whether to write or call the vacation lover.

McMillan charts the very real bewilderment of the older woman trying (a) to know if what happened on her vacation might be love (b) to find the courage to bring home a foreign man and (c) to decide whether to actually marry the dashing young fellow.

The light and heat of fiction

Literary and cinematic treatments of the female sexual adventurer have intersected and re-intersected with reality. Top authors have launched their careers and created fortunes via the muse of romance on the road. At the same time, female authors be they novelists or travel writers have endured savage attacks — sometimes from each other! — for daring to confess to sluttish revels, especially if they broadcast the more hilarious details.

And somewhere in all this writing (and literary backstabbing) about romance on the road lies works of fiction that do what fiction does best, bringing the level of moral imagination and artful rendering deserved by this most vivid and at times magical experience. "The writer is ... shaman to the tribe," Erica Jong has observed (Templin 173).

Jong may be the popular face of travel romance, but the high masters would be E.M. Forster, who saw deeply into how foreign climes freed the heart to pursue its true mate, for Britain's repressed gay men and adventurous women alike, and Paul Theroux, more attuned to raw, animalistic pleasure with strangers as a turbocharged key to knowledge unattainable in a routine life.

Forster's earliest novels, after the dawn of the 20th century, chronicled the Victorian peak of amorous visits by Englishwomen to romantic Italy. And the revival of his novels as films beginning in the 1980s coincided with the current explosion in holiday liaisons (see timeline). Whereas hit movies such as *A Room with a View* project a sweeter, gentler and more subtle vision of searching for love overseas when compared to the cultural milestones *Fear of Flying* and *Stella*, Forster also may be the master of plumbing raw carnality, in the short stories "The Obelisk" and "The Other Boat," written respectively in 1939 and 1958 and published after his death in 1970.

A shy and rather inexperienced homosexual, Forster in his more graphic works drew on a vivid imagination and some exotic encounters while in the employ of an Indian maharaja. Novelist and travel writer Paul Theroux more boldly mines his rambunctious years as a youthful Peace Corps volunteer in Malawi in many of his stories and novels, which might best be called fictional autobiography (Rubin) — in which a character much like the author exaggerates some events and invents others.

In 1964, Theroux visited a leper colony by the shores of Lake Malawi and borrowed from the experience for the startling "Lepers of Moyo" section of *My Other Life*. The extended, 1,500-word sex scene is perhaps the most artful and stirring of his numerous evocations of lust in exotic locales. During a drumming ceremony, Theroux's narrator sneaks off with a young admirer to her blind grandmother's hut for silent but molten foreplay. "[Amina] was pressed so hard against me it was as though we were not two people anymore, but were so penetrated that we were like one wild, tearful creature. She tore at her breasts and then clamped her mouth over the fingers of one hand and wept. I was intent on one drumming rhythm. If sex is knowledge, and I believed it was, I was on the verge of knowing everything" ("Lepers" 86).

In Theroux's "Lepers" and "Homage to Mrs. Robinson" (older woman seduces younger man in a cozy train compartment on the Italian Riviera), E.M. Forster's "The Obelisk" and Suyin's *Mountain*, holy madness possesses near-strangers. They couple urgently as African drums beat or northern seas crash on cliffs. Mediterranean railcars rock as hearts race, and Himalayan mountains glitter in a crystal atmosphere that makes women suddenly lucid, so lucid as to view an impromptu open-air congress as the wisest move of their lives.

Writers such as E.M. Forster and Paul Theroux divine the poetry of travel sex as precisely as social scientists weigh its psychology.

The adventurous woman: comedienne

Hannah Bilton (*Vestal Fire*, 1927) visits the expatriate colony on Capri during the happy-go-lucky era of Scott and Zelda. This quiet, Pennsylvania-bred beauty possesses dark brown hair and a fine profile, but it is her "vivid hot blue eyes" that give her away:

> Her appeal to a libertine was always immediate, because she had the charm of having evidently never experienced love with all its irksome implications of emotional standards. ... Sentiment was wasted upon Miss

Hannah. ... When a woman only draws near to men by the high-road of sex, it is not astonishing that she should become inured to heavy traffic. (292)

Demure in public, Miss Hannah surprised many a dancing partner at villa parties as more of "an accomplished wanton" than "a prim Quakeress" (293). Men readily steered her into the shadows for quickies; what the thin woman "lacked in acreage she made up for by accessibility" (310). When Miss Bilton traveled on to the Far East, wagging tongues told of her "in the harem of a hospitable potentate" and enjoying "familiarity with the Chinese coolies" (321).

This is not your flirtation-only Daisy Miller.

While Henry James let the innocent Daisy wander into tragedy — without even any explicit satisfaction in the boudoir along the way — two generations later, Scottish novelist Compton Mackenzie refused to deny his female characters their trifles. Travel sex, casual liaisons, lesbian frolics — these were precisely their cup of tea.

Notably, Miss Hannah is not blousy or a drunk or even loud, not conflicted or doomed; she merely adores getting laid. Miss Hannah may even have been something like a real person who passed through Capri. Mackenzie lived on the grottoed isle and observed first hand its historically documented sexual roguery (Aldrich preface, xi).

A lust for laughter as well as sex and food, on the order of a Tom Jonesian wench, would seem a logical constellation of personality traits. And without a doubt, Miss Hannah's comic heiresses — Isadora Wing and Shirley Valentine and *The Lunatic's* Inga the German photographer — have sisters in the real world with physical appetites and a light-hearted approach to fulfilling them. We know because Isadora Wing is sister to her creator Erica Jong — and because in real life, the Bay Area bisexual erotica author Susie Bright and the English travel writers Fiona Pitt-Kethley and Anne Cumming have provided us with their comic sexual memoirs — as nonfiction.

Though our focus has been on the novel, female sexual explorers' memoirs complete the portrayal of the carnal adventurer as funster. Here Pitt-Kethley reigns. She is to al fresco fiascos what Eric Newby (*A Short Walk in the Hindu Kush*) and Redmond O'Hanlon (*Into the Heart of Borneo*) are to epicly funny disaster travel. "I think bad sex often makes better copy than good sex," FP-K told one interviewer ("100 Men").

Pitt-Kethley contributes to expeditionary literature her explorations of the vagaries of the Mediterranean penis. A guide to the baths of Venus south of Rome wants necklaces wrapped around Mr. Happy (*Journeys* 26). A Greek motorcyclist's manhood awaits attention while misbehaving prophylactics jet about the roadside trees (*Pan* 151-52). A curly-haired Frenchman, his impressive dimensions waving about the hill-sides above Naples ("I was beginning to have serious doubts about whether we were made for each other, biologically speaking"), smugly asks her whether he is short or long, and whether she likes it short or long (*Journeys* 63). So much for intellectual stimulation. Then, "one millimetre from entry, he said he thought he heard someone coming. It certainly wasn't me."

Which is not to say that Pitt-Kethley's books are unqualified successes. Priceless as they are to the sexual historian, *The Pan Principle* (set mostly in Greece) and *Journeys to the Underworld* (Italy) lack sustained interest when the author wanders into classical history and serious topics. Most critics find her scholarship on classical sites laughable, and her flitting from antiquities to indecencies chaotic; an "amnesiac divide" (Cropper) lies between the two. (I myself on editors' recommendations left sex out of my first book, *An Amateur's Guide to the Planet*. Intimate encounters do suck reader interest away from rival topics and would appear to do better in their own separate books, as Anne Cumming seemed to realize.)

Which brings us to our next topic: the visceral loathing that many critics seem to feel for female authors who write about travel sex — especially when they write in a comic note.

Bonking: Just bunk?

Let's start with *The Pan Principle*. Indeed, the critics panned it on principle.

The poetess was found guilty of that worst of crimes: bonking, sometimes in "grubbily inorgasmic" fashion. "Ms. Pitt-Kethley [is] excessively fond of a bonk," one reviewer wrote (Thompson-Noel), though admitting that another (bonkless) travel book he had to review in conjunction with *The Pan Principle* sat "tamely in the hand" by comparison.

London critics make merry with FP-K's wide-open availability, her "negotiating wayside sex" (Cropper) and carrying "condoms ... so she can copulate with passers-by" (P. Jones). They giggle at references to FP-K washing her "private" parts (Cropper), after she herself made them less than mysterious.

Anne Cumming's missives came under similar fire: "Her writing about sex, while extraordinarily honest, tends to be just one damn bonk after another" (Kenny). Meanwhile, Lucretia Stewart is a stereotypical "middle-aged Anglo-Saxon woman who travels alone to the Caribbean for just one thing — a quick black bonk in the bushes" (Elphinston).

Even just one "damn bonk" can loose swarms of critics. Vindictive reaction toward Dea Birkett's *Serpent in Paradise*, which honestly describes a one-night stand as ruinous of her standing on tiny Pitcairn Island in the remote South Pacific, abounds on Amazon.com. While thousands of men go to Polynesia chasing a chimera of sexual license, when one woman wants to get close to the descendents of *Bounty* mutineers, the sky falls in.

What is going on here? Women who write with wit and frankness about sex have enjoyed the wrath of critics, and not just beginning in the 1960s: "certainly since the Restoration and the 18th century, when English women began to write for money, the writing woman has been a target for abuse of the most virulent kind" (Templin 1). Further, "wit, associated with erotic impropriety, was in itself suspect" and sexual misbehavior in print "indicated it in life."

Suyin and Jong provide contemporary examples. After *A Many-Splendoured Thing* (granted, it was autobiographical) was published, Suyin noted wryly that in Hong Kong circles "a reputation as a loose nymphomaniac was now established for me by some of the more indignant" (*House* 73-74). Similarly, Erica Jong observed, "There is a tendency on the part of a certain type of naive reader to assume that an author who was written this type of book is available for one-night stands" (Templin 125).

Let's now compare the author of *Fear of Flying* and the author of *The Great Railway Bazaar* in greater detail.

Titans clash

The champ in the category of absorbing slings and arrows has been, for three decades, Erica Jong (née Mann), born in New York City in April 1942. "Can It Be Good Literature If It's Funny, Sexy, and Written by a Woman?" Charlotte Templin asks in the title of the first chapter of a book that tackles the topic of the New York author's detractors.

Perhaps predictably, given centuries of punishment of women who write about physicality, coupled with professional rivalry, the most popularly successful writer on travel sex (Jong) has been attacked most savagely by the most literarily successful one (her co-generationist Theroux). In the process of becoming an Anglicized American while living in London, Theroux, a fellow wartime baby born one year and 16 days before Jong and 200 miles away, in Medford, Mass., seemed to have picked up from Martin Amis and other English contemporaries a certain vituperative misogyny. When asked to review *Flying* for a British publication, Theroux ("Hapless") scorched the earth: "Erica Jong's witless heroine looms like a mammoth pudenda, as roomy as the Carlsbad caverns, luring amorous spelunkers to confusion in her plunging grottoes."

Three decades later, the passage is "an insult so revealing that Jong quotes it to this day," the *New York Times* (L. Miller) noted. Not recalling

Fear of Flying as all that rife with spelunkers, lost in an echoing subterranean vastness, I reread the novel and counted Isadora enjoying eight unions blessed by matrimony, with Bennett Wing, and exactly one explicit instance of adultery (156).

Ultimately, the value today to the sexual historian of Theroux's "mammoth pudenda" rebuke is that it inspires a look at just how Jong and Theroux, the two leading lights of the genre, actually portray travel liaisons.

Both find trains a congenial setting for instant ardor. Sex and sexual tension linked to train travel appears in at least five Theroux works (*Bazaar* 336; "Homage to Mrs. Robinson" 152-53; "Strangers on a Train" 129; *Rooster* 267; *The Pillars of Hercules* 109-11) including two (*Pillars*, "Homage") set on the same Mediterranean shores as *Flying*.

Jong, and later Theroux, also agree on the paradoxical virtue and innocence of passion with the foreign stranger.

"There is no power game," Jong wrote, and "no one is trying to prove anything ... the zipless fuck is the purest thing there is" (*Flying* 14).

Four years after *Fear of Flying's* publication, Theroux (unwittingly?) agreed with Jong that a road quickie (especially if involving an older woman) was not only thrilling but noble, for sex was no longer "a means to another end: ... job, money, marriage, power, domination ... strategy or currency" ("Homage" 154).

Whereas Jong tells us, both in her fiction and in interviews, that the zipless fuck is a fantasy she has not experienced, Jong's nemesis makes it clear that he draws on a wealth of personal experience. Theroux's career over the course of three decades drew generously from the mammothly available pudenda of Malawi bar girls and their rural sistren ("African Girls"; "The Lepers of Moyo"; "White Lies"). The bar girls, zipless in the most literal sense, wore no underwear or shoes, Theroux tells us, and could be tipped on their backs without foreplay.

Four works by Theroux deal extensively with African girls — "White Lies" (1979), *My Secret History* (1989 — "although some of the events and places depicted in this novel bear a similarity to those in my own life, the characters all strolled out of my imagination"), *My Other Life* (1996 — "an imaginary memoir") and *Sir Vidia's Shadow* (1998) .

The clues to autobiography include the photo of Theroux on the front cover of *My Other Life*, in such self-evident titles as *My Other Life* and *My Secret History*, the author's own introductory faint disclaimers, and bitter protests lodged by Theroux's ex-wife to counter his portrayals of certain domestic incidents (Rubin). Theroux's settings for overseas capers in Malawi and Uganda mirror his real-life peregrinations. His narrators include a pair with the perfectly transparent names Paul and

Paulie. Another narrator, Julian, who makes thrashing love with a Yoruba tribeswoman from Nigeria with the bearing of a princess, is swiftly revealed for who he really is: "Yomo is Yomo ... but the young man is not Julian Lavalle. It's me, Paul Theroux, and I am shining my light upon the past. I cannot improve on this story" (*Vidia* 17).

As both Jong and Theroux clearly draw on their own curricula vitae, Theroux's more extensive and exotic experiences provide richer material for transmutation into fiction. The authors also arrive at somewhat different themes. For Jong, carnality with the foreign stranger involves an aspect of feminist, and somewhat muddled, rebellion against the constraints of marriage. For Theroux, the revolt is more complicated, involving politics both sexual and racial. He seems to resent Western women, who in contrast to Africans require elaborate negotiations for sex (a theme also seen in Norman Rush's "Alone in Africa," a short story about an expatriate's antics when his wife briefly leaves Botswana). And, Theroux notes, "because this was Africa and they were black [sex] was not only a pleasure, it was also an act of political commitment" (*History* 212). African women thought better of themselves when desired by white men (211).

For both Jong and Theroux, travel sex represents the realization of a dream of effortless intercourse. In Africa, Theroux compares sex to shaking hands, or playing cards, "unlimited and guiltless."

A notable distinction between Jong and Theroux also emerges. In *Flying*, Isadora Wing's travel lover, Adrian Goodlove, suffers from impotence; Theroux's male characters fully salute a cosmos of partners who holler in appreciation.

Absent in Isadora Wing, at least in her appearance in *Flying*, is the more daring sexual connoisseurship of Theroux's narrators, his thinly disguised selves exploring the truly alien lover and the galaxies of wild pleasure the most outré discover. Wing limits herself to her psychoanalyst husband, an impotent Brit and a fantasy Italian. Meanwhile Theroux's Julian Lavelle pushes far more deeply into uncharted territory, lighting candles and getting into bed with the Yoruba aristocrat Yomo, who "howled eagerly in the ecstasy of sex like an addict injected, and her eyes rolled up in her skull and she stared, still howling, with big white eyes like a blind zombie that sees everything" (*Vidia* 5).

Skill matters

Further, it is the caliber and heat of Theroux's words that seize the elusive reality of travel sex, the physical delirium that liberates the spirit: "Sex was magic, mind-expanding. ... it was knowledge too — not blind lust, though wild monkey-lust was part of it, helping to illuminate the act" (*Vidia* 78). For Theroux, itinerant intercourse is vital, life-changing, a genuine exploration of the sexual geography of the world. Physical encounters are too important to be swept under the rug while describing cathedrals, pyramids and mountain ranges, even when honesty about the temptations of infidelity (while married, he made a pass and described same at the close of *The Great Railway Bazaar*) may bring dire consequences on the home front.

Here's a tricky issue. Male authors seem to get a free pass on explicit sexual passages while females suffer unfairly. But at the same time, a literary judge must point out how a Forster, Theroux or Houellebecq brings far more gifts of imagination, moral reflection and prose style than a Jong or McMillan, especially to the task of capturing the incendiary nature of trysts with a near stranger.

Perhaps the truest fictional depiction of casual travel sex occurs in Forster's short story "The Obelisk," too risqué to be published until after the novelist's death in 1970, with Theroux's "The Lepers of Moyo" and "Homage to Mrs. Robinson" also outstanding for burning sensuality, and Houellebecq far out in front in depicting the prerogative of the lonely and less attractive to use their money to seek affection overseas. All are male writers.

Barring Han Suyin and Ruth Prawer Jhabvala (see "An Experience of India"), the other big names among female novelists (and some memoirists) bring their own rope to the hangman with boneheaded, amateurish passages in their prose. Just one example: In course of reading Jong's *Flying* sequel, *Any Woman's Blues*, for purposes of composing a newspaper review, my eyes disbelieved the page where Jong permitted her female protagonist to remark, "I could look up his nostril and see eternity. ... As we coupled, mountain ranges rose and fell" (*Blues* 16). *The Baltimore Sun* book editor didn't believe me either when I rendered the passage in my review, and I had to show him the actual words. One indicator of how time has rendered its verdict on *Blues*, released in 1990: A notice on Amazon.com that 122 new and used copies are available, with a starting price of one cent.

Barely hidden in Theroux's nasty review of *Fear of Flying* is his deduction that he could, and later would, burrow more deeply than Jong into reality of carnality with exotic outsiders at its most transcendent and bring higher talent to its rendering — mixed with resentment that Jong's coinage, the "zipless fuck," not his literary output, would be read by millions and rule the zeitgeist.

Trivial soul-baring?

At least Theroux and Jong agree that travel sex is a significant event in a wanderer's life.

Bizarrely, Fiona Pitt-Kethley, a noted dabbler in foreign men herself, took aim at Lady Jane Digby, a crucial figure at the dawn of female sexual adventuring (see History chapter) in a book review headlined, "A Woman of No Importance." Pitt-Kethley deemed Lady Jane "neither a role model nor a history maker and has nothing to teach us," though over eight decades, six biographers and six (!) novelists (four English, one French — Balzac — and one Greek, see Oddie 339-40) have disagreed.

Even the editor of a collection of erotic tales deemed her own female contributors "recklessly confessional" (de Kretser 7). The editor wondered whether women who explore the globe were by definition less likely to be in home relationships, or whether travel writing had shifted as a genre, reflecting the ingress of more females. Yet she had unwittingly managed to denigrate her essayists. The derogatory label "confessional" has long been applied to women's writing deemed "shameful and too personal," while male authors "are allowed the expression of strong feelings and states of mind" (Templin 2). Jong says "confessional writing ... implies that what these women are doing is just sort of spilling out whatever they have in their guts and that there's no craft involved in the writing" (Templin 66).

There are landmines for even the most popular authors with their fans. While Terry McMillan had enjoyed adulation — screaming, stomping audiences of 1,000 (Trescott) — Erica Jong was devastated when feminists at a San Francisco poetry festival booed and hissed a poem on pregnancy and birth (*Fifty* 284), and June Juska, who wrote a book (*A Round-Heeled Woman*) about the reaction to her personal ad for a sex partner placed when she was 66, endured harsh female criticism at a reading in her home town, in Berkeley, Calif. (Witchel).

The secret lives of travel writers

All the put-downs, by males and females, of lusty confessionals by traveling women do demonstrate a lingering hypocrisy at the core of narratives about journeys.

As Ian Littlewood wrote in *Sultry Climes*, the sex is nearly always there in journeys and if the event doesn't make into print, the trip highlight has been censored. Tourists themselves present the culture and not the sex: "letters home commonly tell of the churches visited, not the brothels" (4-5). Yet "far from being marginal to what tourism is about, the sexual element is vital to it. ... Because we like to pretend they are separate, the history of tourism has left out the sex, and the contemporary responses to sex tourism have left out the history."

Yes, as Littlewood notes, sex is "vital" to the travel narrative. Even if a female reviewer (Kaveney) primly says of Pitt-Kethley's *Journeys*, "The casual screws ... end up being a distraction from *what is important*" (emphasis added).

So, what of the writer who obviously leaves sex (sometimes a lot of it) out? Who renders his heroic expedition as a "fictional world," resembling something by Tolkien, wherein "like children's dolls, the characters have a noticeable absence of genitalia" (Rowell 40).

For example, two British travel writers have died of AIDS. The first to succumb, the bisexual Bruce Chatwin, gelded his books of lovers with unswerving determination. London literary insiders apparently adored praising his work, such as *Songlines* and *In Patagonia*, and being "in the know" on his inverted tastes while telling wire services that he died of a fungal disease contracted in China, as was stated in his obituary.

Chatwin himself acknowledged a problem. *In Patagonia* described the author, a stunning blue-eyed blond, meeting a pianist who played him Beethoven and Chopin. When a friend praised the passage, Chatwin confessed that he'd left out a small detail: At the end of the music, the pair traipsed off to the bedroom. Hemingway "said if you take something OUT of a piece of writing it always shows," Chatwin acknowledged (qtd. in Clapp 42).

Much more must have been taken out of Chatwin's work. Does his illness point to a wealth of assignations between 1962 and 1986 (the year of his AIDS diagnosis), as he visited much of Asia, the Americas, the Caribbean (including Haiti) and Africa (Shakespeare 490-91)? He told his doctors alternative versions of possible contacts, mentioning "an Australian whom he had known between 1978 and 1981" and a 1978 gang rape in Benin.

Were his dalliances really so unimportant to Chatwin himself, aware as he began to deteriorate that as a consequence his voice would be stilled prematurely, at the age of 48?

The second author to succumb, Anne Cumming, made no explicit public mention of her disorder until her last days. Yet her two books contained the truth of her activities (lots of gay and bisexual lovers and travel sex) and her obituary the truth of her demise; dying did not "out" her as a sex traveler.

So we see Cumming and female authors dare to recognize the truth and the importance of their physical travel adventures. In doing so, they often do not reach the pinnacle of literary excellence. Yet who is the better witness to human experience? University of Glasgow professor Richard Cronin (163) looks at "the English girl" (played by Julie Christie in the film version) whose diary makes up the modern section of Ruth Prawer Jhabvala's *Heat and Dust*. His comments about a fictional diarist might well apply to today's female novelists, who lack polish but not veracity:

The English girl ... is the product of a meagre culture. But her gauche, unimaginative prose gropes, however clumsily, in an effort to reach out to her experience. Forster and [fellow Indiaphile writer J.R.] Ackerley are never clumsy, never grope. Their experience never seems to lie outside the language in which they record it. Which is to say, of course, that they are accomplished writers, but which may suggest also that writers are not wholly to be trusted.

Travel sex authors:
their kindest statements come from the bank

Many "confessional" female authors can take consolation in their royalty checks.

Travel romances made Han Suyin's career as an author. In fact, in the early 1950s *A Many-Splendoured Thing* was such a hit that it helped boost her publisher's fortunes following postwar doldrums (Archives), and we may infer that her personal prosperity did not suffer.

Marguerite Duras received circa $500,000 for film rights to her novel *The Lover* (Adler 378). Later in the 1990s, Terry McMillan earned $6 million for the book version of *How Stella Got Her Groove Back* (Skow) and additional millions for the movie rights. And from 1984 to 1992, five film adaptations of E.M. Forster's work, including three novels based on traveling female protagonists in erotic situations, racked up more than $150 million at the box office (Rosenthal).

Ultimately, critics want to find traveling females who describe fleshly entertainments both unseemly and unimportant. They are wrong. Readers have rendered their verdict, and even the cloying memoirist Laurie Gough, with her moonlit Fijian (*Kite Strings*) and Balinese (Bali Moon) boyfriends, has devoted loyalists eagerly posting reviews on Amazon.com.

For the novelists, modestly reworked life experiences have landed solidly on the bulls' eye of what women have liked to read ever since the first novels in English appeared in the 17th century. Namely, love stories involving obstacles overcome.

"Men write stories about heroism and women write stories about men," Helen Hazen wrote in *Endless Rapture* (18). "Over and over—cowboys, spies, starships; romance, gothic, nurse. Probably less than 20 percent of all fiction varies from the norm. ... Men continue to read stories of courage in the adversity of overcoming evil, and women continue to read about courage in the adversity of overcoming men."

Real travel romances indeed fit the bill of what readers like.

Now let's turn our attention from authors to their depictions of female characters.

The adventurous woman: Untamable

We have seen how literature represents the sort of woman who engages in travel sex often as a comedian, or lusty soul. Novels also portray her as married but far more passionate than her husband. Up crops a renegade view, threatening throughout history, that women harbor passion matching the heat of the healthy male and sometimes surpassing it, verging on wildness.

Isadora Wing (*Fear of Flying*) finds herself in a lukewarm marriage, with a depressed husband who killed her love with his silences. Marital dissatisfaction also eats at Anne Ford (*The Mountain Is Young*), Suzanne (*Women of Sand and Myrrh*), Shirley Valentine, and Hilda in "The Obelisk." Even Mrs. Clifton in the film *The English Patient* becomes unhinged in Cairo, dropping her loving but brotherly husband for the edgy sexuality of Count Lazlo: "This is a different world is what I tell myself, a different life, and I'm a different sort of wife."

Other women also find themselves engaged or wedded to constricted or bigoted men, but their true complaint is broader: the restrictions of British society. Lucy Honeychurch's spirit blossoms in Italy, which literally provides her with *A Room with a View,* and India's sensuality unhinges Adela Quested (*A Passage to India*), Olivia Rivers (*Heat and Dust*), the foreign correspondent's wife in Ruth Prawer Jhabvala's "An Experience of India" and the nuns in *Black Narcissus.*

The adventurous woman: Lonely

And some women in literature are fallen but valiant soldiers in the dating war.

Travel sex as a natural response to a collapse in Westerners' attraction to each other figures in Michel Houellebecq's brilliant *Platform*. A Parisian women who works in a travel agency, Valerie, remains celibate for 10 years. On a trip to Thailand, she meets Michel, another wanderer in the gray landscape of the modern desexed workplace. Michel's own celibacy is relieved in swift, gushing encounters with Thai massage girls, who appear to relight the French bureaucrat's pilot light. He now dares to ask Valerie for her number. She is wary, almost frightened, but agrees.

Back in Paris, Michel visits Valerie's apartment, and steam rises from the pages on their instant and exquisite mating of bodies and hearts. Valerie's ability to touch expertly, to excite lust with her fine body, and to love with a shining intelligence, moves Michel.

Platform spurs the reader to realize the colossal extent of the waste of potential loving and caring and physical joy in the lives of even beautiful Frenchwomen, let alone the rest of us. Further, Valerie and Michel cannot find each others' arms by encountering each other in their home city. They must travel 6,000 miles to Thailand to escape icy metropolitan hopelessness and land in a place where they can (a) meet informally and (b) view each other as sexual beings, as they wear bathing suits, swim and drink in resorts where sexual opportunity is omnipresent, as brightly obvious as the glowing neon signs of the massage parlors.

In addition to depicting longterm female celibacy, the commodification of sex and the search for healing, Houellebecq tackles the dating war (84, 104), the attraction of Western males to Asian females, and Western females to black males (167) and the dogmatism of attacks on adult sex tourism (36-37). *Platform* takes a novelistic approach to the themes of the "Reasons" chapter of *Romance on the Road*.

The adventurous woman: as viewed by men

As does the male literary critic, the male novelist, poet or short story writer often turns a baleful eye on the female sex traveler.

• The white tourist in Barbados is a slow-thinking lamb, barely worth the effort and discomfort it takes for an island man to get her drunk enough for sex on a midday picnic. "Her blouse was soaked under the arm-pits and when she lay back on the towel after her third rum punch the outline of her breasts were limned in sweat on her shirt. To tell the truth it was awful. I don't think I ever felt so uncomfortable in my life. ... There were crushed, drowned ants on her legs. I had bits of grass and dirt on me, which itched, and I didn't think I'd ever feel clean again" (Layne 51).

Or ...

• The female tourist is a beautiful model-quality blonde with a thing for black dick. In *The Harder They Come*, record executive Hilton takes a tourist back to her hotel the morning after, watching the "longlegged swinging walk that he had noticed American women affected when they thought they were being watched. 'Fine bitch. What a batti. Boy, these tourist women will do anay-thang. Nothing them won't do.'" Hilton wonders why they "rub up against every little black waiter an' doorman they can find" and "what it was about American white women made them holler so loud. Something was going on up there, the men couldn't be doing their job" (Thelwell 243-44).

• The female expatriate's wife must be badgered into a fixation with black male sexuality that she doesn't feel by a powerful, slightly menacing island bureaucrat. In *The Chosen Place, the Timeless People*, an American WASP, Harriet Amron, on an island much like Barbados, is hectored by local lawyer Lyle Hutson: "Enter into the spirit of life on the island, Mrs. Amron! ... And that shouldn't be too difficult for you. You've obviously overcome much of the narrow thinking to be found up your way. ... You're not, in other words, unalterably opposed to the strange and different, like so many Americans. Well, then, it's time to take yet another step forward and enter fully into the fold — embrace yet another brother, so to speak. It might well be ... to the good of your salvation." (This characterization of male attitudes actually comes from a female novelist, Marshall 423).

• European females who hire Moroccans, "getting screwed in the dunes of the interior," one set of men in the morning, another the same night, are pathetic, desperate creatures, a gay Italian poet (Busi 40-41) rails. The women, he writes, return no happier, with hard eyes and mouths, "typical of the woman who has split sentimentality off from sex, losing thereby. ... What a disaster women are when they join the sexual vanguard. ... They behave exactly like sour, unsatisfied and impotent queers — practically insatiable."

• Beautiful French girls dangle their charms in front of innocent Indian men, young musicians or students. They promise a happiness in love and career almost outside the Indian imagination and then move on to something else, dismissing the encounter as a frivolity all along, in the eye of Indian male novelist Pankaj Mishra in his ironically titled *The Romantics*.

A good number of female sex travelers are targets of complaint by foreign observers, but the accusations are all over the map — are women naive or hardened, capricious or calculating, too blasé or too loyal to their marriage? If there is smoke where there is fire, some women are indeed callous, as will be examined in the next chapter on Ethics. But the scattershot nature of the attacks indicate once more a certain automatic negativity toward sex play by modern women.

Additional views of the sexual explorer

Girl next door. Shirley Valentine is stunningly ordinary, while Stella Payne is a different sort of common denominator, with her black yuppie consumerism. But these women, born of a play and a novel, became the most famous portrayals of travel sex heroines as part of hit movies.

Woman in danger. Menace unnameable in its fearfulness (*A Passage to India*), madness (*The Sheltering Sky*) and death (*Daisy Miller*, Forster's "The Other Boat") may await the sex traveler, for the purity of the experience is only one side of a coin of the awesome and hardly tamable power of animalistic impulse.

In the film version of *The Sheltering Sky*, Kip (Debra Winger) and Port (John Malkovich) visit Morocco just after World War II. After a lengthy struggle with typhoid, Port dies in a mysterious desert fortress. Kip, eyes dead, will to live gone, clutching a single suitcase, waits without expectations by a stream. A Taureg trading party on camels happens by, led by a youthful, virile man. Belqassim, peering from a head covering, smiles at Kip with only his dark eyes. Back in Belqassim's ramparted Sahara town, Kip finds herself in an isolated room.

His head hooded, Belqassim kneels to wash her feet with what looks like a sponge of red straw, as she stands in the bowl. "Hada," he says — her feet. "Enchewa" — toe. "Ahfooda" — knee, and then he moves to her thigh. With golden skin, a head of soft curls and an unthreatening manner, Belqassim smiles with pure sexual joy and reveals his face. Their intercourse is shown at bed level from behind, her legs wrapping around his, moans of pleasure audible. The moment appears to capture the rapture of travel sex so removed from daily experience as to be transforming. Yet this is no consoling, happy ending. Belqassim keeps Kip locked up. She goes mad, decorating her room with her pages torn from her diary, her past life lost to her.

The strangeness of the desert, full of erotic promise, destroys the unwitting Westerner. Foreign climes magnify sexual unease. Cultural disorientation follows attraction, as happened in *A Passage to India* (1924), *Black Narcissus* (1939) as well as *The Sheltering Sky* (novel version, 1949). As in *Daisy Miller* and countless works throughout recorded history, sexual freedom by women can be portrayed only if it leads to disaster.

This now-dated theme of "women in danger" has long been supplanted by a view of female sexual explorers as comic, untamable or the girl next door. As one example of a move to repudiate doomsday consequences, *Heat and Dust* (by Ruth Prawer Jhabvala, a European woman married to an Indian architect) draws its flavor from E.M. Forster's memoirs of working for a maharaja and then turns around to challenge Forster's depiction of female hysteria in *A Passage to India*. The Raj-era Englishwoman in *Heat and Dust*, and her husband's granddaughter, enjoy making love with Indian men.

Travel writers are easy

Memoirists, some not writers by trade, have outpaced novelists in portraying holiday romances. For example, architect Sarah Lloyd wrote of her love affair in India, and other examples would be Corinne Hofmann, a boutique owner who lost her heart in Kenya; Claude Bergeret, a schoolteacher in Cameroon; and Margaret Fountaine, a butterfly collector who roamed the world.

However, many memoirists and essayists are indeed professional authors. Their dominance suggests not only the obvious — writers are more likely to work experience into publishable material — but also that an occupational duty to collect material (or, more loftily, to experience life at its fullest) compels them to sample foreign men.

In other words, while only a small proportion of women, ranging through every profession from hairdressers to university professors, who experience travel sex are writers, the vast majority of female travel writers conduct amorous experiments abroad.

Examples of scribblers are legion among sexual adventurers, beginning with the Englishwomen Cumming, Pitt-Kethley and Lucretia Stewart. Add American journalist Margaret Fuller, travel writers Robyn Davidson (Australian), Dea Birkett (British) and Laurie Gough (Canadian), and perhaps four dozen essayists whose works have been anthologized. Among novelists, we have Terry McMillan, Han Suyin and Erica Jong, to which we may add the interculturally married Ruth Prawer Jhabvala. In fact, the unpublished (in her lifetime) Maryse Holder immersed herself in gratifying well-endowed Mexican men as a path to possible literary immortality (and achieved only limited fame, and that posthumously).

Writers seek experience, and for the young female writer today, who might be surprised to be viewed as a neo- (and very mini-) Hemingway, hunting men rather than sportfish, a foreign boyfriend seems to offer the right balance of risk (less than might first appear) and reward — life-experience material a good bit livelier than how one assembled credits toward a master's degree in creative non-fiction.

The commentator's quest for potential material was perhaps expressed best by Aldo Busi: "Good sex enriches the aesthetic sensibility, bad sex enriches the speculative intelligence and therefore changes in one's career. But either way it is worthwhile" (97).

We've spoken of the echo chamber between fiction and reality as regards female sexual exploration. One almost senses a growing awareness overseas that travel writers are easy lays and will later be tellers of the tale.

After one night together, an Italian pet lover named Guisseppe later sends Fiona Pitt-Kethley a postcard reading, "Bye Bye to the most darling writer in the world" (Journeys 146). A Russian prostitute is disgusted to learn the profession of an American client, for he is not the first writer who has complicated her life (Fallowell). Further, she is not surprised when she learns he doesn't have enough money for her usual rate. And writers freeload in other areas than money (Birkett, Serpent 234); on the speck of Pitcairn in the South Pacific, islanders know visiting writers will spill their confidences, reducing them to curiosities and keeping the advance money.

Foreigners are even justifiably suspicious of non-writers. In the 1995 film Before Sunrise, a French girl, Celine, and an American boy, Jesse, feel drawn to each other on the train from Budapest to romantic Vienna, with its streets teeming with belly dancers, harpsichord players, poets and actors. When they ponder capping the night with lovemaking, Celine resists: "No, that's such a male fantasy. Meet a French girl on the train, fuck her and never see her again. It's a great story to tell. I don't want to be a great story."

After a while, the sexual historian begins to be a bit surprised to find adventure travels either without romance (Dodwell, *New Guinea*), with sternly rebuffed romantic overtures in Morocco (Hubbard) and Tobago (Thomas 592) or with delicious sexual situations, in two cases involving virtuoso, intimate massage, left unconsummated: Isabella Tree ("Souk") with a Moroccan named Najim, and Kira Salak (8-9) with a Tahitian named Coco.

How did they resist?

"It is now almost de rigueur for women travellers to indulge in sexual adventure," British biographer and columnist Byron Rogers wrote, examining how females choose to portray their experience. Victorian butterfly collector Margaret Fountaine was radical to even record her trysts in her diary, he noted: "The result was that *Love among the Butterflies* only came out a century after those travels began, long after her death, for she had broken the ultimate taboo: She had written it all down. What is beginning to happen now is that women travellers in their own lifetime are breaking this taboo, without disguises, or diaries left with instructions for their executors, and with no regrets. They share a recklessness so extreme, it is as though a new literary genre has been born."

Short takes: Movies

Bombay Talkie, 1970. In this first Merchant-Ivory production, primitive compared to their later spectacles, Lucia Lane (Jennifer Kendal), a British writer, appears on the set of a musical in Bollywood. Though shallow and utterly bored with Indian politics and customs, Lucia draws the ardent admiration of both a handsome actor, Vikram (Shashi Kapoor), and a poet and screenwriter, Hari (Zia Mohyeddin), destroying the happiness of both. *Bombay Talkie*, with its lack of introspection, offers few deep insights about romance on the road, unless its points are that Indian men lust in an automatic way after Westerners, and that Western women live up to the stereotype of being loose and available. (Fellow actress Felicity Kendal describes her sister's romantic real-life marriage to gorgeous co-star Kapoor in her memoir, *White Cargo*.)

Echoes of Paradise, 1987. This slow-moving, predictable Australian soap opera describes an unfulfilled wife and her Balinese lover, but at least it documents the availability of beach boys in tourist Asia.

A Winter Tan, 1988. Critics termed the film version of *Give Sorrow*

Words by Maryse Holder a "shocking, unforgettable nightmare." Canadian film director Jackie Burroughs plays Maryse, usually with a fifth of whiskey in her hand, and the script follows Holder's letters closely. At a bullfight, she tells two shocked Canadian men, "Mexicans have huge cocks. Some Indians go down." She falls in love with Miguel Navaro at a dance, meets him in Mexico City for "four days of perfect love" with "sex on the hour." Maryse thinks, "I'm happy! I'm happy!" but she slips away from him and buys a train ticket west. At an ocean-side Pacific village she grabs men and lays a beautiful 14-year-old with a smashing blend of Indian eyes and full Negro lips, for which, along with for her public drunkenness, she is arrested. The film is probably more coherent than the book, with memorable scenes as Maryse toasts, "Here's to a whole new feminism, a sluttish and heterosexual one, one not with virtue, with freedom, pleasure."

The Sheltering Sky, 1990. Perhaps the most beautiful and despairing film on exotic eroticism, Bernardo Bertolucci depicts desperate peril for an American couple in North Africa, as the husband is attacked after visiting a shantytown prostitute, and his wife is kept in a dark room along the ramparts of a desert town, isolated except for visits from her radiant lover. Eight years later, *Hideous Kinky* would explore a more benign Morocco of playful, engaging potential suitors.

The Lunatic, 1992. Paul Campbell shines as Aloysius and Julie T. Wallace as Inga in an exuberant, earthy adaptation of Anthony C. Winkler's novel. Even more starkly than the novel, the film, set in Jamaica, makes it clear that Inga's body rules Aloysius's little world, until the stark reality of money trumps everything. Though it appears that Inga loses out in the end, she unapologetically takes a hefty portion of pleasure with her lover first, and her amiable tolerance of Aloysius's madness changes his life so that his pure heart is ultimately rewarded.

The Lover, 1992. Marguerite Duras's reworked autobiography arrived at the screen lush and beautiful but bereft of the tensions and rawness of her original "novel" describing her affair, during her childhood in Vietnam, as a quasi-prostitute to the son of a Chinese millionaire.

Bezness, 1992. A Tunisian gigolo's life offers a rare look at the male point of view of travel romances. For a discussion, see Hopwood 284-285.

The Old Lady Who Walked in the Sea, 1995. Jeanne Moreau plays Lady M., an aging con artist in Guadeloupe who recruits a young, hunky beach boy, Lambert, to help with her lucrative blackmail and jewelry heists.

Lady M. wants to experience one last love before she dies — and wants him to be a young man. "Dear Lord," she thinks to herself in the film's opening moments, while dressing for seduction, "... keep alive in me forever this dirty desire for love, this throb that saves me from death, this hellish hope that makes my heart beat faster, this lamentable longing for young flesh!" Lambert is a blond Frenchman windsurfing his time away and thus *The Old Lady* does not examine the considerable phenomenon of female sex tourism with Caribbean men. Still, this film zeros in on the dynamics and motivation of older women pursuing younger men in the tropics, away from traditional mores.

Before Sunrise, 1995. Young travelers Jesse (Ethan Hawke), an American, and Celine (Julie Delpy), French, disembark by train in romantic Vienna, in perhaps the film most focused on the modern reality of travel encounters. Jesse wants romantic magic with Celine on their one night together, and sways her with what seems like a self-serving argument, but one that may strike the experienced traveler as valid. He tells her to imagine the future:

"Jump ahead 10, 20 years and you're married. Only your marriage doesn't have the same energy that it used to have, you know? You start to blame your husband. You start to think about all those guys you've met in your life and what might have happened if you picked up with one of them. Well I'm 'one of those guys.' That's me! So think of this as time travel from then to now to find out what you're missing out on."

The Good Woman of Bangkok, 1995. Australian Dennis O'Rourke primarily interviews at length a Bangkok bar girl named Aoi, with big glasses and sad eyes, in a "documentary fictionalized film," whatever that is. Notable for how one baby-cheeked American boy describes the dating war: "I fucked seven girls here in one day. Look at her, 20 bucks! In comparison, I hate to tell you, American woman are fucking bitches and idiots compared to these women. These women are top of the line, their bodies are the best ... you can't beat the attitude of these girls. There's no girl in the world that'll give you a shower and give a blow job, fuck your brains out and fold your clothes with a smile on her face, dammit, nowhere."

How Stella Got Her Groove Back, 1998. Based on Terry McMillan's book, the camera dwells with longing on clothes, home furnishings and kitchen appliances, dragging the book's abundant materialism front and center. Still, the bankability of stars Angela Bassett as Stella and Whoopi Goldberg as her friend Delilah made many viewers more aware of romance tourism in Jamaica and its Caribbean neighbors.

Hideous Kinky, 1998. Kate Winslet plays Julia, the hippie mother of two young girls. She flees a screwy marriage in England for Morocco, where an acrobat named Bilal takes the young family under his wing. Quiet sensuality marks scenes where Bilal listens to a bare-breasted

Portrayals timeline

1856: Walt Whitman's "Song of the Open Road" is published, limning the power of travel to remove restraints on behavior, to be "loos'd of limits and imaginary lines. Going where I list, my own master total and absolute." The poet asks a question to which some readers may answer yes: "Do you know what it is as you pass to be loved by strangers? Do you know the talk of those turning eyeballs? ... What is it I interchange so suddenly with strangers?" Whitman's orientation toward other men is significant, for the theme that exotic sex might be more than a facet of travel, "that sex might be itself the source of enlightenment, belongs to a separate tradition, which runs strongest in those travellers, often women or homosexuals, whose erotic interests at home have been most severely curtailed" (Littlewood 95).

1876-77: First two novels about female travel romances, both written by American men, appear, depicting American women in Rome being courted by various titled but threadbare suitors who seek their money (see History chapter). Mollie Wopsus (J. Miller, *The One Fair Woman*), a gregarious Californian, eventually sees through the dispossessed nobles; the protagonist of *Daisy Miller* (Henry James) does not. A doomed innocent, Daisy eventually dies of malaria as a result of romantic moonlight stroll.

1905: A master of the theme of class and race obstacles to finding the heart's true match arrives on the literary scene. E.M. Forster kicks off trio of female heroines involved in travel romances with Lilia Herriton, a wealthy widow who marries a younger, penniless Italian, in *Where Angels Fear to Tread*. A true story Forster ("Three Countries" 291) heard vacationing in Italy inspired *Angels*. The novel thus offers valuable historical documentation of Victorian travel romance quite apart from its literary and entertainment merit. Next in barely fictional Italy arrives Lucy Honeychurch (**1908**, *A Room with a View*), who also finds a way to reject convention for passion. More darkly, Adela Quested (**1924**, *A Passage to India*) becomes intrigued and then overwhelmed by India's heat, mystery and eroticism with negative repercussions all around.

1919: *The Sheik*, first as a book by E.M. Hull (a female author) and two years later as a popular film starring Rudolph Valentino, depicts a young aristocrat, Diana Mayo, abducted by an Arab sheik, Ahmed, who saves her from a second kidnapping and wins her heart. Female viewers (shades of early Beatles fans) fainted at showings

---

Julia's hopes and fears, and her impoverished lover helps the young family when its fortunes are at its lowest. This adaptation of Esther Freud's memoir depicts the foreign lover as exotically desirable by the mother and at the same time utterly trusted by her children.

Under the Tuscan Sun, 2003. Briefly significant byplay between Frances (Diane Lane), who impulsively buys a villa in Tuscany, and her Positano-based lover on stereotypes involving American women and

of the film. As if to acknowledge that wild raptures between a English lady and a lusty Arab were literally beyond the pale, in the closing scenes Lady Diana learns the sheik, conveniently, was adopted and is really the son of an English lord and a Spanish woman.

1927: An actual lesbian expatriate community on the Italian island of Capri inspires *Vestal Fire* and its followup *Extraordinary Women*. In *Vestal Fire*, Scottish novelist Compton Mackenzie breaks new ground on three levels, as the introduces the durable idea of female travel liaisons as boisterous comedy, describes lesbian unions and depicts the pragmatism of the Italian gigolo in service to paying customers, male or female. The bisexual if-the-price-is-right, who is at heart heterosexual, was later further documented from Baghdad (Cumming, *Love Quest* 71) to Bali (Baranay, *Bali* 98) and is an important current reality in travel sex destinations worldwide. After Mackenzie, lesbian travel hookups as a fictional topic languished for 60 years, until in *Sure of You* San Francisco-based Amistead Maupin documents Lesbos in Greece, the real-world Sapphic successor to the Capri colony.

1939: Rumer Godden, an Englishwoman raised in Bengal and Assam, in *Black Narcissus* revisits the broad theme — Apollonian identity discombobulated by the Dionysian East — of *A Passage to India*, with a similarly disastrous ending. (*The Sheltering Sky* by Bowles will later reprise this theme.) A group of nuns travel to far northeast India to set up a convent school, living in a big building that formerly housed a general's harem. The exotic East infuses their lives with palpable sexuality. A handsome general's son, Dilip, wearing the perfume Black Narcissus, arrives for lessons. A young housegirl, Kanchi, in care of the nuns, touches Dilip's feet and "warm delightful teasing stole upwards;" the pair slip into a stable on convent grounds for a relationship that will eventually make Kanchi a general's concubine (223). The nuns reel with stray thoughts of Dilip, frantic planting of a riotous garden, sexual fixations on a nearby expatriate Englishman (with a fatal result), and a gnawing sense that they can't trust themselves to be nuns anymore.

1958: Han Suyin makes history as a female novelist by depicting travel intimacy in fairly graphic terms in *The Mountain Is Young*, in which Anne Ford makes vigorous love with Unni Menon, in one session "losing herself in a paroxysm of sensuality of which she had not known herself capable" (265).

1969: Authorial viewpoints begin to Italian men, but this visually satisfying film is marred by truly incongruous profanity. *Tuscan Sun* will also puzzle readers of the book version, because the film borrows a substantially unrelated plot from unacknowledged sources, including perhaps Marlena di Blasi's wondrous book *A Thousand Days in Venice* and the far superior film *Bread and Tulips* (2000), about an Italian woman who strays to Venice, abandoning her unappreciative family.

appear from sons and daughters of the Caribbean, beginning with Paul Layne ("Sunny Barbados") and Barbadian-American Paule Marshall (*The Chosen Place, the Timeless People*). A tone of unpleasantness and discomfort marks these early works on sexual tensions involving island men, who are depicted as sleazy predators, and white females, shown as treating the black man as something akin to a lab experiment — a brief dabble allowing the "liberated woman" to add to her sexual résumé. In **1980**, the same dynamic later appears in Jamaican-American Michael Thelwell's *The Harder They Come* (237-45).

1970s: Dawn of era of openness about sexual travel, with posthumous publication of E.M. Forster's explicit short stories (**1972**) and Margaret Fountaine's diaries (**1980**) sandwiching *Fear of Flying* (**1973**), daringly published while Erica Jong was, obviously, alive, and just 32 years old.

1972: Posthumous publication of E.M. Forster's "The Obelisk," originally written in **1939**, three decades before frank writing about travel trysts began to gather momentum. Ernest and Hilda, married, visit an English seacoast town with an Obelisk, an obvious phallic memorial. Hilda feels stirrings as they make their way uphill along a muddy gorge. She

finds herself documenting her balding, smallish husband's physical drawbacks, and her mind wanders to what it would be like for "restless arms to clasp her beyond redemption" (115). They hear a scrambling noise behind them, and two sailors rush up. Hilda notices the "handsome, gallant and educated" one, named Stan. "Almost without her knowing, he guided her off the path and got her down among the bushes." As the sound of footsteps passes, she kisses him. "For the first time in her life she felt worthy. Her humiliation slipped from her, never to return. She had pleased him. ... She took the lead, ordered the mysterious stranger, the film-star, the sheikh, what to do, she was, for one moment, a queen, and he her slave. They came out of the depths together, confederates" (122-23).

Hilda has had the true experience of the best sort of casual travel sex: enjoyable, intense, romantic, and most of all, revealing for the first time a grown woman's ability to lead a handsome men in the physical act, and the heady sense of freedom and confidence that ensues: "her eyes filled with happy tears." Forster provides an inspired O. Henry twist to close "The Obelisk," well worth not spoiling. The piece appears in *The Life to Come and Other Stories* (**1972**).

Plays

Dilemma of a Ghost. 1964, Legon, Ghana. Ama Ata Aidoo takes a remarkably early look at real points of friction between Western women and their foreign, traditional husbands, including physical abuse and limited notions of female independence. Eulalie, a New York City black woman, and her Ghanaian husband, Ato, baffle Ato's family by not immediately having children. And when Ato relays familial criticism of

1973: Erica Jong's cultural milestone, *Fear of Flying*, coins the term "zipless fuck." Mainstream publications covering the 15th, 20th and 30th anniversaries of the novel must still tapdance around her words as "zipless" heat, a "zipless" encounter and "an infamous zipless phrase." In 2003, the *New York Times* admitted that "the novel's most famous term ... can't be printed in this publication without resort to such hideously coy euphemisms as 'fastener-free fornication'" (L. Miller). "The zipless thing will be on my tombstone," Jong acknowledges in a 1994 interview (Olshan).

1974: Verging on soft porn, *Emmanuelle* features a diplomat's wife exploring casual sex. The French film proves valuable by catching the same wave — examining disinhibition away from home — as *Fear of Flying* and exploring Thailand's early emergence as a paid sex playground to a broader clientele than just American G.I.s and Japanese and German males.

1982-91: Beginning with *Heat and Dust* (**1982**) and *A Passage to India* (**1984**), adaptations of a pair of novels with complexly related pedigrees (Cronin 161), a quartet of films grossing in the hundreds of millions revive the themes of E.M. Forster and his revisionist heir, Ruth Prawer Jhabvala.

The formula, presenting a colonial wife, fiancée, widow or step-granddaughter rigid with boredom with her priggish English man and seeking something spicier, continues in *A Room with a View* (**1986**) and finally *Where Angels Fear to Tread* (**1991**).

1987: Jamaican-American Anthony C. Winkler finds commoner ground with Jong and other sexual humorists than with disapproving Caribbean authorial voices in his raucous novel (later film) *The Lunatic*. Lonely, hungry and lacking in "pum-pum" for two years, Aloysius makes a hole in the Jamaican dirt and comes after three thrusts. Later he sleeps in a clearing, and a German tourist named Inga Schmidt photographs him with a hearty erection. She was "short and thick as a tree stump" (41) with powerful muscles and knowledge of kung-fu. Inga, just as horny as Aloysius, lives in a clearing with him and the aptly named Service, wearing out both. Aloysius is not pleased with sharing Inga, whom he comes to love in his own simple way, but in exchange for meals and pum-pum he is willing to go along with everything she wants except bondage. Local attempts to warn Inga that Aloysius is a madman cause her to scream, irrefutably, "I stay vith him because he has a big cock! Vhat you think of that?" (106)

Eulalia's smoking and drinking, she retorts, "Who married me, you or your goddamm people?"

Smile Orange. 1971, Kingston, Jamaica. Trevor Rhone creates Ringo, a Jamaican kitchen staffer and polished gigolo who coaches a resort busboy on how to seduce tourists with rum and a sob story. "You have knee-pad?" Ringo asks laughing. "You ever try and do anything on di sand yet."

Viva Detroit. 1992, London. St. Lucian Derek Walcott's dark comedy

Portrayals timeline (continued)

When Inga leaves the island, Aloysius is rehabilitated to the extent that he can end up with "the farting window Dawkins" who further civilizes him if, in exchange, he will only "prevent her vital passage from closing like a clogged pipe" (218).

1988: Lebanese author Hanan Al-Shaykh, who lived in Egypt and Saudi Arabia before moving to London, portrays four women in an unnamed Gulf state in *Women of Sand and Myrrh*. An American expatriate's wife, Suzanne, estranged from her husband, feels freer to explore her sexuality with Arabs in a restricted society than she would at home, where she would merely be regarded as fat and unattractive. Once rejected by her Arab lover, Suzanne appears to be a pitiful, desperate creature, as trapped as the three Arab female protagonists. A later fictive work by an Arab woman, *The Map of Love* (Soueif 1999), portrays the Western female, in this case an English widow a century ago who falls in love with an Egyptian nationalist, as bold and curious.

1989: *Shirley Valentine* arrives in celluloid, making a big splash in her native Britain. The Liverpool housewife audaciously signs up for a trip sans family to Greece. Her disgusted daughter sees through the plan right away: "I think it's disgrace, my own mother behaving like that." Shirley retorts, "That's right, Milandra, I'm going to Greece for the sex. Sex for breakfast, sex for dinner, sex for tea and sex for supper." Once in the islands, Costas the seducer takes her on a boat ride, promising "on my honor" not to "make fuck with you." Of course, we know what happens next. Though Costas turns out to be a creep, Shirley's boldness is rewarded when her her husband arrives, contrite and attentive. And Costas does provide a healing moment: "He kissed me stretch marks," Shirley marvels.

1991: Shoko Ieda's novel *Iero Kyabu* (Yellow Cab) becomes a sensation in Japan as it chronicles young women who travel and take foreign lovers. In Thailand, medical researchers actually track surge in "yellow cab" arrivals (Vorakitphokatorn 66).

1992-99: What I will call "Bali moped syndrome" illustrates the noisy echo chamber where fiction and real behavior (perhaps inspired in some cases by fiction?) continually ping pong — and how Western women can be suckers for the most clichéd seduction moves. In **1992**, magazine writer Rebekah Ozanne depicts Bali as "a land where the men sing love songs to you by moonlight [and] take you riding on the back of their motorbikes."

---

describes the travails of a Caribbean gigolo named Sonny and his relationship to Pat, a divorced American photographer.

Sex, Chips and Ouzo (original title, Kamaki). 1997, Edinburgh. A pair of Glasgow housewives and a pair of Greek *kamaki* (gigolos) provide different versions the morning-after their frolics in a farce praised as sharply written.

Women on the Verge. 2001, Dublin. Playwright Marie Jones describes

Inez Baranay's novel the same year, *The Edge of Bali*, features the same motorbikes, moonrise and necking by the sea. In 1999, travel writer Laurie Gough (Bali Moon) describes her own romantic interlude when painter Nyoman Bagus "suggested we go for a ride on his motorbike to watch the moonrise. ... I lay back on the sand with him to fall into the sky's naked eternal mystery and its bursting ecstasies. Soon we were kissing each other. I tasted salt water on his lips and knew that one day he would leave the island of Bali. We must have been kissing for hours, lost in the warm scent and skin of each other, because when we looked for the moon, it was high and alone in the sky, conjuring shadows on the beach." Readers await the next installment.

1996: Terry McMillan writes *How Stella Got Her Groove Back* in one month based on her real-life Jamaican vacation romance (Spratling). Critics ("barely qualifies as beach literature" wrote *Time* magazine's John Skow) mowed down her efforts. Female readers loved them — literally stomping and leaping up to cheer at one reading (Trescott). Like the similarly autobiographical and self-revelatory Erica Jong, McMillan laughed all the way to bank, making a fortune on a book that appeared in movie version in 1998.

1998-2000: A crop of anthologies of road romance essays underlines the move of women's voices from fiction to the nonfiction essay, evidenced in *Love & Romance: True Stories of Passion on the Road* (Wylie); *Brief Encounters: Stories of Love, Sex and Travel* (de Kretser); *Lesbian Travels* (Bledsoe), all published in 1998; and *Erogenous Zones* (Stewart), 2000.

2000: Pankaj Mishra in *The Romantics* depicts Indian men as helpless innocents left deflated in the wake of sexually available but casually destructive Western travelers.

2001: Michel Houellebecq's *Plateforme* depicts the French couple Michel and Valerie as once-lost souls brought together by a trip to Thailand and thereafter savvy to the enormous potential for the euphoric love, the ecstatic sex — and the big money to be made off the lonely — implicit in travel sex. The former computer tech's novel aroused the fury of politically correct France, where he was hauled to court (from his home wisely made in distant Ireland) by Islamists unhappy with his plot's tie-in of Muslims to sexual hypocrisy and bloody terrorism. Feminists and a giant publisher of travel guidebooks, mocked for its admonishments against sex tourism, joined the anti-Houellebecq fray (Riding). In 2002, an English translation appeared as *Platform*.

Belfast tourist Anna falling in love with Halif, owner of a bar and cafe 20 years her junior, on a holiday in the Gambia.

§§§

Now let's wrap up by looking at the future: ethics and etiquette, and the futures of sex and power for the traveling woman.

Sex, power, ethics and the future

In June 1998, my husband and I stood on the modest ruins of Emporion on the brilliantly sunwashed coast of Spain.

Long ago, the 2,500-year-old site had seen ancient history's winners, the Greeks and then the Romans, wade ashore. In search of cultural reinvigoration, local women extended sexual hospitality to military men, seen as powerful bringers of luck or magic, or gods in disguise.

As the dashing soldiers left active duty and took up ordinary lives like those of other locals, wives and concubines absorbed the one-time foreigners, who gradually became natives.

From prehistory through the Allied occupations of Japan and Europe, victorious armies have captured the loser's women, either as slaves or as willing partners.

Now, history's winners for the first time include Western women who travel around an Information Age world in economic triumph. Now, it is the foreign man who extends sexual hospitality to the powerful (female) stranger. He becomes a shaman, wielding unfamiliar magic to dispel Western loneliness. He may try to absorb this monied wanderer into his homeland or to reconcile himself to her spiriting him away.

When my Peace Corps friend Rachel returned from Tanzania with her husband, her deed marked her as a New Centurion — one of thousands of middle-class Western women shattering precedent, indicating feminist advancement as they bring home men from half a world away.

In the mid-19th century, some female travelers felt they had to disguise themselves as men or carry pistols to move freely (Birkett, *Spinsters* 116-20). As time went on, it became clear that remote tribes conferred on white women, even in Victorian skirts, the status of honorary men.

And today, traveling women become not just honorary men, but monied conquerors taking a victory lap.

The phenomenon was not unheard of in early history. Two millennia ago, the highly sexed Cleopatra followed her lover Julius Caesar to Rome and later departed Egypt for Asia Minor to seduce Marc Antony. Wealth and power allowed a pharaoh's daughter to behave like a male emperor.

Heirs to the mantle of the Roman Empire, women now create a Romance Empire, which builds on female pre-eminence, and possible superiority, in adapting to foreign cultures. Women in the United States and Japan dominate Study Abroad programs, the Peace Corps, adventure travel and solo travel, and also find themselves overseas more than ever as anthropologists and international health professionals.

For generations, love affairs have been part of women's explorations. Those who bring home a foreign husband — especially from the developing world — mark a radical change in world order. In the 1840s, feminist author Margaret Fuller departed Italy with her aristocrat husband for the United States; in the 1990s, millionaire author Terry McMillan invited a younger Jamaican she met on vacation to her California digs.

They and thousands of other women with their holiday affairs chip away at our scientific understanding of female sexual behavior — and evolutionary imperatives to select similar mates.

Traveling women — and perhaps *only* traveling women — attain sexual freedom equal to men. When they head to poorer regions, womens' wealth gives them a power heretofore limited to men. In the act of travel sex, a woman attains liberation; in marrying a foreigner, a prerogative once belonging only to her most militarily successful brothers.

Are women from the West now in effect men, their participation in the world's dominant economies arming them for the first time with the power of a Caesar to seek pleasure? Not fully, for they remain women, but with a power beyond Cleopatra's to pursue contentment. That helps us understand the exhilaration of the woman in a Caribbean bungalow enjoying an attentive man's pleasures, who sees a vista opening in front of her of just how fun a vacation — and life — can be.

Traveling women also exert new-found muscle in two other ways, as they alter societies by indirectly liberating foreign women and by conferring status on non-white men.

Female travelers: Agents of change

Thousands of years after Greeks and Romans assimilated into coastal Iberia at Emporion and other colonies, a different sort of invader arrived — the sun-seeking female Viking on a 1960s charter flight.

Some of these latter-day conquerors carried off Spanish husbands, who began to appear by the hundreds in Swedish marriage records (Månsson, *Cultural Conflict* 105).

But in the bars of Barcelona and Malaga and Palma, visiting blondes demonstrated another profound impact of female sex tourism as their holiday flings liberated, paradoxically, the Spanish woman.

Lucia Graves, daughter of Robert Graves, the chronicler of Roman emperors (*I, Claudius*), grew up on coastal Spain and watched the revolution first hand. She saw younger women in the early 1960s compare their way of life to the Nordic females' and began "to question the rigidity of their own moral codes. ... I actually saw these changes occurring over a period of two or three years" (151-58). Spanish girls watched the Scandinavian, German and British girls "with a mix of curiosity, disdain and envy." They had been taught to guard their virginity, yet "how could they not see the patriarchal plot behind these rules?"

Latin boys and girls lived in sexual misery. The male waiters and bartenders first found solace with sunburned foreigners. Eventually young Spanish women, left alone in their bedrooms and studying their bodies, listened to awakened physical yearnings for their hot men. They rebelled against both their elders and their foreign female rivals.

Changes took time, but by 1994, Whit Stillman's stylish film *Barcelona* featured an American businessman telling his visiting cousin, "The sexual revolution reached Spain much later than the U.S.," but when the revolution hit Barcelona, "everything was swept aside. ... Spanish girls tend to be really promiscuous."

Admirers of traditional societies may weep at the homogenization tourism brings, but one striking aspect of non-Western areas is the generally low status of women. Thus a loss of "cultural integrity" may mean, in its own lurching, messy way, a lessening of the ability of male elders to run matters with an iron hand.

Tourism has also changed, generally for the better, the lot of local women in Greece, particularly Athens, as well as in Mexico, Costa Rica (Hicks 53), Thailand and even Nepal, to name examples documented in social science. Tourism income has made women who run restaurants and hostelries wealthier (Castelberg-Koulma), demonstrating a link between income, property rights and sexual freedom first seen in the Victorian era.

As in Spain, Greece was a place with a galloping double standard until Athenian women began to copy their Northern female visitors (Mansfield). Tourism made urban Greek women more affluent and contact with foreign tourists has changed their sexual attitudes.

In the Greek capital, young and middle-aged women have begun to dress and behave more like the tourists in terms of sexual freedom, with some now living with their boyfriends. The result: dwindling ranks of the legendary Greek loverman. Journalist Paul Mansfield quoted a Greek friend, Iannis, as saying:

There are no kamakia any more. Maybe still on some islands, because things change slowly there, but not here in Athens. Now, if they want a girlfriend they can find a Greek girl.

The paradoxically positive effect of the Shirley Valentine and her fellow tourists on the young Greek woman has been widely noted: "Here, in her tourist empire, the daughter is in charge" (Zoro 184), running tavernas, bantering in good English or German with her customers as her monolingual parents cook and bus tables.

Western women have attempted in other ways to be a force for the good of their sisters in the developing world. In 19th century Morocco, Englishwoman Emily Keene bathed local infants, setting an example of cleanliness for local mothers, and taught herself how to inoculate babies. In Jordan, Queen Noor has spoken out against "honor killings" sometimes carried out against women who have had sex outside marriage. In India, Sally Holkar, American-born wife of a maharaja's son, has revived the womanly tradition of handlooming textiles.

Then there is the Western woman's impact on foreign men, for her assent to bedroom equality threatens notions of racism.

Accepting the dark man as a peer

In the 1930s, British-American expatriate K'tut Tantri (32) became close to a Balinese prince. A colonial officer scolded her in the clear language of the white supremacist: "We Dutch rule these people by keeping them in their place. What will happen to that, do you think, if once they get the idea that white people regard them as equals? You — a white woman — accepting the hospitality of a native family."

Female sex travelers may act as radicals for fairness, as they bestow affection on foreign men and thus acknowledge the men's humanity. These pairings unite the rainbow couple in a challenge to the old order of white men in charge. North Africa explorer Isabelle Eberhardt (82) vigorously defended "the exceptional nature" of her Algerian husband to a skeptical French colonial. Other Victorian women sang the praises of foreign men to an extent that can only be described as subversive, given the way female praise undercut attempts by colonial men to portray their subjects as childish and incapable of self-government. These female pioneers appear to feel empathy toward foreign men, for both had to struggle against attempts to "keep them in their place."

The film *Heat and Dust*, set in colonial India, has a moment crystallizing the difference in perception. As Olivia washes the back of Douglas, her husband, he opines, "They're so transparent. The Indians, all of them. They're like children."

Olivia replied, "They look like grownup men to me. Certainly the

Nawab does." She sees the local governor as grown up, and they later become lovers.

Anthropologists, including Jill Dubisch and Jean Gearing, realized that to deny the sexual appeal of foreign men is to deny their humanity. Gearing (202) realized that her marriage to a Caribbean man "demonstrated publicly that I viewed Vincentian as my equals in status, not mere 'research subjects,' and also established me as a non-racist."

"Marrying someone from a different status group," sociologist Matthijs Kalmijn (497) observed, "is not only accepting that person as an equal lifetime partner, it is also choosing that the next generation will not continue the distinctions between status groups that currently prevail."

This may be the significance of hundreds of thousands of Westerners, particularly women, bedding non-whites around the world — they confer equality, if not always solving misunderstandings in the process.

Whether sex serves as a rich road to understanding between people of the West and the developing world may be debatable. Interracial sex or marriage is often seen, incorrectly, as a panacea for bigotry (see Belliveau, *Amateur* 243), and travel sex as a means of true cultural breakthrough, the best way to know a country.

Certainly, travel sex may be an avenue out of tourist ghettos, especially in the Caribbean.

But at the same time, gay anthropologist Stephen O. Murray (242-50) points out that the Westerner may not even be getting a clear idea about foreign sexual practices (let alone overall culture) if the alien lover alters his behavior to to ingratiate himself with the tourist as a means of seeking a patron or foreign sponsor. The horrific divorce rate for tourist women who bring home foreign men attests to one aspect of this disconnect.

Still, as my husband, artist and historian Lamont W. Harvey, points out, "sex is intrinsic to travel. You can't have a more learning experience than having sex with someone from another culture. Learning about other cultures is not limited to looking at art and sculptures and ruins."

Ethics

In a world where the female traveler wields power to slowly change human interaction, ethical behavior becomes a more pressing concern. With women's flexing of economic muscle comes questions of ethics and etiquette specific to traveling and meeting relatively vulnerable men. And the emergence of the female cad is not a pretty sight.

As in all love affairs, those involving foreign men may go terribly wrong. Mirella Ricciardi acknowledged how her affair with a Swahili youth essentially wrecked his life. In Nepal, a husband and father of two found himself bankrupt after a Japanese-American female tourist ended their affair; he killed himself (Spano "Trekking"). In Tobago, a female tourist appears to have knowingly spread HIV.

Unethical foreign men have behaved reciprocally: conning Western tourists, preying on their desperation for a different life, entering bigamist relationships, knowingly infecting them with HIV.

Such is the unfortunate state of affairs in which some members of both sexes manage grievous wrongs, easily spotted as unethical.

However, antagonists of sex travel — professors who subscribe to various ideologies (postmodernism, Marxism or anti-sex branches of feminism) or feminist activists (Oppermann, *Sex Tourism* 154-55) — level a broader charge of such behavior as inherently unethical and exploitive of the non-Western partner.

Defending the Western female traveler

Harsh condemnation of sex travel is in error, in my view. In fact, casual travel sex, as Erica Jong and Paul Theroux deduced, can be one of the purest, *least* exploitive relationships.

And even when money changes hands, or race and age barriers are breached, it can be farfetched to charge exploitation — particularly given the near-total absence of Western-style prostitution's middlemen from female sex travel. "Scholars and activists," anthropologist Paulla Ebron (238) wrote, "are often better at pointing to victims than at seeing complex negotiations." A man has a prerogative to hope for a better life and to seek it via the only means at his disposal, if that should be a capacity for companionship. So much the better if his shiny personality attracts a rich woman.

A woman has a prerogative to assuage loneliness, and this right needs to be defended with ferocity.

These travel affairs can be viewed as a quiet refusal by Western women, especially older ones, to accept loneliness as their lot — a move that deserves applause and respect.

Racism and stupidity underlie some charges of exploitation. Hardliners who charge Western women with exploiting poor or non-white men tend to end up sharing the political territory of the white supremacist, for they insinuate that the traveling woman belongs properly only with her own "kind."

At this point I invited my husband, Lamont, into the debate over ethics and travel sex. Though he has never progressed past flirtations with women in Italy, he brings credentials to the question of crossing race and age barriers; there would be no Lamont had not his white father married (illegally, at the time in the state of Maryland) a black woman 10 years his senior.

Lamont began by stressing that it is important not to endorse uncommitted sex as the preferred mode. Then we discussed the proper way to proceed when temporary love does become part of travel.

I read to Lamont an passage from Lucretia Stewart's *The Weather Prophet* (70-71) about a dance party on a Caribbean island. Stewart described "a slender Finnish woman with white-blonde hair" who "twined herself like poison ivy round a young black boy. From behind she looked like a girl but, when you saw her face, it was clear that she was in her fifties." As she "ground her crotch" against the boy, who appeared to be about 17, "an expression of desperate yearning flooded her face. His face registered only grim concentration."

"What — should the youth not do it?" Lamont asked. "A lot of men would like this situation. There's no problem if she doesn't lead him on. Dancing in a club together doesn't mean you are serious." Being able to dance with different partners is "the whole point of an open society."

"We know that black guys like fat women," he added. "Is it wrong for women to take advantage of that?" Conversely, there is no sin in an older white woman either going where she is wanted or preferring a young black male. "People have their standards of selection," Lamont said. "Some white guys go overboard for blondes, even though many brunettes are beautiful. If someone crosses cultural boundaries in the process, I wouldn't read too much into it. They're allowed. People have standards even for their own kind."

Similarly, the Finnish woman has the right to seek company where she is perceived to be attractive. "Maybe the guys in Finland think she's an old hag," Lamont continued. "Maybe these guys on the dance floor have always wanted to have it on with white women and haven't had the chance. He has his fun. She has her fun. Go have your fun! There's nothing wrong unless there's lying.

"I'm willing to defend people having fun in interracial situations," he said. To do otherwise is to "buy into the KKK's ideas of racial purity and the puritanical belief that free sex is always wrong. ... Under what standards is interracial marriage not horrible? If you can't say, that you are looking for intellectual reasons to back up bigotry. Just because you have a Ph.D. doesn't mean you can't be a fancy bigot."

Does God hate the sex traveler?

To condemn the tourist's sexual contacts en bloc is not moral superiority but moral simplification.

Littlewood (94)

God put you on my road.

Alain Hodge, my benefactor on a trip to St. Bart's

Like Lamont I agree that sex is natural, but my views are complicated by the fact that as a woman raised as a Roman Catholic, I have been taught that casual sex is wrong. Clearly I have fundamentally followed and agreed with Catholic teaching in terms of my behavior within the United States — but not overseas. As for my carnal license on foreign shores, I could claim temporary insanity (i.e., "identity loss") and post-divorce cynicism, but that would be only partly true. For I enjoyed my temporary insanity too much for it to be truly such.

Further, in retrospect, my foreign lovers emboldened me to "get back in the game" of dating and to remarry. Gradually I became a more whole person. Could I have come to see Lamont without fear and with hope for our success, had foreign men not rather steadily found me luscious when so many American men clearly did not?

So, what is a Roman Catholic to say? First, that I do see situations when travel sex can be immoral, as when it involves violating the trust of a loving husband, of which more later.

But Fate can deal the modern woman a difficult hand, one in which a foreign man can be as a practical matter her only ace of hearts.

And, as if to prove that no sex is truly casual, love can steal quietly in on the sex act, and the holiday lovers find themselves in a church, temple or mosque having their commitment officially blessed.

Does Jesus not forgive weaknesses of the flesh, as he did with Mary Magdalene? "Her sins are forgiven, for she loved much," he said (Luke 7:47) of a woman who opened herself to men and also Christ himself. Did God not create us with an explosive need for contact with the skin of others, and allow Solomon to sing the praises of top-flight lovemaking, in open air surrounded by blossom scents, in His holy book? Did not God's Son condemn the Pharisees as "blind leaders" for simple judgmentalism not balanced by sympathy or faith?

In many cases, holiday affairs proceed ethically, even offering a sanctified path toward moral living for the fallen female soldier in the dating war. As life provides fewer straightforward avenues to couplehood, perhaps God steers us to the foreign man, either as a husband or as a healing boyfriend who sustains us in a protracted wait for lasting love.

Theologian Harry Abbott Williams (81) describes how virtue may derive from casual travel sex. Men and women whose generosity has been stunted by bad experiences need to relearn grace from giving people, sometimes physically. Williams describes how the prostitute in the film *Never on Sunday* gives her body to a destructively self-doubting young sailor in a way that gives him confidence: "He goes away a deeper fuller person than he came in. What is seen is an act of charity which proclaims the glory of God."

To the traditionally religious, this will sound like trendy situational ethics — the narcissistic human tailoring God's word to fit the "if it feels good, do it" ethos. It is — and yet it isn't. Female believers may want to stick with the Commandments through every situation, but that doesn't help their loneliness when husbands suddenly crack up or run off and available replacements are less forthcoming as they get older.

Respecting mystery

One can see casual sex — practiced in its most reputationally safe form as a travel fling — as a normal human response to longings without subscribing to the school of thought that "anything goes." A woman my age and even with my experience can sit morally appalled by casual "hooking up" on campus, often with both parties drunk.

The pathetic fuck-buddy encounter mocks the mystery, danger, excitement and road to knowledge of sex, while the fiery union of travel unions comes closer to marking the holiness of the physical act.

"The excitement of casual sex at present derives in part from the fact it is not the norm," psychologist Albert Ellis (167) wrote. "... It is plausible to think that if we were completely casual about sex then we should have lost one of the elements in our life that gives it significance."

In effect, casual sex can be sleazy if it routinely results from drinking too much at your local singles bar — and romantic when it results from an almost courageous decision to take a foreign lover.

It may be self-serving to find a paradoxical morality to travel liaisons while condemning the hook-up. But 'tis the "pleasure bond" (as Lionel Tiger described it) that binds couples and helps create stable families. One could almost make the leap to say that civilization is indirectly strengthened by strong erotic ties between couples. And the Baby Boomer sex traveler returned from pilgrimaging may bring a spark into her eventual second marriage, while the blasé collegian isn't even really capable of perceiving the pricelessness of true intimacy.

Let's look at how apparent paganism can help a woman to love, and false orthodoxy can prevent her from forming a mature bond.

Misdirected piety

I personally know of at least one divorced devout Catholic woman who refuses to have recreational (or even potentially premarital) sex. Today's reality is that this stance scares off 99.99 percent of men, including the limited pool of available quality fellows.

As an example I'll describe a friend I'll call Flora. We both had brief painful first marriages. Flora later concluded that "men only want one thing." She remains divorced, bitter and remote from men. Now, when

Flora encounters a bachelor, she rejects the sensual side of his interest. Yet sex is an important part of compatibility for a man and a woman and a dandy repair kit for the rough nicks and scratches of daily life. Meanwhile after my divorce, I kept up some contact with men via sex, even if only slutting around places like Greece. I do believe that bitterness toward the opposite sex is readily detectable and a risk for divorced women. If foreign adventuring provides an antidote, bravo.

So, travel sex can be a pure, non-exploitive activity, oddly respectful of the sacredness and significance of intercourse, and a vehicle toward returning a woman to hope and generosity with the opposite sex.

To the cynic that cannot believe that the promiscuous traveler can also find monogamy paramount, I can only point to my own experience, where mental illness (not an outside affair) killed my first marriage, which arose from a travel romance with an Englishman met in San Francisco. Travel sex for me led directly to a first marriage and then flowed circuitously into a second marriage that hinged on foreign men as agents to prevent permanent post-divorce bitterness. Readers will recall the role of situations in casual travel sex. If one's behavior flows from one's situation, leading to wantonness in the Caribbean with strangers, it can also flow in the reverse direction, into faithfulness to one's husband.

The psychologist Ellis argues, "It may be thought that it is just obvious that if one indulges in casual sex then one will become unable to take sex in general seriously, lose the capacity to have sex as an essential element in a deep and intimate relation, say. But this is not obvious. It is not a priori. There is no contradiction in the idea of someone being able, in different contexts, to regard the same thing both casually and seriously."

Can this be magic?

Denied but lurking in a woman's decision to have travel sex may be a flickering hope of finding her true partner. Evolutionary behaviorists recognize that casual sex does have a base in our female ancestors' sexual repertoire, especially for women thinking of finding or switching mates: "Through sex women can gauge such qualities as a man's sensitivity, his concern with her happiness, and his flexibility" (Buss, *Evolution* 87).

And our culture's sexual priests and priestesses have repeatedly noted how affinity can surprisingly lurk in lust.

Gay writer Edmund White, in words relevant to the traveling woman, told an interviewer "that promiscuity has gotten a very bad name and some of the most intense and poetic and intimate experiences of my life were one-night stands. People who have never lived that life like to imagine that it is very heartless, cold, mechanical and so on — which it can be.

"But Jean Genet, who had a lot of casual sex in his life — I mean, as much as I have — once said, 'I have never experienced my sexuality in a pure state.' By which he meant he'd always been a little bit in love with everybody he'd been to bed with. And I can say as much. ... It means that you have a kind of fantasy that you could imagine that if things clicked with this person, that you could live with him forever. Or you're fascinated by the way he looks, by the way he moves, by his vulnerability, by his homeliness. ... I mean, there's something touching and human about this other person that you have between your hands, suddenly, and who is so vulnerable and exposed — as you are."

As did White, psychologist Ellis argues (161) that lust even toward a near-stranger involves some degree of attraction to the person, not just their body: "One may be aroused by the awareness of a flirtatious manner, or a vivacious personality, or a wanton character, or simply by being the object of lust oneself."

Sex with strangers "is often thought of badly because it's assumed that you and the 'stranger' don't care about each other, that it's cold and unfeeling and exploitative because you don't know where they work or what their mother does or what books have influenced them," bisexual erotica writer Susie Bright (227-28) believes. "This is probably the most ironic myth of all about anonymous sex — that it lacks intimacy — since having sex with someone you've never known before will often leave you with a secret about them that no one else in their familiar life could ever guess. It's similar to being stuck in the elevator with a stranger, when they blurt out a story to you and you confide likewise in them. Then the elevator is fixed and you walk out, never to see that soul again yet feeling intensely grateful to them.

"Sex with strangers is not reliably orgasmic, or happy, or spiritually uplifting; in fact, it can be the absolute opposite. But I would say that it is nearly always intimate, because it is very rare to fuck someone for the first time without being, if only for a moment, scared."

Anonymous sex, paradoxically, also avoids some of the pitfalls of indeterminate relationships, where a Western woman falls into an affair that the foreign man takes seriously and she does not. We have the off-putting example of writer Mary Morris. When she lived in Mexico, a handsome Indian named Alejandro fell deeply for her. He introduced her to his family and his world and treated her with kindness. When she mentions going home, he holds out his empty hands and says, "Yes, but I am in love with you. You may go, but I am in love with you."

"I could never stay here," she wrote (183). "I couldn't stay with you."

There's a touch of stoniness in their tale, not seen in accounts of purely casual encounters.

Apparent indulgence releases the spirit

Can sex with a male stranger allow a traveling woman to acquire deep confidence?

American Jungian analyst Nancy Qualls-Corbett examined the symbolism of the sexy stranger in myths, religion and fairy tales, as well as dreams, as an instigator of change stirring the complacent female. Qualls-Corbett (140) describes a woman named Lisa, in her early 40s, divorced, attractive to men, who had sex with a stranger while traveling overseas.

"I was somewhat alarmed at what was happening to me," Lisa wrote. "I was not out of control, but my control was not as I've always known it, as if something else was intervening. I recall the release I felt in love-making."

According to Qualls-Corbett, Lisa had "allowed her body to respond naturally to the call of love, instead of retreating into her head for an appropriate or clever response" (141). Lisa was unashamed and exhilarated, armed with a new directness and "released from the compulsion to perform in a certain manner so as to gain or keep a man's attention."

Many women mention a feeling of completeness, repair and renewed sexual identity as a result of road romances. Every woman who navigated her way to rambunctious satisfaction with a stranger sees men with changed eyes. The foreign man may have astonished with his eagerness to please her first, his ease with his stellar body, his emotional intelligence in reading women, his generosity and pride in making even a fleeting encounter a happy one.

Sex can be a tremendous discovery process. The exploration involved in any intimate affair increases exponentially with a foreigner or even a stranger.

Casual travel sex can be a legitimate bridge activity for the older woman concerned with her good name at home and aware that her mate search may be a lengthy one. "By my mid-thirties it had become a positive mission to find and have sex with an intelligent man," British sex traveler Fiona Pitt-Kethley wrote ("20 Years"). "Being naturally greedy I wanted good looks, intelligence and good sex all in the same package. It took me half a lifetime to find it."

Etiquette

Years ago, after an exhausting descent of Mount Kenya, a retired American teacher named Hanny Lightfoot-Klein (225) found the local hotel jammed. In the dining room, she encountered a dermatologist who offered to share his quarters. After a shower, she slid into one of the three beds. Her benefactor was snoring at the other end of the room. The next morning, he apologized: "It isn't that you aren't a very attractive woman, but I was totally exhausted last night. I hope I have not been remiss." The dermatologist showed a wry appreciation for the intrinsic relationship between travel and sex, one so potent that he felt obliged to apologize for *not* making a pass at a stranger.

Yes, as carefree as holiday liaisons may appear, these encounters carry their own set of rules, ones the dermatologist acknowledged. The erotic traveler may have to put some thought into behavior guidelines. San Francisco sex researcher Jack Morin (306) notes the likely discovery that "your early moral training was so fundamentally antierotic that it's of limited use to you now." One must go past codes focusing on a host of prohibited acts and must also avoid the other extreme of rejecting "all ethical considerations as antierotic."

Here are seven guidelines for conducting romances on the road.

1. The same ethics apply as at home.

Both parties should take steps to avoid unwanted pregnancy or transmission of disease.

Both parties need to fully agree with proceeding to intercourse, not impaired by severe emotional distress, intellectual impairment, or excessive use of alcohol and other drugs.

And for the woman, especially ...

2. Don't lead men on.

> **If a woman will dress quietly, walk quickly, and look straight ahead of her, she will not be molested; but if one who is strikingly pretty and showily dressed saunters slowly along, looking into shop windows and also staring at the passers-by, she will very likely be followed by some man who is willing to take the chance of possible amusement; not is he altogether to blame, because the nice women whom he has known have not laid themselves open to such misunderstanding.**
>
> *European Travel for Women* by Mary Cadwaller Jones (15-16)

Back in 1900, travel guide author Mary Cadwaller Jones had the right idea about a woman's responsibility for the signals she sends out.

Today chaos reigns on U.S. campuses in terms of sexual etiquette. Young women may blithely hook up or conversely enter compromising situations (letting men in their beds to "just sleep," drinking too much, wearing clothing that exposes midriff, upper thigh and breast; engaging in advanced sex play) and taking umbrage when full intercourse occurs.

Rest assured that no such confusion exists overseas. Women of my generation (coming of age in the early 1970s) had a simple understanding, congruent with how most men think, of how arousal leads (as it was designed to) to intercourse. An invitation to bed is an invite to sex, as one American girl should have known before allowing an Ecuadorian to spend the night with her and later charging rape (Meisch 458).

Young traveling women who DON'T want sex with foreign men should:

• Abandon the foolishness advocated on some college campuses that a woman can invite a man into bed "just for cuddling."

• Never go off alone with your guide unless you either want sex or are prepared to refuse or physically repel advances if you have placed your trust in error.

• "Never bathe topless, and never lose sight of other people on the beach, however solitary and tempting it may appear." Lindsey Hilsum (395) wrote this regarding Lamu in Kenya, but it's good advice along the East African coast or really anywhere.

• Avoid provocative dress and smiling at or even eye contact with men, which can readily be misconstrued as an invitation.

• Avoid public drunkenness, exits at a late hour from night clubs, strolls around bad urban areas and wandering in the moonlight on rape-prone Pacific islands.

• Even in cases where you are not leading men on, be quick to recognize signals of impending problems and respond. Do not assume due to cultural variations that an act obnoxious at home is not the same overseas. Trust your instincts, and if you catch "the indefinable but indisputable scent of danger" (Lightfoot-Klein 125), act or leave. Be willing to think the worst of people if warranted.

For example, in 1980, two female friends and I sunbathed on a beach along the French Riviera. A North African peddler arrived, showed us some carved elephants, dropped to one knee and began stroking the blonde hair of one of my companions. Stunned, she laughed nervously but did not reprimand him. "Go now," I growled in French the instant he touched her, furious that he would violate the personal space of an inexperienced tourist. He left.

If you are in a similar situation, don't hesitate to act icily or even like you are verging on a PMS attack. Feel free to make a scene that attracts the attention of others nearby.

Female travelers should not lead foreign men on emotionally, either.

3. Remember, the man is real, not an actor in your fantasy.

Of all the women's stories I have come across in writing *Romance on the Road*, one that distressed me most involved not a question of exploitation but of mild cruelty masked as romanticism.

Beth Ann Fennelly (26), a poet, wrote of spending three weeks in

Italy, traveling in the wake of a bad breakup. Harassed by men, she felt "more disillusioned than when I left." In Capri, a tall man with curly hair tried to help her, crossing off three of the four pensions listed in her error-riddled guidebook. Later that night, she ran into Massimo at a restaurant. They stole away for a romantic interlude on Mount Tiberio.

They were to meet the next morning for a picnic, but Fennelly "didn't want a new day and the chance that we might wreck things." She wanted the memory of the night forever. She left the island, not stopping when she saw Massimo "waiting at the funicular, clacking the handles of his picnic basket."

As Lamont notes, "It's not a perfect moment if he's out with a picnic basket broken hearted. After that moment he goes on in his life, and he says that's a farce, she set me up."

Were the roles reversed, we would term the man a cad.

Unfortunately, American women seem particularly guilty of hurting men with their narcissistic faux-romanticism. After finding "pure freedom" in Naples with a lover named Mariano, Deb Fellner (34) lacked common decency when the hotel worker developed feelings for her. "Mariano has tried to call me at home. His voice over the crackling line invades my world. I don't return his calls. Good byes at Hotel Zara were final, and I choose to preserve memories as they were. Perfect. Frozen. Finite."

"Beautiful, charming, generous and kind" was Mariano, in Fellner's own words. Oh dear. We can only hope that generous and kind Italians have learned to run at the sight of the starry-eyed American "romantic."

Other Yankees in the Hall of Shame include Maryse Holder, who jilted Miguel in Mexico City; the aforementioned Mary Morris (who termed her lover Alejandro "handsome, charming, kind and loyal;" perhaps foreign men who earn a quartet of laudable adjectives will now realize they are doomed with gringas); and very nearly Laura Fraser (64), tempted to bolt after her romance on an Italian island: "the aesthetic choice would be to never see him again, to keep the memory of your perfect chance meeting intact."

Mean-spirited "aesthetics" prevailed for four of these five American writers. A better example comes from the British, who clearly state:

4. Tell the truth.

Americans exalt their sexual encounters to mythic significance, in part because they see their lovers as innocent and pure of heart (an innocence they seem hellbent on annihilating). No doubt Italian, Mexican and other men detect and respond to the Americans' imbuing the moment with significance. Yet the easy American girl ultimately decides she will somehow preserve a perfect encounter by behaving toward these golden angels with the coldness one might direct to a creep.

British sex travelers Anne Cumming and Fiona Pitt-Kethley, more averse to coating their activities with sentimentality, made it a point of honor never to lie to a casual sex partner. Pitt-Kethley advises how to play it straight: "I never promise permanence to anyone. I believe in honesty. I wouldn't do what the average man does — seduce by lies. I don't pretend to love. I don't swear I'll be there tomorrow" (Journeys 9).

Lamont agrees: "Two consenting adults without disease, in love for the duration of the act, can part without callousness."

5. Do not use a foreign man as a sperm donor.

Western women have entered into affairs with a good number of Jamaican, Thai and Javanese men (and no doubt many others not recorded in the literature) to have pretty brown babies. The pain of the discarded father can be seen in the tale of a young Thai man named Lek, who entertained a vacationing Swedish girl. After she returned home, she learned that she was pregnant. Lek later borrowed money to see his beautiful twin daughters, halfway around the world. But the Swedish woman had a new boyfriend. She was no longer interested in the father of her children and only allowed him to see the girls once (Odzer 272).

Here we see the rather nakedly exercised power of the Western woman to erase the poor man who contributed his exotic looks and self to her offspring. These women prove the point of the traveling woman as the New Centurion, though she collects sperm from far and wide rather than disperses it, as has the male conqueror from time before history.

Fortunately for babies born to wiser mothers, other traveling women even in cases of divorce make certain that the father and the child get together at least annually even if great distances are involved.

While Americans seem to be guilty of jilting sincere men, it seems to be the Europeans leading the trend of treating foreign men as low-cost sperm banks. Though psychologists identify an evolutionary basis for the behavior of women who use casual partners as sperm donors, as women who throughout evolution have wanted better genes and "sexy sons" who themselves will have excellent mating prospects (Buss, Evolution 91), there is something quite calculating about denying fathers any chance of even seeing their offspring.

Following on this point, travelers should ...

6. Be considerate of a poor or younger man.

The Western woman may be the one who is in a position to hurt the man with her economic superiority and power to love him and leave him.

For whatever reason, the problem seems to come arise frequently in India, where Western women may have to grapple with a tough decision on how best to handle additional contact.

Novelist Pankaj Mishra (*The Romantics*) artfully depicts the wreckage left behind by a well-to-do young Frenchwoman in India after her return home, as her letters exhilarate and then devastate her abandoned lover. Sarah Lloyd, in her real-life affair, was more careful. After 18 months with her Sikh lover, with whom she was unable to continue in a relationship that had stagnated, Lloyd described how she returned to England. "We could never have made each other happy, but my guilt still gnawed at my stomach. I knew with absolute certainty that Jungli would love me until his death" (*Indian Attachment* 244).

"I'm not in touch with Jungli any more," Lloyd e-mailed me, "and have no idea what became of him. We corresponded for perhaps a year after I left, but I felt he was still hoping that I would come back, so I felt it might be kinder in the long run to stop writing."

In dating a poorer or younger person, Lamont noted, "you have a responsibility with them. Be careful of their feelings. With that said, they are prone to irrational changes and actually they may end up hurting you.

"The younger man if he's with someone older also has to bear in mind that you can hurt her. You're dumping someone who may not be able to find someone else. If you were a Norwegian with another Norwegian, you'd have to deal with this. These issues are not confined to crosscultural or age differences or interracial relationships. The difficulties are greater but the issues are the same."

7. Avoid infidelity.

Even a woman in a contented marriage may be tempted by a lovestruck Tahitian with flowers in his hair telling her she is beautiful, as happened to a Los Angeles writer. Beth Clark (138, 140) became enthralled with Hiro to the extent "that I almost forgot something important: I'm married. Happily married for four years, to a wonderful guy who happened to be 3,600 miles away. ... Suddenly I identified with all those millions of people who slip off their wedding rings ... ." It was a struggle, but she kept her holiday relationship at the level of a school crush.

While travel romances play a valuable role in the single or divorced woman's love life, returning her to the land of physicality, such partnerships do not have a place as being ethical — or even very bright — for the contentedly married.

Erica Jong, creator of the zipless fuck, touched on the line between right and wrong when asked her own views of casual sex. "I think it doesn't usually work except as a fantasy. I scarcely think it's a viable kind of sex for a mature woman, although maybe, from time to time, it's fun to do when you're feeling a little bit crazy and Bacchic and abandoned. ... We all need stable relationships in order to grow and do work and raise families and do all the things that keep civilization going" (Fleming 89-90).

As much as females have evolved in step with gay men in seeking sexual opportunity and freedom overseas, at a certain point it is the heterosexual woman who guards the future of marriage by taming men and drawing a boundary against infidelity to preserve the stability needed to raise children. As Jong indicates, this is the role of the mature woman. There is a time and a place for everything, and travel sex is something to get out of the system before becoming a wife and mother.

Yet married women — some with their husbands along for the trip! — often manage to sneak off with willing beach boys, especially in Caribbean (de Albuquerque, *Sex, Beach Boys* 95), to the point that beach boys realize that as long as the husband is not right there on the sand, the wife is fair game (Karch 252; Herold, "Female Tourists" 988).

See dat woman dere? I wanna foop she. Her husband wants me to do it too. I mean it.

Judo, a beach boy on Barbados (Press 114)

Husbands and boyfriends — on trips anywhere — would be wise not to nap or fall sick in their hotel room, given copious tales of wives sneaking out for hot action, including in Jerusalem (Bowman 85-87) and India (Dreir). In Kenya, a puzzled snorkeling guide in the coastal town of Watamu told a friend of mine about wives *and* husbands sneaking out for affairs with Africans. "He didn't understand why people professed to be in a marriage and yet slept around with opposite or same-sex natives," my friend said.

In Greece, a female writer even described a tale, possibly apocryphal, of having casual sex while her boyfriend slept nearby (Sinnott).

A pair of surveys found that from 3 percent ("That Holiday Romance") to 7 percent (Carter 337) of travelers who had casual sex did so with their regular sex partner stashed elsewhere, presumably back at their lodging.

Probably most unfaithful wives are unhappy, while some are happy but subject to crushes as Clark described, and a few are crazy about their husbands but born to be sex travelers. The latter was the case with English translator Anne Cumming, who screwed around Morocco "and made the important discovery that my sexual organs did not necessarily require love to set them in motion. Up till then, I had felt ... one fell in love every, every time. Now I knew that satisfactory fucking does not always affect the deeper emotions" (*Love Quest* 52).

Wisely, she "did not expect Charles [a pseudonym for her husband] to understand that. I was nervous about our reunion." Cumming was correct to fear her husband's reaction. They eventually divorced. Casual sex "is not a wise move if adopted as an exclusive mating strategy because men do prize fidelity in a mate" (Buss, *Evolution* 92).

Marriages depend on honesty and trust. Travel infidelity is to be avoided by the loving wife.

Still, flings may appeal to women either in a foundering marriage or those who have made a practical decision that they need to keep their family together but, given a sexually distant husband, will quietly fly away for affairs — and again, travel sex provides the most responsible avenue for those wishing to avoid reputational damage or perhaps even divorce. In Greece, one female vacationer told an interviewer: "I like sex ... but not with my husband" (Wickens, "Hedonistic" 821). Indeed, some married British women report planning to have sex abroad and taking condoms as a precaution (Bloor, Feasibility Study sec. 14.11).

For married women looking to hold on to a good thing, Beth Clark (142) provides her insight, as she realized, "I should never expect to have complete control over my emotions, just my choices. When I married Sam, I didn't vow not to get wild crushes, I just promised not to do anything about them."

The Future

We've talked about sex and power, and how the economically powerful traveling woman must develop a sense of ethics and etiquette in dealing with the foreign man.

Next let's see how these changes affect the future, beginning with studies of human behavior.

Tourist women: Confounding the social scientists

Traveling females knock out the pillars supporting cherished notions of the social sciences on psychology, sexual conduct, mate selection and evolution-directed behavior. The wanton actions of reasonably normal female travelers flatly contradict scientists whose simplistic study designs fail to account for how much fear of social disapproval reins in women's sexual behavior.

Only the disciplines of demography and economics seem to have models correctly anticipating how lonely women with enough money for airfares will zoom themselves to areas of male surplus, as though the latter had "love for sale" banners plastered on every beach.

For example, holiday affairs should prompt revisions of our understandings of:

• **Instant sex.** Sociologist David Buss (*Evolution* 78) wrote that "for most women, sex after just one hour is a virtual impossibility." Yet the

Experiences chapter describes how some veterans of travel sex can get busy with strangers within minutes.

- **Casual sex**. Many suppositions rest on a famous but highly flawed study (R. Clark 776) at Florida State University. In the experiment, an attractive man said to campus co-eds, "I have been noticing you around campus. Would you go to bed with me tonight?" All female students approached said no, but in the reverse situation, when an attractive woman asked men to bed, 69 percent of the fellas said yes.

The study was said to show that, as a result of evolutionary imperatives, men want to spread sperm far and wide while women are selective and wait for committed mates who help her raise offspring. Yet women happily engage in casual sex when they can avoid the "slut" label (Hodgkinson, Einon) and when they can engage a foreign man in a mutual mating dance built on quiet cues of willingness rather than a stark offer for sex. Obviously, the authors needed to make a short flight from Florida State to a Bahamas beach to better test their hypothesis.

- **Sex involving multiple partners**. As seen in the What's Going On chapter, women are exploring the outer limits of sexual freedom by taking numerous partners in a day or week or month of traveling. Sex researchers will have their hands full trying to understand extreme female behavior more in common with gay male tricking than with straight male sex tourism, which often involves loyalty to a single Thai bar girl through repeated visits and financial support in the interim. Lying hidden in plain view, the female connoisseur will become a topic of investigation for her overall confidence gained via sexual experience, a link previously identified only in males (Newcomb).

The overall question for social scientists again circles back to the opening of this chapter: Does money make women de facto men, even in the arena of casual sex?

Differences in sexual behavior are narrowing, in a way that defies human evolutionary theory in one sense (women now pick up men, pay them for sex and bed complete strangers) and affirms it in another (women seek the warrior hero, the man who will attend to their deep romantic need for a confident gent).

Social scientists April Gorry and David Buss have noticed the paradigm shifts in female mating behavior. Casual sex can be rational and beneficial to women; the wildest of passion may possess "a crystalline logic, precise purpose, and supreme sensibility" (Buss, *Dangerous Passion* 2).

Never pursued in a vacuum, casual sex "is influenced by development, personal appeal, sex ratio, cultural traditions, legal sanctions, and the strategies pursued by others," Buss wrote (*Evolution* 95).

"Casual sexual strategies of both sexes are deeply founded in human evolutionary history. ... And the fact that women shift to brief liaisons under predictable circumstances, such as a dearth of men capable of investing in them or an unfavorable ratio of women to men, tells us that women have specific psychological mechanisms designed for temporary mating."

21 predictions

From what we now know about the past and the present of women travelers and their foreign lovers, let's speculate about what may lie ahead. We are at the curtain raising of Act 3 of a play that began with Victorian explorers and reached a middle stage between 1960 and 2000.

What female travel sex will signify

1. Historians and feminists will recognize the deeper meaning of females seeking intimacy via travel. Because of the nexus between sexual freedom, travel and power, intimate adventures by women will come to be seen as a reliable marker of feminist advance, beginning in the middle of the Victorian era and soaring after the 1960s.

How women will behave

2. Many aging Baby Boomer women will continue to travel to find sex partners. The Boomers are a pro-sex generation, but the marriage gap, as discussed in the Reasons chapter, leaves many without partners.

3. Travel sex will continue to evolve from being taboo to being trendy, as is already evidenced by foreign language phrasebooks with translations of graphic sex acts and literary anthologies of essays on the topic.

Women will continue to become more like men in terms of:

4. Enjoying casual sex, especially as an interim undertaking for the lonely divorced or widowed woman traveling overseas, where she can avoid most reputational consequences.

5. Paying for affectionate companionship, as happens in the Caribbean, Africa and Southeast Asia.

Women will continue to become more like gay men in terms of:

6. Experimenting with rawer sex. In 1991, sex traveler Anne Cumming (*Love Quest* 144) could say that "most women prefer romance to sex. They want ambience and all the little attentions. They like the by-products of sex rather than its stark reality. Only queers appreciate the pure animal ingredients. That's why Arab countries are riddled with ageing European pederasts." Events have partly overtaken this view, as traveling women experiment with wildly hedonistic behavior. And ...

7. Western women will soften their dealings with men, seeing some merit to the way Japanese and Thai women consider it no crime to make a man happy, by smiling, listening to them and holding high standards of grooming, blending femininity with economic emancipation.

How men will behave

8. Some of the novel arrangements explored via travel sex will become part of the domestic landscape. Young men in the West will, like foreign men, begin to value the older woman (now seen via her travel adventures as a sexy and fun creature), easing the demographic problem of the marriage gap. Highly educated women will free freer to opt for husbands (similar to their overseas lovers) of modest achievement but kindly demeanor.

9. Foreign men are bound to become bolder and bolder with tourist women, as fewer maintain either genuine innocence or feel bound by the colonial idea that European women were off-limits.

10. Western and especially Japanese men will become more companionable as a result of rejection by their own women. Given existence of female Japanese sex travelers, "I think it is time for overworked Japanese men to start changing. ... I don't care how rich Japan has become; any country that has to export women's frustrations is just not right" (Kajiwara Hazuki qtd. in Kelsky, *Verge* 139).

Who will go where

11. The European Union's easing of rules on migration will continue to increase marriages, reflecting current patterns where Belgian, Danish, German, French and Irish women work in Spain, Italy and Greece (Ackers) and meet and marry men there.

12. Much as women from Latin countries (Venezuela, Portugal, Spain) and rapidly advancing nations (Taiwan, South Korea) have begun to pursue travel romances, even more females of means from an ever broadening ripple of places will be seen in sex tourism destinations. Incredibly, a handful of indigenous women in remote Borneo have begun to travel moderate distances across the jungle to become mistresses by choice to Korean and Chinese timber company executives — activity that mirrors local love songs extolling "the glamour of the powerful stranger" (Tsing 227). As a book reviewer noted, the logic of travel in search of sexual freedom and variety ultimately "points to a time when dark-skinned rich women from hot countries will come seeking the exotic experience of sex with muscular white boys from Britain's housing estates" (J. Adams).

Indeed, in 2003, Lina M. Wong (39), a Fijian of part-Chinese descent, described meeting her German husband when she traveled to Australia! "I love people of my own color," she wrote, "but in my imagination, white guys were different, challenging, more exciting."

13. India will eventually be a popular destination for Western females

seeking erudite, handsome and English-speaking husbands among a surplus of 32 million males. The subcontinent, which within a decade or two may finally surge into the world's top economic tier, could become a one-stop solution to loneliness in the West all on its own.

14. Despite similar male surpluses, the men of China, Japan and Korea will be the last to see significant interactions with white Western females. The Zone of Sexual Winter will continue to be marked by a lack of mutual interest, with the exception of some Japanese male peacocks.

15. Much as adventure travelers enjoy one-upsmanship of going to boutique destinations (Madagascar) vs. exotic but well-attended spots on the backpacker trail (Nepal), **female connoisseurs will go beyond Jamaica, Greece and Thailand to find men in more remote areas, as has begun in the strange tropics of Melanesia.**

How the social landscape will change

16. Foreign marriages will have a greater success rate as more Third World men become educated and share the internationalist outlook of cosmopolitan Western women. Many women now date uneducated, poor foreign men, but as education improves in the developing world they will find more lettered men, and these will be the more promising long-term husbands.

We will see additional affirmation of a classic psychological study finding that whites prefer minorities "who agree with them to whites who disagree with them" (Rokeach 140). In other words, shared values will trump race in mating.

17. The dating war will ameliorate as a post-feminist world returns to rewarding the best aspects of masculinity and femininity. More distinct sex roles will allow Westerners to once more become exotic to each other and to rediscover the treasure of shared cultural shorthand. Maturing one-time sex tourists, male and female, may (as the author did) ultimately return home, armed with the courage to date outside their group, better able to appreciate a meeting of minds with a compatriot.

18. The generally positive impact of Western tourists on women's liberation in the Roman Catholic and Orthodox Mediterranean will remain less obvious in Muslim areas, where tourism is limited and where local women face far higher punishments for copying laissez-faire sexuality.

19. Similarly, female tourists will bring little balm to the the profound wounds of men and women in the English-speaking Caribbean. Some island women belittle their men as worthless, and some island men attack their women as lacking in intelligence and tenderness, meanwhile displaying "the insatiable, and apparently indiscriminate desire, of black men for white women" (Stewart, *Weather* 145). Still, a Caribbean made more affluent were tourist receipts to remain in the islands, rather than flowing to foreign concerns, might enjoy softer relations between its men and women. A Western woman of the future might no longer find so many island men needy for money, status and emotional fulfillment and so many island women resentful, if the Caribbean's daughters can copy their sisters in Greece and Mexico by making money in tourism.

20. Tourist women will make a difference in the standard of living of their male lovers as well as that of foreign female entrepreneurs. Western "foreign aid" reaches the poor around the world as a result of holiday romances, with gifts handed out one to one, body to body and hand to hand. Tens of thousands of Western females in relationships with foreign men form a nexus between the West and the less developed world, a connection that forges marriages and creates international children.

21. The female travelers of North America, Europe, Japan and Australia will continue to dismantle a millennia-old cultural imperative requiring them to consort with and marry someone of the same color. Perhaps a switch has been thrown where now a substantial minority seek simple but kind and available men of any shade. Or perhaps they have a sense that these times call for reinvigoration from the mysterious stranger, in the same way sacred priestesses from ancient Emporion and Babylon to modern Polynesia have physically welcomed the heroic traveler.

May you live in interesting times

> In pre-modern Europe, only among aristocratic groups was sexual licence openly permitted among "respectable" women. Sexual freedom follows power and is an expression of it ... .
>
> Giddens (39)

> Never pass up a chance for sex and never pass up a chance to do your laundry.
>
> Hanny Lightfoot-Klein advising the woman taking an extended journey (115)

Romance on the road can be both a radical act of sexual anarchy and a deeply traditional attempt to rediscover customary feminine roles by liaising with a man of primal masculinity.

Joana McIntyre Varawa stood the natural order on its ear when in 1985 she "did what only a few dreamers — all men — had done before her: She moved to a South Pacific island and married a good-looking native 30 years her junior" (Shapiro). A revolutionary move — to a place of timeless custom.

Western women now live in an exciting time of choice. Travel has opened all the world's models of courtship and love to the modern woman. The 21st century girl can forge a challenging but rewarding life with her foreign man; binational couples have run Himalayan trekking companies, African safari operations and Indonesian island hostelries.

Wishing you luck

I hope you have enjoyed *Romance on the Road* — and that you travel with love or find it on the way.

Perhaps my own exile in the sexual desert was unnecessarily too long. But perhaps this was not for nothing. One astute reader of *Romance* in manuscript form suggested, "You are a different and more interesting person as a result of all your experiences, and your husband Lamont likes you for them."

She added, "Your book reads like a love letter to Lamont."

Romance may also be a letter of a different sort, one of encouragement to lonely women. I have been motivated in the large task of writing this book by a number of emotions, including fear, anger and fascination. Fear of recriminations from those would would be unhappy with my secret life as a sex tourist, a fear that greatly slowed my progress in the early stages of writing a manuscript. Anger, as I began to delve into social science literature, at a lack of empathy for women, left alone by the cruel dictates of demography, who let loose on vacations. And a fascination bordering on the obsessive with how vivid and dominating travel romances stood in my memory.

In the end, fascination won over fear, as it did with my instance of sex with a stranger in Greece. My body dictated following a mysterious path, and the human urge to couple and share intimacy won over emotions bruised in the dating war.

Such is the way travel and interested strangers allow us to break free of both routine and ultimately isolation. World traveler Paul Theroux lamented, after recently revisiting Africa, how "in the past, people tried to make things work and struggled in hard times — in Asia, in Latin America, in Africa. In the past 15 years people have given up struggling at home and tried to emigrate" (Coyne, "Talking"). Implicit in this observation is that ambitious men in the developing world have made a simple decision, which looks irreversible in the near term, to leave; tourist women can be agents of their desires on many levels.

As for the tourist women, locked in routines back home that don't fulfill their desire for closeness, a foreign trip may hold the key that unlocks them from a virtual jail, smashing bars that pin them down like the tumbling digits in *The Matrix*.

An Affection Deficit Disorder grips much of the world, and the solution may be an airplane ticket away.

Bibliography

Note: All Lexis-Nexus down-
loads unless listed otherwise
were conducted at the Milton S.
Eisenhower Library at Johns
Hopkins University, Baltimore,
Md.

"Anne Cumming." *The Times*
London 2 Sept. 1993, sec.
Features (obituary). Lexis-Nexus.
8 June 2001.

Archives of Jonathan Cape Ltd. 9
July 2003. U of Reading.
Available: <http://www.library.
rdg.ac.uk/colls/special/cape.ht
ml>. 30 Aug. 2003.

Art and Adventure: Mali and
Burkina Faso, Feb 5-21, 2003.
2003. Online posting. Women's
Travel Club. Available:
<http://www.womenstravel-
club.com/trips/mali2003.html>.
2 July 2003.

Bangkok by Night: Gay and
Lesbian Scene. n.d. Thailand.
com: Gay Thailand. Available:
<http://www.thailand.com/tra
vel/nightlife/nightlife_bangkok
_gayscene.htm>. 11 July 2002.

Best to Avoid the Kuta Cowboys.
17 Aug. 2002. Online posting.
Balitravelforum. Available:
<http://www.balitravelforum.c
om/archive200208/44903.html>.
21 Nov. 2002.

Bukit Lawang Is "Bangkok in
Reverse." 9 Dec. 2000. Online
posting. Lonely Planet Thorn
Tree. Available: <http://thorn-
tree.lonelyplanet.com/>. 10 May
2001.

C'est La Vie! 17 May 2001.
Online posting. Lonely Planet
Thorn Tree. Available:
<http://thorntree.lonelyplanet.
com/>. 23 May 2001.

"A Cycle of Exploitation: Sri
Lanka's 'Beach Boys'." *Bangkok
Post* Bangkok 14 Jan. 1996.
Available: <http://www.chula.
ac.th/institute/arcm/jan96.htm>.

Free Holidays in South Cyprus!
Aug. 1998. Turkish Cypriot
Network News. Available:
<http://www.tcn-cy.freeuk.

com/Tcn30.htm>. 15 Oct. 2002.

"Hail Caesar: Augustus, First of
the Emperors." New York: New
Video Group, 1998. Ed. BBC.

Indonesian Diversity. 5 Jan. 2001.
Online posting. Lonely Planet
Thorn Tree. Available:
<http://thorntree.lonelyplanet.
com/>. 10 May 2001.

Israeli Men as Lovers. 19 May-15
June 2003. Online posting.
Lonely Planet Thorn Tree.
Available: <http://thorntree.
lonelyplanet.com/>. 3 July 2003.

"Japan Mulls Travel Warning for
Women Visiting Bali." Deutsche
Presse-Agentur 19 March 2002.
Lexis-Nexus.

Lebanese Men. 24 May-10 June
2003. Online posting. Lonely
Planet Thorn Tree. Available:
<http://thorntree.lonelyplanet.
com/>. 17 July 2003.

Lesvos. 18 June 1999. Online
posting. Lonely Planet Thorn
Tree. Available: <http://thorn-
tree.lonelyplanet.com/>. 9 May
2002.

"Local Casanovas Preying on
Women Tourists." Bernama
(Malaysian National News
Agency) 3 June 1998. Lexis-
Nexus. 12 Jan. 2004.

Middle East. 3-4 May 2001.
Online posting. Lonely Planet
Thorn Tree. Available: <http://-
thorntree.lonelyplanet.com/>. 10
May 2001.

Middle East — Mixed
Marriages. 7 July-30 Sept. 2001.
Online posting. Lonely Planet
Thorn Tree. Available: <http://
thorntree.lonelyplanet.com/>. 9
May 2002.

Morocco.Com Discussion Forum
— Moroccan Men Dating
American Women??? 2001.
Online posting. Morocco.com.
Available: <http://www.moroc-
co.com/forums/showthread.ph
p3?threadid=3249&pagenum-
ber=1>. 2 July 2003.

The Opposite of Progress: The
Arabian Nights Harem Girl
Fantasy. Jolly Roper. Available:

<http://www.jollyroper.com/no
bondz.harem/harem.html>. 10
Apr. 2003.

Phuket Thailand — a Newbie
Guide: Women Sex Tourists. 7
Oct. 2000. Available:
<http://sabailand.bizland.com/
Phuket_Thailand_A_Newbie_
Guide.htm>. 6 Feb. 2003.

Preconceptions — Removed. 6-8
July 2003. Online posting.
Lonely Planet Thorn Tree.
Available: <http://thorntree.
lonelyplanet.com/>. 17 July
2003.

"Re: Pleasantly Surprised --
Smile." E-mail to the author. 1
June 2001.

"Reisenotizen: Sextouristinnen?
[Travel Notes: Female Sex
Tourists?]." *Taz, Die Tageszeitung*
Berlin 7 Sept. 1996: 24. Lexis-
Nexus. U Maryland McKeldin,
College Park. 2 Feb. 2003.

"Romeo Waiter Fired for
Bigamy." Press Association
Newsfile London 4 Oct. 1996.
Lexis-Nexus. 26 Aug. 2001.

"The Sex Industry: Giving the
Customer What He Wants."
Economist 14 Feb. 1998: 21-23.

Sex on the Road. 20 Dec. 2001.
Online posting. Lonely Planet
Thorn Tree. Available: <http://
thorntree.lonelyplanet.com/>. 28
Dec. 2001.

Sex ... or a Misplaced Need for
Affection. 2 May 2001. Online
posting. Lonely Planet Thorn
Tree. Available: <http://thorn-
tree.lonelyplanet.com/>. 10 May
2001.

Sexiest Men in South America?
19 Sept. 1999. Online posting.
Lonely Planet Thorn Tree.
Available: <http://thorntree.
lonelyplanet.com/>. 10 May
2001.

A Shame on the Dykes. 23 Oct.
1999. Online posting. Lonely
Planet Thorn Tree. Available:
<http://thorntree.lonelyplanet.
com/>. 9 May 2002.

Skala Eressos/Lesvos. 11 Apr.
1999. Online posting. Lonely

Planet Thorn Tree. Available: <http://thorntree.lonelyplanet.com/>. 9 May 2002.

"Stay Away, Gambia Warns 'Sex Tourist' Women." *Daily Mail* London 22 Aug. 1994: 7. Lexis-Nexus. 7 Mar. 2001.

Sumatran Men. 8 Aug.-23 Aug. 2001. Online posting. Lonely Planet Thorn Tree. Available: <http://thorntree.lonelyplanet.com/>. 24 Aug. 2001.

Thailand Lesbian and Women's Resources by Utopia. 2003. Utopia-Asia. Available: <http://www.utopia-asia.com/womthai.htm>. 6 Feb. 2003.

"That Holiday Romance Still Has Sex Appeal." Press Association Newsfile London 7 July 1991. Lexis-Nexus. 23 Mar. 2001.

Thomas Cook — a Brief History. Available: <http://www.thomascook.info/tck/de/en/tcw/0,2773,0-0-402186,00.html>. 29 Apr. 2003.

True Confessions of a Frustrated TEFL Teacher. 23 Oct. 2000. Online posting. Lonely Planet Thorn Tree. Available: <http://thorntree.lonelyplanet.com/>. 22 Jan. 2001.

Turkish Men :). 14-17 May 2003. Online posting. Lonely Planet Thorn Tree. Available: <http://thorntree.lonelyplanet.com/>. 3 July 2003.

What Is It About Black Men. 22 April 2001. Online posting. Lonely Planet Thorn Tree. Available: <http://thorntree.lonelyplanet.com/>. 10 May 2001.

"Where Men Are for Sale." *Marie Claire* Dec. 2001: 100. Infotrac. Enoch Pratt Free Library, Baltimore. 1 Apr. 2003.

The World Factbook: Country Listing. 2002. U.S. Central Intelligence Agency. Available: <http://www.odci.gov/cia/publications/factbook/indexgeo.html>. 7 June 2002.

Yes It's Sex. 2 May 2001. Online posting. Lonely Planet Thorn Tree. Available: <http://thorntree.lonelyplanet.com/>. 10 May 2001.

Ackerman, Diane. *A Natural History of Love*. New York: Random House, 1994.

Ackers, Louise. Women, Citizenship and European Community Law: The Gender Implications of the Free Movement Provisions: Centre for the Study of Law in Europe, Brussels 1996. Available: <http://www.leeds.ac.uk/law/csle/textw1-1.htm>. 31 Aug. 2002

Adams, Jad. "Entering the Territory." Rev. of *Sultry Climates: Travel and Sex Since the Grand Tour* by Ian Littlewood. *Guardian* London 9 June 2002. Available: <http://books.guardian.co.uk/Print/0,3858,420 0765,00.html>. 8 Apr. 2002.

Adams, Vincanne. *Tigers of the Snow and Other Virtual Sherpas*. Princeton, N.J.: Princeton UP, 1996.

Adler, Laure. *Marguerite Duras: A Life*. Trans. Anne-Marie Glasheen. Chicago: U of Chicago P, 2000.

Ahmad, Mahmoud. "Campaign to Dissuade Saudi Men from Taking Foreign Wives." *Arab News* Jeddah, Saudi Arabia 9 July 2003. Available: <http://www.arabnews.com/?page=1&section=0&article=28565&d=9&m=7&y=2003>. 9 July 2003.

al-Shaykh, Hanan. *Women of Sand and Myrrh*. New York: Doubleday, 1988.

Aldrich, Robert. *The Seduction of the Mediterranean: Writing, Art, and Homosexual Fantasy*. London, New York: Routledge, 1993.

Allegra, Donna. "Dancing Home a Stranger." Bledsoe 1998 138-55.

Allen, Charles, and Sharada Dwivedi. *Lives of the Indian Princes*. New York: Crown, 1984.

Amber, Jeannine. "Sex on the Beach: What Is It About Island Guys That Makes Grown Women Go Gaga?" *Essence* Oct. 1997: 101-04, 161-64.

Anderson, Patricia. *When Passion Reigned: Sex and the Victorians*. New York: Basic, 1995.

Apt, Carol, and David Farley Hurlbert. "The Female Sensation Seeker and Marital Sexuality." *Journal of Sex and Marital Therapy* 18.4 (1992): 315-24.

Arvidson, Maria, Dan Hellberg and Per-Anders Mardh. "Sexual Risk Behavior and History of Sexually Transmitted Diseases in Relation to Casual Travel Sex During Different Types of Journeys." *Acta obstetricia et gynecologica Scandinavica* 75.5 (1996): 490-94.

Arvidson, Maria, et al. "Risky Behavior in Women with History of Casual Travel Sex." *Sexually Transmitted Diseases* 24.7 (1997): 418-21.

Asian lover. Re: Re: Okay, the Truth About White Women/Asian Men. 4 Aug. 1998. Online posting. Korealink. Available: <http://www.korealink.com/public/general/messages/663.shtml>. 6 Nov. 2001.

Aziz, Christine. "Seeking Sex in the Gambia." *Marie Claire* (London) 1994: 10-18.

Baer, Barbara. "The Veil of Kachenjunga." Wylie 1998 245-53.

Bagus, Mary Ida. "Sows on Heat and Disoriented Boars — Straight Sex from Bali to Melbourne." *Melbourne Journal of Politics* 24 (1997): 69-93. Infotrac. Enoch Pratt Free Library, Baltimore. 1 Apr. 2003.

Bahbehanian, Laleh. Policing the Illicit Peripheries of Egypt's Tourism Industry. Fall. 2000. *Middle East Report* 216. Available: <http://www.merip.org/mer/mer216/216_behbehenian.html>. 15 Oct. 2002.

Baker, Aryn. "Desperately Seeking Survival: Bali's Living Are Casualties of a Dead Economy." *Time International* 2 Dec. 2002: 7+. Infotrac. Enoch Pratt Free Library, Baltimore. 1 Apr. 2003.

Balentine, Sharon. "Walking Her Sorrow into Life." McCauley 1998 174-84.

Ballantine, Derek. "Pacific: All the Trouble under the Sun." *Sunday Herald Sun* Melbourne, Australia 28 May 2000, sec. News: 14. Lexis-Nexus. 19 Aug. 2003.

Ballhatchet, Kenneth. *Race, Class and Class under the Raj*. London: Weidenfeld, 1980.

Baranay, Inez. *The Saddest Pleasure*. Sydney, Australia: Collins, 1989.

---. *The Edge of Bali.* Pymble, Australia: Angus, 1992.

Barbara, Augustin. *Marriage across Frontiers.* Trans. David E. Kennard. Philadelphia, Pa.: Multilingual Matters, 1989.

---. "Mixed Marriages: Some Key Questions." *International Migration* 32.3 (1994): 571-86.

Barr, Emily. *Backpack.* New York: Plume, 2002.

Barrett, Michael, et al. "Canada." *International Encyclopedia of Sexuality.* Ed. Robert T. Francoeur. Vol. 1. New York: Continuum, 1997. 221-343. 1.

Barrowclough, Anne. "The Truth About Love on the Gigolo Coast: Much Has Been Written About the British Women Who Flock to the Gambia Seeking Romance. But What Becomes of Those Who Find It? Too Often, Women Go Off in Search of Partners, Only to Find Themselves Trapped in Squalid Prisons of Their Own Making." *Daily Mail* London 27 Sept. 1994: 18-19. Lexis-Nexus. 22 Mar. 2001.

Batten, Mary. *Sexual Strategies: How Females Choose Their Mates.* New York: Putnam, 1992.

Bauer, Thomas G., and Bob McKercher, ed. *Sex and Tourism: Journeys of Romance, Love and Lust.* Binghamton, N.Y.: Hapworth, 2003.

Bay, Lisa. "In the Eyes of Ahmad." Wylie 1998 143-44.

Beauman, Nicola. *E.M. Forster: A Biography.* New York: Knopf, 1994.

Becker, Gary S. "A Theory of Marriage: Part I." *Journal of Political Economy* 82.4 (1973): 813-46.

Beddoe, Christine. "Beachboys and Tourists: Links in the Chain of Child Prostitution in Sri Lanka." Oppermann 1998 42-50.

Bell, Alan P., and Martin S. Weinberg. *Homosexualities: A Study of Diversity among Men and Women.* New York: Simon, 1978.

Bell, Gertrude. *The Desert and the Sown.* New York: Dutton, 1907.

Belliveau, Jeannette. *An Amateur's Guide to the Planet.* Baltimore, Md.: Beau Monde, 1996.

Belliveau, Jeannette. *Sexual Geography.* Baltimore, Md.: Beau Monde, forthcoming.

Bem, Daryl J., and Andrea Allen. "On Predicting Some of the People Some of the Time: The Search for Cross-Situational Consistencies in Behavior." *Psychological Review* 81.6 (1974): 506-21.

Bengis, Ingrid. "A Journey to Self-Destruction." Rev. of *Give Sorrow Words: Maryse Holder's Letters from Mexico.* *New York Times* New York 10 June 1979, sec. Book Review: 11.

Berer, Marge. *Women and HIV/AIDS — An International Sourcebook.* 1993. Bigchalk Library. Enoch Pratt Free Library, Baltimore. Contemporary Women's Issues Database. 11 Oct. 2002.

Beveridge, Lord. *India Called Them.* London: Allen, 1947.

Bindel, Julie. "The Price of a Holiday Fling." *Guardian* London 17 July 2003. Available: <http://www.guardian.co.uk/weekend/story/0,3605,990237,00.html>.

Birkett, Dea. *Spinsters Abroad: Victorian Lady Explorers.* New York: Blackwell, 1989.

---. "Journey Woman: Out of India, Robyn Davidson Is Struggling to Make a Life in London. Dea Birkett Talks to the Camel Lady Who Has Redrawn the Map." *Scotland on Sunday* Edinburgh 26 May 1996, sec. Spectrum: 11. Lexis-Nexus.

---. *Serpent in Paradise.* New York: Anchor, 1997.

Black, Paula. "Sex and Travel: Making the Links." Clift and Carter 2000 250-63.

Blackwell, Debra, and Daniel T. Lichter. "Mate Selection among Married and Unmarried Couples." *Journal of Family Issues* 21 (2000): 271-302.

Blackwood, Evelyn. "Falling in Love with an-Other Lesbian." Kulick 1995 51-75.

Bledsoe, Lucy Jane, ed. *Lesbian*

Travels: A Literary Companion. San Francisco: Whereabouts, 1998.

Bloor, Michael, et al. Feasibility Study for Co-Ordinated Community Action on the Improved Targeting of HIV/AIDS Prevention Campaigns among International Travellers: Final Report: Cardiff: School of Social and Administrative Studies, University of Wales 1997.

Bloor, Michael, et al. "Differences in Sexual Risk Behaviour between Young Men and Women Travelling Abroad from the UK." *The Lancet* 352 (1998): 1664-68.

Boissevain, Jeremy. "Tourism and Development in Malta." *Development and Change* 8.4 (1977): 523-38.

Boltwood, Alana. Alana's Involuntary Celibacy Project. 2002. Available: <http://www.ncf.ca/~ad097/ic-home.html>. 10 Sept. 2002.

Bonneux, Luc, et al. "Risk Factors for Infection with Human Immunodeficiency Virus among European Expatriates in Africa." *British Medical Journal* 297 (1988): 591-94.

Borzello, Lynn. "Living without Fear." Jansz and Davies 1995 624-30.

Bowden, Robert. "Point, Click, Matrimony. Web Sites That Display 'Net-Order Brides' Are Praised by Some as Places to Find Love and Disparaged by Others as Places That Exploit Foreign Women and Defraud Men." *Tampa Tribune* Tampa, Fla. 10 June 1996, sec. Baylife: 1.

Bowles, Paul. *The Sheltering Sky.* New York: New Directions, 1949.

Bowles, Paul. "Preface." Trans. Paul Bowles. *The Oblivion Seekers.* Isabelle Eberhardt. San Francisco: City Lights, 1972. 7-17. 1897-1904.

Bowman, Glenn. "Fucking Tourists: Sexual Relations and Tourism in Jerusalem's Old City." *Critique of Anthropology* 9.2 (1989): 77-93.

Bradt, Hilary. "Travel: Weather's Here, Wish You Were

Wonderful. Traveller's Tale: Look Out, It's the Muleteers from Hell! Hilary Bradt on Why the Worst People Seem to Go on the Best Holidays." *Daily Telegraph* London 29 Jan. 1994: 30. Lexis-Nexus. 6 Apr. 2001.

Bramlett, M.D., and Mosher, W.D. Cohabitation, Marriage, Divorce and Remarriage in the United States: National Center for Health Statistics. Vital and Health Statistics, Atlanta, Ga. 2002. Available: <http://www.cdc.gov/nchs/data/series/sr_23/sr_23_021.pdf>

Blanch, Lesley. *The Wilder Shores of Love*. New York: Simon, 1954.

Bright, Susie. *Susie Bright's Sexual State of the Union*. New York: Simon, 1997.

Brook, Elaine, and Julie Donnelly. *The Windhorse*. New York: Paragon House, 1986.

Brown, Naomi. "Beachboys as Culture Brokers in Bakau Town, the Gambia." *Community Development Journal* 27.4 (1992): 361-370.

Brown, Rebecca. "Foreword." Bledsoe 1998 i-iii.

Brueggemann, Rudy. Fear and Loathing on the Mzungu Trail. 1997. Available: <http://www.rudyfoto.com/SafariStory.html>. 24 Aug. 2001.

Bryce, Jane. "A Very Nigerian Coup." Jansz and Davies 1990 349-53.

Buck, Ross. *Human Motivation and Emotion*. 2nd ed. New York: Wiley, 1988.

Bullough, Caroline. "A Student in Alexandria." Jansz and Davies 1995 200-03.

Bullough, Vern, and Bullough, Bonnie. *Women and Prostitution: A Social History*. Revised ed. Buffalo, N.Y.: Prometheus Books, 1987.

Burton, Richard F. *The Book of the Thousand Nights and a Night*. Vol. X. X vols. Benares, India: Kamashastra Society. Published for private subscribers only, 1886.

Busi, Aldo. *Sodomies in Elevenpoint*. Trans. Stuart Hood. London: Faber, 1992.

Buss, David M. "Human Mate Selection." *American Scientist* 73 (1985): 47-51.

---. "Sex Differences in Human Mate Preferences: Evolutionary Hypotheses Tested in 37 Cultures." *Behavioral and Brain Sciences* 12 (1989): 1-49 (including peer comments).

---. "Conflict in Married Couples: Personality Predictors of Anger and Upset." *Journal of Personality* 56.4 (1991): 663-88.

---. *The Evolution of Desire: Strategies of Human Mating*. New York: Basic, 1994.

---. *The Dangerous Passion: Why Jealousy Is as Necessary as Love and Sex*. New York: Free Press, 2000.

Butt, Leslie. The Social and Political Life of Infants among the Baliem Valley Dani, Irian Jaya. McGill University, 1998. Montreal. Available: <http://www.papuaweb.org/dlib/s123/butt/phd.pdf>. 19 Aug. 2003.

Buyers, Christopher. India: Salute States: Patiala. 2001. Available: <http://www.dreamwater.net/regiment/RoyalArk/India/patiala3.htm>. 6 Feb. 2002.

---. India: Salute States: Kapurthala. 2001. Available: <http://www.dreamwater.net/regiment/RoyalArk/India/kaputh2.htm>. 6 Feb. 2002.

---. India: Salute States: Indore. 2001. Available: <http://www.dreamwater.net/regiment/RoyalArk/India/indore4.htm>. 6 Feb. 2002.

---. "Re: Chapter Excerpt on India." E-mail to the author. 20 July 2003.

Cabezas, Amalia L. "Women's Work Is Never Done: Sex Tourism in Sosúa, Dominican Republic." Kempadoo 1999 93-124.

Caldwell, John C. AIDS in Melanesia: Australian Agency for International Development 2000. Available: <http://www.ausaid.gov.au/publications/pdf/caldwell.pdf>. 18 Aug. 2003

Calkins, Fay G. *My Samoan Chief*. Honolulu: U of Hawaii P, 1962.

Campbell, Howard. "Negril's Beach Boys: Gigolos Showing Single Tourist Women a Good Time." *Jamaica Observer* Kingston, Jamaica 21 July 2001. Available:

<http://www.jamaica-observer.com/news/html/20020720T220000-0500_29170_OBS_NEGRIL_S_BEACH_BOYS.asp>. 4 Feb. 2003.

Campbell, Shirley, Althea Perkins and Patricia Mohammed. " 'Come to Jamaica and Feel All Right:' Tourism and the Sex Trade." Kempadoo 1999 125-56.

Carpenter, Mary Thorn. *In Cairo and Jerusalem: An Eastern Note-Book*. New York: Randolph, 1894.

Carter, Simon, et al. "The Sexual Behaviour of International Travellers at Two Glasgow GUM Clinics." *International Journal of STD & AIDS* 8.5 (1997): 336-8.

Castelberg-Koulma, Mary. "Greek Women and Tourism: Women's Co-Operatives as an Alternate Form of Organization." *Working Women: International Perspectives on Gender and Labour Ideology*. Ed. N. Redclift and M.T. Sinclair. New York: Routledge, 1991. 197-213.

Caulfield, Annie. *Kingdom of the Film Stars: Journey into Jordan*. Melbourne, Australia: Lonely Planet, 1997.

Cesara, Manda [Karla Poewe]. *Reflections of a Woman Anthropologist*. New York: Academic, 1982.

Chalmers, Sarah. "Why I Gave up My BMW and Our £600,000 House for a Tin Shack and a Penniless Man Called Dembo; Femail on the Incredible Story of a Middle-Class Woman Who Had the Courage to Fulfil Her African Dream." *Daily Mail* London 23 June 1998: 18. Lexis-Nexus. 16 April 2002.

Chancellor, Alexander. "The Ultimate Equaliser." *Guardian* London 23 Feb. 2002. Available: <http://www.guardian.co.uk/weekend/story/0,3605,653661,00.html>. 3 July 2003.

Chapkis, Wendy. *Live Sex Acts: Women Performing Erotic Labor*. News York: Routledge, 1997.

Chapple, Steve. "The Peripatetic Heart." *New York Times* New York 20 July 1997: Travel, 25.

Chevannes, Barry. "Sexual Behavior of Jamaicans: A Literature Review." *Social and Economic Studies* 42.1 (1993): 1-45.

Chidester, Dianne Lynn. Women in Turkey: An Introductory Report. 1998. Available: <http://socialscience.tjc.edu/mkho/fulbright/1998/turkey/chidester.htm>. 8 July 2003.

Chipperfield, Faith. *The Life and Death of Margaret Fuller*. New York: Coward McCann, 1957.

Clapp, Susannah. *With Chatwin*. New York: Knopf, 1997.

Clark, Beth. "Tropical Temptation." Wylie 1998 138-44.

Clark, Russell D. "The Impact of AIDS on Gender Differences in Willingness to Engage in Casual Sex." *Journal of Applied Social Psychology* 20.9 (1990): 771-82.

Clarke, John I. *The Human Dichotomy: The Changing Numbers of Males and Females*. New York: Pergamon, 2000.

Clift, Stephen, and Simon Forrest. "Factors Associated with Gay Men's Sexual Behaviours and Risk on Holiday." *AIDS Care* 11.3 (1999): 281-95.

Clift, Stephen, and Simon Carter, ed. *Tourism and Sex: Culture, Commerce and Coercion*. London: Pinter, 2000.

Coates, Stephen. "Attacks on Tourists Shatter Thailand's 'Land of Smiles' Image." Agence France Press 9 Feb. 1998. Lexis-Nexus. 22 Mar. 2001.

Cohen, Erik. "Arab Boys and Tourist Girls in a Mixed Jewish-Arab Community." *International Journal of Comparative Sociology* 12 (1971): 217-233.

---. "Sensuality and Venality in Bangkok: The Dynamics of Cross-Cultural Mapping." *Deviant Behavior* 8 (1987): 223-34.

Cohen, Stanley, and Laurie Taylor. "Free Areas, Escape Routes and Identity Sites." *Escape Attempts: The Theory and Practice of Resistance to Everyday Life*. 2nd ed. New York: Routledge, 1992. 112-53.

Comerford, Patrick. "The Real Shirley Valentines: Patrick Comerford Meets Irish Women Who Stayed to Work and Live in Greece after the Holiday Was Over." *Irish Times* Dublin 6 Aug. 1997, sec. Features: 8. Lexis-Nexus. 30 June 2002.

Conlin, Michelle. "Valley of No Dolls: Silicon Valley Has 10 Zillion Nerds to Every One Woman." *Business Week* 6 Mar. 2000. Lexis-Nexus. 28 Aug. 2002.

Cooke, Hope. *Time Changes*. New York: Simon, 1980.

Copland, Ian. *The Princes of India in the Endgame of Empire, 1917-47*. Cambridge, England: Cambridge UP, 1997.

Cottrell, Ann Baker. "Cross-National Marriage as an Extension of an International Life Style: A Study of Indian-Western Couples." *Journal of Marriage and the Family* 35.4 (1973): 739-41.

---. "Cross-National Marriages, a Review of the Literature." *Journal of Comparative Family Studies* 21.2 (1990): 151-69.

Coyne, John, ed. *Living on the Edge: Fiction by Peace Corps Writers*. Willimantic, Conn.: Curbstone, 1999.

---. Talking with Paul Theroux. 2003. Peace Corps Writers. Available: <http://www.peacecorpswriters.org/pages/2003/0303/303talkthero4.html>. 29 Oct. 2003.

Craft, Robert. "Bali H'ai." Rev. of *Colin McPhee: Composer in Two Worlds* by Carol J. Oja and *A House in Bali* by Colin McPhee. *New York Review of Books* 24 Oct. 1991: 56-59.

Cripps, Rebecca. "A Different Rhythm." Jansz and Davies 1990 64-67.

Cronin, Richard. *Imagining India*. London: Macmillan, 1989.

Cropper, Martin. "No Panic: It's Only a Poet in the Woodland; Martin Cropper Finds That Wildlife Intrudes Everywhere on a Search for the Seats of the Muses." Rev. of *The Pan Principle* by Fiona Pitt-Kethley. *Daily Telegraph* London 26 Feb. 1994, sec. Books: 5. Lexis-Nexus. 10 May 2002.

Crossette, Barbara. "Women Harassed on Tours in Asia." *New York Times* New York 28 Jan. 1990, Late ed., sec. Foreign: 9. Lexis-Nexus. 14 Nov. 2001.

Culross, Trudy. *It Gets Better after Cairo*. London: Mandarin, 1988.

Cumming, Anne. *The Love Habit: The Sexual Confessions of an Older Woman*. New York: Bobbs, 1977.

---. *The Love Quest: A Sexual Odyssey*. London: Owen, 1991.

Cummings-Yeates, Rosalind. "Journey to Yard: A Jamaican Cultural Experience." Jansz, et al, 1999 313-18.

Curtin, J. Sean. International Marriages in Japan: Part Four — Basic Data on International Marriage in 2002. 28 Jan. 2003. GLOCOM Platform. Available: <http://www.glocom.org/special_topics/social_trends/20021112_trends_s16/>. 21 Feb. 2003.

Cuthbertson, Ken. *Nobody Said Not to Go: The Life, Loves, and Adventures of Emily Hahn*. New York: Faber, 1998.

D'Cunha, Cyril. "Goa High on HIV Prevalence List." Asia Africa Intelligence Wire 8 June 2002. Infotrac. Enoch Pratt Free Library, Baltimore. 1 Apr. 2003.

D'Elia, Gregory. "Parallel Lives: Jacqueline Roumeguère: Masai and Parisian." *The World and I* [*Washington Times*] 1995: 346-55.

Dahles, Heidi. "Of Birds and Fish: Street Guides, Tourists, and Sexual Encounters in Yogyakarta, Indonesia." Oppermann 1998 30-41.

Dahles, Heidi, and Karin Bras. "Entrepreneurs in Romance Tourism in Indonesia." *Annals of Tourism Research* 26.2 (1999): 276-293.

Dalby, Liza Crihfield. *Geisha*. Berkeley: U of California P, 1983.

Daniels, Lizz. "Rajasthan: Sex in the Sand." *In Focus: Magazine of Tourism Concern* 1998/99. Available: <http://www.tourismconcern.org.uk/magazine/rajasthan.htm>. 9 Apr 2002.

Dann, Graham. *The Barbadian Male: Sexual Attitudes and Practice*. London: Macmillan Caribbean, 1987.

Darlington, Shasta. "Vatican

Warns Catholics against Marrying Muslims." Reuters 14 May 2004. Available: <http://www.reuters.com/print erFriendlyPopup.jhtml?type=top News&storyID=5150255>. 14 May 2004.

Davidson, Robyn. *Tracks*. 1980. New York: Vintage, 1995.

---. *Desert Places*. New York: Viking, 1996.

Davis, Kingsley, and Pietronella van den Oever. "Demographic Foundations of Sex Roles." *Population and Development Review* 8.3 (1982): 495-511.

de Albuquerque, Klaus. "Sex, Beach Boys and Female Tourists in the Caribbean." *Sexuality & Culture*. Ed. Barry M. Dank. Vol. 2. New Brunswick, N.J.: Transaction, 1998. 87-111. 2.

---. "In Search of the Big Bamboo: How Caribbean Beach Boys Sell Fun in the Sun." *The Utne Reader* Jan.-Feb. 2000: 82-86.

de Albuquerque, Klaus, and Jerome L. McElroy. "Tourist Harassment." *Annals of Tourism Research* 28.ER2 (2001): 477-92.

de Graaf, Ron, et al. "Sexual Risk of HIV Infection among Expatriates Posted in AIDS Endemic Areas." *AIDS* 11.9 (1997): 1173-81.

---. "Underlying Reasons for Sexual Conduct and Condom Use among Expatriates Posted in AIDS Endemic Areas." *AIDS Care* 10.6 (1998): 651-65.

de Kretser, Michelle, ed. *Brief Encounters: Stories of Love, Sex and Travel*. Oakland, Calif.: Lonely Planet, 1998.

de Moya, E. Antonio, and Rafael Garcia. "Three Decades of Male Sex Work in Santo Domingo." *Men Who Sell Sex: International Perspectives on Male Prostitution and AIDS*. Ed. Peter Aggleton. London: UCL, 1999. 127-40.

Dennis, Steve. "Travel 2000 Mexico: Jumpin' Beings; Beautiful Acapulco Has Been Reborn — but Steve Dennis Revels in Its Star-Studded History." *Mirror* London 15 Jan. 2000, sec. Features: 26. Lexis-Nexus. 30 June 2002.

Derr, Deandre. Before the Crackdown Part 2. Stickman's Guide to Bangkok. Available: <http://www.stickmanbangkok.com/reader/reader72.html>. 11 July 2002.

di Blasi, Marlena. *A Thousand Days in Venice (An Unexpected Romance)*. Chapel Hill, N.C.: Algonquin, 2002.

Diamond, Jared. *Guns, Germs and Steel: The Fate of Human Societies*. New York: Norton, 1997.

Djelantik, Anak Agung Madé. *The Birthmark: Memoirs of a Balinese Prince*. Hong Kong: Periplus, 1997.

Dodson, Betty. Dr. Betty Dodson Transcript: Looking at Women's Orgasm over the Last Thirty Years. 1998. Available: <http://www.sexuality.org/dodson98.html>. 1 Aug. 2002.

Dodwell, Christina. *In Papua New Guinea*. Yeovil, Somerset, England: Oxford Illustrated, 1983.

---. Interview with Giles Milton. "Pushing Back the Feminine Frontiers: Roam-Alone Women Who Stride into the Unknown." *Mail on Sunday* London 21 Mar. 1993: 66. Lexis-Nexus. 22 Mar. 2001.

Donnelly, Denise, et al. "Involuntary Celibacy: A Life Course Analysis." *Journal of Sex Research* 38.2 (2001): 159-69.

Donnelly, Denise. "Review of Draft Chapter." Letter to the author. Dec. 2002.

Donner, Florinda. *Shabono*. New York: Delacorte, 1982.

Dougary, Ginny. "Wish You Were Here, Darling." *Times* London 21 Jan. 1995, sec. Features. Lexis-Nexus. 30 June 2002.

Dowling, Denise. "The Kuta Cowboys." Jansz, et al., 1999 276-84.

Dreir, Lisa. The Heart of a Tourist Hustler. 1998. Salon.com. Available: <http://www.salon.com/wlust/feature/1998/09/18feature.html>. 9 Nov. 2001.

du Cros, Hilary, and Dominique de Cros. "Romance, Retsina and Reality in Crete." Bauer 2003 43-55.

Dubisch, Jill. "Lovers in the Field." Kulick 1995 26-50.

Duff Gordon, Lady [Lucie]. *Letters from the Cape*. 1861. Ed. John Purves. London: Milford, 1921.

---. *Letters from Egypt (1862-69)*. New York: Praeger, 1969.

Duras, Marguerite. *The Lover*. New York: Harper, 1985.

---. *The North China Lover*. Trans. Leigh Hafrey. New York: New, 1992.

Dwyer, Jim. "Exuberant Crowd's Most Urgent Request: Water." *New York Times* New York 3 Apr. 2003. Available: <http://www.nytimes.com/2003/04/03/international/worldspecial/03AIRB.html>. 3 Apr. 2003.

Eberhardt, Isabelle. *Prisoner of the Dunes*. Trans. Sharon Bangert. London, Chester Springs, Pa.: Owen, 1995.

Ebron, Paulla. "Traffic in Men." *Gendered Encounters: Challenging Cultural Boundaries and Social Hierarchies in Africa*. Ed. Maria Grosz-Ngaté, and Omari H. Kokole. New York: Routledge, 1997. 223-44.

Edwards, Amelia. *A Thousand Miles Up the Nile*. New York: Scribner, 1877.

Edwards, Tamala M. "Flying Solo: More Women Are Deciding That Marriage Is Not Inevitable, That They Can Lead a Fulfilling Life as a Single. It's an Empowering Choice, but for Many Not an Easy One." *Time* 28 Aug. 2001: 46. Infotrac. Enoch Pratt Free Library, Baltimore. 16 Sept. 2002.

Einon, Dorothy. "Are Men More Promiscuous Than Women?" *Ethology and Sociobiology* 15 (1994): 131-43.

Eiser, J. Richard, and Nicholas Ford. "Sexual Relationships on Holiday: A Case of Situational Disinhibition?" *Journal of Social and Personal Relationships* 12.3 (1995): 323-39.

Ellis, Albert. "Casual Sex." *International Journal of Moral and Social Studies* 1.2 (1986): 157-69.

Ellis, Bruce J. "The Evolution of Sexual Attraction: Evaluative Mechanisms in Women." *The Adapted Mind*. Ed. J.H. Barkow , L. Cosmidese, and J. Tooby. New York: Oxford UP, 1992. 267-88.

Ellis, Lee. "Re: Question Relating to 'Sexually Aggressive Women'." E-mail to the author. 3 Jan. 2000.

Elmore, James L., and James T. Quattlebaum. "Female Sexual Stimulation During Antidepressant Treatment." *Pharmacotherapy* 17.3 (1997): 612-16.

Elphinston, Anita. "Letter to the Editor: Trouble in the Caribbean." *Daily Telegraph* London 31 Oct. 1995: 26. Lexis-Nexus. 18 June 2002.

Emily, Shareefa of Wazan. *My Life Story*. London: Arnold, 1911.

Eng, Thomas R., et al. "HIV-1 and HIV-2 Infections among U.S. Peace Corps Volunteers Returning from West Africa." *Journal of Travel Medicine* 2.3 (1995): 174-77.

Englebert, Victor. "The Otavalo Weave a Niche: The Age-Old Textile Tradition of These Ecuadorean Indians Has Bonded Families and Community While Attracting an International Tourist Market." *Americas* Nov.-Dec. 2001: 6, 10. Infotrac. Enoch Pratt Free Library, Baltimore. 1 Apr. 2003.

Enloe, Cynthia. *Bananas, Beaches & Bases: Making Feminist Sense of International Politics*. Berkeley, Calif.: U of California P, 1990.

Errington, Liz. "Greek Twist: A Trip to Sappho's Birthplace Is a Holiday with a Difference." *The Pink Paper* Oct. 1999. Available: <http://www.gay-circle.co.uk/HTMLDocs/greece.htm>. 7 May 2002.

Essock, Susan M. "Spouse Preference Shifts with Age." *Behavioral and Brain Sciences* 12 (1989): 19-20.

Fallowell, Duncan. "One Hot Summer in St. Petersburg." *Stewart* 2000 43-47.

Faul, Michele. " 'Stella' the Movie Attracting Single Women to Jamaica." Associated Press New York 6 Dec. 1998. Lexis-Nexus. 2 Sept. 2003.

Fellner, Deb. "American Girls Are Easy." *Maiden Voyages* Fall 1997: 32-34.

Fennelly, Beth Ann. "Day in Capri." *Wylie* 1998 26-31.

Ferrin, Lynn. "Sex, Yams and the Kula Ring." *A Woman's Passion for Travel*. Ed. Marybeth Bond and Pamela Michael. San Francisco, Calif.: Travelers' Tales, 1999. 86-93.

Fields, Jason and Lynne M. Casper. America's Families and Living Arrangements: March 2000: Current Population Reports, P20-537, U.S. Census Bureau, Washington, D.C. 2001. Available: <http://www.census.gov/population/www/socdemo/hh-fam.html>. 23 Aug. 2002

Fineman, Mark. "A Parent's Hell in a Bit of Paradise." *Los Angeles Times* Los Angeles 10 July 2000. Available: <http://www.latimes.com/travel/la-071000missing.story>. 4 Feb. 2003.

Fleming, Karl, and Anne Taylor Fleming. *The First Time*. New York: Simon, 1975.

Fonda, Daren. The Male Minority: As Men Slip to 44 Percent of Undergrads, Some Colleges Actively Recruit Them. 2 Dec. 2000. Time.com. Available: <http://www.time.com/time/education/article/0,8599,-90446,00.html>. 16 Sept. 2002.

Forster, E.M. *A Room with a View*. London: Arnold, 1908.

---. *A Passage to India*. London: Arnold, 1924.

---. "The Obelisk." *The Life to Come and Other Stories*. New York: Norton, 1972. 113-29. 1939.

---. "The Other Boat." *The Life to Come and Other Stories*. New York: Norton, 1972. 166-197. 1957-58.

---. "Three Countries." 1953. Ed. The *Hill of Devi and Other Indian Writings*. Vol. 14. The Abinger Edition of E.M. Forster. Suffolk, England: Arnold, 1983. 289-96. 1953.

---. "Kanaya." 1953. Ed. *The Hill of Devi and Other Indian Writings* (see above).

Forsythe, Steven, et al. "Protecting Paradise: Tourism

and AIDS in the Dominican Republic." *Health Policy and Planning* 13.3 (1998): 277-86.

Forsythe, Steven. "Re: Thanks for the Information!" E-mail to the author. 4 June 2001.

---. E-mail to the author. 30 May 2001.

Fountaine, Margaret. *Love among the Butterflies*. Ed. W.F. Cater. Boston: Little, 1980.

---. *Butterflies and Late Loves: The Future Travels and Adventures of a Victorian Lady*. Ed. W.F. Cater. Topsfield, Mass.: Salem House, 1987.

Frank, Katherine. *A Passage to Egypt: The Life of Lucie Duff Gordon*. Boston: Houghton, 1994.

Fraser, Laura. *Italian Affair*. New York: Pantheon, 2001.

Frawley, Maria H. *A Wider Range: Travel Writing by Women in the Victorian Era*. Cranbury, N.J.: Associated UP's, 1994.

---. Letter to the author. 16 June 2000.

Freud, Esther. *Hideous Kinky*. New York: Harcourt, 1992.

Freud, Esther. "The Joy of Souks: Hideous Kinky Was the Acclaimed Story of Esther Freud's Moroccan Childhood. Now It's Been Made into a Film, She Goes on Location in Marrakesh to See Kate Winslet in a Kaftan Playing Her Mum." *Observer* London 17 Jan. 1999, sec. Review: 5. Lexis-Nexus. 26 Aug. 2001.

Friday, Nancy. *My Secret Garden: Women's Sexual Fantasies*. New York: Pocket, 1973.

---. *Women on Top: How Real Life Has Changed Women's Sexual Fantasies*. New York: Simon, 1991.

Fukuyama, Frances. What Divides America: Conservatives Lose If Voters Chose Politicians on Cultural Issues. 15 Nov. 2000. Available: <http://www.opinionjournal.com/>. 15 Nov. 2000.

Gagneux, Olivier P., et al. "Malaria and Casual Sex: What Travelers Know and How They Behave." *Journal of Travel Medicine* 3.1 (1996): 14-21.

Gaunt, Mary. *Alone in West Africa*. London: Laurie, 1912.

Gearing, Jean. "Fear and Loving in the West Indies." Kulick 1995 186-218.

Gibbings, Wesley. "Trinidad and Tobago Health: The High Cost of Sex Tourism." InterPress News Service Rome 24 Mar 1997. Available: <http://www.aegis.com/news/ips/1997/IP970305.html>. 14 Apr 2002.

Giddens, Anthony. *The Transformation of Intimacy*. Stanford, Calif.: Stanford UP, 1992.

Gillies, P., et al. "HIV-Related Risk Behaviour in UK Holiday-Makers." *AIDS* 6.3 (1992): 339-341.

Gillmore, Mary Rogers, Pepper Schwartz and Diane Civic. "The Social Context of Sexuality: The Case of the United States." Holmes 1999 95-105.

Glickauf-Hughes, Cheryl L., George B. Hughes and Marolyn C. Wells. "A Developmental Approach to Treating Dual-Career Couples." *American Journal of Family Therapy* 14.3 (1986): 254-263.

Godden, Rumer. *Black Narcissus*. Boston: Little, 1939.

Goldberg, Herb. *The New Male: From Macho to Sensitive but Still All Male*. New York: Signet, 1979.

Golde, Peggy. "Odyssey of Encounter." Golde 1986 65-93.

---, ed. *Women in the Field: Anthropological Experiences*. Berkeley, Calif.: U of California P, 1986.

Golden, Marita. *Migrations of the Heart*. New York: Anchor, 1983.

Gornick, Vivian. *In Search of Ali Mahmoud: An American Woman in Egypt*. New York: Dutton, 1973.

Gorry, April Marie. Leaving Home for Romance: Tourist Women's Adventures Abroad. Diss. U of California, Santa Barbara, 1999. Ann Arbor: UMI 9958930, 2000.

Gough, Laurie. Bali Moon: A Wanderer Enjoys the Night Sky with a New Friend. 5 May 1999. Salon.com. Available: <http://www.salon.com/travel/feature/1999/05/05/excerpt

>. 6 Nov. 2001.

---. *Kite Strings of the Southern Cross: A Woman's Travel Odyssey*. Travelers' Tales. Ed. Larry Habegger James O'Reilly. San Francisco: Travelers' Tales, 1999.

Graves, Lucia. *A Woman Unknown: Voices from a Spanish Life*. Washington, D.C.: Counterpoint, 2000.

Griest, Stephanie Elizondo. "Sweet Thing." *Cuba: True Stories*. Ed. Tom Miller. San Francisco: Travelers' Tales, 2001. 46-50.

Grossbard-Schechtman, Amyra. "Marriage Squeezes, Cohabitation, and the Feminist Revolution." *Contemporary Marriage: Comparative Perspectives in a Changing Institution*. Ed. Kingsley Davis. New York: Sage, 1985. 375-95.

Grossman, Sarah. "Adios Paraguay." Bledsoe 1998 113-26.

Gurumurthy, S. Not Foreign Hands Any More, but Its Head. 4 May 1999. Indian Express. Available: <http://www.ofbjp.org/news/0599/13.html>. 7 July 2003.

Guttentag, Marcia, and Paul F. Secord. *Too Many Women? The Sex Ratio Question*. New York: Sage, 1983.

Haddad, George. "He Man Hookers." *Adam* 1977: 56-58, 90, 96.

Hahn, Emily. *China to Me*. Philadelphia: Blakiston, 1944.

---. "The Big Smoke." *No Hurry to Get Home: The Memoir of the New Yorker Writer Whose Unconventional Life and Adventures Spanned the Twentieth Century*. New York: First Seal, 2000. 220-40.

Hall, C. Michael. "Gender and Economic Interests in Tourism Prostitution: Thailand: 'Land of Smiles' or 'the Brothel of Asia'." Kinnaird and Hall 1994 154-58.

Hall, Unity. *Emily: The Moroccan Princess from Elephant and Castle*. London: Souvenir, 1971.

Hamilton, Annette. "Primal Dream: Masculinism, Sin, and Salvation in Thailand's Sex Trade." *Sites of Desire, Economies of Pleasure: Sexualities in Asia and

the Pacific*. Ed. Lenore Manderson and Margaret Jolly. Chicago: U of Chicago P, 1997. 145-165.

Hancock, Louise, and Gerard Couzens. "How the Child Bride Grew Up: She Was a Naive Tourist of 13 and He Was a Dark-Eyed Turkish Waiter When Her Parents Let Them Wed. Five Years on They Reveal How the Shocking Affair Changed Their Lives." *Sunday Mirror* London 17 Dec. 2000, sec. Features: 16, 17. Lexis-Nexus. 18 Oct. 2002.

Harrell-Bond, Barbara. "A Window on the Outside World:" Tourism as Development in the Gambia. Vol. 19. Hanover, N.H.: American Universities Field Staff, 1978.

Harvey, Claire. "'Kuta Cowboys' Strutting Their Stuff for Lovelorn Visitors." *Jakarta Post* Jakarta, Indonesia 5 May 2002. EBSCOHost. Enoch Pratt Free Library, Baltimore. 11 Oct. 2002.

Hawkes, Sarah J., et al. "Risk Behaviour and HIV Prevalence in International Travellers." *AIDS* 8.2 (1994): 247-52.

Hazen, Helen. *Endless Rapture: Rape, Romance and the Female Imagination*. New York: Scribner, 1983.

Hector. Thai Story. 2000. Clubbing.com: The Global Guide to Clubland. Available: <http://www.clubbing.com/guest/feat1.asp>. 11 July 2002.

Hellberg, Dan, et al. "Casual Travel Sex, Sex Tourism and International Prostitution." *Travel Medicine International* 15.4 (1997): 142-49.

Hellicar, Martin. "AIDS Lover Freed." *Cyprus Mail* Nicosia 1 Jan. 1998. Available: <http://-www.hri.org/news/cyprus/cm news/1998/98-01-01.cmnews.html>. 20 June 2002.

---. "Waiter Charged with AIDS Crime." *Cyprus Mail* Nicosia 16 May 1998. Available: <http://-www.hri.org/news/cyprus/cm news/1998/98-05-16.cmnews.html>. 15 Oct. 2002.

Herman, Deb. "A Lesbian Holiday." Jansz, et al., 1999 238-43.

Herold, Edward, Rafael Garcia and Tony DeMoya. "Female Tourists and Beach Boys:

Romance or Sex Tourism?" *Annals of Tourism Research* 28.4 (2001): 978-997.

Herold, Edward S., and Dawn-Marie Mewhinney. "Gender Differences in Casual Sex and AIDS Prevention: A Survey of Dating Bars." *Journal of Sex Research* 30.1 (1993): 36-42.

Herz, Steve, J.D. Robinson and Rod Gibson. "Bin Laden Had Diana Murdered: Princess Was Targeted Because of Her Influence on Women in the Muslim World." *Globe* Boca Raton, Fla. 18 Dec. 2001.

Hicks, Shawna A. "Women in Tourism: Impacts from Tourism on the Women of Quepos, Costa Rica." 19 June 2003. 1996. Wallace vol. 1. Available: <http://www4.ncsu.edu:8030/~twallace/1996rpts.htm>.

Hilsum, Lindsey. "Knowing Nairobi." Jansz and Davies 1995 394-99.

Hirsch, Jane Brown. *Alhaji: A Peace Corps Adventure in Nigeria*. Santa Barbara, Calif.: Fithian, 1994.

Hodgkinson, Liz. "Shirley Valentine Is Alive and Well; Men Like to Brag, but Women May Be Having More Partners — Because It Is Far Easier for Them to Have a Fling on Holiday." *Independent* London 14 Mar. 1994: 18. Lexis-Nexus. 29 June 2003.

Hofmann, Corinne. *La Massaï Blanche* [the White Masai]. *Die weisse Massai* (1999; Munich). Trans. Anne Weber (from German). French ed. Paris: Plon, 2000.

---. Interview with Ursula Sautter. No Regrets. Time Talks with 'the White Masai' Author Corinne Hofmann. 4 Aug. 2000. Available: <http://www.time.com/time/europe/webonly/europe/2000/08/hofmann.html>. 18 Mar. 2002.

---. Home Page. 2002. Available: <http://www.massai.ch/>. 20 Nov. 2002.

Holder, Maryse. *Give Sorrow Words: Maryse Holder's Letters from Mexico*. New York: Grove, 1979.

Holland, Patrick, and Graham

Huggan. *Tourists with Typewriters: Critical Reflections on Contemporary Travel Writing*. Ann Arbor, Mich.: U of Michigan P, 1998.

Hollander, Dore. "Many Americans Still Practice High-Risk Sexual Behavior." *Human Sexuality: Opposing Viewpoints*. Ed. Brenda Stalcup. Opposing Viewpoints. San Diego, Calif.: Greenhaven, 1995. 226-29.

Hollander, Xaviera. *The Happy Hooker: My Own Story*. 1972. 30th anniversary ed. New York: Regan, 2002.

Holmes, King K., et al., ed. *Sexually Transmitted Diseases*. 3rd ed. New York: McGraw Hill, 1999.

Hopwood, Derek. *Sexual Encounters in the Middle East: The British, the French and the Arabs*. Reading, England: Ithaca, 1999.

Horney, Karen. *The Neurotic Personality of Our Time*. New York: Norton, 1937.

Hottola, Petri. *The Intercultural Body: Western Woman, Culture Confusion and Control of Space in the South Asia Travel Scene*. Joensuu, Finland: Publications of the Dept. of Geography, U of Joensuu, no. 7, 1999.

---. "Your... 2nd." E-mail to the author. 5 Mar. 2002.

Houellebecq, Michel. *Platform*. Trans. Frank Wynne. New York: Knopf, 2002.

Houweling, Hans, and Roel A. Coutinho. "Risk of HIV Infection among Dutch Expatriates in Sub-Saharan Africa." *International Journal of STD & AIDS* 2 (1991): 252-57.

Howard, Jane. *Margaret Mead: A Life*. New York: Simon, 1984.

Howard, Philip. "Lays of the Great God Pan." Rev. of *The Pan Principle* by Fiona Pitt-Kethley. *Times* London 10 Feb. 1994, sec. Features. Lexis-Nexus. 9 June 2001.

Hoxie, Elizabeth F. "Mrs. Grundy Adopts Daisy Miller." *New England Quarterly* Dec. 1946: 474-84.

Hubbard, Margaret. "Running through Fes." Jansz, et al., 1999 421-25.

Hull, E.M. *The Sheik*. London: E. Nash, 1919.

Hulme, Debbie. Interview with Carmen Bruegman. "Destroyed by a Masai Monster: Like So Many before Her, This Career Woman Thought She'd Found Love with a Masai Warrior. But When She Left Britain to Live with Him, She Was Walking into a Nightmare That Was to Wreck Her Life and Leave Her Destitute." *Daily Mail* London 12 Aug. 2000: 24-25. Lexis-Nexus. 22 Mar. 2001.

Hunt, J.M. "Traditional Personality Theory in the Light of Recent Evidence." *American Scientist* 53 (1965): 80-96.

Hunter, Eileen, with Narisa Chakrabongse. *Katya and the Prince of Siam*. Bangkok: River, 1994.

I.M. "Letter from Paris Correspondent." *Nation* 18 Apr. 1878: 257-59.

Ieda, Shoko. *Iero Kyabu* (Yellow Cab). Tokyo: Koyushuppan, 1991.

Ilaw, Marianne. "Oh, Oh, Those West Indian Men!" E. Lee 1997 133-38.

---. Telephone interview with the author. 8 June 2001.

Irvine, Lucy. *Castaway*. New York: Random, 1983.

---. *Faraway*. London: Corgi, 2000.

Iyer, Pico. *The Lady and the Monk: Four Seasons in Kyoto*. New York: Knopf, 1991.

J.P.T. "American Women Abroad." *Nation* 30 May 1878: 355-56.

James, Henry. "Daisy Miller: A Study." 1878. Stafford 1963 43-102.

James, Laurie. *Why Margaret Fuller Ossoli Is Forgotten*. Dix Hills, N.Y.: Golden Heritage, 1988.

Jamison, Kay Redfield. *Touched with Fire*. New York: Free, 1993.

Jammeh, Lt. Yahya. Interview with Susan d'Arcy. "Moral Yearnings." *Sunday Times* London 4 Sept. 1994. Lexis-Nexus. 22 Mar. 2001.

Jansz, Natania, and Miranda Davies, ed. *Women Travel:*

Adventures, Advice and Experience: A Real Guide Special. New York: Prentice Hall, 1990.

---, ed. More Women Travel: Adventures and Advice from More Than 60 Countries. London: Rough Guides, 1995.

Jansz, Natania, et al., ed. Women Travel: First-Hand Accounts from More Than 60 Countries. London: Rough Guides, 1999.

Jayawardena, Kumari. The White Woman's Other Burden: Western Women and South Asia During British Rule. London: Routledge, 1995.

Jhabvala, Ruth Prawer. Heat and Dust. New York: Harper, 1976.

---. "An Experience of India." Out of India: Selected Stories. New York: Morrow, 1986. 125-46.

Johnson, Anne M., et al. Sexual Attitudes and Lifestyles. Oxford, England: Blackwell, 1994.

---. "Sexual Behaviour in Britain: Partnerships, Practices, and HIV Risk Behaviours." The Lancet 358 (2001): 1835-42.

Jones, F.L. "Convergence and Divergence in Ethnic Divorce Patterns: A Research Note." Journal of Marriage and the Family 58 (1996): 213-18.

Jones, Mary Cadwalader. European Travel for Women. New York: Macmillan, 1900.

Jones, Michael E. "HIV and the Returning Expatriate." Journal of Travel Medicine 6 (1999): 99-106.

Jones, Peter. "An Ignoramus in Arcadia: Pan Was Absolutely Right to Hide from Fiona Pitt-Kethley, Says Peter Jones." Rev. of The Pan Principle by Fiona Pitt-Kethley. Sunday Telegraph London 6 Feb. 1994, sec. Books: 11. Lexis-Nexus. 10 May 2002.

Jones, Rose. "Husbands and Lovers: Gender Construction and the Ethnography of Sex Research." Markowitz 1999 25-42.

Jong, Erica. Fear of Flying. New York: Holt, 1973.

---. Any Woman's Blues: A Novel of Obsession. New York: Harper, 1990.

---. Fear of Fifty: A Midlife Memoir. New York: Harper, 1994.

Josephy, Helen, and Mary Margaret McBride. Paris Is a Woman's Town. New York: Coward McCann, 1929.

Juska, Jane. A Round-Heeled Woman: My Late-Life Adventures in Sex and Romance. New York: Villard, 2003.

Kalmijn, Matthijs. "Status Homogamy in the United States." American Journal of Sociology 97.2 (1991): 496-523.

Karch, Cecilia A. , and G.H.S. Dann. "Close Encounters of the Third World." Human Relations 34.4 (1981): 249-68.

Kaveney, Roz. "Mortifying Record of Wanderlust on a Roman Holiday." Rev. of Journeys to the Underworld by Fiona Pitt-Kethley. Sunday Times London 6 Nov. 1988, sec. Books: G14.

Kay, John. "Mob Rape Holiday Brit, 43, on Beach." Sun London 27 May 2000. Lexis-Nexus. 22 Mar. 2001.

Kelley, Cornelia Pulsifer. The Early Development of Henry James. Rev. ed. Urbana, Ill.: U of Illinois P, 1965.

Kelsky, Karen. "Intimate Ideologies: Transnational Theory and Japan's 'Yellow Cabs'." Public Culture 6 (1994): 465-478.

---. Women on the Verge: Japanese Women, Western Dreams. Durham, N.C.: Duke UP, 2001.

Kemp, Charlotte. "My Toyboy Tours: Pat's Guide to Finding Love in the Sun: Growing Trend of Women Holidaying on Their Own." Mirror London 15 Aug. 1998, sec. Features: 26. Lexis-Nexus. 10 May 2002.

Kempadoo, Kamala, ed. Sun, Sex and Gold: Tourism and Sex Work in the Caribbean. Lanham, Md.: Rowman, 1999.

Kendal, Felicity. White Cargo. London: Michael Joseph, 1998.

Kennedy, Dominic. "European Widows Exploit Sri Lanka Teenagers for Sex." Times London 29 Aug. 1996, sec. Overseas. Lexis-Nexus. 22 Mar. 2001.

Kennedy, Ruby Jo Reeves. "Premarital Residential Propinquity and Ethnic Endogamy." American Journal of Sociology 48.5 (1943): 580-84.

Kenny, Mary. "People: The Lessons of a Life Devoted to Sex." Appreciation of Anne Cumming. Sunday Telegraph London 5 Sept. 1993: 2. Lexis-Nexus. 7 June 2001.

Kernahan, Mel. White Savages in the South Seas. London, New York: Verso, 1995.

Khatib-Chahidi, Jane, Rosanna Hill and Renée Paton. "Chance, Choice and Circumstance: A Study of Women in Cross-Cultural Marriages." Cross-Cultural Marriage: Identity and Choice. Ed. Rosemary Breger and Rosanna Hill. New York: Berg, 1998. 49-66.

Kimball, Camilla. "Ticos and Tourists: Cross-Cultural Gender Relations in Quepos, Costa Rica." 1999. Wallace. Available: <http://www4.-ncsu.edu:8030/~twallace/Kimball.pdf>. 19 June 2003.

Kingsley, Mary. Travels in West Africa. London: Macmillan, 1897.

Kinnaird, Vivian, and Derek Hall, ed. Tourism: A Gender Analysis. New York: Wiley, 1994.

Kleiber, Dieter, and Martin Wilke. AIDS, Sex und Tourismus: Ergebnisse Einer Befragung Deutscher Urlauber und Sextouristen. Baden-Baden, Germany: Nomos-Verlagsgesellschaft, 1995.

Kobak, Annette. Isabelle: The Life of Isabelle Eberhardt. New York: Knopf, 1989.

Kousis, Maria. "Tourism and the Family in Rural Crete." The Sociology of Tourism. Ed. Yiargos Apostolopoulos. New York: Routledge, 1996. 219-32.

Kruhse-MountBurton, Suzy. "Sex Tourism and Traditional Male Identity." International Tourism: Identity and Change. Ed. Marie-Françoise Lanfant, et al. London: Sage, 1995. 192-204.

Kulick, Don, and Margaret Wilson, ed. Taboo: Sex, Identity and Erotic Subjectivity in Anthropological Fieldwork. London and New York: Routledge, 1995.

Kurosawa, Susan. "Advance of the Vulgar Boatmen." Weekend Australian Sydney 11 May 2002, sec. Travel: R23. Lexis-Nexus. 29 June 2002.

Kurtz, Howard. "From Naked

News to Naked Fiction." *Washington Post* Washington, D.C. 6 Aug. 2003. Available: <http://www.washington-post.com/wp-dyn/articles/A22725-2003Aug6.html>. 6 Aug. 2003.

Labbate, Lawrence A. "Bupropion-Sr-Induced Increased Libido and Spontaneous Orgasm." *Canadian Journal of Psychiatry* 43.6 (1998): 644-45. Available: <http://www.cpa-apc.org/Publications/-Archives/CJP/1998/Aug/let-ters2.html>. 23 Oct. 2002.

Laner, Mary Riege. "Competition and Combativeness in Courtship: Reports from Women." *Journal of Family Violence* 4.2 (1989): 181-95.

Langewiesche, William. *Sahara Unveiled*. New York: Pantheon, 1996.

Lapsley, Hilary. *Margaret Mead and Ruth Benedict*. Amherst, Mass.: U of Massachusetts P, 1999.

Laumann, Edward O., et al. *The Social Organization of Sexuality: Sexual Practices in the United States*. Chicago: U of Chicago P, 1994.

Lawrence, D.H. *Lady Chatterley's Lover*. 1930. Ed. Michael Squires. Cambridge, England: Cambridge UP, 1993.

Layne, Paul. "Sunny Barbados." *BIM* 1969: 46-51.

Lee, Elaine, ed. *Go Girl! The Black Woman's Book of Travel and Adventure*. Portland, Ore.: Eighth Mountain, 1997.

Lee, Gary. "Crime in the Caribbean: A Reality Check." *Washington Post* Washington, D.C. 8 Apr. 2001: E01. Available: <http://www.wash-ingtonpost.com/ac2/wp-dyn?pagename=article&node=&contentId=A45699-2001Apr5&notFound=true>. 4 Feb. 2003.

Leed, Eric J. *The Mind of the Traveler*. New York: Basic, 1991.

Leheny, David. "A Political Economy of Asian Sex Tourism." *Annals of Tourism Research* 22.2 (1995): 367-84.

Lerner, Gerda. "The Origin of Prostitution in Ancient Mesopotamia." *Signs: Journal of Women in Culture and Society* 11 (1986): 236-54.

Lett, James W. "Ludic and Liminoid Aspects of Charter Yacht Tourism in the Caribbean." *Annals of Tourism Research* 10 (1983): 35-56.

Levenstein, Harvey. *Seductive Journey: American Tourists in France from Jefferson to the Jazz Age*. Chicago: U of Chicago P, 1998.

Lewis, Jane. *Women in England, 1870-1950: Sexual Divisions and Social Change*. Bloomington, Ind.: Indiana UP, 1984.

Lewis, Richard Jr., George Yancey and Siri S. Bletzer. "Racial and Nonracial Factors That Influence Spouse Choice in Black/White Marriages." *Journal of Black Studies* 28.1 (1997): 60-78.

Lichter, Daniel T. "Delayed Marriage, Marital Homogamy, and the Mate Selection Process among White Women." *Social Science Quarterly* 71.4 (1990): 802-11.

Lightfoot-Klein, Hanny. *A Woman's Odyssey into Africa*. New York: Haworth, 1992.

Lindsey, Timothy. *The Romance of K'tut*. Kuala Lumpur: Oxford UP, 1997.

Lines, Andy. "War on Terror: On Holiday in Sweden He Was 'Such a Nice Boy' ... But at University a Hate-Filled Tutor Poisoned His Mind; the Mirror Investigates How Bin Laden Went from Likeable Youth to a Fanatic." *Mirror* London 24 Sept. 2001, sec. Features: 12, 13. Lexis-Nexus. 7 July 2003.

Lipton, Shereé. *Fiji, I Love You, Full Speed*. Wellington, N.Z.: Seven Seas, 1972.

Litt, Iris. "Leaving Las Pájaros." Wylie 1998 3-7.

Littlewood, Ian. *Sultry Climates: Travel and Sex*. Cambridge, Mass.: Da Capo, 2001.

Lloyd, Sarah. *An Indian Attachment: The True Story of an Englishwoman's Haunting Love Affair with a Young Sikh*. New York: Morrow, 1984.

---. "Re: Fao Jeanette Belliveau." E-mail to the author. 28 Feb. 2001.

Long, Rosemary. *Under the Baobab Tree*. Orpington, Kent: Dobby, 1993.

---. "The Holiday Love Affair That Lasted: My Mother Thought Africans Wore Grass Skirts. When I Said I Wanted to Marry Ray, She Cried." *Daily Mail* London 12 Apr. 1993: 18. Lexis-Nexus. 21 July 2001.

---. Interview with Catriona Wrottesley. "Lovers Who Come out of Africa." *Scotsman* Edinburgh 20 Jan. 1998: 11. Lexis-Nexus. 8 Mar. 2001.

Lord Monson. Interview with Andrew Evans. "Women Are Sex Tourists Too, Claims Peer." Press Association Newsfile London 3 Apr. 1995. Lexis-Nexus. 23 Mar. 2001.

Lovell, Mary. *Rebel Heart : The Scandalous Life of Jane Digby*. New York: Norton, 1995.

Lowe, Nigel. "International Child Abduction: The English Experience." *International and Comparative Law Quarterly* 48 (1999): 127-55.

Lucke, Jayne C. "Gender Roles and Sexual Behavior among Young Women." *Sex Roles* 39.3/4 (1998): 273-97.

Lynch, Barbara. "The Foreigner and the Shepherd." Jansz, et al., 1999 521-28.

Lyons, Douglas C. "Where the Men Are: The 10 Best Cities." *Ebony* July 1993: 30. InfoTrac Web. Enoch Pratt Free Library, Baltimore. 26 Feb. 2001.

Ma, Karen. *The Modern Madame Butterfly: Fantasy and Reality in Japanese Cross-Cultural Relationships*. Tokyo: Tuttle, 1996.

Mabbett, Hugh. *In Praise of Kuta: From Slave Port to Fishing Village to the Most Popular Resort in Bali*. Wellington, N.Z.: January, 1987.

Mackay, Lindsey. Interview with Karen Mcveigh. "The Kiss That Ruined My Life." *Scottish Daily Record & Sunday Mail* Glasgow 28 May 1999: 37-39. Lexis-Nexus. 18 Apr. 2002.

Mackenzie, Compton. *Vestal Fire*. 1927. The New Phoenix Library. London: Chatto, 1951.

---. *Extraordinary Women*. 1928.

London: Hogarth, 1986.

Mackinnon, Angus. "Bin Laden: The Saudi Dissident Waging Holy War on the US." Agence France Press 16 Sept. 2001. Lexis-Nexus. 7 July 2003.

Macklovich, Katya. "Paris in Pink." Northam 1999 237-241.

Macy, Marianne. *Working Sex: An Odyssey into Our Cultural Underworld*. New York: Carroll and Graf, 1996.

Maddox, Brenda. "Shirley Decides She's Had Enough." *New York Times* New York 12 Feb. 1989, Late City Final ed., sec. 2: 1. Lexis-Nexus. 29 June 2002.

Mahmoody, Betty. *Not without My Daughter*. 1987. New York: St. Martin's, 1987. Large print.

Maltz, Wendy, and Suzie Boss. *In the Garden of Desire: The Intimate World of Women's Sexual Fantasies*. New York: Broadway, 1997.

Manning, Frank E. "The Caribbean Experience." *Cultural Survival Quarterly* 6.3 (1982): 13-14.

Mansfield, Paul. "Why Macho Men Left Athens: For the First Time, Young Women Can Stroll around Athens without Being Harassed by an Oversexed 'Kamaki'." *Sunday Telegraph* London 17 Aug. 1997: 19. Lexis-Nexus. 22 Mar. 2001.

Månsson, Sven-Axel. *Cultural Conflict and the Swedish Sexual Myth: The Male Immigrant's Encounter with Swedish Sexual and Cohabitation Culture*. Månsson, Sven-Axel. New York: Hanover House, 1993.

---. "Divorce Rates." E-mail to the author. 12 Dec. 2002.

Mardh, Per-Anders, Maria Arvidson and Dan Hellberg. "Sexually Transmitted Diseases and Reproductive History in Women with Experience of Casual Travel Sex Abroad." *Journal of Travel Medicine* 3.3 (1996): 138-42. Abstract. Available: <http://www.opus-lu.se/Opus/abstracts/absgyn/p eranders.html>. 17 Oct. 2002.

Markowitz, Fran. "Sexing the Anthropologist: Implications for Ethnology." Markowitz and Ashkenazi 1999 161-74.

Markowitz, Fran, and Michael Ashkenazi, ed. *Sex, Sexuality and the Anthropologist*. Urbana, Ill.: U of Chicago P, 1999.

Marong, Carina. "Love through Open Eyes." Jansz, et al., 1999 208-13.

Marshall, Paule. *The Chosen Place, the Timeless People*. New York: Harcourt, 1969.

Martin, Susan Z. Subject: Places to See (Rajasthan, Bombay, Others). 11 July 1995. Online posting. Stego's FAQ on India travel. Available: <http://www.-geocities.com/TheTropics/1814/ind_place1.html>. 21 Nov. 2001.

Mason, Cheryl. Interview with Louise Daly. "We May Look an Odd Couple, but My Masai Warrior Is No Sex Slave." *Daily Mail* London 7 Sept. 1995: 44. Lexis-Nexus. 22 Aug. 2001.

---. Interview with Sarah Chalmers. "Our Bizarre Love Defied All Odds: When Housewife Cheryl Mason Left Her Husband for a Masai Warrior, No One Expected It to Last. Yet Six Years on, the Odd Couple Are Still Together Despite Some All Too Predictable Problems." *Daily Mail* London 14 June 1999: 20. Lexis-Nexus. 23 Aug. 2001.

---. Interview with Helen Weathers. "How I Killed My Masai Marriage; When Cheryl Mason, a Middle Class Married Mother of Three, Fell for a Masai Warrior Six Years Ago, She Vowed to Defy the Cynics. But Now, He Is Returning to Kenya, Broken by Her Demands That He Should Behave Like an Englishman. This Is Her Cautionary Tale." *Daily Mail* London 20 Jan. 2000: 34. Lexis-Nexus. 22 Aug. 2001.

Mason, Michael. *The Making of Victorian Sexuality*. New York: Oxford UP, 1994.

Mather, Ian. "Question: Which of These Three Men Rules a 'Kernel' of Terror? (Answer: King Fahd of Saudi Arabia)." *Scotsman* Edinburgh 11 Aug. 2002: 14. Lexis-Nexus. 7 July 2003.

Matthews, Harry G. *International Tourism: A Political and Social Analysis*. Cambridge, Mass.: Schenkman, 1978.

Maupin, Armistead. *Sure of You*. New York: Harper, 1987.

McCauley, Lucy, ed. *Women in the Wild*. San Francisco, Calif.: Travelers' Tales, 1998.

McDowell, Edwin. "Jamaica Sweeps Off Its Welcome Mat." *New York Times* 21 June 1998: Travel section. Lexis-Nexus. 4 Jan. 2000.

McElroy, Colleen J. *A Long Way from St. Louie: Travel Memoirs*. Minneapolis, Minn.: Coffee House, 1997.

McKibbin, Kerry. "Friendships Confused." Jansz, et al., 1999 139-49.

McLynn, Frank. *Burton: Snow Upon the Desert*. London: Murray, 1990.

McMillan, Terry. *How Stella Got Her Groove Back*. New York: Viking, 1996.

McVeigh, Tracy, and Jonathan Watts. "How Women Are Lured into Japan's Vice Dens." *Observer* London 16 July 2000, sec. News: 9. Lexis-Nexus. 28 Jan. 2003.

Mead, Margaret. "Field Work in the Pacific Islands, 1925-1967." Golde 1986 291-331.

---. *Male and Female*. 1949. New York: Perennial, 2001.

Meisch, Lynn A. "Gringas and Otavaleños: Changing Tourist Relations." *Annals of Tourism Research* 22.2 (1995): 441-62.

Melchett, Sonia. "Elaine Brook." *Passionate Quests: Five Modern Women Travellers*. Boston: Faber, 1992. 183-208.

Mendelsohn, R., et al. "Sexual Behaviour in Travellers Abroad Attending an Inner-City Genitourinary Medicine Clinic." *Genitourinary Medicine* 72.1 (1996): 43-46.

Mewhinney, Dawn M., Edward S. Herold and Eleanor Maticka-Tyndale. "Sexual Scripts and Risk-Taking of Canadian University Students on Spring Break in Daytona Beach, Florida." *Canadian Journal of Human Sexuality* 4.4 (1995): 273-88.

Michael, Robert T., et al. *Sex in America: A Definitive Survey*. Boston: Little, 1994.

Mikach, Sarah M., and J. Michael Bailey. "What Distinguishes Women with Unusually High Numbers of Sex Partners?" *Evolution & Human Behavior* 20.3 (1999): 141-50.

Miller, Henry, and Erica Jong. "Two Writers in Praise of Rabelais and Each Other." *New York Times* New York 7 Sept. 1974: 27.

Miller, Joaquin. *The One Fair Woman.* New York; Chapman and Hall, London: Carleton, 1876.

Miller, Laura. "Taking Wing." *New York Times* Book Review New York 1 June 2003: 39. 31 Aug. 2003.

Minney, R.J. *Fanny and the Regent of Siam.* New York: World, 1962.

Mirza, Humayun. *From Plassey to Pakistan: The Family History of Iskander Mirza, the First President of Pakistan.* Lanham, Md.: UP of America, 1999.

Mischel, Walter. *Personality and Assessment.* New York: Wiley, 1968.

Mishra, Pankaj. *Butter Chicken in Ludhiana.* New Delhi: Penguin, 1995.

---. *The Romantics.* New York: Random House, 2000.

Momsen, Janet Henshall. "Tourism, Gender and Development in the Caribbean." Kinnaird and Hall 1994 106-120.

Moore, Christopher G. *A Haunting Smile.* Bangkok: White Lotus, 1993.

Moore, Jan, et al. "HIV Risk Behavior among Peace Corps Volunteers." *AIDS* 9.7 (1995): 795-9.

Morin, Jack. *The Erotic Mind: Unlocking the Inner Sources of Sexual Passion and Fulfillment.* New York: HarperCollins, 1995.

Morris, Mary. *Nothing to Declare: Memoirs of a Woman Traveling Alone.* Boston: Houghton, 1988.

Morrow, Ann. *Highness: The Maharajahs of India.* London: Grafton, 1986.

Morton, Helen. "My Chastity Belt: Avoiding Seduction in Tonga." Kulick 1995 168-85.

Mulhall, Brian P. "Sex and Travel: Studies of Sexual Behaviour, Disease and Health Promotion in International Travellers — a Global Review." *International Journal of STD & AIDS* 7 (1996): 455-65.

Mullings, Beverley. "Fantasy Tours: Exploring the Global Consumption of Caribbean Sex Tourisms." *New Forms of Consumption: Consumers, Culture and Commodification.* Ed. Mark Gottdiener. Lanham, Md.: Rowman, 2000. 227-250.

Murphy, Dervla. *The Ukimwi Road: From Kenya to Zimbabwe.* Woodstock, N.Y.: Overlook, 1993.

Murray, Stephen O. "Male Homosexuality in Guatemala: Possible Insights and Certain Confusions from Sleeping with the Natives." *Out in the Field: Reflections of Lesbian and Gay Anthropologists.* Ed. Ellen Lewin and William L. Leap. Urbana, Ill.: U of Illinois P, 1996. 236-58.

Myers, Wayne A. "Addictive Sexual Behavior." *Journal of the American Psychoanalytic Association* 42.4 (1994): 1159-82.

Nettleford, Rex. The Cultural [and Environmental] Impact of Tourism: Caribbean Tourism Research Centre, Christ Church, Barbados 1977.

Newberry, Julia. *Julia Newberry's Diary.* 1869-71. New York: Norton, 1933.

Newcomb, Michael D. "Sexual Experience among Men and Women: Associations within Three Independent Samples." *Psychological Reports* 56.2 (1985): 603-14.

Newman, Barbara. *The Covenant: Love and Death in Beirut.* New York: Crown, 1989.

Nieves, Evelyn. "For Women in Silicon Valley, It Seems Like Strikeout.com." 10 April 2000. Available: <http://www.nytimes.com/>. 10 Apr. 2000.

Nilan, Pam. Young People as Embodied Subjects in Bali: Ritual, Politics and Risk/Profit: U of Newcastle, Callaghan, Australia 2001. Available: <http://www.capstrans.edu.au/nilan1.pdf>. 4 Feb. 2003

---. "Re: Question Related to Your Area of Expertise!" E-mail to the author. 12 Feb. 2003.

Njiké-Bergeret, Claude. *Ma Passion Africaine.* Paris: Lattès, 1997.

Noakes, Katy. "Ruff Spots and Rent-a-Dreads." Jansz, et al., 1999 318-24.

Norfolk, Andrew. "Career Woman Quits to Marry Fiji Chief's Son." *Times* London 15 March 2003, sec. News: 5.

North, Nic. "Anguish of Brit Widow." *Mirror* London 5 June 2001, sec. News: 5. Lexis-Nexus. 28 Jan. 2003.

Northam, Bruce, and Brad Olsen, ed. *In Search of Adventure: A Wild Travel Anthology.* San Francisco: Consortium of Collective Consciousness, 1999.

Nozedar, Beryl. Adventures of a Mid-Life Psychic. 1998. Online article. Berkeley Psychic Institute. Available: <http://www.berkeleypsychic.com/Reader/archive/November98/berylnozedar.html>. 2 July 2003.

O'Connell Davidson, Julia, and Jacqueline Sánchez Taylor. "Fantasy Islands: Exploring the Demand for Sex Tourism." Kempadoo 1999 37-54.

O'Connell Davidson, Julia, and Jacqueline Sánchez Taylor. Child Prostitution and Sex Tourism: Goa: ECPAT International, Bangkok, Thailand 1995. Available: <http://www.ecpat.net/eng/Ecpat_inter/projects/sex_tourism/sex_tourism.asp>. 5 Feb. 2003

O'Connell Davidson, Julia. "Sex Tourism in Cuba." *Race and Class* 38.1 (1996): 39-48.

O'Connell Davidson, Julia, and Jacqueline Sánchez Taylor. Child Prostitution and Sex Tourism: Venezuela: ECPAT International, Bangkok 1996. Available: <http://www.ecpat.net/eng/Ecpat_inter/projects/sex_tourism/sex_tourism.asp>. 19 June 2003

Oddie, E.M. [Elinor Mary O'Donoghue]. *The Odyssey of a Loving Woman.* New York,

London: Harper, 1936.

Odzer, Cleo. *Patpong Sisters: An American Woman's View of the Bangkok Sex World*. New York: Blue Moon, 1994.

Olshan, Joseph and Kurt Pitzer. "Bawdy by Jong: Once Outspokenly Zipless, the '70s Free Spirit Who Promoted Guiltless Sex Simmers Down — a Bit — in a Memoir." *People* 12 Sept. 1994: 77-78.

The Onion. Report: Economically Disadvantaged Men More Skilled at Communicating Attraction to Women. 28 Nov. 2001. Online newspaper. Available: <http://www.theonion.com/>. 28 Nov. 2001.

Oppenheimer, Valerie Kincade. "A Theory of Marriage Timing." *American Journal of Sociology* 94.3 (1988): 563-91.

Oppermann, Martin, ed. *Sex Tourism and Prostitution: Aspects of Leisure, Recreation and Work*. Elmsford, N.Y.: Cognizant, 1998.

---. "Sex Tourism." *Annals of Tourism Research* 26.2 (1999): 251-66.

Orso, Ethelyn G. *The Macha of Chira: Confessions of an Anthropologist*. New Orleans: Lakeview, 1991.

Ortner, Sherry B. *Life and Death on Mt. Everest: Sherpas and Himalayan Mountaineering*. Princeton, N.J.: Princeton UP, 1999.

Owen, Richard. "Casanovas Preparing to Woo by the Book." *Times* London 10 Apr. 2002, sec. Overseas news: 19. EBSCOHost. Enoch Pratt Free Library, Baltimore. 11 Oct. 2002.

Ozanne, Rebekah. "Falling in Love in Bali." *Inside Indonesia* (1992): 17.

Paglia, Camille. *Vamps and Tramps*. New York: Vintage, 1994.

Palmer, Catherine A. "Tourism and Colonialism: The Experience of the Bahamas." *Annals of Tourism Research* 21.4 (1994): 792-811.

Passman, Kristina M. "Veil." *Women's Studies Encyclopedia*. Ed. Helen Tierney. Westport, Conn.: Greenwood, 1999. 1449-50.

Patrick, Diane. *Terry McMillan: The Unauthorized Biography*. New York: St. Martin's, 1999.

Patta, Debora. "Racist Threats and Animal Sacrifices: The Perils of Marrying a Zulu Prince." *Sunday Times* London 13 Dec. 1998. Lexis-Nexus. 26 Aug. 2001.

Pattullo, Polly. *Last Resorts: Tourism in the Caribbean*. London: Cassell, 1996.

Paul, Chandrika. "Uncaging the Birds: The Movement to Allow Bengali Women into the Medical Profession: 1870-1880s." *Journal of South Asia Women Studies* 7.1 (2001). Available: <http://www.asiatica.org/publications/jsaws/vol7_no1-/paper2.asp>. 11 Dec. 2001.

Peake, Robert. "Swahili Stratification and Tourism in Malinda Old Town, Kenya." *Africa* 59.2 (1989): 209-20.

Pearce, Philip L. *The Social Psychology of Tourist Behavior. International Series in Experimental Social Psychology*. Vol. 3. Oxford, New York: Pergamon, 1982.

Pemble, John. *The Mediterranean Passion*. Oxford, England: Clarendon, 1987.

Perry, Michael. "Paradise Lost in South Pacific." Reuters Sydney 2 Apr. 2002. Lexis-Nexus. 19 Aug. 2003.

Phillips, Joan L. "Tourist-Oriented Prostitution in Barbados: The Case of the Beach Boy and the White Female Tourist." Kempadoo 1999 183-200.

Pirages, Dennis. "Microsecurity: Disease Organisms and Human Well-Being." *Washington Quarterly* 18.4 (1995): 7-11.

Pitt-Kethley, Fiona. *Journeys to the Underworld*. London: Chatto, 1988.

---. *The Pan Principle*. London: Sinclair-Stevenson, 1994.

---. "After 20 Years of Way Laying Male Bimbos, Fiona Pitt-Kethley Vows Today to Stay a One-Man Woman." *Guardian* London 16 Dec. 1995, sec. Features: 25. Lexis-Nexus. 30 Apr. 2002.

---. "A Woman of No Importance." Rev. of *A Scandalous Life* [U.K. title of *Rebel Heart*] by Mary S. Lovell. *Times* London 17 June 1995, sec. Features. Lexis-

Nexus. 18 Jan. 2001.

---. "After 100 Men, Is This the Real Thing?" Interview with Mackenzie, Susan. *Evening Standard* London 28 Feb. 1994: 12. Lexis-Nexus. 2 Sept. 2003.

Poewe, Karla. Anthro-L: August-1994: Re: Reflections of a Woman Anthropologist. 30 Aug. 1994. Online posting. Available: <http://www.ucalgary.ca/~kpo ewe/index.htm>. 13 Mar. 2002.

---. Dresden and Life under the Russians. 1995. Available: <http://www.anatomy.usyd. edu.au/danny/anthropology/a nthro-l/archive/august-1994/0144.html>. 2 Mar. 2001.

Pohl, Otto. "Kenya Cracking Down on 'Beach Boys,' Gigolos Serving Tourists." *New York Times* New York 14 Feb. 2002, Late ed., sec. Foreign: A12. Lexis-Nexus. 18 Oct. 2002.

Population Reference Bureau. 2001 World Population Data Sheet. Available: <http://www.-prb.org/Content-/NavigationMenu/Other_ reports/2000-2002/sheet5.html>. 27 Sept. 2002.

Press, Clayton M. Jr. "Reputation and Respectability Reconsidered: Hustling in a Tourist Setting." *Caribbean Issues* IV.1 (1978): 109-20.

Price, Neil. *Lower Class Response to Marginality in Bequia Island, St. Vincent*. London: Macmillan Caribbean, 1988.

Pruitt, Deborah, and Suzanne LaFont. "For Love and Money: Romance Tourism in Jamaica." *Annals of Tourism Research* 22.2 (1995): 422-40.

Pulsifer, Gary. "Love Quest of a Liberated Woman: Obituary: Anne Cumming." *Guardian* London 1 Sept. 1993: 10. Lexis-Nexus. 8 June 2001.

Purvis, June, ed. *Women's History: Britain, 1850-1954*. London: UCL, 1995.

Qualls-Corbett, Nancy. *The Sacred Prostitute: Eternal Aspect of the Feminine*. Toronto: Inner City, 1988.

Qian, Zhenchao. "Breaking Racial Barriers: Variations in Interracial Marriage between 1980 and 1990." *Demography* 34.2

(1997): 263-76.

Ranny. Looking for Hot!! Sizzling!! Female Tourists!!!! 2001. Online posting. Mumbai-central.com. Available: <http://mumbai-central.-com/cgi-sys/cgiwrap/hch-haya/mboards/bbs_forum.cgi?forum=people.20s&read=00081 0-000000.msg&use_last_read=-on&last_read=0>. 24 Aug. 2001.

Ratnapala, Nandasena. "Male Sex Work in Sri Lanka." *Men Who Sell Sex: International Perspectives on Male Prostitution and AIDS*. Ed. Peter Aggleton. London: UCL, 1999. 127-40.

Reid, Melanie. "Dream Holiday Where the Souvenir Is a Hunky Greek Boyfriend: Patricia Cowley Who Is a Real Life Shirley Valentine." *Scottish Daily Record & Sunday Mail* Glasgow 13 Oct. 1996: 32. Lexis-Nexus. 10 May 2002.

Reuters. "Emirate Offers Loan for Grooms to Wed Locals." *Toronto Star* Toronto 19 June 1992, sec. Life: C9. Lexis-Nexus. 7 July 2003.

Rhone, Trevor. "Smile Orange." *Old Story Time and Smile Orange*. Kingston, Jamaica: Longman, 1981. 89-155. 1971.

Ricciardi, Mirella. *African Saga*. 1982. London: Collins, 1985.

---. *African Visions: The Diary of an African Photographer*. London: Cassell, 2000.

Rice, Edward. *Captain Sir Richard Francis Burton*. New York: Scribner, 1990.

Richardson, John H. "The Restless Man: The Long Way Home (Part 1)." *Esquire* Nov. 2001: 82. Bigchalk Library. Enoch Pratt Free Library, Baltimore. 7 Apr. 2004.

Ricketts, Kevin. "Tribesmen Jailed over the Assault of American Couple." AAP Newsfeed [Australian Associated Press] Sydney 26 Apr. 2001. Lexis-Nexus. 18 Aug. 2003.

Ridout, Lucy. "Just One Big Service Industry." Jansz and Davies 1995 594-98.

Rigoglioso, Marguerite. "Preying: A Sicilian Tuna Slaughter Conjures a Drama of Sex, Death and Betrayal." McCauley 1998 129-37.

Roach, Denise. "So Why Am I European?" Jansz and Davies 1995 247-52.

Robinson, Adam. "Bin Laden: The Saudi Dissident Waging Holy War on the US." *Daily Mail* London 10 Nov. 2001: 36. Lexis-Nexus. 7 July 2003.

Robinson, Hilary. "Behind the Picture Postcards." Jansz and Davies 1990 248-50.

Robinson, Jane. *Wayward Women*. New York: Oxford UP, 1990.

---. *Unsuitable for Ladies: An Anthology of Women Travellers*. New York: Oxford UP, 1994.

---. Letter to the author. 23 April 2001.

Robinson, Kim, Harclyde Walcott and Trevor Fearon. *The How to Be Jamaican Handbook*. 11th printing ed. Kingston, Jamaica: Jamrite, 1987.

Rogers, Byron. "Travelling Just a Little Bit Too Far: As Channel Four Announces a Holiday Programme with a Difference — Young Women on a Manhunt — Byron Rogers Identifies a New Breed of Female Travel Writers Who Believe Sex Is Part of the Jaunt." *Daily Telegraph* London 20 Oct. 1995: 25.

Rohit, Zaveri. Insight India: 25b. 15 Nov. 2001. Online posting. Mumbai-central.com. Available: <http://www.mum-bai-central.com/nukkad/nov-2001/msg00226.html>. 10 Apr. 2003.

Rokeach, Milton, Patrica W. Smith and Richard I. Evans. "Two Kinds of Prejudice or One?" *The Open and Closed Mind: Investigations into the Nature of Belief Systems and Personality Systems*. Ed. Milton Rokeach. New York: Basic, 1960. 132-68.

Roloff, Juliane. "Marriages with and Divorces from Foreigners in Germany [Eheschließungen und Ehescheidungen von und mit Ausländern in Deutschland]." *Zeitschrift für Bevölkerungswissenschaft* 23.3 (1998): 319-34.

---. "Re: Question Related to Your Area of Expertise." E-mail to the author. 11 Dec. 2002.

Romano, Dugan. *Intercultural Marriage: Promises and Pitfalls*. 2nd ed. Yarmouth, Mass.: Intercultural, 1997.

Rosenthal, Daniel. "A Long Way from Howards End." *Times* London 18 May 1995, sec. Features. Lexis-Nexus. 13 Sept. 2000.

Ross, Michael W. "Psychological Perspectives on Sexuality and Sexually Transmitted Diseases." Holmes 1999 107-13.

Roumeguère, Carolyn. Interview with Laura Campbell. "Style: Masai Mara Meets the Fulham Road. You Can Hear Carolyn Roume-guere's Jewellery Long before You See It; In Fact, It Is Dramatic Enough to Hang on the Wall as Art." *Daily Telegraph* London 25 Aug. 1997: 12. Lexis-Nexus. 22 Aug. 2001.

---. "Growing up with the Maasai." Carolyn Roumeguère press kit for Nomad Jewellery n.d.

Roumeguère, Jacqueline. *Quand Le Python Se Déroule*. Paris: Laffont, 1988.

Rowell, Galen. *In the Throne Room of the Mountain Gods*. San Francisco: Sierra Club, 1977.

Rubin, Martin. "Masquerading as Fiction." Rev. of *My Other Life* by Paul Theroux. *Los Angeles Times* Los Angeles, Calif. 20 Oct. 1996, Home ed., sec. Book Review: 6. Lexis-Nexus. 8 Apr. 2002.

Runciman, Steven. *A Traveller's Alphabet: Partial Memoirs*. New York: Thames, 1991.

Rush, Norman. "Alone in Africa." Coyne 1999 (orig. published 1984) 295-317.

Rushing, Andrea Benton. "Goin' There and Knowin' There." E. Lee 1997 13-24.

Rushton, J. Philippe. "Epigenesis and Social Preference." *Behavioral and Brain Sciences* 12 (1989): 31-32.

Russell, R.J.H., and J. Bartrip. "Homo Sociobiologicus Not Found." *Behavioral and Brain Sciences* 12 (1989): 32-33.

Ryan, Chris, and C. Michael Hall. *Sex Tourism: Marginal People and Liminalities.* New York: Routledge, 2001.

Ryan, Chris. "Re: Right on Target." E-mail to the author. 15 May 2001.

Saardchom, Narumon. Marriage Markets across Countries. Available: <http://www.casact.org/coneduc/reinsure/astin/2000/saardchom1.doc>. 17 Sept. 2002.

Sadat, Jehan. *A Woman of Egypt.* New York: Simon, 1987.

Saheed, Alison. "An Uneasy Path." Jansz and Davies 1990 198-202.

Salak, Kira. *Four Corners: One Woman's Solo Journey into the Heart of Papua New Guinea.* Washington, D.C.: Counterpoint, 2001.

Salmon, Catherine and Donald Symons. *Warrior Lovers: Erotic Fiction, Evolution and Female Sexuality.* London: Weidenfeld, 2001.

Sánchez Taylor, Jacqueline. "Tourism and 'Embodied' Commodities: Sex Tourism in the Caribbean." Clift and Carter 2000 41-53.

---. "AIDS Risk to 'Shirley Valentine' Tourists." *Independent* London 16 July 2000: 7. Lexis-Nexus. 29 June 2002.

---. "Dollars Are a Girl's Best Friend? Female Tourists' Sexual Behaviour in the Caribbean." *Sociology* 35.3 (2001): 749-764.

---. "Re: Very Interested in Your Dr and Jamaica Work!" E-mail to the author. 16 May 2001.

Sanger, William W. *The History of Prostitution: Official Report to Board of Alms-House Governors by Resident Physician at Blackwell's Island (New York).* New York: Arno, 1972.

Sargent, Wyn. *People of the Valley: Life with a Cannibal Tribe in New Guinea.* New York: Random, 1974.

Schmidt, Margaret Fox. *Passion's Child: The Extraordinary Life of Jane Digby.* New York: Harper, 1976.

Schneebaum, Tobias. *Where the Spirits Dwell: An Odyssey in the Jungle of New Guinea.* New York: Grove, 1988.

Seal, A., Victor Minichiello and M. Omodei. "Young Women's Sexual Risk Taking Behaviour: Re-Visiting the Influences of Sexual Self-Efficacy and Sexual Self-Esteem." *International Journal of STD & AIDS* 8.3 (1997): 159-65.

Selanniemi, Tom. E-mail to the author. 19 June 2001.

Shaffer, Kate. "Tica and Gringa Relationships: A Study of Acculturation." 1996. Wallace vol. 1. Available: <http://www4-.ncsu.edu:8030/-~twallace/FinalReport96.pdf>. 19 June 2003.

Shaffer, Tanya. *Somebody's Heart Is Burning: A Woman Wanderer in Africa.* New York: Vintage, 2003.

Shakespeare, Nicholas. *Bruce Chatwin: A Biography.* New York: Doubleday, 1999.

Shapiro, Laura. "Under the South Pacific Stars." *Newsweek* 17 July 1989: 54. Lexis-Nexus. 21 July 2003.

Sheridan, Michael. "Lucie and a Japanese Heart of Darkness." *Sunday Times* London 8 July 2001, sec. Overseas news. Lexis-Nexus. 28 Jan. 2003.

Sherpa, Donna M. *Living in the Middle: Sherpas of the Mid-Range Himalayas.* Prospect Heights, Ill.: Waveland, 1994.

Sherwood, Mrs. John. "American Girls in Europe." *North American Review* June 1890: 681-91.

Shibuya, Ikuzo. Zimbabwe: The Streets of Shames by Female Foreign Tourists. 1997. Available: <http://www03.u-page.so-net.ne.jp/yc4/ikuzo798/english-index2.html>. 24 Aug. 2001.

Shoko, Rangarirai. "Zimbabwean Gigolos Prey on Rich White Foreign Women." Africa News Service 19 Nov. 2000. Infotrac. Enoch Pratt Free Library, Baltimore. 7 Apr. 2004.

Sikstrom, Bo, et al. "Sexual Risk Behavior in Women with Cervical Human Papillomavirus Infection." *Archives of Sexual Behavior* 25.4 (1996): 361-72. Infotrac. Bradford College, Mass. 29 Sept. 1999.

Simons, Eleanor. "How Safe Are You on Holiday? Sexual Assault on Holiday." *Sun* London 12 July

2000. Lexis-Nexus. 18 Oct. 2002.

Simpson, Mona. "Ramadan." de Kretser 1998 139-64.

Sinclair, James. "Re: How Interesting!" E-mail to the author. 9 Dec. 2001.

---. "Re: Hi James -- Question Regarding the Meerzas." E-mail to the author. 2 Aug. 2003.

Sinclair, Zena Meerza. "Petals in the Dust." Memoir excepts sent as e-mail from her son, James Sinclair, to the author. 12 Dec. 2001.

Singh, Sagar. "Love, Anthropology and Tourism." *Annals of Tourism Research* 29.1 (2001): 261-64.

Sinnott, Abby. "Santorini Style." Northam 1999 246-251.

Sircar, Sanjay. E-mail to the author. 11 Dec. 2000.

Skow, John. "Some Groove." *Time* 6 May 1996: 77.

Smith, Helena. "Another Side of Paradise: The Sky Is Blue, the Sun Is Hot, the Guys Are Gorgeous. But What Happens When the Summer's Gone? Can You Take the Zorba out of the Greek? Helena Smith Talks to the Women Who Stayed On." *Guardian* London 17 Nov. 1993, sec. Features: 2. Lexis-Nexus. 29 June 2002.

---. "Shirley Valentine Man Jailed." *Guardian* London 12 June 2002, sec. Home pages: 7. Lexis-Nexus. 30 June 2002.

Smith, Sally Bedell. *Reflected Glory: The Life of Pamela Churchill Harriman.* New York: Simon, 1996.

Snyder, Mark, and Jeffry A. Simpson. "Self-Monitoring and Dating Relationships." *Journal of Personality and Social Psychology* 47.6 (1984): 1281-91.

Soueif, Adhaf. *The Map of Love.* New York: Anchor, 1999.

South, Scott J. "Sex Ratios, Economic Power, and Women's Roles: A Theoretical Extension and Empirical Test." *Journal of Marriage and Family* 50.1 (1988): 19-31.

---. "Sociodemographic Differentials in Mate Selection Preferences." Journal of Marriage and the Family 53

(1991): 928-40.

---. "Re: Thank You! Section Draft Attached." E-mail to the author. 26 Sept. 2002.

Spalt, Lee. "Sexual Behavior and Affective Disorders." *Diseases of the Nervous System* 36.12 (1975): 644-47.

Spano, Susan. "Romance on a Trip: Love in a New Zone." *Star Tribune* (reprinted from Los Angeles Times) Minneapolis, Minn. 27 Sept. 1998: 1G. Lexis-Nexus. 14 Nov. 2001.

---. "Trekking to Cloud 9 in Nepal: Some U.S. Women Find Love, Even Marriage, with Their Sherpas. But Often, the Romances in the Himalayas Have Led to Broken Hearts." *Los Angeles Times* 8 Sept. 2000: A1. Lexis-Nexus. 14 Nov. 2001.

Spathias, Moira. "Beware the Dark, Handsome Stranger: Moira Spathias Blows the Whistle on the Reality of Holiday Romance." *Guardian* London 16 July 1992, sec. Features: 34. Lexis-Nexus. 30 June 2002.

Spira, Alfred, Nathalie Bajos and the ACSF Group. *Sexual Behaviour and AIDS*. Aldershot, England: Avebury, 1994.

Spratling, Cassandra. "How Terry McMillan Got Her Groove Back." Knight-Ridder/-Tribune News Service 22 May 1996. Infotrac. Enoch Pratt Free Library, Baltimore. 6 Sept. 03.

Spuhler, J.N., and Philip J. Clark. "Migration into the Human Breeding Population of Ann Arbor, Michigan, 1900-1950." *Human Biology* 33 (1961): 223-36.

Stafford, William T., ed. *James's Daisy Miller, the Story, the Play, the Critics*. New York: Scribner, 1963.

Stanley, David. Moon Handbooks: A Closer Look: Fiji Customs. Available: <http://-www.moon.com/closer/fiji_customs.html>. 17 July 2003.

Stanton, Maureen. "Piranha." de Kretser 1998 85-94.

Stapley, Mildred. "Is Paris Wise for the Average American Girl?" *Ladies' Home Journal* April 1906: 16, 54.

Stephens, Harold. *At Home in Asia: Expatriates in Southeast Asia and Their Stories*. Miranda, Calif.: Wolfenden, 1995.

Stern, Madeleine B. *The Life of Margaret Fuller*. New York: Greenwood, 1991.

Stevenson, Catherine Barnes. *Victorian Women Travel Writers in Africa*. Boston: Twayne, 1982.

Stewart, Lucretia. *The Weather Prophet: A Caribbean Journey*. London: Chatto, 1995.

---, ed. *Erogenous Zones: An Anthology of Sex Abroad*. New York: Modern Library, 2000.

Strobel, Margaret. *European Women and the Second British Empire*. Bloomington, Ind.: Indiana UP, 1991.

Sumner, Melanie. *Polite Society*. Boston: Houghton, 1995.

Susanne K. "Infos" and "Your E-Mail Dd 21/06/01." E-mails to the author. 17 and 29 June 2001.

Susman, Ed. "AIDS: Is 'Paradise' Next?" United Press International 10 Dec. 2003. Lexis-Nexus. 12 Jan. 2004.

Sussman, Ellen. "How Would My Rape Shape My Kids' Lives?" *Newsweek* Dec. 8 2003: 16.

Suyin, Han. *The Mountain Is Young*. New York: Putnam, 1958.

---. *My House Has Two Doors*. New York: Putnam, 1980.

Symons, Donald. "Your Manuscript." E-mail to the author. 28 Jan. 2003.

Tantri, K'tut. *Revolt in Paradise*. New York: Harper, 1960.

Teasdill, Wendy. "Om Mani Padme Hum." Jansz and Davies 1995 604-11.

Templin, Charlotte. *Feminism and the Politics of Literary Reputation: The Example of Erica Jong*. Lawrence, Kan.: U Press of Kansas, 1995.

Terwiel, B.J. *A History of Modern Thailand, 1767-1942*. St. Lucia: U of Queensland P, 1983.

Thanh-Dam, Truong. "The Dynamics of Sex Tourism: The Case of Southeast Asia." *Development and Change* 14 (1983): 533-553.

Thelwell, Michael. *The Harder They Come*. New York: Grove, 1980.

Theobald, Stephanie and Michael Howard. "Women: Lesbians Go Mad in Lesbos. Well, That Was the Plan for the Package Trip to Sappho's Home Town. But Then the Local Mayor Stepped In and Tried to Tone Down the Festivities." *Guardian* London 14 Sept. 2000, sec. Features: 8. Lexis-Nexus. 10 May 2002.

Theodoulou, Mike. "For Shirleys Everywhere." *Times* London 21 Nov. 1998, sec. Features. Lexis-Nexus. 10 May 2002.

Therival, Riki. "Finding a Place in Kyoto." Jansz and Davies 1990 268-71.

Theroux, Paul. "White Lies." Coyne 1999 (orig. published 1979) 3-15.

---. "Hapless Organ." Rev. of *Fear of Flying* by Erica Jong. *New Statesman* 19 Apr. 1974: 554.

---. *The Kingdom by the Sea: A Journey around Great Britain*. Boston: Houghton, 1983.

---. "Homage to Mrs. Robinson." *Sunrise with Seamonsters*. Boston: Houghton, 1985. 152-55. 1977.

---. "Strangers on a Train." *Sunrise with Seamonsters*. Boston: Houghton, 1985. 126-35. 1976.

---. *The Great Railway Bazaar*. 1975. New York: Washington Square, 1985.

---. *Riding the Iron Rooster: By Train through China*. New York: Putnam, 1988.

---. *My Secret History*. New York: Putnam, 1989.

---. "African Girls." *My Secret History*. New York: Putnam, 1989. 191-209.

---. *The Happy Isles of Oceania: Paddling the Pacific*. New York: Putnam, 1992.

---. *The Pillars of Hercules*. New York: Putnam, 1995.

---. *My Other Life*. Boston: Houghton, 1996.

---. "The Lepers of Moyo." *My Other Life*. Boston: Houghton, 1996. 14-89.

---. *Sir Vidia's Shadow: A Friendship across Five Continents.* Boston: Houghton, 1998.

---. *Dark Star Safari: Overland from Cairo to Cape Town.* Boston: Houghton, 2003.

Thomas, Michelle. "Exploring the Contexts and Meanings of Women's Experiences of Sexual Intercourse on Holiday." Clift and Carter 2000 200-20.

Thomas, Polly. "A Funny Old Place." Jansz, et al., 1999 589-95.

Thompson, Thomas. *Serpentine.* New York: Doubleday, 1979.

Thompson-Noel, Michael. "In Search of Pan and the People of Thrace." Rev. of *The Pan Principle* by Fiona Pitt-Kethley. *Financial Times* London 19 Feb. 1994, sec. Books: XXII. Lexis-Nexus. 2 Sept. 2003.

Tolmacheva, Marina A. "Ibn Battuta on Women's Travel in the Dar Al-Islam." *Women and the Journey: The Female Travel Experience.* Ed. Bonnie Frederick and Susan H. McLeod. Pullman, Wash.: Washington State UP, 1993. 118-40.

Townsend, John Marshall. "Mate Selection Criteria: A Pilot Study." *Ethology and Sociobiology* 10 (1989): 241-253.

Toynbee, Polly. "'Where Are My Children?'" *Times* London 20 Dec. 1990, sec. Features. Lexis-Nexus. 22 Feb. 2002.

Tree, Isabella. *Islands in the Clouds.* Hawthorn, Australia: Lonely Planet, 1996.

Tree, Isabella. Culture Shock. Travel Intelligence. Available: <http://www.travelintelligence.net/wsd/articles/art_520.html>. 18 Aug. 2003.

---. Souks and the Single Girl. Travel Intelligence. Available: <http://www.travelintelligence.net/wsd/articles/art_444.html>. 25 Aug. 2003.

Trescott, Jacqueline. "Terry McMillan, Breathing Easy: A Jamaican Vacation Did the Author a World of Good." *Washington Post* Washington, D.C. 1 June 1996, Final ed., sec. Style: H1. NewsBank InfoWeb. 10 Sept. 2003.

Tsing, Anna Lowenhaupt. *In the Realm of the Diamond Queen.* Princeton, N.J.: Princeton UP, 1993.

Twedwr-Moss, Robert. "Salons of Tea and Empathy." *Times* London 24 Oct. 1992: Features. Lexis-Nexus. 8 June 2001.

U.N. Population Division. World Marriage Patterns 2000. 2000. Available: <http://www.un.org/esa/population/publications/worldmarriage/worldmarriage.htm>. 23 Aug. 2002.

U.N. Statistics Division. Indicators on Population. 2002. Available: <http://unstats.un.org/unsd/demographic/social/population.htm>. 6 Aug. 2002.

U.S. Census Bureau. Educational Attainment of the Population 15 Years and over, by Marital Status, Age, Sex, Race, and Hispanic Origin: March 2000. 19 Dec. 2000. Available: <http://www.census.gov/population/www/socdemo/education/p20-536.html>. 23 Aug. 2002.

---. International Data Base. 10 May 2000. Available: <http://www.census.gov/ipc/www/idbsprd.html>. 21 Aug. 2002.

---. *County and City Data Book: 2000.* May 2001. Available: <http://www.census.gov/prod/www/ccdb.html>. 8 Aug. 2002.

---. Statistical Abstract 2001. Washington, D.C., 2001.

---. Table P-48 Occupation of Longest Job — Full-Time, Year-Round Workers by Median Earnings and Sex: 1982 to 2000. 18 Apr. 2002. Available: <http://www.census.gov/hhes/income/histinc/p48.html>. 21 July 2002.

U.S. Centers for Disease Control. "Table 9. Median and Mean Age of Bride and Groom by Previous Marital Status: Marriage-Registration Area, 1964-90." *Monthly Vital Statistics Report* 43.12(S) (1995): 16. Available: <http://www.cdc.gov/nchs/fastats/pdf/4312s-t9.pdf>. 23 Aug. 2002.

---. "Table 3. Provisional Number of Marriages and Divorces: Each Division and State, December 1996b and 1997, and Cumulative Figures, 1995-97." Monthly Vital Statistics Report 46.12 (1998): 8. Available: <http://www.cdc.gov/nchswww/data/mvs46_12.pdf>. 1 Aug. 2000.

---. Marriage, Fastats A-Z. 11 Sept. 2002. Available: <http://www.cdc.gov/fastats/marriage.htm>. 24 Dec. 2002.

U.S. Immigration and Naturalization Service. Immigrants Admitted to the United States, 1972 (Computer Files): ICPSR version. Washington, D.C.: U.S. Dept. of Justice, Immigration and Naturalization Service [producer], 1972. Ann Arbor, Mich: Inter-university Consortium for Political and Social Research [distributor], 1988. Additional computer files in this series analyzed for 1980, 1990, 1996.

---. Immigrants Admitted to the United States (Codebooks). 1976, 1980, 1990, 1996. Available: <http://www.icpsr.umich.edu:8080/ICPSR-STUDY/08952.xml, http://www.icpsr.umich.edu:8080/ICPSR-STUDY/08960.xml, http://www.icpsr.umich.edu:8080/ICPSR-STUDY/06164.xml, http://www.icpsr.umich.edu:8080/ICPSR-STUDY/02534.xml>. 7 Oct. 2002.

UNAIDS. Report on the Global HIV/AIDS Epidemic 2002: Table of Country-Specific HIV/AIDS Estimates and Data, End 2001. 2002. Available: <http://www.unaids.org/barcelona/presskit/report.html>. 27 Sept. 2002.

United Nations. *Demographic Yearbook 1999.* New York, 2001.

Valero, Helena, as told to Ettore Biocca. *Yanoáma: The Narrative of a Woman Abducted by Brazilian Indians.* London: Allen & Unwin, 1969.

Varawa, Joana McIntyre. *Changes in Latitude: An Uncommon Anthropology.* New York: Atlantic Monthly, 1989.

---. Interview with the author. 29 Sept. 1990.

Vorakitphokatorn, Sairudee, et al. "AIDS Risk in Tourists: A Study on Japanese Female Tourists in Thailand." *Journal of Population and Social Studies* 5.1-2 (1993-94): 55-84.

Wagatsuma, Hiroshi. "The Social Perception of Skin Color in Japan." *Daedalus* 96.2 (1967): 407-43.

Wagner, Ulla. "Out of Time and Space — Mass Tourism and Charter Trips." *Ethnos* 42.1-2 (1977): 39-49.

Wagner, Ulla, and Bawa Yamba. "Going North and Getting Attached: The Case of the Gambians." *Ethnos* 51.3 (1986): 199-222.

Waldron, D'Lynn. War in the Himalayas. Available: <http://www.dlynnwaldron. com/HimalayaWar.html>. 8 May 2003.

Walker, Alice, and Pratibha Parmar. *Warrior Marks: Female Genital Mutilation and the Sexual Blinding of Women*. San Diego, Calif., New York, London: Harcourt, 1996.

Wallace, Tim, ed. Tourism and Its Consequences: Case Studies from Quepos/Manuel Antonio, Costa Rica. Raleigh, N.C.: NCSU Ethnographic Field School, North Carolina State U. Available: <http://www4.ncsu.edu:8030/~twallace/study A.html>.

Ward, Tim. A*rousing the Goddess*. Toronto: Somerville, 1996.

Ware, Vron. "Purity and Danger: Race, Gender and Tales of Sex Tourism." *Back to Reality? Social Experience and Cultural Studies*. Ed. Angela McRobbie. Manchester, England: Manchester UP, 1997. 133-51.

Wasserstrom, William. *Heiress of All the Ages: Sex and Sentiment in the Genteel Tradition*. Minneapolis, Minn.: U of Minnesota P, 1959.

Weaver, Tony. Malindi: The Inside Story. 1999. Available: <http://www.go2africa.com/ kenya/_articles/article_28.asp> . 24 Aug. 2001.

Wengle, John L. "Death and Rebirth in Fieldwork: A Case Study." *Culture, Medicine and Psychiatry* 11 (1987): 357-85.

Wetherall, Sarah. "A Cautious Enjoyment." 1990. Jansz and Davies. 370-73.

Wheat, Sue. "Women Are Sex Tourists Too: Is It the Romance That Women Are Paying for in Jamaica? Or Is It a Feeling of Power That They Can't Get at

Home?" *Independent* London 1999.

Wheeler, Tony. *Papua New Guinea: A Travel Survival Kit*. 2nd ed. South Yarra, Australia: Lonely Planet, 1981.

White, Edmund. Interview with David Tuller. "States of Desire Then and Now." *Chronicle* San Francisco 5 Oct. 1997: 3.

Whitman, Walt. "Song of the Open Road." *Walt Whitman: Complete Poetry and Selected Prose and Letters*. Ed. Emory Halloway. London: Nonesuch, 1967. 136-46. 1856.

Whyte, Martin King. *The Status of Women in Preindustrial Societies*. Princeton, N.J.: Princeton UP, 1978.

Wickens, Eugenia. "Consumption of the Authentic: The Hedonistic Tourist in Greece." *Tourism: The State of the Art*. Ed. A.V. Seaton. New York: Wiley, 1994. 818-24.

---. "Licensed for Thrills: Risk-Taking and Tourism." *Tourism and Health: Risks, Research and Responses*. Ed. Stephen Clift and Peter Grabowski. London: Pinter, 1997. 153-64.

---. "Review of Draft Chapter." Letter to the author. 12 June 2001.

Wiederman, Michael W., and Elizabeth Rice Allgeier. "Gender Differences in Mate Selection Criteria: Sociobiological or Socioeconomic Explanation?" *Ethology and Sociobiology* 13.2 (1992): 115-24.

Williams, Donna Marie. *Sensual Celibacy*. New York: Fireside, 1999.

Williams, Harry Abbott. "Theology and Self-Awareness." *Soundings: Essays Concerning Christian Understanding*. Ed. A.R. Vidler. Cambridge: Cambridge UP, 1966. 67-102.

Williams, Zoe. "Lesbos in a Twist over Lesbians from London." *Evening Standard* London 15 Sep. 2000: 7. Lexis-Nexus. 10 May 2002.

Wilmshurst, Joan. "Re: Question Re: 'N.C.D.'" E-mail to the author. 23 Jan. 2002.

. "Mixed Marriages." E-mail to

the author. 25 Feb. 2002.

Wilson, Wade T. *Fantasy Islands: A Man's Guide to Exotic Women and International Travel*. 2nd ed. Alameda, Calif.: Roam, 1998.

Windo, Pamela. "Re: Good to Talk to You!" E-mail to the author. 25 Aug. 2002.

---. "Agadir." E-mail to the author. 22 Aug. 2002.

---. Interview with the author. 22 Aug. 2002.

Winkler, Anthony C. *The Lunatic*. Secaucus, N.J.: Stuart, 1987.

Winstone, H.V.F. *Gertrude Bell*. London: Cape, 1978.

Witchel, Alex. "Sex and the Single Senior." *New York Times* New York 27 April 2003. Available: <http://www.nytimes.-com/2003/04/27/fashion/27J ANE.html>. 1 May 2003.

Wolf, Yapady. "The World of the Kuta Cowboy." *Inside Indonesia* (1993): 15-17.

Wolfenstein, Martha, and Nathan Leites. *Movies: A Psychological Study*. Glencoe, Ill.: Free, 1950.

Wong, Lina M. "Island Girl." Bauer 2003 35-42.

Wood, Ben. "Surf Culture and Tourism in the Quepos/Manuel Antonio Area." 19 June 2003. 1997. Wallace vol. 2. Available: <http://www4.ncsu.edu:8030- /~twallace/97CRrpt.pdf>.

Wright, John. "Geoffrey Vaki — Crusader of Hope." *Post-Courier* Port Moresby, Papua New Guinea 8 Apr. 2003. Available: <http://www.postcouri-er.com.pg/20030408/focus.htm >. 18 Aug. 2003.

Wright, Tiffany Marie. *Female Sexual Behavior: Analysis of Big Five Trait Facets and Domains in the Prediction of Sociosexuality*. Diss. U of California Riverside, 1999. Abstract, PsychInfo. 26 Nov. 2002.

WuDunn, Sheryl. "Their Men? Boring and Sexist, Japanese Women Declare; Gradual Rebellion / Feminism in Japan." *International Herald Tribune* Neuilly-sur-Seine, France 10 July 1995. Lexis-Nexus. 22 Mar. 2001.

Index

Bibliography, con't

Wylie, Judith Babcock, ed. *Love & Romance: True Stories of Passion on the Road*. San Francisco, Calif.: Travelers' Tales, 1998.

Yamashita, Shinji. *Bali and Beyond : Explorations in the Anthropology of Tourism*. Trans. J.S. Eades. New York: Berghahn, 2003.

---. The Japanese Encounter with the South: Japanese Tourists in Palau: Conference on "Moving Cultures: Remaking Asia-Pacific Studies", Honolulu 1998. Available: <http://www.hawaii.edu/~movingcultures/papers/confl_papers/Yamashita.html>.

Young, Cathy. *Ceasefire! Why Men and Women Must Join Forces to Achieve True Equality*. New York: Free, 1999.

Younger, Coralie. *Wicked Women of the Raj: European Women Who Broke Society's Rules and Married

Indian Princes*. New Delhi: HarperCollins, 2003.

Zinovieff, Sofka. "Hunters and Hunted: Kamaki and the Ambiguities of Sexual Predation in a Greek Town." *Contested Identities: Gender and Kinship in Modern Greece*. Ed. Peter Loizos et al. Princeton, N.J.: Princeton UP, 1991. 203-20.

Zoro, Janet. "A Lasting Idyll." Jansz and Davies 1990 182-85.

About the author

Jeannette Belliveau was born in 1954 in Washington, D.C., and grew up in Rockville, Md. She graduated in 1976 as a journalism major from the University of Maryland.

Belliveau has worked as a newspaper reporter, editor and designer in Maryland, Alaska and Britain (*Montgomery Journal, Tundra Drums, Surrey Advertiser*) and as a financial and graphics editor at the *Baltimore Sun* and *Washington Post*. From 1985 through 1994, she traveled in six continents. In 1991, she revisited Asia as a Jefferson Fellow, sponsored by the East-West Center in Honolulu, Hawaii.

Her first book, *An Amateur's Guide to the Planet*, described adventure travels to 12 countries, and became a surprise hit as an popular college geography text.

Belliveau lives in the maritime district of Fells Point in Baltimore, Md., with her husband, artist and historian Lamont W. Harvey, and their Shetland sheepdogs and cats.

For details on her presentations, visit www.beaumonde.net.

Index, con't